Lecture Notes in Computer Science 6513

Commenced Publication in 1973
Founding and Former Series Editors:
Gerhard Goos, Juris Hartmanis, and Jan van Leeuwen

Yongwha Chung
Moti Yung (Eds.)

Information
Security Applications

11th International Workshop, WISA 2010
Jeju Island, Korea, August 24-26, 2010
Revised Selected Papers

 Springer

Volume Editors

Yongwha Chung
Korea University
Department of Computer and Information Science
Jochiwon-eup, Yeongi-gun
Chungnam-do, 339-700, Korea
E-mail: ychungy@korea.ac.kr

Moti Yung
Google Inc. and Columbia University
Computer Science Department
Room, 464, S.W. Mudd Building
New York, NY 10027, USA
E-mail: moti@cs.columbia.edu

Library of Congress Control Number: 2010941098

CR Subject Classification (1998): C.2, K.6.5, E.3, D.4.6, J.1, H.4

LNCS Sublibrary: SL 4 – Security and Cryptology

ISSN   0302-9743
ISBN-10   3-642-17954-1 Springer Berlin Heidelberg New York
ISBN-13   978-3-642-17954-9 Springer Berlin Heidelberg New York

springer.com

© Springer-Verlag Berlin Heidelberg 2011
Printed in Germany

Typesetting: Camera-ready by author, data conversion by Scientific Publishing Services, Chennai, India
Printed on acid-free paper   06/3180

Preface

The 11th International Workshop on Information Security Applications (WISA 2010)was held on Jeju Island, Korea, during August 24–26, 2010. The workshop was hosted by the Korea Institute of Information Security and Cryptology (KIISC), supported by the Electronics and Telecommunications Research Institute (ETRI) and the Korea Internet and Security Agency (KISA), sponsored by the Ministry of Public Administration and Security (MoPAS) and the Korea Communications Commission (KCC).

The aim of the workshop was to serve as a forum for presenting new research and experimental results in the area of information security applications from academic communities as well as from industry. The workshop program covered a wide range of security aspects, from cryptography to systems and network security as well as experimental work.

It was our great pleasure and honor to serve as the Program Committee Co-chairs of WISA 2010. This year, too, the proceedings of the workshop were published in the LNCS series of Springer. The WISA 2010 Program Committee received 107 papers from14 countries. The submissions were exceptionally strong, and the committee accepted 25 papers for the full-paper presentation track. All the papers were carefully evaluated through blind peer-review by at least three members of the Program Committee.We would like to say that acceptance is a great achievement since the selection process was highly competitive, and many good papers were not accepted.

In addition to the contributed papers, the workshop had four invited talks. Hong Sun Kim, Soung-Ju Kang, Jungwoo Ryoo and Moti Yung gave us distinguished special talks entitled "Security Challenges Posed by Mobile Internet Services," "Information Security Policy for Smart Korea," "Software Security by Design,"and "Embedding Cryptographic Components in Complex System," respectively.

Many people helped and worked hard to make WISA 2010 successful. We would like to thank all the people involved in the technical program and in organizing the workshop. We are very grateful to the Program Committee members and external referees for their time and efforts in reviewing the submissions and selecting the accepted papers. We should also express our special thanks to the Organizing Committee members and the General Chair, Jongin Lim, for their hard work in managing the workshop.

Finally, on behalf of all those involved in organizing the workshop, we would like to thank the authors of all the submitted papers, for sending and contributing their interesting research results to the workshop, and the invited speakers. Without their submissions and support, WISA 2010 could not have been a success.

October 2010   Yongwha Chung
                                                                       Moti Yung

Organization

Advisory Committee

Hideki Imai	Chuo University, Japan
Hee-Jung Kim	KISA, Korea
Heung-Nam Kim	ETRI, Korea
Kwangjo Kim	KAIST, Korea
Sehun Kim	KAIST, Korea
Hong-sub Lee	Soonchunhyang University, Korea
PilJoong Lee	POSTECH, Korea
Sang-Jae Moon	Kyungpook National University, Korea
Kil-Hyun Nam	Korea National Defense University, Korea
Bart Preneel	Katholieke University Leuven, Belgium
Man-Young Rhee	Kyung Hee University, Korea
Min-Sub Rhee	Dankook University, Korea
Young-Dong Son	NSRI, Korea
Joo-Seok Song	Yonsei University, Korea
Dong-Ho Won	Sungkyunkwan University, Korea

General Chair

Jongin Lim	Korea University, Korea

Steering Committee

Heung-Youl Youm	Soonchunhyang University, Korea
Hyun-Sook Cho	ETRI, Korea
Jae-Cheol Ryou	Chungnam National University, Korea
Hyung-Woo Lee	Hanshin University, Korea
Jae-Kwang Lee	Hannam University, Korea
Dong-Il Seo	ETRI, Korea
Kyo-Il Chung	ETRI, Korea
Kiwook Sohn	NSRI, Korea

Organizing Committee

Chair

Sang-Choon Kim	Kangwon National University, Korea

Members

Jaehoon Nah	ETRI, Korea
Ji-Young Ahn	KIISC, Korea
Byoungcheon Lee	Joongbu University, Korea
Hyun-Cheol Jeong	KISA, Korea
Daesung Kwon	NSRI, Korea
Jihoung Kim	Semyung University, Korea
KeunHee Han	MoPAS, Korea
Kangbin Yim	Sooncounhyang University, Korea
Taenam Cho	Woosuk University, Korea
Heuisu Ryu	Gyeongin National University of Education, Korea
Khi Jung Ahn	Cheju National University, Korea

Program Committee

Co-chairs

Yongwha Chung	Korea University, Korea
Moti Yung	Google Inc. and Columbia University, USA

Members

Susan Pancho-Festin	University of the Philippines, Phillippines
Frederik Armknecht	Ruhr University Bochum, Germany
Feng Bao	Institute for Infocomm Research, Singapore
Rodrigo Roman Castro	University of Malaga, Spain
Debbie Cook	Columbia University, USA
Ed Dawson	Queensland University of Technology, Australia
Stefan Katzenbeisser	Technical University Darmstadt, Germany
Brian King	Purdue University, USA
Dongdai Lin	Chinese Academy of Sciences, China
Michael Locasto	George Mason University, USA
Masahiro Mambo	University of Tsukuba, Japan
Atsuko Miyaji	JAIST, Japan
Koji Nakao	KDDI&NICT, Japan
Rolf Oppliger	eSecuriry Technologies, Switzerland
Dan Page	University of Bristol, UK
Namje Park	UCLA, USA
Vassilis Prevelakis	AEGIS Research Center, Greece
Willy Susilo	University of Wollongong, Australia
Tsuyoshi Takagi	Future University Hakodate, Japan

Tzong-Chen Wu	National Taiwan University of Science and Technology, Taiwan
Chung-Huang Yang	National Kaohsiung Normal University, Taiwan
Rui Zhang	AIST, Japan
Joonsang Baek	Institute for Infocomm Research, Singapore
SeongHan Shin	AIST, Japan
Bart Preneel	Katholieke University Leuven, Belgium
Mark Manulis	University of Darmstadt, Germany
H. Kikuchi	Tokai University, Japan
Yanjiang Yang	Institute for Infocomm Research, Singapore
PilJoong Lee	POSTECH, Korea
JaeCheol Ha	Hoseo University, Korea
Jin Kwak	Soonchunhyang University, Korea
Dong Kyue Kim	Hanyang University, Korea
Howon Kim	Pusan National University, Korea
Jung-Chan Na	ETRI, Korea
Yoojae Won	KISA, Korea
Kiwook Sohn	NSRI, Korea
Sung Bum Pan	Chosun University, Korea
Okyeon Yi	Kookmin University, Korea
Sang-Uk Shin	Pukyong National University, Korea
Seungjoo Kim	Sungkyunkwan University, Korea
Jung Hee Cheon	Seoul National University, Korea
Mun-Kyu Lee	Inha University, Korea
Hyung Jong Kim	Seoul Women's University, Korea
Taekyoung Kwon	Sejong University, Korea

Table of Contents

Attack

Biometrics

Secure Protocol

Construction of Identity Based Signcryption Schemes

Sumit Kumar Pandey and Rana Barua

Indian Statistical Institute
Kolkata -700108
{rana,sumit_r}@isical.ac.in

Abstract. In this paper, we show how to construct an Identity Based Signcryption Scheme (IBSC) using an Identity Based Encryption (IBE) and an Identity Based Signature (IBS) schemes. We show that the security of the IBSC scheme–indistinguishability as well as unforgeablity–is derived from the security of the underlying IBE and IBS schemes. Moreover, we show that under mild (reasonable) assumptions, the scheme is both space and time efficient compared to the Sign-then-Encrypt approach.

1 Introduction

In order to simplify key management, Shamir proposed an Identity Based Cryptosystem [18] in 1984. In this cryptosystem, unambiguous identity of a user(such as email address, social security number etc.) is used as a public key and the secret key corresponding to a user is issued by a third party called the Private Key Generator (PKG). Since 1984, although Shamir proposed the first Identity Based Signature (IBS) scheme in his proposal of Identity Based Cryptosystem, there were several proposals for Identity Based Encryption (IBE) schemes. However none fulfilled the demands posed by IBE until 2000 when Sakai-Ohgishi-Kashara [17]and 2001 when Boneh and Franklin [3] proposed an IBE scheme from bilinear pairing on Elliptic Curves. In 2001 again, Cocks [7] proposed an IBE scheme based on quadratic residuosity problem modulo an RSA composite modulus.

In 1997, Zheng[20] proposed a new primitive *viz* signcryption in which encryption and signature are done simultaneously at a much lower computational cost and communication overhead than the Sign-then-Encrypt approach. The scheme in [20] was not formally proved to be secure since no formal notion of security was proposed then. It was only in EUROCRYPT 2002 that An, Dodis and Rabin [1] introduced a formal notion of security for signcryption.

Since the introduction of the primitive, several schemes have been proposed. Very recently, Matsuda-Matsuura-Schuldt [15] gave several simple but efficient contructions of signcryption schemes using existing primitives. In one of the constructions, they inroduced the notion of *signcryption composable* and show how, in this case, a signature scheme and an encryption scheme can be combined to achieve higher efficiency than a simple composition. (Also, [15] gives a nice account of some prevous work on signcryption and has an extensive bibliography.)

Y. Chung and M. Yung (Eds.): WISA 2010, LNCS 6513, pp. 1–14, 2011.
© Springer-Verlag Berlin Heidelberg 2011

In this paper, we consider an efficient construction of an *Identity Based* Signcryption scheme. We will show how to construct an Identity Based Signcryption (IBSC) scheme using any Identity Based Encryption (IBE) scheme and Identity Based Signature (IBS) scheme. Our construction differs from those of [15] in the sense that we do not use the sign-then-encrypt or encrypt-then-sign paradigm. In fact, our construction allows signature and encryption to be done in parallel for increased efficiency. Security of the resulting IBSC scheme is inherited from the security results of the underlying IBE and IBS schemes in the random oracle model. We illustrate our construction by first combining the Boneh-Franklin IBE scheme[3] and the IBS scheme of Shamir[18]. Then we obtain another IBSC scheme by combining Boneh-Franklin IBE with the Kurasawa-Heng IBS ([11], page 113 of [13]). We then compare these schemes with the existing schemes which are known to be efficient and secure and show how the resulting schemes compare with the existing ones.

2   Preliminaries

2.1   Formal Models for Identity Based Encryption

An IBE scheme consists of four algorithms which are the following:

- **Setup:** A probabilistic polynomial time algorithm run by a private key generator (PKG) that takes security parameter as input and outputs a master key msk and public parameters $params$.
- **KeyGen:** A deterministic polynomial time algorithm run by PKG which takes master secret key msk, identity ID and public parameters $Params$ as input and outputs a secret key d_{ID} associated to the identity ID.
- **Encrypt:** A probabilistic polynomial time algorithm that takes a message m, the recipient identity ID_{Rec}, and public parameters $Params$ and outputs a ciphertext $C = Encrypt(m, ID_{Rec}, Params)$.
- **Decrypt:** A deterministic polynomial time algorithm that takes a ciphertext C, recipient identity ID_{Rec}, recipient secret key $d_{ID_{Rec}}$ and public parameters $Params$ as input and outputs m if C is the valid ciphertext of message m else $\perp$.

2.2   Security Notion of IBE Scheme

An IBE scheme is said to be adaptively chosen-ciphertext (IND-CCA2) secure if no probabilistic polynomial time algorithm adversary has a non-negligible advantage in the following game.

- The Challenger runs the Setup algorithm on input of a security parameter and gives the public parameters $Params$ to adversary $\mathcal{A}$.
- Find Stage: $\mathcal{A}$ starts probing the following oracles:
  - KeyGen: returns private keys for arbitrary identities.

- Decryption: given an identity ID_R and a ciphertext C, it generates the receiver's private key $d_{ID_R} = KeyGen(ID_R)$ and returns either plaintext m if C is the valid encryption of m else $\perp$.

$\mathcal{A}$ can submit her queries adaptively in the sense that each query may depend on the previous queries. Once $\mathcal{A}$ decides that above stage is over, she produces two plaintexts m_0, m_1 and an identity ID_R for which she has not extracted the secret key while probing KeyGen oracle. Challenger then chooses a random bit $b \in \{0, 1\}$ and returns the ciphertext $C = Encrypt(m_b, ID_R, Params)$ and sends it to A.

- Guess Stage: A issues new queries same as in the Find stage but she cannot ask for the private key of ID_R. Finally, $\mathcal{A}$ outputs a bit b' and wins if $b' = b$. $\mathcal{A}$'s advantage is defined as $Adv(\mathcal{A}) = |\Pr(b' = b) - \frac{1}{2}|$.

2.3   Formal Models for Identity Based Signature

An IBS scheme consists of four algorithms which are the following:

- **Setup:** A probabilistic polynomial time algorithm run by a private key generator (PKG) that takes security parameter as input and outputs a master key msk and public parameters $params$.
- **KeyGen:** A deterministic polynomial time algorithm run by PKG which takes master secret key msk, identity ID and public parameters $Params$ as input and outputs a secret key d_{ID} associated to the identity ID.
- **Sign:** A probabilistic polynomial time algorithm that takes a message m, the sender's identity ID_{Sen}, sender's secret key $d_{ID_{sen}}$ and public parameters $Params$ and outputs a signature $\sigma = Sig(m, ID_{Sen}, d_{ID_{Sen}}, Params)$.
- **Verify:** A deterministic polynomial time algorithm that takes message m, a signature σ and sender's identity ID_S as input and outputs *accept* if σ is the valid signature of message m else outputs *reject*.

2.4   Security Notion of IBS Scheme

An IBS scheme is said to be existentially unforgeable against chosen message attack if no probabilistic polynomial time algorithm adversary has a non-negligible advantage in the following game:

- The Challenger runs the Setup algorithm on input of a security parameter and gives the public parameters $Params$ to adversary $\mathcal{A}$.
- $\mathcal{A}$ starts probing the following oracles:
  - KeyGen: returns private keys for arbitrary identities.
  - Sign: given an identity ID_S and a message m, it generates the sender's private key $d_{ID_S} = KeyGen(ID_S)$ and returns signature σ on message m associates to the identity ID_S.

Once $\mathcal{A}$ decides that this stage is over, $\mathcal{A}$ produces a triple (m^*, ID_S^*, σ^*) where private key corresponding to ID_S^* has not been extracted before and a message-signature pair (m^*, σ^*) such that (m^*, ID^*) was never submitted to the Sign oracle. $\mathcal{A}$ wins the game if σ^* is the valid signature on message m^* associated to the identity ID_S^*. $\mathcal{A}$'s advantage is defined as the probability of winning the above game.

2.5 Formal Models for Identity Based Signcryption

An IBSC scheme consists of the following four algorithms:

- **Setup:** A probabilistic polynomial time algorithm run by a private key generator (PKG) that takes security parameter as input and outputs a master secret key msk and public parameters $params$ that include a system wide public key.
- **KeyGen:** A deterministic polynomial time algorithm run by the PKG which takes master secret key msk, identity ID and public parameters $Params$ as input and outputs a secret key d_{ID} associated to the identity ID.
- **Signcryption:** A probabilistic polynomial time algorithm that takes a message m, the recipient identity ID_{Rec}, sender's identity ID_{Sen}, sender's private key $d_{ID_{Sen}}$ and public parameters $Params$ as input and outputs a ciphertext $C = Signcryption(m, ID_{Rec}, ID_{Sen}, d_{ID_{Sen}}, Params)$.
- **Designcryption:** A deterministic polynomial time algorithm that takes a ciphertext C, the recipient's identity ID_{Rec}, sender's identity ID_{Sen}, receiver's secret key $d_{ID_{Rec}}$ and public parameters $Params$ as input and outputs either a message $m = $ Designcryption$(C, ID_{Rec}, ID_{Sen}, d_{ID_{Rec}}, Params)$ if C is a valid ciphertext of m or an error symbol $\perp$.

For consistency, it is required that if $C = $ Signcryption$(m, ID_{Rec}, ID_{Sen}, d_{ID_{Sen}}, Params)$ then the output of the Designcryption$(C, ID_{Rec}, ID_{Sen}, d_{ID_{Rec}}, Params)$ is m (and sometimes an additional information that allows receiver to convince a third party that plaintext actually emanates from the sender).

2.6 Security Notion of IBSC Scheme

There are several models of security. We shall consider the strongest notion of confidentiality and unforgeability below.

Confidentiality. An IBSC is said to be indistinguishable against chosen ciphertext attack (IND-IBSC-CCA) if no probabilistic poynomial time adversary has a non-negligible advantage in the following game between the adversary and a challenger.

- The Challenger runs the Setup algorithm on input of security parameters and sends the public parameters, $Params$, to the adversary $\mathcal{A}$.
- Find Stage: $\mathcal{A}$ starts probing the following oracles:
  - KeyGen: returns private key for arbitrary identities.
  - Signcryption: given a pair of identities ID_{Rec}, ID_{Sen} and a plaintext m, it returns an encryption under the receiver's identity ID_{Rec} of the message m signed in the name of the sender ID_{Sen}.
  - Designcryption: given a pair of identities (ID_{Rec}, ID_{Sen}) and a ciphertext C, it generates the receiver's secret key $d_{ID_{Rec}} = $ KeyGen(ID_{Rec}) and returns either a pair (m, s) made of a plaintext m and a transferable authenticating information for the sender's identity ID_{Sen} or the $\perp$ symbol if C does not properly decrypt under the secret key $d_{ID_{Rec}}$.

Once $\mathcal{A}$ decides that this stage is over, it produces two plaintexts m_0, m_1 and identities ID_{Rec} and ID_{Sen} and sends to the challenger. $\mathcal{A}$ should not have extracted the secret key of ID_{Rec} before. Challenger then returns $C = Signcryption(m_b, ID_{Rec}, ID_{Sen}, d_{ID_{Sen}}, Params)$ to $\mathcal{A}$ for a random $b \in \{0,1\}$.

- Guess Stage: $\mathcal{A}$ issues new queries. This time $\mathcal{A}$ may not issue a key extraction request on ID_{Rec}. Finally, $\mathcal{A}$ output a bit b' and wins if $b' = b$.

$\mathcal{A}'s$ advantage is defined as $Adv(\mathcal{A}) = |\Pr(b' = b) - \frac{1}{2}|$.

A weaker notion of *outsider* security does not allow the attacker to corrupt the private key of $ID*_S$ at any time.

Unforgeability. An IBSC scheme is said to be existentially ciphertext unforgeable against adaptive chosen message attacks (ECUF-IBSC-CMA) if no probabilistic polynomial time adversary has a non-negligible advantage in the following game:

- The Challenger runs the Setup algorithm on input of security parameters and sends the public parameters, $Params$, to the adversary $\mathcal{A}$.
- Find Stage: $\mathcal{A}$ starts probing the following oracles:
  - KeyGen: returns private key for arbitrary identities.
  - Signcryption: given a pair of identities ID_{Rec}, ID_{Sen} and a plaintext m, it returns an encryption under the receiver's identity ID_{Rec} of the message m signed in the name of the sender ID_{Sen}.
  - Designcryption: given a pair of identities (ID_{Rec}, ID_{Sen}) and a ciphertext C, it generates the receiver's secret key $d_{ID_{Rec}} = \text{KeyGen}(ID_{Rec})$ and returns either a pair (m, s) made of a plaintext m and a transferable authenticating information for the sender's identity ID_{Sen} or the $\perp$ symbol if C does not properly decrypt under the secret key $d_{ID_{Rec}}$
- Finally, $\mathcal{A}$ produces a triple $(C^*, ID^*_{Rec}, ID^*_{Sen})$ that was not obtained from the Signcryption oracle during find stage and for which the secret key of ID^*_{Sen} was not extracted. The adversary (forger) wins the game if the result of $Designcryption(C^*, ID^*_{Rec}, ID^*_{Sen}, d_{ID^*_{Sen}}, Params)$ is not $\perp$.

The adversary's advantage is its probability of winning the game.

3   Proposed Scheme

Notation:

- $S_{IBE} \rightarrow$ Identity Based Encrytion Scheme.
  - $ENC.S_{IBE}(., \ldots, .) \rightarrow$ Encryption algorithm of S_{IBE}.
  - $DEC.S_{IBE}(., \ldots, .) \rightarrow$ Decryption algorithm of S_{IBE}.
- $S_{IBS} \rightarrow$ Identity Based Signature Scheme.
  - $SIG.S_{IBS}(., \ldots, .) \rightarrow$ Sign algorithm of S_{IBS}.
  - $VER.S_{IBS}(., \ldots, .) \rightarrow$ Verification algorithm of S_{IBS}.

- $SecParam \rightarrow$ Security Parameter.
- $\mathcal{R} \rightarrow$ Random number space.
- $\mathcal{M} \rightarrow$ Message space.
- $\mathcal{C}' \rightarrow$ Ciphertext space of S_{IBE}
- $\mathcal{S}' \rightarrow$ Signature space of S_{IBS} corresponding to message space $\mathcal{M}$.
- $Params_{IBE} \rightarrow$ Public parameters of S_{IBE}.
- $Params_{IBS} \rightarrow$ Public parameters of S_{IBS}.
- $Params \rightarrow$ Public parameters of our signcryption scheme.
- $msk_{IBE} \rightarrow$ Master key of S_{IBE}.
- $msk_{IBS} \rightarrow$ Master key of S_{IBS}.
- $msk \rightarrow$ Master key of our signcryption scheme.
- $KeyGen_{IBE}(.) \rightarrow$ Key generation algorithm of S_{IBE}.
- $KeyGen_{IBS}(.) \rightarrow$ Key generation algorithm of S_{IBS}.

Bit length of message space $\mathcal{M}$, public parameters of S_{IBE}, $Params_{IBE}$, public parameters of S_{IBS}, $Params_{IBS}$, msk_{IBE} and msk_{IBS} depends upon the security parameter. It can be safely assumed that any element from $\mathcal{R}$, $\mathcal{M}$, $\mathcal{C}'$, $\mathcal{S}'$, $Params_{IBE}$, $Params_{IBS}$, msk_{IBE} and msk_{IBS} can be encoded into string of $\{0,1\}$. Let l_1 be the bit-length of message m. We require that bit-length of random number $r \in \mathcal{R}$ should be equal to the bit-length of message m. Let l_2 be the bit length of signature $s \in S'$. Moreover, $Params_{IBE} \cap Params_{IBS} = \phi$.

Setup($SecParam$)

Let $H_1 : \{0,1\}^* \rightarrow \{0,1\}^{l_1}$, $H_2 : \{0,1\}^* \rightarrow \{0,1\}^{l_2}$, $H_3 : \{0,1\}^* \rightarrow \{0,1\}^{l_1}$ be secure hash functions. The public parameter, $Params$, consists of ($Params_{IBE}$, $Params_{IBS}, H_1, H_2, H_3$) and the master key, msk, is (msk_{IBE}, msk_{IBS}).

Key Generation(ID)

Let $sk_{IBE} \leftarrow KeyGen_{IBE}(ID)$ and $sk_{IBS} \leftarrow KeyGen_{IBS}(ID)$. The secret key corresponding to identity ID will be (sk_{IBE}, sk_{IBS}).

Signcryption($m, ID_{Rec}, ID_{Sen}, sk_{ID_{Sen}}, Params$)

1. Choose r randomly from $\mathcal{R}$.
2. Let $c' \leftarrow ENC.S_{IBE}(r, ID_{Rec}, Params_{IBE})$.
3. Compute $h_1 = H_1(r, c', ID_{Sen})$.
4. Compute $h_2 = H_2(m, c', h_1, ID_{Rec}, ID_{Sen})$.
5. Compute $c = H_3(h_1, ID_{Sen}) \oplus m$.
6. Let $sk_{ID_{Sen}} = (sk_{ID_{Sen}IBE}, sk_{ID_{Rec}IBS})$.
   Let $(m, s) \leftarrow SIG.S_{IBS}(m, sk_{ID_{Sen}IBS}, Params_{IBS})$.
7. Compute $d = h_2 \oplus s$.

The Ciphertext will be $C \equiv (c, c', d)$.

Designcryption($C, ID_{Rec}, ID_{Sen}, sk_{ID_{Rec}}, Params$)

1. Let $sk_{ID_{Rec}} = (sk_{ID_{Rec}IBE}, sk_{ID_{Rec}IBS})$.
   Let $r' \leftarrow DEC.S_{IBE}(c', sk_{ID_{Rec}IBE}, Params_{IBE})$.

2. Compute $h'_1 = H_1(r', c', ID_{Sen})$.
3. Compute $m' = H_3(h'_1, ID_{Sen}) \oplus c$.
4. Compute $h'_2 = H_2(m', c', h'_1, ID_{Rec}, ID_{Sen})$.
5. Compute $s' = h'_2 \oplus d$.
6. Let $x \leftarrow VER.S_{IBS}(m', s', ID_{Sen}, Params_{IBS})$.
   - If above step is correctly verified, then $VER.S_{IBS}(., \ldots, .)$ returns m', else $\perp$.
7. Return x.

4 Security

4.1 Message Cofidentiality

We will prove our scheme to be IND-IBSC-CCA secure under the random oracle model if the underlying Identity Based Encryption scheme is IND-ID-CCA secure. Security proof will assume that the *Signcryption* algorithm always takes different identities in the input.

Theorem 1. *In the random oracle model, if there exists an IND-IBSC-CCA adversary $\mathcal{A}$ which is able to distinguish ciphertexts with an advantage ϵ, then there exists an IND-ID-CCA adversary $\mathcal{B}$ that has advantage $\frac{\epsilon}{2}$ against the underlying Identity Based Encryption scheme S_{IBE}.*

Proof. We shall show how to construct an IND-ID-CCA adversary $\mathcal{B}$ that uses $\mathcal{A}$ to gain advantage $\frac{\epsilon}{2}$ against S_{IBE}. Suppose Algorithm $\mathcal{B}$ receives public parameters $Params_{IBE}$ from S_{IBE}. $\mathcal{B}$ chooses an Identity Based Signature scheme S_{IBS} whose public parameters $Params_{IBS}$ are independently generated from the public parameters of S_{IBE}. We can safely assume that $Params_{IBE} \cap Params_{IBS} = \phi$. $\mathcal{B}$ maintains lists L_1, L_2 and L_3 for queries on hash functions H_1, H_2 and H_3. Besides these, $\mathcal{B}$ maintains two other lists $\mathcal{S}_1$ and $\mathcal{S}_2$ for queries on secret keys of different identities corresponding to S_{IBE} and S_{IBS}.

We now explain how requests from $\mathcal{A}$ are treated by $\mathcal{B}$ who plays the role of a challenger to $\mathcal{A}$.

- H_1 queries: For inputs $r_i \in \mathcal{R}$, $c'_i \in \mathcal{C}'$ and $ID_i \in \{0, 1\}^*$ from $\mathcal{A}$, $\mathcal{B}$ searches list L_1 for tuple $(r_i, c'_i, ID_i, h_{1i})$. If such tuple exists $\mathcal{B}$ returns h_{1i} to $\mathcal{A}$, else $\mathcal{B}$ chooses a string uniformly at random from $\{0, 1\}^{l_1}$, say h_{1i}. $\mathcal{B}$ then adds the tuple $(r_i, c'_i, ID_i, h_{1i})$ into the list L_1 and returns h_{1i} to $\mathcal{A}$.
- H_2 queries: For input $m_i \in \mathcal{M}$, $c'_i \in \mathcal{C}'$, $h_i \in \{0, 1\}^{l_1}$, and ID_{1i}, $ID_{2i} \in \{0, 1\}^*$ from $\mathcal{A}$, $\mathcal{B}$ searches the list L_2 for tuple $(m_i, c'_i, h_i, ID_{1i}, ID_{2i}, h_{2i})$. If such a tuple exists, B returns h_{2i} to $\mathcal{A}$, else $\mathcal{B}$ chooses a string uniformly at random from $\{0, 1\}^{l_2}$, say h_{2i}. $\mathcal{B}$ then adds the tuple $(m_i, c'_i, h_i, ID_{1i}, ID_{2i}, h_{2i})$ to the list L_2 and returns h_{2i} to $\mathcal{A}$.
- H_3 queries: For inputs $h_i \in \{0, 1\}^{l_1}$ and $ID_i \in \{0, 1\}^*$ from $\mathcal{A}$, $\mathcal{B}$ searches the list L_3 for a tuple (h_i, ID_i, h_{3i}). If such a tuple exists, $\mathcal{B}$ returns h_{3i} to $\mathcal{A}$, else $\mathcal{B}$ chooses a string h_{3i} uniformly at random from $\{0, 1\}^{l_1}$. $\mathcal{B}$ then adds the tuple (h_i, ID_i, h_{3i}) to the list L_3 and returns h_{3i} to $\mathcal{A}$.

- Secret key queries: For an input ID_i from $\mathcal{A}$, algorithm $\mathcal{B}$ responds to $\mathcal{A}$ in two steps:
  1. $\mathcal{B}$ sends ID_i to S_{IBE}. Let S_{IBE} returns the corresponding secret key sk_{IBE_i}. $\mathcal{B}$ then adds (ID_i, sk_{IBE_i}) into the list $\mathcal{S}_1$.
  2. As the constituent Identity Based Signature scheme, S_{IBS}, is chosen by $\mathcal{B}$, so $\mathcal{B}$ generates the secret key sk_{IBS_i} corresponding to ID_i. $\mathcal{B}$ then adds (ID_i, sk_{IBS_i}) into the list $\mathcal{S}_2$.

  $\mathcal{B}$ finally returns (sk_{IBE_i}, sk_{IBS_i}) to $\mathcal{A}$.
- Signcryption queries: The response to signcryption query for message $m_i \in \mathcal{M}$ corresponding to the receiver's identity ID_{Rec_i} and sender's identity $ID_{Sen_i} \in \{0,1\}^*$ is as follows:
  1. $\mathcal{B}$ searches the list $\mathcal{S}_2$ for the secret key corresponding to identity ID_{Sen_i}. If it does not exist, $\mathcal{B}$ generates the secret key corresponding to ID_{Sen_i} using S_{IBS}. Let sk_{IBS_i} be the corresponding secret key.
  2. $\mathcal{B}$ then runs $Signcryption(m_i, ID_{Rec_i}, ID_{Sen_i}, sk_{IBS_i}, Params)$. Let $C_i \equiv (c_i, c_i', d)$ be the output of the $Signcryption$ algorithm. Then $\mathcal{B}$ returns C_i to $\mathcal{A}$.

  Note that to signcrypt the message corresponding to receiver's identity ID_{Rec}, the secret key of ID_{Rec} is not required. Hence a valid ciphertext can be generated without any secret key query for the receiver's identity to S_{IBE}
- Designcryption queries: For input $C = (c_i, c_i', d)$ where $c_i \in \mathcal{C}$, $c_i' \in \mathcal{C}'$ and $d \in \{0,1\}^{l_2}$, ID_{Rec_i}, $ID_{Sen_i} \in \{0,1\}^*$ (receiver's and sender's identities are ID_{Rec_i} and ID_{Sen_i} respectively), $\mathcal{B}$ sends (c_i', ID_{Rec_i}) to S_{IBE} to decrypt. Let r_i be the output from the decryption algorithm of S_{IBE}. Then $\mathcal{B}$ searches the list L_1 for tuple $(r_i, c_i', ID_{Sen_i}, h_{1i})$. If such a tuple does not exist, $\mathcal{B}$ chooses uniformly at random a string h_{1i} from $\{0,1\}^{l_1}$ and adds $(r_i, c_i', ID_{Sen_i}, h_{1i})$ to the list L_1. Now, $\mathcal{B}$ searches the list L_3 for a tuple $(h_{i1}, ID_{Sen_i}, h_{3i})$. If such a tuple does not exist, $\mathcal{B}$ chooses h_{3i} uniformly at random from $\{0,1\}^{l_1}$ and adds $(h_{1i}, ID_{Sen_i}, h_{3i})$ to the list L_3. $\mathcal{B}$ then computes $m_i = h_{3i} \oplus c_i$. Then, $\mathcal{B}$ searches the list L_2 for tuple $(m_i, c_i', h_{1i}, ID_{Rec_i}, ID_{Sen_i}, h_{2i})$. If such tuple not exist, $\mathcal{B}$ chooses a random string, say h_{2i}, uniformly at random from $\{0,1\}^{l_2}$ and adds $(m_i, c_i', h_{3i}, ID_{Rec_i}, ID_{Sen_i}, h_{2i})$ to the list L_2. $\mathcal{B}$ then returns the appropriate output, consistent with the verification algorithm of S_{IBS}, to $\mathcal{A}$.

Once $\mathcal{A}$ decides to enter the challenge phase, it chooses two messages m_0, m_1 of same length and two indentities ID_R and ID_S corresponding to receiver's and sender's identity respectively and sends them to $\mathcal{B}$. $\mathcal{B}$ then chooses two random strings $r_0, r_1 \in \{0,1\}^{l_1}$ and receiver's identity ID_R and sends them to S_{IBE}. S_{IBE} then chooses a bit, say b, uniformly at random from $\{0,1\}$ and computes the ciphertext c' associated to receiver's identity. S_{IBE} then sends the ciphertext c' to $\mathcal{B}$. $\mathcal{B}$ then chooses a bit $v \in \{0,1\}$ uniformly at random. $\mathcal{B}$ then searches the list L_1 for tuple (r_v, c', ID_S, h_1). If such tuple does not exist, $\mathcal{B}$ chooses uniformly at random h_1 from $\{0,1\}^{l_1}$ and adds (r_v, c', ID_S, h_1) into the list L_1.

Now, $\mathcal{B}$ searches the list L_2 for tuple $(m_v, c', h_1, ID_R, ID_S, h_2)$. If such tuple does not exist, $\mathcal{B}$ chooses a random string, say h_2, uniformly at random from $\{0,1\}^{l_2}$ and adds $(m_v, c', h_3, ID_R, ID_S, h_2)$ into the list L_2. Then $\mathcal{B}$ searches the list L_3 for tuple (h_1, ID_S, h_3). If such tuple doesn't exist, $\mathcal{B}$ chooses a number, say h_3 uniformly at random from $\{0,1\}^{l_1}$ and adds (h_1, ID_S, h_3) into the list L_3. Then $\mathcal{B}$ searches the list $\mathcal{S}_2$ for secret key corresponding to identity ID_S. Let secret key be sk_{IBS}. After that $\mathcal{B}$ runs S_{IBS} on message m_v and identity ID_S to get signature. Let $(m_v, s') = S_{IBS}(m_v, sk_{IBS})$. Now, $\mathcal{B}$ computes $c = h_3 \oplus m_v$ and $d = h_2 \oplus s'$ and sends the ciphertext $C \equiv (c, c', d)$ to $\mathcal{A}$.

$\mathcal{A}$ then performs a second series of queries (except secret key query on identity ID_R) which is treated in the same way.

Note that in the above game, $\mathcal{B}$ interacts with S_{IBE} as in the real game. Secret key query for identity ID_R has not been asked by $\mathcal{A}$ to $\mathcal{B}$, hence by $\mathcal{B}$ to S_{IBE}.

At the end of the simulation, $\mathcal{B}$ will use the bit guessed by $\mathcal{A}$ to guess the challenge bit with S_{IBE}. If $\mathcal{A}$ guesses $w \in \{0,1\}$, $\mathcal{B}$ will also guess the same bit *viz* w. At challenge phase,

- If $b = v$, the simulation is perfect and the ciphertext, C, produced by $\mathcal{B}$ will be the valid ciphertext of message m_v corresponding to ID_R (receiver's identity) and ID_S (sender's identity). Consequently,

$$\Pr(\mathcal{B} \text{ wins} \mid b = v) = \Pr(\mathcal{A} \text{ wins} \mid C \text{ is a valid ciphertext})$$

- If $b \neq v$, then r_v can be thought of as chosen uniformly at random from $\{0,1\}^{l_1} \setminus \{r_b\}$. To $\mathcal{A}$'s view r_v and c' are independent. Hence, the output from H_1 and hence from H_2 and H_3 are, to $\mathcal{A}$'s view, strings uniformly chosen at random from $\{0,1\}^{l_2}$ and $\{0,1\}^{l_1}$ respectively. Thus XOR of h_2 and h_3 with s' and message m_v, i.e. $d = h_2 \oplus s'$ and $c = h_3 \oplus m_v$, results in strings with uniformly distribution in $\{0,1\}^{l_2}$ and $\{0,1\}^{l_1}$ respectively. Thus to $\mathcal{A}$'s view, $C = (c, c', d)$ is a random ciphertext chosen uniformly from the ciphertext space. Hence, in this case

$$\Pr(\mathcal{B} \text{ wins} \mid b \neq v) = \Pr(\mathcal{A} \text{ wins} \mid C \text{ is a random ciphertext}) = 1/2$$

Therefore,
$$\Pr(\mathcal{B} \text{ wins}) = \Pr(\mathcal{B} \text{ wins} \mid b = v) \times \Pr(b = v) +$$
$$\Pr(\mathcal{B} \text{ wins} \mid b \neq v) \times \Pr(b \neq v)$$
$$= \tfrac{1}{2}(\Pr(\mathcal{B} \text{ wins} \mid b = v)) + \tfrac{1}{2}(\tfrac{1}{2})$$
$$= \tfrac{1}{2}(\Pr(\mathcal{B} \text{ wins} \mid b = v) + \tfrac{1}{2})$$

Hence, advantage of
$\mathcal{B} = Adv(\mathcal{B}) = |\Pr(\mathcal{B} \text{ wins}) - \tfrac{1}{2}|$
$= \tfrac{1}{2}(|(\Pr(\mathcal{B} \text{ wins} \mid b = v) - \tfrac{1}{2})|) = \tfrac{1}{2}(|\Pr(\mathcal{A} \text{ wins}) - \tfrac{1}{2}|) = \tfrac{1}{2}(Adv(\mathcal{A})) = \tfrac{\epsilon}{2}$

4.2 Ciphertext Unforgeability

We can similarly prove ciphertext unforgeability. We show that our scheme is ECUF-IBSC-CMA secure under the random oracle model provided the underlying IBS scheme is secure under adaptive chosen message attack.

Theorem 2. *In the random oracle model, if there exists an ECUF-IBSC-CMA forger $\mathcal{A}$ which is able to produce a forged ciphertext with an advantage ϵ, then there exists an algorithm $\mathcal{B}$ for an adaptively chosen message attack which can forge the IBS scheme S_{IBS} with advantage ϵ.*

Proof. Suppose algorithm $\mathcal{B}$ receives public parameters $Params_{IBS}$ from S_{IBS}. Then $\mathcal{B}$ will choose an Identity Based Encryption scheme S_{IBS} whose public parameters $Params_{IBE}$ are independently generated from the public parameters of S_{IBS}. We assume that $Params_{IBS} \cap Params_{IBE} = \phi$. $\mathcal{B}$ maintains lists L_1, L_2 and L_3 for queries on hash functions H_1, H_2 and H_3. Besides these, $\mathcal{B}$ maintains two other lists $\mathcal{S}_1$ and $\mathcal{S}_2$ for queries on secret keys of different identities corresponding to S_{IBE} and S_{IBS} .

We now explain how requests from $\mathcal{A}$ are treated by $\mathcal{B}$. The response to H_1, H_2 and H_3 queries are exactly as in th proof of Theorem 4.1.

- Secret key queries: To a query for ID_i from $\mathcal{A}$, $\mathcal{B}$ responds to $\mathcal{A}$ in two steps:

  1. $\mathcal{B}$ sends ID_i to S_{IBS}. Let S_{IBS} return the corresponding secret key sk_{IBS_i}. $\mathcal{B}$ then adds (ID_i, sk_{IBS_i}) to the list $\mathcal{S}_2$ corresponding to entry ID_i.
  2. As the constituent Identity Based Encryption scheme, S_{IBE}, is chosen by $\mathcal{B}$, so $\mathcal{B}$ generates the secret key sk_{IBE_i} corresponding to ID_i. $\mathcal{B}$ then adds (ID_i, sk_{IBE_i}) to the list $\mathcal{S}_1$ corresponding to entry ID_i.

  $\mathcal{B}$ finally returns (sk_{IBE_i}, sk_{IBS_i}) to $\mathcal{A}$.
- Signcryption queries: For input $m_i \in \mathcal{M}$, ID_{Rec_i}, $ID_{Sen_i} \in \{0,1\}^*$ (receiver's and sender's identities are ID_{Rec_i} and ID_{Sen_i} respectively), $\mathcal{B}$ sends (m_i, ID_{Sen_i}) to S_{IBS} to get a signature for m_i. Let s_i be the output from the signature algorithm of S_{IBS}. $\mathcal{B}$ then chooses some $r_i \in \mathcal{R}$ and runs the Encryption algorithm of S_{IBE} corresponding to input (r_i, ID_{Rec_i}). Let c_i' be the output of the encryption algorithm of S_{IBE}. Then $\mathcal{B}$ searches the list L_1 for a tuple $(r_i, c_i', ID_{Sen_i}, h_{1i})$. If such a tuple does not exist, $\mathcal{B}$ chooses a a string uniformly at random, say h_{1i}, from $\{0,1\}^{l_1}$ and adds $(r_i, c_i', ID_{Sen_i}, h_{1i})$ to the list L_1. Now, $\mathcal{B}$ searches the list L_3 for tuple $(h_{1i}, ID_{Sen_i}, h_{3i})$. If no such tuple exists, $\mathcal{B}$ chooses h_{3i}, say, uniformly at random from $\{0,1\}^{l_1}$ and adds $(h_{1i}, ID_{Sen_i}, h_{3i})$ to the list L_3. $\mathcal{B}$ then computes $c_i = h_{3i} \oplus m_i$. Then, $\mathcal{B}$ searches the list L_2 for tuple $(m_i, c_i', h_{1i}, ID_{Rec_i}, ID_{Sen_i}, h_{2i})$. If such tuple does not exist, $\mathcal{B}$ chooses a random string, say h_{2i}, uniformly at random from $\{0,1\}^{l_2}$ and adds $(m_i, c_i', h_{3i}, ID_{Rec_i}, ID_{Sen_i}, h_{2i})$ into the list L_2. $\mathcal{B}$ then computes $d_i = h_{2i} \oplus s_i$ and returns $C_i = (c_i, c_i', d_i)$ to $\mathcal{A}$.
- Designcryption queries: Designcryption query for ciphertext $C_i = (c_i, c_i', d_i)$ where $c_i \in \mathcal{C}, c_i' \in \mathcal{C}'$ and $d \in \{0,1\}^{l_2}$ corresponding to the receiver's identity ID_{Rec_i} and sender's identity $ID_{Sen_i} \in \{0,1\}^*$ is executed as follows:

  1. $\mathcal{B}$ searches the list $\mathcal{S}_1$ for the secret key corresponding to identity ID_{Rec_i}. If it does not exist, $\mathcal{B}$ generates the secret key corresponding to ID_{Rec_i} using the key generation algorithm of S_{IBE}. Let sk_{IBE_i} be the corresponding secret key.

2. $\mathcal{B}$ then runs Designcryption($C_i, ID_{Rec_i}, ID_{Sen_i}, sk_{IBE_i}, Params$). Let x be the output of the Designcryption algorithm. $\mathcal{B}$ then returns x to $\mathcal{A}$.

Note that to designcrypt the message associated to sender's identity ID_{Sen}, only the receiver's secret key is required. One does not require the secret key of ID_{Sen}.

Once this game is over, $\mathcal{A}$ submits a ciphertext $C = (c, c', d)$ corresponding to the receiver's identity ID_{Rec} and the sender's identity ID_{Sen} such that the secret key corresponding to ID_{Sen} have not been queried earlier. $\mathcal{B}$ then decrypts c' corresponding to the receiver's identity ID_{Rec}. Let r be the output of the decryption algorithm. $\mathcal{B}$ then searches the list L_1 for a tuple of the form (r, c', ID_{Sen}, h_1). If no such tuple exists, $\mathcal{B}$ chooses a uniformly at random a string, say h_1, from $\{0,1\}^{l_1}$ and adds (r, c', ID_{Sen}, h_1) to the list L_1. Then $\mathcal{B}$ searches the list L_3 for tuple (h_1, ID_S, h_3). If such a tuple does not exist, $\mathcal{B}$ chooses h_3, say, uniformly at random from $\{0,1\}^{l_1}$ and adds (h_1, ID_{Sen}, h_3) to the list L_3 and then computes $m = c \oplus h_3$. $\mathcal{B}$ then searches the list L_2 for a tuple $(m, c', h_1, ID_{Rec}, ID_{Sen}, h_2)$. If such a tuple does not exist, $\mathcal{B}$ chooses h_2 uniformly at random from $\{0,1\}^{l_2}$ and adds $(m, c', h_3, ID_{Rec}, ID_{Sen}, h_2)$ to the list L_2 and computes $s = d \oplus h_2$. Finally, $\mathcal{B}$ submits (m, s) corresponding to the sender's identity ID_{Sen}.

It is clear if $C = (c, c', d)$ is a valid ciphertext corresponding to receiver's identity ID_{Rec} and sender's identity ID_{Sen}, then (m, s) is a valid message-signature pair for the sender's identiy ID_{Sen}.

Hence, advantage of $\mathcal{B} = \mathcal{A}dv(\mathcal{B}) = \Pr(\mathcal{B} \text{ wins}) = \epsilon$.

5   Efficiency

1. Time Efficiency: Our proposed scheme is based upon Encrypt and Sign paradigm, where a random number is encrypted instead of a message. Hence, encryption amd signature can be done in parallel in the signcryption algorithm. Let t_E, t_S and t_H be the time taken by the encryption, sign and hash algorithms respectively. Then, assuming that the signature and encryption are computed concurrently, the time taken by our scheme will be $T = \max(t_E, t_S) + 3t_H$; whereas in the Sign-then-Encrypt approach, the total time taken will be $t_E + t_S$. In general, $t_H << (t_E \text{ or } t_S)$.

2. Space Efficiency: In many cases, in practice, the ciphertext length bears (approx.) a constant ratio with the plaintext. This is also the case with many signature schemes. Let the output length of the encryption algorithm be (at most) αl_1, where l_1 is the bit length of message m. Let the output length of the signature corresponding to a l_1 bit message be (at most) $l_2 = \beta l_1$. Hence, the total length of ciphertext will be (at most) $(\alpha + \beta + 1)l_1$. But in the Sign-then-Encrypt approach, ciphertext length will be, roughly, $\alpha(\beta + 1)l_1$. Hence, our scheme is likely to produce a shorter ciphertext length compared to the Sign-then-Encrypt approach if $\alpha \geq \frac{1}{\beta} + 1$.

Table 1. Efficiency Comparisons

Scheme	Signcryption			Designcryption			Ciphertext Overhead
	E	P	SM	E	P	SM	
Boyen IBSC [5]	1	1	3	0	4	2	$2|G_1| + |ID| + |M|$
Chen-Malone-Lee IBSC [6]	0	1	3	0	3	1	$2|G_1| + |ID| + |M|$
Barreto et. al. IBSC [2]	1	0	3	1	2	1	$2|G_1| + |M|$
Different IBSC constructed using our generic method							
BF-IBE [3] + SH-IBS [18]	1	1	1	2	1	1	$|G_1| + 2|Z_N^*| + 3|M|$
BF-IBE [3] + KH-IBS ([11], [13])	1	1	2	1	2	1	$2|G_1| + |Z_q^*| + 3|M|$

- E denotes number of exponentiation.
- P denotes number of pairing. We assume $e : G_1 \times G_1 \rightarrow G_T$, if e is a symmetric bilinear map, else $e : G_1 \times G_2 \rightarrow G_T$, in case of asymmetric bilinear map.
- SM denotes number of scalar multiplication of a point on elliptic curve.
- $|G_1|$ denotes the bit length of an element in group G_1 used in pairing.
- $|G_2|$ denotes the bit length of an element in group G_2 used in pairing.
- $|G_T|$ denotes the bit length of an element in group G_T used in pairing.
- $|ID|$ denotes the bit length of an identity.
- $|M|$ denotes the message length.
- $|Z_N^*|$ denotes the length of an element in Z_N^* where $N = pq$ is the product of two prime numbers p and q.
- $|Z_q^*|$ denotes the length of an element of Z_q^*. Here q is a prime number.
- BF-IBE denotes Boneh-Franklin Identity Based Encryption scheme [3].
- SH-IBS denotes Shamir Identity Based Signature scheme [18].
- KH-IBS denotes Kurosawa-Heng Identity Based Signature scheme ([11],[13]).

6   Comparisons

Using our generic method, we composed two IBSC scheme - first one by composing Boneh-Franklin Identity Based Encryption (BF-IBE) [3] with Shamir's Identity Based Signature (SH-IBS) [18] scheme and the second one by composing Boneh-Franklin IBE [3] with Kurosawa-Heng Identity Based Signature (KH-IBS) ([11], page 113 of [13]) scheme. We compared these schemes with the Identity Based Sgncryption (IBSC) schemes proposed by Boyen [5], Chen-Malone-Lee [6] and Barreto et. al. [2]. BF-IBE + SH-IBS (Boneh-Franklin IBE and Shamir IBS) has more than double ciphertext overhead and BF-IBE + KH-IBS (Boneh-Franklin IBE and Kurosawa-Heng IBS) has almost double ciphertext overhead than IBSC schemes proposed by Boyen, Chen-Malone-Lee and Barreto. In case of time efficiency, both schemes (BF-IBE + SH-IBS and BF-IBE + KH-IBS) take less time in signcryption (note to remember that in our method, in signcryption, encryption and signature algorithm can be run in parallel) and designcryption compared to Boyen and Chen-Malone-Lee IBSC scheme. Barreto's scheme has lower cost of computation in signcryption than that of BF-IBE + SH-IBS and BF-IBE + KH-IBS but in designcryption, BF-IBE + SH-IBS has lower and BF-IBE + KH-IBS has almost equal cost of computation than that of Barreto. Summary of the efficiency comparisons has been given in table 1.

References

1. An, J.H., Dodis, Y., Rabin, T.: On the security of joint signature and encryption. In: Knudsen, L.R. (ed.) EUROCRYPT 2002. LNCS, vol. 2332, pp. 83–107. Springer, Heidelberg (2002)
2. Barreto, P.S.L.M., Libert, B., McCullagh, N., Quisquater, J.-J.: Efficient and provably-secure identity-based signatures and signcryption from bilinear maps. In: Roy, B. (ed.) ASIACRYPT 2005. LNCS, vol. 3788, pp. 515–532. Springer, Heidelberg (2005)
3. Boneh, D., Franklin, M.: Identity-based encryption from the Weil pairing. In: Kilian, J. (ed.) CRYPTO 2001. LNCS, vol. 2139, pp. 213–229. Springer, Heidelberg (2001)
4. Boneh, D., Gentry, C., Hamburg, M.: Space-Efficient Identity Based Encryption Without Pairings. In: FOCS 2007, pp. 647–657. IEEE Computer Society, Los Alamitos (2007)
5. Boyen, X.: Multipurpose identity-based signcryption: A swiss army knife for identity-based cryptography. In: Boneh, D. (ed.) CRYPTO 2003. LNCS, vol. 2729, pp. 383–399. Springer, Heidelberg (2003)
6. Chen, L., Malone-Lee, J.: Improved identity-based signcryption. In: Davida, G.I., Frankel, Y., Rees, O. (eds.) InfraSec 2002. LNCS, vol. 2437, pp. 260–275. Springer, Heidelberg (2002)
7. Cocks, C.: An Identity-based encryption based on quadratic residues. In: Honary, B. (ed.) Cryptography and Coding 2001. LNCS, vol. 2260, pp. 360–363. Springer, Heidelberg (2001)
8. Gentry, C.: Practical Identity-Based Encryption without Random Oracles. In: Vaudenay, S. (ed.) EUROCRYPT 2006. LNCS, vol. 4004, pp. 445–464. Springer, Heidelberg (2006)
9. Gentry, C., Peikert, C., Vaikuntanathan, V.: Trapdoors for hard lattices and new cryptographic constructions. In: STOC 2008, pp. 197–206. ACM, New York (2008)
10. Hess, F.: Efficient Identity Based Signature Schemes based on Pairings. In: Nyberg, K., Heys, H.M. (eds.) SAC 2002. LNCS, vol. 2595, pp. 310–324. Springer, Heidelberg (2003)
11. Kurosawa, K., Heng, S.H.: Identity-based identification without random oracles. In: Gervasi, O., Gavrilova, M.L., Kumar, V., Laganá, A., Lee, H.P., Mun, Y., Taniar, D., Tan, C.J.K. (eds.) ICCSA 2005. LNCS, vol. 3481, pp. 603–613. Springer, Heidelberg (2005)
12. Libert, B., Quisquater, J.J.: New identity based signcryption schemes from pairings, http://eprint.iacr.org/2003/023.pdf
13. Libert, B.: New Secure Applications of Bilinear Maps in Cryptography. Ph.D. Thesis, Catholic University, Louvain (2006)
14. Malone-Lee, J.: Identity Based Signcryption, http://eprint.iacr.org/2002/098.pdf
15. Matsuda, T., Matsuura, K., Schuldt, J.C.N.: Efficient Constructions of Signcryption Schemes and Signcryption Composability. In: Roy, B., Sendrier, N. (eds.) INDOCRYPT 2009. LNCS, vol. 5922, pp. 321–342. Springer, Heidelberg (2009)
16. Paterson, K.G., Schuldt, J.C.N.: Efficient Identity-based Signatures Secure in the Standard Model, http://eprint.iacr.org/2006/080.pdf

17. Sakai, R., Ohgishi, K., Kasahara, M.: Cryptosystems Based on Pairing. In: Symposium on Cryptography and Information Security-SCIS (2000)
18. Shamir, A.: Identity Based Cryptosystems and Signature Schemes. In: Blakely, G.R., Chaum, D. (eds.) CRYPTO 1984. LNCS, vol. 196, pp. 47–53. Springer, Heidelberg (1985)
19. Waters, B.: Efficient Identity-Based Encryption Without Random Oracles. In: Cramer, R. (ed.) EUROCRYPT 2005. LNCS, vol. 3494, pp. 114–127. Springer, Heidelberg (2005)
20. Zheng, Y.: Digital Signcryption or how to achieve Cost(Signature & Encryption) << Cost(Signature)+Cost(Encryption). In: Kaliski Jr., B.S. (ed.) CRYPTO 1997. LNCS, vol. 1294, pp. 165–179. Springer, Heidelberg (1997)

Predicate-Based Authenticated Key Exchange Resilient to Ephemeral Key Leakage

Atsushi Fujioka, Koutarou Suzuki, and Kazuki Yoneyama

NTT Information Sharing Platform Laboratories
3-9-11 Midori-cho Musashino-shi Tokyo 180-8585, Japan
{fujioka.atsushi,suzuki.koutarou,yoneyama.kazuki}@lab.ntt.co.jp

Abstract. We provide the first eCK security model for predicate-based authenticated key exchange (AKE) to guarantee resistance to leakage of ephemeral secret keys. We also propose an two-pass attribute-based AKE protocol secure in the proposed predicate-based eCK security model based on a attribute-based encryption. The proposed protocol has advantages in security against leakage of ephemeral secret keys and the round complexity compared to the previous predicate-based AKE protocol.

Keywords: predicate-based AKE, eCK security.

1 Introduction

Authenticated key exchange (AKE) protocols allow each user to establish a common session key secretly and reliably with the intended peer based on each user's static secret keys. Recently, studies on ID-based AKE [8,11] have received much attention in usable sense regarding the management of certificates. Moreover, predicate-based AKEs [9,4], in which the user identifies the peer by *specifying the attributes*, were proposed as a natural extension of ID-based AKE. For example, user U wants to establish a session key with someone who offers a service, but U may not want to reveal any information except whether U has a right to receive the service or not. In another situation, U is not concerned with the peer's ID but with the peer's condition (i.e., attributes or policy) specified by U. For such situations where ID-based AKE is not applicable, predicate-based AKE is quite useful.

In the predicate-based AKE scenario, each user U is first given a static secret key based on his condition γ_U by the key generation center (KGC). Next, U (U') specifies the condition δ_U (δ'_U), which the peer U' (U) is expected to satisfy, and exchanges ephemeral information with U' (U), respectively. Then, a session key between users U with the condition γ_U and U' with the condition $\gamma_{U'}$ can be established if and only if γ_U satisfies $\delta_{U'}$ and $\gamma_{U'}$ satisfies δ_U, where γ_U and $\gamma_{U'}$ are the conditions which the user expects the other to satisfy. We represent whether γ satisfies δ with a predicate $P : \{0,1\}^l \times \{0,1\}^l \to \{0,1\}$, where l is a positive integer. When two users U and U' perform predicate-based AKE, both user can compute the session key if and only if $P(\gamma_U, \delta_{U'}) = 1$ and $P(\gamma_{U'}, \delta_U) = 1$. These conditions γ_U and δ_U can be implemented as an access policy and a set of attributes. Note that, the identity is a kind of policy or attribute.

Y. Chung and M. Yung (Eds.): WISA 2010, LNCS 6513, pp. 15–30, 2011.
© Springer-Verlag Berlin Heidelberg 2011

1.1   Motivation

In the context of the secret handshake protocols, some protocols can be used to achieve the predicate-based AKE scenario. Ateniese, Kirsch and Blanton [1] proposed a secret handshake protocol with dynamic and fuzzy matching, where users specify the attribute of the peer. However, their protocol can deal with only the simple authentication condition of whether the attributes match more than a threshold.

Wang, Xu and Ban [16], and Wang, Xu and Fu [17,18] proposed simple variants of predicate-based AKE. In their protocols, attributes are regarded as identification strings, and there is no mechanism for evaluating policy predicates. Thus, their protocols are a kind of ID-based AKE rather than predicate-based AKE.

Gorantla, Boyd and Nieto [9] proposed attribute-based AKE protocol (GBN10). Their protocol provides users with access control based on the users' attributes. However, the condition is common for all users. Thus, the GBN10 protocol does not fit in the predicate-based AKE scenario since each user cannot specify the condition in which the peers are expected to satisfy each other in the protocol. The GBN10 protocol is constructed based on the predicate-based key encapsulation mechanism (KEM) and security is proved in the security model based on the Bellare-Rogaway (BR) model [3].

Birkett and Stebila (BS10) [4] proposed predicate-based AKE protocol (BS10). Their protocol is generically constructed with a predicate-based signature. They prove security of their protocol without random oracles in the security model based on the BR model [3].

However, security in [9] and [4] cannot guarantee resistance to *leakage of ephemeral secret keys*, because the BR model does not capture the leakage of ephemeral secret keys. Leakage of ephemeral secret keys will occur due to various factors, e.g., the pseudo-random generator implemented in the system is poor, the ephemeral secret key itself is leaked by physical attacks such as side channel attacks. Thus, resistance to leakage of ephemeral secret keys is regarded as essential for AKE protocols, and the extended Canetti-Krawzcyk (eCK) security model [13], which captures leakage of ephemeral secret keys, is widely used for security proofs of recent AKE protocols. As Birkett and Stebila stated in their conclusion [4], there is no predicate-based AKE protocol that satisfies resistance to leakage of ephemeral secret keys, and finding such a protocol has been an open problem.

To prove the security in the eCK model (eCK security), it is known that the NAXOS technique [13] is effective. The NAXOS technique involves that each user applying a hash function to the static and ephemeral secret keys, and computing an ephemeral public key by using the output of the function as the exponent of the ephemeral public key. An adversary cannot know the output of the function as long as the adversary cannot obtain the static secret key even if the ephemeral secret key is leaked. Here, it is may be worth to note that the BS10 protocol does not become secure against leakage of ephemeral secret keys because we have no predicate-based signature, which is secure against revealing the randomness used in signing, and the NAXOS technique cannot be applied the underlying signature trivially.

Another problem of the BS10 protocol is in the communication round. Most eCK secure AKE protocols only need two-pass message transmission with no key confirmation, where key confirmation means that each user can explicitly verify that the session key is common with the peer. If necessary, key confirmation is easily obtained by sending confirmation information as the last pass. In the BS10 protocol, key confirmation is mandatory, and so the protocol always needs three passes. On some applications, predicate-based AKE is not necessarily required to have key confirmation. Since the construction of the BS10 protocol is based on the signed-DH paradigm [7], the third pass (for key confirmation) in the BS10 protocol cannot be removed for the security proof. Hence, the construction of two-pass eCK secure predicate-based AKE with no key confirmation has certain significance.

1.2 Contribution

In this paper, we have mainly two contributions: the first definition of predicate-based eCK security model, and the first construction of attribute-based AKE protocol, which needs only two-pass message transmission and is secure in the predicate-based eCK security model.

Predicate-Based eCK Security Model. In contrast with the security model used by Birkett and Stebila [4] (based on the BR model), we allow the adversary to obtain static secret keys, the master key, and ephemeral secret keys individually to make the eCK model suitable to the predicate-based AKE setting. Of course, if the adversary obtains the ephemeral secret key and the static secret key of an user (or the master key) together, the session key can be justly computed by the adversary. Thus, we have to consider the *freshness* of the session. Freshness is the condition of the session in which the adversary cannot trivially break the secrecy of the session key. Although the adversary is not allowed to reveal any secret information of the fresh session in the security model used in [4], we allow the adversary to take most malicious behaviors concerned with revealing secret information in the proposed security model. In the predicate-based AKE setting, especially, a static secret key corresponding to condition γ may also be usable as the static secret key corresponding to another condition γ' if γ' implies γ. Thus, our freshness definition is defined carefully in such am implication.

Moreover, compared with the security models for AKE and ID-based AKE, the role of the static key is different. In AKE and ID-based AKE, the static public key is directly used to construct the session key. On the other hand, there is no notion of the static public key and the static secret key is only used to give access control in predicate-based AKE. Thus, the security model does not require that the session identity contains static keys.

Notice that our definition of predicate-based eCK security model captures only *payload hiding* and does not capture *attribute hiding*. since we consider *payload hiding* is basic property for predicate-based AKE following [12], which says in the introduction that payload hiding is considered 'the "basic" level of security' and attribute hiding is considered 'a stronger notion of security' for predicate-based encryption. Comparing with our definition, the definition of Birkett and Stebila [4] captures both payload hiding and attribute hiding, however does not capture leakage of secret keys.

Birkett and Stebila [4] says that if attribute hiding is not needed, one can trivially construct predicate-based AKE by combining credential and public key based AKE. This is the case for *explicitly* authenticated key exchange with three-pass of [4]. However, for our *implicitly* authenticated key exchange with two-pass, this is not the case, so attribute hiding is not necessary.

Two-Pass Attribute-Based AKE Protocol. We proposes an two-pass attribute-based authenticated key exchange (AKE) protocol based on a attribute-based encryption [14,10]. The attribute-based AKE is a specific case of predicate-based AKE, where a predicate $P(\gamma, \delta)$ is implemented as follows; the first input γ of P corresponds to an access tree on the attribute set and the second input δ of P corresponds to a subset of the attribute set, and the output of P corresponds to whether the subset δ of the attribute set satisfies the access tree γ on the attribute set. And we prove that the proposed two-pass attribute-based AKE is secure in the predicate-based eCK security model as predicate-based AKE.

Birkett and Stebila [4] proposed generic construction of predicate-based AKE from predicate-based signature. However, their concrete implementation uses attribute-based signature, so the resulting AKE scheme is attribute-based AKE.

In attribute-based encryption schemes [14,10], the receiver's secret key is generated from an access policy of the receiver, and a set of attributes is embedded in the ciphertext. Thus, when the set of attributes of the ciphertext satisfies the access policy of the secret key, the receiver can decrypt the ciphertext. To apply this mechanism [10] to attribute-based AKE, we adapt the access policy to condition γ and the set of attributes to condition δ. Hence, the proposed protocol allows each user to specify the set of attributes the peer is expected to satisfy and user's secret key is generated from user's access policy, i.e., the proposed protocol is key-policy attribute-based AKE. And notice that the proposed protocol is the first key-policy attribute-based AKE.

Next, to guarantee resistance to leakage of ephemeral secret keys, we apply the NAXOS technique [13] to our protocol. Thus, even if an adversary obtains the ephemeral secret key, the session key established in the session is concealed from the adversary. In contrast with the BS10 protocol, our protocol can match the NAXOS technique because our scheme does not use a attribute-based signature as a building block but uses attribute-based encryption.

The proposed protocol is achieves efficiency in two-pass message transmission, though the BS10 protocol needs three passes. Our protocol does not have key confirmation, but it is not essential for AKE. If key confirmation is required, it is easy to change the ordinary two-pass AKE protocol to have key confirmation by sending confirmation information as the third pass. Generally, since a session using the session key follows after the AKE session, we can simultaneously send confirmation information in the first pass of the following session.

In Section 2, we define the predicate-based eCK security model. In Section 3, we propose our two-pass attribute-based AKE protocol, which is secure in the predicate-based eCK security model. In Section 4, we conclude the paper.

Related Work. Models for key agreement were introduced by Bellare and Rogaway [3] and Blake-Wilson, Johnson and Menezes [5], in the shared- and public-key settings, respectively. Recent developments in two-party certificate-based AKE in the public-key infrastructure (PKI) setting have improved the security models and definitions, i.e., Canetti-Krawzcyk security model [7] and LaMacchia, Lauter and Mityagin's eCK security model [13].

There are ID-based AKE protocols, see for example [8,15]. Boyd and Choo [6] state that many existing ID-based AKE protocols are not as secure as we expect them to be. Furthermore, security analysis for ID-based AKE protocols do not formally analyze ephemeral private key leakage. The only protocol that formally considers this scenario is that proposed by Huang and Cao [11].

2   eCK Security Model for Predicate-Based AKE

In this section, we provide an eCK security model for predicate-based AKE. Our predicate-based eCK security model is an extension of the eCK security model for PKI-based AKE by LaMacchia, Lauter and Mityagin [13] to predicate-based AKE.

The proposed eCK security model for predicate-based AKE is different from the original eCK security model for PKI-based AKE in the following points: 1) the session is identified by the string γ_i of user U_i, 2) freshness conditions for StaticKeyReveal queries are different, and 3) MasterKeyReveal query is allowed for the adversary same as in ID-based AKE.

Algorithms. Predicate-based AKE protocol Π consists of the following algorithms. We denote a user as U_i and the user's associated string as γ_i. User U_i and other parties are modeled as a probabilistic polynomial-time Turing machine. Predicate $P : \{0,1\}^l \times \{0,1\}^l \to \{0,1\}$, where l is an integer, is given as a part of the public parameters. Predicate P takes two input strings γ and δ and outputs a bit $P(\gamma, \delta) = 1$ or 0.

Key Generation. The key generation algorithm KeyGen takes a security parameter 1^k as input, and outputs a master secret key msk and a master public key mpk, i.e., KeyGen(1^k) $\to (msk, mpk)$.

Key Extraction. The key extraction algorithm KeyExt takes the master secret key msk, the master public key mpk, and a string γ_i given by user U_i, which encode the user's condition, and outputs a static secret key ssk_{γ_i} corresponding to the string γ_i, i.e., KeyExt(msk, mpk, γ_i) $\to ssk_{\gamma_i}$.

Key Exchange. Users U_A and U_B share a session key by performing the following n-pass protocol. User U_A (U_B) selects string δ_A (δ_B), which encode the user's attribute.

User U_A starts the protocol by computing the 1st message m_1 by using the algorithm Message, which takes the master public key mpk, the string γ_A, the static secret key ssk_{γ_A}, and the string δ_A, and outputs 1st message m_1, i.e., Message$(mpk, \gamma_A, ssk_{\gamma_A}, \delta_A) \to m_1$. User U_A sends the 1st message m_1 to the other user U_B.

For $i = 2, ..., n$, upon receiving the $(i-1)$-th message m_{i-1}, user U_X ($X = A$ or B) computes the i-th message by using the algorithm Message, which takes the master public key mpk, the string γ_X, the static secret key ssk_{γ_X}, the string δ_X, and the sent and received messages $m_1, ..., m_{i-1}$, and outputs the i-th message m_i, i.e., Message$(mpk, \gamma_X, ssk_{\gamma_X}, \delta_X, m_1, ..., m_{i-1}) \to m_i$. User U_X sends the i-th message m_i to the other user U_Y ($Y = B$ or A).

Upon receiving or after sending the final n-th message m_n, user U_X ($X = A$ or B) computes a session key by using the algorithm SessionKey, which takes the master public key mpk, the string γ_X, the static secret key ssk_{γ_X}, the string δ_X, and the sent and received messages $m_1, ..., m_n$, and outputs session key K, i.e., SessionKey$(mpk, \gamma_X, ssk_{\gamma_X}, \delta_X, m_1, ..., m_n) \to K$.

Both users U_A and U_B can compute the same session key if and only if $P(\gamma_A, \delta_B) = 1$ and $P(\gamma_B, \delta_A) = 1$.

Session. An invocation of a protocol is called a *session*. Session activation is done by an incoming message of the forms $(\Pi, P, \mathcal{I}, \gamma_A, \gamma_B)$ or $(\Pi, P, \mathcal{R}, \gamma_B, \gamma_A, m_1)$, where we equate Π with a protocol identifier, P with a predicate identifier, $\mathcal{I}$ and $\mathcal{R}$ with role identifiers, and γ_A and γ_B with associated strings of users U_A and U_B. If U_A was activated with $(\Pi, P, \mathcal{I}, \gamma_A, \gamma_B)$, then U_A is called the session *initiator*. If U_B was activated with $(\Pi, P, \mathcal{R}, \gamma_B, \gamma_A, m_1)$, then U_B is called the session *responder*. After being activated by an incoming message of the forms $(\Pi, P, \mathcal{I}, \gamma_A, \gamma_B, m_1, ..., m_{2k-2})$ from the responder U_B, the initiator U_A outputs m_{2k-1}, then may be activated by an incoming message of the forms $(\Pi, P, \mathcal{I}, \gamma_A, \gamma_B, m_1, ..., m_{2k})$ from the responder U_B. After being activated by an incoming message of the forms $(\Pi, P, \mathcal{R}, \gamma_B, \gamma_A, m_1, ..., m_{2k-1})$ from the initiator U_A, The responder U_B outputs m_{2k}, then may be activated by an incoming message of the forms $(\Pi, P, \mathcal{R}, \gamma_B, \gamma_A, m_1, ..., m_{2k+1})$ from the initiator U_A. Upon receiving or after sending the final n-th message m_n, both users U_A and U_B compute a session key K.

If U_A is the initiator of a session, the session is identified by $\mathtt{sid} = (\Pi, P, \mathcal{I}, \gamma_A, \gamma_B, m_1)$, $(\Pi, P, \mathcal{I}, \gamma_A, \gamma_B, m_1, m_2, m_3)$,..., $(\Pi, P, \mathcal{I}, \gamma_A, \gamma_B, m_1, ..., m_n)$. If U_B is the responder of a session, the session is identified by $\mathtt{sid} = (\Pi, P, \mathcal{R}, \gamma_B, \gamma_A, m_1, m_2)$ $(\Pi, P, \mathcal{I}, \gamma_A, \gamma_B, m_1, m_2, m_3, m_4)$,..., $(\Pi, P, \mathcal{I}, \gamma_A, \gamma_B, m_1, ..., m_n)$. We say that a session is *completed* if a session key is computed in the session. The *matching session* of a completed session $(\Pi, P, \mathcal{I}, \gamma_A, \gamma_B, m_1, ..., m_n)$ is a completed session with identifier $(\Pi, P, \mathcal{R}, \gamma_B, \gamma_A, m_1, ..., m_n)$ and vice versa.

Adversary. The adversary $\mathcal{A}$, which is modeled as a probabilistic polynomial-time Turing machine, controls all communications between parties including session activation, by performing the following adversary query.

- Send(message): The message has one of the following forms: $(\Pi, P, \mathcal{I}, \gamma_A, \gamma_B, m_1, ..., m_{2k-1})$, or $(\Pi, P, \mathcal{R}, \gamma_B, \gamma_A, m_1, ..., m_{2k})$. $\mathcal{A}$ obtains the response from the user.

A user's secret information is not accessible to $\mathcal{A}$. However, leakage of secret information is captured via the following adversary queries.

- SessionKeyReveal(sid): $\mathcal{A}$ obtains the session key for the session sid, provided that the session is completed.
- EphemeralKeyReveal(sid): $\mathcal{A}$ obtains the ephemeral secret key associated with the session sid.
- StaticKeyReveal(γ_i): $\mathcal{A}$ learns the static secret key associated with string γ_i.
- MasterKeyReveal: $\mathcal{A}$ learns the master secret key of the system.
- EstablishParty(U_i, γ_i): This query allows $\mathcal{A}$ to register a static public key corresponding to string γ_i on behalf of the party U_i; $\mathcal{A}$ totally controls that party. If a party is established by an EstablishParty(U_i, γ_i) query issued by $\mathcal{A}$, then we call the party U_i *dishonest*. If not, we call the party *honest*.

Freshness. For the security definition, we need the notion of freshness.

Definition 1 (Freshness). *Let* sid* $= (\Pi, P, \mathcal{I}, \gamma_A, \gamma_B, m_1, ..., m_n)$ *or* $(\Pi, P, \mathcal{R}, \gamma_B, \gamma_A, m_1, ..., m_n)$ *be a completed session between honest user U_A with string γ_A and U_B with string γ_B. If the matching session exists, then let $\overline{\text{sid}^*}$ be the matching session of* sid*. *Define session* sid* *as fresh if none of the following conditions hold:*

1. *$\mathcal{A}$ issues a* SessionKeyReveal(sid*), *or* SessionKeyReveal($\overline{\text{sid}^*}$) *query if $\overline{\text{sid}^*}$ exists,*
2. $\overline{\text{sid}^*}$ *exists and $\mathcal{A}$ makes either of the following queries*
   - *both* StaticKeyReveal(γ) *s.t. $P(\gamma, \delta_B) = 1$ and* EphemeralKeyReveal(sid*),
   - *or both* StaticKeyReveal(γ) *s.t. $P(\gamma, \delta_A) = 1$ and* EphemeralKeyReveal($\overline{\text{sid}^*}$),
3. $\overline{\text{sid}^*}$ *does not exist and $\mathcal{A}$ makes either of the following queries*
   - *both* StaticKeyReveal(γ) *s.t. $P(\gamma, \delta_B) = 1^*$ and* EphemeralKeyReveal(sid*),
   - *or* StaticKeyReveal(γ) *s.t. $P(\gamma, \delta_A) = 1$,*

where if $\mathcal{A}$ issues MasterKeyReveal() *query, we regard that $\mathcal{A}$ issues* StaticKeyReveal(γ) *s.t. $P(\gamma, \delta_B) = 1$ and* StaticKeyReveal(γ) *s.t. $P(\gamma, \delta_A) = 1$ queries.*

Security Experiment. For our security definition, we describe the following security experiment. Initially, $\mathcal{A}$ is given a set of honest users, and makes any sequence of the queries described above. During the experiment, $\mathcal{A}$ makes the following query.

- Test(sid*): Here, sid* must be a fresh session. Select random bit $b \in_U \{0,1\}$, and return the session key held by sid* if $b = 0$, and return a random key if $b = 1$.

---

* δ_B is defined by the adversary $\mathcal{A}$.

The experiment continues until $\mathcal{A}$ makes a guess b'. $\mathcal{A}$ *wins* the game if the test session sid^* is still fresh and if $\mathcal{A}$'s guess is correct, i.e., $b' = b$. The advantage of $\mathcal{A}$ in the AKE experiment with predicate-based AKE protocol Π is defined as $\text{Adv}_{\Pi}^{\text{predAKE}}(\mathcal{A}) = \Pr[\mathcal{A} \ wins] - \frac{1}{2}$. We define the security as follows.

Definition 2 (Security). *We say that predicate-based AKE protocol Π is secure in the predicate-based eCK model, if the following conditions hold:*

1. *If two honest parties complete matching Π sessions and $P(\gamma_A, \delta_B) = 1$ and $P(\gamma_B, \delta_A) = 1$ hold, then, except with negligible probability, they both compute the same session key.*
2. *For any probabilistic polynomial-time adversary $\mathcal{A}$, $\text{Adv}_{\Pi}^{\text{predAKE}}(\mathcal{A})$ is negligible.*

Moreover, we say that predicate-based AKE protocol Π is selective-condition secure *in the predicate-based eCK model, if the adversary $\mathcal{A}$ outputs (δ_A, δ_B) at the beginning of the security experiment.*

3   Proposed Two-Pass Attribute-Based AKE Protocol

We constructed a attribute-based AKE protocol based on attribute-based encryption schemes [14,10]. By applying the NAXOS technique [13], the proposed protocol can satisfy the predicate-based eCK security, under the gap Bilinear Diffie-Hellman (BDH) assumption [2] in the random oracle model.

3.1   Assumption

Let k be the security parameter and p be a k-bit prime. Let G be a cyclic group of a prime order p with a generator g, and G_T be a cyclic group of the prime order p with a generator g_T. Let $e : G \times G \to G_T$ be a polynomial-time computable bilinear non-degenerate map called pairing. We say that G, G_T are bilinear groups with the pairing e.

The gap Bilinear Diffie-Hellman (BDH) problem [2] is as follows. Define the computational BDH function $\text{BDH} : G^3 \to G_T$ as $\text{BDH}(g^a, g^b, g^c) = e(g, g)^{abc}$ and the decisional BDH predicate $\text{DBDH} : G^4 \to \{0, 1\}$ as a function which takes an input $(g^a, g^b, g^c, e(g, g)^d)$ and returns the bit one if $abc = d \bmod p$ or the bit zero otherwise. An adversary $\mathcal{A}$ is given input $g^a, g^b, g^c \in_U G$ selected uniformly randomly and can access the $\text{DBDH}(\cdot, \cdot, \cdot, \cdot)$ oracle, and tries to compute $\text{BDH}(g^a, g^b, g^c)$. For adversary $\mathcal{A}$, we define advantage

$$Adv^{\text{gap BDH}}(\mathcal{A}) = \Pr[g^a, g^b, g^c \in_U G, \mathcal{A}^{\text{DBDH}(\cdot,\cdot,\cdot,\cdot)}(g^a, g^b, g^c) = \text{BDH}(g^a, g^b, g^c)],$$

where the probability is taken over the choices of g^a, g^b, g^c and the random tape of adversary $\mathcal{A}$.

Definition 3 (gap BDH assumption). *We say that G satisfies the gap BDH assumption, if for any probabilistic polynomial-time adversary $\mathcal{A}$, advantage $Adv^{\text{gapBDH}}(\mathcal{A})$ is negligible in security parameter k.*

3.2   Access Tree

In the proposed attribute-based AKE protocol, we use a predicate $P(\gamma, \delta)$, where the output of P corresponds to whether a set of attributes δ satisfies an access tree γ, i.e., the first input γ of P corresponds to the access tree and the second input δ of P corresponds to the set of attributes. Thus, a static secret key of user U_A is represented as an access tree γ_A, and a ephemeral public key of user U_B is represented as a set of attributes δ_B. We show an explanation of the access tree and the set of attributes below.

Let γ be a tree and let $L(\gamma)$ be the set of all leaf nodes of γ. Let c_u be the number of child nodes of non-leaf node u, and we set $c_u = 1$ for leaf node u. Threshold value k_u ($1 \leq k_u \leq c_u$) is assigned to each node u, and thus $k_u = c_u = 1$ for each node u. For each node u, we assign $index(u) \in \{1, \ldots, c_w\}$, where w is the parent of u and u is the $index(u)$-th child of w. Then, each node u of the tree is associated with the k_u-out-of-c_u threshold gate. Let $\mathcal{U} = \{1, 2, \ldots, n\}$ be the universe of attributes, and we assign $att(u) \in \mathcal{U}$ for each leaf node u. Then, each leaf node u of the tree is associated with an attribute. We call the tree γ with $(k_u, index(u), att(u))$ *access tree*.

We define that the set of attributes $\delta \subset \mathcal{U}$ satisfies access tree γ as follows: For each leaf node u, we say u is satisfied if and only if $att(u) \in \delta$. For non-leaf node u, we say u is satisfied if and only if the number of satisfied child nodes of u is equal to or greater than k_u. Then, we say the set of attributes satisfies the access tree if and only if the (non-leaf) root node u_r is satisfied.

By using the above access tree, we can describe any monotone circuit consists of OR and AND gates, since a threshold gate implies an OR gate when $k_u = 1$ and implies an AND gate when $k_u = c_u$. Moreover, the access tree enables us to describe any general circuit by adding attribute $\bar{a}$ representing NOT of each attribute a to the universe $\mathcal{U}$ of attributes, since a NOT gate can be moved to a leaf node of the access tree by using De Morgan's laws.

3.3   Proposed Two-Pass Attribute-Based AKE Protocol

In this section, we describe the proposed attribute-based AKE protocol.

Parameters. Let k be the security parameter and G, G_T be bilinear groups with pairing $e : G \times G \to G_T$ of order k-bit prime p with generators g, g_T, respectively. Let $H : \{0,1\}^* \to \{0,1\}^k$ and $H' : \{0,1\}^* \to \mathbb{Z}_p$ be cryptographic hash functions modeled as random oracles. In addition, let $\Delta_{i,S}$ for $i \in \mathbb{Z}_p$ and a set S of elements in $\mathbb{Z}_p$ be the Lagrange coefficient such that $\Delta_{i,S}(x) = \prod_{j \in S, j \neq i} \frac{x-j}{i-j}$.

Key Generation. The key generator (algorithm) randomly selects a master secret key $z \in_U \mathbb{Z}_p$ and $\{t_i \in_U \mathbb{Z}_p\}_{i \in \mathcal{U}}$ for each attribute. Also, the key generator publishes the master public key $Z = g_T^z \in G_T$ and $\{T_i = g^{t_i}\}_{i \in \mathcal{U}}$.

Key Extraction. For a given access tree γ_A of user U_A, the key extractor (algorithm) computes the static secret key $\{D_u\}_{u \in L(\gamma_A)}$ by choosing a polynomial q_u for each node u in γ_A as follows:

First, the key extractor sets the degree of the polynomial q_u to be $d_u = k_u - 1$. For the root node u_r, $q_{u_r}(0) = z$ and other d_{u_r} points of q_{u_r} are randomly chosen from $\mathbb{Z}_p$. Thus, q_{u_r} is fixed and other $c_{u_r} - d_{u_r}$ points are determined. For any other node u, set $q_u(0) = q_{u'}(index(u))$, where u' is the parent node of u and other d_u points of q_u are randomly chosen from $\mathbb{Z}_p$. Polynomials of all nodes are recursively determined with this procedure. Next, the key extractor computes a secret value for each leaf node u as $D_u = g^{\frac{q_u(0)}{t_i}}$, where $i = att(u)$. Finally, the key extractor returns the set $\{D_u\}_{u \in L(\gamma_A)}$ of the above secret values as the static secret key.

The static secret key $\{D_u\}_{u \in L(\gamma_B)}$ for an access tree γ_B of user U_B is derived from the same procedure.

Key Exchange. In the following description, user U_A is the session initiator and user U_B is the session responder. User U_A has static secret keys $\{D_u\}_{u \in L(\gamma_A)}$ corresponding to an access tree γ_A, and user U_B has static secret keys $\{D_u\}_{u \in L(\gamma_B)}$ corresponding to an access tree γ_B. Then, user U_A sends to user U_B ephemeral public keys $(X, \{T_i^x\}_{i \in \delta_A})$ corresponding to the set of attributes δ_A, and user U_B sends to user U_A ephemeral public keys $(Y, \{T_i^y\}_{i \in \delta_B})$ corresponding to the set of attributes δ_B. Finally, both users U_A and U_B compute the shared key K if and only if $P(\gamma_A, \delta_B) = 1$ and $P(\gamma_B, \delta_A) = 1$, i.e., the set of attributes δ_B satisfies the access tree γ_A and the set of attributes δ_A satisfies access tree γ_B.

1. First, U_A determines a set $\delta_A \subset \mathcal{U}$ of attributes in which he hopes δ_A satisfies the access tree γ_B of U_B. U_A randomly chooses an ephemeral private key $\tilde{x} \in_U \mathbb{Z}_p$. Then, U_A computes $x = H'(\{D_u\}_{u \in L(\gamma_A)}, \tilde{x})$, and the ephemeral public key $X = g^x$ and $\{T_i^x\}_{i \in \delta_A}$. U_A sends X, $\{T_i^x\}_{i \in \delta_A}$ and the set of attributes δ_A to U_B.

2. Upon receiving $X = g^x$, $\{T_i^x\}_{i \in \delta_A}$, and δ_A, U_B determines a set of attributes δ_B in which he hopes δ_B satisfies the access tree γ_A of U_A. U_B randomly chooses an ephemeral private key $\tilde{y} \in_U \mathbb{Z}_p$. Then, U_B computes $y = H'(\{D_u\}_{u \in L(\gamma_B)}, \tilde{y})$, and the ephemeral public key $Y = g^y$ and $\{T_i^y\}_{i \in \delta_B}$. U_B sends Y, $\{T_i^y\}_{i \in \delta_B}$ and the set of attributes δ_B to U_A.

   U_B computes the shared secrets as follows: First, for each leaf node u in γ_B, U_B computes $e(D_u, T_j^x) = e(g^{\frac{q_u(0)}{t_j}}, g^{xt_j}) = e(g, g)^{xq_u(0)}$, where $j = att(u)$, if $att(u) \in \delta_A$. Next, for each non-leaf node u in γ_B, set $\tilde{S}_u' = \{u_c | u_c$ is a child node of u s.t. $e(g, g)^{xq_{u_c}(0)}$ is obtained.$\}$. If $|\tilde{S}_u'| \geq k_u$, U_B sets $\tilde{S}_u \subset \tilde{S}_u'$ s.t. $|\tilde{S}_u| = k_u$ and $S_u = \{index(u_c) | u_c \in \tilde{S}_u\}$, and computes

$$\prod_{u_c \in \tilde{S}_u} (e(g, g)^{xq_{u_c}(0)})^{\Delta_{i, S_u}(0)} = \prod_{u_c \in \tilde{S}_u} e(g, g)^{xq_u(i) \cdot \Delta_{i, S_u}(0)} = e(g, g)^{xq_u(0)},$$

   where $i = index(u_c)$. This computation validly works by using polynomial interpolation. On the output of the root node u_r of γ_B, U_B obtains $e(g, g)^{xq_{u_r}(0)} = e(g, g)^{xz}$ if δ_A satisfies the access tree γ_B.

   Then, U_B sets the shared secrets $\sigma_1 = e(g, g)^{xz}$, $\sigma_2 = Z^y$, $\sigma_3 = X^y$, and the session key $K = H(\sigma_1, \sigma_2, \sigma_3, \Pi, P, (\delta_A, X, \{T_i^x\}_{i \in \delta_A}), (\delta_B, Y, \{T_i^y\}_{i \in \delta_B}))$. U_B completes the session with session key K.

3. Upon receiving Y, $\{T_i^y\}_{i \in \delta_B}$ and δ_B, U_A computes the shared secrets as follows: First, for each leaf node u in γ_A, U_A computes $e(D_u, T_j^y) = e(g^{\frac{q_u(0)}{t_j}}, g^{yt_j}) = e(g, g)^{yq_u(0)}$, where $j = att(u)$, if $att(u) \in \delta_B$. Next, for each non-leaf node u in γ_A, U_B computes if $|\tilde{S}_u'| \geq k_u$.

$$\prod_{u_c \in \tilde{S}_u} (e(g,g)^{yq_{u_c}(0)})^{\Delta_{i,S_u}(0)} = \prod_{u_c \in \tilde{S}_u} e(g,g)^{yq_u(i) \cdot \Delta_{i,S_u}(0)} = e(g,g)^{yq_u(0)},$$

where $i = index(u_c)$. On the output of the root node u_r of γ_A, if δ_B satisfies the access tree γ_A, U_A obtains $e(g,g)^{yq_{u_r}(0)} = e(g,g)^{yz}$.
Then, U_A sets the shared secrets $\sigma_1 = Z^x$, $\sigma_2 = e(g,g)^{yz}$, $\sigma_3 = Y^x$, and the session key $K = H(\sigma_1, \sigma_2, \sigma_3, \Pi, P, (\delta_A, X, \{T_i^x\}_{i \in \delta_A}), (\delta_B, Y, \{T_i^y\}_{i \in \delta_B}))$. U_A completes the session with session key K.

The shared secrets are $\sigma_1 = g_T^{xz}, \sigma_2 = g_T^{yz}, \sigma_3 = g^{xy}$, and therefore they can compute the same session key K if $P(\gamma_A, \delta_B) = 1$ and $P(\gamma_B, \delta_A) = 1$.

3.4 Security

The proposed attribute-based AKE protocol is selective-condition secure in the predicate-based eCK security model under the gap BDH assumption and in the random oracle model.

Theorem 1. *If G is a group, where the gap BDH assumption holds and H and H' are random oracles, the proposed attribute-based AKE protocol is selective-condition secure in the predicate-based eCK model described in Section 2.*

Proof of Theorem 1 is provided in Appendix A. Here, we provide sketch of the proof. Adversary $\mathcal{A}$ can reveal the master secret key, static secret keys and ephemeral secret keys in the test session according to Definition 2.

First, when $\mathcal{A}$ poses an EphemeralKeyReveal query, $\tilde{x}$ and $\tilde{y}$ may be revealed. However, using the NAXOS technique (i.e. $H'(\{D_u\}_{u \in L(\gamma_A)}, \tilde{x})$ for x and $H'(\{D_u\}_{u \in L(\gamma_B)}, \tilde{y})$ for y), x and y are not revealed as long as $\{D_u\}_{u \in L(\gamma_A)}$ and $\{D_u\}_{u \in L(\gamma_B)}$ are not revealed respectively. Since $\mathcal{A}$ cannot pose EphemeralKeyReveal and StaticKeyReveal queries for the same user in the test session as in Definition 2, an EphemeralKeyReveal query gives no advantage to $\mathcal{A}$.

Next, we consider the case when the StaticKeyReveal query for party U_A is posed and there is no matching session. Then, the simulator cannot embed the BDH instances (g^u, g^v, g^w) into the static secret key of U_A and the ephemeral public key of the peer. However, the simulator can still embed $e(g^u, g^v)$ into the master public key $Z = e(g,g)^z$ and g^w into T_i^x for all i as $g^{w\beta_i}$, where $T_i = g^{\beta_i}$, because $\mathcal{A}$ cannot pose the MasterKeyReveal query and reveal x for U_A. Thus, the simulation successfully works, and the simulator can obtain $e(g,g)^{uvw}$ from $\sigma_1 = e(g,g)^{xz}$.

Finally, we consider the case when the MasterKeyReveal query or both StaticKeyReveal queries for the test session and its matching session is posed. Then, the simulator cannot embed the BDH instances into the static secret keys of the test session owner and its peer, and the master secret key. However, the simulator can still embed g^u into the ephemeral public key X and g^v into the ephemeral public key Y because $\mathcal{A}$ cannot reveal x and y for U_A and U_B. Thus, the simulation successfully works, and the simulator can obtain $e(g,g)^{uvw}$ by computing $e(g^w, \sigma_3) = e(g^w, g^{xy})$. This is the reason why our protocol needs to exchange X and Y as well as $\{T_i^x\}_{i\in\delta_A}$ and $\{T_i^x\}_{i\in\delta_B}$ and σ_3 is needed.

4   Conclusion

We first defined the eCK security model, which captures leakage of ephemeral secret key, for predicate-based AKE by extending the eCK security model [13] for AKE. We also proposed an eCK secure two-pass attribute-based AKE protocol based on attribute-based encryptions [14,10], using the NAXOS technique [13]. Our proposed protocol is selective-condition secure in the predicate-based eCK security model under the gap BDH assumption and in the random oracle model.

References

1. Ateniese, G., Kirsch, J., Blanton, M.: Secret handshakes with dynamic and fuzzy matching. In: NDSS 2007 (2007)
2. Baek, J., Safavi-Naini, R., Susilo, W.: Efficient multi-receiver identity-based encryption and its application to broadcast encryption. In: Vaudenay, S. (ed.) PKC 2005. LNCS, vol. 3386, pp. 380–397. Springer, Heidelberg (2005)
3. Bellare, M., Rogaway, P.: Entity authentication and key distribution. In: Stinson, D.R. (ed.) CRYPTO 1993. LNCS, vol. 773, pp. 232–249. Springer, Heidelberg (1994)
4. Birkett, J., Stebila, D.: Predicate-based key exchange. In: Steinfeld, R., Hawkes, P. (eds.) ACISP 2010. LNCS, vol. 6168, pp. 282–299. Springer, Heidelberg (2010)
5. Blake-Wilson, S., Johnson, D., Menezes, A.: Key agreement protocols and their security analysis. In: 6th IMA International Conference, pp. 30–45 (1997)
6. Boyd, C., Choo, K.-K.R.: Security of two-party identity-based key agreement. In: Dawson, E., Vaudenay, S. (eds.) Mycrypt 2005. LNCS, vol. 3715, pp. 229–243. Springer, Heidelberg (2005)
7. Canetti, R., Krawczyk, H.: Analysis of key-exchange protocols and their use for building secure channels. In: Pfitzmann, B. (ed.) EUROCRYPT 2001. LNCS, vol. 2045, pp. 453–474. Springer, Heidelberg (2001)
8. Chen, L., Cheng, Z., Smart, N.P.: Identity-based key agreement protocols from pairings. Int. Journal of Information Security 6(4), 213–241 (2007)
9. Gorantla, M.C., Boyd, C., Nieto, J.M.G.: Attribute-based authenticated key exchange. In: Steinfeld, R., Hawkes, P. (eds.) ACISP 2010. LNCS, vol. 6168, pp. 300–317. Springer, Heidelberg (2010)
10. Goyal, V., Pandey, O., Sahai, A., Waters, B.: Attribute-based encryption for fine-grained access control of encrypted data. In: ACM Conference on Computer and Communications Security 2006, pp. 89–98 (2006)
11. Huang, H., Cao, Z.: An id-based authenticated key exchange protocol based on bilinear diffie-hellman problem. In: ASIACCS 2009, pp. 333–342 (2009)
12. Katz, J., Sahai, A., Waters, B.: Predicate encryption supporting disjunctions, polynomial equations, and inner products. In: Smart, N.P. (ed.) EUROCRYPT 2008. LNCS, vol. 4965, pp. 146–162. Springer, Heidelberg (2008)

13. LaMacchia, B.A., Lauter, K., Mityagin, A.: Stronger security of authenticated key exchange. In: Susilo, W., Liu, J.K., Mu, Y. (eds.) ProvSec 2007. LNCS, vol. 4784, pp. 1–16. Springer, Heidelberg (2007)
14. Sahai, A., Waters, B.: Fuzzy identity-based encryption. In: Cramer, R. (ed.) EUROCRYPT 2005. LNCS, vol. 3494, pp. 457–473. Springer, Heidelberg (2005)
15. Smart, N.P.: Identity-based authenticated key agreement protocol based on weil pairing. Electronic Letters 38(13), 630–632 (2002)
16. Wang, H., Xu, Q., Ban, T.: A provably secure two-party attribute-based key agreement protocol. In: Fifth International Conference on Intelligent Information Hiding and Multimedia Signal Processing, pp. 1042–1045 (2009)
17. Wang, H., Xu, Q., Fu, X.: Revocable attribute-based key agreement protocol without random oracles. Journal of Networks 4(8), 787–794 (2009)
18. Wang, H., Xu, Q., Fu, X.: Two-party attribute-based key agreement protocol in the standard model. In: ISIP 2009, pp. 325–328 (2009)

A   Proof of Theorem 1

We show that if polynomially bounded adversary $\mathcal{A}$ can distinguish the session key of a fresh session from a randomly chosen session key, we can solve the gap BDH problem. Let κ denote the security parameter, and let $\mathcal{A}$ be a polynomially (in κ) bounded adversary. We use $\mathcal{A}$ to construct a gap BDH solver $\mathcal{S}$ that succeeds with non-negligible probability. Adversary $\mathcal{A}$ is said to be successful with non-negligible probability if $\mathcal{A}$ wins the distinguishing game with probability $\frac{1}{2} + f(\kappa)$, where $f(\kappa)$ is non-negligible, and the event M denotes a successful $\mathcal{A}$.

Let the test session be $\mathtt{sid}^* = (\Pi, P, \mathcal{I}, \gamma_A, \gamma_B, \hat{\delta}_A, \hat{\delta}_B)$ or $(\Pi, P, \mathcal{R}, \gamma_A, \gamma_B, \hat{\delta}_B, \hat{\delta}_A)$ that is a completed session between honest user U_A with string γ_A and U_B with string γ_B, where users U_A and U_B are the initiator and responder of the test session $\mathtt{sid}^*$. We denote the message sent from U_A to U_B by $\hat{\delta}_A$ and the message sent from U_B to U_A by $\hat{\delta}_B$. Let H^* be the event in which $\mathcal{A}$ queries $(\sigma_1, \sigma_2, \sigma_3, \Pi, P, \hat{\delta}_A, \hat{\delta}_B)$ to H. Let $\overline{H^*}$ be the complement of event H^*. Let $\mathtt{sid}$ be any completed session owned by an honest user such that $\mathtt{sid} \neq \mathtt{sid}^*$ and $\mathtt{sid}$ is non-matching to $\mathtt{sid}^*$. Since $\mathtt{sid}$ and $\mathtt{sid}^*$ are distinct and non-matching, the inputs to the key derivation function H are different for $\mathtt{sid}$ and $\mathtt{sid}^*$. Since H is a random oracle, $\mathcal{A}$ cannot obtain any information about the test session key from the session keys of non-matching sessions. Hence, $\Pr(M \wedge \overline{H^*}) \leq \frac{1}{2}$ and $\Pr(M) = \Pr(M \wedge H^*) + \Pr(M \wedge \overline{H^*}) \leq \Pr(M \wedge H^*) + \frac{1}{2}$, whence $f(\kappa) \leq \Pr(M \wedge H^*)$. Henceforth, the event $M \wedge H^*$ is denoted by M^*.

We denote the master secret and public keys by $z, Z = g^z$. For user U_i, we denote the string by γ_i, the static secret key by $D_i = \{D_u\}_{u \in L(\gamma_i)}$, the ephemeral secret key by $\tilde{x}_i$, and the exponent of the ephemeral public key by $x_i = H'(\{D_u\}_{u \in L(\gamma_i)}, \tilde{x}_i)$. We also denote the session key by K. Assume that $\mathcal{A}$ succeeds in an environment with n users and activates at most s sessions within a user.

We consider the following events.

- Let D be the event in which $\mathcal{A}$ queries the static secret key $\{D_u\}_{u \in L(\gamma)}$ to H', *before* asking StaticKeyReveal queries or the MasterKeyReveal query or *without* asking StaticKeyReveal queries or the MasterKeyReveal query.
- Let $\overline{D}$ be the complement of event D.

We consider the following events, which cover all cases of adversary $\mathcal{A}$'s behavior.

- Let E_1 be the event in which test session $\mathtt{sid}^*$ has no matching session $\overline{\mathtt{sid}}^*$ and $\mathcal{A}$ queries $\mathsf{StaticKeyReveal}(\gamma)$ s.t. $P(\gamma, \delta_B) = 1$.
- Let E_2 be the event in which test session $\mathtt{sid}^*$ has no matching session $\overline{\mathtt{sid}}^*$ and $\mathcal{A}$ queries $\mathsf{EphemeralKeyReveal}(\mathtt{sid}^*)$.
- Let E_3 be the event in which test session $\mathtt{sid}^*$ has matching session $\overline{\mathtt{sid}}^*$ and $\mathcal{A}$ queries $\mathsf{MasterKeyReveal}()$ or queries $\mathsf{StaticKeyReveal}(\gamma)$ s.t. $P(\gamma, \delta_B) = 1$ and $\mathsf{StaticKeyReveal}(\gamma)$ s.t. $P(\gamma, \delta_A) = 1$.
- Let E_4 be the event in which test session $\mathtt{sid}^*$ has matching session $\overline{\mathtt{sid}}^*$ and $\mathcal{A}$ queries $\mathsf{EphemeralKeyReveal}(\mathtt{sid}^*)$ and $\mathsf{EphemeralKeyReveal}(\overline{\mathtt{sid}}^*)$.
- Let E_5 be the event in which test session $\mathtt{sid}^*$ has matching session $\overline{\mathtt{sid}}^*$ and $\mathcal{A}$ queries $\mathsf{StaticKeyReveal}(\gamma)$ s.t. $P(\gamma, \delta_B) = 1$ and $\mathsf{EphemeralKeyReveal}(\overline{\mathtt{sid}}^*)$.
- Let E_6 be the event in which test session $\mathtt{sid}^*$ has matching session $\overline{\mathtt{sid}}^*$ and $\mathcal{A}$ queries $\mathsf{EphemeralKeyReveal}(\mathtt{sid}^*)$ and $\mathsf{StaticKeyReveal}(\gamma)$ s.t. $P(\gamma, \delta_A) = 1$.

To finish the proof, we investigate events $D \wedge M^*$, $E_i \wedge \overline{D} \wedge M^*$ ($i = 1, ..., 6$), which cover all cases of event M^*, in the following.

Here, we only consider the event $E_1 \wedge \overline{D} \wedge M^*$, due to the page limitation. Details of the other cases is provided in the full paper version of this parer.

In event E_1, test session $\mathtt{sid}^*$ has no matching session $\overline{\mathtt{sid}}^*$, and $\mathcal{A}$ queries $\mathsf{StaticKeyReveal}(\gamma)$ s.t. $P(\gamma, \delta_B) = 1$, and $\mathcal{A}$ does not query $\mathsf{EphemeralKeyReveal}(\mathtt{sid}^*)$ and $\mathsf{StaticKeyReveal}(\gamma)$ s.t. $P(\gamma, \delta_A) = 1$ by the condition of freshness. We embed the instance as $Z = e(g, g)^z = e(U, V)$, $T_i^x = W^{\beta_i}$ where $T_i = g^{\beta_i}$, and extract $e(g, g)^{uvw}$ from $\sigma_1 = e(g, g)^{xz}$. In event $E_1 \wedge \overline{D} \wedge M^*$, $\mathcal{S}$ performs the following steps.

Setup. The gap BDH solver $\mathcal{S}$ begins by establishing n honest users that are assigned random static key pairs. In addition to the above steps, $\mathcal{S}$ embeds instance $(U = g^u, V = g^v, W = g^w)$ of the gap BDH problem as follows.

Let δ_A and δ_B be the target conditions selected by $\mathcal{A}$. $\mathcal{S}$ sets the public master key as $Z = e(U, V) = g_T^{uv}$, $T_i = g^{\beta_i}$ for $i \in \delta_A$, and $T_i = V^{\beta_i} = g^{v\beta_i}$ for $i \notin \delta_A$, where $\mathcal{S}$ selects $\beta_i \in_U \mathbb{Z}_q$ randomly.

$\mathcal{S}$ randomly selects two users U_A and U_B and integers $j_A \in_R [1, s]$, that becomes a guess of the test session with probability $1/n^2 s$. $\mathcal{S}$ sets the ephemeral public key of j_A-th session of user U_A as $T_i^x = W^{\beta_i} = g^{w\beta_i}$ for $i \in \delta_A$ and $X = W$.

The solver $\mathcal{S}$ activates $\mathcal{A}$ on this set of users and awaits the actions of $\mathcal{A}$. We next describe the actions of $\mathcal{S}$ in response to user activations and oracle queries.

Simulation. The solver $\mathcal{S}$ simulates oracle queries as follows. $\mathcal{S}$ maintains list L_H that contains queries and answers of H oracle, and list L_S that contains queries and answers of $\mathsf{SessionKeyReveal}$,

1. $\mathsf{Send}(\Pi, P, \gamma_i, \gamma_j)$: $\mathcal{S}$ selects a string δ_i, picks ephemeral secret key $x \in_U \mathbb{Z}_q$, honestly computes ephemeral public key $\hat{\delta}_i$, records $(\Pi, P, \gamma_i, \gamma_j, \hat{\delta}_i)$, and returns it.

2. $\mathsf{Send}(\Pi, P, \gamma_i, \gamma_j, \hat{\delta}_i)$: $\mathcal{S}$ selects a string δ_j, picks ephemeral secret key $y \in_U \mathbb{Z}_q$, honestly computes ephemeral public key $\hat{\delta}_j$, records $(\Pi, P, \gamma_i, \gamma_j, \hat{\delta}_i, \hat{\delta}_j)$, and returns it.

3. $\mathsf{Send}(\Pi, P, \gamma_i, \gamma_j, \hat{\delta}_i, \hat{\delta}_j)$: If $(\Pi, P, \gamma_i, \gamma_j, \hat{\delta}_i)$ is not recorded, $\mathcal{S}$ records the session $(\Pi, P, \gamma_i, \gamma_j, \hat{\delta}_i, \hat{\delta}_j)$ as not completed. Otherwise, $\mathcal{S}$ records the session as completed.

4. $H(\sigma_1, \sigma_2, \sigma_3, \Pi, P, \hat{\delta}_i, \hat{\delta}_j)$:

   (a) If $(\sigma_1, \sigma_2, \sigma_3, \Pi, P, \hat{\delta}_i, \hat{\delta}_j)$ is recorded in list L_H, then return recorded value K.

   (b) Else if $(\Pi, P, \hat{\delta}_i, \hat{\delta}_j)$ is recorded in list L_S, $\mathrm{DBDH}(X, U, V, \sigma_1) = 1$, $\mathrm{DBDH}(Y, U, V, \sigma_2) = 1$, and $e(X, Y) = e(g, \sigma_3)$, then return recorded value K and record it in list L_H.

   (c) Else if $\mathrm{DBDH}(X, U, V, \sigma_1) = 1$, $\mathrm{DBDH}(Y, U, V, \sigma_2) = 1$, $e(X, Y) = e(g, \sigma_3)$, $i = A, j = B$, and the session is the j_A-th session of user U_A, then $\mathcal{S}$ stops and is successful by outputting the answer of the gap BDH problem instance $\sigma_1 = \mathrm{BDH}(U, V, W)$.

   (d) Otherwise, $\mathcal{S}$ returns random value K and records it in list L_H.

5. $\mathsf{SessionKeyReveal}(\mathtt{sid})$:

   (a) If the session $\mathtt{sid}$ is not completed, return error.

   (b) Else if $\mathtt{sid}$ is recorded in list L_S, then return recorded value K.

   (c) Else if $(\sigma_1, \sigma_2, \sigma_3, \Pi, P, \hat{\delta}_i, \hat{\delta}_j)$ is recorded in list L_H, $\mathrm{DBDH}(X, U, V, \sigma_1) = 1$, $\mathrm{DBDH}(Y, U, V, \sigma_2) = 1$, and $e(X, Y) = e(g, \sigma_3)$, then return recorded value K and record it in list L_S.

   (d) Otherwise, $\mathcal{S}$ returns random value K and records it in list L_S.

6. $H'(\{D_u\}_{u \in L(\gamma_i)}, \tilde{x})$: If $\{D_u\}_{u \in L(\gamma_i)}, \tilde{x}$ is used in the j_A-th session of user U_A, $\mathcal{S}$ aborts with failure. Otherwise, simulate this random oracle in the usual way.

7. $\mathsf{EphemeralKeyReveal}(\mathtt{sid})$: $\mathcal{S}$ returns random value $\tilde{x}$ and records it.

8. $\mathsf{StaticKeyReveal}(\gamma_i)$: First, we consider the case that γ_i is an access tree with height 1. By the condition $P(\gamma_i, \delta_A) \neq 1$, we have $|\gamma_i \cap \delta_A| < k$, where k is the threshold. Thus, we have a set Γ s.t. $\gamma_i \cap \delta_A \subset \Gamma \subset \delta_A$ and $|\Gamma| = k - 1$.

   For $u \in \Gamma$, $\mathcal{S}$ selects random $q(i)$ and sets $D_u = V^{q(i)/\beta_i} = g^{vq(i)/\beta_i} = g^{Q(i)/\beta_i}$, where $i = index(u)$. $\mathcal{S}$ also sets $g^{vq(0)} = g^{uv}$, and this implicitly defines degree $k - 1$ polynomial $q(x)$ and $Q(x) = vq(x)$.

   For $u \notin \delta_A$, $\mathcal{S}$ sets $D_u = [\prod_{j=index(v), v \in \Gamma} g^{q(j)\Delta_{j, \Gamma}(i)} U^{\Delta_{0, \Gamma}(i)}]^{1/\beta_i} = g^{q(i)/\beta_i} = g^{Q(i)/v\beta_i}$, where $i = index(u)$.

   Finally, $\mathcal{S}$ returns $\{D_u\}_{u \in L(\gamma_i)}$.

   If the height is more than 1, $\mathcal{S}$ creates $\{D_u\}_{u \in L(\gamma_i)}$ as follows. By the condition $P(\gamma_i, \delta_A) \neq 1$, attributes δ_A do not satisfy access tree γ_i, so the root node u_r is not satisfied, i.e., the number of satisfied nodes is less than threshold k_{u_r} of the root node u_r. Thus, we have a set Γ of nodes that contains all satisfied nodes and $|\Gamma| = k_{u_r} - 1$.

   For $u \in \Gamma$, $\mathcal{S}$ selects random $q(index(u))$ and assigns it to the node $u \in \Gamma$. $\mathcal{S}$ also sets $g^{q(0)} = D_{u_r} = g^{uv}$, and this implicitly defines degree

$k_{u_r} - 1$ polynomial $q(x)$. For each node $u \in \Gamma$, $\mathcal{S}$ performs secret sharing iteratively, i.e., makes shares of $q(index(u))$ then makes shares of the share and so on, until reaching a leaf node.

For $u \notin \Gamma$, $\mathcal{S}$ computes $D_u = g^{q(index(u))}$ and assigns it to the node $u \notin \Gamma$, which is unsatisfied by the definition of Γ.

For each unsatisfied node $u \notin \Gamma$, $\mathcal{S}$ applies the above procedure recursively. Finally, $\mathcal{S}$ reaches unsatisfied node u that has leaf nodes as its children. Then $\mathcal{S}$ computes $\{D_u\}_{u \in L(\gamma_i)}$ the same as in the case that γ_i is an access tree with height 1.

9. MasterKeyReveal(): $\mathcal{S}$ aborts with failure.
10. EstablishParty(U_i, γ_i): $\mathcal{S}$ responds to the query faithfully.
11. Test(sid): If ephemeral public key X is not W in session sid, then $\mathcal{S}$ aborts with failure. Otherwise, respond to the query faithfully.
12. If $\mathcal{A}$ outputs a guess γ, $\mathcal{S}$ aborts with failure.

Analysis. The simulation of the adversary environment is perfect except with negligible probability. The probability that $\mathcal{A}$ selects the session, where ephemeral public key X is W, as the test session sid* is at least $\frac{1}{n^2 s}$. Suppose this is indeed the case, $\mathcal{S}$ does not abort in Step 11.

Suppose event E_1 occurs, $\mathcal{S}$ does not abort in Step 9, since MasterKeyReveal() is not queried. Suppose event E_1 occurs, $\mathcal{S}$ does not abort in Step 6 except with negligible probability, since EphemeralKeyReveal(sid*) is not queried.

Under event M^*, $\mathcal{A}$ queries correctly formed $\sigma_1, \sigma_2, \sigma_3$ to H. Therefore, $\mathcal{S}$ is successful as described in Step 4c and does not abort as in Step 12.

Hence, $\mathcal{S}$ is successful with probability $Pr(S) \geq \frac{p_1}{n^2 s}$, where p_1 is the probability that $E_1 \wedge \overline{D} \wedge M^*$ occurs.   □

A New Efficient Construction for Non-Malleable Zero-Knowledge Sets*

Wenpan Jing, Haixia Xu, and Bao Li

State Key Laboratory of Information Security,
Graduate University of Chinese Academy of Sciences,
No.19A Yuquan Road, 100049 Beijing, China
{wpjing,hxxu,lb}@is.ac.cn

Abstract. The idea of Zero-Knowledge Sets (ZKS) was firstly proposed by Micali, Rabin and Kilian. It allows the prover to commit to a secret set and then prove either "$x \in S$" or "$x \notin S$" without revealing any more knowledge of the set S. Afterwards, R.Gennaro defined the concept of independence for ZKS and gave two tree-based constructions. In this paper, we define the independence property for ZKS in a more flexible way than the definition of Gennaro's and prove that for ZKS, our independence implies non-malleability and vice versa. Then an independent ZKS scheme is constructed in an algebraic way by mapping values to unique primes, accumulating the set members and hiding the set. Comparing with the tree-based constructions: our scheme is more efficient while proving a value belongs (resp. not belongs) to the committed set; furthermore, the committed set is easier to update.

Keywords: zero-knowledge set, commitment, non-malleability, independence.

1 Introduction

Two roles are involved in a *zero-knowledge sets* (ZKS) protocol, known as the *prover* and the *verifier*. The main purpose of ZKS is that for any finite set S, which consists of some finite strings, the prover can produce a commitment of the set and prove either "$x \in S$" or "$x \notin S$" ($x \in \{0, 1\}^*$ is an arbitrary string) without revealing any more knowledge of the set S, even the size of the set. Furthermore, the verifier could not be cheated, which means that any prover can not successfully prove both "$x \in S$" and "$x \notin S$", once the commitment is fixed.

One can see that ZKS is a basic cryptographic primitive which is highly related to commitment scheme and zero-knowledge proof protocol. A ZKS protocol can be regarded as a special commitment scheme that commits to multiple strings, requiring "hiding" and "binding" properties as a normal commitment scheme, but can be partially opened (only revealing one string each time). It also can be regarded as a special zero-knowledge argument system which not only gives a proof when "$x \in L$", but also gives a proof when "$x \notin L$", where L is a language. Besides, ZKS has a brilliant application perspective in protecting the security of database access [12].

---

* Supported by the National Natural Science Foundation of China (No.60673073), the National High-Tech Research and Development Plan of China (863 project) (No.2006AA01Z427) and the National Basic Research Program of China (973 project)(No.2007CB311201).

Y. Chung and M. Yung (Eds.): WISA 2010, LNCS 6513, pp. 31–43, 2011.
© Springer-Verlag Berlin Heidelberg 2011

1.1 Background

The idea of Zero-Knowledge Sets was first proposed by Micali, Rabin and Kilian [12]. A very creative construction of ZKS was given in the same issue. They used Pederson's commitment scheme and Merkle tree to generate the commitment to a set S. They claimed that if discrete logarithm problem was hard, then their construction was a ZKS scheme. Moreover, Micali et al. introduced the notion of "Fake" commitment to prune the tree and greatly reduced the complexity. A new variety of commitment, which is called "Mercurial Commitment", was abstracted by Chase et al. in [3] from the idea of "Fake" commitment. Mercurial Commitment is a trapdoor commitment with relaxation in binding property. With the notion of mercurial commitment abstracted, to build ZKS falls into a routine job: one needs only to combine any mercurial commitment and any collision-resistant hash function together. Afterwards, Catalano et al. in [1] studied further on mercurial commitment, especially on their constructions.

Gennaro and Micali gave the notion of *independent ZKS* [8]. They claimed that *independence* is a security requirement which is at least as secure as *non – malleablity*. A cryptographic system is non-malleable means that it could resist the so-called man-in-the-middle attack [7]. In the ZKS system particularly, any adversary could not correlatively produce commitments of sets or proofs after interact with the prover. They constructed commitment schemes both being non-malleable and mercurial, and built independent zero-knowledge sets from them.

Catalano, Fiore and Messina proposed a ZKS scheme with short proofs [2]. They used tree-based structure with a new mercurial commitment called "trapdoor q-mercurial commitment" which allowed a sequence of elements to be committed at one time. As a result, the depth of the tree was effectively reduced and consequently the proofs of each element was shortened.

All of the ZKS schemes above are based on mercurial commitment and collision-resistant hash functions. They all use the tree-based structure which has lots of advantages, e.g., the design is modularized; the commitment of the set is easy to generate and efficient to store. However, the proof to each x grows along with the increase of the depth of the tree; moreover, the tree based structure makes the ZKS hard to be updated. Unfortunately, these flaws are fatal while coming into practice and hard to conquer with this specific structure.

Xue et al. proposed a completely different algebraic construction of ZKS based on strong RSA assumption [15]. They introduced a new collision-free hash function which mapped each natural number to a unique prime number, then built the commitment using an accumulator like construction. The scheme has many advantages: easy to be updated; easy to be programmed; the commitment and the proofs are all very short; the elements in the set do not need to be ordered, etc. However, the scheme could not resist malleability attack.

1.2 Our Contributions

A new definition of independence for zero-knowledge sets is presented. Comparing with the definition in [8], our definition is more simplified and fixes a slight flaw of the definition in [8]. Moreover, the author of [8] claimed independence was at least as strong as non-malleability without proof and leaved whether non-malleability implies independence an open problem. We prove that if a ZKS is independent then it is non-malleable with respect to opening and vice versa.

We build an independent ZKS protocol satisfying our definition afterwards. Our construction is different from the existing independent ZKS constructions for not using the tree-based structure. It inherits the structure of [15] so that it is easy to update and the proof for a value can be very short. Moreover, our scheme achieves independence by eliminating the homomorphism property of the constructions in [15].

1.3 Road Map

The paper is organized as follows. In section 2, we provide several preliminaries and notions. Section 3 is the definition of ZKS. In section 4, we redefine non-malleability and independence for ZKS. A proof for the equivalence of non-malleability and independence for ZKS is also provided. In section 5, we show our construction of non-malleable ZKS based on the strong RSA assumption.

2 Preliminaries

2.1 Notations

We say a function is *negligible* if it vanishes faster than any polynomial of the security parameter, and a function v *non-negligible* if there exists a polynomial p such that for all sufficient large k's it holds that $v(k) > 1/p(k)$. $\mathbb{Z}$ is the ring of integers, and for positive integer n, $\mathbb{Z}_n$ is the ring of integers modulo n, and $\mathbb{Z}_n^*$ is the corresponding multiplicative group of units. We write $y \leftarrow A(x)$ to denote that algorithm A takes x as input and outputs y, and $y \leftarrow_R A(x)$ means the algorithm A is a randomized algorithm. We write $y \leftarrow A^{O(\cdot)}(x)$ to denote the algorithmic action of running A on input x, with oracle access to O, and outputting y finally.

2.2 Definitions

Definition 1 (Strong RSA Assumption[14]). *For every probabilistic polynomial-time algorithms $\mathcal{A}$,*

$$Pr[n \leftarrow G(1^k), x \leftarrow_R \mathbb{Z}_n, (y, e) \leftarrow \mathcal{A}(n, x) : y^e = x \pmod{n} \cap 1 < e < n] \le neg(k),$$

where $G(1^k)$ is a algorithm generating RSA modulus, and neg(k) is a negligible function.

Lemma 1. *[15]: For any integer n,given integers $u, v \in \mathbb{Z}_n^*$ and $a, b \in \mathbb{Z}$, such that $u^a = v^b \pmod{n}$ and $gcd(a, b) = 1$, one can efficiently compute $x \in \mathbb{Z}_n^*$ such that $x^a = v \pmod{n}$.*

Definition 2 (Equivocable Commitment schemes [6]). *Let $(\mathcal{TTP}, \mathcal{S}, \mathcal{R})$ be a commitment scheme in the public parameter model over message space $\mathcal{M}$. com and dec be the commitment and decommitment outputted by $\mathcal{S}$. We say that $(\mathcal{TTP}, \mathcal{S}, \mathcal{R})$ is equivocable if there exists a probabilistic polynomial time equivocable commitment simulator **Equiv** such that:*

(1) **Equiv**$_1$(1^k) *outputs* (σ, *com*, *s*) *(where σ is the public parameter, s represents state information).*
(2) *For all m $\in$ M,* **Equiv**$_2$(s, m) *outputs dec such that:*
  (a) $R(\sigma, com, dec) = m$.
  (b) *The following two random variables are computational indistinguishable:*
    $\{\sigma \leftarrow \mathcal{TTP}(1^k); (com, dec) \leftarrow S(\sigma, m) : (\sigma, com, dec)\}$.
    $\{(\sigma, com, s) \leftarrow$ **Equiv**$_1$(1^k); dec $\leftarrow$ **Equiv**$_2$(s, m) : (σ, com, dec)$\}$.

3   Zero-Knowledge Sets

Our definition of zero-knowledge set follows [8,12,15]. A zero-knowledge set protocol involves a prover and several verifiers. In the public parameter model, they share public parameters which we denote as σ in the following context. σ could be given by a $\mathcal{TTP}$. The prover secretly holds a set S, which is a subset of $\{0, 1\}^*$. There are two stages afterwards. On the first stage, the prover commits to the set S and sends the commitment to the verifier. On the second stage, several sessions can be initiated by the verifier. A verifier can query the prover with any $x \in \{0, 1\}^*$ in each session. The prover returns a proof π_x for either $x \in S$ or $x \notin S$. The verifier will output either "accept" or "reject".

A zero-knowledge set protocol should satisfy three security requirements: completeness, soundness and zero-knowledge. Informally, completeness means that if the prover give the verifier a correct and honest proof, the verifier is always convinced. Soundness means that the prover could not cheat the verifier: the prover could not efficiently give proofs for both $x \in S$ and $x \notin S$ for any x. Zero-knowledge means that whatever the verifier can efficiently compute after interacting with the prover can also be efficiently compute before, or in other words, the verifier is not able to gain any knowledge other than what the prover gave him. Especially, he could not know whether a value he had not queried is in S or not. Moreover, he could not know about the size of S.

Definition 3. *(Zero-Knowledge Sets) A zero-knowledge set consists of four efficient algorithms: ZKS = (setup, commit, prove, verify).*
setup.   *Generate the public parameter. This algorithm is running by a TTP. Input: Security parameter* 1^k. *Output:* σ.
commit.   *The prover commit to a set S. Input: σ and a set S. Output: A commitment C to the set S, and some private information dec to decommit.*
prove.   *The verifier queries the prover with $x \in \{0, 1\}^k$. The prover outputs a proof π_x with input$\{\sigma, x, S, C, dec\}$.*
verify.   *With input $\{\sigma, C, x, \pi_x\}$, the verifier outputs either* accept *or* reject.

The algorithms should satisfy following three properties:
(1) *(Perfect Completeness with an Effecient Prover) The* **ZKS** *algorithm satisfies completeness, if for $\forall S$ and $\forall x$ holds that:*

$$Pr\begin{bmatrix} \sigma \leftarrow_R \textbf{setup}(1^k); \\ (C, dec) \leftarrow \textbf{commit}(\sigma, S); \\ (\pi_x) \leftarrow \textbf{prove}(\sigma, x, S, C, dec) : \\ \textbf{verify}(\sigma, C, x, \pi_x) = accept \end{bmatrix} = 1.$$

(2) (Computational Soundness)The ZKS algorithm satisfies soundness, if for ∀S and ∀x and any probabilistic polynomial time algorithm P holds that:

$$Pr\left[\begin{array}{l} \sigma \leftarrow_R \text{\textbf{setup}}(1^k), (C, x, \pi_x, \pi'_x) \leftarrow \textbf{P}(\sigma, S): \\ \text{\textbf{verify}}(\sigma, C, x, \pi_x) = accept \cap \text{\textbf{verify}}(\sigma, C, x, \pi'_x) = accept \end{array}\right] = neg(k)$$

where π_x is the proof for $x \in S$, π'_x is the proof for $x \notin S$ and neg(k) is a function negligible in k.

(3) (Zero-Knowledge) The ZKS algorithm satisfies zero-knowledge property, if for any efficient adversary $\mathcal{A}$, and any set S there exists a probabilistic polynomial time simulator $\textbf{sim} = \{\textbf{sim}_1, \textbf{sim}_2\}$ that, the outputs of the two experiments following are computational indistinguishable, where the outputs of the two experiments are actually the views of the adversary interacting with a real world prover and a simulator respectively.

$Exp^{ZK-Real}_{\mathcal{A},ZKS}$	$Exp^{ZK-Fake}_{\mathcal{A},Sim}$
$\sigma \leftarrow_R \textbf{setup}(1^k)$;	$(\sigma', C, s) \leftarrow_R \textbf{sim}_1(1^k)$
$(C, dec) \leftarrow \textbf{commit}(\sigma, S)$;	*(where s represents state information)*;
For any sufficient large number m,	*For any sufficient large number m,*
for $1 \le i \le m$:	*for* $1 \le i \le m$:
$(x_1, \omega_1) \leftarrow \mathcal{A}(\sigma, C)$,	$(x_1, \omega'_1) \leftarrow \mathcal{A}(\sigma', C')$,
$(\pi_{x_1}) \leftarrow \textbf{prove}(\sigma, x_1, S, C, dec)$,	$(\pi'_{x_1}) \leftarrow \textbf{sim}_2{}^S(\sigma', x_1, C', s)$
$(x_i, \omega_i) \leftarrow \mathcal{A}(\sigma, C, \{x_1, \omega_1\}, ...\{x_{i-1}, \omega_{i-1}\})$,	$(x_i, \omega'_i) \leftarrow \mathcal{A}(\sigma', C', \{x_1, \omega'_1\}, ...\{x_{i-1}, \omega'_{i-1}\})$,
$(\pi_{x_i}) \leftarrow \textbf{prove}(\sigma, x_i, S, C, dec)$;	$(\pi'_{x_i}) \leftarrow \textbf{sim2}{}^S(\sigma', x_i, C', s)$;
return:	*return:*
$\sigma, C, x_1, \pi_{x_1}, ..., x_i, \pi_{x_i}, ..., x_m, \pi_{x_m}$	$\sigma', C', x_1, \pi'_{x_1}, ..., x_i, \pi'_{x_i}, ..., x'_m, \pi_{x_m}$

ω_i *means the private information yielded while $\mathcal{A}$ picks the element x_i.*

Lemma 2. *The algorithm "**commit**" in ZKS as definition 5 is equivocable.*

Proof. Note that the ZKS simulator of Definition 3 for the zero-knowledge property is actually working the same way as the simulator of Definition 2. Therefore, this lemma is straightforward.

4   Non-malleability for ZKS

Under some circumstances, the security described above is not sufficient. For instance, there might be a man-in-the-middle attack. During the man-in-the-middle attack, an adversary simultaneously participates in two executions. In one execution, the adversary acts as a verifier and gets commitments from the prover and queries elements for proofs. In the other one it acts as a prover who composes a zero-knowledge set which is related to the real prover's set. An honest verifier would not be able to tell the difference between interaction with a real prover and with the adversary.

Typically, in the man-in-the-middle attack, the adversary takes advantage of the malleability of the ciphertext, which in ZKS is the commitment to the set. The adversary produces legitimate ciphertext directly from one known ciphertext without knowing a corresponding plaintext. Since the ciphertext is related, the plaintext will also be related.

In this section, we define non-malleable ZKS after the definition of non-malleable commitment [6]. Then we give a definition of independence which is slightly different from the original definition from [8], and use the technique of [6] to prove that the independence is as strong as non-malleability for ZKS. The proof also shows the way to prove the non-malleability of a ZKS.

Definition 4. *(Non-malleability for ZKS) Let **ZKS** = (**setup, commit, prove, verify**) be a zero-knowledge sets protocol, and k be the security parameter. A ZKS protocol is non-malleable with respect to opening if for any probabilistic polynomial time adversary $\mathcal{A}$, there exists a polynomial time simulator $\mathcal{A}'$, such that for all valid relations R (see the following remark):*

$$Pr[\textbf{Exp}^{Real}_{\mathcal{A}, ZKS} = 1] - Pr[\textbf{Exp}^{Sim} = 1] \leqslant neg(k)$$

where:

$\textbf{Exp}^{Real}_{\mathcal{A}, ZKS}$
$\sigma \leftarrow \textbf{setup}(1^k); \ S \leftarrow_R \{0,1\}^k;$
$(C, dec) \leftarrow \textbf{commit}(\sigma, S);$
$C_{\mathcal{A}} \leftarrow \mathcal{A}^{prove(\sigma,.,C,S,dec)}(\sigma, C);$
$S_{\mathcal{A}} \leftarrow \mathcal{A}^{prove(\sigma,.,C,S,dec)}(\sigma, C, S);$
$return \ R(S, S_{\mathcal{A}})$

$\textbf{Exp}^{Sim}_{\mathcal{A}'}$
$S \leftarrow_R \{0,1\}^k;$
$S_{\mathcal{A}'} \leftarrow \mathcal{A}'(1^k);$
$return \ R(S, S_{\mathcal{A}'})$

Remark. We have several restrictions here about the experiments: we assume that $S_{\mathcal{A}}$ is really a decommitment of $C_{\mathcal{A}}$ in this definition and the following context (we assume the experiment will not be going on if $S_{\mathcal{A}}$ is not a decommitment of $C_{\mathcal{A}}$); and if $\mathcal{A}$ outputs "⊥" in any step, the experiment will be repeated from the beginning until the experiment is successfully finished; the experiments which is not successfully finished does not count.

By "valid relation", we mean that the relationship is able to describe in polynomial times and not trivial. For instance, "$S_{\mathcal{A}}$ containing the values that $\mathcal{A}$ queried before" is not considered as a "valid relation".

Independence for ZKS. The independence of our definition follows [8]. The notion of independence requires that after seeing a commitment C, the adversary produces its own commitment $C_{\mathcal{A}}$. Afterwards, no matter what set the commitment is opened to, the decommitment of $C_{\mathcal{A}}$ could not be changed. In other words, after the adversary outputs its commitment, the set corresponds to the commitment is fixed. $\mathcal{A}$ itself is unable to equivocate its commitment. So the set committed by the adversary is independent from the set committed by the prover with respect to opening.

Definition 5. *(Independence for ZKS) Let **ZKS** = (**setup, commit, prove, verify**) be a zero-knowledge sets protocol, and k be the security parameter. We say that ZKS protocol is independence, if for any set S, any probabilistic polynomial time adversary*

$\mathcal{A} = (\mathcal{A}_1, \mathcal{A}_2)$, *there exists a polynomial time simulator* $sim = \{sim_1, sim_2\}$ *such that* $Pr[\mathbf{Exp}_{\mathcal{A},ZKS}^{Independence} = 1] \leqslant neg(k)$, *where:*

$\mathbf{Exp}_{\mathcal{A},ZKS}^{Independence}$

$(\sigma, C) \leftarrow sim_1(1^k);$

$(C_{\mathcal{A}}, \tau) \leftarrow \mathcal{A}_1^{sim_2^S(C,Q_i)}(\sigma);$

$S' \leftarrow_R \{0, 1\}^k$ and $S' \cap S = \{x \mid x \text{ has been queried before.}\};$

$(x, \pi_x) \leftarrow \mathcal{A}_2^{sim_2^S(C,Q_i)}(\sigma, C_{\mathcal{A}}, \tau);$

$(x, \pi'_x) \leftarrow \mathcal{A}_2^{sim_2^{S'}(C,Q_i)}(\sigma, C_{\mathcal{A}}, \tau);$

(*where one of* π_x *and* π'_x *is proof for* $x \in S$ *and the other for* $x \notin S$;):

if $\mathbf{verify}(\sigma, C, x, \pi_x) = accept \cap \mathbf{verify}(\sigma, C, x, \pi'_x) = accept,$

return 1;

else, return 0

Where τ *is the private information* $\mathcal{A}_1$ *produced to help.* Q_i *is the* i^{th} *query to the commitment* C. *Moreover,* $sim_2^S(C, Q_i)$ *means that* sim_2 *has oracle access to set* S *to help it answering the query* Q_i.

Remark. Simulated prover is used here because we need to open the same commitment to different sets. Since a simulator or a real prover seems indistinguishable for the adversary, this definition makes sense.

We do not require $C_{\mathcal{A}} \neq C$, so the definition of non-malleability here is stronger than that of [6]. Also, our definition of non-malleability and independence has several differences with the definitions in [8]. First of all, the authors of [8] allows the adversary access to several sets $S_1, S_2, ... S_n$ before outputting his own commitment. For simplicity, we use a weaker definition here. However, we stress that the scheme we constructed in section 5 is independent with respect to the stronger definition. Moreover, in our definition of independence, sets S' is generated adaptively after adversary gave its commitment, while in the definition and proof of schemes of [8], they assume both of the two database at the beginning. Since sets S' is clearly relative with the adversary's queries before giving its commitment, our definition is more reasonable.

Theorem 1. *If a ZKS protocol is independent, then it is non-malleable with respect to opening, and vice versa.*

Proof. The zero-knowledge simulator of ZKS (cf. definition 7) is a key ingredient in this proof. The simulator generates public parameters which are distributed identically to the real execution. The knowledge of the trapdoor makes it capable of proving any value both in and not in a set from a commitment.

Assuming a real set S and a ZKS algorithm, we consider the probability of any probabilistic polynomial algorithm $\mathcal{A} = (\mathcal{A}_1, \mathcal{A}_2)$, which is also known as the adversary, outputting a set $S_{\mathcal{A}}$ that $R(S, S_{\mathcal{A}}) = 1$. Four cases exist here:

Case 1. $\mathcal{A}$ interacting with a real prover, which is the $\mathbf{Exp}_{\mathcal{A}, ZKS}^{Real}$.(cf. definition 4).

Case 2. $\mathcal{A}$ interacting with a probabilistic simulator $sim = \{sim_1, sim_2\}$. The simulator has oracle access to the set S. It commits to a random string and answers $\mathcal{A}$'s query by checking if the value is in S and generate proofs using the trapdoor information. The experiment is the $\mathbf{Exp}_{\mathcal{A},Sim}^{Fake_1}$ described in Fig.1.

Case 3. $\mathcal{A}$ interacting with a probabilistic simulator $\mathbf{sim} = \{\mathbf{sim}_1, \mathbf{sim}_2\}$. The simulator commits to a random string and answers $\mathcal{A}$'s query by checking if the value is in S before $\mathcal{A}$ generates its own commitment. And then, it answers $\mathcal{A}$'s query with another set S', where $S' \cap S = \{x \mid x$ has been queried before.}.The experiment is the $\mathbf{Exp}_{\mathcal{A},Sim}^{Fake_2}$ described in Fig.1.

Case 4. $\mathcal{A}$ gains nothing from the simulator. It is the situation of $\mathbf{Exp}^{Sim}$(cf. definition 4).

$\mathbf{Exp}_{\mathcal{A},Sim}^{Fake_1}$	$\mathbf{Exp}_{\mathcal{A},Sim}^{Fake_2}$
$(\sigma,C) \leftarrow \mathbf{sim}_1(1^k);$	$(\sigma,C) \leftarrow \mathbf{sim}_1(1^k);$
$(C_{\mathcal{A}},\tau) \leftarrow \mathcal{A}_1^{\mathbf{sim}_2^S(C,Q_i)}(\sigma);$	$(C_{\mathcal{A}},\tau) \leftarrow \mathcal{A}_1^{\mathbf{sim}_2^S(C,Q_i)}(\sigma);$
$S_{\mathcal{A}} \leftarrow \mathcal{A}_2^{\mathbf{sim}_2^S(C,Q_i)}(\sigma,C_{\mathcal{A}},\tau,C,S);$	$S_{\mathcal{A}} \leftarrow \mathcal{A}_2^{\mathbf{sim}_2^{S'}(C,Q_i)}(\sigma,C_{\mathcal{A}},\tau,C,S');$
return R $(S,S_{\mathcal{A}})$	*return R* $(S,S_{\mathcal{A}})$

Fig. 1. Where $S_{\mathcal{A}} \leftarrow \mathcal{A}_2^{\mathbf{sim}_2^S(C,Q_i)}(\sigma,C_{\mathcal{A}},\tau,C,S)$ means that $\mathcal{A}_2$ queries the set with several values and $\mathbf{sim}_2$ provides the proofs of the values according to set S. Afterwards, with input of $\sigma,C_{\mathcal{A}},\tau,C,S$, $\mathcal{A}_2$ outputs set $S_{\mathcal{A}}$ which is the decommitment of $C_{\mathcal{A}}$.

Comparing these four cases, $\mathcal{A}$ gets less and less information of the set S. Therefore the the probabilities of outputting 1 of each adjacent case (which is the success probability of the adversary) is decrease. We have:

$$Pr[\mathbf{Exp}_{\mathcal{A},ZKS}^{Real} = 1] \geq Pr[\mathbf{Exp}_{\mathcal{A},Sim}^{Fake_1} = 1] \geq Pr[\mathbf{Exp}_{\mathcal{A},Sim}^{Fake_2} = 1] \geq Pr[\mathbf{Exp}^{Sim} = 1].$$

Since case 1 and 4 are the experiments from the definition of non-malleability, to prove a ZKS algorithm is non-malleable, we have to prove the difference of the probabilities of outputting 1 between each adjacent cases is negligible.

If the probabilities of outputting 1 of case 1 and 2 are non-negligibly different, we can have a algorithm $\mathcal{B}$ which invokes $\mathcal{A}$ as a subroutine and contradicts the zero-knowledge property of ZKS. It runs $\mathcal{A}$ in both the experiments several times, then decides that the experiment with higher probabilities of outputting 1 is the experiment with the real prover. The advantage of $\mathcal{B}$ to distinguish a real prover and a simulator would be non-negligible. Therefore, we have :

$$Pr[\mathbf{Exp}_{\mathcal{A},ZKS}^{Real} = 1] - Pr[\mathbf{Exp}_{\mathcal{A},Sim}^{Fake_1} = 1] \leq neg(k) \tag{1}$$

Also obviously, the probabilities of outputting 1 in case 3 and 4 are the same. Since during case 3, the simulator knows noting about S except the values $\mathcal{A}$ queried before committing. No knowledge could be provided by the simulator to $\mathcal{A}$. Therefore:

$$Pr[\mathbf{Exp}_{\mathcal{A},Sim}^{Fake_2} = 1] - Pr[\mathbf{Exp}^{Sim} = 1] \leq neg(k) \tag{2}$$

Now let us focus on case 2 and 3. We will show that:

$$Pr[\mathbf{Exp}_{\mathcal{A},Sim}^{Fake_1} = 1] - Pr[\mathbf{Exp}_{\mathcal{A},Sim}^{Fake_2} = 1] \leq Pr[\mathbf{Exp}_{\mathcal{A},ZKS}^{Independence} = 1] \tag{3}$$

If the same $S_{\mathcal{A}}$ is generated by the adversary during both of the experiments, the probabilities of outputting 1 of both cases are the same. So if $Pr[\mathbf{Exp}_{\mathcal{A},Sim}^{Fake_1} = 1] -$ $Pr[\mathbf{Exp}_{\mathcal{A},Sim}^{Fake_2} = 1] \geq neg(k)$, then different $S_{\mathcal{A}}$ is generated by the adversary in both cases. Since the procedures are exactly the same before $\mathcal{A}$ outputs its commitment. It is reasonable to assume $\mathcal{A}$ outputs the same commitment in both cases. If $S_{\mathcal{A}}$ is different and $S_{\mathcal{A}}$ is truly the decommitment of $C_{\mathcal{A}}$, then there must be at least one element x which belongs to one of the $S_{\mathcal{A}}$ but not the other. Therefore, in one case, $\mathcal{A}$ is able to prove that $x \in S_{\mathcal{A}}$, and in the other case it is able to prove that $x \notin S_{\mathcal{A}}$ for the same commitment. We can have that $Pr[\mathbf{Exp}_{\mathcal{A},ZKS}^{Independence} = 1] \geq neg(k)$. Equation 3 is proved.

From equation 1, 2 and 3, we have: if $Pr[\mathbf{Exp}_{\mathcal{A},ZKS}^{Independence} = 1] \leq neg(k)$ then $Pr[\mathbf{Exp}_{\mathcal{A},ZKS}^{Real} = 1] - Pr[\mathbf{Exp}^{Sim} = 1] \leq neg(k)$. That is to say, if a ZKS protocol is independent, then it is non-malleable with respect to opening.

Furthermore, if $Pr[\mathbf{Exp}_{\mathcal{A},ZKS}^{Independence} = 1] \geq neg(k)$, then during case 2 and case 3 different $S_{\mathcal{A}}$ are outputted by $\mathcal{A}$, which we denote as $S_{\mathcal{A}_2}$ and $S_{\mathcal{A}_3}$ respectively. Furthermore, $\mathcal{A}$ is able to equivocate its commitment and make it related to the set it has queried. Therefore, there exists a relationship R' that $R'(S, S_{\mathcal{A}_2}) = 1$ and $R'(S, S_{\mathcal{A}_3}) = 0$. We have:

$$Pr[\mathbf{Exp}_{\mathcal{A},Sim}^{Fake_1} = 1] - Pr[\mathbf{Exp}_{\mathcal{A},Sim}^{Fake_2} = 1] \geq Pr[\mathbf{Exp}_{\mathcal{A},ZKS}^{Independence} = 1] \geq neg(k)$$

So that:

$$Pr[\mathbf{Exp}_{\mathcal{A},ZKS}^{Real} = 1] - Pr[\mathbf{Exp}^{Sim} = 1] \geq neg(k)$$

Therefore, if a ZKS protocol is non-malleable with respect to opening , it is independence. $\square$

Note that from the proof it is easy to figure that the theorem is true while the protocol is equivocable.

5 Constructions

In this section, we first briefly show our assumptions and the basic build blocks to construct our protocol. Then, a non-malleable ZKS is constructed.

5.1 Assumptions and Build Blocks

We construct our scheme under the public parameter model. The security of our scheme is based on the strong RSA assumption[14]. The *non-interactive zero-knowledge proof of knowledge* (NIZKoK) constructed in [5] is used while proving each value.

We modify the hash function constructed in [15] to a collision-free hash function and use it as a basic build block. The hash function H is a bijective map mapping each element to a unique prime like follows:

$H(x) = p$, where for any element $x \in \{0, 1\}^k$, p is the smallest prime number greater than $(x + 1)^2$.

According to the Cramer-Granville Conjecture, [10] has proved that there is at least one prime number between t^2 and $(t + 1)^2$, where t is a positive integer, so hash function

H is a bijective map. And even we test every integer with a polynomial promality test starting from t^2 until a prime is found, the time complicity is $\mathbb{O}(logt)$ [15]. Therefore, the hash function H is an efficiently computable.

Finally, we assume the existence of secure signature scheme (**sig,ver**) with a pair of key (sk, vk) [4]. sk and algorithm **sig** are used to sign on a message and vk and algorithm **ver** are used to verify it. A commitment protocol $Com_r(m)$ satisfying hiding and binding property is also assumed.

5.2   Construction of ACCUMU-ZKS

In this subsection, we construct a ZKS protocol and prove its independence. We call our protocol **ACCUMU-ZKS**.

ACCUMU-ZKS = (**setup, commit, prove, verify**):

setup.   Generate the public parameter σ. On input 1^k, select a k-bit RSA modulus n and a $g \leftarrow_R QR_n$. Output $\sigma = (n, g)$.

commit.   With the input of a finite set $S = \{x_1, x_2, ..., x_n\}$, the prover chooses random string r, s and computes:

$u = H(x_1)H(x_2)...H(x_n)$, $v = G(r)G(vk)$;
$C_S = g^{u+v} \pmod{n}$, $C_r = Com_s(r)$;
(sk, vk) is a pair of keys for a signature scheme.

Then it outputs $C = (C_S, C_r)$ as its commitment of the set S and publishes vk. It keeps $dec = (r, u, v, s, S, sk)$ as private information to generate proofs in the proving stage. G is a collision-resistant one-way hash function. Com is a commitment scheme.

prove.   While a verifier starts a session to query the set S, and its legitimate identity has been verified, the prover secretly chooses a random string r_i as the session random input. Then it computes $C_{r_i} = Com_{s_i}(r_i)$ (where s_i is the randomness used to generate the ith commitment) and a signature of C, C_{r_i}. It transfers $C_{r_i}, sig_{sk}(C, C_{r_i})$ to the verifier (i is the index to mark a session).

The verifier verifies the signature with vk. If it is valid, he query prover with some element x.

If $x \in S$: The prover computes $C_x = g^{u/H(x)+G(r_i)} \pmod{n}, d = g^{G(r_i)H(x)-G(r)G(vk)}$ (mod n). It also generates a NIZKoK proof π_x that the prover knows r and r_i satisfies d and r, r_i is the decommitment of C_r and C_{r_i}. The prover outputs $\{C_x, d, \pi_x\}$ as the proof for $x \in S$.

If $x \notin S$: Then $gcd(u + G(r_i)H(x), H(x)) = 1$. The prover computes two integers a and b such that $a(u + G(r_i)H(x)) + bH(x) = 1$. The prover computes $C_x = g^{u+G(r_i)H(x)}$ (mod n), $C_x' = C_x^a \pmod{n}$, $d = g^{(-b)} \pmod{n}$, $m = g^{G(r_i)H(x)-G(r)G(vk)} \pmod{n}$. Then it generates a NIZKoK proof π_x that the prover knows a, b, r, r_i such that $m = g^{G(r_i)H(x)-G(r)G(vk)} \pmod{n}, d = g^{(-b)} \pmod{n}, C_x' = C_x^a \pmod{n}$, and r, r_i is the decommitment of C_r and C_{r_i}. Finally the prover outputs $\{C_x', C_x, m, d, \pi_x\}$ as the proof for $x \notin S$.

verify.   If the prover claims $x \in S$, the verifier checks if $(C_x^{H(x)} = C_S \cdot d)$, and verifies the NIZKoK proof π_x. If the NIZKoK proof is accepted, the verifier outputs *accept*, otherwise, it outputs *reject*.

If the prover claimed $x \notin S$, the verifier checks if $C_x' = d^{H(x)}g \pmod{n}$, $m = C_x^{H(x)}/C_S \pmod{n}$ and if the NIZKoK proof is accepted. If yes, the verifier outputs *accept*, otherwise, he outputs *reject*.

Remark. Comparing with the tree-based constructions, this scheme is easier to update: To adding (resp. eliminating) a value, the tree-based commitment of a set is re-calculated by resetting all the nodes along the path and for each node a committing and hashing operation is involved; while in our scheme, you just have to multiply the corresponding prime to u (resp. divide u by the prime) to achieve this. Moreover, the length of the proof for a value increases with the growth of the depth of the tree for the tree-based construction, while the complexity of the proof algorithm in our scheme remains the same.

Theorem 2. *ACCUMU-ZKS is a non-malleable ZKS protocol with respect to opening under the strong RSA assumption.*

Proof. To prove that the **ACCUMU-ZKS** is a non-malleable ZKS protocol, we need to prove that it is a ZKS scheme first and then prove its independence property.

The completeness is quite obvious. The soundness property relies on the strong RSA assumption. Because if any adversary $\mathcal{A}$ has the ability to generate solid proofs both for $x \in S$ and $x \notin S$, we have (in the following equations, we uses the same symbol with the construction above, only with extra marks " $\in S$ " or " $\notin S$ " for distinguishing):

$$C_{x \in S}{}^{H(x)}/d_{x \in S} = C_S \pmod{n}; C_{x \notin S}{}^{H(x)} = mC_S \pmod{n}; C_{x \notin S}' = d_{x \notin S}^{H(x)}g \pmod{n};$$

Also, from the NIZKoK of $C_{x \notin S}' = C_{x \notin S}{}^a$ and $d_{x \notin S} = g^{-b}$, we can have a knowledge extractor that extracts α, β from the NIZKoK such that:

$$C_{x \notin S}' = C_{x \notin S}{}^\alpha; d_{x \notin S} = g^\beta$$

From the equations above, we have:

$$(mC_{x \in S}{}^{H(x)}/d_{x \in S})^\alpha = (g^{\beta H(x)}g)^{H(x)} \pmod{n}$$

According to Lemma 1, if $gcd(\alpha, (1 + H(x)\beta)^{H(x)}) = 1$, we can find $y, e \in Z_n$ such that $y^e = g \pmod{n}$. The probability is non-negligible after several queries. Therefore, if any adversary $\mathcal{A}$ has the ability to generate solid proofs both for $x \in S$ and $x \notin S$, we can use it to break the strong RSA assumption with non-negligible advantage. The soundness property is proved.

To prove the zero-knowledge property, we need to construct a ZKS simulator that acts like a real prover and produces views which are computational indistinguishable with real ones. However, the simulator knows only what the verifier should know, which is "whether an element $x \in S$". Then the ZK property could be proved. Before describing the ZKS simulator, we define an oracle O, which with query x, tells whether $x \in S$. Then we specify the behavior of the simulator for the protocol:

$\mathbf{sim_1}$: With input 1^k, $\mathbf{sim_1}$ chooses two prime p and q and compute $n = pq$, $g \in QR_n$, then sets the public parameter $\sigma = \{n, g\}$, stores (p, q) as internal state (where (p, q)

is the trapdoor to help sim_2 generate valid proofs). Then it chooses random string r and a prime p, generates a pair of key (sk, vk) of a signature scheme and computes $C_S = g^{p+G(r)G(vk)}$ (mod n) and $C_r = Com_s(r)$. Finally, it outputs $C = \{\{C_S, C_r\}$ and $vk\}$.

sim_2: When the adversary starts a session, it computes $C_{r_i}, \text{sig}_{sk}(C, C_{r_i})$ like a real prover. Then sim_2 queries the oracle O if $x \in S$.

If O answers yes, sim_2 computes $H(x), H(x)^{-1}$ with the knowledge of (p, q), and $C_x = g^{pH(x)^{-1}+G(r_i)}$ (mod n), $d = g^{G(r_i)H(x)-G(r)G(vk)}$ (mod n). Then it generates a NIZKoK proof π_x the same way as the real prover. It outputs $\{C_x, d, \pi_x\}$.

If O answers no, and the corresponding prime to x is not p, sim_2 works the same way as the real prover and outputs$\{C_x', C_x, m, d, \pi_x\}$. (It could simply output $\perp$ while the corresponding prime to x is p and re-simulate.)

The simulator is basically having the same properties with the simulator in [15], so the proof for the computational indistinguishability of the views is alike. ZKS property is preserved. We leave the details due to the length limit. One can refer to [15] for a full proof.

Therefore, **ACCUMU-ZKS** is a ZKS protocol for satisfying the completeness, soundness and zero-knowledge property.

Now let us prove the independence property of **ACCUMU-ZKS**. Assume there is a set S and an adversary $\mathcal{A} = \{\mathcal{A}_1, \mathcal{A}_2\}$ which contradicts the independence condition in Definition 5. We run sim_1 to get the public parameter σ and the commitment $C = \{\{C_S, C_r\}$ and $vk\}$ to the set S. $\mathcal{A}_1$ queries some values on the commitment and sim_2 answers the queries with oracle access to set S. At last, $\mathcal{A}_1$ outputs a commitment of its own $C_{\mathcal{A}} = \{\{C_{S_{\mathcal{A}}}, C_{r_{\mathcal{A}}}\}, vk_{\mathcal{A}}\}$. And we generate a random sets S' which only meets set S with the values $\mathcal{A}_1$ has queried.

Then we run two copies of $\mathcal{A}_2$ to get a proof of a element x. One answers $\mathcal{A}_2$'s queries to the by running sim_2 with oracle access to set S. The other one answers $\mathcal{A}_2$'s queries to the by running sim_2 with oracle access to set S'. Finally, $\mathcal{A}_2$ outputs $\{x_{\mathcal{A}}, (C_{x_{\mathcal{A}}}, d_{\mathcal{A}}, \pi_{x_{\mathcal{A}}})\}$ and $\{x_{\mathcal{A}}, (C'_{x_{\mathcal{A}}}, C_{x_{\mathcal{A}}}, m_{\mathcal{A}}, d_{\mathcal{A}}, \pi_{x_{\mathcal{A}}})\}$ in different executions. From the structure of both proofs, we can see that one of them is a proof for $x_{\mathcal{A}} \in S$ and the other for $x_{\mathcal{A}} \notin S$. Both of them will be accept by the verifier. (Without loss of generality and to simplify the proof here, we can assume that in both executions, $\mathcal{A}_2$ chooses the same session random string $r_{i_{\mathcal{A}}}$, because different $r_{i_{\mathcal{A}}}$ would not affect the validity of proof $\mathcal{A}_2$ outputs.) We have two cases here:

Case 1: $vk_{\mathcal{A}} \neq vk$. In this case, with a randomly chosen $r_{i_{\mathcal{A}}}$, the possibility of getting $v_{\mathcal{A}} = v$ by coincidence is negligible. The advantage of computing r from the commitment or NIZKoK proof is negligible. Therefore the probability that $C_{\mathcal{A}} = C$ is negligible. While $C_{\mathcal{A}} \neq C$, if $\mathcal{A}_2$ outputs $\{x_{\mathcal{A}}, (C_{x_{\mathcal{A}}}, d_{\mathcal{A}}, \pi_{x_{\mathcal{A}}})\}$ and $\{x_{\mathcal{A}}, (C'_{x_{\mathcal{A}}}, C_{x_{\mathcal{A}}}, m_{\mathcal{A}}, d_{\mathcal{A}}, \pi_{x_{\mathcal{A}}})\}$ in different executions and the verifier accepts, the soundness proof shows how to uses such proofs to break the strong RSA assumption.

Case 2: $vk_{\mathcal{A}} = vk$. In this case, if $C_{\mathcal{A}} = C$, $\mathcal{A}_2$ must chooses different $r_{i_{\mathcal{A}}}$ from sim_2's, we have $C_{r_{i_{\mathcal{A}}}} \neq C_{r_i}$; and if $\mathcal{A}$ uses the same C_{r_i}, it must be $C_{\mathcal{A}} \neq C$. Otherwise, giving different proofs for $x_{\mathcal{A}}$ would be incurious, since $\mathcal{A}$ just copies whatever sim_2 does. In both situation, we could break the signature scheme. That is, assuming $\mathcal{A}$ wants to forge the prover's signature. It acts as following: $\mathcal{A}$ queries the prover with some values and gets signature on $\{C, C_{r_i}\}$ (where i represents the index mark the queries). We want to get a signature of the prover on a different message from what we already got during the query. Since $\mathcal{A}$ chooses $vk_{\mathcal{A}} = vk$. And either $C_{\mathcal{A}} \neq C$, or $C_{r_{i_{\mathcal{A}}}} \neq C_{r_i}$, the message $\mathcal{A}$ has signed is different from that he has got from the queries. It succeeds.

We have that **ACCUMU-ZKS** is a non-malleable ZKS with respect to opening.   □

References

1. Catalano, D., Dodis, Y., Visconti, I.: Mercurial Commitments: Minimal Assump-tions and Efficient Constructions. In: Halevi, S., Rabin, T. (eds.) TCC 2006. LNCS, vol. 3876, Springer, Heidelberg (2006)
2. Catalano, D., Fiore, D., Messina, M.: Zero-knowledge Sets with Short Proofs. In: Smart, N.P. (ed.) EUROCRYPT 2008. LNCS, vol. 4965, pp. 433–450. Springer, Heidelberg (2008)
3. Chase, M., Healy, A., Lysyanskaya, A., Malkin, T., Reyzin, L.: Mercurial Commitments and Zero-Knowledge Sets based on general assumptions. In: Cramer, R. (ed.) EUROCRYPT 2005. LNCS, vol. 3494, pp. 422–439. Springer, Heidelberg (2005)
4. Cramer, R., Shoup, V.: Signature Schemes Based On the Strong RSA Assumption. In: Proc. the 6th ACM Conference on Computer and Communications Security, Singapore, pp. 46–51 (November 1999)
5. De Santis, A., Persiano, G.: Zero-knowledge Proofs of Knowledge Without Interaction. In: Proceedings of the 33rd Annual Symposium on Foundations of Computer Science, pp. 427–436 (1992)
6. Di Crescenzo, G., Katz, J., Ostrovsky, R., Smith, A.: Efficient and Non-interactive Non-malleable Commitment. In: Pfitzmann, B. (ed.) EUROCRYPT 2001. LNCS, vol. 2045, pp. 40–59. Springer, Heidelberg (2001)
7. Dolev, D., Dwork, C., Naor, M.: Non-malleable Cryptography. SIAM J. Comp. 30(2), 391–437 (1991)
8. Gennaro, R., Micali, S.: Independent zero-knowledge sets. In: Bugliesi, M., Preneel, B., Sassone, V., Wegener, I. (eds.) ICALP 2006. LNCS, vol. 4052, pp. 34–45. Springer, Heidelberg (2006)
9. Goldreich, O.: Foundations of Cryptography: Basic Tools. Cambridge University Press, Cambridge (2001) ISBN 0-521-79172-3
10. Granville, A.: Harold Cramer and the Distribution of Prime Numbers. Scandanavian Actuarial Journal 1, 12–28 (1995)
11. Liskov, M.: Updatable zero-knowledge databases. In: Roy, B. (ed.) ASIACRYPT 2005. LNCS, vol. 3788, pp. 174–198. Springer, Heidelberg (2005)
12. Micali, S., Rabin, M.O., Kilian, J.: Zero-Knowledge Sets. In: Proc. of FOCS 2003, pp. 80–91 (2003)
13. Sahai, A.: Non-Malleable Non-Interactive Zero Knowledge and Adaptive Chosen-Ciphertext Security. In: 40th FOCS, pp. 543–553 (1999)
14. Shamir, A.: On the Generation of Cryptographically Strong Pseudorandom Sequences. ACM Transactions on Computer Systems 1(1), 38 (1983)
15. Xue, R., Li, N., Li, J.: Algebraic Construction for Zero-knowledge Sets. Journal of Computer Science and Technology 23(2), 166–175 (2008)

Distributed Paillier Cryptosystem without Trusted Dealer

Takashi Nishide and Kouichi Sakurai

Department of Informatics, Kyushu University,
744 Motooka, Nishi-ku, Fukuoka, 819-0395, Japan
{nishide,sakurai}@inf.kyushu-u.ac.jp

Abstract. We propose a distributed key generation protocol for the threshold Paillier cryptosystem. Often in the multiparty computation based on the threshold Paillier cryptosystem, the existence of a trusted dealer is assumed to distribute secret key shares, but it can be a single point of attack, so it is not preferable. Building on the threshold Paillier cryptosystem with a trusted dealer, we show how to eliminate the trusted dealer by robust distributed key generation without using safe primes.

Keywords: Distributed Key Generation, Multiparty Computation, Secret Sharing, Threshold Paillier Cryptosystem.

1 Introduction

Many multiparty computation (MPC) protocols using threshold homomorphic cryptosystems are Paillier-based [32] constructions (e.g., [13,3,28,36,26]). Therefore, the distributed key generation (DKG) protocol for the threshold Paillier cryptosystem is one of the most important applications of MPC because we can eliminate the trusted dealer of the key and it is the main purpose of MPC.

The DKG protocol (e.g., [33,27]) for discrete-log based cryptosystems (e.g., ElGamal cryptosystem) is relatively efficient and simple. However, the DKG protocol for RSA-based cryptosystems is a non-trivial task. Boneh and Franklin [5,6] proposed the first DKG protocol for the RSA cryptosystem. Unfortunately it cannot be applied to the threshold RSA cryptosystem [38] because for a technical reason the RSA modulus for [38] must be a special type of RSA modulus that is a product of two large safe primes where a prime $p(= 2p' + 1)$ is a safe prime if p' is also a prime. For the same technical reason, the threshold Paillier cryptosystem [23] also needs an RSA modulus that is a product of two safe primes.

Fouque and Stern [24] proposed how to use an RSA modulus that is not a product of two safe primes in order to relax the condition and the security proof of their scheme is based solely on the standard complexity assumption, but the scheme is not so efficient because it still uses fairly restricted RSA moduli and one party needs to generate several zero-knowledge proofs for decryption.

On the other hand, Damgård and Koprowski [19] also proposed how to use an RSA modulus that is not a product of two safe primes, and the scheme seems practical because it can accept a wider class of RSA moduli, which means a fewer number of iterations are necessary for distributed key generation and one party

Y. Chung and M. Yung (Eds.): WISA 2010, LNCS 6513, pp. 44–60, 2011.

has only to generate one zero-knowledge proof for decryption. Though the security proof of their scheme is based on the non-standard complexity assumption, the assumption seems reasonable in the real-life applications.

Though there are several existing distributed key generation protocols [5,25,19,24,1,20,31] for the RSA cryptosystem, as pointed out in [39], they are not enough for the Paillier cryptosystem because the decryption procedure of the Paillier cryptosystem is different from that of the RSA cryptosystem, so we need different protocols for the Paillier cryptosystem.

Our Results. Building on [5,19], we show how the scheme of [23] that needs a trusted dealer can be realized without relying on the trusted dealer of the key that can be a single point of attack. In our scheme, the RSA modulus does not need to be a product of two safe primes. Our protocols are secure against an active and static adversary corrupting any minority of the parties and assume the random oracle model as in [19,24] for non-interactive zero-knowledge proofs.

The proposed protocols are robust without relying on the common reference string (CRS) model that is needed in [20]. In [24], the protocol to generate a prime candidate p such that $p-1$ is not divisible by small factors was proposed, but it is not robust and incomplete as mentioned in Sect. 4.1, so we give the protocol that works in a secure and robust way. Also we show how to generate the verification keys in a robust way that are necessary for decryption, which was not explicitly described in the previous work such as [5,19,24,1].

Related Work. Algesheimer, Camenisch, and Shoup [1] proposed a novel DKG protocol that can generate such a special type of RSA modulus directly. However, the protocol is not robust and finding safe primes can be very time-consuming and we are not aware whether there are infinitely many safe primes, so it will be more flexible for us to be able to use a wider class of RSA moduli as in [19].

Damgård and Jurik proposed a generalized Paillier cryptosystem [17] and another homomorphic cryptosystem [18] that can be considered as a mix of ElGamal and Paillier cryptosystems and both the threshold versions of [17,18] need RSA moduli that are products of two safe primes. One advantage of [18] over the Paillier cryptosystem is that because the secret key of [18] can be generated at random without the knowledge of the factors of the RSA modulus, the RSA modulus can be system-wide and reused by any set of parties that performs MPC. The part of our protocols will be applicable to realize the DKG protocols for both [17] and [18].

Damgård and Dupont [14] proposed how to use general RSA moduli for the threshold RSA signature scheme with the observation that resultant signatures can be verified with the public key (i.e., self-verifiable) after they are generated from partial signature shares even if an adversary has a non-negligible chance of giving valid zero-knowledge proofs for bad partial signature shares. However, the technique in [14] requires that we can recognize that the threshold signature generation or threshold decryption is done correctly and the techinique will not be applied to the context of our threshold decryption in the worst case because we may not be able to recognize the correct subset of partial decryption shares in case of $t < n/2$ (rather than $t < n/3$) where n is the number of parties and t is the number of parties the adversary can corrupt. Also, the part of our protocols will still be useful for [14] because we can guarantee that $(p-1)/2$ and $(q-1)/2$ do not contain small factors where $N = pq$ is the RSA modulus and this is the requirement for the most efficient variant in [14].

[20] proposed a novel and robust protocol that uses replicated integer secret sharing [21], but it is restricted in that the protocol is only for three parties and assumes the CRS model in which an RSA key N_{CRS} used for integer commitments must be given with a trusted setup.

2   Building Blocks

2.1   Threshold Paillier Cryptosystem

The threshold Paillier cryptosystem was proposed in [23], which uses the technique similar to the threshold RSA signature scheme [38]. The decryption scheme is a bit different from that of the original Paillier cryptosystem. We describe the $(t + 1, n)$ threshold Paillier cryptosystem [23] with a trusted dealer.

<u>Key Generation and Distribution Phase:</u>

1. The trusted dealer generates an RSA modulus $N = pq$ where p and q are safe primes. That is, $p = 2p' + 1$, and $q = 2q' + 1$ where p' and q' are also prime, and $\gcd(N, \varphi(N)) = 1$.
2. The dealer picks up $\beta \in \mathbb{Z}_N^*$ at random, and computes the values, $m = p'q'$, $\theta = m\beta \bmod N$, $\Delta = n!$. Because $\lambda(N^2) = \operatorname{lcm}(\varphi(p^2), \varphi(q^2)) = 2Nm$, note that $\forall x \in \mathbb{Z}_{N^2}^*$, $x^{2Nm} \equiv 1 \bmod N^2$.
3. The public key PK and the decryption key SK are $PK = (N,\ G,\ \theta)$ and $SK = \beta m$ where $G = N + 1$. The ciphertext c of a message M is defined as $c = G^M x^N \bmod N^2$ where $x \in \mathbb{Z}_N^*$ is random.
4. In order to share the decryption key $SK = \beta m$, the dealer generates a polynomial f with a_i chosen at random from $\{0, 1, \ldots, Nm - 1\}$, $f(x) = \beta m + a_1 x + a_2 x^2 + \cdots + a_t x^t \bmod Nm$, and sends $f(i)$ to each party P_i $(1 \le i \le n)$ through the secure channel.

   Also the dealer picks up a random value $r \in \mathbb{Z}_{N^2}^*$ and publishes the verification keys VK and VK_i for P_i as $VK = v = r^2 \bmod N^2$, and $VK_i = v^{\Delta f(i)} \bmod N^2$. These verification keys are necessary for the parties to prove that the decryption procedure is done correctly. For a technical reason, $v^{\Delta f(i)}$ is used instead of $v^{f(i)}$ for VK_i.

<u>Decryption Phase:</u>

Now the parties decrypt a ciphertext $c = G^M x^N \bmod N^2$ where M is the plaintext.

1. Each party P_i publishes $c_i = c^{2\Delta f(i)} \bmod N^2$ by using its secret share, which we call the partial decryption share. Also P_i publishes the zero-knowledge proof of equality that $f(i) = \log_{v^\Delta} VK_i = \log_{c^{4\Delta}}(c_i)^2$. We accept only the partial decryption shares with the valid zero-knowledge proofs of equality.

The reason we use $f(i) = \log_{c^{4\Delta}}(c_i)^2$ instead of $f(i) = \log_{c^{2\Delta}} c_i$ is to make sure that we are working in Q_{N^2} as in [38] where Q_{N^2} is the subgroup of squares in $\mathbb{Z}_{N^2}^*$.

2. By combining $t + 1$ valid partial decryption shares of the subset S of the parties, we can obtain $M = L(\prod_{i \in S} c_i^{2\mu_i} \bmod N^2) \times \frac{1}{4\Delta^2 \theta} \bmod N$ where $\mu_i = \Delta \times \lambda_{0,i}^S \in \mathbb{Z}$, $\lambda_{x,i}^S = \prod_{i' \in S \setminus \{i\}} \frac{x-i'}{i-i'}$, and $L(u) = \frac{u-1}{N}$.

Proof of correctness

$$\prod_{i \in S} c_i^{2\mu_i} = c^{4\Delta \sum_{i \in S} f(i)\mu_i} = c^{4\Delta \sum_{i \in S} \Delta f(i)\lambda_{0,i}^S}$$

$$= c^{4\Delta^2 m\beta} = (G^M x^N)^{4\Delta^2 m\beta}$$

$$= G^{4\Delta^2 m\beta M} \quad (\because \forall x, \ x^{2Nm} = 1 \bmod N^2)$$

$$= 1 + 4\Delta^2 m\beta MN \bmod N^2 \quad (\because G = N + 1).$$

Therefore, $L(\prod_{i \in S} c_i^{2\mu_i} \bmod N^2) = 4\Delta^2 m\beta M = M \times 4\Delta^2 \theta \bmod N$.

Δ and θ are public information. Thus, we have $M = L(\prod_{i \in S} c_i^{2\mu_i} \bmod N^2) \times \frac{1}{4\Delta^2 \theta} \bmod N$. $\square$

2.2 Secret Sharing over the Integers

In addition to a polynomial secret sharing scheme over a prime finite field, we need a secret sharing scheme over the integers [35], which is a variant of [37]. We describe the $(t+1, n)$ secret sharing over the integers where $t < n/2$ and an adversary can corrupt up to t parties.

Suppose the dealer wants to share a secret integer $s \in [-I, I]$ where I is the interval for s. Then the dealer of the secret generates a polynomial, $f(x) = \Delta s + a_1 x + a_2 x^2 + \cdots + a_t x^t$ where $\Delta = n!$, random values $a_i \in_R^1 [-K\Delta^2 I, K\Delta^2 I]$ and K is chosen such that $1/K$ is negligible (say $K = 2^{128}$) and distributes $f(i)$ to the i-th party P_i for $1 \le i \le n$. If $s \in [0, I]$, then a_i can be chosen such that $a_i \in_R [0, K\Delta^2 I]$. The proof of the security can be found, for instance, in [35].

2.3 Pedersen's VSS over the Integers

To make the protocol robust, we need verifiable secret sharing (VSS) over the integers. We use the Pedersen's VSS scheme [34] over the integers introduced in [10,31] that works with a group of large known order. There exists a VSS scheme over the integers based on a composite (RSA) number such as [16], but as pointed out in [2,20], we need a trusted setup to obtain such a shared composite number which is a product of two safe primes and we want to avoid the trusted setup. As in [25], the RSA moduli for VSS can be generated by each verifier and the provers can generate different commitments and zero-knowledge proofs for each verifier, but the computational cost is quite high as mentioned in [20]. Therefore, we use the Pedersen's VSS scheme that works with a group of large known order.

---

[1] This means that an element is chosen uniformly at random.

In the Pedersen's VSS, we use generators g and h of a subgroup of $\mathbb{Z}_P^*$ where P and P' are primes, $P' \mid P - 1$, and the order of g and h is P'. The discrete log of h over base g is unknown and such h can be jointly generated by using, for instance, [27], or can be generated as, say, $h = H(g, P, P')$ where H is a hash function modeled as a random oracle. Note that in this paper, $\mathbb{Z}_{P'}$ is considered to be a set $\{x \mid -\frac{(P'-1)}{2} \le x \le \frac{(P'-1)}{2}\}$ to be able to handle negative values. That is, all modular arithmetic is done centered around 0. To share a secret integer $s \in [-I, I]$ where I is the interval for s, the dealer of the secret generates a polynomial over the integers $f(x) = \Delta s + a_1 x + a_2 x^2 + \cdots + a_t x^t$ and a random companion polynomial $f'(x) = s' + a_1' x + a_2' x^2 + \cdots + a_t' x^t \bmod P'$ where $s', a_i' \in_R \mathbb{Z}_{P'}$ and publishes verification shares of a pair of polynomials $f(x), f'(x)$, $C_0 = g^{\Delta s} h^{s'} \bmod P$ and $C_j = g^{a_j} h^{a_j'} \bmod P$ for $1 \le j \le t$ with zero-knowledg range proofs [7,30] that $s \in [-I, I]$ and $a_i \in [-K\Delta^2 I, K\Delta^2 I]$ where the expansion rate of [7,30] is 3. For the commitment $C_0 = g^{\Delta s} h^{s'} \bmod P$, the dealer generates $g^s h^{s''} \bmod P$ with a zero-knowledge range proof that $s \in [-I, I]$ and compute $C_0 = (g^s h^{s''})^\Delta \bmod P$. Each P_i receives $f(i)$ and $f'(i)$ from the dealer and does the share verification by checking whether $g^{f(i)} h^{f'(i)} = \prod_{j=0}^t (C_j)^{i^j} \bmod P$ holds. If the share verification fails, P_i complains publicly. If more than t parties complain, the dealer is disqualified. Also P_i checks whether $|f(i)| \le (\Delta I + tn^t K\Delta^2 I)$. If the check fails, P_i exposes its share. If the share verification is corret but the size of the share is invalid, the dealer is disqualified. Because $f(x)$ is defined over the integers and the relation about $f(i)$ should hold over the integers rather than modulo P', the order of g, P' must be chosen such that it at least satisfies $P' > 2(2\Delta I + 2tn^t K\Delta^2 I)$. Note that of course $f(x)$ can be shared modulo P' rather than over the integers if necessary.

3   DKG Protocol for RSA Modulus Generation

The protocols [5,29] describe how to generate an RSA modulus and share the secret key in a distributed way. [29] describes the implementation and optimization of [5] in detail. We follow the RSA modulus generation in [5] with our modifications. We need this protocol to construct our threshold Paillier cryptosystem without a trusted dealer.

3.1   High-Level Overview of [5]

The n parties perform the following basic steps to compute an RSA modulus $N = pq$. We assume that the parties need at least $2k$ bits for the security level of the RSA modulus.

1. Every party P_i except P_1 picks up random secrets $p_i, q_i \in [2^{k-1}, 2^k - 1]$ such that $p_i \equiv q_i \equiv 0 \bmod 4$ (say $k = 1024$). P_1 also picks up random secrets $p_1, q_1 \in [2^{k-1}, 2^k - 1]$ such that $p_1 \equiv q_1 \equiv 3 \bmod 4$. The distributions of p and q are not uniform but as shown in [5], the distributions have at least k bits of entropy. We assume that $t < n/2$ where t is the degree of a polynomial used for secret sharing. The protocol here is designed to be t private. That is, any subset of t or less than t parties cannot reveal the factorization of N.

2. The parties agree on some large prime P' such that it at least satisfies that $P' > \{n(3 \times 2^{k-1})\}^2 > 2N$ where n is the number of parties. P' is the order of g and h described in Sect. 2.3.

3. By using the BGW protocol [4], the n parties compute $N = p \times q = \sum_{i=1}^{n} p_i \times \sum_{i=1}^{n} q_i \bmod P'$ without revealing p and q. Because $N < P'$, the parties can compute N.

4. The parties perform biprimality test for checking if N is a product of two primes in a distributed way. If the test fails, the protocol is restarted.

3.2 Distributed Computation of RSA Modulus N by BGW Protocol

We show how the parties compute and publish $N = (\sum p_i) \times (\sum q_i)$ by using the BGW protocol in detail.

1. Each party P_i generates two random t-degree polynomials f_i, g_i over the integers and random companion polynomials f_i', g_i' such that

$$f_i(x) = p_i + a_1 x + a_2 x^2 + \cdots + a_t x^t \bmod P',$$

$$f_i'(x) = p_i' + a_1' x + a_2' x^2 + \cdots + a_t' x^t \bmod P',$$

$$g_i(x) = q_i + b_1 x + b_2 x^2 + \cdots + b_t x^t \bmod P',$$

$$g_i'(x) = q_i' + b_1' x + b_2' x^2 + \cdots + b_t' x^t \bmod P',$$

where $p_i, q_i \in_R [2^{k-1}, 2^k - 1]$ and $a_i, b_i, p_i', q_i', a_i', b_i' \in_R \mathbb{Z}_{P'}$. Also, P_i generates a random $2t$-degree polynomials $h_i, h_i' \in \mathbb{Z}_{P'}[x]$ such that

$$h_i(x) = c_0 + c_1 x + c_2 x^2 + \cdots + c_{2t} x^{2t} \bmod P',$$

$$h_i'(x) = c_0' + c_1' x + c_2' x^2 + \cdots + c_{2t}' x^{2t} \bmod P'$$

where $c_0 = 0$. Note that $f_i(0) = p_i$, $g_i(0) = q_i$, and $h_i(0) = 0$. $h_i(x)$ is necessary for randomization in the BGW protocol.

2. P_i computes the following values: $p_{i,j} = f_i(j)$, $p_{i,j}' = f_i'(j)$, $q_{i,j} = g_i(j)$, $q_{i,j}' = g_i'(j)$, $h_{i,j} = h_i(j)$, $h_{i,j}' = h_i'(j)$ for $j = 1, \ldots, n$. P_i sends the tuple $\langle p_{i,j}, p_{i,j}', q_{i,j}, q_{i,j}', h_{i,j}, h_{i,j}' \rangle$ to P_j through the secure channel. P_i also publishes verification shares for pairs of polynomials $(f_i(x), f_i'(x))$, $(g_i(x), g_i'(x))$, $(h_i(x), h_i'(x))$.

   We need to add zero-knowledge range proofs for the zero-coefficient verification shares (i.e., p_i, q_i) for robustness. P_i except P_1 generates $g^{p_i} h^{p_i'} \bmod P$ as follows. P_i picks up random $p_i = 4k_{p_i} \in [2^{k-1}, 2^k - 1]$ and $r_{p_i} \in_R \mathbb{Z}_{P'}$ and publishes $g^{k_{p_i}} h^{r_{p_i}}$ with the zero-knowledge range proof that $k_{p_i} \in [2^{k-3}, 2^{k-2} - 1]$ by using [7,30] that are based on only the discrete logarithm problem and much more efficient than the classical bitwise proof. The verification share is computed as $g^{p_i} h^{p_i'} = (g^{k_{p_i}} h^{r_{p_i}})^4 \bmod P$. Though the range proofs in [7,30] are not tight (i.e., the expansion rate is 3), it will not be a problem because p_i chosen by a malicious party is guaranteed to be in

$[0, 3 \times 2^{k-1}]$. P_i also generates the zero-knowledge proof that $c_0 = 0$ for the verification share $g^{c_0} h^{c'_0}$. These zero-knowledge proofs can be easily turned into a non-interactive one using the Fiat-Shamir heuristic [22]. The verification share for q_i can be generated similarly and also P_1 can generate the verification shares similarly.

3. After receiving the above tuple from other parties, P_i does the share verification and if the shares are inconsistent, P_i broadcasts a complaint against the malicious party. If the share verification succeeds, P_i computes $N_i = \left(\sum_{j=1}^{n} p_{j,i} \right) \left(\sum_{j=1}^{n} q_{j,i} \right) + \sum_{j=1}^{n} h_{j,i} \bmod P'$, and P_i publishes N_i and its companion share N'_i. Since the Pedersen commitments for $\sum_{j=1}^{n} p_{j,i}$, $\sum_{j=1}^{n} q_{j,i}$, and $\sum_{j=1}^{n} h_{j,i}$ are publicly available, P_i can generate a Pedersen commitment C'_i for N_i such that $C'_i = g^{N_i} h^{N'_i} \bmod P$ with a zero-knowledge proof of a multiplicative relation by using the standard techniques such as [12].

4. Now we consider the following polynomial, $\alpha(x) = \left(\sum_{j=1}^{n} f_j(x) \right) \left(\sum_{j=1}^{n} g_j(x) \right) + \sum_{j=1}^{n} h_j(x) \bmod P'$. Note that $N_i = \alpha(i)$ and $\alpha(0) = N$. Because $\alpha(x)$ is a 2t-degree polynomial, and we have n $(> 2t)$ shares, we can compute coefficients of $\alpha(x)$ by using Lagrange interpolation. Thus, we can obtain $N = \alpha(0) = \sum_{i \in S} N_i \lambda_{0,i}^S \bmod P'$ where $|S| = 2t + 1$.

3.3   Distributed Biprimality Test for N

Boneh and Franklin [5] showed how the parties can check if N is a product of two primes without revealing p and q. Their novel distributed biprimality test assumes that $p \equiv q \equiv 3 \bmod 4$. This condition can be assured by having P_1 pick up the secrets $p_1 \equiv q_1 \equiv 3 \bmod 4$, and all other parties pick up the secrets $p_i \equiv q_i \equiv 0 \bmod 4$. The parties perform the following steps.

1. The parties agree on a random g' such that the Jacobi symbol $\left(\frac{g'}{N} \right) = 1$.

2. Note that each party P_i has a commitment in the form of $C_{0,i} = g^{p_i + q_i} h^r \bmod P$. P_1 publishes $Q_1 = g'^{(N+1-p_i-q_i)/4} \bmod N$ with a zero-knowledge proof that $\log_{g'} Q_1$ is equal to the committed value in $g^{N+1}/C_{0,1}$ with the bases g^4 and h. Similary for $2 \leq i \leq n$, P_i publishes $Q_i = g'^{(p_i+q_i)/4} \bmod N$ with a zero-knowledge proof that $\log_{g'} Q_i$ is equal to the committed value in $C_{0,i}$ with the bases g^4 and h. We can use the zero-knowledge proofs similar to the one in Appendix B.

3. The parties check that $Q_1 / \prod_{i=2}^{n} Q_i \stackrel{?}{\equiv} \pm 1 \bmod N$. If it does not hold, N is discarded.

4   Relaxing Condition on Safe Primes

As we have seen in Sect. 2.1, the trusted dealer needs two safe primes to generate an RSA modulus $N = pq$ for the threshold Paillier cryptosystem. That is, $p = 2p' + 1$, $q = 2q' + 1$ where p', and q' are also primes. The reason we need safe primes is to make Q_{N^2} a cyclic group and have sufficiently large number of generators in Q_{N^2}. By choosing a generator for the verification key VK, each VK_i can completely determine the party's secret share mod Nm, and prevent the party from publishing the bad partial decryption share. Furthermore, if N is a product of two safe primes, an element chosen at random from Q_{N^2} is a generator with overwhelming probability.

As mentioned in Sect. 1, [24] and [19] proposed alternative ways to avoid using safe primes. Compared with [24], [19] seems more practical because it needs a fewer number of zero-knowledge proofs though it relies on the non-standard complexity assumption (which is similar to the small order assumption in [15]), so we follow the approach of [19] where the assumption is used in $\mathbb{Z}_N$, while we use the assumption in $\mathbb{Z}_{N^2}$ because we deal with the Paillier cryptosystem. By following [19], we can accept a prime p that satisfies the condition that $(p-1)/2$ is not divisible by any prime less than n where n is the number of the parties even if p is not a safe prime.

4.1   How to Check a Prime Candidate with Trial Division

Now let $p(= \sum_{i=1}^{n} p_i)$ be a prime candidate. Let $n_i(\leq n)$ be a public prime. In order to check whether $p-1$ is not divisible by n_i in a robust way, the parties compute and reveal $\gamma = (p-1)R_a + n_i R_b$ where $R_a = \sum_{i=1}^{n} R_{a,i}$, $R_b = \sum_{i=1}^{n} R_{b,i}$, and $R_{a,i} \in [0, Kp_{\max}], R_{b,i} \in [0, K^2 p_{\max}^2]$ are secret random values chosen by P_i, and $p_{\max} = n(3 \times 2^{k-1})$ and $1/K$ is negligible and the computation of γ can be done with random $2t$-degree polynomials similarly as described in Sect. 3.2. If $\gcd(\gamma, n_i) = 1$, then $(p-1)/2$ is not divisible by n_i and p is accepted. It may hold that $n_i \mid R_a$, and then the good candidate p may be discarded. However, if we compute γ's a number of times with fresh random values R_a and R_b, the probability that at least one of R_a's is coprime to n_i will be relatively high. For the zero-knowledge range proofs of $R_{a,i}$ and $R_{b,i}$, we can use [7,30]. When $n_i = 2$, the parties compute and reveal $\gamma = (p-1)R_a + 4R_b$. If $\gcd(\gamma, 4) = 2$, then $(p-1)/2$ is not divisible by 2 and p is accepted. In our case, since $p \equiv 3 \bmod 4$, this is unnecessary. We can assume $|\gamma| < \gamma_{\max} = 2p_{\max}nKp_{\max} + 2n^2 K^2 p_{\max}^2$ and then P' must be chosen such that it at least satisfies $P' > 2\gamma_{\max}$.

As proven in Appendix A, the information about p does not leak from γ when p is accepted.

This trial division can also be used for p and q before computing $N = pq$.

The trial division protocol in [6,1] is non-robust because it is in the honest-but-curious model. In [24], γ is computed as $(p-1)+n_i R_b$, but it leaks the information $p-1 \bmod n_i$ about p and the value $\varphi(N) + (N-1)R_b$ is also computed to check that $\gcd(N-1, \varphi(N)) = 4$, but this leaks the entire information about $\varphi(N)$ because $\varphi(N) < N-1$. Also in [19], the information about p is leaked slightly by revealing $p_i \bmod n_i$ for the trial division.

5   Threshold Paillier without Trusted Dealer

We show how to construct the threshold Paillier cryptosystem without a trusted dealer building on the protocols described so far. We revisit the threshold

Paillier cryptosystem with a trusted dealer. As we have seen in Sect. 2.1, the dealer has to pick up a random $\beta \in \mathbb{Z}_N^*$ and compute $\theta = m\beta \bmod N$ where $m = p'q'$. Also, the dealer distributes the secret shares for βm by using the polynomial $f(x) = \beta m + a_1 x + a_2 x^2 + \cdots + a_t x^t \bmod Nm$. In order to eliminate the dealer, the parties must compute $\theta = m\beta \bmod N$ so that no parties can know β or m, and share βm over the integers instead of mod Nm because no parties should know m. We use the simple observations that $\varphi(N) = (p-1)(q-1) = 4m$ is a multiple of m, and the parties have the polynomial sharing of $\varphi(N)$ after the computation of N. Actually, we have $\varphi(N) = (N - p - q + 1) = (N + 1 - \sum_{i=1}^n (p_i + q_i))$ and $\sum_{i=1}^n (p_i + q_i)$ is already shared modulo P' as observed in [6]. We denote $\varphi(N)$ by φ. As mentioned in Sect. 4, N does not need to be a product of two safe primes here. In order to realize the $(t+1, n)$ threshold Paillier cryptosystem, the parties perform the following steps. The full security proof can be found in the full version of this paper with the modified decisional composite residuosity (DCR) assumption similar to the modified RSA security assumption introduced in [25]. In the proof, basically our simulator plays the roles of honest parties, obtains all the shares of the adversary, and exploits the adversary's power to break the modified DCR assumption and other assumptions.

Key Generation Phase:

1. The n parties perform the distributed RSA modulus generation protocol in Sect. 3.2 with the biprimality test and the additional protocol in Sect. 4.1 to make sure that $(p-1)/2$ and $(q-1)/2$ are not divisible by any prime less than n. As a result, they publish N and have a polynomial sharing of φ modulo P'.

2. Each party P_i picks up a random $\beta_i \in_R [0, KN]$ and $R_i \in_R [0, K^2 N]$ where K is chosen such that $1/K$ is negligible. By using the protocol in Sect. 4.1, the parties compute and reveal $\theta' = \Delta\varphi \left(\sum_{i=1}^n \beta_i \right) + N \left(\sum_{i=1}^n \Delta R_i \right)$ where only ΔR_i is shared over the integers by using the technique in Sect. 2.3. For the zero-knowledge range proofs about β_i, R_i and the coefficients of the polynomial to share ΔR_i, we can use [7,30] as mentioned in Sect. 2.3. Let β be $\sum_{i=1}^n \beta_i$. The value $\theta' \bmod N (= \Delta\varphi\beta \bmod N)$ becomes part of the public key PK. Note that the parties now have a polynomial sharing of $-\Delta\varphi\beta$ over the integers by a polynomial sharing of $N \left(\sum_{i=1}^n \Delta R_i \right) - \theta'$ over the integers. We can assume $|\theta'| < \Delta N \times 2nKN + N\Delta 2nK^2 N < \theta'_{\max} = 2n\Delta K(1 + K)N_{\max}^2$ where $N_{\max} = p_{\max}^2$ and then P' must be chosen such that it at least satisfies $P' > 2\theta'_{\max}$. We can prove that the information about φ does not leak from θ' similarly as in Appendix A.

3. In the previous step, each party P_i generates and distributes the verification shares for sharing ΔR_i. Let $f_1(x)$ be the polynomial over the integers for sharing $\sum_{i=1}^n \Delta R_i$ and then $g^{f_1(i)} h^{f_1'(i)} \bmod P$ is publicly available for $1 \leq i \leq n$. Because $-\Delta\varphi\beta$ is shared by the polynomial $f(x) = N f_1(x) - \theta'$, $g^{f(i)} h^{f'(i)} \bmod P$ is also publicly computable for $1 \leq i \leq n$. Because the share $f_1(i)$ is bounded by $2n(\Delta K^2 N + tn^t K \Delta^2 K^2 N)$, the share $|f(i)|$ is

bounded by $2N_{\max}n(\Delta K^2 N_{\max} + tn^t K \Delta^2 K^2 N_{\max}) + \theta'_{\max}$ (we call this value T and T is $O(K^3 N_{\max}^2)$). Therefore, P' must be chosen such that it at least satisfies $P' > 2T$.

With the commitment $g^{f(i)} h^{f'(i)} \bmod P$ of $f(i)$, P_i generates and distributes a commitment $VK_i = v^{\Delta f(i)} \bmod N^2$ with a zero-knowledge proof that $\log_{v^\Delta} VK_i = f(i)$ where $v \in_R Q_{N^2}$ is an agreed random value and VK_i is a verification key for P_i. The details of how to create such zero-knowledge proofs are given in Appendix B.

Decryption Phase:
The parties decrypt ciphertext $c = G^M x^N \bmod N^2$ of plaintext M.

1. P_i publishes the partial decryption share $c_i = c^{2\Delta f(i)} \bmod N^2$ by using its secret share $f(i)$. Also P_i publishes the zero-knowledge proofs of equality that $f(i) = \log_{c^{4\Delta}}(c_i)^2 = \log_{v^\Delta} VK_i$. We accept only the partial decryption shares with the valid zero-knowledge proofs of equality. The reason we use $f(i) = \log_{c^{4\Delta}}(c_i)^2$ instead of $f(i) = \log_{c^{2\Delta}} c_i$ is to make sure that we are working in Q_{N^2}. Now N is not a product of two safe primes, so we apply the similar technique used in [19] to construct the zero-knowledge proofs for the partial decryption shares. The details of how to create such zero-knowledge proofs are given in Appendix C.

2. By combining $t + 1$ valid partial decryption shares of the subset S of the parties, we can obtain $M = L(\prod_{i \in S} c_i^{2\mu_i} \bmod N^2) \times \frac{1}{-4\Delta^2 \theta'} \bmod N$ where $\mu_i = \Delta \times \lambda_{0,i}^S \in \mathbb{Z}$, and $L(u) = \frac{u-1}{N}$.

Proof of correctness

$$\prod_{i \in S} c_i^{2\mu_i} = c^{4\Delta \sum_{i \in S} f(i)\mu_i} = c^{4\Delta \sum_{i \in S} \Delta f(i)\lambda_{0,i}^S}$$

$$= c^{-4\Delta^3 \beta\varphi} = (G^M x^N)^{-4\Delta^3 \beta\varphi}$$

$$= G^{-4\Delta^3 \beta\varphi M} \quad (\because {}^\forall x, \ x^{N\varphi} = 1 \bmod N^2)$$

$$= 1 - 4\Delta^3 \beta\varphi MN \bmod N^2 \quad (\because G = N + 1).$$

Therefore, $L(\prod_{i \in S} c_i^{2\mu_i} \bmod N^2) = -4\Delta^3 \beta\varphi M = M \times (-4\Delta^2 \theta') \bmod N$.

Δ and θ' are public information. Thus, we have $M = L(\prod_{i \in S} c_i^{2\mu_i} \bmod N^2) \times \frac{1}{-4\Delta^2 \theta'} \bmod N$. $\qquad\square$

Acknowledgements

This research is (partially) supported by JAPAN SCIECE AND TECHNOL-OGY AGENCY (JST), Strategic Japanese-Indian Cooperative Programme on Multidisciplinary Research Field, which combines Information and Communications Technology with Other Fields, entitled "Analysis of Cryptographic Algorithms and Evaluation on Enhancing Network Security Based on Mathematical Science."

References

1. Algesheimer, J., Camenisch, J., Shoup, V.: Efficient computation modulo a shared secret with application to the generation of shared safe-prime products. In: Yung, M. (ed.) CRYPTO 2002. LNCS, vol. 2442, pp. 417–432. Springer, Heidelberg (2002)

2. Bangerter, E., Camenisch, J., Krenn, S.: Efficiency limitations for $Sigma$-protocols for group homomorphisms. In: Micciancio, D. (ed.) Theory of Cryptography. LNCS, vol. 5978, pp. 553–571. Springer, Heidelberg (2010)

3. Baudron, O., Fouque, P.-A., Pointcheval, D., Poupard, G., Stern, J.: Practical multi-candidate election system. In: Proc. 20th ACM PODC, pp. 274–283 (2001)

4. Ben-Or, M., Goldwasser, S., Wigderson, A.: Completeness theorem for non-cryptographic fault-tolerant distributed computation. In: Proc. 20th Annual ACM Symposium on Theory of Computing (STOC), pp. 1–10 (1988)

5. Boneh, D., Franklin, M.: Efficient generation of shared RSA keys. In: Fumy, W. (ed.) EUROCRYPT 1997. LNCS, vol. 1233, pp. 425–439. Springer, Heidelberg (1997)

6. Boneh, D., Franklin, M.: Efficient generation of shared RSA keys. J. ACM 48(4), 702–722 (2001)

7. Brickell, E., Chaum, D., Damgård, I., Graaf, J.: Gradual and verifiable release of a secret. In: Pomerance, C. (ed.) CRYPTO 1987. LNCS, vol. 293, pp. 156–166. Springer, Heidelberg (1988)

8. Cachin, C.: An asynchronous protocol for distributed computation of RSA inverses and its applications. In: Proc. ACM PODC, pp. 153–162 (2003)

9. Camenisch, J., Michels, M.: Proving in zero-knowledge that a number is the product of two safe primes. In: Stern, J. (ed.) EUROCRYPT 1999. LNCS, vol. 1592, pp. 107–122. Springer, Heidelberg (1999)

10. Catalano, D., Gennaro, R., Halevi, S.: Computing inverses over a shared secret modulus. In: Preneel, B. (ed.) EUROCRYPT 2000. LNCS, vol. 1807, pp. 190–207. Springer, Heidelberg (2000)

11. Chan, A., Frankel, Y., Tsiounis, Y.: Easy come - easy go divisible cash. In: Nyberg, K. (ed.) EUROCRYPT 1998. LNCS, vol. 1403, pp. 561–575. Springer, Heidelberg (1998); Updated version with corrections, GTE Tech. Report available at http://www.ccs.neu.edu/home/yiannis/

12. Cramer, R., Damgård, I.: Zero-knowledge proofs for finite field arithmetic or: Can zero-knowledge be for free? In: Krawczyk, H. (ed.) CRYPTO 1998. LNCS, vol. 1462, pp. 424–441. Springer, Heidelberg (1998)

13. Cramer, R., Damgård, I., Nielsen, J.B.: Multiparty computation from threshold homomorphic encryption. In: Pfitzmann, B. (ed.) EUROCRYPT 2001. LNCS, vol. 2045, pp. 280–300. Springer, Heidelberg (2001)

14. Damgård, I., Dupont, K.: Efficient threshold RSA signatures with general moduli and no extra assumptions. In: Vaudenay, S. (ed.) PKC 2005. LNCS, vol. 3386, pp. 346–361. Springer, Heidelberg (2005)

15. Damgård, I., Fujisaki, E.: An integer commitment scheme based on groups with hidden order. Cryptology ePrint Archive 2001/064 (2001)

16. Damgård, I., Fujisaki, E.: A statistically-hiding integer commitment scheme based on groups with hidden order. In: Zheng, Y. (ed.) ASIACRYPT 2002. LNCS, vol. 2501, pp. 125–142. Springer, Heidelberg (2002)

17. Damgård, I., Jurik, M.: A generalisation, a simplification and some applications of Paillier's probabilistic public-key system. In: Kim, K.-c. (ed.) PKC 2001. LNCS, vol. 1992, pp. 119–136. Springer, Heidelberg (2001)

18. Damgård, I., Jurik, M.: A length-flexible threshold cryptosystem with applications. In: Safavi-Naini, R., Seberry, J. (eds.) ACISP 2003. LNCS, vol. 2727, pp. 350–364. Springer, Heidelberg (2003)
19. Damgård, I., Koprowski, M.: Practical threshold RSA signatures without a trusted dealer. In: Pfitzmann, B. (ed.) EUROCRYPT 2001. LNCS, vol. 2045, pp. 152–165. Springer, Heidelberg (2001)
20. Damgård, I., Mikkelsen, G.L.: Efficient robust and constant-round distributed RSA key generation. In: Micciancio, D. (ed.) Theory of Cryptography. LNCS, vol. 5978, pp. 183–200. Springer, Heidelberg (2010)
21. Damgård, I., Thorbek, R.: Linear integer secret sharing and distributed exponentiation. In: Yung, M., Dodis, Y., Kiayias, A., Malkin, T.G. (eds.) PKC 2006. LNCS, vol. 3958, pp. 75–90. Springer, Heidelberg (2006)
22. Fiat, A., Shamir, A.: How to prove yourself: practical solutions to identification and signature problems. In: Odlyzko, A.M. (ed.) CRYPTO 1986. LNCS, vol. 263, pp. 186–194. Springer, Heidelberg (1987)
23. Fouque, P.-A., Poupard, G., Stern, J.: Sharing decryption in the context of voting or lotteries. In: Frankel, Y. (ed.) FC 2000. LNCS, vol. 1962, pp. 90–104. Springer, Heidelberg (2001)
24. Fouque, P.A., Stern, J.: Fully distributed threshold RSA under standard assumptions. In: Boyd, C. (ed.) ASIACRYPT 2001. LNCS, vol. 2248, pp. 310–330. Springer, Heidelberg (2001)
25. Frankel, Y., MacKenzie, P.D., Yung, M.: Robust efficient distributed RSA-key generation. In: Proc. 30th ACM STOC, pp. 663–672 (1998)
26. Franklin, M.K., Gondree, M., Mohassel, P.: Improved efficiency for private stable matching. In: Abe, M. (ed.) CT-RSA 2007. LNCS, vol. 4377, pp. 163–177. Springer, Heidelberg (2006)
27. Gennaro, R., Jarecki, S., Krawczyk, H., Rabin, T.: Secure distributed key generation for discrete-log based cryptosystems. J. Cryptology 20(1), 51–83 (2007)
28. Hirt, M., Nielsen, J.B.: Robust multiparty computation with linear communication complexity. In: Dwork, C. (ed.) CRYPTO 2006. LNCS, vol. 4117, pp. 463–482. Springer, Heidelberg (2006)
29. Malkin, M., Wu, T., Boneh, D.: Experimenting with shared RSA key generation. In: Proc. Internet Society's 1999 Symposium on Network and Distributed System Security (SNDSS 1999), pp. 43–56 (1999)
30. Okamoto, T.: An efficient divisible electronic cash scheme. In: Coppersmith, D. (ed.) CRYPTO 1995. LNCS, vol. 963, pp. 438–451. Springer, Heidelberg (1995)
31. Ong, E., Kubiatowicz, J.: Optimizing robustness while generating shared secret safe primes. In: Vaudenay, S. (ed.) PKC 2005. LNCS, vol. 3386, pp. 120–137. Springer, Heidelberg (2005)
32. Paillier, P.: Public-key cryptosystems based on composite degree residuosity classes. In: Stern, J. (ed.) EUROCRYPT 1999. LNCS, vol. 1592, pp. 223–238. Springer, Heidelberg (1999)
33. Pedersen, T.: A threshold cryptosystem without a trusted party. In: Davies, D.W. (ed.) EUROCRYPT 1991. LNCS, vol. 547, pp. 522–526. Springer, Heidelberg (1991)
34. Pedersen, T.: Non-interactive and information-theoretic secure verifiable secret sharing. In: Feigenbaum, J. (ed.) CRYPTO 1991. LNCS, vol. 576, pp. 129–140. Springer, Heidelberg (1992)
35. Rabin, T.: A simplified approach to threshold and proactive RSA. In: Krawczyk, H. (ed.) CRYPTO 1998. LNCS, vol. 1462, pp. 89–104. Springer, Heidelberg (1998)

36. Schoenmakers, B., Tuyls, P.: Efficient binary conversion for Paillier encrypted values. In: Vaudenay, S. (ed.) EUROCRYPT 2006. LNCS, vol. 4004, pp. 522–537. Springer, Heidelberg (2006)

37. Shamir, A.: How to share a secret. Communications of ACM 22(11), 612–613 (1979)

38. Shoup, V.: Practical threshold signatures. In: Preneel, B. (ed.) EUROCRYPT 2000. LNCS, vol. 1807, pp. 207–220. Springer, Heidelberg (2000)

39. SecureSCM Project. Secure computation models and frameworks. Technical Report D9.1, D9.1_SecureSCM_V1.0.pdf (2008), http://www.securescm.org/

A   Proof of Sect. 4.1

In Sect. 4.1, the parties compute and reveal $\gamma = (p - 1)\left(\sum_{i=1}^{n} R_{a,i}\right) + n_i\left(\sum_{i=1}^{n} R_{b,i}\right)$ where $p = \sum_{i=1}^{n} p_i$ is a shared secret and n_i is a public value and $R_{a,i} \in [0, Kp_{\max}]$ and $R_{b,i} \in [0, K^2 p_{\max}^2]$.

We prove that the information about p does not leak from γ when p is accepted, that is, $\gcd(p - 1, n_i) = 1$, following [8], but obtaining a new bound. To do so, we consider the most advantageous situation to the adversary where the adversary knows the values of all the parties except one honest party. That is, without loss of generality, we can assume that the adversary knows $p' = \sum_{i=1}^{n-1} p_i$, $R'_a = \sum_{i=1}^{n-1} R_{a,i}$, and $R'_b = \sum_{i=1}^{n-1} R_{b,i}$. We can think of $\gamma = (p_n + p' - 1)(R_{a,n} + R'_a) + n_i(R_{b,n} + R'_b)$ as a random variable where p_n, $R_{a,n}$, and $R_{b,n}$ are also random variables determined by the honest party. We prove that whatever p_n is, the distribution of γ is statistically indistinguishable. Let $f_1, f_2 \in [2^{k-1}, 2^k - 1]$ and $f_1 > f_2$ without loss of generality. Let $\gamma_1 = (f_1 + p' - 1)(R_{a,n} + R'_a) + n_i(R_{b,n} + R'_b) = f'_1(R_{a,n} + R'_a) + n_i(R_{b,n} + R'_b)$ where $f'_1 = f_1 + p' - 1$ and $f'_1 < p_{\max}$. Similarly let $\gamma_2 = (f_2 + p' - 1)(R_{a,n} + R'_a) + n_i(R_{b,n} + R'_b) = f'_2(R_{a,n} + R'_a) + n_i(R_{b,n} + R'_b)$ where $f'_2 = f_2 + p' - 1$ and $f'_2 < p_{\max}$. We prove that the distribution of the random variable γ_1 is statistically indistinguishable from that of γ_2 where f'_1 and f'_2 are not random variables but certain fixed numbers and $\gcd(f'_1, n_i) = \gcd(f'_2, n_i) = 1$.

To simplify γ_1 and γ_2, we consider $\gamma'_1 = \gamma_1 - n_i R'_b = f'_1(R_{a,n} + R'_a) + n_i R_{b,n}$ and $\gamma'_2 = \gamma_2 - n_i R'_b = f'_2(R_{a,n} + R'_a) + n_i R_{b,n}$ because $n_i R'_b$ is a constant where $R_{a,n}$ and $R_{b,n}$ are random variables. Let $d(\gamma'_1, \gamma'_2)$ be the statistical distance between γ'_1 and γ'_2. Then $d(\gamma'_1, \gamma'_2) = \sum_{x=f'_2 R'_a}^{f'_1(Kp_{\max}+R'_a)+n_i K^2 p_{\max}^2} |\Pr[\gamma'_1 = x] - \Pr[\gamma'_2 = x]|$.

We split the range of x into the following ranges:

$x \in [f'_2 R'_a, f'_2(Kp_{\max} + R'_a)]$,
$x \in [f'_2(Kp_{\max} + R'_a), f'_1(Kp_{\max} + R'_a)]$,
$x \in [f'_1(Kp_{\max} + R'_a), n_i K^2 p_{\max}^2]$,
$x \in [n_i K^2 p_{\max}^2, f'_1(Kp_{\max} + R'_a) + n_i K^2 p_{\max}^2]$.

We call these ranges, range1, range2, range3, range4 respectively. Then for range1, we have $\Pr[\gamma'_1 \in \text{range1}] < \Pr[n_i R_{b,n} < f'_2 Kp_{\max}] = \frac{f'_2 Kp_{\max}}{n_i K^2 p_{\max}^2}$, and $\Pr[\gamma'_2 \in \text{range1}] < \Pr[n_i R_{b,n} < f'_2 Kp_{\max}] = \frac{f'_2 Kp_{\max}}{n_i K^2 p_{\max}^2}$.

For range2, we have $\Pr[\gamma'_1 \in \text{range2}] < \Pr[n_i R_{b,n} < f'_1 Kp_{\max}] = \frac{f'_1 Kp_{\max}}{n_i K^2 p_{\max}^2}$

and $\Pr[\gamma_2' \in \text{range2}] = \sum_{x=f_2'(Kp_{\max}+R_a')}^{f_1'(Kp_{\max}+R_a')} \Pr[\gamma_2' = x]$

$= \sum_{x=f_2'(Kp_{\max}+R_a')}^{f_1'(Kp_{\max}+R_a')} \Pr[f_2'(R_{a,n}+R_a')+n_iR_{b,n} = x]$

$= \sum_{x'=f_2'Kp_{\max}}^{f_1'Kp_{\max}+(f_1'-f_2')R_a'} \Pr[f_2'R_{a,n}+n_iR_{b,n} = x']$

$= \sum_{x'=f_2'Kp_{\max}}^{f_1'Kp_{\max}+(f_1'-f_2')R_a'} \sum_{y'=0}^{f_2'Kp_{\max}} \Pr[f_2'R_{a,n} = y', n_iR_{b,n} = x'-y']$

$= \sum_{x'=f_2'Kp_{\max}}^{f_1'Kp_{\max}+(f_1'-f_2')R_a'} \sum_{\substack{0 \le y' \le f_2'Kp_{\max} \\ f_2'|y' \\ n_i|x'-y'}} \frac{1}{K^2p_{\max}^2} \Pr[f_2'R_{a,n} = y']$

$\approx (f_1'-f_2')(Kp_{\max}+R_a')\frac{Kp_{\max}}{n_i}\frac{1}{K^2p_{\max}^2}\frac{1}{Kp_{\max}} = \frac{(f_1'-f_2')(Kp_{\max}+R_a')}{n_iK^2p_{\max}^2}$

where $0 \le f_1'-f_2' < 2^k < p_{\max}$ and $0 \le R_a' \le nKp_{\max}$.

For range3, let $x \in \text{range3}$, and then we have $\Pr[\gamma_1' = x] = \Pr[f_1'(R_{a,n}+R_a')+n_iR_{b,n} = x]$

$= \Pr[f_1'R_{a,n}+n_iR_{b,n} = x-f_1'R_a']$

$= \sum_{y'=0}^{f_1'Kp_{\max}} \Pr[f_1'R_{a,n} = y', n_iR_{b,n} = x-f_1'R_a'-y']$

$= \sum_{\substack{0 \le y' \le f_1'Kp_{\max} \\ f_1'|y' \\ n_i|x-f_1'R_a'-y'}} \frac{1}{K^2p_{\max}^2} \Pr[f_1'R_{a,n} = y'] \approx \frac{Kp_{\max}}{n_i}\frac{1}{K^2p_{\max}^2}\frac{1}{Kp_{\max}}$

Similarly, we have $\Pr[\gamma_2' = x] \approx \frac{Kp_{\max}}{n_i}\frac{1}{K^2p_{\max}^2}\frac{1}{Kp_{\max}}$. Since $|\Pr[\gamma_1' = x] - \Pr[\gamma_2' = x]| \le \frac{1}{K^2p_{\max}^2}\frac{1}{Kp_{\max}}$, we have $\sum_{x \in \text{range3}} |\Pr[\gamma_1' = x] - \Pr[\gamma_2' = x]| < n_iK^2p_{\max}^2\frac{1}{K^2p_{\max}^2}\frac{1}{Kp_{\max}} = \frac{n_i}{Kp_{\max}}$

For range4, we have $\Pr[\gamma_1' \in \text{range4}] < \Pr[n_iR_{b,n} \ge n_iK^2p_{\max}^2 - f_1'(Kp_{\max}+R_a')] = \frac{f_1'(Kp_{\max}+R_a')}{n_iK^2p_{\max}^2}$ and $\Pr[\gamma_2' \in \text{range4}] < \Pr[n_iR_{b,n} \ge n_iK^2p_{\max}^2 - f_2'(Kp_{\max}+R_a')] = \frac{f_2'(Kp_{\max}+R_a')}{n_iK^2p_{\max}^2}$.

Let $d(\gamma_1', \gamma_2')\text{range}$ be $\sum_{x \in \text{range}} |\Pr[\gamma_1' = x] - \Pr[\gamma_2' = x]|$. Then we have

$d(\gamma_1', \gamma_2')_{\text{range1}} < \Pr[\gamma_1' \in \text{range1}] + \Pr[\gamma_2' \in \text{range1}],$
$d(\gamma_1', \gamma_2')_{\text{range2}} < \Pr[\gamma_1' \in \text{range2}] + \Pr[\gamma_2' \in \text{range2}],$
$d(\gamma_1', \gamma_2')_{\text{range3}} < \frac{n_i}{Kp_{\max}},$
$d(\gamma_1', \gamma_2')_{\text{range4}} < \Pr[\gamma_1' \in \text{range4}] + \Pr[\gamma_2' \in \text{range4}]$

that are all negligible. Therefore, $d(\gamma_1', \gamma_2')$ is negligible and this concludes the proof.

For simplicity, we implicitly assumed that $R_a' > 0$, but it can happen that $R_a' < 0$ because the zero-knowledge range proof [7,30] is not tight (i.e., the expansion rate is 3) and malicious parties may succeed in using $R_{a,i}(< 0)$. However, even if $R_a' < 0$, we can prove that the statistical distance $d(\gamma_1', \gamma_2')$ is negligible with the similar discussion by choosing the ranges of x appropriately.

In Sect. 5, the parties compute and reveal $\theta' = \Delta\varphi\left(\sum_{i=1}^{n}\beta_i\right) + N\left(\sum_{i=1}^{n}\Delta R_i\right)$. We can prove that the distribution of $\Delta\varphi\left(\sum_{i=1}^{n}\beta_i\right) + N\left(\sum_{i=1}^{n}\Delta R_i\right)$ is statistically indistinguishable from that of $\Delta(N-1)\left(\sum_{i=1}^{n}\beta_i\right) + N\left(\sum_{i=1}^{n}\Delta R_i\right)$ with the similar discussion again by choosing $\beta_i \in_R [0, KN]$ and $R_i \in_R [0, K^2N]$ because $\gcd(\varphi, N) = \gcd(N-1, N) = 1$ and thus the information about φ does not leak from θ'.

B   How to Create Verification Key

Given $x, g, h, C_0 = g^x h^y \bmod P \in \mathbb{Z}_P$ and $v \in \mathbb{Z}_{N^2}$, the party P_i generates a commitment $VK_i = v^{\Delta x} \bmod N^2$ with a zero-knowledge proof of equality that $x = \log_g C_0/h^y = \log_{v^\Delta} VK_i$ where $|x| < T$ as follows. This interactive proof can be easily turned into a non-interactive one using the Fiat-Shamir heuristic [22]. We follow the approach used in [11,9].

1. P_i sends, to the verifier, $(R_{j,1} = g^{r_j} h^{r'_j} \bmod P)_{1 \leq j \leq h}$ and $(R_{j,2} = v^{\Delta r_j} \bmod N^2)_{1 \leq j \leq h}$ where $r_j \in_R [0, 2^\ell T]$, $r'_j \in \mathbb{Z}_{P'}$, and h, ℓ are security parameters chosen such that $1/2^h$ and $1/2^\ell$ are negligible.
2. The verifier sends $(c_j \in_R \{0,1\})_{1 \leq j \leq h}$ to P_i.
3. P_i replies by sending $(z_j = r_j + c_j x)_{1 \leq j \leq h}$ in $\mathbb{Z}$ and $(z'_j = r'_j + c_j y)_{1 \leq j \leq h}$ in $\mathbb{Z}_{P'}$.
4. The verifier checks that $g^{z_j} h^{z'_j} \stackrel{?}{\equiv} R_{j,1} C_0^{c_j} \bmod P$, $v^{\Delta z_j} \stackrel{?}{\equiv} R_{j,2}(VK_i)^{c_j} \bmod N^2$, and $z_j \stackrel{?}{\in} [0, 2^\ell T]$ for $1 \leq j \leq h$.

This statistical zero-knowledge proof succeeds with probability greater than $1 - \frac{1}{2^\ell}$ if $|x| < T$ and a cheating prover can succeed with probability less than $\frac{1}{2^h}$. This proof convinces the verifier that $x \in [-2^\ell T, 2^\ell T]$ and thus to make this zero-knowledge proof work, note that P' must be chosen such that it at least satisfies $P' > 2^{\ell+1} T$.

C   How to Create Zero-Knowledge Proof for Partial Decryption Share

Given $x, v, VK_i = v^{\Delta x}, c \in \mathbb{Z}_{N^2}$, the party P_i generates a partial decryption share $c_i = c^{2\Delta x} \bmod N^2$ with a zero-knowledge proof of equality that $x = \log_{c^{4\Delta}}(c_i)^2 = \log_{v^\Delta} VK_i$ where $|x| < T$ as follows. This interactive proof can be easily turned into a non-interactive one using the Fiat-Shamir heuristic [22]. We follow the approach used in [19].

1. P_i sends, to the verifier, $R_1 = v^{\Delta r} \bmod N^2$ and $R_2 = c^{4\Delta r} \bmod N^2$ where $r \in_R [0, 2^{t+\ell} T]$, and t, ℓ are security parameters chosen such that $1/2^t$ and $1/2^\ell$ are negligible.
2. The verifier sends $c' \in_R [0, 2^t]$ to P_i.
3. P_i replies by sending $z = r + c'x$ in $\mathbb{Z}$.
4. The verifier checks $v^{\Delta z} \stackrel{?}{\equiv} R_1(VK_i)^{c'} \bmod N^2$ and $c^{4\Delta z} \stackrel{?}{\equiv} R_2 c_i^{2c'} \bmod N^2$.

To explain the computational assumption we need, we consider a group of squares in $\mathbb{Z}^*_{N^2}$ and denote it by Q_{N^2}. We can represent an element $u \in Q_{N^2}$ by (u_p, u_q) such that $u \equiv g_{p^2}^{u_p} \bmod p^2$ and $u \equiv g_{q^2}^{u_q} \bmod q^2$ where g_{p^2} and g_{q^2} are generators of squares in $\mathbb{Z}^*_{p^2}$ and $\mathbb{Z}^*_{q^2}$ respectively. Furthermore, if the order of g_{p^2} is $\prod_{j=1}^{j_p} p_j^{v_j}$ and the order of g_{q^2} is $\prod_{j=1}^{j_q} q_j^{v'_j}$, u_p and u_q can be represented by tuples $(u_{p,1}, \ldots, u_{p,j_p})$ and $(u_{q,1}, \ldots, u_{q,j_q})$ by considering the Chinese remainder theorem where $u_{p,j} \in \mathbb{Z}_{p_j^{\nu_j}}$ and $u_{q,j} \in \mathbb{Z}_{q_j^{\nu_j'}}$. Therefore, any u can be represented uniquely by $[(u_{p,1}, \ldots, u_{p,j_p}), (u_{q,1}, \ldots, u_{q,j_q})]$.

We describe our computational assumption that is similar to the one introduced in [19], but adapted to $\mathbb{Z}_{N^2}^*$ instead of $\mathbb{Z}_N^*$ with a refinement and show, for soundness, the probability that a cheating prover can succeed in creating a valid zero-knowledge proof for an invalid partial decryption share is negligible based on this assumption.

Assumption 1. We consider any polynomial-time algorithm that outputs a square $a \bmod N^2$, given $N = pq$ generated in the distributed key generation where where $p = q = 3 \bmod 4$. Let Q be the largest prime factor in $\mathrm{lcm}(p-1, q-1)$ and assume that the output a is represented as $[(a_{p,1}, \ldots, a_{p,j_p}), (a_{q,1}, \ldots, a_{q,j_q})]$. Suppose $p_j = Q$ and then we assume that for any such algorithm, the probability that $a \not\equiv 1 \bmod N$ and that $a_{p,j} \equiv 0 \bmod p_j (= Q)$, is negligible. We use the notation $(a)_Q = 0$ when $a \not\equiv 1 \bmod N$ and $a_{p,j} \equiv 0 \bmod Q (= p_j)$. We also assume that $1/Q$ is negligible.

Intuitively this assumption implies that $\mathrm{lcm}(p-1, q-1)$ includes at least one large (superpolynomial) prime factor Q with overwhelming probability and it is infeasible to guess Q.

Lemma 1. *Suppose that a cheating prover generates a partial decryption share c_i for c and that c_i is incorrect, that is, $c_i^2 \not\equiv c^{4\Delta x} \bmod N^2$. Then either $(c_i^2/c^{4\Delta x})_Q = 0$ or the probability that the cheating prover can generate a valid zero-knowledge proof is negligible.*

Proof. Let α be $c^{4\Delta}$, β be c_i^2, $\tilde{v}$ be v^{Δ}, and $w(= \tilde{v}^x)$ be VK_i and then $\alpha^x \not\equiv \beta \bmod N^2$. Because $\alpha^x \not\equiv \beta \bmod N^2$, we can assume $\alpha_{p,j} x \not\equiv \beta_{p,j} \bmod p_j^{\nu_j}$ for some j without loss of generality (that is, there should be a difference in either $\mathbb{Z}_{p^2}^*$ or $\mathbb{Z}_{q^2}^*$ or in both). For $p_j = Q$, we should have $\alpha_{p,j} x \not\equiv \beta_{p,j} \bmod p_j^{\nu_j}$ and otherwise $(\alpha^x/\beta)_Q = 0$. We prove the following claim.

Claim. When $\alpha_{p,j} x \not\equiv \beta_{p,j} \bmod p_j^{\nu_j}$ where $p_j = Q$, then for any choice of R_1 and R_2 the cheating prover makes in the first step of the zero-knowledge protocol, there is at most one value of $c' \bmod p_j$ for which the cheating prover can generate a valid response z.

We need to consider two cases to prove this claim. First suppose there is no y such that $\alpha_{p,j} y \equiv \beta_{p,j} \bmod p_j^{\nu_j}$. Assume that the cheating prover can reply to two challenges c_1' and c_2' with z_1 and z_2 where $c_1' \not\equiv c_2' \bmod p_j$ and the same R_1 and R_2 are used for two challenges. Then we have $\alpha_{p,j}(z_1 - z_2) \equiv \beta_{p,j}(c_1' - c_2') \bmod p_j^{\nu_j}$. Because $c_1' - c_2'$ has an inverse modulo $p_j^{\nu_j}$, $\alpha_{p,j}(z_1 - z_2)(c_1' - c_2')^{-1} \equiv \beta_{p,j} \bmod p_j^{\nu_j}$ and this is a contradiction. Next assume that $\alpha_{p,j} \tilde{x} \equiv \beta_{p,j} \bmod p_j^{\nu_j}$ where $\tilde{x} \not\equiv x \bmod \mathrm{ord}(\alpha_{p,j})$ and the order of $\alpha_{p,j} \bmod p_j^{\nu_j}$, $\mathrm{ord}(\alpha_{p,j})$ is some power of p_j. Then we can also assume $\tilde{x} \not\equiv x \bmod p_j$ because otherwise we have $(\alpha^x/\beta)_Q = 0$.

Again assume that the cheating prover can reply to two challenges c_1' and c_2' with z_1 and z_2 where $c_1' \not\equiv c_2' \bmod p_j$ and the same R_1 and R_2 are used for two challenges. Then we have $\alpha_{p,j}(z_1 - z_2) \equiv \beta_{p,j}(c_1' - c_2') \bmod p_j^{\nu_j}$ and $\tilde{v}_{p,j}(z_1 - z_2) \equiv w_{p,j}(c_1' - c_2') \bmod p_j^{\nu_j}$. Because $c_1' - c_2'$ has an inverse modulo $p_j^{\nu_j}$, there exists d such that $d = (c_1' - c_2')^{-1} \bmod p_j^{\nu_j}$. Therefore, we have $\alpha_{p,j}d(z_1 - z_2) \equiv \beta_{p,j} \bmod p_j^{\nu_j}$ and $\tilde{v}_{p,j}d(z_1 - z_2) \equiv w_{p,j} \bmod p_j^{\nu_j}$. Thus we have $\tilde{x} \equiv d(z_1 - z_2) \bmod \mathrm{ord}(\alpha_{p,j})$ and $x \equiv d(z_1 - z_2) \bmod \mathrm{ord}(\tilde{v}_{p,j})$. Both $\mathrm{ord}(\alpha_{p,j})$ and $\mathrm{ord}(\tilde{v}_{p,j})$ are some power of p_j, so we have $\tilde{x} \equiv x \bmod p_j$ and this is a contradiction. This concludes the proof of the claim.

From the above discussion, when the prover is cheating, $((c_i)^2/c^{4\Delta x})_Q = 0$ holds or the probability that the cheating prover can generate a valid zero-knowledge proof for an invalid partial decryption share is $1/Q (= 1/p_j)$ that is negligible. This concludes the proof of Lemma 1.   □

Fast Scalar Multiplication for ECC over GF(p) Using Division Chains

Colin D. Walter⋆

Information Security Group, Royal Holloway, University of London,
Egham, Surrey, TW20 0EX, United Kingdom
`Colin.Walter@rhul.ac.uk`

Abstract. There have been many recent developments in formulae for
efficient composite elliptic curve operations of the form $dP+Q$ for a small
integer d and points P and Q where the underlying field is a prime field.
To make best use of these in a scalar multiplication kP, it is necessary
to generate an efficient "division chain" for the scalar where divisions of
k are by the values of d available through composite operations.

An algorithm-generating algorithm for this is presented that takes
into account the different costs of using various representations for curve
points. This extends the applicability of methods presented by Longa
& Gebotys at PKC 2009 to using specific characteristics of the target
device. It also enables the transfer of some scalar recoding computation
details to design time. An improved cost function also provides better
evaluation of alternatives in the relevant addition chain.

One result of these more general and improved methods includes a
slight increase over the scalar multiplication speeds reported at PKC.
Furthermore, by the straightforward removal of rules for unusual cases,
some particularly concise yet efficient presentations can be given for
algorithms in the target device.

Keywords: Scalar multiplication, multibase representation, addition chain,
division chain, exponentiation, DBNS, elliptic curve cryptography.

1 Introduction

Exponentiation has been the subject of much study over the years. Classic sum-
maries of the state of the art a decade ago are Knuth and Gordon [14,12]. The
aim of these methods is almost always minimising the operation count in an addition chain for the exponent. This is an NP-hard problem. More recent work has
concentrated on wider optimisation issues, such as those imposed by constraints
on the size of any pre-computed table of values, the working space required,
the relative costs of squaring and multiplication, and reducing the side channel
leakage generated by a particular operation sequence.

⋆ The work described in this paper has been supported [in part] by the European
Commission through the ICT programme under contract ICT-2007-216676 ECRYPT
II.

Recently, efficient composite elliptic curve operations of the form $dP+Q$ have been developed for double-and-add ($d = 2$), triple-and-add ($d = 3$) and quintupling ($d = 5$) etc. over $\mathbb{F}_p$ [6,18,16]. By careful choice of curve formulae and affine coordinates for the table entries, these become faster than equivalent combinations of the normal point addition and doubling formulae, and so should lead to faster scalar multiplication. With each application of the operation $dP+Q$ to the accumulating scalar multiple, the part of the key which has yet to be processed is reduced by a factor d using integer division. This is exactly the process for generating a division chain, and so division chains are the natural setting for optimising scalar multiplication when these composite operations are available.

Division chains were first defined in [19] and [20] where the author uses them to derive efficient addition chains in the context of limited table and working space. The resulting chains are significantly shorter than those for binary exponentiation when using just one more register. Without cheap inversion (as is the case for RSA), exponentiation by k can be performed in a right to left direction using an average of about $1.4 \log_2(k)$ operations using divisors $d = 2$ and $d = 3$ (*op. cit.* §5). This improves on the usual $\frac{3}{2} \log_2(k)$ operations using only the divisor $d = 2$ but is less efficient than the $\frac{4}{3} \log_2(k)$ for sliding 2-bit windows[1] which also uses space equivalent to one more register than binary methods. Although with more divisors the speed can be improved to under $\frac{5}{4} \log_2(k)$ operations using the same space, this requires much more pre-processing of the exponent and applies only to the right to left direction for which the composite elliptic curve operations $dP+Q$ do not have more efficient forms. Figures are not provided in [19] for the addition-subtraction chains relevant for elliptic curves, nor are they provided for the left-to-right direction which is marginally less efficient for space constrained implementations but which is of relevance here where the composite operations provide increased efficiency. One aim of the present work is to fill this gap.

For application to elliptic curves, it is the number of field operations which particularly determines the time efficiency of scalar point multiplication. This number depends to a large extent on the form of the curve equation and the coordinate representations chosen for the table entries and intermediate points during processing[2] [13]. The resulting cost of point doublings, additions, triplings etc., rather than the length of the addition sub-chain, is the natural input to the cost evaluation function from [19] which is used to compare competing alternative divisors. This explicit function enables the design time derivation of the algorithm for choosing divisors at run time in a more refined manner than in [17]. Moreover, it transfers *all* of the search for the best divisor to design time.

---

[1] k is partitioned from right to left into "digit" subsequences 0, 01 and 11. Exponentiation is performed left to right using table entries for 01 and 11. Even digits 0 occur with probability $\frac{1}{2}$ whereas the odd digits 01 and 11 occur with probability $\frac{1}{4}$. So an exponent bit has probability $\frac{1}{3}$ of being associated with digit 0, and $\frac{2}{3}$ with digit 01 or 11. Thus the average cost per exponent bit is asymptotically $\frac{1}{3} \cdot \frac{1}{1} + \frac{2}{3} \cdot \frac{3}{2} = \frac{4}{3}$ operations.

[2] Some speed-ups require additional space for four or more coordinates per point.

The less structured double base and multibase representations of Dimitrov *et al.* [4,5,6] represent the scalar k as a signed sum of powers of two (or more) numbers. The extra freedom there allows the use of a slower, greedy algorithm to obtain a very compact representation. However, compactness is not the aim here and extra conditions are required to provide the structure required here for an efficient conversion to a fast addition sequence. These extra conditions are those of a *randomary* representation [22]. Similar representations have been created more recently by Ciet, Longa *et al.* [3,15,17] but restricted to cases in which all digits are zero except those associated with divisor 2 (or its powers).

Here those restrictions are lifted to give a very general setting which encompasses all this previous work on the more structured multibase forms. A side effect of the generality is a modest increase in the speed records achieved in [17]. But the results are also applicable in wider contexts than the particular devices targetted there. For example, the relatively cheap cost of tripling on DIK3 curves [10] makes use of the new availability of non-zero digits associated with base 3.

The main body of the paper describes the above in more detail: division chains and their notation are covered initially; then a discussion on selecting divisor and digit sets followed by details of the cost function for determining the recoding process, and results to evaluate a variety of parameter choices. Finally, Appendix B contains an explicit and very straightforward example algorithm for generating an efficient division chain in the case of divisor set $\{2,3\}$.

2   Addition Chains

The concept of addition chains and addition-subtraction chains needs extending to the context here. Let $\mathcal{OP}$ be the set of "distinguished" operations which we wish to use in exponentiations schemes. For convenience only unary or binary operations are considered. For the (additive) group G of interest, they combine one or two multiples of a given $g \in G$ into a higher multiple of g. So, for each $p \in \mathcal{OP}$ there will be a pair $(\lambda, \mu) \in \mathbb{Z}^2$ such that $p(g, h) = \lambda g + \mu h$ for all $g, h \in G$. As special cases, $(1, 1)$ yields $g + h$ (an addition), $(2, 0)$ yields $2g$ (a doubling) and $(-1, 0)$ provides $-g$ (an inversion). Thus $\mathcal{OP}$ can be viewed as a subset of $\mathbb{Z}^2$. Recent research has provided double-and-add, triple-and-add and even quintuple operations [18,16] to help populate $\mathcal{OP}$. These are of the type $p = (2, d)$ or $p = (3, d)$ etc. where the d-th multiple of the initial point g is in the pre-computed table. These operations lead to a more general addition chain:

Definition 1. *For a set $\mathcal{OP}$ of linear binary operators on an additive group, an $\mathcal{OP}$-addition chain for $k \in \mathbb{Z}$ of length n is a sequence of quadruples $(a_i, b_i, k_i, p_i) \in \mathbb{Z}^3 \times \mathcal{OP}$, $0 \leq i \leq n$, such that, for all $i > 0$,*

- $k_i = \lambda_i a_i + \mu_i b_i$ for $p_i = (\lambda_i, \mu_i) \in \mathcal{OP}$
- $a_i = k_{s_i}$ and $b_i = k_{t_i}$ for some s_i and t_i with $0 \leq s_i < i$ and $0 \leq t_i < i$
- $(a_0, b_0, k_0, p_0) = (1, 0, 1, (1, 0))$
- $k_n = k$.

3 Representations from Division Chains

Addition chains are too general for use in devices with limited memory. The standard left-to-right binary exponentiation algorithm overwrites all previous calculations with the latest value and so its operations can only access the most recent value and the initial input. Hence its addition chain can only contain triples of the form $(k_{i-1}, k_{i-1}, 2k_{i-1})$ (a squaring) or $(k_{i-1}, 1, k_{i-1}+1)$ (a multiplication). Schemes with pre-computed tables are similarly restricted.

The natural extension of this restriction allows only quadruples of the form $(k_{i-1}, 1, \lambda_i k_{i-1}+\mu_i 1, (\lambda_i, \mu_i))$ in an $\mathcal{OP}$-addition chain, i.e. $k_i = \lambda_i k_{i-1}+\mu_i$. Consequently, just as the sequence of squares and multiplications completely determines the exponent k in binary exponentiation, so the sequence of operations (λ_i, μ_i) also determines k. Given k, we can obtain such a sequence (in reverse order) by iteratively choosing $(\lambda_i, \mu_i) \in \mathcal{OP}$ such that μ_i lies in the residue class of $k_i \bmod \lambda_i$, and then performing the division $k_{i-1} = (k_i - \mu_i)/\lambda_i$. The process starts with $k = k_n$ and finishes with $k_0 = 0$. This defines a *division chain* for an integer k, and it is specified by the list of pairs (λ, μ) corresponding to the constituent operations. This is clear from the presentation of k as

$$k = (((\mu_1\lambda_2 + \mu_2)\lambda_3 + ... + \mu_{n-2})\lambda_{n-1} + \mu_{n-1})\lambda_n + \mu_n \qquad (1)$$

Subscripts for addition chains are used in the opposite direction from those in digit representations of numbers. In order to obtain the customary notation for the latter, let us re-number the pairs (λ, μ) by defining $(r_i, d_i) = (\lambda_{n-i}, \mu_{n-i})$. Then the division chain determines a *randomary* representation[3] of k [19]:

$$k = (((d_{n-1}r_{n-2} + d_{n-2})r_{n-3} + ... + d_2)r_1 + d_1)r_0 + d_0 \qquad (2)$$

in which the r_i are called *bases* and the d_i are called *digits*. If all the divisors r_i were equal, then this would simply be a representation in radix $r = r_i$. Digits would be chosen in $[0..r-1]$ to yield the standard representation. Here the bases will belong to some small set $\mathcal{B} \subset \mathbb{N}$ such as $\{2,3,5\}$ and the digits will lie in a subset $\mathcal{D} \subset \mathbb{Z}$ which may contain negative values and may depend on the base.

An example from [22] is

$$235_{10} = (((((1)3 + 0)2 + 1)5 + 4)2 + 0)3 + 1.$$

Following standard subscript notation for specifying the base, this is written $235_{10} = 1_2 0_3 1_2 4_5 0_2 1_3$. Digit/base pairs are obtained using the usual *change of base* algorithm except that the base may be varied at each step: for $i = 0, 1, ...$ extract digit d_i by reducing modulo r_i, and divide by r_i. In the example of 235_{10},

---

[3] Developed from the words *binary, ternary, quaternary* etc. to indicate the apparent random nature of base choices as used in, for example, [21]. This is a not a multi-base (or mixed base) representation in the original sense of that term, and so "randomary" may be useful to distinguish the two forms. A double base (DBNS) example is writing $k = \sum_i \pm 2^{b_i} 3^{t_i}$, which has a different structure.

the first base is 3 and 235 mod 3 = 1 is the first digit (that of index 0). The algorithm continues with input $(235 - 1)/3 = 78$ to determine the next digit.

Such representations determine a left-to-right exponentiation scheme using Horner's rule (which follows the bracketing above from the inside outwards). In an additive group G the iterative step is

$$k_i g = r_{n-i}(k_{i-1}g) + (d_{n-i}g) \qquad (3)$$

using table entry $d_{n-i}g$ and starting at the most significant, i.e. left, end.

4   Choosing the Base Set $\mathcal{B}$

This section considers the choice of base set when the scalar k is used just once and the full cost of creating the multibase representation must be counted. If a cryptographic token were to use the same key throughout its lifetime then more effort could be spent on optimising the representation offline before initialisation, and so different rules would apply. Such a situation is not covered here.

Application of base r reduces the key by a factor of almost exactly r and so shortens k by close to $\log_2 r$ bits. If this requires c_r group operations when used, then its approximate cost for comparing with other bases is $c_r / \log_2 r$ (when neglecting other benefits). Apart from powers of 2 this ratio is lowest for numbers of the form $r' = 2^{n'} \pm 1$ as these consume very close to n' scalar bits for a cost of only $n'+1$ or $n'+2$ operations according to whether the digit is zero or represented in the pre-computed table. For large n' this is going to be better than the average cn for the whole algorithm on a key of n bits, where c is typically in the region of 1.2 to 1.25. With a table of T entries such bases can be used in about $2T+1$ out of r' cases. $k \bmod r'$ must be computed every time to check the usability of r' and, for k in binary, the effort involved in this is proportional to $n' \log(k)$. However, the saving to the scalar multiplication is less than $(c-1)n'$ group operations per use, giving an average of $(2T+1)(c-1)n'2^{-n'}$ per calculation of $k \bmod r'$. Hence, as n' increases the re-coding cost will quickly outweigh any benefit obtained from its use. The same reasoning applies to any large non-2-power radix. Hence $\mathcal{B}$ should only contain small numbers.

Generation of addition-subtraction chains for all small integers shows that, with few exceptions, exponentiation by most bases r requires close to $1.25 \log_2 r$ operations[4] without counting the extra one for any point addition. With an aim of achieving an average of fewer than 1.25 operations per bit, such base choices are not going to be of much use unless the associated digit is zero or there is foreseeable benefit, such as a zero digit in the immediate future.

An investigation of small bases was carried out. It was noted first that no base r below 2^9 required more than two registers for executing a shortest addition

---

[4] The distribution is much more uniform than for NAF, and the 1.25 operations per bit slowly decreases. NAF gives a chain with an asymptotic average of $\frac{4}{3} \log_2 r$ operations. 27 is the first number with an add/sub chain shorter than the NAF, and 427 is the first number with an add/sub chain two operations shorter than the NAF. 31 is the first that needs a subtraction for its shortest chain.

chain for r – the minimum possible for numbers other than powers of 2. So space is not an issue. For the most part, only prime candidates need be considered for the following reason. Suppose radix $r = st$ is composite and it is to be used on k with digit d. Then k would be reduced to $(k-d)/st$. However, application of the base/digit pairs $(s, 0)$, (t, d) has the same effect. Consequently, the value of including r as a divisor depends on whether or not a minimal addition chain for r is shorter than the sum of the chain lengths for any factorisation of r. As an example, no powers of 2 above 2 itself need be included. Thus, the pair $(4, 3)$ can be replaced without cost by $(2, 0)$ followed by $(2, 3)$. However, 33 should be kept in as it has a chain of length 6 which is less than the combined chain lengths for 3 and 11. The investigation revealed $\{33, 49, 63, 65, 77, 95, 121, 129, 133, 143, \ldots\}$ to be the sequence of composite numbers having shorter addition/subtraction chains (by sequence length) than the sum of those of any factorisation.

In fact, *shorter* needs to be interpreted at a finer level of detail. Powers of 3 then become more interesting: two applications of base 3 requires two point doublings and two point additions but one application of base 9 can be achieved with three doublings and one addition. This is the same number of point operations, but should be cheaper since a doubling ought to have a lower cost than a point addition. Similarly, 15 is cheaper than 3 and 5 separately.[5]

After omissions for the above reasons and because of poor ratios $c_r / \log_2 r$, there remains only the initial part of the sequence

$$\{2, 3, 5, 9, 15, 17, 31, 33, 47, 63, 65, 77, 97, 127, 129, \ldots\}.$$

In particular, 7, 11 and 13 have been removed. They have among the very highest costs of any base, with $c_r / \log_2 r$ well above $\frac{4}{3}$. This high cost holds even when the relative cost of a doubling is accounted for and has a value anywhere between 0.5 and 1.0 times the cost of an addition. As the ratio approaches 0.5 the popular base 3 also becomes extremely expensive under this measure, whereas bases 5 and 9 are consistently good. 3 is better than 5 only once the ratio is above 0.87.

An exhaustive search was made for shortest divisor chains using choices from the above sequence to determine which bases were the most useful since any resource-constrained device can only allow a few possibilities. Shortest was measured assuming point doubling to have a cost between half and one times the cost of an addition (*see* [17], Table 1). The digit set was allowed to be any subset of $\{-7, \ldots, +7\}$. In all cases, the frequency of use was close to, in descending order, $\{2; 3; 5; 9, 7; 17, 13, 11; 33, 31, 23, 19; 65, 63, \ldots; 129, 127, \ldots\}$ which is 2 concatenated with the sequences $2^{n+1}+1, \ldots, 2^n+3$ for $n = 0, 1, 2, \ldots$[6] As expected, the frequencies of bases r decrease as r increases. Consequently, it is reasonable to consider only bases in the set $\{2, 3, 5, 9, 17\}$[7] since, with such low frequencies, more bases can only give negligible speed-up to a scalar multiplication. Furthermore, extra bases would require more code and more pre-computation. In fact,

---

[5] The finer detail of gains from using composite operations is treated below.

[6] This listing assumes that bases r of interest have minimal addition chains of length $1 + \lceil \log_2(r-2) \rceil$, which is true for the range of interest and the above restrictions.

[7] In order of decreasing frequency when doubling is half the cost of addition.

the decrease in frequencies is much greater when the cost of doubling approaches that of point additions. In this case, it is hardly worth considering more than just $\{2, 3, 5, 17\}$.[8] However, when doubling is just half the cost of adding, note that 7, 11 and 13 are still possible options. Despite the heavy average cost per bit by which these bases reduce k, they can lead to future values of k which have cheaper than average reductions and enable the extra cost to be recovered. The search for optimal chains also revealed that odd bases rarely make use of non-zero digits. This was the case even when the addition of a table element was assigned just half the cost of the additions used in multiplying by a base. Thus almost no extra speed is likely to be achieved if non-zero digits are allowed for odd bases when composite curve operations are introduced.

This leads to the most sensible base choices for embedded cryptosystems being $\mathcal{B} = \{2, 3\}$ or $\mathcal{B} = \{2, 3, 5\}$. They were first considered in [21,22] and more recently by [18,17] where non-zero digits are only allowed for base 2. Larger sets provide virtually no reasonable advantages and might only be considered out of vanity for attaining a rather marginal increase in speed.

5   Choosing the Digit Set $\mathcal{D}$

Using the very rough cost function given by addition chain length in the previous section it became clear that the fastest scalar multiplication methods would use non-zero digits almost exclusively with the base 2. Consequently, digits which are multiples of 2 can be eliminated as follows. Applying the base/digit pair $(r, 0)$ followed by $(2, 2d)$ is equivalent to applying the (r, d) followed by $(2, 0)$. So the table need not contain even digit multiples of the initial point to cover this case. Similarly, $(2, d')$ followed by $(2, 2d)$ is equivalent to $(2, d+d')$ followed by $(2, 0)$, but the new expression saves one point addition. If $d+d'$ is not an acceptable digit, $(2, d+d')$ could be implemented as a double and add (of multiple d) followed by an extra addition (of multiple d'), thereby again eliminating the need for any even digit multiples in the table or any further adjustment to the representation. Alternatively, $d+d'$ could be split into an acceptable digit and a carry up to the preceding base/digit pair as in the constant base case, with this process repeated until the digit problem is resolved at no additional cost.

As in the case of NAF, and confirmed by the search in §4, the choice of a non-zero digit is almost always going to be made to make the next one or more digits zero. By taking the digit set $\mathcal{D} = \{0, \pm 1, \pm 2, \ldots, \pm(2T-1)\}$ for given table size T, it is possible to maximise the power of 2 achievable as a factor of the next value of k during recoding. Because the composite operators work equally well for any table entry, the desired operation set now has the form $\mathcal{OP} = \mathcal{B} \times \mathcal{D}$ where the two factors are now known.

6   Optimising the Representation

As just noted, a primary aim in the multibase algorithm is to select bases for which the digit is zero as this saves the point addition. When this is not possible,

---

[8] In order of decreasing frequency when doubling has the same cost as addition.

the recoding strategy should make a base/digit choice to ensure it happens next time or as soon as possible thereafter. This requires knowing the key modulo a power of each available base. Let π be a common multiple of the elements in the base set $\mathcal{B}$ which contains only primes dividing available bases and in which it is helpful to have a high power of two because of the frequency with which 2 will be chosen as a base. Decisions will be based on $k_i \bmod \pi$. Indeed, for arbitrary p prime to all base choices, the value of $k_i \bmod p$ can clearly have no influence on the choice of base. However, if π were picked large enough (e.g. larger than k) we would have complete knowledge of k and so there would be enough information to determine an optimal division chain.

Divisor choices are not independent. The choice of the first divisor is partly affected by the best choice for the next, and less so by subsequent ones. After a chain of four or more, simulations show that the effect is minimal. Hence we want to pick the first divisor to minimise the average cost of the addition sub-chain formed by the next four or so divisors. So let λ be the length of sub-chain to be investigated. This would be the window size if the base were fixed. Initially, let π be the least common multiple of the λth powers of each base in $\mathcal{B}$. If the pre-computed table has T elements and δ is minimal such that $T \leq 2^\delta$ then a base 2 digit can sometimes be chosen to guarantee divisibility by at least $2^{\delta+2}$. (For example, with $T = 3$ and table entries for $\{\pm 1, \pm 3, \pm 5\}$, we have $\delta = 2$ and, when $k_i \equiv 5 \bmod 8$, either of the digits $-3, 5$ might be used, but one will make $k_i - d_i \equiv 0 \bmod 16$.) In such cases, in effect, we have a base of $2^{\delta+2}$. Thus the base 2 digits cannot be chosen accurately towards the end of the window unless π is augmented by another factor of at least $2^{\delta+1}$. Moreover, this example shows that the cost benefits of digit choices continue beyond the end of the window.

For each residue mod π, all possible sub-chains of length λ are generated. The first pair (r, d) is then chosen from the "best" sub-chain and assigned to be the choice whenever k_i has that value modulo π. Explicit code for this is presented in the first algorithm of Appendix A. Since the search takes a total of $O(\pi \{T \sum_{r \in \mathcal{B}} \frac{1}{r}\}^\lambda)$ time, $\lambda = 3$ is easily achievable with reasonable resources.

In the next section, the device-specific definition of "best" is given properly. However, the above association of pairs (r, d) with residues mod π is obtained from an off-line search and yields a simple algorithm for programming into the target device, such as the second algorithm in Appendix A. Most divisor choices are determined by very simple rules such as selecting the pairs $(2, 0)$ and $(3, 0)$ respectively when the residue mod π is divisible by 2 or 3. So the table of data can generally be converted to a much more compact set of simple rules. The full set of rules mod π may contain many exceptional cases. They become less critical to the performance of the algorithm as the number of residues affected decreases, and so some very small cases can be absorbed into larger ones with very little loss in performance, thereby reducing code size. Appendix B contains two examples of the recoding algorithm's iterative step showing just how compact the resulting code can be and yet still provide a very efficient scheme.

6.1   The Detailed Cost Function

In §4 the cost per bit of applying base r is given as $c_r/\log_2 r$ where c_r was initially taken as the length of the addition chain used for r in order to ascertain which were the best values to put in $\mathcal{B}$. From now on, costs $c_{r,d}$ are taken at the accuracy required to differentiate successfully between competing choices for (r,d). If reading and writing operations, field additions and scalar field multiplications are relatively cheap, $c_{r,d}$ is given by the appropriately weighted sum of field multiplication and squaring counts. They depend on the form of the equation and the coordinate representation chosen for the elliptic curve and its points. The reader is referred to [17], Table 1, for examples covering the specialised efficient doubling, tripling and quintupling operations of interest here.

A sequence of λ iterative steps of the type (3) can be composed into a single operation of the same type, represented by a base/digit pair (r,d) where the new base r is the product of those of the constituent pairs. The cost function $c_{r,d}$ can be extended to this by adding the costs of the component pairs. However, the per bit cost $c_{r,d}/\log_2 r$ is no longer a good estimate of the relative value of the choice of either (r,d) or the first pair in the window. The reduction achieved by any sub-chain is typically followed by an average reduction. Suppose c is the average cost per bit and an alternative sub-chain has cost $c_{r',d'}$ to achieve a reduction by (r',d'). Removing a further factor of r/r' from $(k_i-d')/r'$ costs an average of $c\log_2(r/r')$, giving a total of $c_{r',d'}+c\log_2(r/r')$ for reducing k_i by a factor of r. So the first choice is better on average if $c_{r,d} < c_{r',d'}+c\log_2(r/r')$, i.e. if $c_{r,d}-c\log_2 r < c_{r',d'}-c\log_2 r'$. Thus the "best" sub-chain is taken to be the one minimising

$$c_{r,d} - c\log_2 r \tag{4}$$

This is simply the extra work required above the average expected. Although use of (4) requires advance knowledge of the average cost per bit c, various values can be tried in practice, of course, in order to converge on the smallest.

Finally, no choice of base/digit sequence for the window makes full use of the value $k_i \bmod \pi$. For a sub-chain equivalent to (r,d), $c_{r,d}$ does not take into account properties of $(k_i-d)/r \bmod \pi/r$. As noted above, the final digit in the window is usually chosen, like the others, to give exact divisibility in the following digit when that possible. So the sub-chain pair (r,d) in (4) should be augmented to include pairs $(r',0)$ representing any remaining divisibility in $k_i-d \bmod \pi$.

6.2   A Markov Process

An interesting consequence of specifying the divisor/digit pair to choose given the residue of k_i modulo π is that these residues become non-uniform after the first iteration and, after about half a dozen choices, have settled close to their asymptotic probabilities. This is a Markov process which, in the limit, leads to a precise value for the work c per bit required when evaluating (4).

The process is described by a $\pi \times \pi$ transition probability matrix $P = (p_{ij})$ where p_{ij} is the probability that an input of $i \bmod \pi$ will generate an output of $j \bmod \pi$. If the pair (r_i, d_i) is associated with $i \bmod \pi$ then the output j

will be one of the r_i values $(i-d_i+t\pi)/r_i \bmod \pi$ for $0 \le t \le r_i-1$. As these are all equally likely, each of these p_{ij} has the value r_i^{-1} and for other values of j, p_{ij} is zero. The matrix P^m contains entries $p_{ij}^{(m)}$ which are the probabilities of input $i \bmod \pi$ resulting in an output of $j \bmod \pi$ after m divisors are applied to k using the algorithm. Averaging over all i gives the probability of residue $j \bmod \pi$ after m iterations. This converges very quickly to a steady state in which the probabilities typically lie in a range between $\frac{3}{4}\pi^{-1}$ and $\frac{5}{4}\pi^{-1}$.

If p_j is the asymptotic probability for residue class $j \bmod \pi$ and c_j the cost of the pair (r_j, d_j) associated with that class, then the average cost per bit is

$$c = \frac{\sum_{j=0}^{\pi-1} p_j c_j}{\sum_{j=0}^{\pi-1} p_j \log_2(r_j)} \tag{5}$$

In fact, using a slightly more aggressive (smaller) value for c in (4) seems to yield the best value for c in (5). Our overall objective is, of course, to minimise this.

The transition matrix is usually too big for practical calculations. Instead, a Monte Carlo simulation can be performed. A large number of random keys k is generated, written in base π for convenience, and recoded to find the probabilities. Since (4) may have failed to capture all the useful information in the associated residue modulo π, this process can be repeated on neighbouring schemes to identify the local minimum for c: for each residue $i \bmod \pi$ alternative pairs (r_i, d_i) can be tried to improve c. The same process can also be used to evaluate potential simplifications to the scheme.

7   Test Results and Evaluation

Table 1 shows figures comparing the above algorithm with the best earlier results as provided by the refined NAF method of Longa and Gebotys in [17], Table 4. It illustrates the speed-ups for three sets of projective coordinate systems. These are standard Jacobian coordinates (with $a = -3$), inverted Edwards coordinates [7,1] and extended coordinates on the Jacobi Quartic form [2,13]. The cost per operator columns give the number of field multiplications or equivalents (counting 0.8 for each squaring) which are used for doubling (D), tripling (T), quintupling (Q) and the addition of a table entry (A) within a double-add, triple-add etc. operation in the given coordinate system. The stored points were the first few of 1, 3, 5, 7,... times the initial point. The number of them is recorded in the third column group, and the cost of initialising them is included in the operator count totals. In order to make scaling to other key lengths easier, an initialisation optimisation [17,8,16] which saves 10 to 12 field multiplications has not been applied to either set of results. The final column is the asymptotic number of field multiplications (or equivalents) per bit of k, calculated as in §6.2. This is the value of c in (5).

The methodology here performs a systematic search at design time to determine the best run-time choice. This choice is wider than that in [17] because, for example, 2 is not automatically the divisor when k is even (see Appendix B for an example), bases which divide k exactly need not be chosen as divisors,

Table 1. Comparative Point Multiplication Speeds for 160-bit Scalar (*cf* [17], Table 4)

Method	Coords	D	T	Q	A	$\mathcal{B}$	#Stored Pts	π	Op. Count Sq = 0.8M	Cost/Bit c
[17]	JQuart	6.0	11.2		8.4	{2,3}	8		1229.2	7.50
"	"	"	"		"	"	1		1288.4	8.10
"	InvEdw	6.2	12.2		8.8	"	8		1277.1	7.79
"	Jacobian	7.0	12.6		10.2	"	8		1445.1	8.91
Here	JQuart	6.0	11.2		8.4	{2,3}	8	$2^{13}3^3$	1207.1	7.32
"	"	"	"		"	"	4	$2^{13}3^3$	1212.0	7.52
"	"	"	"		"	"	2	$2^{17}3^4$	1253.8	7.84
"	"	"	"		"	"	1	$2^{17}3^4$	1287.6	8.10
"	InvEd	6.2	12.2		8.8	"	8	$2^{13}3^3$	1242.5	7.55
"	Jacobian	7.0	12.6		10.2	"	8	$2^{13}3^3$	1414.9	8.57
[17]	JQuart	6.0	11.2	17.2	8.4	{2,3,5}	8		1226.5	7.48
"	Jacobian	7.0	12.6	19.6	10.2	"	8		1435.2	8.84
Here	JQuart	6.0	11.2	17.2	8.4	{2,3,5}	8	$2^93^25^2$	1203.7	7.30
"	Jacobian	7.0	12.6	19.6	10.2	"	8	$2^93^25^2$	1409.8	8.53

and divisors other than 2 can have non-zero digits associated with them. All this automatically leads to the possibility of faster scalar multiplication. However, the tabulated results here represent a less deep search – a larger value for π is necessary to uncover all the conditions listed in [17], Tables 2 and 3. Further computation could have been used to obtain them. There is no clear cost function in [17] but an explicit cost function has been given above in (4). This is not the obvious one (which is sub-optimal) but arguments have been presented to justify the conclusion that it is better. This difference probably also contributes to the greater speeds here, which are asymptotically 2.5% faster than [17].

The best value for money seems to occur with tables of 4 points, being under 1% slower than their 8 point counterparts. For the fastest times, observe that the Jacobi Quartic coordinate representation [13] can be used to perform 160-bit scalar multiplication with divisors 2 and 3 and a table of 8 pre-computed points using, on average, the equivalent of fewer than 1200 field multiplications when the optimisations of [8,16] are applied. This can be achieved with very straightforward code, which is given in the first example of Appendix B.

8   Conclusion

A detailed methodology has been presented for deriving compact, device-specific algorithms which perform very efficient scalar multiplication for elliptic curves in modestly resource constrained environments when the scalar is an unseen fresh, random, cryptographic key. The method is based on multibase representations of the scalar and careful construction of a cost function for evaluating alternatives. A valuable output demonstrating the efficacy of the approach is the fastest known algorithm in certain contexts, such as when composite curve operations are available. Another output is a couple of examples which illustrate the compactness of resulting code for the iterated recoding step.

With an initial recoding cost equivalent to two or three field multiplications, the exponentiation algorithm is efficient and avoids an expensive run-time search by resolving the search questions at design time. Part of the speed-up is derived from a much fuller choice of base/digit pairs at each step than prior algorithms and part from a new, explicit device-specific cost function for evaluating different options in the search for the most efficient addition chain. That function can, and should moreover, use detailed knowledge of the times for various field operations. Exactly the same methods can be applied with more extensive preparatory computation to generate still faster or compact algorithms than tabulated here.

References

1. Bernstein, D., Lange, T.: Analysis and Optimization of Elliptic-Curve Single-Scalar Multiplication. Cryptology ePrint Archive, Report 2007/455, IACR 2007 (2007)
2. Billet, O., Joye, M.: The Jacobi Model of an Elliptic Curve and Side-Channel Analysis. In: Fossorier, M.P.C., Høholdt, T., Poli, A. (eds.) AAECC 2003. LNCS, vol. 2643, pp. 34–42. Springer, Heidelberg (2003)
3. Ciet, M., Joye, M., Lauter, K., Montgomery, P.: Trading Inversions for Multiplications in Elliptic Curve Cryptography. Designs, Codes and Cryptography 39(2), 189–206 (2006)
4. Dimitrov, V., Cooklev, T.: Two Algorithms for Modular Exponentiation using Non-Standard Arithmetics. IEICE Transactions on Fundamentals of Electronics, Communications and Computer Sciences E78-A(1), 82–87 (1995)
5. Dimitrov, V.S., Jullien, G.A., Miller, W.C.: Theory and Applications for a Double-Base Number System. In: Proc. 13th IEEE Symposium on Computer Arithmetic, Monterey, July 6-9, pp. 44–51. IEEE, Los Alamitos (1997)
6. Dimitrov, V.S., Imbert, L., Mishra, P.K.: Efficient and Secure Elliptic Curve Point Multiplication using Double-Base Chains. In: Roy, B. (ed.) ASIACRYPT 2005. LNCS, vol. 3788, pp. 59–78. Springer, Heidelberg (2005)
7. Edwards, H.: A Normal Form for Elliptic Curves. Bull. Amer. Math. Soc. 44, 393–422 (2007)
8. Elmegaard-Fessel, L.: Efficient Scalar Multiplication and Security against Power Analysis in Cryptosystems based on the NIST Elliptic Curves over Prime Fields, Masters Thesis, University of Copenhagen (2006)
9. Fouque, P.-A., Valette, F.: The Doubling Attack – Why upwards is better than downwards. In: Walter, C.D., Koç, Ç.K., Paar, C. (eds.) CHES 2003. LNCS, vol. 2779, pp. 269–280. Springer, Heidelberg (2003)
10. Doche, C., Icart, T., Kohel, D.R.: Efficient Scalar Multiplication by Isogeny Decompositions. In: Yung, M., Dodis, Y., Kiayias, A., Malkin, T.G. (eds.) PKC 2006. LNCS, vol. 3958, pp. 191–206. Springer, Heidelberg (2006)
11. Giessmann, E.-G.: Ein schneller Algorithmus zur Punktevervielfachung, der gegen Seitenanalattacken resistent ist. In: Workshop über Theoretische und praktische Aspekte von Kryptographie mit Elliptischen Kurven, Berlin (2001)
12. Gordon, D.M.: A Survey of Fast Exponentiation Algorithms. Journal of Algorithms 27, 129–146 (1998)
13. Hisil, H., Wong, K., Carter, G., Dawson, E.: Faster Group Operations on Elliptic Curves. Cryptology ePrint Archive, Report 2007/441, IACR (2007)

14. Knuth, D.E.: The Art of Computer Programming, 2nd edn. Seminumerical Algorithms, vol. 2, §4.6.3, pp. 441–466. Addison-Wesley, Reading (1981)
15. Longa, P.: Accelerating the Scalar Multiplication on Elliptic Curve Cryptosystems over Prime Fields, Masters Thesis, University of Ottawa (2007)
16. Longa, P., Miri, A.: New Composite Operations and Precomputation Scheme for Elliptic Curve Cryptosystems over Prime Fields. In: Cramer, R. (ed.) PKC 2008. LNCS, vol. 4939, pp. 229–247. Springer, Heidelberg (2008)
17. Longa, P., Gebotys, C.: Fast Multibase Methods and Other Several Optimizations for Elliptic Curve Scalar Multiplication. In: Jarecki, S., Tsudik, G. (eds.) PKC 2009. LNCS, vol. 5443, pp. 443–462. Springer, Heidelberg (2009)
18. Mishra, P.K., Dimitrov, V.: Efficient Quintuple Formulas for Elliptic Curves and Efficient Scalar Multiplication using Multibase Number Representation. In: Garay, J.A., Lenstra, A.K., Mambo, M., Peralta, R. (eds.) ISC 2007. LNCS, vol. 4779, pp. 390–406. Springer, Heidelberg (2007)
19. Walter, C.D.: Exponentiation using Division Chains. In: Proc. 13th IEEE Symposium on Computer Arithmetic, Monterey, CA, July 6-9, pp. 92–98. IEEE, Los Alamitos (1997)
20. Walter, C.D.: Exponentiation using Division Chains. IEEE Transactions on Computers 47(7), 757–765 (1998)
21. Walter, C.D.: MIST: An Efficient, Randomized Exponentiation Algorithm for Resisting Power Analysis. In: Preneel, B. (ed.) CT-RSA 2002. LNCS, vol. 2271, pp. 53–66. Springer, Heidelberg (2002)
22. Walter, C.D.: Some Security Aspects of the MIST Randomized Exponentiation Algorithm. In: Kaliski Jr., B.S., Koç, Ç.K., Paar, C. (eds.) CHES 2002. LNCS, vol. 2523, pp. 276–290. Springer, Heidelberg (2003)
23. Yao, A.C.-C.: On the Evaluation of Powers. SIAM J. Comput. 5(1), 100–103 (1976)

Appendix A. Pseudo-Code for the Recoding Scheme

The algorithm in Fig. 1 determines the base/digit pairs to associate with each residue i mod π of the key k during generation of the multibase representation. Its inputs include a choice of base set $\mathcal{B}$ and digit set $\mathcal{D}$ suitable for the target device, the window width λ and the value of π (the λth power of the lcm of bases in $\mathcal{B}$ times a power of 2 determined by the table size). The output is deposited in two arrays, Base and Digit. The function $Cost$ is that in (4), and it is described in detail in §6.1.

The algorithm in Fig. 2 uses the arrays Base and Digit to recode the key k, storing the resulting multibase representation in an array MB. Usually the array accesses in the loop body will be replaced by coded rules as in Appendix B.

Appendix B. Code for the Iterative Step

The very simple code of Figure 3 provides mod $2^6 3^2$ rules for selecting the next divisor/ residue pair (r, d) for k with base set $\mathcal{B} = \{2, 3\}$ and a precomputed table of 8 points containing 1, 3, 5,..., 15 times the input point. Once the pair (r, d) is chosen, k is then reduced to $(k-d)/r$ for the next application of the rules. The rules were obtained using a sub-chain length of $\lambda = 2$ with $c = 7.328$

```
For i: 0 ≤ i < π do
{  BestCost ← MaxCost
   For all r1 in B and all d1 in D do
   If (i-d1) mod r1 = 0 then
   {  i1 = (i-d1)/r1
      For all r2 in B and all d2 in D do
      If (i1-d2) mod r2 = 0 then
      {  ...
         If Cost((r1,d1),(r2,d2),...,(rλ,dλ)) < BestCost then
         {  BestCost ← Cost((r1,d1),(r2,d2),...,(rλ,dλ))
            Base[i] ← r1
            Digit[i] ← d1
         }
      }
   }
}
```

Fig. 1. Algorithm to determine Base/Digit pairs for each Residue mod π

```
n ← 0
While k ≠ 0 do
{  i ← k mod π
   MB[n].r ← Base[i]
   MB[n].d ← Digit[i]
   k ← (k-Digit[i])/Base[i]
   n ← n+1
}
MB.len ← n
```

Fig. 2. Algorithm to recode k to a Division Chain Representation

```
If k = 0 mod 9 and k ≠ 0 mod 4 then
        r ← 3, d ← 0
else if k = 0 mod 2 then
        r ← 2, d ← 0
else if k = 0 mod 3 and 18 < (k mod 64) < 46
        and ((k mod 64)-32) ≠ 0 mod 3 then
        r ← 3, d ← 0
else    r ← 2, d ← ((k+16) mod 32) - 16.
```

Fig. 3. A Choice of Mod $2^6 3^2$ Recoding Rules for a Table Size of 8

in (4) and the Jacobi Quartic form costs of the composite operations as listed in Table 1. This generated the same value for c in (5). Increasing λ by 1 only saves 1 more multiplication per 160-bit scalar.

Similar conditions are given in [17], Tables 2 and 3. The main difference here is that some multiples of 2 are assigned the divisor 3 rather than the 2 forced by [17]. This enables the next residue to be modified by a large table entry to make it much more highly divisible by 2. Note, however, that divisor 3 is not

```
If k = 0 mod 9 and k ≠ 0 mod 4
and (16 < (k mod 256) < 240) then
        r ← 3, d ← 0
else if k = 0 mod 2 then
        r ← 2, d ← 0
else if k = 0 mod 3 and 8 < (k mod 32) < 24
        and ((k mod 32)-16) ≠ 0 mod 3 then
        r ← 3, d ← 0
else    r ← 2, d ← ((k+8) mod 16) - 8.
```

Fig. 4. A Choice of Mod $2^8 3^2$ Recoding Rules for a Table Size of 4

used with a non-zero digit although the generating algorithm could have allowed it. Including the pre-computations for table entries, the total field multiplication count for 160-bit scalars is just under 1208 (at 1 squaring = 0.8 multiplications). This was obtained by a Monte Carlo simulation. The optimisations referred to in [17,16] enable a further 10-12 multiplications to be saved during initialisation using [8], §4.2.2, thereby taking the total to under 1200.

In the same context as the above except for having a pre-computed table of four instead of eight points, the code in Fig. 4 works with $\pi = 2^8 3^2$ and generates a recoding which requires 1214.2 field multiplications on average. This is over 22.7 multiplications better than code with no triplings.

Design of a Novel Pseudo-Random Generator Based on Vectorial FCSRs

Boufeldja Allailou[1], Abdelaziz Marjane[2], and Abdellah Mokrane[2]

[1] LAGA, UMR CNRS 7539, Université Paris 8, Saint-Denis, France
allailou@math.univ-paris13.fr
[2] LAGA, UMR CNRS 7539, Université Paris 13, Villteneuse, France
marjane@math.univ-paris13.fr,
mokrane@math.univ-paris13.fr

Abstract. Feedback with carry shift registers (FCSRs) have been introduced first by Goresky and Klapper, particularly as an alternative to linear feedback shift registers (LFSRs). Similarly to LFSRs, FCSRs have an underlying algebraic structure that facilitates their analysis, and their output sequences have many desirable statistical properties. Besides their direct applications as pseudorandom number generators, they have proven useful as building blocks for stream ciphers, but an FCSR should never be used by itself as keystream generator. To ovoid this problem, Arnault an Berger proposed to use Filtred FCSR. Weakness related to the representation structure allowded an efficient attack developed by Hell and Johansson.

In this paper, we propose a new stream cipher based on a novel conception of pseudorandom generators Vectorial FCSR (VFCSR). This configuration allows an efficient resistance the above attack.

Keywords: VFCSR, FCSR, Stream cipher.

1 Introduction

Feedback with carry shift registers (FCSRs) are a class of nonlinear sequences generator and were first introduced by M. Goresky and A. Klapper in[1]. The maximal length of FCSR sequences are called l-sequences. It is widely belived that l-sequences have very good pseudorandom properties, but, as LFSRs, should never be used by themselves as a keystream [7]. To avoid this problem, F. Arnault and T. P. Berger proposed to use a linear filter to FCSRs. And later proposed two algorithms called F-FCSR-8 and F-FCSR-H. The hardware oriented version F-FCSR-H v2 was one of eSTREAM hardware-oriented finalists.

Weakness in F-FCSRs family was first described in [7]. Recently, Hell and Johansson in [9], have exploited this way, for which the quadratic appearance of the transition function becomes linear, to mount a very powerful attack against the F-FCSR stream cipher familly. Due to this attack, F-FCSR-H v2 has been removed from the eSTREAM portfolio since September 8, 2008[15]. however, Breaking F-FCSR-H, does not mean FCSRs are dead[10]. Very recently, in [11], F. Arnault and all have presented a new approch for FCSRs based on a representation called "ring", which is viewed as a generalization of the Fibonacci and

Y. Chung and M. Yung (Eds.): WISA 2010, LNCS 6513, pp. 76–91, 2011.
© Springer-Verlag Berlin Heidelberg 2011

Galois representations. As sited in [11], Ring FCSRs have many advantages over the previous representations and one of them is that they can be used to prevent the attack of Hell and Johansson [9].

In this paper, we present a new design of a peudorandom generator, which call it F-VFCSR. It's based on the new conception called Vectorial FCSRs [2]. This approch prevent the attack of Hell and Johansson. This paper is organized as follows, in section 2, we briefly review FCSR automaton [7][12]. In section 3 we give an introduction to the new conception VFCSR[2], then we represent the VFCSR Automaton in section 4. Section 5 is devoted to the attack on F-FCSR-H and the new conception's properties, and in section 6 as an application, we present a new stream ciphers oriented hardwar F-VFCSR-H.

2   Recalling the FCSR Automaton

2.1   Binary FCSRs

Goresky and Klapper have introduced FCSRs in 1993 in "2-adic Shift Registers"[1]. These registers rely over a 2-adic elegant structure which is an alternative to the linear architecture of LFSRs. They differ from LFSRs for adding memory and for the calculations from the register located in $\mathbb{Z}$. By associating the output sequence in $\mathbb{F}_2$ to 2-adic integer, which is formally a power series $s = \sum_{i=0}^{\infty} s_i 2^i$ with $s_i \in \{0, 1\}$, Goresky and Klapper shows that this 2-adic integer is a rational, which is equivalent to say, according to the 2-adic theory, that the output sequence is eventually periodic. The denominator of the rational is always the connection integer of the FCSR $q = q_r 2^r + \ldots + q_1 2^1 - 1$ where q_i are the connection coefficients. If we note $(s_i)_i$ the output sequence and $\frac{p}{q}$ the associated rational (p and q coprime), the period is therefore the order of 2 modulo q. The period is maximal if q is prime and 2 is primitive root modulo q. In this case, the period is $q - 1$. These sequences are called l-sequences (longer sequences). They look like the m-sequences of LFSRs in terms of distribution properties (the balanced property ...) and of cross-correlation (cross-correlation of 2 or 3 levels). As for LFSRs, FCSRs have two different representations: the Fibonacci representation and Galois representation.

2.2   Description of the Automaton[7][8]

Let $q = 1 - 2d$ be a negative integer. The FCSR generator with connection integer q can be described, in Galois representation, as a circuit containing two registers:

- The main register $\mathcal{M}$ with k binary memories (one for each cell), where k is the bit length of d.
- The carry register $\mathcal{C}$ with l binary memories where $l + 1$ is the Hamming weight of d. Using the binary expansion $\sum_{i=0}^{k-1} d_i 2^i$ of d, we put

$$I_d = \{i | 0 \leq i \leq k - 2 \text{ and } d_i = 1\}.$$

We also put $d^* = d - 2^{k-1}$. The integer l is then the cardinality of I_d and the Hamming weight of d^*.

We will say that the main register contains the integer $m = \sum_{i=0}^{k-1} m_i 2^i$ when it contains the binary values $(m_0, ..., m_{k-1})$. The content m of the main register always satisfies $0 \leq m \leq 2^k - 1$. In order to use similar notation for the carry register, we can think of it as a k bit register where the $k - l$ bits of rank not in I_d are always 0. The content $c = \sum_{i \in I_d} c_i 2^i$ of the carry register always satisfies $0 \leq c \leq d^*$.

2.3   Transition Function

As described above, the FCSR circuit with connection integer q is an automaton with 2^{k+l} states corresponding to the $k + l$ binary memories of main and carry registers. We say that the FCSR circuit is in state (m, c) if the main and carry registers contain, respectively, the binary expansion of m and of c.

Suppose that, at time t, the FCSR circuit is in state $(m(t), c(t))$ with $m = \sum_{i=0}^{k-1} m_i(t) 2^i$ and $c = \sum_{i=0}^{k-1} c_i(t) 2^i$. The state $(m(t+1), c(t+1))$ at time $t+1$ is computed using:

- For $0 \leq i \leq k - 2$
  - if $i \notin I_d$, $m_i(t+1) := m_{i+1}(t)$.
  - if $i \in I_d$, Fig.(5-e)

$$m_i(t+1) := m_{i+1}(t) \oplus c_i(t) \oplus m_0(t) \qquad (1)$$
$$c_i(t+1) := m_{i+1}(t)c_i(t) \oplus c_i(t)m_0(t) \oplus m_0(t)m_{i+1}(t)$$

- For the case $i = k - 1$, $m_{k-1}(t+1) := m_0(t)$.

Note that this transition function is described with quadratic Boolean functions and that, for all three cases, $m_i(t+1)$ can be expressed with a single formula: $m_i(t+1) := m_{i+1}(t) \oplus d_i c_i(t) \oplus d_i m_0(t)$ if we put $m_k(t) = 0$ and $c_{k-1}(t) = 0$.

Example 1. Let q = 349, so d = 175, k = 8, and l = 5. The diagram shown in Fig.1 , shows these two registers[1].

3   Vectorial FCSR Theoritical

The VFCSRs or vectorial FCSRs are FCSRs with vectorial conception of the objects and the spaces. This conception can grow so far the analysis. Klapper introduced this idea in "FCSR over finite fields (1994)" describing the finite field $\mathbb{F}_{2^n}$ as a vectorial space of n dimensions over $\mathbb{F}_2$. Indeed, $\mathbb{F}_{2^n} = \mathbb{F}_2[\bar{\beta}]$ where β is a root of a primitive irreducible polynomial on $\mathbb{Z}$ and $\bar{\beta}$ is the reduction modulo

---

[1] Often, in papers related to the F-FCSR stream cipher, the FCSR example have q = 347. In our example we have choosen q = 349 in order to show difference between the two designs: FCSR and Vectoriel FCSR in the quadratic case with $\tilde{q} = 349$.

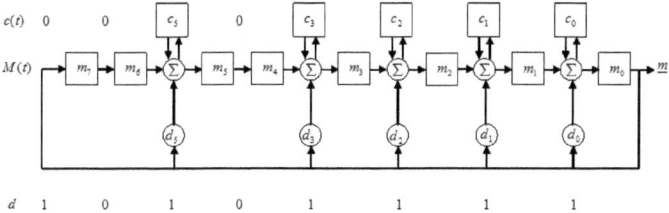

Fig. 1. Galois-FCSR automaton example

2 of β. However, Klapper develops a formal analysis by associating the output sequence $(m_i)_i$ to the element $\sum_i m_i 2^i$ in $(\mathbb{Z}[\beta])_2$ and shows that it corresponds to a "rational" $\frac{s}{q}$ where s and q are in $\mathbb{Z}[\beta]$.

In "Vectorial Conception of FCSR" [2], A. Marjane and B. Allailou have developped vectorial analysis of FCSR basing on this vectorial conception We calculate the period, the behavior of the memory, the vectorial exponential representation, the pseudo-randomness basic properties...

Operation in the register: Let P a primitive irreducible polynomial over $\mathbb{Z}$ form $X^n - \cdots - 1$. Let $\beta \in \mathbb{C}$ a root of P. We consider $\mathbb{Z}[\beta]$ the free $\mathbb{Z}$-module of rank n. Let $\overline{\beta}$ the reduction modulo 2 of β and let $\overline{P}$ the reduction modulo 2 of P. We have $\mathbb{F}_2\left[\overline{\beta}\right] = \mathbb{F}_2[X]/(\overline{P})$ a vectorial space over $\mathbb{F}_2$ of dimension n. Let $\mathcal{B} = \left\{1, \beta, \cdots, \beta^{n-1}\right\}$ the canonical basis of $\mathbb{Z}[\beta]$. Let $r \in \mathbb{N}^*$ and the initial state $(m_0, \cdots, m_{r-1}, c_{r-1}) \in (\mathbb{F}_2\left[\overline{\beta}\right])^r \times \mathbb{Z}[\beta]$. Let $(q_1, q_1, ..., q_r) \in (\mathbb{F}_2\left[\overline{\beta}\right])^r$ the connection coefficients. We write all these elements in the basis $\mathcal{B}$.

$$(m_0, ..., m_{r-1}, c_{r-1}) = \left(\begin{pmatrix} m_0^0 \\ \vdots \\ m_{n-1}^0 \end{pmatrix}, \cdots, \begin{pmatrix} m_0^{r-1} \\ \vdots \\ m_{n-1}^{r-1} \end{pmatrix}, \begin{pmatrix} c_0^{r-1} \\ \vdots \\ c_{n-1}^{r-1} \end{pmatrix} \right).$$

$$(q_1, q_1, \cdots, q_r) = \left(\begin{pmatrix} q_0^1 \\ \vdots \\ q_{n-1}^1 \end{pmatrix}, \begin{pmatrix} q_0^2 \\ \vdots \\ q_{n-1}^2 \end{pmatrix}, \cdots, \begin{pmatrix} q_0^r \\ \vdots \\ q_{n-1}^r \end{pmatrix} \right)$$

We take the canonical lift of $(m_0, ..., m_{r-1})$ and $(q_1, q_1, ..., q_r)$ in $\mathbb{Z}[\beta]$ and we compute $\sigma_r = q_1 m_{r-1} + \cdots + q_r m_0 + c_{r-1}$. Here multiplication and addition are located in $\mathbb{Z}[\beta]$ and definided by P. Next we compute $m_r = \sigma_r (\mathrm{mod}\ 2)$, we take the canonical lift of m_r and we compute $c_r = \sigma_r (div2)$. Finally, we leave m_0 and c_{r-1} and enter m_r and c_r. The vectorial expression of these elements in the basis $\mathcal{B}$ is:

$$\sigma_r = \begin{pmatrix} \sigma_0^r \\ \vdots \\ \sigma_{n-1}^r \end{pmatrix}, a_r = \begin{pmatrix} \sigma_0^r (\mathrm{mod}\ 2) \\ \vdots \\ \sigma_{n-1}^r (\mathrm{mod}\ 2) \end{pmatrix} \text{ and } m_r = \begin{pmatrix} \frac{\sigma_0^r - m_0^r}{2} \\ \vdots \\ \frac{\sigma_{n-1}^r - m_{n-1}^r}{2} \end{pmatrix}$$

Definition 1. *We call this register a VFCSR over* $(\mathbb{F}_2, P, \beta)$. *The vectorial sequence* $\underline{m} = (m_0, \cdots, m_{r-1}, m_r, \cdots) \in \mathbb{F}_2$ *is called the output sequence of the VFCSR. The vectorial sequence* $(c_{r-1}, c_r, \cdots) \in \mathbb{Z}^{\mathbb{N}}$ *is called the memory sequence.* $(q_1, q_2, \cdots, q_r)$ *are called connection coefficients.* r *is the size of the VFCSR and* $(m_0, \cdots, m_{r-1}, c_{r-1})$ *the initial state.*

Analysis: We associate the output sequence to the following 2-adic vector $\alpha =$
$$(\alpha_j)_{0 \leq j \leq n-1} = \left(\sum_{i=0}^{+\infty} m_j^i 2^i \right)_{0 \leq j \leq n-1} \in \mathbb{Z}_2{}^n,$$ and we associate the connection coefficient to the following *connection vector*

$$(q_1, \cdots, q_r) \rightarrow \left(\tilde{q}_j = q_j^r 2^r + \ldots + q_j^1 2 \right)_{0 \leq j \leq n-1} \in \mathbb{Z}^n.$$

Through simple calculations, we find recurrence relations that link the vectorial component of m_r with the component of initial state and of c_r. Using these recurrence relations, we show that α verify a linear system. The matrix representation of this system in the basis $\mathcal{B}$ has an odd diagonal and all other coefficients are even. We note M this matrix and we have $M \, \alpha = (\tilde{p}_j)_{0 \leq j \leq n-1} \Leftrightarrow \alpha = \frac{1}{\det M} comat(M) \cdot (\tilde{p}_j)_{0 \leq j \leq n-1}.^2$. So $\alpha \in \frac{1}{|\det M|} \mathbb{Z}^n$. M is called the *connection matrix of the VFCSR in the basis* $\mathcal{B}$. We set $q = \sum_{i=1}^{r} q_i 2^i - 1$ belonging to $\mathbb{Z}[\beta]$ and being written in the basis $\mathcal{B}$

$$q = \begin{pmatrix} \tilde{q}_0 \\ \tilde{q}_1 \\ \vdots \\ \tilde{q}_{n-1} \end{pmatrix} - \begin{pmatrix} 1 \\ 0 \\ \vdots \\ 0 \end{pmatrix}.$$

We find that $|\det M| = \left| \mathbf{N}_{\mathbb{Q}}^{\mathbb{Q}(\beta)}(q) \right|$. q is called the *connection integer* of the VFCSR and we note $\tilde{q}$ the value $|\mathbf{N}_{\mathbb{Q}}^{\mathbb{Q}(\beta)}(q)|$. q and $\tilde{q}$ don't depend on the basis.

Properties: According to the 2-adic theory, the sequences $(m_j^0, \cdots, m_j^n, \cdots)$ are eventually periodic. The period divides $ord_{\tilde{q}}(2)$. We set $\alpha_j = \frac{\tilde{s}_j}{\tilde{q}}$. If $\tilde{q}$ divides $\tilde{s}_j$, then $per(\alpha_j) = 1$. If $\tilde{q}$ does not divide $\tilde{s}_j$, then $per(\alpha_j) = ord_{\frac{\tilde{q}}{p \gcd(\tilde{q}, \tilde{s}_j)}}(2)^3$, $per(\underline{m}) = lcm \{per(\alpha_j); 0 \leq j \leq n - 1 \text{ et } \tilde{q} \nmid \tilde{s}_j\}$. $\underline{m}$ is periodic if and only if for all j, $-\tilde{q} \leq \tilde{s}_j \leq 0$. The period is maximal if $\tilde{q}$ is a prime number, 2 is primitive root modulo $\tilde{q}$ and $\underline{m}$ is not trivial (i.e. $per(\underline{m}) = 1$). Then $\underline{m}$ is a vectorial *l*-sequence. With this vectorial conception, $\underline{m}$ can be viewed as a vector of binary FCSR-sequences with the same integer connection $\tilde{q}$. The basic properties of distribution are verified. A *VFCSR-sequence* has a vectorial exponential representation: $\forall i, \ m_i = 2^{-i} \left(\sum_{t=0}^{n-1} y_t \beta^t \right) (mod \, \tilde{q}) (mod \, 2)$ for some vector

---

^{2} *comat* is the comatrix.

^{3} *per* =: the period of.

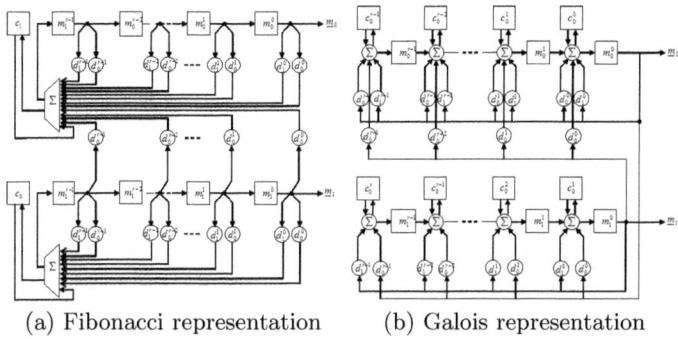

(a) Fibonacci representation   (b) Galois representation

Fig. 2. VFCSR representation for a triplet connection $(\tilde{q}, u, v)$

Table 1. Theoritical models of VFCSRs

	Quadratic Case	Cubic Case
Vectoriel FCSR	$(\mathbb{F}_2, X^2 - X - 1, \mathcal{B})$	$(\mathbb{F}_2, X^3 - X - 1, \mathcal{B})$
Connection Matrix	$\mathcal{M} = \begin{pmatrix} u & v \\ -v & -u-v \end{pmatrix}$	$\begin{pmatrix} -u & -w & -v \\ -v & -v-w & -v-w \\ -w & -v & -u-w \end{pmatrix}$
Norm of integer connection	$\tilde{q} = \lvert u^2 + uv - v^2 \rvert$	$\tilde{q} = -u^3 - v^3 - w^3 + 3uvw$ $+uv^2 - uw^2 - 2u^2w + vw^2$
Vectoriel coordinates of q	$q(u,v)$	$q(u,v,w)$
	$u = \tilde{q}_0 - 1$ and $v = \tilde{q}_1$	$u = \tilde{q}_0 - 1$, $v = \tilde{q}_1$ and $w = \tilde{q}_2$

$(y_t, \cdots, y_{n-1}) \in \mathbb{Z}^n$. Finally, in [2], we develop further results about behavior of memory, initialisation, statistical tests and pseudoradomness properties of VFCSRs.

Our interest in this paper is for the quadratic case (Table 1), which is defined as follows:

1. Form integers σ_1^z and σ_0^z,

$$\sigma_0^z = \sum_{i=1}^{i=r} \left(d_0^i m_0^{z-i} + d_0^i m_1^{z-i} + d_1^i m_0^{z-i} \right) + c_0^{z-1}, \forall z \geq r, \qquad (2)$$

$$\sigma_1^z = \sum_{i=1}^{i=r} \left(d_1^i m_1^{z-i} + d_0^i m_0^{z-i} \right) + c_1^{z-1}.$$

2. Schift the content of the first element register and the second element register on step to the right, while outputing the rightmost bits m_0^{z-i} and m_1^{z-i} as shown in Fig.(2-a),
3. Put $m_0^{z-i} = \sigma_0^z \pmod 2$ and $m_1^{z-i} = \sigma_1^z \pmod 2$, $\forall z \geq r$
4. Replace memorys integer as below: $c_1^z = \frac{\sigma_1^z - m_1^z}{2}$ and $c_0^z = \frac{\sigma_0^z - m_0^z}{2}$.

4   VFCSR Automaton

This section is dedicated to the description of the VFCSR automaton in Galois representation. To do so, we follow the same approach given in section (2.2).

4.1   Description of the Automaton

Let $(\widetilde{q}, u, v)$ the triplet connection, with $\widetilde{q} = u^2 + uv - v^2$ the norm connection, with vectoriels coordinates connection $u = 1 - 2d_0$ (an odd integer) and $v = -2d_1$ (an even integer). The VFCSR with norm connection $\widetilde{q}$ can be described as a module containing two circuits, each of which contain two registers:

Circuit 1

- The main register $\mathcal{M}_0$ with k_0 binary memories (one for each cell), where k_0 is the bit length of d_0, that is $2^{k_0-1} \leq d_0 \leq 2^{k_0}$.
- The carry register $\mathcal{C}_0$ with L memories in $\mathbb{Z}$ (one for each cell with a $\boxplus$ at its left), where $L = W_H(D)$ is the Hamming weigth of $D = (d_0 \vee d_1)_2{}^4$. Using the binary expansion $\sum_i = 0^k - 1 d_0 2^i$ of d_0, we put

$$I_{d_0} = \{i|0 \leq i \leq k_0 - 1 \text{ and } d_0 = 1\}, \tag{3}$$
$$I_D = \{i|0 \leq i \leq k_0 - 1 \text{ and } d_0 = d_1 = 1, d_0 \neq d_1\}.$$

Circuit 2

- The main register $\mathcal{M}_1$ with k_1 binary memories (one for each cell), where k_1 is the bit length of d_1, that is $2^{k_1-1} \leq d_1 \leq 2^{k_1}$.
- The carry register $\mathcal{C}_1$ with L memories in $\mathbb{Z}$, where $L = W_H(D)$. Using the binary expansion $\sum_{i=0}^{k-1} d_1 2^i$ of d_1, we put

$$I_{d_1} = \{i|0 \leq i \leq k - 1 \text{ and } d_1 = 1\}, \tag{4}$$
$$I_D = \{i|0 \leq i \leq k_0 - 1 \text{ and } d_0 = d_1 = 1, d_0 \neq d_1\}.$$

4.2   Transition Function

As described above, the VFCSR module with norm connection $\widetilde{q}$ is an automaton with $2^{2(k+L)}$ states corresponding to the $k + L$ binary memories of main and carry registers in each circuit. We say that the VFCSR circuits is in state $((m_0, c_0); (m_1, c_1))$ if the main and carry registers contain, respectively, the binary expansion of m and of c.

Suppose that, at time t, the VFCSR module circuits are in state $((m_0(t), c_0(t)); (m_1(t), c_1(t)))$, the state $((m_0(t+1), c_0(t+1)); (m_1(t+1), c_1(t+1)))$ at time $t + 1$ is computed using:

---

[4] $D = (d_0 \vee d_1)_2$ is the result of logical "Or" operation on binary representation of d_0 and d_1.

– For $0 \leq i \leq k - 2$ and $i \notin I_D$,

$$m_0^i(t+1) := m_0^{i+1}(t) \tag{5}$$
$$m_1^i(t+1) := m_1^{i+1}(t)$$

– For $0 \leq i \leq k - 2$

  • if $i \in I_{d_0}$, Fig.(5-c) and Fig.(5-d)

$$m_0^i(t+1) := m_0^{i+1}(t) + c_0^i(t) + m_0^0(t) + m_1^0(t)(\text{mod } 2) \tag{6}$$
$$c_0^i(t+1) := m_0^{i+1}(t) + c_0^i(t) + m_0^0(t) + m_1^0(t)(\text{div } 2)$$
$$m_1^i(t+1) := m_1^{i+1}(t) + c_1^i(t) + m_0^0(t)(\text{mod } 2)$$
$$c_1^i(t+1) := m_1^{i+1}(t) + c_1^i(t) + m_0^0(t)(\text{div } 2)$$

  • if $i \in I_{d_1}$, Fig.(5-e) and Fig.(5-f)

$$m_0^i(t+1) := m_0^{i+1}(t) + c_0^i(t) + m_1^0(t)(\text{mod } 2) \tag{7}$$
$$c_0^i(t+1) := m_0^{i+1}(t) + c_0^i(t) + m_1^0(t)(\text{div } 2)$$
$$m_1^i(t+1) := m_1^{i+1}(t) + c_1^i(t) + m_1^0(t)(\text{mod } 2)$$
$$c_1^i(t+1) := m_1^{i+1}(t) + c_1^i(t) + m_1^0(t)(\text{div } 2)$$

  • if $i \in I_{(d_0 \wedge d_1)}$[5], Fig.(5-a) and Fig.(5-b)

$$m_0^i(t+1) := m_0^{i+1}(t) + c_0^i(t) + 2m_0^0(t) + m_1^0(t)(\text{mod } 2) \tag{8}$$
$$c_0^i(t+1) := m_0^{i+1}(t) + c_0^i(t) + 2m_0^0(t) + m_1^0(t)(\text{div } 2)$$
$$m_1^i(t+1) := m_1^{i+1}(t) + c_1^i(t) + m_0^0(t) + m_0^0(t)(\text{mod } 2)$$
$$c_1^i(t+1) := m_1^{i+1}(t) + c_1^i(t) + m_0^0(t) + m_0^0(t)(\text{div } 2)$$

– For $i = k - 1$

  • if $i \in I_{d_0}$, Fig.(5-g), case $k_1 > k_2$

$$m_0^{k-1}(t+1) := c_0^{k-1}(t) + m_0^0(t) + m_1^0(t)(\text{mod } 2) \tag{9}$$
$$c_0^{k-1}(t+1) := c_0^{k-1}(t) + m_0^0(t) + m_1^0(t)(\text{div } 2)$$
$$m_1^{k-1}(t+1) := m_0^0(t)$$

  • if $i \in I_{d_1}$, (case $k_1 < k_2$)

$$m_0^{k-1}(t+1) := m_0^0(t) \tag{10}$$
$$m_1^{k-1}(t+1) := m_1^0(t)$$

---

[5] $(d_0 \wedge d_1)_2$: The logical operation "*And*" on binary representation of d_0 and d_1.

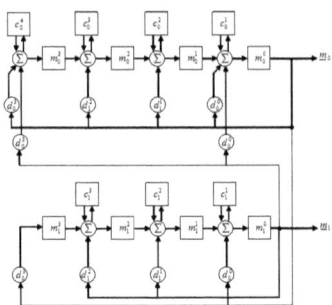

Fig. 3. VFCSR Galois representation for $(\widetilde{q}, u, v) = (349, 17, 12)$

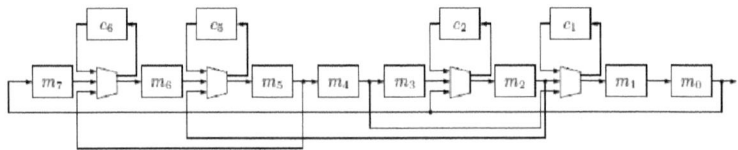

Fig. 4. An example of a ring FCSR (q = -347)

- if $i \in I_{(d_0 \wedge d_1)}$, Fig.(5-i) and Fig.(5-h), case $k_1 = k_2$

$$m_0^{k-1}(t+1) := c_0^{k-1}(t) + 2m_0^0(t) + m_1^0(t)(\text{mod } 2) \qquad (11)$$
$$c_0^{k-1}(t+1) := c_0^{k-1}(t) + 2m_0^0(t) + m_1^0(t)(\text{div} 2)$$
$$m_1^{k-1}(t+1) := c_1^{k-1}(t) + m_1^0(t) + m_0^0(t)(\text{mod } 2)$$
$$c_1^{k-1}(t+1) := c_1^{k-1}(t) + m_1^0(t) + m_0^0(t)(\text{div} 2)$$

$m_0^i(t+1)$ and $m_1^i(t+1)$ can be expressed respectively with a single formula:

$$m_0^i(t+1) = m_0^{i+1}(t) + D^i c_0^i(t) + d_0^i m_0^0(t) + d_1^i m_0^0(t) + d_0^i m_1^0(t)(\text{mod } 2)$$
$$m_1^i(t+1) = m_1^{i+1}(t) + D^i c_1^i(t) + d_0^i m_0^0(t) + d_1^i m_1^0(t)(\text{mod } 2)$$

if we put $(m_0^k(t), m_1^k(t)) = (0, 0)$.

Example 2. Let $(\widetilde{q}, u, v) = (349, 17, 12)$, so for circuit 1 $d_0 = 9 = (1001)_2$ and for circuit 2 $d_1 = 6 = (0110)_2$. Then $D = (1111)_2$ and $L = W_H(D) = 4$ memories in each circuit. The diagram shown in Fig.(3) shows these two circuits for a Galois VFCSR.

5   New Conception Analysis

The main key observation on F-FCSR-H v2 structur in [9], is the fact that the carry bits in the carries register, behave very far from random and they all have one common input variable, the feedback bit (m_0), Fig.(5-e). It has been seen that when the feedback bit is zero then a carry bit that is zero must remain zero whereas if the carry bit is one then by probability $1/2$ it will turn to zero and, If the feedback bit is zero a few consecutive time instances. Then it is very likely that the carry bit is pushed to zero, this can make the carry register in a known sate. To resist to this attack, inventors of F-FCSR-H v2 recently have proposed a new representation called ring, Fig.(4)[11], it is based upon matrix definition. The difference with Fibonacci and Galois FCSRs representation is that any cell in the main register can be used as a feedback for any other cell. In ring representation, connection integer is defined by $q = det(I - 2T)$, with q is prime and 2 is a primitive root modulo q and T is $n \times n$ random binary matrix.

The main differences between galois FCSR, ring FCSR and the galois VFCSR are respectively: all the feedback functions defined by (1) are controlled by a one commun input, all the feedback functions defined by the matrix transition T are controlled by different inputs and for VFCSR, all the feedback functions defined for circuit 1 and circuit 2 respectively by (3) and (4) are controlled either

- by two differents inputs in both circuits Fig.(5-c) and Fig.(5-b),
- in circuit 1: by one input from cictuit 2 Fig.(5-e),
- in circuit 2: by one input Fig.(5-f) or by one input from cictuit 1, Fig.(5-d).

In addition, carries in VFCSRs are not all in $\{0,1\}$ as in FCSRs but they takes values in $\{0,1,2,\cdots,2^n - 1\}$ where n is the dimension of the vectorial space. In the quadratic case where $n = 2$, boxes additions , hardware point of vue, are classified into three categories:

1. In Fig.(5-j), the addition boxe is like that of the galois FCSRs and $c \in \{0,1\}$,
2. in Fig.(5-k), $c \in \{0,1,2\}$ and is coded on two bits (Most significant bit c^M and Least significant bit c^L. In this case the probability that c is zero when the feedback bit is zero is not $1/2$,
3. in Fig.(5-l), $c \in \{0,1,2,3\}$ and that same remark as for second categorie.

The VFCSR circuits interdependance, represents the major obstacle to the attack [9]. Controling carries, to manage the control of a part of the main register in one of the two circuits, correspond to the controling carries in the two circuits at the same time.

5.1 Randomness Property of Galois VFCSR

Pseudorandom property of sequences generated by VFCSR in Galois representation shown in Fig. 2-b, have been investigated by package NIST (National Institute of Standardization and Technology) STS [16]. These tests are useful in detecting deviations of a binary sequence from randomness [17]. This package consists of 15 different statistical tests, which allow accepting (or rejecting) the hypothesis about randomness of the testing sequence. NIST framework, like

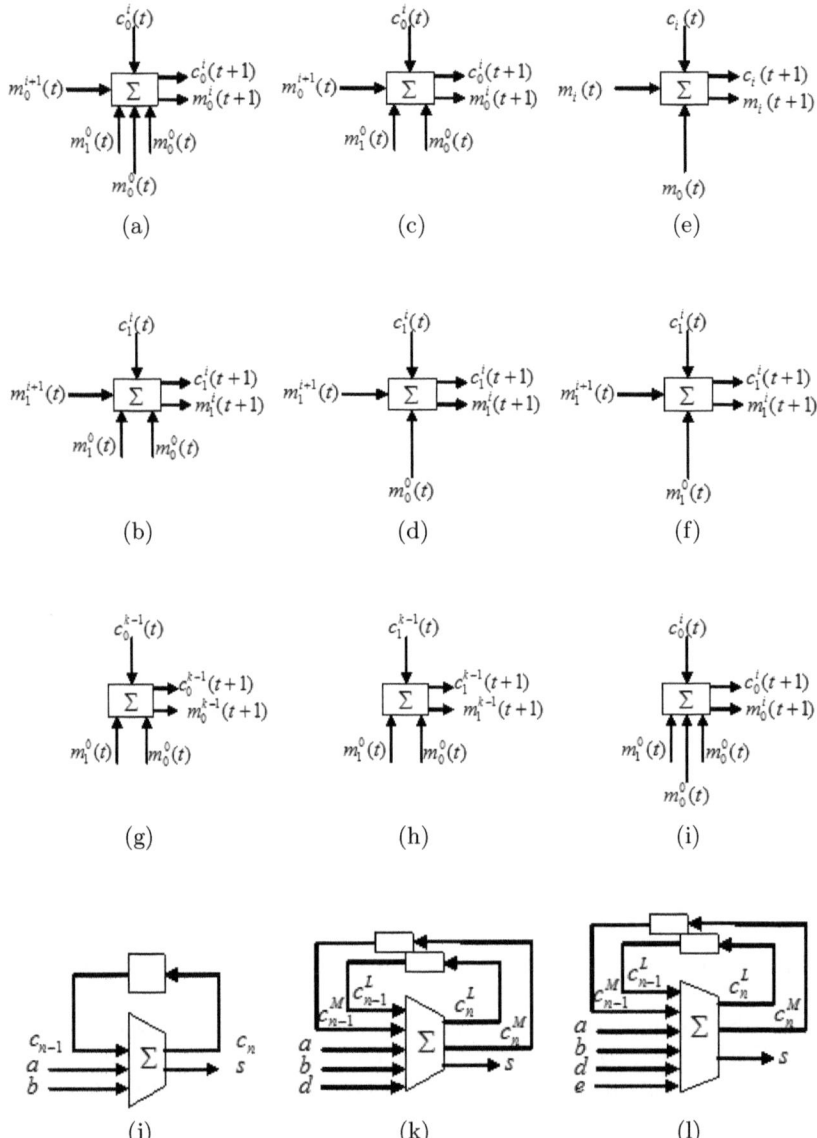

Fig. 5. Types of addition boxes in Galois VFCSR Architecture

many tests, is based on hypothesis testing. Testing result is $P - value \in [0, 1]$. If $P - value \geq 0.01$, the tested sequence is considered to be random (accepted).

Table 2, presents the results of the statistical analysis of sequences $\underline{m}_0$ and $\underline{m}_1$ from the Galois representation by the package NIST, for a sample of 2200000 bits. Parameter used is the triplet connection (1) in Table 4. All tests were passed

Table 2. Results statistical tests

Statisticals Tests	Tests parameters	Sequence m_0 P-value	Task	Sequence m_1 P-value	Task
Frequency	-	0.774985	Pass	0.178398	Pass
Block Frequency	m=128	0.805492	Pass	0.440320	Pass
Runs	-	0.264820	Pass	0.714705	Pass
Longest Run	M=10000	0.063204	Pass	0.933766	Pass
Rank	-	0.833143	Pass	0.322493	Pass
DFT	-	0.980256	Pass	0.891733	Pass
Non-Overlapping Template	m=9, B=110100010	0.465025	Pass	0.030875	Pass
Overlapping Template	m=9	0.464561	Pass	0.351158	Pass
Universal	L=8, Q=2456	0.099817	Pass	0.662900	Pass
Linear Complexity	M=500	0.165002	Pass	0.734850	Pass
Serial	m=16, $\nabla \psi_m^2$	0.977832	Pass	0.801563	Pass
	m=16, $\nabla^2 \psi_m^2$	0.981500	Pass	0.551655	Pass
Approximate Entropy	m=10	0.828275	Pass	0.278716	Pass
Cumulative	Forward	0.503953	Pass	0.221351	Pass
Sums	Reverse	0.761476	Pass	0.137620	Pass
Random Excursions	X=3	0.401433	Pass	0.794891	Pass
Random Excursions Variant	X=1	0.074490	Pass	0.480395	Pass

Table 3. One module quadratique VFCSR compared to two circuits FCSRs

	Two FCSRs	One VFCSR
Circuits	Two *independent* circuits	Two *interdependent* circuits
Integer connection	q	
Norm connection		$\widetilde{q} = u^2 + uv - v^2$ with $u = q$
Outputs	Tow sequences	Two sequences
Period	$q - 1$	$\widetilde{q} - 1 \simeq q^2$
Cel numbers	2^{k+l}	$2^{2(k+L)}$
Carries Value	$c_i \in \{0, 1\}$	$c_0^i, c_1^i \in \{0, 1, 2, 3\}, \{0, 1, 2\}, \{0, 1\}$

successfully , and for tests where there's more $P - value$ (which all passed), and to not clutter the table, we put one result as for Non-Overlapping Template, Random Excursions and Random Excursions Variant. As a result of conducted experiments it has been noticed very good pseudorandom properties of output sequences, m_0 and m_1.

5.2 Appearance of Equivalence

It appears at first sight that a VFCSR module is equivalent to two FCSRs circuits, while this is not correct. To clarify this ambiguity, some differences are summarized in Table 3 and to explain this, we take the case, two (circuits) FCSRs with connection integer q and one (module) VFCSR with the triplet connection $(\widetilde{q}, u, v)$, where $u = q$ and v such as $\widetilde{q} = u^2 + uv - v^2$.

Table 4. Somme triplet connection

triplet	$\tilde{q} =$	3974140296190695420616004753553979604200521434082 0825272689327902761723128526374726419918065389949
Connection (1)	$u =$	19935245913182750153280416113442150364601400879963
	$v =$	19935245913182750153280416113442150364601400879860
triplet	$\tilde{q} =$	4266994849918554052261353866090907339418780356791 9447365495441931015659537243024973441786752485001
Connection (2)	$u =$	19935245913182750153280416113442150364601400879963
	$v =$	18338289120761436060978627722716643152500711340996

6   Stream Cipher Conception

In this section, we propose as application for VFCSR pseudorandom generator, a new familly of Stream ciphers based on Interdependance in Filtred Register. In this paper we present the quadratique case, that said, a quadratique VFCSR with triplet connection $(\tilde{q}, u, v)$ and the stream cipher is the Q-SIFR[6].

6.1   Proposed Parameters

We propose for Q-SIFR steam cipher, the triplet connection $(\tilde{q}, u, v)$ defined in Table 4. u was choosen equal to the integer connection q

$$u = q = 19935245913182750153280416113442150364601400879963$$

as for F-FCSR-H stream cipher in [7] and v to satisfies $\tilde{q} = u^2 + uv - v^2$, where $\tilde{q}$ is prime and 2 primitive root modulo $\tilde{q}$.

6.2   Design of the Filter

From secutity point of view, this new conception inherits all advantages of F-FCSR-H stream cipher. Since an VFCSR (vs. FCSR) automaton is nonlinear, there is no need to use a Boolean function with a high nonlinearity for filtering the output [6][7]. Then, the best functions for filtering an VFCSR generator are linear functions.

$$f : \mathbb{F}_2^n \to \mathbb{F}_2$$
$$f(x_1, ..., x_n) = \overset{n}{\underset{i=1}{\oplus}} f_i x_i, \ f_i \in \mathbb{F}_2.$$

The VFCSR length (size of the main register in both circuits) is the length of $D = (d_0 \vee d_1)_2$, where D value based on the vectoriel coordinates chosen is

$$D = (49838114782956875383201040283605375911503502199\mathbf{1})_{10}.$$

---

[6] Q-SIFR: pronounced quadratic *şifr*.

Fig. 6. Deployment of the Q-SIFR stream cipher

With $k = length(D) = 160$, addition boxes and carries cells are present at the positions matching the ones in the 160 bits of $(D)_2$ (which has Hamming weigth 84) for each circuits. To extract pseudorandom byte, we use the static filter. Then the filter is known and not key-dependent[7].

$$F = D = (574C2EFF\,9330CFE2\,C311EE45\,57A36AC8\,1EEA12A7)_{16}$$

Using the designers notation [18], this means that the filter F splits in 8 subfilters (subfilter j is obtained by selecting the bit j in each byte of F) is given by

$$F_0 = (0011.0111.0100.1010.1011)_2, \quad F_4 = (0111.0010.0010.0011.1100)_2,$$
$$F_1 = (1001.1010.1101.1100.0001)_2, \quad F_5 = (1001.1100.0100.1000.1010)_2,$$
$$F_2 = (1011.1011.1010.1110.1111)_2, \quad F_6 = (0011.0101.0010.0110.0101)_2,$$
$$F_3 = (1111.0010.0011.1000.1001)_2, \quad F_7 = (1101.0011.1011.1011.0100)_2.$$

6.3 Pseudorandom Data Extraction

Before pseudorandom data extraction, the setup of the Key and the Initial Vector (IV) should be donne, who is a crucial step in keystream generators [13]. For this, we follow the same procedure difined in [14] for the F-FCSR-H v2. After setup phase, the bit z_0^i (with $0 \le i \le 7$) of each extracted byte from Circuit 1 (respectively, the bit z_1^i (with $0 \le i \le 7$) of each extracted byte from Circuit 2) are expressed by

$$z_0^i = \bigoplus_{j=0}^{19} f_i^{(j)} m_0^{8j+i}, \quad F_i = \sum_{j=0}^{7} f_i^{(j)} 2^j$$

$$z_1^i = \bigoplus_{j=0}^{19} f_i^{(j)} m_1^{8j+i}, \quad F_i = \sum_{j=0}^{7} f_i^{(j)} 2^j.$$

So the *Quadratic* Filtred VFCSR Keystream generator outputs *two bytes* every time instance t, $z_t = (z_0^i \| z_1^i)_t$. The deployment of the Q-SIFR stream cipher, given seed S the cancatenation of a key k and an initial vector IV, allow us to use an ecryption function $E(S, P) = z_t \oplus p_t = c_t$ and a corresponding decryption function $D(S, C) = z_t \oplus c_t = p_t$ as described in Fig.(6).

---

[7] In the case where filter is constructed from the Key, dynamic filter.

7   Conclusion and Future Work

In this paper, we have presented a new stream cipher design based on a filtred quadratic VFCSR automaton. Illustrated numerical experiments conducted utilizing NIST Statistical Tests Suite, confirm the good randomness propertys of the *Quadratic* VFCSRs in Galois representation.

The main differences compared to the FCSRs are addition boxes and carries cells types. Direct result noticed, that this attack [9] carried out on F-FCSR is infeasible on F-VFCSR.

VFCSR structure allowed in the case of filtred quadratic VFCSR to extract two bytes every time the keystream generator is clocked. Implementation of Q-SIFR stream cipher is as simple in software and hardware as that for F-FCSR, also we keep key and IV setup same for F-FCSR-H v2.

References

1. Klapper, A., Goresky, M.: 2-adic shift registers. In: Anderson, R. (ed.) FSE 1993. LNCS, vol. 809, pp. 174–178. Springer, Heidelberg (1994)
2. Marjane, A., Allailou, B.: Vectorial Conception of FCSR. In: Carlet, C., Pott, A. (eds.) SETA 2010. LNCS, vol. 6338, pp. 240–252. Springer, Heidelberg (2010)
3. Goresky, M., Klapper, A.: 2-adic shift registers. In: Anderson, R. (ed.) FSE 1993. LNCS, vol. 809, pp. 174–178. Springer, Heidelberg (1994)
4. Klapper, A.: Feedback with Carry Shift Registers over Finite Fields (extended abstract). In: Preneel, B. (ed.) FSE 1994. LNCS, vol. 1008, pp. 170–178. Springer, Heidelberg (1995)
5. Goresky, M., Klapper, A.: Feedback shift registers, 2-adic span, and combiners with memory. Journal of Cryptology 10, 111–147 (1997)
6. Arnault, F., Berger, T.P.: Design of new pseudo random generators based on a filtered FCSR automaton. In: SASC, Bruges, Belgium (October 2004)
7. Arnault, F., Berger, T.P.: Design and properties of a new pseudo-random generator based on a filtered FCSR automaton. IEEE Transactions on Computers 54(11), 1374–1383 (2005)
8. Arnault, F., Berger, T.P., Minier, M.: On the security of FCSR-based pseudorandom generators. In: SASC, the State of the Art of Stream Ciphers, pp. 179–190 (January 2007)
9. Hell, M., Johansson, T.: Breaking the F-FCSR-H stream cipher in real time. In: Proceeding of 14th International Conference on the Theory and Application of Cryptology and Information Security: Advances in Cryptology, December 07-11 (2008)
10. Tian, T., Qi, W.-F.: Linearity properties of binary FCSR sequences. Designs, Codes and Cryptography 52(3) (September 2009)
11. Arnault, F., Berger, T.P., Lauradoux, C., Minier, M., Pousse, B.: A new approach for FCSRs. In: Jacobson Jr., M.J., Rijmen, V., Safavi-Naini, R. (eds.) SAC 2009. LNCS, vol. 5867, pp. 433–448. Springer, Heidelberg (2009)
12. Berger, T.P., Arnault, F., Lauradoux, C.: Description of F-FCSR-8 and F-FCSR-H stream ciphers. In: SKEW - Symmetric Key Encryption Workshop, An ECRYPT STVL event, Aarhus, Danemark (May 2005)

13. Jaulmes, E., Muller, F.: Cryptanalysis of ECRYPT candidates F-FCSR-8 and F-FCSR-H. eSTREAM, ECRYPT Stream Cipher Project, Report 2005/046 (2005), http://www.ecrypt.eu.org/stream
14. Arnault, F., Berger, T., Lauradoux, C.: Update on F-FCSR stream cipher. eSTREAM, ECRYPT Stream Cipher Project, Report 2006/025 (2006), http://www.ecrypt.eu.org/stream
15. http://www.ecrypt.eu.org/stream/
16. http://csrc.nist.gov/groups/ST/toolkit/rng/documents/sts-2.0.zip
17. http://csrc.nist.gov/publications/nistpubs/800-22-rev1/ SP800-22rev1.pdf
18. Arnault, F., Berger, T.P., Lauradoux, C.: Update on F-FCSR stream cipher. ECRYPT - Network of Excellence in Cryptology, Call for stream Cipher Primitives - Phase 2 (2006), http://www.ecrypt.eu.org/stream/

Low-Resource Hardware Design of an Elliptic Curve Processor for Contactless Devices

Erich Wenger[1], Martin Feldhofer[1], and Norbert Felber[2]

[1] Institute for Applied Information Processing and Communications,
Graz University of Technology
[2] Integrated Systems Laboratory,
Swiss Federal Institute of Technology Zürich
{erich.wenger,martin.feldhofer}@iaik.tugraz.at,
felber@iis.ee.ethz.ch

Abstract. Hardware implementations for contactless devices like NFC or RFID tags face fierce constraints concerning the chip area and the power consumption. In this work, we present the low-resource hardware implementation of a 16-bit microprocessor that is able to efficiently perform Elliptic Curve Cryptography (ECC). The highly optimized design features the calculation of the Elliptic Curve Digital Signature Algorithm (ECDSA) using the standardized NIST curve in the finite field $\mathbb{F}_{p_{192}}$. We carefully selected the underlying algorithms to minimize the required memory resources while also keeping the required runtime within reasonable limits. In total, the microprocessor requires a chip area of 11686 gate equivalents and performs the ECDSA within 1377k clock cycles, which is to our knowledge the smallest implementation of ECDSA using the NIST P-192 curve published so far.

Keywords: Low-Resource Hardware Implementation, Microprocessor, Elliptic Curve Cryptography, ECDSA.

1 Introduction

With the introduction of contactless technologies like Near Field Communication (NFC) and Radio Frequency Identification (RFID) the vision of the Internet of Things (IoT), where arbitrary objects communicate with each other, becomes reality. Until now, a major roadblock for large-scale use of this pervasive technology is the lack of security concepts and the missing low-resource implementations of cryptographic algorithms and protocols. With the introduction of security services like authentication and confidentiality the consumer acceptance can be improved. In our opinion, using strong cryptographic algorithms with a high security level and which are standardized is essential. This becomes comprehensible by looking at recently published attacks against proprietary solutions like the Mifare system [26].

A very suitable method of preventing attacks like forgery of goods is to use an authentication protocol with a digital signature scheme like the Elliptic Curve

Y. Chung and M. Yung (Eds.): WISA 2010, LNCS 6513, pp. 92–106, 2011.

Digital Signature Algorithm (ECDSA). Elliptic Curve Cryptography (ECC) can be used as a very efficient public-key scheme for low-resource processing because it requires far less resources than the widely known RSA scheme. With the ECDSA on a passive tag a proof-of-origin application can be easily established with the following approach. In principle, the passive tag stores a certificate in its non-volatile memory that has been signed by a central authority. First the reader retrieves the certificate from the tag and verifies the validity of the public key. Then it sends a random challenge to the tag. The tag uses its private key within the ECDSA to sign this challenge to prove the knowledge of the private key. The signature returned to the reader allows the verification of the authenticity of the tag.

Passively powered devices like NFC cards or RFID tags have fierce constraints concerning the chip area and power consumption. This is due to the low-cost requirement and the contactless operation, where the tag gets supplied from the electromagnetic field of a reader device. However, Elliptic-Curve operations with its underlying finite-field arithmetic is computational very intensive. Hence, a hardware module that performs ECDSA has to be highly optimized. In literature, implementations of ECDSA use one of three different design approaches. The first is to use an 8-, 16- or 32-bit general-purpose microprocessor [5, 9, 10, 13, 15]. In contactless devices where the application is fixed this approach is rather inefficient. The second possibility is to implement instruction-set extensions to an existing processor. The work of Großschädl et al. [8] evaluates this method. The third approach is to implement dedicated hardware modules with the single purpose to calculate ECDSA [3, 7, 14, 23–25].

In this paper we incorporate the ideas of building an optimized dedicated hardware module with the flexible approach of a general-purpose processor by designing a customized processor for calculating ECDSA. This approach combines the advantages of both implementation concepts. First, it can be extended with further functionality like protocol handling and other administrative tasks in a contactless device, but it is optimized for low-resource requirements, especially low chip area. In order to achieve the ambitious design goal to build the smallest hardware module for calculating ECDSA using the standardized NIST curve in $\mathbb{F}_{p_{192}}$, the instruction set and the used algorithms have been optimized. For that optimization, a multiply-accumulate unit is used in the ALU of the processor, the memory access to the RAM macro has been improved and the used algorithms are very memory and time efficient.

This paper is composed to show which measures have been taken to implement the smallest ECDSA hardware module. Section 2 presents a system overview, explains why the NIST P-192 curve has been selected and why a the implementation of a microprocessors is the best approach. Section 3 shows the selected algorithms used for ECC calculations and the underlying finite-field operations. In Section 4, the architecture of the microprocessor is depicted and the results of the design are shown in Section 5. Finally, conclusions are drawn in Section 6.

2   System Overview

In the following, we answer a few questions that allow a better understanding of the system and give insights to the most important design decisions.

2.1   Why Are Prime Fields Used as Underlying Fields?

The Elliptic Curve Digital Signature Algorithm can be performed, using various different elliptic curves and parameters. Binary extension fields $\mathbb{F}_{2^m}$ are used for many area-optimized ASICs. Unfortunately for an ECDSA signature, prime-field $\mathbb{F}_p$ operations are needed for the final operations, independent whether binary or primary fields are used as underlying field of the elliptic curve. So there are two solutions for this problem: either build an ASIC that is optimized for binary fields and extend it to be capable of calculating the final prime-field operations, or use prime-field only ECDSA parameters. In the second case, only prime-field arithmetic is required throughout the algorithms. As a result, the number of necessary arithmetic hardware components can be minimized. We think that the smallest implementations are processors that only use prime fields.

2.2   Is a Microprocessor Required?

A common application for elliptic curve signatures are smart cards. A future application for elliptic curve signatures are RFID tags, which today only have dedicated finite state machines. Both of those technologies have defined wireless interfaces (e.g. ISO-14443 [19] or ISO-15693 [18]). Those protocols can easily be implemented using a microprocessor. By having a small microprocessor managing the protocol and a co-processor handling the ECDSA signature introduces the problem of redundant hardware. Using the microprocessor for both tasks reduces the total chip-area requirement of an RFID tag. We think that a design using a processor will be used for the future ECC-capable RFID tags.

2.3   Why Is a Custom Designed Microprocessor Necessary?

A good starting point would be to modify an existing processor. But in order to have maximum security, flexibility and performance, a custom processor has been designed. As a result, the functionality and the instruction set of the processor can be chosen freely. The requirements for such a processor are listed in the order of their importance:

- **Security** is more important than any other attribute. Nobody wants to pay for an insecure design. In the presented design, security is achieved by selecting secure, standardized and performance-efficient algorithms. Measures to counteract side-channel attacks have been implemented.
- **Low-Area.** The most important factor for electronic bulk commodity, using RFID systems are the costs of the tag. The price is mainly defined by the used manufacturing process and the required chip area. Fulfilling the low

area requirement is achieved by using a small set of registers and a rather small, 16-bit multiplier. In general, the memory is the largest module of an ECDSA design. So, in order to keep the memory requirements low, curve parameters with a small prime size are selected: NIST-P192.

- **Low-Power.** The power for RFID tags is supplied by an electromagnetic field that is transmitted by a reader. The available power of such an electromagnetic field is limited by international regulations and decreases proportional to the distance between the tag and the reader antenna. As a result, the available power for an RFID tag is very low. For the implemented processor shown in this paper, we have concentrated our efforts on the low-area requirement and used methods like clock gating (for the registers) and operand isolation (for the multiplier) to reduce the power consumption.

- **Reusability.** A processor that does not at least support a minimum set of operations is practically useless. Such a processor would not be very flexible and nobody would use it. In our design the operations provided by the Thumb [1] and AVR [2] instruction sets are used as references. Both use a small, 16-bit instruction word. The resulting instruction set is extended and optimized for ECDSA and still supports the most important general-purpose instructions.

- **Performance** is a very important factor for every design. The special properties of the selected NIST-P192 parameters, make a fast reduction procedure possible. To further increase the performance of the presented processor, the memory access has been optimized and the instruction set has been parallelized.

2.4 Why Is the Signature Verification Algorithm Implemented?

First of all, it is important to understand that the shown design is optimized for the ECDSA signature generation algorithm. Adding the extra functionality of a signature verification is very cheap. Only a few extra assembler functions and a bit more memory is required. However, having a signature verification algorithm on an embedded tag, greatly extends the usability of such a tag. In the case of an RFID reader-and-tag scenario, the tag could proof the authenticity of the reader, before actually sending his own digital signature.

With the hope that all the important questions are answered at this point, a more detailed discussion of the used algorithms is possible.

3   Implemented Algorithms

In order to calculate an elliptic curve signature, various algorithms need to be implemented. We decided not to cover an introduction to elliptic curves, point and field arithmetic, but we want to encourage the interested reader to take a look into [12]. The elliptic curve digital signature and verification algorithms are shown in Algorithm 1 and Algorithm 2.

Algorithm 1. ECDSA signature generation

Require: Domain parameters, private key d, message m.
Ensure: Signature (r, s).
 1: Select $k \in_R [1, n-1]$.
 2: Compute $kP = (x_1, y_1)$ and convert x_1 to an integer $\bar{x}_1$.
 3: Compute $r = \bar{x}_1 \bmod n$. If $r = 0$ then go to step 1.
 4: Compute $e = H(m)$.
 5: Compute $s = k^{-1}(e + dr) \bmod n$. If $s = 0$ then go to step 1.
 6: Return(r, s).

Algorithm 2. ECDSA signature verification

Require: Domain parameters, public key Q, message m, signature (r, s).
Ensure: Acceptance or rejection of the signature.
 1: Verify that r and s are integers in the interval $[1, n-1]$. If any verification fails
    then return("Reject the signature").
 2: Compute $e = H(m)$.
 3: Compute $w = s^{-1} \bmod n$.
 4: Compute $u_1 = ew \bmod n$ and $u_2 = rw \bmod n$.
 5: Compute $X = u_1 P + u_2 Q$.
 6: If $X = \infty$ then return("Reject the signature");
 7: Convert the x-coordinate x_1 of X to an integer $\bar{x}_1$; compute $v = \bar{x}_1 \bmod n$.
 8: If $v = r$ then return("Accept the signature");
    Else return("Reject the signature").

3.1   Scalar Point Multiplication

The majority (about 95%) of the ECDSA's execution time is spent on the elliptic curve point multiplication (line 2 in Algorithm 1 and line 5 in Algorithm 2). This point multiplication algorithm needs to be save from simple and differential power analysis attacks. So it is necessary to use a point multiplication scheme as it is shown in Algorithm 3. In this scheme, point addition and point doubling is performed for every bit of the scalar. The only difference between a one and a zero bit in the scalar are some address bits. Because of this small change, we posture that a simple power analysis is not possible. A differential power analysis is also not possible because the ephemeral key k is changed in every request. Nevertheless, information about the point multiplication is additionally masked with a method called Randomized Projective Coordinates introduced by Coron [6]. This very cheap and effective countermeasure multiplies the initial base point $P = (X, Y, Z)$ with a random integer λ so that $P = (\lambda X, \lambda Y, \lambda Z)$.

The point multiplication, as it is presented in Algorithm 3 can be further improved with the following methods:

 – The Montgomery ladder introduced by Izu et al. [20] can be used to calculate a multiplication without the y-coordinates of the points. Let x_1, x_2 be x-coordinate values of two points P_1, P_2 of an elliptic curve $E : y^2 = x^3 + ax + b$.

Algorithm 3. SPA-safe point multiplication

Require: $k = (k_{t-1}, ..., k_1, k_0)_2$, $k_{t-1} = 1$, $P \in E(\mathbb{F}_q)$.
Ensure: kP.
 1: $Q[0] \leftarrow P$.
 2: $Q[1] \leftarrow 2P$.
 3: **for** i from $t - 2$ to 0 **do**
 4:     $Q[1 \oplus k_i] \leftarrow Q[k_i] + Q[1 \oplus k_i]$
 5:     $Q[k_i] \leftarrow 2Q[k_i]$
 6: **end for**
 7: Return(Q).

Then the x-coordinate value x_3 of the sum $P_3 = P_1 + P_2$ is given by

$$x_3 = \frac{2(x_1 + x_2)(x_1 x_2 + a) + 4b}{(x_1 - x_2)^2} - x_3' \tag{1}$$

where x_3' is the x-coordinate value of $P_3' = P_1 - P_2$. On the other hand, the x-coordinate value of x_4 of the doubled point $P_4 = 2P_1$ is given by

$$x_4 = \frac{(x_1^2 - a)^2 - 8bx_1}{4(x_1^3 + ax_1 + b)}. \tag{2}$$

- The doubling and add operations can be combined into a single function. As a result, intermediate results do not have to be calculated separately.
- In order to calculate Equations (1) and (2) efficiently, the base point $P = (x, y)$ needs to be transformed to the standard projective representation $P = (X, Y, Z)$, where $x = X/Z$ and $y = Y/Z$. As a result the inversions needed in Equations (1) and (2) can be avoided during the double-and-add algorithm. Note that one final inversion is still needed for the reversion of the standard projection.
- The z-coordinates of both points can be represented by a common z-coordinate. As a result, an 192-bit memory register can be saved.

All those optimizations have also been applied by Hutter [17] to create an efficient double-and-add algorithm that only requires seven 192-bit registers. This algorithm is based on the formulas by Izu et al. [20] and requires 16 field multiplications and 16 field additions.

This efficient multiplication scheme is used for the signature as well as for the verification algorithm. For that, the original algorithm needed some modifications. First of all, it cannot be assumed that the most significant bit of u_1 or u_2 is always set (as it is for signing). But with a simple loop, the parameter t of Algorithm 3 can be easily found. Secondly, the base point P of the signature algorithm is always fixed. In this case, $x_3' = P_x$ and $Q[1] \leftarrow 2P$ are both fixed parameters that can be stored as constants. The verification algorithm performs a point multiplication with the public key Q. Q varies from signature to signature. Therefore x_3' and the initial $Q[1]$ vary. As a result, additional data memory is required for the storage of x_3'. The initial point doubling $Q[1] \leftarrow 2P$ has to be done once per verification. This is implemented very efficiently using Equation 2 and standard projective coordinates, resulting in 2 multiplications, 2 squarings and 10 additions. Two more functions are needed for a successful verification: a y-recovery and a point addition. The point addition as shown in Equation 1 cannot be used, because it assumes a constant difference between P_1 and P_2. So, the more general formula

$$x_3 = \left(\frac{y_2 - y_1}{x_2 - x_1} \right)^2 - x_1 - x_2 \tag{3}$$

which also uses the y-coordinates of the points is used. As a result a y-recovery has to be performed after each point multiplication. The y-recovery is done within the projected coordinates and needs 9 multiplications, 2 squarings, 9 additions and *no inversion*. The point addition algorithm needs 8 multiplications, 2 squarings and 4 additions. It takes advantage of the fact that only the x-coordinate is needed for the verification algorithm.

Up to now, it has been assumed that efficient field operations are available. Those operations are described in the following subsection.

3.2   Finite-Field Arithmetic

The finite-field operations build the basics for the point multiplication and are the most time-critical algorithms. They are performed modulo the prime $p_{192} = 2^{192} - 2^{64} - 1$. Whereas the field addition and subtraction operations can hardly be optimized, there are a lot of possibilities to improve the field multiplication. Most importantly, we designed our processor with a multiply-accumulate unit as central arithmetic logic unit. As a result, a fast product scanning multiplication algorithm can be applied. Secondly, contradicting the low-area requirement, all loops are unfolded. By doing so, no cycles for in/decreasing memory reference registers or variable range checks are wasted. Thirdly, the reduction of the upper half of the multiplication result is done in-place. This behavior has hardly any effect on the execution time but reduces the requirement for any temporary memory. Table 1 shows the big difference between the native and the highly optimized instruction set. For the native implementation, very simple instructions have been used. By modifying those instructions and parallelizing data load and calculation instructions, the runtime has been improved by a factor of 2.5. Furthermore, by using the available work registers as Cache, the runtime has been reduced to 328 cycles. This renders very effective because a single-port memory is used due to the the the low area requirement.

At this point it is interesting to note that the squaring operation has been omitted. By adding such a function to the design, the runtime improves by 7.6%, whereas the area increases by 15.5%. Hence, we decided to use the standard multiplication for squaring. Most of that area increase is resulted by having a program memory with more entries.

Further necessary operations are field addition, multiplication and inversion algorithms that use a general integer n as modulo (lines 3-5 in Algorithm 1 and 3-4 in Algorithm 2). The prime used for those operations is not as nice as p_{192}. More general algorithms need to be used. For the multiplication, the Finely Integrated Product Scanning Form (FIPS) of a Montgomery multiplication algorithm by Koc et al. [22] is used. Table 1 shows a short comparison of three different implementations: Using a native instruction set with unfolded loops, using the optimized instruction set for the same implementation and using the optimized instruction set and loops in order to reduce the code size. Because the Montgomery Multiplications are less relevant concerning the runtime, the smallest implementation is used.

Table 1. Comparison of different multiplication functions. IS stands for Instruction Set. The bold implementations have been used.

Method	Cycles	Code Size
NIST P-192		
Native IS	997	997
Optimized IS	401	401
Registers as Cache	**328**	**328**
Montgomery Multiplication		
Native IS	1580	1580
Optimized IS	651	651
Optimized Loops	**2021**	**84**

The slowest of all algorithms is the inversion algorithm. This algorithm is needed for the reversion of the projective point coordinates (inversion of the z-coordinate) and the inversion of k and s in the ECDSA algorithm. For that a Montgomery inverse algorithm (see [21]) with final Montgomery multiplication (see [11]) is used. Because the speed is of minor importance, the focus has been on a small (program-memory efficient) implementation.

Generally, its a balancing act to choose which resources are spent on performance and which hardware is rather omitted. The next section covers a discussion of the used hardware architecture.

4   Hardware Architecture

All the previously described algorithms are implemented on a brand new processor architecture (see Figure 1). This processor is fully custom designed to perfectly suit the elliptic curve algorithms. Because of the aspired RFID application, the processor is ought to run on a relatively low frequency (less than 20MHz) and be as area efficient as possible. The design is based on a Harvard architecture (separated program and data memory). Investigation showed that a 16-bit word size is a good compromise between a low-area design and still being able to compute an ECDSA signature within a reasonable time.

Many implementations (see [3, 14]) have the problem of an excruciating large data memory. They make use of synthesized dual-port memories. Although a

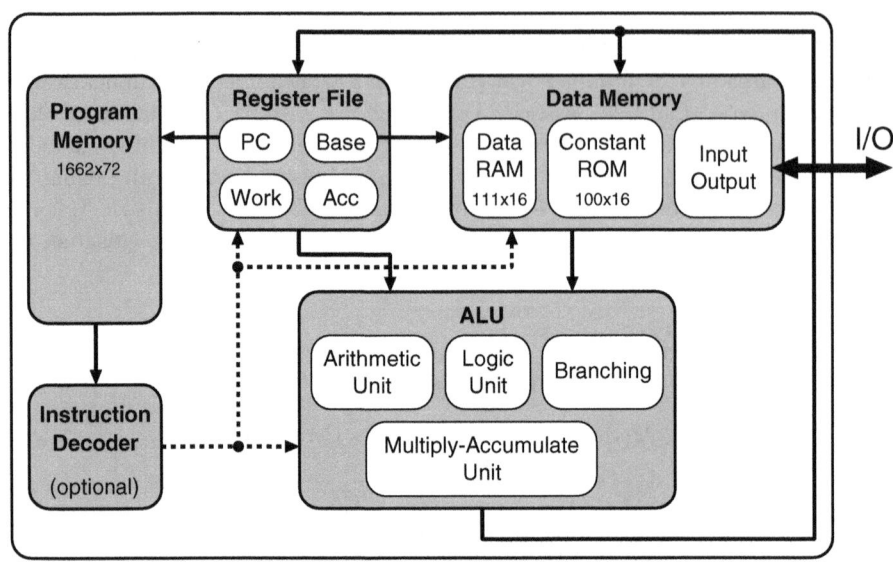

Fig. 1. Block diagram of the implemented processor with register file, ALU, data memory and program memory with the instruction decoder

dual-port memory improves the runtime of a signature generation by a factor of two, it has been decided to use a much smaller, single-port RAM macro. As a result, the data memory is implemented very area efficiently.

The data memory is split in three parts. One is the already mentioned RAM macro. A second part is a look-up table for constants. The third part are memory mapped inputs and outputs (I/O). Those I/O modules can be any memory logic necessary for the design. In the case of an RFID tag an interface such as ISO-14443 or ISO-15693 (see [18, 19]) would be such an I/O module.

The program memory is a synthesized look-up table. All 72 control signals are directly encoded in each entry of the table. Two other implementations with an optimized instruction set that use a 16-bit look-up table or a 16-bit ROM macro need more chip area. Those implementations would use the instruction decoder shown in Figure 1. The index for the selection of the control vector is the program counter (PC) of the CPU.

The CPU is equipped with a small register file. Like every other processor, it comes with a program counter and a stack pointer register. Because of the multiply-accumulate unit embedded within the ALU, an accumulator register is part of the design. This accumulator is actually implemented as three 16-bit registers. Further required registers are three 'base' registers, used to reference memory locations, and four work registers. Those work registers are the only registers without any special purpose. The CPU also contains status bits (Carry, Zero, Overflow, Negative) that are found in every microprocessor.

With this basic information, it is possible to look at some details. The most important feature of the processor is that it can process data loaded from the memory very efficiently. Unlike other designs, where the data from the memory needs to be stored in a register before it can be used, our processor can process the newly loaded data directly. This is especially important for the memory intensive field-multiplication algorithms. Another important feature is that the result of an ALU operation can be directly stored in a register *and* the memory. Such features in connection with the parallelized instruction set is the perfect environment for a fast and efficient calculation of an ECDSA signature. In this case, 'parallelized' means that several operations are encoded within one instruction and therefore they can be performed within the same cycle. As an example, a multiply-accumulate instruction that processes the read data can also request new data from the RAM within the same cycle. A short example that combines all those advantages is shown in Figure 2. The results of those optimizations has already been shown in Table 1.

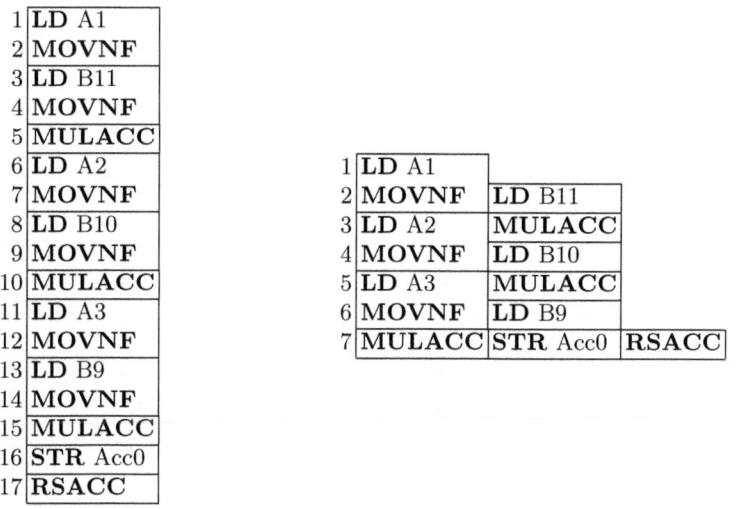

Fig. 2. Part of a field multiplication algorithm. It stores and right shifts the result of the following equation: $A1 \cdot B11 + A2 \cdot B10 + A3 \cdot B9$. On the left hand side is the un-optimized code. On the right hand side is the resulting optimized code. **MOVNF** stores the previously loaded data into a register.

5   Results

The results of our implementation are summarized in Table 2. For achieving these results, we used the UMC-L180 technology in connection with the synthesis tool Design-Compiler from Synopsys. As already mentioned, the signature verification algorithm can be easily implemented based on the signature generation algorithm. Hence, we compare the sign-only version with the sign-and-verify implementation in the following.

Table 2. Comparison of two processor implementations. One is used for the ECDSA signature generation, the other one for the verification of an ECDSA signature.

Part	Sign	Verify (+ Sign)	Difference
Execution Time [kCycles]:			
Field multiplication	1003	2013	+100.7%
Field add/subtract	196	392	+100.0%
Montgomery inverse	95	95	-
Total	1377	2645	+92.1%
Number of words/entries:			
Data RAM	111	149	+34.2%
Program memory	1662	2321	+39.7%
Constants	100	148	+48.0%
Area [Gate Equivalents]:			
Program memory	4092	5441	+33.0%
CPU	4354	4354	-
Data RAM	2553	2988	+17.0%
Other	687	837	+21.8%
Total	11686	13620	+16.5%

Because the verification algorithm needs two point multiplications, the execution time differs greatly. Almost twice as much cycles are required for the field multiplications and additions used within the verification algorithm. The total cycles spent on the Montgomery inversion is roughly the same because both implementations need two inversions. Although larger memories and look-up tables are required for the verification design, this results in a small increase of the total area requirement by only 12.4%.

Relative to the total runtime of the signature generation algorithm, 73% of the runtime is spent on the field multiplications, 14% on the field additions and subtractions and 6.9% on two executions of the Montgomery inverse. Also an investigation on the used instructions has been made. The five most used commands (of 46 in total) are in connection with the memory. Four of them are parallelized instructions. Compared to dedicated co-processors, the **CALL** and **RET** instructions are a sign of overhead of the presented processor. Both instructions cover 44412 cycles, which is three percent of the total runtime. In other words, the runtime overhead of the presented processor is very small compared to a dedicated co-processor.

In many other ASIC designs, the control logic is the smallest part. However, the largest part of our processor is the program memory. It takes up 4092GE of the total chip area. This is because the implemented ECDSA signature algorithms needs a lot of different sub-functions. The major part of the CPU is the ALU with 2608GE.

Table 3 gives a comparison of our work with various other publications. All of those implementations have been optimized for low area and low power requirements. Some implementations use the binary extension field $\mathbb{F}_{2^{163}}$ (according to NIST). This field provides a big advantage over the NIST prime fields $\mathbb{F}_{p_{192}}$. The

Table 3. Comparison of our implementation with related work

	Area [GE]	Cycles [kCycles]	ECC Curve	VLSI technology	Processor
Kumar 2006 [23]	15094	430	B-163	AMI C35	NO
Hein 2008 [14]	13685	306	B-163	UMC L180	NO
Yong Ki Lee 2008 [24]	12506	276	B-163	UMC L130	YES
Bock 2008 [4]	12876	80	B-163	220nm	NO
Leinweber 2009 [25]	8756	191	B-163	IBM L130	YES
Auer 2009 [3]	24750	1031	P-192	AMS C35	NO
Fürbass 2007 [7]	23656	500	P-192	AMS C35	NO
Hutter 2010 [17]	19115	859	P-192	AMS C35B4	YES
This work	**11686**	**1377**	**P-192**	**UMC L180**	**YES**

computational complexity of a field multiplication is a lot lower. Hence the total number of cycles required for a point multiplication is a lot simpler. So it is not unexpected that the designs by Kumar, Hein, Yong Ki Lee, Bock and Leinweber (see [4, 14, 23–25]) are better in terms of area and execution time. But none of those designs implemented a full ECDSA signature. All of them concentrated on an efficient point multiplication.

Our implementation covers the ECDSA and SHA-1 algorithms and even so, it is 40% smaller than the smallest NIST P-192 implementation by Fürbass [7].

Because our created processor does not only outperform the shown dedicated hardware modules we also compare our work with implementations on other processor platforms. The comparison shown in Table 4 only lists papers which provide results for a NIST P-192 point multiplication.

Table 4. Comparison of the performance of different processors

	Processor	Word size [bit]	Cycles [kCycles]
Gura 2004 [10]	AVR ATmega128	8	9920
Hu 2004 [16]	Trimedia TM1300	32	2955
This work		**16**	**1377**

Our processor performs better than the implementation by Gura et al. [10] on an 8-bit AVR processor. This probably is due to the small word size of that processor. But our design is also twice as fast than the implementation by Hu et al. [16] on a 32-bit Trimedia processor. This is especially spectacular, because the word size of the Trimedia processor is twice the word size of our implementation.

Using the tool First Encounter, a power simulation of the placed and routed design resulted in a power dissipation of $193\mu W$ at a frequency of $1.695MHz$. This is an eight of the carrier frequency used for a ISO-14443 RFID tag.

6   Conclusion

In this paper we have presented the hardware design of a low-resource micro-processor that has been optimized for the implementation of Elliptic Curve Cryptography. We have investigated the required algorithms to perform ECDSA signature generation and verification for the NIST P-192 curve which is defined over the prime field $\mathbb{F}_{p_{192}}$. The 16-bit microprocessor in Harvard architecture features a multiply-accumulate unit and has optimized access to the data memory in order to perform fast finite-field operations and hence allows fast ECC point multiplication. The processor has a chip area of 11686 gate equivalents including program memory, data memory, register file and ALU. It requires for the calculation of one ECDSA signature 1377k clock cycles. Our solutions outperforms all published software solutions and dedicated hardware modules in terms of chip area and allows an efficient calculation of ECDSA in authentication applications for contactless devices.

Acknowledgements

We would like to thank the team working at the Microelectronics Design Center at the Swiss Federal Institute of Technology Zürich (especially Frank Gürkaynak and Beat Muheim) for their helpful comments concerning chip design and the team at the Institute for Applied Information Processing and Communications at Graz University of Technology (especially Michael Hutter) for their help concerning the elliptic curve algorithms and the related power analysis counter measures.

This work has been supported by the Austrian Government through the research program FIT-IT Trust in IT Systems under the project number 825743 (project PIT).

References

1. ARM Corporation: 16-bit Thumb Instruction Set (May 2010),
   http://infocenter.arm.com/help/topic/com.arm.doc.qrc0006e/
   QRC0006_UAL16.pdf
2. Atmel Corporation. 8-bit AVR Instruction Set (May 2008), http://www.atmel.
   com/dyn/resources/prod_documents/doc0856.pdf
3. Auer, A.: Scaling hardware for electronic signatures to a minimum. Master's thesis,
   TU Graz (October 2008)
4. Bock, H., Braun, M., Dichtl, M., Hess, E., Heyszl, J., Kargl, W., Koroschetz, H.,
   Meyer, B., Seuschek, H.: A Milestone Towards RFID Products Offering Asymmetric Authentication Based on Elliptic Curve Cryptography. Invited talk at RFIDsec
   2008 (July 2008)
5. Brown, M.K., Hankerson, D.R., Hernández, J.C.L., Menezes, A.J.: Software Implementation of the NIST Elliptic Curves Over Prime Fields. In: Naccache, D. (ed.)
   CT-RSA 2001. LNCS, vol. 2020, pp. 250–265. Springer, Heidelberg (2001)

6. Coron, J.-S.: Resistance against Differential Power Analysis for Elliptic Curve Cryptosystems. In: Koç, Ç.K., Paar, C. (eds.) CHES 1999. LNCS, vol. 1717, pp. 292–302. Springer, Heidelberg (1999)
7. Fürbass, F., Wolkerstorfer, J.: ECC Processor with Low Die Size for RFID Applications. In: Proceedings of 2007 IEEE International Symposium on Circuits and Systems. IEEE, Los Alamitos (May 2007)
8. Großschädl, J., Savaş, E.: Instruction Set Extensions for Fast Arithmetic in Finite Fields GF(p) and GF(2^m). In: Joye, M., Quisquater, J.-J. (eds.) CHES 2004. LNCS, vol. 3156, pp. 133–147. Springer, Heidelberg (2004)
9. Guajardo, J., Blümel, R., Krieger, U., Paar, C.: Efficient Implementation of Elliptic Curve Cryptosystems on the TI MSP430x33x Family of Microcontrollers. In: Kim, K.-c. (ed.) PKC 2001. LNCS, vol. 1992, pp. 365–382. Springer, Heidelberg (2001)
10. Gura, N., Patel, A., Wander, A., Eberle, H., Shantz, S.C.: Comparing Elliptic Curve Cryptography and RSA on 8-Bit CPUs. In: Joye, M., Quisquater, J.-J. (eds.) CHES 2004. LNCS, vol. 3156, pp. 119–132. Springer, Heidelberg (2004)
11. Hachez, G., Quisquater, J.-J.: Montgomery Exponentiation with no Final Subtractions: Improved Results. In: Paar, C., Koç, Ç.K. (eds.) CHES 2000. LNCS, vol. 1965, pp. 91–100. Springer, Heidelberg (2000)
12. Hankerson, D., Menezes, A.J., Vanstone, S.: Guide to Elliptic Curve Cryptography. Springer, Heidelberg (2004)
13. Hasegawa, T., Nakajima, J., Matsui, M.: A Practical Implementation of Elliptic Curve Cryptosystems over GF(p) on a 16-Bit Microcomputer. In: Imai, H., Zheng, Y. (eds.) PKC 1998. LNCS, vol. 1431, pp. 182–194. Springer, Heidelberg (1998)
14. Hein, D., Wolkerstorfer, J., Felber, N.: ECC is Ready for RFID - A Proof in Silicon. In: Workshop on RFID Security 2008 (RFIDsec 2008) (July 2008)
15. Hu, Y., Li, Q., Kuo, C.: Efficient implementation of elliptic curve cryptography (ECC) on VLIW-micro-architecture media processor. In: 2004 IEEE International Conference on Multimedia and Expo, ICME 2004, vol. 2 (2004)
16. Hu, Y., Li, Q., Kuo, C.C.J.: Efficient implementation of elliptic curve cryptography (ecc) on vliw-micro-architecture media processor. In: ICME, pp. 879–882 (2004)
17. Hutter, M., Feldhofer, M., Plos, T.: An ECDSA Processor for RFID Authentication. In: Ors, B. (ed.) 6th Workshop on RFID Security - RFIDsec 2010, June 7-9. LNCS. Springer, Heidelberg (2010)
18. International Organisation for Standardization (ISO). ISO/IEC 15693-3: Identification cards - Contactless integrated circuit(s) cards - Vicinity cards – Part 3: Anticollision and transmission protocol (2001)
19. International Organization for Standardization (ISO). ISO/IEC 14443: Identification Cards - Contactless Integrated Circuit(s) Cards - Proximity Cards (2000)
20. Izu, T., Möller, B., Takagi, T.: Improved Elliptic Curve Multiplication Methods Resistant against Side Channel Attacks. In: Menezes, A., Sarkar, P. (eds.) INDOCRYPT 2002. LNCS, vol. 2551, pp. 296–313. Springer, Heidelberg (2002)
21. Kaliski, B.: The Montgomery Inverse and its Applications. IEEE Transactions on Computers 44(8), 1064–1065 (1995)
22. Koç, Ç.K., Acar, T., Kaliski Jr., B.S.: Analyzing and Comparing Montgomery Multiplication Algorithms. IEEE Micro 16(3), 26–33 (1996)
23. Kumar, S.S., Paar, C.: Are standards compliant Elliptic Curve Cryptosystems feasible on RFID? In: Workshop on RFID Security 2006 (RFIDSec 2006), Graz, Austria, July 12-14 (2006)

24. Lee, Y.K., Sakiyama, K., Batina, L., Verbauwhede, I.: Elliptic-Curve-Based Security Processor for RFID. IEEE Transactions on Computers 57(11), 1514–1527 (2008)
25. Leinweber, L., Papachristou, C., Wolff, F.: Efficient Architectures for Elliptic Curve Cryptography Processors for RFID. In: International Conference on Computer Design, ICCD (2009)
26. Nohl, K., Evans, D., Starbug, Plötz, H.: Reverse-Engineering a Cryptographic RFID Tag. In: Proceedings of USENIX Security Symposium, San Jose, CA, USA, July 31, pp. 1–9. USENIX (2008)

A Design Procedure for Oscillator-Based Hardware Random Number Generator with Stochastic Behavior Modeling

Takehiko Amaki, Masanori Hashimoto, Yukio Mitsuyama, and Takao Onoye

Dept. Information Systems Engineering, Osaka University, Japan JST CREST
{amaki.takehiko,hasimoto,mituyama,onoye}@ist.osaka-u.ac.jp

Abstract. This paper presents a procedure in designing an oscillator-based hardware random number generator (HRNG) which generates highly random bitstreams even under the deterministic noises. The procedure consists of two parts; HRNG design without considering deterministic noises followed by randomness evaluation under deterministic noises. A stochastic behavior model to efficiently decide the design parameters is proposed, and it is validated by measurement of HRNGs fabricated in 65nm CMOS process. The proposed model directly calculates approximate entropy of output without generating bitstream, which make it easier to explore design space. A simulator considering the power supply noise is also developed for evaluation under deterministic noises.

Keywords: Stochastic model, Hardware random number generator.

1 Introduction

Hardware random number generation, which is indispensable for secret and public key generation and challenge and response authentication, is a fundamental underlying technology to realize highly secure systems.

Oscillator-based hardware random number generator (HRNG)[1][2][3] is a popular circuit which produces hardware random numbers. Figure 1 depicts a block diagram of basic oscillator-based HRNG. The HRNG consists of a sampler and two distinct oscillators; one is fast and the other is slow. The sampler acquires bits from fast oscillator (D in Fig. 1) using the signal of slow oscillator as clock (CK in Fig. 1). The oscillators inherently have jitter because of internal noises, and hence a rise timing of slow oscillator signal fluctuates from the viewpoint of rising edges of fast oscillator. In this paper, random period jitter, which is defined as the standard deviation of periods, is called 'jitter' shortly. Oscillator-based HRNG generates random numbers exploiting this fluctuation as a random source.

To design a HRNG that satisfies given specification, it is necessary to estimate randomness of designed HRNG and procure appropriate design parameters. It is, however, difficult to simulate oscillator-based HRNGs, because jitters of oscillators are not directly considered in ordinary simulators. Additionally, long simulation time with small time step are required, since the oscillation periods of the two oscillators and their jitters are on different orders of magnitude while randomness tests require long bitstreams.

Y. Chung and M. Yung (Eds.): WISA 2010, LNCS 6513, pp. 107–121, 2011.

Therefore, an efficient behavior model and simulation method for evaluating randomness of oscillator-based HRNG are necessary to guide design space exploration and meet the design specification.

References [4][5] modeled a slow oscillator under random noises and deterministic signals as a voltage-controlled oscillator (VCO). Required jitter to produce sufficient randomness and effects of deterministic noises were discussed with poker test [6].Frequency ratio of two oscillators is also discussed when it is small (about 15). Although [4] claimed that a larger frequency ratio results in better randomness, this tendency is derived from a supposition about the behavior of oscillator-based HRNG and quantitative evaluation in terms of frequencies is not sufficiently provided. In addition, the proposed model in [4] cannot evaluate the effect of deterministic noises exactly when the noise frequencies are higher than the slow oscillator. Moreover, the model was not validated with hardware measurement. Reference [2] introduced a numerical formula that gives transition probability between successive bits as a function of average and standard deviation of oscillation cycles and initial phase difference of two oscillators. However, rigorous randomness tests [6][7][9] were not performed, and deterministic noises were not considered. Reference [10] modeled a chaotic oscillator which is used as a slow oscillator, and provided a design guideline based on entropy estimation. The developed model is, however, tailored for chaotic oscillator and VCO, and hence it cannot be used for other types of oscillator-based HRNG. Though reference [11] proposed a stochastic model for a HRNG, it discuss a HRNG with shift registers and oscillators presented in [12] and the target is different from this paper.

This paper proposes a design procedure for oscillator-based HRNG using a stochastic behavior model. Key design parameters are explored and determined first by the proposed model without considering deterministic noises. Next, its robustness is verified by simulation taking into account deterministic noises, and the design is finalized if the randomness under deterministic noises is satisfactional.

The proposed behavioral model utilizes Markov chain, which is one of stochastic process, and quickly estimates approximate entropy (defined in NIST test set[7]) without generating bitstream. Guided by the estimated approximate entropy and target entropy, principal design and behavioral parameters, that are average periods, and requirement of jitters and duty cycles of oscillators, are determined. The quality of HRNG outputs can be quantitatively evaluated by other standard randomness tests as well if necessary, since the proposed model can also generate bitstream. Finally, its randomness under deterministic noise is confirmed using a HRNG simulator developed for that purpose. Because the simulator calculates each stage delay considering random and deterministic fluctuation, the deterministic noises are reasonably evaluated even when the noise frequency is higher than those of oscillators. It should be noted that the proposed procedure is applicable to any types of oscillator, since the parameters of interest are independent from topology or type of the oscillator. Furthermore, in this work, we validate the proposed model with hardware measurement of oscillator-based HRNG implemented in 65nm CMOS process.

The rest of this paper is organized as follows. Section 2 outlines the proposed design procedure. In section 3, a behavior model with Markov chain and a procedure of randomness evaluation are proposed and validated with hardware measurement. An

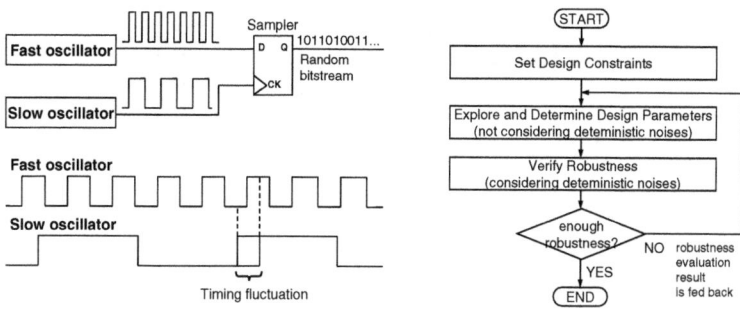

Fig. 1. Basic oscillator-based HRNG   **Fig. 2.** HRNG design procedure

example of parameter determination is also presented. Section 4 discusses the robustness evaluation under deterministic noises. Conclusion is given in section 5.

2 Proposed HRNG Design Procedure

This section introduces a design procedure with the proposed Markov model (section 3) and simulation considering deterministic noise (section 4).

Figure 2 shows the design procedure. The first step is to set design constraints that include required throughput and randomness. Also, basic circuit information, such as achievable frequencies and jitter characteristics of various oscillators, is given. Second, design parameters, such as oscillator frequencies, are explored and determined so that the given constraints are satisfied. Then, the robustness of the HRNG designed above is verified through a simulation under deterministic noise. If the HRNG has enough robustness to the deterministic noises, the HRNG design finishes, otherwise the result of robustness test is fed back to the second step, and redesign is carried out.

3 Proposed Stochastic Behavior Model

In this section, a behavior model of oscillator-based HRNGs using Markov chain is proposed. The model is validated with hardware measurement results. Also, the proposed design procedure using approximate entropy as randomness metric is exemplified.

3.1 Behavior Model of Oscillator-Based HRNG

Markov chain is a discrete-state/discrete-time stochastic process $\{X_n\} = \{X_0, X_1, X_2, \ldots\}$ where $\{X_n\}$ is a sequence of random variables, which satisfies, for each r, the Markov property, that is[14]

$$P(X_r = x_r | X_{r-1} = x_{r-1}, X_{r-2} = x_{r-2}, \ldots, X_0 = x_0) = P(X_r = x_r | X_{r-1} = x_{r-1}). (1)$$

This means that next state X_{n+1} depends only on current state X_n and is independent from past states $X_0, X_1, \ldots, X_{n-1}$.

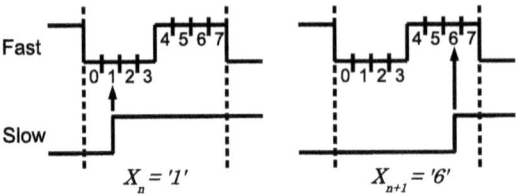

Fig. 3. An example of application

Before explaining the proposed model, we describe some assumptions for the model. We assume that jitters of oscillators are temporally uncorrelated, which means that we consider thermal noise, shot noise and/or 1/f noise and do not consider deterministic noises (will be considered in section 4) like power supply noise, substrate noise, and external noise. Given the assumption above, Markov chain is applicable to behavior modeling of oscillator-based HRNG.

In the proposed model, the fast oscillator waveform of one cycle is divided into m spans and each span is regarded as a state. Thus, a Markov chain that has m-state space is constructed. Let us suppose the n-th rising edge of the slow oscillator. We here define this timing as time n. At this rise timing, the fast oscillator is staying in one state among m states defined above. X_n denotes the state at time n. HRNG generates n-th bit corresponding to X_n, since each state corresponds to LOW or HIGH. Figure 3 illustrates an example that the proposed model is applied to a HRNG where $m = 8$. HRNG takes state 1 at time n and state 6 at time $n+1$, and then $X_n = 1$ and $X_{n+1} = 6$. In this example, since states $0, 1, 2$, and 3 correspond to LOW and states $4, 5, 6$ and 7 are HIGH, the n-th output is 0 and $(n + 1)$-th output is 1.

3.2 Model Construction and Usage

Figure 4 shows the randomness evaluation process with the Markov model. There are two ways for randomness evaluation. One generates bitstreams and then evaluates them with statistical randomness tests. The other directly calculates approximate entropy which is a popular metric of randomness. Each step is explained in the following.

Transition Matrix Calculation. This step constructs a transition matrix $\boldsymbol{P}$ that characterizes state transition of Markov chain. The matrix size is $m \times m$ when the model has m-state space. An element of the matrix $p_{i,j}$ is the probability of transition from i to j ($0 \leq i, j \leq m - 1$). Transition step a is the number that the state proceeds and is defined as $\{(j-i)+m\}\%m$. Let $q_{(a)}$ denote the probability that the next state advances by a from the current state. Supposing a Gaussian distribution, $p_{i,i+a}$ is calculated as

$$p_{i,i+a} = \sum_{l=-\infty}^{\infty} q_{(a+l \cdot m)} = \sum_{l=-\infty}^{\infty} \int_{l \cdot t_{\text{fast}}+a \cdot t_{\text{span}}}^{l \cdot t_{\text{fast}}+(a+1)t_{\text{span}}} f(x)dx, \qquad (2)$$

$$f(x) = \frac{1}{\sqrt{2\pi}\sigma} \exp\left(-\frac{(x-\mu)^2}{2\sigma^2}\right), \qquad (3)$$

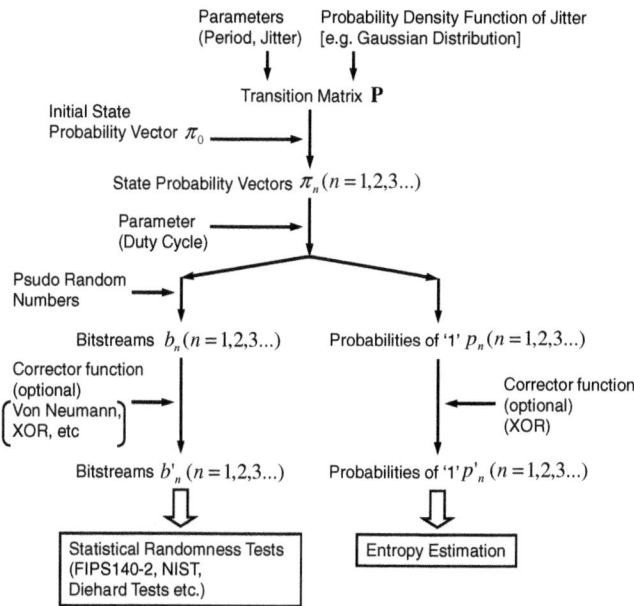

Fig. 4. Evaluation process with the Markov model

where t_{fast} is the average period of fast oscillator, and t_{span} is the time range of one state and is defined as t_{fast}/m. $f(x)$ is the probability density function of Gaussian distribution. Note that any other distribution shapes can be handled by the proposed model as long as they are independent on time, though Gaussian distribution is adopted as a representative shape in this paper. A remainder in case that average period of slow oscillator t_{slow} is divided by that of fast oscillator is denoted as μ. It is the most likely that the next timing of sampling is advanced by μ from the current. To easily take into consideration jitters of both oscillators, we derive an equivalent jitter of slow oscillator from the viewpoint of fast oscillator. The equivalent jitter σ is expressed as $\sqrt{\sigma_{\text{slow}}^2 + \sigma_{\text{fast}}^2 \frac{t_{\text{slow}}}{t_{\text{fast}}}}$, where σ_{slow} and σ_{fast} are the jitters of oscillators. The next sampling timing distributes more uniformly as σ increases. $p_{i,j}(i > j)$ can also be obtained by Eq. (2) since $p_{i,j+m}$ is equal to $p_{i,j}$ with extending the maximum range of j. Thus, P can be derived with Eq. (2).

Let us explain Eq. (2) using the situation in Fig. 3 as a simple example, where m is 8, X_n is '1' and X_{n+1} is '6'. Figure 5 explains the summation and integration in Eq. (2). When t_{fast} is sufficiently large, i.e. $t_{fast} >> \sigma$ (upper case in Fig. 5), $p_{1,6}$ is approximately obtained as $q(6 - 1) = \int_{5 \cdot t_{span}}^{6 \cdot t_{span}} f(x)dx$. On the other hand, t_{fast} is comparable to or smaller than σ (bottom case in Fig. 5), $q(5+8\times(-1)), q(5+8\times1), \cdots$ should be considered. As σ becomes relatively larger compared to t_{fast}, more terms of q should be summed up, and finally Eq. (2) is obtained.

The parameter of m affects the accuracy and the run time of evaluation. To precisely model the behavior, $t_{span}(= t_{fast}/m)$ should be sufficiently smaller than σ. The size of m will be experimentally discussed in section 3.4.

State Probability Vector Calculation. Given the transition matrix, the next state probability vector π_{n+1} is calculated from the current state probability vector π_n;

$$\pi_{n+1} = \begin{pmatrix} P\{X_n = 0\} \\ P\{X_n = 1\} \\ \vdots \\ P\{X_n = m-1\} \end{pmatrix}^T \begin{pmatrix} p_{0,0} & p_{0,1} & \cdots & p_{0,m-1} \\ p_{1,0} & p_{1,1} & \cdots & p_{1,m-1} \\ \vdots & \vdots & \ddots & \vdots \\ p_{m-1,0} & p_{m-1,1} & \cdots & p_{m-1,m-1} \end{pmatrix} = \pi_n \mathbf{P}. \quad (4)$$

Transition matrix $\mathbf{P}$ is independent on time n because of the Markov property, and hence π_n can be calculated with initial state probability vector π_0; $\pi_n = \pi_0 \mathbf{P}^n$. Figure 6 shows an example of π_n transition in case that the initial state is 0.

Bit Generation and Randomness Tests. Duty cycle d is defined as the ratio of number of states which are HIGH to the number of all states m. For example, when state 0 to 29 are LOW and state 30 to 99 are HIGH($m = 100$), d is $(70/100) \times 100 = 0.7$. When the next state probability vector, which can be obtained from the current state, and the duty cycle are given, the next state and the next output are stochastically decided with pseudo random numbers generated by a computer. Repeating this process generates a successive bitstream. Randomness is evaluated by testing the generated bitstream with arbitrary statistical tests.

Entropy Estimation. Approximate entropy [7] can be directly calculated by the proposed model without bit generation. The probabilities of '1' occurrence at successive outputs, $p_1, p_2, \cdots$, are calculated with the corresponding state probability vectors and duty cycle. Note that p_n is not independent from $p_1, p_2, \cdots p_{n-1}$ and consider the correlation to the past bitstream in a similar way to π_n. Approximate entropy ApEn is then computed as follows:

$$\text{ApEn} = \phi^{(m_b)} - \phi^{(m_b+1)}, \quad \phi^{(m_b)} = \sum_{i=0}^{2^{m_b}-1} \xi_i \log \xi_i, \quad (5)$$

where m_b is block length and a typical value of 10 is employed in this paper. ξ_i is the probability that the successive m_b bits are equal to i. For instance, ξ_{13} is the probability

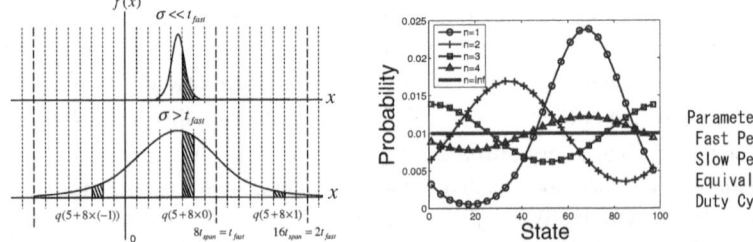

Fig. 5. An example of transition matrix calculation

Fig. 6. State probability vectors with the time proceeding

of $(0000001101)_2$ and described as $(1 - p_1)(1 - p_2)(1 - p_3)(1 - p_4)(1 - p_5)(1 - p_6)p_7 p_8(1 - p_9)p_{10}$. With the Markov model, ξ_i can be calculated from the probabilities of '1' or '0' occurrence, which differs from the conventional way of counting each i in generated long bit sequences. Because ApEn slightly varies depending on the initial state, ApEns are calculated for all initial states and the average is adopted.

Corrector Consideration. Postprocessing with corrector (XOR corrector[8], Von Neumann corrector[1] and etc.) is a popular technique to improve the randomness. When the bitstream is generated from the model, arbitrary correctors can be simply applied to the random numbers and then the statistical tests are executed.

For entropy estimation, the probabilities of '1' occurrence after the correction, p'_n, need to be estimated from p_n. In the case of XOR corrector, p'_n can be computed as $p'_n = p_{2n-1}p_{2n} + (1 - p_{2n-1})(1 - p_{2n})$, whereas Von Neumann corrector is difficult to apply since it may discard the bits boundlessly and p'_n computation is not easy.

3.3 Model Validation with Hardware Measurement

The proposed Markov model is implemented with MATLAB and validated with measurement. Two oscillator-based HRNGs are fabricated in 65nm CMOS process, and approximate entropy and poker test of acquired bitstreams are utilized for validation.

Test Structures. Two HRNGs (TEG A and TEG B), of which chip photos and block diagrams are shown in Fig. 7, were fabricated in 65nm process. 5-, 7- and 15-stage ring oscillator(RO)s are implemented as fast oscillators, and a 251-stage RO, which consists of transistors with 10nm longer channel length, and 4-, 64-, 512- and 4096-frequency-dividers are implemented as slow oscillators in TEG A. 7-, 15- and 31-stage ROs are implemented as fast oscillators, and a 251-stage RO and 16-, 64-, 256- and 1024-frequency-dividers are implemented as slow oscillators in TEG B. All stage elements of ROs are static CMOS inverters and 2-input NAND gates.

Body biasing technique is adopted to finely tune the duty cycle of fast oscillators. Although the duty cycle might be adjusted by a frequency divider, the perfect duty cycle of 50% does not necessarily result in the balance of 1/0 occurrence due to the input offset of the sampler. Figure 8 exemplifies the duty cycle adjustment when four body voltages (VNW_A, VNW_B, VPW_A and VPW_B) are given to every other inverter in 5-stage RO. The time when **inout** is HIGH depends on the delay of the NMOSs of the 1st, 3rd and 5th inverters, and the PMOSs of the 2nd and 4th inverters. The time of LOW is affected by the other MOSs complementarily. The duty cycle gets larger when the forward biases are applied to VNW_A and VPW_B, and reverse biases are applied to VNW_B and VPW_A, so that the time of HIGH increases and the time of LOW decreases. Thus, the duty cycle can be chosen freely by changing the four voltages.

Validation with Poker Test. 100 sequences of 20k random bitstream were generated by TEG A and measured. The same amount of bitstream was also generated using the proposed model. The parameters for the model are decided as follows. The average period of the fast oscillators were derived from circuit simulation. The average period of

the slow oscillator was obtained by measurement, and the duty cycle of the fast oscillators is set to 0.5. The equivalent jitter was first estimated from the standard deviation of
the measured slow oscillator periods, and then slightly adjusted so that the absolute χ
value of the simulation results became close to that of the measurement where χ is the
score of poker test and smaller χ means higher randomness. The size of state space is
set to 100.

Figure 9 shows the measurement and simulation results of poker test with 5- and
15-stage fast oscillators. Pass mark of χ is $2.16 < \chi < 46.17$[6]. The horizontal axis
is the period of the slow oscillator, and it is varied by changing the configuration of the
frequency divider. The duty cycle of the fast oscillators, which was estimated assuming
that 1/0 probability represented the duty cycle[10], was adjusted to within 50±3% by
body biasing. We can see from the results of both simulation and measurement in Fig. 9
that increasing sampling sparseness s, which means that the sampler captures data once
per s rising edges of the clock, namely enlarging jitter of the slow oscillator[13], improves the quality of random bitstream. In case of 5-stage oscillator, χ reaches to the
bottom more quickly as the period of slow oscillator increases. This means the decrease
in the average period of fast oscillator reduces the necessary amount of jitter for sufficient randomness.

Figure 10 shows the poker test result changing the duty cycle of the fast oscillators.
7-stage ring oscillator was used as the fast oscillator and 512-frequency-divider was
enabled. The duty cycle of the fast oscillator was varied from 44% to 58%. Figure 10
shows that unbalanced duty cycle of the fast oscillator degrades the randomness. The
results of simulation and measurement are well correlated in Fig.10, which means the
analysis result using the proposed model is valid.

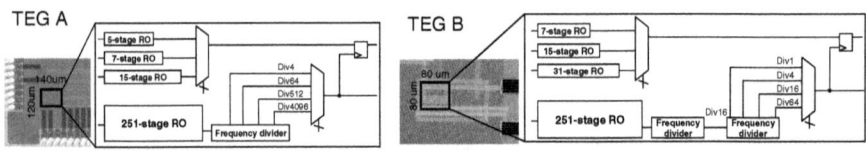

Fig. 7. Chip photos and block diagrams of HRNGs

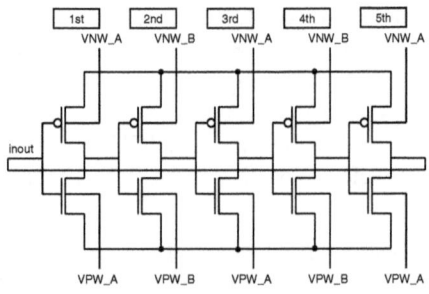

Fig. 8. Example of duty cycle adjustment with body biasing technique

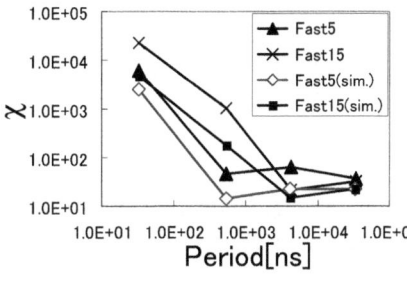

Fig. 9. Randomness vs. sampling sparseness and fast average period

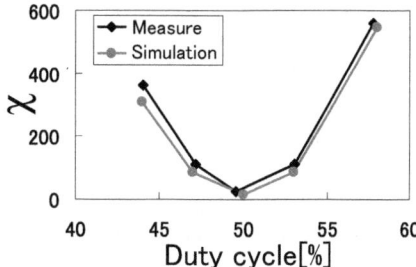

Fig. 10. Randomness vs. duty cycle

Validation with Approximate Entropy. 128 sequences of 2^{18} bits were measured from TEG B, and then approximate entropy of them was computed. Approximate entropy was also calculated by the proposed model without generating bitstreams. Calculation of one entropy for a set of parameters takes about 100 seconds with Opteron 8224SE(3.2 GHz) when the size of state space m is 1000 and sampling sparseness s is 1. The average period of the oscillators and the duty cycle of the fast oscillators are determined similarly to the prior section. The equivalent jitter was estimated from the standard deviation of the measured slow oscillator periods. Below, the size of state space is set to 1000.

P-value of approximate entropy test is numerically computed from the ApEn[7]. The pass mark of ApEn is set to 0.691 or higher here, because the pass mark of p-value is defined as 0.01 and it corresponds to 0.691 of ApEn.

Table 1 lists PASS/FAIL of approximate entropy test when the number of stage of fast RO was changed. 16-frequency-divider was employed at slow oscillator. The duty cycle of the fast oscillators is adjusted to within 50±0.5%. The results of the proposed model in Table 1 indicates that 9- or smaller stage RO is needed for PASS, and the results of the measurement are consistent with the model. Thus, the required period of the fast oscillator is estimated with the model.

Table 2 shows PASS/FAIL of approximate entropy test when the sampling sparseness varies. When the fast oscillator is 7-stage RO, the results of both model and measurement are the same. With the 15-stage RO, the model suggests that at least 2 sampling sparseness is necessary while the measurement shows that 4-frequency-divider is enough to pass the test. Thus, the necessary frequency division is estimated.

3.4 Design Space Exploration with Proposed Model

In section 3.3, the proposed Markov model is experimentally proved to reproduce HRNG behavior. This section illustrates a design space exploration with the model and approximate entropy. Here, ApEn pass mark of 0.691 is given as a HRNG specification.

An oscillator is composed of stage elements (hereafter called gates), such as inverters, and the jitter characteristics of each gate is an important design factor. To discuss that factor, we here define variance constant r_d as the variance of the stage delay divided by the average of the stage delay. Thanks to this definition, the variance constant of an oscillator composed of n gates with r_d variable constant is handily equal to r_d.

Table 1. PASS/FAIL estimation when fast period is changed

Fast Stages	5	7	9	11	13	15	17	19	21	23	25	27	29	31
Model	o	o	o	×	×	×	×	×	×	×	×	×	×	×
Meas.	-	o	-	-	-	×	-	-	-	-	-	-	-	×

Table 2. PASS/FAIL estimation when sampling sparseness is changed (Slow RO is first divided by 16-frequency-divider and then inputted to further frequency dividers)

Sampling Sparseness(x16)		1	2	3	4	5	6	...	16	...	64	...	256
Fast 7	Model	o	o	o	o	o	o	...	o	...	o	...	o
	Meas.	o	-	-	o	-	-	...	o	...	o	...	o
Fast 15	Model	×	o	o	o	o	o	...	o	...	o	...	o
	Meas.	×	-	-	o	-	-	...	o	...	o	...	o

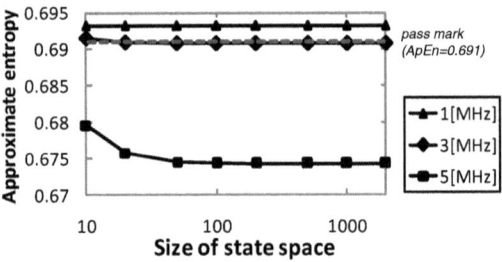

Fig. 11. Approximate entropy vs. size of state space

Size of State Space. The size of state space m affects the model accuracy as referred in section 3.2. Figure 11 show the estimated entropy when m is varied and the other parameters are unchanged. r_d is 1.77×10^{-14} s, the period and the duty cycle of fast oscillator are 1.0 ns and 0.5, which are also used as typical values in the following experiments, and the frequency of slow oscillator are 1 MHz, 3 MHz and 5 MHz. Figure 11 indicates that large state space is necessary on the condition that the estimated entropy is low. It is also suggested that 100 of m is effective for a rough quality estimation and 1000 of m is sufficient for a precise analysis here. The slow jitter from the viewpoint of fast oscillator corresponding to σ in Eq. (3) and $t_{span} = t_{fast}/m$ are 84 ps and 10 ps in case where m is 100 and the slow frequency is 5 MHz, and then σ/t_{span} is 8.4. Consequently, a guideline could suggest that t_{span} should be less than about $\sigma/10$ for effective evaluation. Therefore, the following experiments in this section employ 1000 as the size of state space.

Required Jitter Characteristics of Each Stage Component. Figure 12 plots the approximate entropy as a function of the average period of fast oscillator, and three curves correspond to $r_d=0.89 \times 10^{-14}$ s, 1.77×10^{-14} s and 3.54×10^{-14} s, respectively. Here, the average period of slow oscillator is set to 0.1 μs for 10Mbps throughput. It can be seen from Fig. 12 that smaller r_d requires smaller period of fast oscillator to pass the randomness test. If the minimum period of oscillator is limited to 0.4 ns

(2.5 GHz) by process and circuit implementation, gates whose variance constant is larger than 0.89×10^{-14}s are necessary.

Throughput to Fast Oscillator Period. Figure 13 depicts the entropy variation when the frequency of slow oscillator is changed. Here, r_d is 1.77×10^{-14}s, and the average period of fast oscillators is set to 0.8 ns, 1 ns and 1.25 ns. We can see that slower oscillator is necessary to satisfy ApEn=0.691 as the period of fast oscillator becomes longer. This means that the achievable throughput of HRNG is restricted by the period of fast oscillator.

Effect of XOR Corrector. Figure 14 depicts the entropy estimation with and without XOR corrector. rd is 1.77×10^{-14} s, and the periods of fast and slow oscillators are 1 ns and 1 us (1 MHz). These parameters achieve the entropy more than the pass mark as Fig. 13 shows. Under this condition, the duty cycle is varied from 0.5 to 0.7, where the duty cycle below 0.5 is not evaluated because of the symmetry. Figure 14 indicates that the unbalance of duty cycle limits the achievable entropy. Although the duty cycle must be less than 0.53 without any corrector, the upper limit of duty cycle is relaxed to 0.62 with XOR corrector. Thus, XOR corrector improves the approximate entropy when the duty cycle is unbalanced.

Figure 15 shows the entropy variation with XOR corrector as the frequency of slow oscillator changes. rd is 1.77×10^{-14} s and the period of fast oscillators is 1 ns, and the duty cycle of fast oscillator is set to be 0.50 and 0.56. Figure 15 points out that the estimated entropy fluctuates depending on the frequency of slow oscillator, especially in the case of unbalanced duty cycle. This comes from the difference of the average periods of two oscillators, which is referred as μ in section 3.2. μ affects the correlation of the bitstream, for example, the successive two bits are likely to the same when $\mu = 0$. This correlation between the bits varies the balance of 1/0, and hence μ, which is swept by the average period of slow oscillator in this case, causes the entropy fluctuation in Fig. 15. Therefore, the HRNG with corrector should be designed with some margin to take into account the dip of entropy.

Fast and Slow Oscillators Design. We here design fast and slow oscillators for HRNG with the following constraints and circuit information referring to a 65nm CMOS process. Variance constant of each gate r_d is 1.44×10^{-14}s, which was derived from the

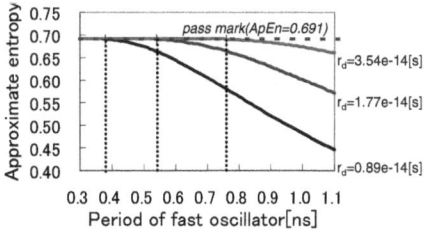

Fig. 12. Approximate entropy vs. fast period

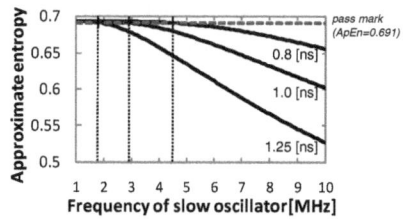

Fig. 13. Approximate entropy vs. slow frequency

measurement of RO in 65nm process. The duty cycle of fast RO is within 50±1 %, and 10 Mbps, which is a typical value in a smart card[15], or higher throughput is required. Any correctors are not employed here.

First, the periods of several oscillators which can be used as fast ROs are estimated by circuit simulation. Here, fast oscillators with different numbers of stages (13, 15, 17 and 19) are evaluated for simplicity. Second, entropies of HRNGs with each of fast ROs are evaluated by the Markov model varying the frequencies of slow ROs.

Figure 16 shows the estimated entropies. The duty cycle is set to 51% assuming the worst case. Achievable throughputs for each fast RO are estimated. Now that 10 Mbps throughput is required, the number of stages of fast RO should not exceed 17. When 15-stage RO is adopted, the number of stages of slow RO is determined so that the slow oscillator frequency is 12.5 MHz or less. On the other hand, in the case of 17-stage RO, the frequency should be 10MHz, which means larger number of stages, that is larger area is necessary.

In actual designs, different oscillator topologies and logic styles, such as current mode logic for faster ROs, are also explored. In this case, power consumption in addition to area becomes a key performance metric and more complex design space must be explored. For such a purpose, the proposed randomness evaluation using approximate entropy is effective in terms of CPU time.

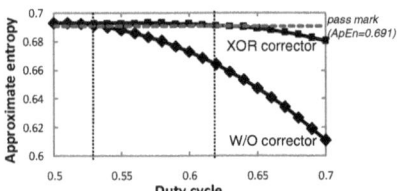

Fig. 14. Improvement of approximate entropy with XOR corrector

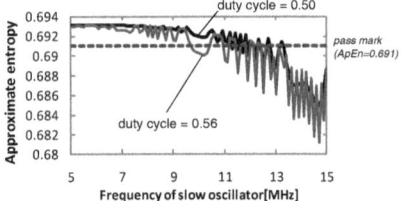

Fig. 15. Approximate entropy vs. slow frequency (XOR corrector is adopted)

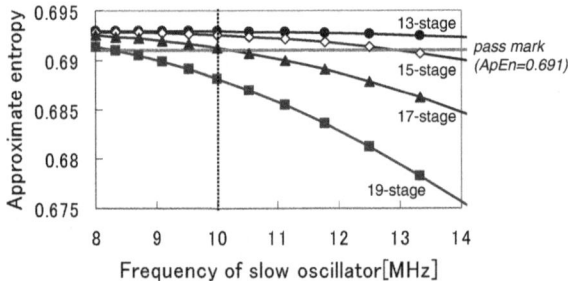

Fig. 16. Randomness evaluation to design fast and slow oscillators

4   Randomness Evaluation under Deterministic Noise

In section 3, HRNG is designed with the randomness evaluation using the stochastic behavior model. This evaluation, however, does not consider deterministic noises such as power supply noise, substrate noise, external noise and malicious attacks. For an actual security system with HRNG, robustness to deterministic noises is necessary. Therefore, focusing on power supply noise that is thought to be the most influential, randomness under deterministic noise is evaluated in this section.

4.1 Simulation Method

A gate-level simulator considering the fluctuation of each gate delay is developed for robustness evaluation. As a preliminary, each gate delay is denoted as $t_{d,(gate)}$.

$$t_{d,(gate)}(t) = t_{d,offset,(gate)}(Vdd(t)) + t_{d,random}, \tag{6}$$

$$t_{d,offset,(gate)}(t) = a_{(gate)} \frac{1}{(Vdd(t) - Vth_{(gate)})^{\alpha_{(gate)}} + b_{(gate)}}, \tag{7}$$

where (gate) denotes gate type. $t_{d,random}$ represents random timing fluctuation originating from random noises, and its average is 0. $t_{d,offset,(gate)}$ is the gate delay without random noises. To express the delay dependency on supply noise, we use a gate delay model (Eq. (7)) based on alpha-power law MOSFET model [16]. Parameters $a_{(gate)}$, $b_{(gate)}$, $\alpha_{(gate)}$ and $Vth_{(gate)}$ are obtained by fitting to circuit simulation results. $Vdd(t)$ represents the function of deterministic noise waveform.

Now that the first rise timings of fast and slow ROs are $t_{(1)FAST}$ and $t_{(1)SLOW}$ and the timings of n-th rising edges are $t_{(n)FAST}$, $t_{(n)SLOW}$, Fig. 17 explains three-step bit generation. 1) Calculate the next timing of rising edge of slow RO $t_{(2)SLOW}$ from the current rising timing $t_{(1)SLOW}$. 2) From $t_{(1)FAST}$ and $t_{(1)SLOW}$, find $t_{(n)FAST}$ which satisfies equalities $t_{(n-1)FAST} < t_{(2)SLOW} < t_{(n)FAST}$. 3) Generate one bit from $t_{(2)SLOW}$, $t_{(n-1)FAST}$, $t_{(n)FAST}$ and duty cycle of the fast RO.

The time interval between successive rising edges is the sum of $t_{d,(gate)}(t)$ multiplied by 2. Additionally, it is multiplied by sampling sparseness when a frequency dividers are used.

4.2 Simulation Results

Randomness evaluation is executed with the simulator which is implemented with C language. Figure 18 depicts the results of poker test under the power supply noise. 100 sequences of 20k bits were generated for test. Sinusoidal noise whose amplitude is 100 mV is added to DC supply voltage of 1.2 V for fast and slow ROs ("Both"). Another result ("Slow Only") is also plotted supposing that the noise is superposed only to slow RO. This situation corresponds to a case that the power supplies are separated to avoid the interaction between ROs. 251-stage RO with 8-frequency-divider, whose average period is 58.6 ns, and 7-stage RO are used as slow and fast ROs. σ of $t_{d,random}$ is set to 0.55 ps referring to the measurement result of RO fabricated in 65nm process.

Figure 18 indicates that the randomness of bitstream depends on the frequency of the deterministic noise. The randomness is insensitive to the period of deterministic noise when the period of sinusoidal noise is large.

Figures 19 and 20 show the influence of σ of $t_{d,random}$ to the randomness. σ is 0.55 ps in Fig. 19 and σ is multiplied by 4 (2.2 ps) in Fig. 20, which means the jitter of ROs is enlarged. In Fig. 19, the randomness in the case that the deterministic noise

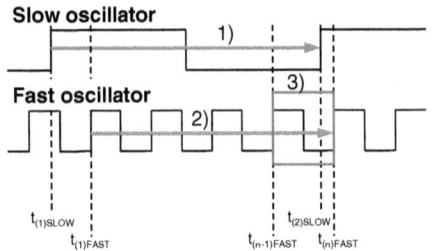

Fig. 17. Concept of simulation

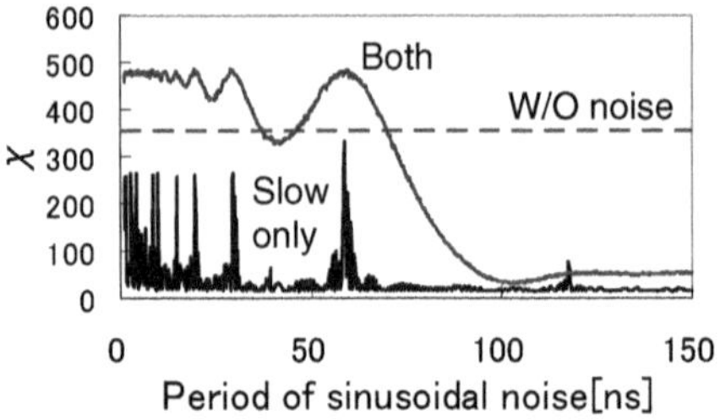

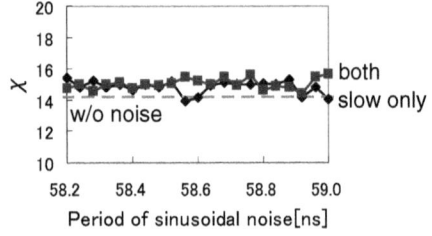

Fig. 18. Randomness evaluation under deterministic noise

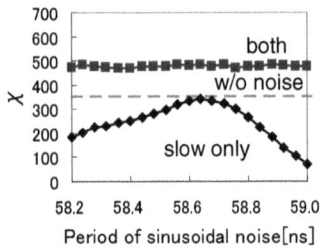

Fig. 19. Randomness evaluation under deterministic noise (σ=0.55 ps)

Fig. 20. Randomness evaluation under deterministic noise (σ=2.2 ps)

is injected to both oscillators is worse than that without noise. Also, the randomness is unstable especially when the supply noise is applied only to slow oscillator. On the other hand, Fig. 20 shows that the χ of poker test without deterministic noise are comparable to that with noises. This reveals that the HRNG with large random jitter is more robust to deterministic noise. After HRNG design explained in section 3, the robustness to the deterministic noise should be evaluated by this simulation.

4.3   Implication from Simulation Results

As referred in chapter 4.2, the randomness of outputs varies depending on the frequency of deterministic noises. Figure 18 indicates that the randomness is sensitive to the high frequency noises, whereas low frequency noises are less harmful, or rather effective to improve the randomness. The frequency of power supply noise externally injected by malicious attacks is relatively low, and hence the effect of such noises are less influential. Low-pass filter is expected to further enhance the robustness. It is also important to investigate the noise coming from other circuits integrated on the same chip. High frequency components included in such noise should be shunted via on-chip decoupling capacitance.

5   Conclusion

This paper presented a behavior model for oscillator-based HRNG and a randomness evaluation method that are suitable for design space exploration. The proposed model can directly estimate approximate entropy in addition to bit stream generation. The presented model was confirmed with hardware measurement. We also developed a HRNG simulator tailored for deterministic noise and carried out the randomness evaluation under deterministic noise. The randomness evaluation with the model and the HRNG simulator enable to design a HRNG that satisfies performance specification.

Acknowledgments. The VLSI chip in this study has been fabricated in the chip fabrication program of VLSI Design and Education Center(VDEC), the University of Tokyo in collaboration with STARC, e-Shuttle, Inc., and Fujitsu Ltd.

References

1. Jun, B., Kocher, P.: The Intel random number generator, cryptography research inc., white paper prepared for Intel corporation (April 1999)
2. Bucci, M., Germani, L., Luzzi, R., Trifiletti, A., Varanonuovo, M.: A high-speed oscillator-based truly random number source for cryptographic applications on a smart card IC. IEEE Transactions on Computers 52(4) (April 2003)
3. Balachandran, G.K., Barnett, R.E.: A 440-nA true random number generator for passive RFID tags. IEEE Transactions on Circuits and Systems 55(11) (December 2008)
4. Petrie, C.S., Connelly, J.A.: Modeling and simulation of oscillator-based random number generators. In: IEEE International Symposium on Circuits and Systems, vol. 4, pp. 324–327 (May 1996)
5. Petrie, C.S., Connelly, J.A.: A noise-based IC random number generator for applications in cryptography. IEEE Transactions on Circuits and Systems 47(5) (May 2000)
6. Security requirements for cryptographic modules, FIPS pub. 140-2 (May 2001)
7. A statistical test suite for the validation of random number generators and pseudorandom number generators for cryptographic applications, NIST, pub. 800-22 (May 2001)
8. Davies, R.B.: Exclusive OR (XOR) and hardware random number generators, pp. 1–11 (February 2002), http://www.robertnz.net/pdf/xor2.pdf
9. Marsaglia, G.: Diehard battery of tests of randomness (1995), http://stat.fsu.edu/pub/diehard/
10. Ergün, S.: Modeling and analysis of chaos-modulated dual oscillator-based random number generators. In: European Signal Processing Conference, pp. 1–5 (August 2008)
11. Schindler, W.: Stochastical model and its analysis for a physical random number generator. In: Paterson, K.G. (ed.) Cryptography and Coding 2003. LNCS, vol. 2898, pp. 276–289. Springer, Heidelberg (2003)
12. Tkacik, T.E.: A hardware random number generator. In: Kaliski Jr., B.S., Koç, Ç.K., Paar, C. (eds.) CHES 2002. LNCS, vol. 2523, pp. 875–876. Springer, Heidelberg (2003)
13. Schellekens, D., Preneel, B., Verbauwhede, I.: FPGA vendor agnostic true random number generator. In: IEEE Proceedings of the International Conference on Field Programmable Logic and Applications, pp. 1–6 (2006)
14. Ledermann, W.: Handbook of applicable mathematics, vol. 6. John Wiley & Sons, Chichester (1980)
15. Matsumoto, M., Yasuda, S., Ohba, R., Ikegami, K., Tanamoto, T., Fujita, S.: $1200\mu m^2$ physical random-number generators based on SiN mosfet for secure smart-card application. In: IEEE International Solid-State Circuits Conference, pp. 414–624 (2008)
16. Sakurai, T., Newton, A.R.: Alpha-power law mosfet model and its applications to cmos inverter delay and other formulas. IEEE Journal of Solid-State Circuits 25(2), 584–594 (1990)

Using Special Use Cases for Security in the Software Development Life Cycle

Jean-Marie Kabasele Tenday

Ecole Polytechnique de Louvain, University of Louvain
Place St-Barbe, 2 - 1348 Louvain-la-Neuve, Belgium
jeanmarie.kabasele@axa.be

Abstract. The goal of this paper is to propose the use of the Misuse Case and Obligation use case concepts in the Software Development Life Cycle (SDLC) in order to position security concerns at the very beginning of this process and to get "secure applications". These concepts are built upon the "use case" concept which is well known by the community of application developers in companies and by the application sponsors. The application sponsors are the key business stakeholders that fund and/or rely on the application for their business benefits. As stated in [1] and [3], the use case concept has proven helpful for the elicitation of, communication about and documentation of requirements [4]. So, we think it is easier to introduce security requirements in the development lifecycle by reusing and/or constructing security requirement artifacts around the use case and UML approach.

Keywords: Secure system development, secure application, misuse case, obligation use case, security in lifecycle.

1 Introduction

Analyzing the «Practice of Building Secure Systems», Wing [23] pointed out four layers that determine the way the security is built in a computing system. Those are: cryptography, protocols, systems/languages and applications. While the first three have almost mature results, the finding was that there was not much for the application level.

A few years later, Devambu and Stubbelbine [3] highlighted the need for securing software and not only the focus on security of communications, and posed the challenge of integrating security concerns with requirements engineering, and in particular with UML. Firesmith [4] stressed the same point when he pointed out the fact that the analysis and the documentation of security threats and security requirements received considerably too little attention, and that the emphasis on security engineering has rather been on the development and use of numerous security mechanisms to protect vulnerable assets and services by countering known security threats.

The goal of this paper is to position security concerns at the very beginning of the process of building "secure applications" in a way to be backed by the application

Y. Chung and M. Yung (Eds.): WISA 2010, LNCS 6513, pp. 122–134, 2011.

owners despite the budget cut pressure. Our strategy is to avoid reinventing the wheel and use common standards. Therefore, we propose to reuse the Unified Modeling Language (UML) and the Rationale Unified Process (RUP) frameworks by readapting and/or enriching the use case artifact. Beside the special security constructs called "Misuse Case" which has been introduced so far in [4] and [21], we also introduce the concept of the Obligation Use Case to capture threats related to the lack of compliance to the obligation requirements. Using a concrete example, we will extend the use case model with these new security concepts and position them as the deliverables of the inception phase in RUP that represents the Software Development Life Cycle (SDLC). These concepts are built upon the "use case" concept well known by the community of application developers in companies and the business sponsors. Our assumption is that it is easier to introduce security requirements by reusing flavors of UML like misuse case and obligation use case.

Simply stated, a misuse case, also known as an abuse case, denotes functionality not desired in the system. It captures an unwanted state as introduced in [11], unlike a normal use case that represents an accepted functionality or a wanted state [11]. An obligation use case is a special use case introduced to enforce an obligation expressed in the requirements. So far, security specification has been more focusing on "permission" whereas few requirements include "obligation".

This paper is organized as follows: after this introductory section, the next section overviews the state-of-the-art of security in the SDLC in general. The third section will remind the SDLC based on the Rational Unified Process and we will introduce a concrete example and its use case model. The fourth section defines the concepts of "Misuse Case", "security use case" and "obligation use case", their possible usage and the way we propose to use them to capture security requirements. The fifth section will be dedicated to the enhancement of "security use cases" in the SDLC. Then we will present the lessons learned and the conclusion.

2 Overview of Security in the SDLC

The findings raised in [3] have been addressed in research and in literature. In the first International Workshop on Information Security, a session has been dedicated to security management, and [11] and [16] proposed frameworks to specify and manage information security.

Both the requirement engineering and the security research communities have maintained effort and proposed solutions to integrate security in the design process. Giorgini et al. ([7] and [8]) extended the Tropos meta-model with security needs and capabilities. In parallel, [14] and [15] integrated security concepts in the KAOS meta-model. The UML has been updated as well. In fact, the UMLsec language was introduced in [9] and [10] as an extension of the UML, using the UML stereotypes, for modeling security related objectives, such as confidentiality, integrity and access control in analysis. On the other hand, [17] defined the secureUML to specify authorization security requirement using the Role Based Access Control models.

Beside all these works, [12] has suggested a new model that provides solutions to specify contextual security policies. This model, called Organization Based Access Control (OrBAC), is based on a formal language and is built around the concept of organization. Likewise, [13] extended the OrBAC model with the Multi-OrBAC to cope with the distributed and collaborative organizations.

On top of all this research, [20] has gathered the fundamental concepts in the information risk management domain to propose the Information System Security Risk Management (ISSRM) model. The ISSRM reference model addresses risk management at three different levels, combining asset, risk, and risk treatment views, called security requirement, and it is rather a kind of formalization of concepts defined in the common criteria standards in a UML like representation view.

Tropos, KAOS and OrBAC are high level frameworks and languages. They are suitable at the pre-study stage of the development process, in other words when the problem is under definition, before the real development starts. To bridge this definition stage with the development process, [18] has achieved this by readapting the secure Tropos and using the ISSRM model. They have applied the same approach to align Misuse Case with the Risk Management [19].

Despite outstanding results, they remain kind of proprietary languages as quoted in [7] and [8], classifying them as the off-the-shelves frameworks. Hence without a huge training effort, it is quite tough to use them and not easy to get the buy-in of security matters from the business stakeholders in companies which are facing competition and budget reduction pressure.

Another finding comes from [1] who points out the fact that the ability to deliver reliable and secure software systems of higher quality within budget and schedule continues to challenge most IT organizations. He argues that this is due to many factors among which the lack of security expertise among software engineers resulting in a software design with no security consideration. In addition, he points out the fact that software developers are usually not provided with the information on how to develop secure applications, and employers neither require it from their employees nor (usually) do they provide any remedial training on how to develop secure applications. We experiment this as well from the field. Some companies have developed their own security related processes; but most of them lack guidance or even information from which they can learn and that they can use as a guideline. The models we have been discussing so far are useful, but awareness effort is still to be expected.

To close the gap, we choose to push security solutions around the UML because it is recognized as a de-facto standard, as outlined in [1]. Thus, developers do not require specific training.

3   RUP – The Software Development Life Cycle

3.1   Inception and Use Case Model

Briefly, the Rational Unified Process (RUP) is a Software Engineering Process that provides a disciplined approach to assigning tasks and responsibilities within a development organization. The process is described in two dimensions as shown on the figure below. Readers who are interested in further details can consult many available literatures and white papers.

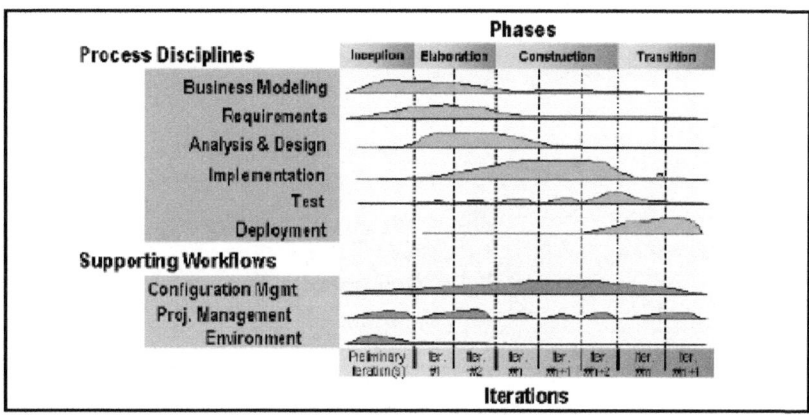

Fig. 1. Rational Unified Process

At the very beginning of the process, during the inception phase when the business stakeholders meet the development team, a business case for the system is established and the project scope delimited. To accomplish this one must identify all external entities (actors) with which the system will interact and define the nature of this inter-action at a high-level. This involves identifying all use cases and describing a few significant ones.

Thus, from our perspective, the relevant outcome of this inception phase is:

- *A vision document*: a general vision of the core project's requirements, key features, and main constraints.
- *An initial use-case model* (about 20% of functional requirements).
- *An initial business case*, which includes business context, success criteria (revenue projection, market recognition, and so on), and financial forecast.

To illustrate this, let us assume the business stakeholder is a Financial Institution operating on the Financial Instrument – a.k.a securities – market and whose strategic goal would be to increase his market share by selling transaction - shares, bonds or other investment products - through an Internet Portal. This is the way the business sponsors are behaving today. They come not only with the problem, but they also have a platform, a specific technology or tool in mind.

In this context, the initial use case model might include the following use-cases:

In this use-case model, two actors are identified, i.e. is the Customer and the Back Office Clerk. They interact with the system by mean of use cases. This denotes the functional view that is often at stake at the beginning and it often happens that the project starts without security goals.

3.2 Security in RUP

While the RUP process is widely used in enterprises, the security workflow is not clearly identified as part of the core engineering workflow. The way security is

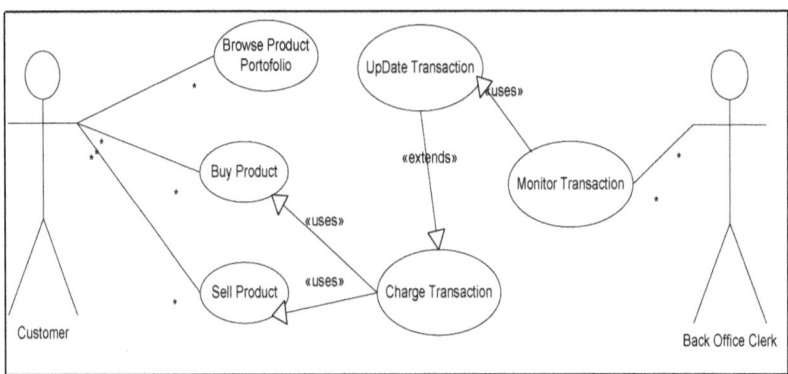

Fig. 2. Use Case model

treated as non-functional requirements or quality attributes like maintainability, usability, etc. The non-functional requirements are expressed with text at this stage and are refined in the software design document during the analysis and design activities whose output is the use case realization diagrams. The success of enhancing security feature is based on the security mindset of the project team.

The extension of the UML with security features introduced here above can not be used at this inception stage. As explained here above and in [9], UMLsec extends the UML for modeling security related features, such as confidentiality and access control. It proposes concepts for specifying requirements on confidentiality and integrity in the Analysis phase and not during the Inception. On the other hand, SecureUML focuses on modeling the authorization requirement and the access control policies and integrating them into a model-driven software development process. It is as well suitable for the analysis and design phase and not during the inception.

But, the challenge is: why do we need confidentiality, integrity, access control etc.? What threat do we need to counter with these security mechanisms? The candidate to address is the Misuse Case concept and its impact on the business.

4   Special Use Case Model

4.1   Misuse Case

The Misuse Case model, also called Abuse Case, was introduced by [21] by the adaptation of the UML use cases. A Misuse Case is defined as an interaction between a system and one or more actors, where the results of the interaction are harmful to the system, or one of the stakeholders of the system. A few years later, [22] proposed to model security by defining misuse cases which describe functionalities that the system should not allow. This new construct makes it possible to represent actions that the system should prevent together with those actions which it should support.

A Mis-Actor concept has been introduced and it denotes the inverse of an actor in a use case identification. It represents someone who will initiate the misuse cases [22].

Because the success criteria for a misuse case is a successful attack against an application, misuse cases are highly effective ways of analyzing security threats but are inappropriate for the analysis and specification of security requirements. To remind, a requirement stands for a statement the system should meet or achieve. To deal with this, [4] has proposed to use intermediate use cases to capture security requirements that would prevent or detect the occurrences of misuse cases. The intermediate use case that prevents or detect is called "Security Use Case".

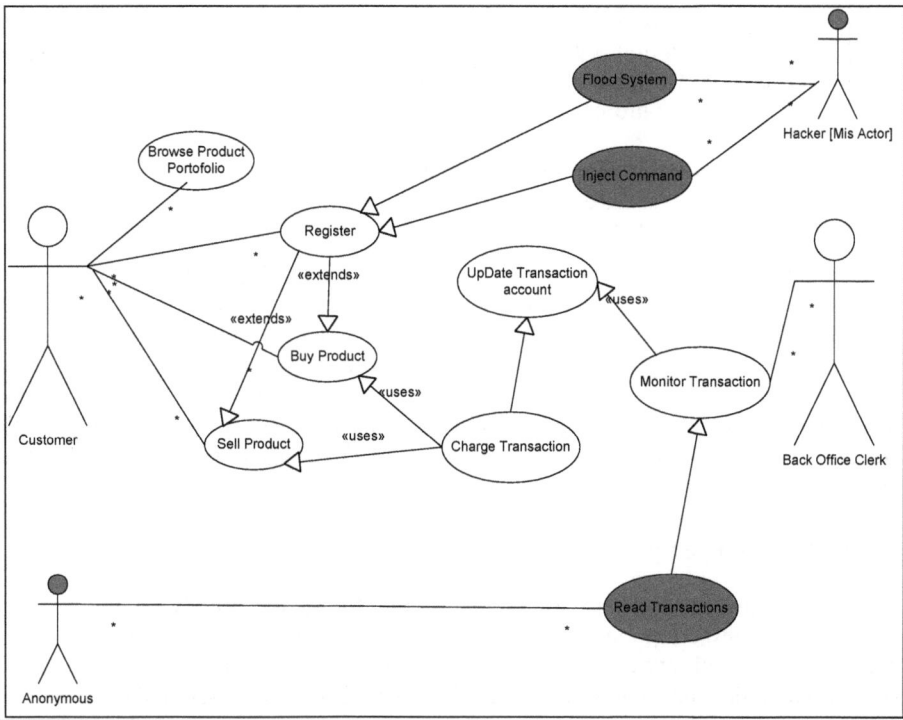

Fig. 3. Use Case model extended with Misuse Cases

As we can see from this picture, the abnormal or non required system behaviors and their mis-actors can be captured at this early stage of development. It is an opportunity for the business stakeholders to be sensitized at the threats and risks that could endanger the system.

4.2 Security Use Case

As seen so far, the success criteria for a misuse case will be a successful attack against a system. Thus, misuse cases are highly effective ways of analyzing security threats but they are inappropriate for the analysis and the specification of security requirements that, if implemented, should prevent from the occurrences of misuse cases.

As pointed out in the previous section, [4] recommends using *security use cases* to specify requirements such that the application will successfully protect itself from its relevant security threats.

Misuse cases are related to threats and vulnerabilities whereas security use cases are related to mitigation controls or security requirements. In the requirement document, we propose to capture the security use case using the following format:

```
Security Use Case:
    ID: {security use case identifier}
    Name: {security use case name}
    Short Description: {short description}
    Rationale: { [Prevent / Detect] << Misuse case concerned >>} or
               {[Enforce] << Obligation Use Case>>}
    …
    Success criteria: {The success criteria predicate}
End_Security Use Case
```

One can reuse whatever template available in literature [22]. However, we recommend two additional fields, more relevant in our view. They are the *"rationale"* and the *"success criteria"*, beside other common fields like name, author, etc.

The rationale field captures the Misuse case that drives the security use case and their relationship or the Obligation Use case as will be shown hereunder. The success criteria field defines the condition – a predicate - under which the security use case achieves its goal, i.e. to "prevent" or "detect" the occurrence of the misuse case or to "enforce" an obligation use case. An example of the usage is provided in a next section.

4.3 Obligation Use Case

A use case typically describes some function that the system should be able to perform. Hence, they are good for working with so-called functional requirements, but not necessarily with extra-functional ones. By nature, they concentrate on what the system *should* do, and we have presented the misuse cases that describe the opposite.

In this section, we propose to focus on what the system *"must"* do. This requirement is referred to as an *obligation*. It has been addressed in many requirement frameworks or models referenced so far [12]. We define an *obligation* as a mandatory requirement or functionality that must be fulfilled by either the users or the system. An example of such is a regulatory requirement as we will see in the case hereunder.

For example in the Financial Institutions, we have encountered the two following obligations [5] and [6], which by the way are real in the financial trading businesses:

Obligation 1 [MiFID - Client categorization][5]:
Clear procedures must be in place to categorize clients and assess their suitability for each type of investment product transaction.

This obligation denotes the fact that prior to starting doing e-trade business; the financial institution must assess the customer trading and/or financial skills (bond, share, future, etc.) as well as his suitability to make trading transactions. The goal is the protection of customers.

This obligation implies that an action or series of actions should be implemented in the system and be executed each time a new customer tries to register to the system. Thus, it can be captured as a use case. We call it an obligation use case that will be bound to the "register use case" through the "includes" relationship. For the sake of simplicity, let us name it "Assess customer skills and categorize".

Obligation 2 [Anti-Money Laundering Act] [6]:

The Anti-Money Laundering and Counter-Terrorism Financing Act requires that any financial institution and any "non-financial trade or business" must file a report concerning a transaction (or series of related transactions) in excess of $10,000 in currency.

This obligation is quite understandable and aims at avoiding the usage of well-known financial institutions as vehicle of terror money. In our framework, it implies a reporting obligation use case in the "extends" relationship with the "Buy" use case if the transaction amount is higher that $10,000.

To remind, an "extends" relationship between use cases means one use case optionally adds the functionality of the other use case when certain conditions are met. An *"includes"* relationship means one use case completely encompasses all the functionality of another use case.

Because the success criteria of the obligation use case match the success of the application as it is the case for the security use case, we propose to treat them as a flavor of security use cases, with the same layout.

In the rationale field of the security use case bound to an obligation, we have proposed here above to use *"enforce"* and not "prevent/avoid".

Fig. 4. Use Case model extended with "Security Use Cases"

5   Extending the SDLC with Special Use Cases

5.1   Use Case – Obligation Use Case and Misuse Case Identification

While reminding the RUP here above, we have seen that about 20% of the use cases are captured in the business analysis and are part of the first deliverables of the inception phase in the requirement elicitation process.

From these use cases, we propose that misuse cases be identified to highlight security risks of the system to be built. Referencing to previous works, use cases denote the wanted states in the system. This is roughly: a genuine agent, or actor, has actual access right to the right asset. On the opposite, a misuse case denotes an unwanted state of the system; in other word it implies the negation of the wanted state.

From the legal and/or business domain requirements, obligation use cases can be identified as discussed here above. However, it is worth noting that they are candidate to misuse case as well. For example, to avoid being reported in for a transaction with more than 10K\$, one would divide the normal amount and execute two or three times the transaction.

Once misuse cases are identified, security use cases need to be proposed to get a secure system with only wanted states. Templates have been discussed, we recommend making a clear reference to misuse cases it prevents or detects and obligation use case they enforce in the field we name "rationale".

Examples:

Security Use Case:
  ID: SUC 01
  Name: Block_Repeated_Registration
  Short Description: Bla bla
  Rationale: Prevent << MUC Flood System >>
  ...
  Success criteria: " The Same input as the previous one is rejected"
End_Security Use Case

Security Use Case
  ID: SUC02
  Name: Control Access
  Short Description: Bla bla
  Rationale: *Prevent* << MUC Read Transaction >>
  ...
  Success criteria: "Only authorized user have read access to the transaction file"
End_Security Use Case

Security Use Case
   <u>ID:</u> SUC03
   <u>Name</u>: Report_More_Than_10K
   <u>Short Description</u>: Bla bla
   <u>Rationale</u>: *Enforce* << AML Act. >>
   ...
   <u>Success criteria</u>: "Report Transaction more than 10 K Euros"
End_Security Use Case

5.2 Refinement

From one use case, multiple misuse cases can be deducted:

- A wrong agent, a hacker for example, accessing assets in the system;
- A right agent, an internal officer for example, having access to data he should not,
- An internal agent, not having access to an asset he should, etc.

Thus, while use cases will be refined through different iterations in the system, misuse cases will be subject to the risk management process – threat and vulnerability assessment - to retain those ones having the high likelihood of occurrence with a high impact on assets. This is a pragmatically way to keep only relevant misuse cases.

5.3 Next Steps

So far, we have identified security use case during the inception phase that involves a huge workload in the business modeling and the requirement analysis processes. The elaboration phase follows the inception and it introduces the analysis and design processes.

The analysis model represents the system in terms of objects that domain experts know and the design model represents the same system at a level of abstraction closer to the source code. The key concept that introduces the analysis & design processes in RUP is the "use-case realization" model, which represents the design perspective of the use case model.

Likewise, the use cases realization of a security use case will represent the design of this security use case. It will be made up with security concepts, protocols and models that will be used in the analysis and design phases to realize the security use case.

For example, the realization use case of the security use case "access control" will be defined using an access control model like the Mandatory Access Control (MAC) model or the Role Based Access Control (RBAC) model and implemented accordingly with identification and authorization schemes. This is the place UMLsec and secureUML are suitable.

The discussion about the mapping of use case realization of security use cases is out of the scope of this paper, but it is worth noting that we have a link between the business goal captured through the use case model and the security mechanisms that one can find in a system.

6 Lesson Learned

We have implemented this model in an enterprise and here are a few findings:

1. The misuse case and the security use case concept are security awareness tool towards the business stakeholders during the business case definition. As a consequence, security tasks are budgeted during the negotiation phase between the sponsors and the development team.
2. The identification and the definition of security use cases make it easier to plan security testing in the project plan. If the success criteria of a security use case fail, it is quite easy to the project team to understand why the production phase can be delayed.
3. The security use cases and their realization can be reused for different development projects in the Enterprise, which contributes to the Return on Investment. Another advantage of the reuse capability is that the security requirement elicitation activity can be delegated to non-expert analysts.
4. Since our development community uses UML and the RUP processes, we did not experiment any resistance while introducing the security use case concept in the development process.
5. The security perspective section in the design document contains security functions that are the realization of identified security use cases and/or obligation use cases.

7 Conclusion

In this paper, we have revisited the misuse case and security use case concepts, and introduced the notion of the obligation use case; after that, we have positioned them at the beginning of the software development lifecycle, namely at the inception phase during which the business use case is built. Among advantages that are presented in the above section, we would stress the fact that deriving security requirements from the business use case, security will be viewed as a business facilitator and not as a constraint as it is in many organizations. Furthermore, the link between the business goals, the security objectives and security mechanisms in the system become clear and straightforward, making security investment easier.

The future work that is of interest in line with this paper would be the construction of a library of security use cases with the alternative realization use cases for each other along with their security mechanisms that implement them. Another direction of research would be the formal construction to define the realization use case of the security use case using the formal languages like UMLsec, secureUML, OrBAC, etc.

References

1. Al-Azzani, S.: Security Testing - RSMG 2 (2009), http://www.cs.bham.ac.uk
2. Bettini, C., Jajodia, S., Wang, S., Wijesekera, D.: Provisions and obligations in policy management and security applications. In: Proceedings of the 28th International Conference on Very Large Data Bases, VLDB Endowment, Hong Kong, pp. 502–513 (2002)
3. Devambu, P.T., Stubbelbine, S.: Software engineering for security: a roadmap. In: Future of Software Engineering, Special volume of the Proceedings of the 22nd Int. Conf. on Software Engineering (ICSE 2000), pp. 227–239 (2000)
4. Firesmith, D.: Security Use Cases. Journal of Object Technology 2(3), 53–64 (2003)
5. European Union: Directive 2004/39/EC on The Markets in Financial Instruments Directive (MiFID). Official Journal of the European Union (2004), http://eurlex.europa.eu
6. European Union : Directive 2005/60/EC on the prevention of the use of the financial system for the purpose of money laundering and terrorist financing; Official Journal of the European Union (2005), http://eurlex.europa.eu
7. Giorgini, P., Massacci, F., Mylopoulos, J.: Requirement Engineering meets Security: A Case Study on Modelling Secure Electronic Transactions by VISA and Mastercard. In: 22th of International Conference on Conceptual Modeling (2003)
8. Giorgini, P., Massacci, F., Zannone, N.: Security and Trust Requirements Engineering; survey. In: Aldini, A., Gorrieri, R., Martinelli, F. (eds.) FOSAD 2005. LNCS, vol. 3655, pp. 237–272. Springer, Heidelberg (2005)
9. Jürjens, J.: Modelling audit security for smart-card payment schemes with UMLsec. In: 16th Int. Conf.on Inf. Security (IFIP/SEC 2001). Kluwer AP, Dordrecht (2001)
10. Jürjens, J.: Towards secure systems development with umlsec. In: FASE/ETAPS 2001. LNCS, vol. 2029, pp. 187–200. Springer, Heidelberg (2001)
11. Kabasele-Tenday, J.-M.: Specifying Security in a Composite System. In: Okamoto, E. (ed.) ISW 1997. LNCS, vol. 1396, pp. 246–255. Springer, Heidelberg (1998)
12. Kalam, E., et al.: Organization based access control. In: Proceedings of the 4th Int. Workshop on Policies for Distributed Systems and Networks (POLICY 2003). IEEE, Los Alamitos (2003)
13. Kalam, E., et al.: Multi-OrBAC: un modèle de contrôle d'accès pour les systèmes multi-organisationnels. Centre pour la Communication Scientifique Directe (2006), http://www.ccsd.cnrs.fr/
14. van Lamsweerde, A., Letier, E.: Handling Obstacles in Goal-Oriented Requirements Engineering. TSE 26(10), 978–1005 (2000)
15. van Lamsweerde, A., Brohez, S., De Landtsheer, R.: Janssens. D.: From System Goals to Intruder Anti-Goals: Attack Generation and Resolution for Security Requirements Engineering. In: Proceedings of RHAS 2003, pp. 49–56 (2003)
16. Leiwo, J., Zheng, Y.: A Framework for the Management of Information Security. In: Okamoto, E. (ed.) ISW 1997. LNCS, vol. 1396, pp. 232–245. Springer, Heidelberg (1998)
17. Lodderstedt, T., Basin, D., Doser, J.: SecureUML: A UML-Based Modeling Language for Model-Driven Security. In: Li, J., Hussmann, H., Cook, S. (eds.) UML 2002. LNCS, vol. 2460, pp. 426–441. Springer, Heidelberg (2002)
18. Matulevičius, R., Mayer, N., Mouratidis, H., Dubois, E., Heymans, P., Genon, N.: Adapting Secure Tropos for Security Risk Management in the Early Phases of Information Systems Development. In: Bellahsène, Z., Léonard, M. (eds.) CAiSE 2008. LNCS, vol. 5074, pp. 541–555. Springer, Heidelberg (2008)

19. Matulevicius, R., Mayer, N., Heymans, P.: Alignment of Misuse Cases with Security Risk Management. In: ARES Proceedings of the 2008 Third Int. Conf. on Availability, Reliability and Security. IEEE, Los Alamitos (2008)
20. Mayer, N., Heymans, P., Matulevičius, R.: Design of a Modelling Language for Information System Security Risk Management. In: Proceedings of the 1st International Conf. on Research Challenges in Information Science (RCIS 2007), pp. 121–131 (2007)
21. McDermott, J., Fox, C.: Using Abuse Case Models for Security Requirements Analysis. In: Proc. of ACSAC 1999, pp. 55–66. IEEE Press, Los Alamitos (1999)
22. Sindre, G., Opdahl, A.L.: Eliciting security requirements with misuse cases. Requirements Engineering 10(1), 34–44 (2005)
23. Wing, J.M.: A Symbiotic Relationship Between Formal Methods and Security, CMU-CS-98-188, Pittsburgh, PA (1998)

Efficient and Optimally Secure In-Network Aggregation in Wireless Sensor Networks

Atsuko Miyaji and Kazumasa Omote

Japan Advanced Institute of Science and Technology (JAIST)
{miyaji,omote}@jaist.ac.jp

Abstract. In many wireless sensor network applications, the data collection sink (base station) needs to find the aggregated statistics of the network. Readings from sensor nodes are aggregated at intermediate nodes to reduce the communication cost. However, the previous optimally secure in-network aggregation protocols against multiple corrupted nodes require two round-trip communications between each node and the base station, including the *result-checking phase* whose *congestion* is $\mathcal{O}(\log n)$ where n is the total number of sensor nodes.

In this paper[1], we propose an efficient and optimally secure sensor network aggregation protocol against multiple corrupted nodes by a *weak adversary*. Our protocol achieves one round-trip communication to satisfy optimal security without the result-checking phase, by conducting aggregation along with the verification, based on the idea of TESLA technique. Furthermore, we show that the congestion is constant. This means that our protocol suits large-scale wireless sensor networks.

1 Introduction

In many wireless sensor network applications, the data collection sink (base station) needs to find the aggregate statistics of the network. Readings from sensor nodes are aggregated at intermediate nodes to reduce the communication cost. This process is called in-network aggregation [1–6, 18–20]. Since aggregation reduces the amount of data to be transmitted through the network, it consequently decreases bandwidth consumption and energy depletion.

Security is a critical requirement in data aggregation, since sensor nodes are typically deployed in unsecured locations and are not equipped with tamper-resistant hardware. An adversary is able to replay, modify, delay, drop, and deliver protocol messages out of order as well as inject own messages. However, most aggregation protocols assume that all intermediate nodes are trusted [3–14, 16–19, 21–23] except [1, 2, 15, 20]. A corrupted node can easily modify its own sensor reading. It is difficult to detect such a dishonest act in data aggregation,

---

[1] This study is partly supported by Grant-in-Aid for Scientific Research (A)i21240001), Grant-in-Aid for Young Scientists (B) (22700066), and IT Specialist Program of Ministry of Education, Culture, Sports, Science and Technology, Japan (MEXT).

Y. Chung and M. Yung (Eds.): WISA 2010, LNCS 6513, pp. 135–149, 2011.

since the modified sensor reading is indistinguishable from the legitimate reading. Such a dishonest act is called *direct data injection attack* [1, 15], where even one small modification might influence a total aggregated value. It is, thus, important to minimize the damage by direct data injection attacks. Such a security model is called *optimal security* [1, 20] (See Definition 1). We also employ the same security model. Optimal security means that the harmful influence on the final aggregation result is proportional to only the number of corrupted nodes which perform direct data injection attacks.

It is important to achieve constant congestion in large-scale wireless sensor networks. Sensors are usually resource-limited and power-constrained. They suffer from restricted computation, communication, and power resources. The energy savings of performing in-network aggregation are crucial for energy-constrained sensor networks. Since the nodes with the heaviest traffic are typically the nodes which are most essential to the connectivity of the network, their failure may cause the network to partition. Although several protocols [1, 2, 20] satisfy optimal security against multiple corrupted nodes, the congestion of these protocols is $\mathcal{O}(\log n)$ where n is the total number of sensor nodes.

In this paper, we propose an efficient and optimally secure sensor network aggregation protocol against multiple corrupted nodes by a *weak adversary*. Our protocol achieves one round-trip communication between each node and the base station to satisfy optimal security without the result-checking phase, by conducting aggregation along with the verification based on the idea of TESLA technique. Furthermore, we show that the congestion (maximum amount of per-node communication) in our protocol is constant. In other words, the amount of the per-node communication does not increase even if the number of nodes becomes huge. This means that our protocol suits large-scale wireless sensor networks.

The rest of this paper is organized as follows. In the next Section 2 we review a survey of other approaches to secure aggregation in sensor networks. Some requirements and preliminary items are provided in Section 3. We review the CPS protocol in Section 4. We propose our protocol in Section 5 and discuss the security and efficiency analysis of our protocol in Section 6. We finally conclude this paper in Section 7.

2   Related Work

There has been many works on preserving integrity in aggregation protocols. The simplest approach is a single-aggregator model [7–10] where each node sends its sensor reading directly to the aggregator (e.g., base station), and then the aggregator computes the final aggregation result. However, these protocols suffer from having a single node with high congestion. Also, several protocols do not assume corrupted nodes that are trying to disturb the aggregation result [11–14].

Recently several researchers have examined security issues in aggregation. Although some aggregation protocols [5, 6] are (optimally) secure against a single corrupted node without corruption of intermediate nodes, these protocols are not optimally secure against multiple corrupted nodes. Some aggregation protocols [1, 2, 20] are optimally secure against multiple corrupted nodes even if intermediate nodes are corrupted. These protocols addressed the issue of measuring and bounding corrupted node's contribution to the final aggregation result. In these protocols [1, 2, 20] related to our protocol, a network forms an aggregation tree, and then each node sends the aggregate up its parent node in the aggregation tree. The commitment is generated for the aggregate in a manner similar to a Merkle tree [24]. The schemes [16, 17] enhance the availability of the above schemes [1, 2], but do not discussed optimal security which is only discussed in [1, 20]. Wagner [15] performed a quantitative study measuring the effect of direct data injection attack on various aggregates.

Chan, Perrig and Song [1] defined optimal security for the first time. The CPS protocol uses two kinds of trees: aggregation tree and commitment tree. The commitment tree can be converted to a virtual binary tree for efficiency. As a result, the congestion for commitment verification is minimized.

Manulis and Schwenk [20] designs the data aggregation protocol in wireless sensor networks, called MS protocol, that satisfies optimal security. They provide a rigorous proof of optimal security against node corruption for the first time. The MS protocol aggregates all children data and sends it to parent node. It has two round-trip communications between each node and the base station including the result-checking phase, similar to the CPS protocol [1]. While the CPS protocol can convert an arbitrary tree to a binary commitment tree, the MS protocol does not consider such a conversion. As a result, the congestion of the MS protocol [20] is less efficient compared with the CPS protocol.

There have been several protocols introduced for preserving the confidentiality of aggregate results [10, 18, 19, 21–23]. This issue is orthogonal to our protocol and is not considered in this paper.

3   Preliminaries

3.1   Requirements

The following requirements need to be considered when designing secure in-network aggregation in wireless sensor networks.

- **Optimal security [1, 20].** Optimal security is the concept to minimize the damaging impact of corrupted nodes on the overall aggregation result and assume the integrity of only data except for data modified by direct data injection attacks. The total aggregation result is modified only as long as the direct data injection attack is performed. It is usually difficult to find direct data injection attacks, and hence it is important not to expand the damage of direct data injection attacks.
- **Low congestion.** As a metric for communication overhead, we usually consider node congestion which is the worst case communication load on any single sensor node during the algorithm. Since the nodes with the heaviest traffic are typically the nodes which are most essential to the connectivity of

the network, their failure may cause the network to partition. Thus, lower communication traffic on the nodes with the heaviest traffic is desirable. Especially, node congestion should not depend on the total number of sensor nodes in large-scale wireless sensor networks.

- **Small number of communication rounds.** The communication between sensor nodes is not so reliable, owing to resource-limited and power-constrained. Thus, one round-trip communication for aggregation between each node and the base station is desirable, i.e., each node has only to send the aggregation messages to its parent node after receiving the query by the base station.
- **Low computational and storage costs.** A sensor node suffers from restricted computation and storage, hence the small computational and storage costs of a node are required. Especially, such costs should not depend on the total number of sensor nodes in large-scale wireless sensor networks. Of course, a node supports only the lightweight operations such as hash functions and symmetric-key encryption.

3.2   Network Assumptions

A sensor network might contain hundreds or thousands of tiny sensor nodes which suffer from restricted computation, communication, and power resources. Most architecture also employs more powerful base station, which is in one-to-many association with sensor nodes. We assume a general multi-hop network with a set $S = \{s_1, \ldots, s_n\}$ of n sensor nodes and a single trusted base station (BS). The sensor network is mostly static with a topology known to BS. This appears to be true of many modern sensor network applications such as a building management.

We also assume that aggregation is performed over an aggregation tree, which is the directed tree formed by the union of all the paths from the sensor nodes to BS (See Section 5). An aggregation transaction begins by broadcasting a query down the tree from BS to the leaves. Then, the sensor nodes measure their environment, and send their measurements back up the tree to BS. A large building with a control network that regulates inside temperatures by measuring the temperature in each room is one example of a hierarchical structure described in [15].

Each node can evaluate both the inputs and outputs of aggregation as mentioned in [20], defined as *Boolean predicates*. Restricting each sensor to read a value $v_i \in [v_{min}, v_{max}]$, the *inputs predicate* outputs *true* if and only if $v_{min} \leq v_i \leq v_{max}$. This means that a sensor node can evaluate the readings of other nodes. In the case of SUM aggregate, consequently, the *output predicate* outputs *true* if and only if $nv_{min} \leq a \leq nv_{max}$, where a is some intermediate aggregation result and n is the total number of sensor nodes which have already contributed into a. For instance, when each sensor node s_i senses temperature in the room, we may set the legitimate sensed value as $v_i \in [0, 50]$ (°C).

3.3 Security Infrastructure

For the purpose of authentication we consider that every sensor node s_i is in possession of some secret key denoted k_i shared between s_i and BS. Each sensor node s_i has a unique identifier I_i. We assume that the sensor nodes have the ability to perform computations of a collision-resistant cryptographic hash function H and secure message authentication code $\mathrm{MAC}_K(\cdot)$ where K is the cryptographic secret key.

3.4 Adversary Model

The primary concern of this paper are *stealthy attacks* as defined in [7]. In this type of attack, the adversary controls one or more nodes, and the goal of the adversary is to cause BS to accept a false aggregate by stealth. We refer to nodes that deviate from the protocol (including benign failures) as faulty nodes. An adversary tries to not only inject its own messages (i.e., direct data injection attacks) but also replay or modify the message sent by s_i or BS. Furthermore, we consider node corruption. We do not assume any tamper-resistance property. Upon corrupting s_i, the adversary obtains full control over s_i and reveals all information kept in s_i including its secret key k_i. We do not consider denial-of-service (DoS) attacks where the goal of the adversary is to prevent BS from getting any aggregation result at all. Such an attack will easily expose the adversary's presence.

We assume a "weak adversary model", i.e., an adversary cannot obtain the secret keys of adjoining two nodes (e.g., a node s_i and its child node). In other words, if the adversary can compromise a node s_i, then he does not obtain the secret key of s_i's children. This means that the adversary can manipulate the commitment of neither s_i's children nor s_i's parent when s_i is compromised. Here, we define the direct data injection attack [1, 15] as follows.

Direct data injection attack: The attack which modifies the data readings reported by the nodes under its direct control, under the constraint that the inputs predicate outputs true, is called "direct data injection attack" [1]. If a secure aggregation scheme has Boolean predicates, it can limit the adversary's capability to perform direct data injection.

Optimal security is the concept to minimize the damaging impact of corrupted nodes on the overall aggregation result and assume the integrity of only data except for data modified by direct data injection attacks. Optimal security means that the harmful influence on the final aggregation result is proportional to only the number of corrupted nodes which perform direct data injection attacks. We can thus define an optimal level of aggregation security as follows:

Definition 1 (Optimal security [1]). *An aggregation algorithm is optimally secure if, by tampering with the aggregation process, an adversary is unable to induce the base station to accept any aggregation result which is not already achievable by direct data injection attacks.*

4   The CPS Protocol

The CPS protocol [1], which was proposed by Chan, Perrig and Song in 2006, computes the sum aggregate by three phases: *query-dissemination, aggregation-commitment* and *result-checking*. The protocol [2] is the modification of the CPS protocol. These schemes assume that the sensor network is mostly static, with a topology known to the base station (BS). The CPS protocol has been already proved to satisfy "optimal security" in [1]. The CPS protocol uses two kinds of trees: aggregation tree and commitment tree. The commitment tree can be converted to a virtual binary tree for efficiency, i.e., all nodes are set to leaf nodes in such a virtual binary tree.

4.1   Protocol Description

Query-dissemination phase. To initiate a query in the aggregation tree, BS originates a query request message and distributes it to the aggregation tree. The query request message contains an attached nonce N to prevent replay of messages belonging to a prior query. Note that this request message can be sent without an authenticated broadcast, as described in [17].

Aggregation-commitment phase. Every node calculates a message based on its own sensor reading, and sends it to its parent node. This message consists of ⟨count, value, commitment⟩, where count is the number of nodes in the subtree rooted at a node, value is the sum of all node values in the subtree, and commitment is the cryptographic commitment tree over the data values and the aggregation process in the subtree. Let v_i be a sensor reading of a node s_i. For a leaf node s_i, the message has the format $\langle 1, v_i, h_i \rangle$, where $h_i = H(N||v_i||ID_i)$ [2]. For an intermediate node, the message has the format $\langle c, v, h \rangle$ with $c = \sum c_j$, $v = \sum v_j$ and $h = H(N||c||v||\ell_1|| \ldots ||\ell_q)$, where its children have the following messages $\ell_1, \ell_2, \ldots, \ell_q$, where $\ell_j = \langle c_j, v_j, h_j \rangle$. Note that the intermediate node regards its own sensor reading as the reading from its child. In other words, the intermediate node sets a virtual leaf node as its child node. This means that all nodes are deployed as real leaf nodes and virtual leaf nodes in a binary tree. Nodes store the messages from their children, which will be used in the next result-checking phase. This result-checking phase ends with BS receiving the final message, including the final aggregate and the final commitment.

Result-checking phase. This phase has the following three steps: dissemination, check and acknowledgement.

- **Dissemination.** BS disseminates the final message to the network in an authenticated broadcast. Every node uses this message to verify that its own sensor reading was aggregated correctly. A node s_i is provided with not only the final message but also the messages of its *off-path* nodes from its parent (s_p). s_i's off-path nodes are the set of all the siblings of the nodes on

---

[2] We employ $h_i = H(N||v_i||ID_i)$ to prevent replay of messages from a leaf node, instead of $h_i = ID_i$ described in [1].

the path from s_i to BS. These are forwarded across the aggregation tree: s_p provides every child s_i with the messages of s_i's siblings in the commitment tree (an intermediate node has two children in the commitment tree), along with every off-path message received from s_p.

- **Check.** Using all off-path messages, s_i recomputes the messages of all its ancestors in the aggregation tree all the way to BS, and compares the result to the final message provided by BS.
- **Acknowledgement.** If the check succeeds, then s_i acknowledges by releasing an authentication code: $MAC_{k_i}(N\|OK)$, where OK is a unique message identifier and k_i is the secret key shared between s_i and BS. Leaf nodes send their *acks* while intermediate nodes wait for *acks* from all their children, compute the XOR of those *acks* with their own *ack*, and forward the resultant aggregated *ack* to their parent. Finally, BS has received the aggregated *ack*. If this aggregated *ack* is valid, then BS declares the aggregation successful.

4.2 Drawbacks

The CPS protocol has the following drawbacks:

- The communication overhead on each node is large. The CPS protocol requires two round-trip communications between each node and BS (one round-trip for query-dissemination phase and aggregation-commitment phase, and another round-trip for the result-checking phase) to do one aggregation procedure. Especially, the result-checking phase has the congestion of $\mathcal{O}(\log n)$.
- The computational cost at each sensor node is great. Not only BS but also each sensor node has to compute the final commitment in order to verify the integrity of its own sensor reading in the result-checking phase. Especially, a leaf node has the computational cost of $\mathcal{O}(\log n)$ in the result-checking phase.

4.3 Checking Mechanism

The result-checking phase enables the CPS protocol to satisfy "optimal security". All the honest nodes can check the validity of the own sensor reading in this phase after the final aggregation result is committed. This implies that the adversary cannot modify the sensor readings of honest nodes.

5 Our Protocol

5.1 Underlying Idea

Our goal is to do aggregation with one round-trip communication in wireless sensor networks. Our protocol achieves one round-trip communication by conducting aggregation along with the verification, based on the idea of basic tool of TESLA [25]. Also, a nonce is unnecessary in our protocol owing to one-time

MAC-key to each session, and thus it protects our protocol against replay attacks. Note that the verification delay happens because of the TESLA-like verification done by the next session, although our protocol assumes a scene that regularly needs the aggregation.

Since our protocol uses *hash chain* technique in TESLA, the number of message authentication is restricted. However, such restriction is not so significant problem because the theft of sensor nodes increases with time and moreover the sensor node works on batteries. We assume that the operating time of the sensor node is innately limited.

5.2   The Format of Message

The message in our protocol consists of ⟨count, value, identifier, commitment, confirmation⟩, where count and value are the same as the CPS protocol. The identifier of node s_i is computed as $I_i = k_{i,0} = H^\ell(k_{i,\ell})$, where ℓ is the maximum number of sessions and $k_{i,\ell}$ is the secret key of the node s_i, shared between s_i and BS. Then, $k_{i,t} = H^{\ell-t}(k_{i,\ell})$ is the secret key of MAC at session t $(1 \leq t \leq \ell - 1)$ and is also treated as a kind of identifier of s_i at the next session $t+1$, which can be verified by $I_i \stackrel{?}{=} H^t(k_{i,t})$. The commitment is the cryptographic commitment and the confirmation is the confirmation result of MAC in the previous session. For a node s_i and its descendant nodes $\{s_j\}$, the message at session t has the following message format:

$$M_{i,t} = \langle c, v, k_{i,t-1}, \mu_{k_{i,t}}, (\bigoplus_j \lambda_{k_{j,t}}) \oplus \lambda_{k_{i,t}} \rangle, \tag{1}$$

$$\text{with} \quad \mu_{k_{i,t}} = MAC_{k_{i,t}}(c||v) \quad and \quad \lambda_{k_{j,t}} = MAC_{k_{j,t}}(p_{j,t-1}),$$

where c and $v = v_{i,t} + \sum_j v_{j,t}$ are the total number of nodes and the total value of sensor readings in the subtree rooted at this node s_i, respectively. $v_{j,t}$ is a sensor reading of s_j and $p_{j,t} \in \{OK, NG\}$ is the verification result of MAC of s_j at session t. Note that if a node s_i is a leaf node then $c = 1$, $v = v_{i,t}$ and the confirmation $= \phi$ (null). Also, if the children node $(s_{j_1}, \ldots, s_{j_q})$ are all nodes on leaves then we set $c = q + 1$ including the number of s_i. Even if $k_{i,t-1}$ is exposed from $M_{i,t}$, the secret key $k_{i,t}$ of MAC cannot be computed from $k_{j,t-1}$ owing to one-wayness of H. An intermediate node s_i sends its own message and forwards its children's messages to its parent. These messages have the format: $\langle M_{i,t}, M_{j_1,t}, \ldots, M_{j_q,t} \rangle$ with s_i's message $M_{i,t}$ and its children messages $M_{j_1,t}, \ldots, M_{j_q,t}$.

5.3   Protocol Description

Our protocol starts with query-dissemination phase, which is the same as the CPS protocol, then ends with aggregation-commitment phase. It does not need the result-checking phase. In aggregation-commitment phase, two steps of confirmation and aggregation are executed. If s_i is a leaf node then it executes neither confirmation process nor aggregation process. s_i has only to send the own message M_i to its parent. Here, we assume that an intermediate node s_i with a secret key $k_{i,\ell}$ has a set of its descendant nodes $\{s_j\}$ and its children and grandchildren nodes $\{s_m\} \subset \{s_j\}$. Let t be the number of a current session. We show only the aggregation-commitment phase since the query-dissemination is the same as the CPS protocol.

Example (Aggregation-commitment phase):

- **Confirmation.** Let s_3 be a present intermediate sensor node at session t deployed in Fig.1. s_3 has preserved the information $\langle$count, value, identifier, commitment$\rangle$ of s_4, s_5, s_6 and s_7 of the previous session $t-1$. The node s_3 receives four messages $M_{4,t}$, $M_{5,t}$, $M_{6,t}$ and $M_{7,t}$ at session t. We consider the confirmation of s_6 by s_3 in this example, similar to s_4, s_5 and s_7. At first, s_3 verifies the identifier $k_{6,t-1}$ by $k_{6,t-2} \overset{?}{=} H(k_{6,t-1})$. If the verification of this identifier is valid then s_3 verifies the previous commitment $\mu_{k_{6,t-1}}$. If the verification of four commitments is valid then s_3 computes $\lambda_{k_{3,t}} = MAC_{k_{3,t}}(OK)$ and then computes $\bigoplus_{j=3}^{7} \lambda_{k_{j,t}}$ to include $M_{3,t}$. After computing the confirmation, s_3 discards $\langle$count, value, identifier, commitment$\rangle$ of s_4, s_5, s_6 and s_7 of the previous session $t-1$.

- **Aggregation.** s_3 uses these four messages to check three sensor readings $v_{4,t}$, $v_{5,t}$ and $v_{6,t}$. For checking the range of $v_{6,t}$, the node s_3 computes the difference between $(v_{6,t}+v_{7,t})$ in $M_{6,t}$ and $v_{7,t}$ in $M_{7,t}$. If $v_{min} \leq v_{4,t}, v_{5,t}, v_{6,t} \leq v_{max}$, then s_3 computes its own message:

$$M_{3,t}=\langle 5, \textstyle\sum_{j=3}^{7} v_{j,t}, \ k_{3,t-1}, \ MAC_{k_{3,t}}\big(5||\textstyle\sum_{j=3}^{7} v_{j,t}\big), \ \bigoplus_{j=3}^{7} MAC_{k_{j,t}}(p_{j,t-1})\rangle, \qquad (2)$$

where $k_{3,t-1} = H(k_{3,t})$. Then, s_3 sends its own message $M_{3,t}$ and forwards its children's messages $M_{4,t}$, $M_{5,t}$ and $M_{6,t}$ to its parent node s_1. When s_3's task is completed, s_3 preserves the information, $(1, v_4, k_{4,t-1}, \mu_{k_{4,t}})$, $(1, v_5, k_{5,t-1}, \mu_{k_{5,t}})$, $(2, v_6, k_{6,t-1}, \mu_{k_{6,t}})$ and $(1, v_7, k_{7,t-1}, \mu_{k_{7,t}})$ until the next session $t+1$. Note that s_3 need not forward $M_{7,t}$ to s_1 since $v_{7,t}$ is included in $M_{6,t}$ in Fig.1.

Protocol (Aggregation-Commitment Phase)

- **Confirmation.** The node s_i has preserved the information $\langle$count, value, identifier, commitment$\rangle$ of $\{s_m\}$ at the previous session $t-1$. When s_i receives messages from its children at session t, these messages contain both children's and grandchildren's messages. At first, s_i verifies the identifier $k_{m,t-1}$ by $k_{m,t-2} \overset{?}{=} H(k_{m,t-1})$ of $\{s_m\}$. If the verification of all identifiers of $\{s_m\}$ is valid then s_i verifies the previous commitments $\mu_{k_{m,t-1}}$ of $\{s_m\}$. If the verification of all commitments of $\{s_m\}$ is valid then s_i computes $\lambda_{k_{i,t}} = MAC_{k_{i,t}}(OK)$ and then computes $(\bigoplus_m \lambda_{k_{m,t}}) \oplus \lambda_{k_{i,t}}$ to include $M_{i,t}$. Otherwise, s_i computes the confirmation as $MAC_{k_{i,t}}(NG)$. After computing such confirmation, s_i discards $\langle$count, value, identifier, commitment$\rangle$ of the previous session $t-1$.

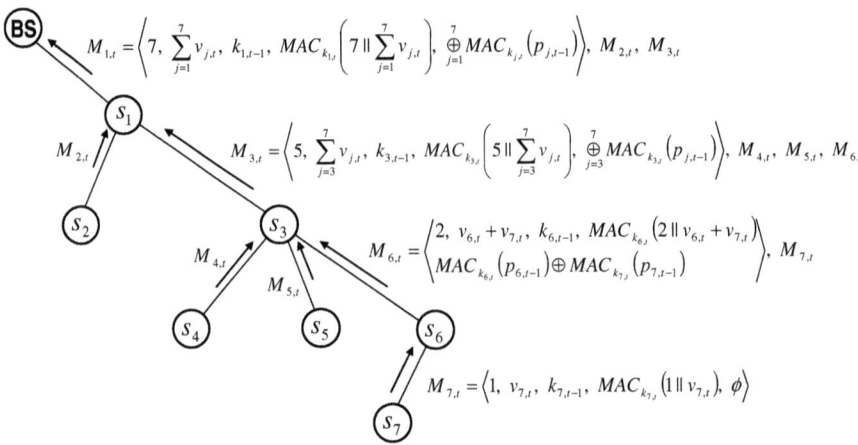

Fig. 1. Example of our protocol (session t)

- **Aggregation.** At first, s_i checks the sensor readings of children nodes using Boolean predicates (See Section 3.2). If s_i's child is a leaf node then
  s_i can directly check whether its child's sensor reading is in the range of
  $[v_{min}, v_{max}]$. Otherwise, s_i can check the range of its child's sensor reading
  by computing the difference between its child's aggregate and its grandchildren's aggregates. If sensor readings of s_i's children are out of range, then
  s_i rejects it. Otherwise, s_i computes its own message, which includes the
  aggregate at s_i (root of the subtree). Of course, s_i can obtain the values
  from its children's messages. Then, s_i sends its own message and forwards
  its children's messages to its parent. However, the node s_i need not forward
  its grandchildren's messages to its parent, because grandchildren's information is included in their children's messages. When s_i's task is completed,
  s_i preserves the information $\langle$count, value, identifier, commitment$\rangle$ of $\{s_m\}$
  until the next session $t + 1$. Finally, BS checks whether its children's sensor
  readings are in the range of $[v_{min}, v_{max}]$ in the same way as an intermediate
  node when BS has received the final messages. BS can compute the final
  commitments and the final confirmation using the secret key of each node.
  BS compares the computed confirmation with the received confirmation. If
  these results match, then BS accepts the aggregation result of the previous
  session $t - 1$. Furthermore, if the final commitments are valid, then BS preserves the aggregation result until the next session. Otherwise, BS rejects
  the result.

A node receives the messages of its children and grandchildren at most. This
means that the congestion of a node s_i is proportional to only the total number
of $\{s_m\}$.

Remark. While the CPS protocol checks the validity of the own sensor readings
in the result-checking phase, our protocol checks the validity of the children

sensor readings in the aggregation-commitment phase. In our protocol, although the node s_i cannot verify the commitment of children and grandchildren at once, we achieves one round-trip communication by conducting aggregation along with the verification, based on the idea of TESLA.

6 Analysis

In this section, we discuss security and efficiency of our protocol. In the security analysis, we prove that our protocol is optimally secure. In the efficiency, we show that the congestion (maximum amount of per-node communication) in our protocol is constant. Also, we show that the computational cost of each node in our protocol is smaller than the CPS protocol.

6.1 Security

As mentioned in Section 3.4, an adversary should have only a limited influence on the result of the aggregation computation. We show that the SUM aggregate of our protocol satisfies "optimal security" described in Definition 1, similar to the CPS protocol. We show the following lemmas before showing theorems about "optimal security". If the values are in the range of $[v_{min}, v_{max}]$, then the values can be shifted to make a range of the form $[0, r]$.

Lemma 1. *Let v_a be a sensor reading of a node s_a. If s_a's parent accepts v_a then $0 \le v_a \le r$ is satisfied in our adversary model.*

Proof. Suppose s_p, v_p $\{s_b\}$ and $\sum v$ are s_a's parent node, s_p's sensor reading, a set of s_a's children and the sum of $\{s_b\}$'s aggregates, respectively. If s_a is honest and s_p accepts v_a, then $0 \le v_a \le r$ is naturally satisfied. We consider only the case that s_a is corrupted and s_p is honest. If s_a is a leaf node then s_p can easily check v_a. In this case, if s_p accepts v_a then $0 \le v_a \le r$. If s_a is an intermediate node then s_p can check v_a by computing the difference between $(v_a + \sum v)$ and $\sum v$, where $(v_a + \sum v)$ is s_a's aggregate. Hence if s_p accepts v_a then $0 \le v_a \le r$. Consequently, if s_p accepts v_a then $0 \le v_a \le r$.   □

Lemma 2. *Suppose there are m nodes with committed (honest) sensor values $v_1, \dots, v_m$ in an aggregation subtree T_m. Then the total of aggregation values by honest nodes at the root of T_m is $\sum_{i=1}^{m} v_i$.*

Proof. We show the result of three generations: a similar reasoning applies for arbitrary m nodes. Suppose s_p, v_p $\{s_h\}$ and $\sum v$ are s_a's parent node, s_p's sensor reading, a set of s_a's honest children and the sum of $\{s_h\}$'s aggregates, respectively. When the aggregate $\sum v$ is sent to s_p at session j, s_a cannot modify $\sum v$ because s_a does not know $\{s_h\}$'s secret keys. As a result, the legitimate aggregation $\sum v$ is included in s_p's aggregate even if s_a is computed. Therefore, the total of aggregation values by honest nodes at the root of T_m is $\sum_{i=1}^{m} v_i$.   □

Theorem 1. *Let the final SUM aggregate received by BS be S. If BS accepts S then $S_L \leq S \leq (S_L + \mu r)$ where S_L is the sum of the data values of all the legitimate nodes, μ is the total number of malicious nodes, and r is the upper bound on the range of allowable values on each node.*

Proof. Let $s_1, \ldots, s_\mu$ be the nodes compromised by an adversary. The compromised node s_i $(1 \leq i \leq \mu)$ cannot manipulate the aggregates of s_i's children but it can manipulate its own sensor reading v_i. The sensor reading v_i satisfies $0 \leq v_i \leq r$ by Lemma 1. Hence it satisfies $0 \leq \mu(v_1 + \cdots + v_\mu) \leq \mu r$. Since S_L should be included in the total of aggregation values by Lemma 2, the SUM result S satisfies $S_L \leq S \leq (S_L + \mu r)$. ☐

Theorem 2. *Our protocol is optimally secure.*

Proof. Let the sum of the data values of all the legitimate nodes be S_L. Consider an adversary with μ malicious nodes which perform direct data injection attacks. An adversary causes the nodes under its control to report a sensor reading within the legal range $[0, r]$. If the adversary sets all μ nodes to have data value 0, the computed aggregate is S_L. If the adversary sets all μ nodes to have data value r, the computed aggregate is $S_L + \mu r$. Any aggregation value between these two extremes is achievable by both attacks. So, the bound of $S_L \leq S \leq (S_L + \mu r)$ by Theorem 1 is exactly on the range of possible results achievable by both attacks. Therefore, our protocol is optimally secure by Definition 1. ☐

6.2   Congestion Complexity

We now consider the congestion induced by the secure SUM aggregate. Congestion is a big problem for large-scale wireless sensor networks, so it is necessary to decrease congestion complexity. Our protocol aims to achieve the constant node congestion not to depend on the total number of nodes (n) owing to one round-trip communication without the result-checking phase. More specifically, we aim to stabilize the maximum amount of information that a single node sends and receives.

While the congestion in the CPS protocol is $\mathcal{O}(\log n)$ (strictly $\mathcal{O}(\log^2 n)$ in [1] and $\mathcal{O}(\log n)$ in [2]), the congestion of our protocol is constant, i.e., the congestion of a node s_a is proportional to only the total number of s_a's children and s_a's grandchildren. This means that our protocol is more scalable and efficient than the CPS protocol. Note that we do not mention the protocol [20] in our efficiency analysis since its congestion is less efficient compared with the CPS protocol.

Node congestion in our protocol eventually depends on the number of children nodes. Hence, the smaller the number of children nodes becomes, the lower the node congestion complexity gets in our protocol. Therefore, if the aggregation tree is composed not to grow the number of children then our protocol is more effective. Note that node congestion in our protocol does not depend on the height of aggregation tree.

Table 1. The communicational complexity and computational cost of each node at each session

		Communicational complexity		Computational cost	
		Leaf node	Intermediate node	Leaf node	Intermediate node
CPS	AC	$|H|$	$|H|(\alpha+1)$	H	H
	RC	$|M|$	$2|H|\log n_{lower} + |M|$	$H\log n + M$	$H\log n_{upper} + M$
Ours	AC	$|H|+|M|$	$(|H|+2|M|)(2\alpha+\beta+1)$	$H+M$	$(H+M)(\alpha+\beta+1)+M$

6.3 Communication Complexity

One round-trip communication between each node and BS for aggregation is desirable. While the CPS protocol required two round-trip communications, our protocol indeed requires only one round-trip communication. Here, we explain the communication complexity of an intermediate node (A leaf node is also included in Table 1.). Let n_{lower} be the number of nodes which are deployed in lower part (only descendant nodes) of a current intermediate node ($n_{lower} \leq n$), and let $|H|$ and $|M|$ be the size of H and MAC, respectively. In the aggregation-commitment phase (AC), while the size of message in the CPS protocol is almost $|H|(\alpha + 1)$ which is mainly the size of commitments that a node sends and receives, the size of message in our protocol is almost $(|H|+2|M|)(2\alpha+\beta+1)$ which is mainly the size of messages a node sends and receives, described in Table 1, where α and β are the number of children and grandchildren nodes, respectively. However, the size of message additionally requires $2|H|\log n_{lower} + |M|$ in the result-checking phase (RC) of the CPS protocol. Therefore, the communication complexity of our protocol is smaller than that of the CPS protocol in large-scale wireless sensor networks.

6.4 Computational and Storage Costs

The computational and storage costs should not depend on the total number of sensor nodes n because of its restricted computation and storage. Here, we explain the computational cost of an intermediate node (A leaf node is also included in Table 1.). We compare our protocol with the CPS protocol by the per-node computational cost described in Table 1. Let n_{upper} be the number of nodes which are deployed in upper level of a current intermediate node ($n_{upper} \leq n$), and let H and M be the computation of H and MAC, respectively. Both the CPS protocol and our protocol employ only the lightweight computation like hash function. However, the computational cost of the CPS protocol depends on the number of nodes n_{upper}, i.e., $H\log n_{upper} + M$ (a leaf node has the worst case of computational cost of $H\log n + M$), while that of our protocol does not depends on the total number of nodes, i.e., it is the constant value $(H+M)(\alpha+\beta+1)+M$ in the aggregation-commitment phase (AC). Thus, our protocol is more effective than the CPS protocol for the per-node computational cost in large-scale wireless sensor networks.

The size of extra storage in our protocol is $(|H| + |M|)(\alpha + \beta)$ compared with the CPS protocol, because a node has to preserve the messages of its children and grandchildren of the previous session. Note that a leaf node need not have such storage. However, it is not so significant problem in large-scale wireless sensor networks since the size of storage is constant, i.e., it does not depend on n.

6.5   Other Operations

The SUM aggregate is easily used to compute the total number of votes in the network, where all the nodes have value either 1 or 0. Also, the average can be easily computed by dividing the SUM aggregate by the total number of nodes. Furthermore, the proposed protocol can use the verification of Φ-quantile aggregate, as described in [1].

7   Conclusion

We proposed an efficient and optimally secure sensor network aggregation protocol for general networks and multiple corrupted nodes. Our protocol satisfies "optimal security" which guarantees that the harmful influence on the final aggregation result is proportional to only the number of corrupted nodes which perform direct data injection attacks. As a result, the influence on the total aggregate can be optimally controlled within a certain range. Furthermore, since our protocol is one round-trip communication without the result-checking phase, both the node congestion complexity and the computational cost of each node are constant in our protocol. Therefore, our protocol suits large-scale wireless sensor networks.

References

1. Chan, H., Perrig, A., Song, D.: Secure hierarchical in-network aggregation in sensor networks. In: CCS 2006, pp. 278–287. ACM, New York (2006)
2. Frikken, K.B., Dougherty, J.A.: An efficient integrity-preserving scheme for hierarchical sensor aggregation. In: WiSec 2008, pp. 68–76. ACM, New York (2008)
3. Madden, S., Franklin, M., Hellerstein, J., Hong, W.: TAG: a tiny aggregation service for ad-hoc sensor networks. In: Proc. ACM SIGOPS Operating Systems, pp. 131–146. ACM, New York (2002)
4. Yao, Y., Gehrke, J.: The cougar approach to in-network query processing in sensor networks. In: Proc. ACM SIGMOD Record, vol. 31, pp. 9–18. ACM, New York (2002)
5. Hu, L., Evans, D.: Secure aggregation for wireless networks. In: SAINT 2003, pp. 27–31. IEEE, Los Alamitos (2003)
6. Jadia, P., Mathuria, A.: Efficient secure aggregation in sensor networks. In: Bougé, L., Prasanna, V.K. (eds.) HiPC 2004. LNCS, vol. 3296, pp. 40–49. Springer, Heidelberg (2004)
7. Przydatek, B., Song, D., Perrig, A.: SIA: Secure information aggregation in sensor networks. In: SenSys 2003, pp. 255–265. ACM, New York (2003)

8. Du, W., Deng, J., Han, Y.S., Varshney, P.: A Witness-Based Approach for Data Fusion Assurance in Wireless Sensor Networks. In: GLOBECOM 2003, pp. 1435–1439. IEEE, Los Alamitos (2003)
9. Mahimkar, A., Rappaport, T.S.: SecureDAV: a secure data aggregation and verification protocol for sensor networks. In: GLOBECOM 2004, pp. 2175–2179. IEEE, Los Alamitos (2004)
10. Yang, Y., Wang, X., Zhu, S., Cao, G.: SDAP: A secure hop-by-hop data aggregation protocol for sensor networks. In: MobiHoc 2006, pp. 356–367. ACM, New York (2006)
11. Gupta, I., Van Renesse, R., Birman, K.P.: Scalable fault-tolerant aggregation in large process groups. In: DSN 2001, pp. 433–442. IEEE, Los Alamitos (2001)
12. Nath, S., Gibbons, P.B., Seshan, S., Anderson, Z.R.: Synopsis diffusion for robust aggregation in sensor networks. In: SenSys 2004, pp. 250–262. ACM, New York (2004)
13. Chen, J.Y., Pandurangan, G., Xu, D.: Robust computation of aggregates in wireless sensor networks: distributed randomized algorithms and analysis. In: IPSN 2005, pp. 348–355. IEEE, Los Alamitos (2005)
14. Manjhi, A., Nath, S., Gibbons, P.B.: Tributaries and deltas: efficient and robust aggregation in sensor network streams. In: Proc. 2005 ACM SIGMOD International Conference on Management of Data, pp. 287–298. ACM, New York (2005)
15. Wagner, D.: Resilient aggregation in sensor networks. In: SASN 2004, pp. 78–87. ACM, New York (2004)
16. Haghani, P., Papadimitratos, P., Poturalski, M., Aberer, K., Hubaux, J.P.: Efficient and robust secure aggregation for sensor networks. In: NPSec 2007, pp. 1–6. IEEE, Los Alamitos (2007)
17. Chan, H., Perrig, A.: Efficient security primitives derived from a secure aggregation algorithm. In: CCS 2008, pp. 521–534. ACM, New York (2008)
18. Zhang, W., Wang, C., Feng, T.: GP2S: Generic Privacy-Preservation Solutions for Approximate Aggregation of Sensor Data. In: PerCom 2008, pp. 179–184. IEEE, Los Alamitos (2008)
19. Castelluccia, C., Mykletun, E., Tsudik, G.: Efficient aggregation of encrypted data in wireless sensor networks. In: MOBIQUITOUS 2005, pp. 109–117. IEEE, Los Alamitos (2005)
20. Manulis, M., Schwenk, J.: Security model and framework for information aggregation in sensor networks. ACM Transactions on Sensor Networks (TOSN) 5(2) (2009)
21. Westhoff, D., Girao, J., Acharya, M.: Concealed data aggregation for reverse multicast traffic in sensor networks: encryption, key distribution, and routing adaptation. IEEE Transactions on Mobile Computing 5(10), 1417–1431 (2006)
22. He, W., Liu, X., Nguyen, H., Nahrstedt, K., Abdelzaher, T.: PDA: Privacy-preserving data aggregation in wireless sensor networks. In: INFOCOM 2007, pp. 2045–2053. IEEE, Los Alamitos (2007)
23. Ren, S.Q., Kim, D.S., Park, J.S.: A secure data aggregation scheme for wireless sensor networks. In: Thulasiraman, P., He, X., Xu, T.L., Denko, M.K., Thulasiram, R.K., Yang, L.T. (eds.) ISPA Workshops 2007. LNCS, vol. 4743, pp. 32–40. Springer, Heidelberg (2007)
24. Merkle, R.C.: Protocols for public key cryptosystems. In: IEEE S&P, pp. 122–134. IEEE, Los Alamitos (1980)
25. Perrig, A., Canetti, R., Tygar, J.D., Song, D.: Efficient Authentication and Signing of Multicast Streams over Lossy Channels. In: IEEE S&P, pp. 56–73. IEEE, Los Alamitos (2000)

An IP Traceback Mechanism against Mobile Attacker for IPv6 and PMIPv6

Jae-hoon Jang[*], Don-Gu Yeo, Dong-hee Lee, and Heung-Youl Youm

Department of information security engineering, Soonchunhyang University,
Sinchang-myeon, Asan-si, Chungcheongnam-do, Korea
{pure,h7ei,leemeca,hyyoum}@sch.ac.kr

Abstract. Many IP traceback mechanisms have been proposed to identify the source of cyber-attacks in the IPv4-based network, the so-called Internet. However, most of existing traceback work is focused on responding to cyber-attacks in the IPv4-based network. Currently, the IPv4-based network is gradually transitioning to the Next Generation Network based on IPv6. In addition, considering the importance of mobility of a portable computer and/or machine, practical traceback techniques applicable to IPv6 and Mobile IPv6 environment will become more important in the near future. In this paper, we review typical existing traceback mechanisms and PMIPv6 technique briefly and propose a traceback mechanism which can identify the source of mobile attackers in IPv6 and PMIPv6 network.

Keywords: IPv6, PMIPv6, Traceback, IP Traceback.

1 Introduction

Internet becomes essential part of everyday living of modern people. With Internet technology getting better, attacking techniques abusing vulnerabilities of hosts in the Internet have also been advanced. The security techniques like IDS (Intrusion Detection System) or IPS (Intrusion Prevention System), so-called passive security systems, have been developed to respond to these attacks. It is difficult to protect against recent attacks with only these passive security systems. Many traceback mechanisms have been proposed to identify location of various attacks which are launched in the Internet. Especially, most of IP traceback techniques have been used for post-mortem countermeasures. But, most of existing traceback mechanisms is used to trace source of attackers in the IPv4 network. Even though some traceback mechanisms that are applicable to IPv6-based network have been proposed, they still have room for improvement in terms of performance and stability. For actively responding to up-to-date attacks in NGN (Next Generation Network), efficient traceback techniques that

---

[*] "This research was supported by the MKE(Ministry of Knowledge Economy), Korea, under the ITRC(Information Technology Research Center) support program supervised by the NIPA(National IT Industry Promotion Agency)" (NIPA-2010-(C1090-1031-0005)).

Y. Chung and M. Yung (Eds.): WISA 2010, LNCS 6513, pp. 150–159, 2011.
© Springer-Verlag Berlin Heidelberg 2011

are applicable to MIPv6 (Mobile IPv6)[1] should be developed. Recent years, PMIPv6 (Proxy MIPv6)[2] that is able to support mobility of a computing device in IPv6-based network has been received lots of attention.

In this paper, we propose a traceback mechanism that is applicable to PMIPv6 environment in order to identify the source of mobile attackers moving in PMIPv6 network.

To our best knowledge, there are no traceback mechanisms which are applicable to identify attacks in PMIPv6. Our contributions are as follows;

- A novel traceback mechanism applicable to PMIPv6 environment.
- Traceback data structure for identifying mobile attackers in PMIPv6.
- Comparison results of proposed scheme with existing traceback schemes.

The rest of this paper is organized as follows. In section 2, typical existing IP traceback techniques are surveyed. In section 3, we propose a traceback mechanism for IPv6 and PMIPv6 environment. In section 4, comparison results of the proposed traceback scheme with typical existing schemes are presented. Finally, we conclude this paper with section 6.

2 Background

In this section, we briefly survey typical traceback mechanisms and PMIPv6.

2.1 Relevant Traceback Mechanisms

A traceback is defined as a technique to identify the location of attacker(s) and the partial or entire attack path over which attacks have happened.

2.1.1 iTrace (ICMP Traceback)
IETF had tried to standardize iTrace[3]. The iTrace constructs traceback data into message body field in ICMP (Internet Control Message Protocol) message with probabilistically sampling and transfer it to a victim.

Since this mechanism generates additional data traffic for traceback, it sends additional traffic overhead to network. But, this mechanism provides very good compatibility since it is based on using ICMP which can be generated at any network nodes such as routers. ICMP is widely used in existing network environment, and ICMPv6 can be also used in IPv6 environment. Therefore, it gives very good scalability and extensibility and is comparatively easy to implement and is easily applicable to existing Internet environment.

2.1.2 Hash-Based Traceback
A hash-based traceback[4, 5] can trace the attacker using single packet for attack. This mechanism uses the so-called SPIE (Source Path Isolation Engine).The SPIE consists of DGA (Data Generation Agent), SCARs (SPIE Collection and Reduction

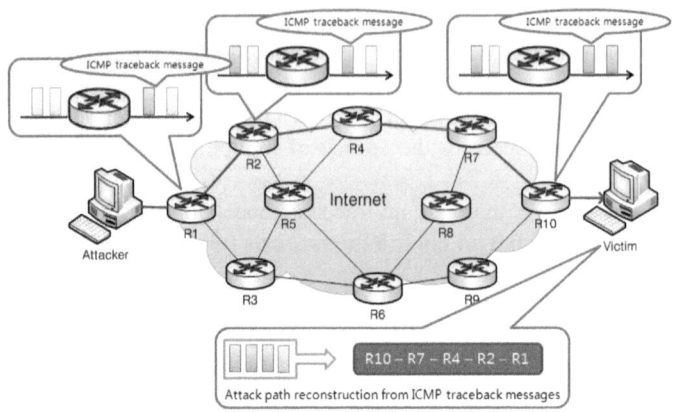

Fig. 1. iTrace (ICMP Traceback)

Agents) and STM (SPIE Traceback Manager). A DGA computes three different hash values and saves them in bloom filter form. A SCAR manages DGAs in specific network area and helps to trace the packet which passes through the network. A STM dispatches the traceback request from a victim to suitable SCAR, reconstructs attack path and manages each elements of SPIE.

2.1.3 Notification Mechanism for MIPv6 Traceback

This scheme[6] is also called signaling mechanism. In this paper, authors dealt with the traceback issues for IPv6 and MIPv6. Especially, they well described the attack scenario among MN (Mobile Node), HA (Home Agent) and CN (Correspondent Node). This scheme is not a new traceback mechanism for IPv6 and MIPv6. This scheme fundamentally uses the SPIE. In addition, authors mentioned it is improvement of SPIE. The key idea of this mechanism is based on the method that a MN notifies HA of being attacked when a MN detects attack. At this time, the ICMPv6 is used in traceback request and reply.

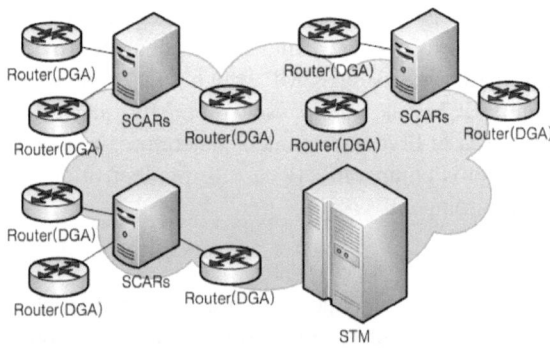

Fig. 2. SPIE for Hash-based Traceback

Type	Code	Checksum
IPv6 packet that HA tunnels to MN		

Fig. 3. ICMPv6 traceback request message for MIPv6

Type	Code	Checksum
Source address of attacker		

Fig. 4. ICMPv6 traceback reply message for MIPV6

Several IPv6-based traceback mechanisms such as [7, 8] have proposed the new traceback mechanisms for IPv6 network using notification mechanism for mobile IPv6 environment.

2.2 Overview of Proxy MIPv6

On MIPv6 standardized as IETF RFC 3775, most actions for mobility support are performed at MN (mobile node). So MIPv6 is a client-based mobility support protocol on the other hand, PMIPv6 is a network-based mobility support protocol. On PMIPv6 standardized as IETF RFC 5213, most actions for mobility support are performed at an access router or a gateway.

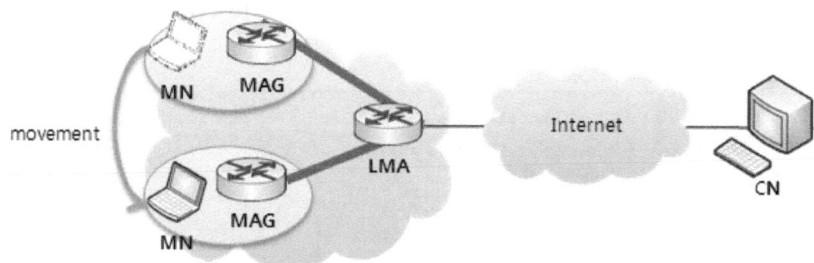

Fig. 5. Mobility for Proxy MIPv6

On PMIPv6, mobility is supported by LMA (Local Mobility Anchor) and MAG (Mobile Access Gateway). LMA can have many MAGs in a domain. MN creates own address by receiving network prefix from MAG. All of communications between inside and outside of LMA are transferred via LMA, and connections between LMA and MAGs are tunneled. LMA has global address called LMAA (LMA Address).

MAG is a first router that MN is connected to and has global address called Proxy-CoA (Proxy Care-of Address). MAG must be able to catch the attached and detached signal when MN is connected and disconnected.

In this paper, the *p-MAG* is the MAG to which attacker was connected previously and the *c-MAG* is the MAG to which attacker being connected.

3 Proposal for Traceback Mechanism in IPv6 and PMIPv6 Environment

The signaling traceback mechanism describes well the attack scenario among MN (Mobile Node), HA (Home Agent) and CN (Correspondent Node) based on SPIE. If a MN is moving in mobile IP environment in which traceback based on SPIE is supported, attack path can be reconstructed. But, it does not ensure that SPIE can identify the moving mobile attacker.

In this section, we propose an IP traceback mechanism for IPv6 and PMIPv6 to support mobility.

For the proposed traceback mechanism, following assumptions are required:

- A victim host can detect the attack(s) from mobile attacker and send a traceback request message to LMA using ICMPv6. Attack detection method is beyond the scope of this paper.
- Pass-through routers and LMAs can construct traceback data in ICMPv6 form and transfer it to victim. At this time, general pass-through router and LMA construct traceback data probabilistically, and LMAs construct traceback data for mobile attacker on PMIPv6 when receive traceback request message.

- Ingress filtering technique[9] is used. So if attack packet from invalid source is received, the packet can be discarded.

3.1 Traceback Message Structure of Proposed Mechanism

In proposed mechanism, the type field in ICMPv6 is set to 170, and a traceback data is constructed into message body in ICMPv6.

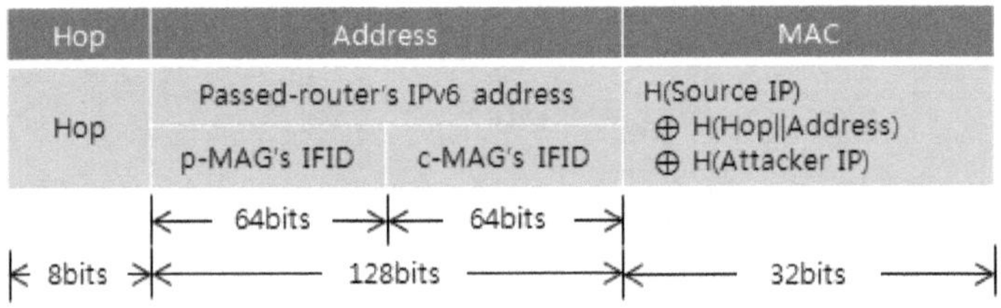

Fig. 6. Traceback message structure of proposed mechanism

Figure 6 is an overall traceback message structure for the proposed mechanism. It can be subdivided into traceback message structure in Figure 7 and Figure 8.

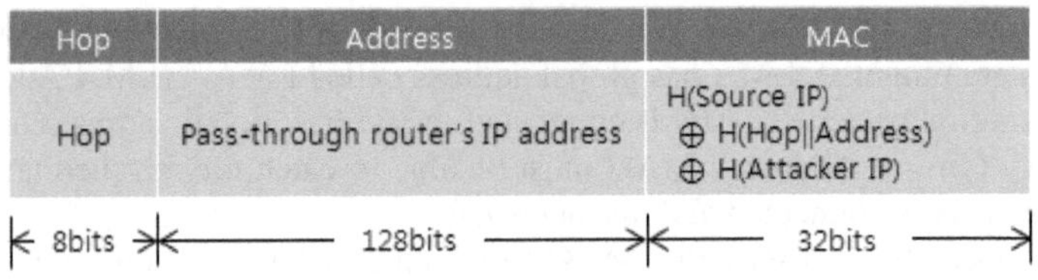

Fig. 7. Traceback message structure of proposed mechanism for IPv6

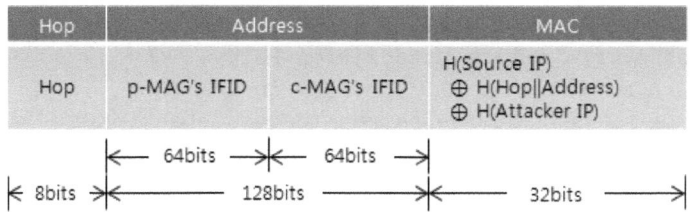

Fig. 8. Traceback message structure of proposed mechanism for PMIPv6

- Hop
  A value of Hop_Limit field in IPv6 header is used.
- Address
  In the proposed mechanism, a traceback data is transferred to a victim by using ICMPv6. So, the source address is an address of the router which constructs traceback data. At this time, *Address* field can be processed as follows:

  1. If *Address* field is equal to source address, it is a traceback data to be sent from general IPv6 router.
  2. If *Address* field is NOT equal to source address, the source address can be seen LMAA. If the interface address of *p-MAG* and *c-MAG* are combined with the network address of LMAA, they are migration path of mobile attacker.

- MAC
  MAC is provided to confirm an attacker and availability of the traceback data. *MAC* field contains result of XORing of hash values of the following three parameters:

  1. Source address (address of router or LMA which constructs traceback data)
  2. A values of *Hop* and *Address* field in traceback data
  3. An attacker's IP address

Following is a pseudo-code of a traceback data construction process.

Traceback data construction procedure

```
At pass-through router R:
    Let S be a sampled attack packet with probability p
    Let I be an ICMPv6 message for traceback data
    Let T be a traceback data
    Write 170 into I.Type
    Write S.Hop_Limit into T.Hop
    Write R.IP into T.Address
    Compute R.MAC = Hash(R.IP)
                  ⊕ Hash(T.Hop||T.Address)
                  ⊕ Hash(S.SourceIP)
    Write R.MAC into T.MAC
```

```
At LMA received traceback request from victim:
   Let A be a mobile attacker on PMIPv6
   IF A move from p-MAG to c-MAG in LMA THEN
      Let I be a ICMPv6 packet for traceback data
      Let T be a traceback data
      Write 170 into I.Type
      Write S.Hop_Limit into T.Hop
      Write p-MAG.IFID||c-MAG.IFID into T.Address
      Compute LMA.MAC = Hash(LMA.IP)
                        ⊕ Hash(T.Hop||T.Address)
                        ⊕ Hash(S.SourceIP)
      Write LMA.MAC into T.MAC
   ENDIF
```

3.2 Attack Path Reconstruction Process

Figure 9 illustrates attack path reconstruction process based for our proposed traceback mechanism.

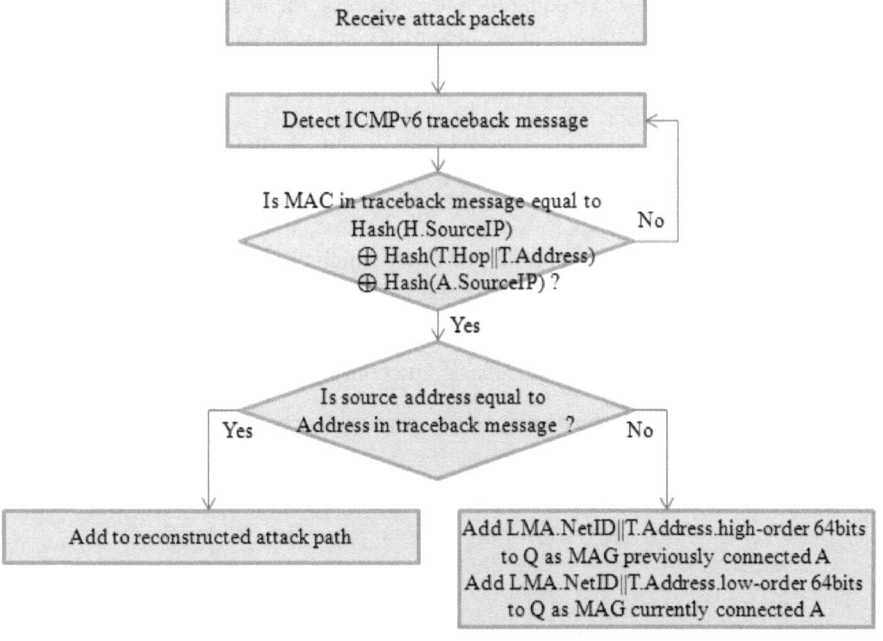

Fig. 9. Attack path reconstruction process

As shown in Figure 7 and Figure 8, a proposed traceback mechanism has different field structures when are used on general pass-through router or MAGs. Once a victim has received traceback data, it can distinguish the type of message fields. In a proposed mechanism, source address is an address of the router because a traceback data is transferred in ICMPv6 form.

Following is a pseudo-code of the attack path reconstruction process.

Attack path reconstruction procedure at victim V:

```
IF detect an attack from attacker A
  For each packet X containing traceback data
    Let Q be a reconstructed attack path
    Let H be a IPv6 header in X
    Let I be a ICMPv6 message in X
    Let T be a traceback data in X
    IF I.Type = 170 THEN
      Extract all of elements from T
      Classify H by T.Hop
      Compute V.MAC = Hash(H.SourceIP)
                    ⊕ Hash(T.Hop||T.Address)
                    ⊕ Hash(A.SourceIP)
      IF T.MAC = V.MAC THEN
        IF T.Address = H.SourceIP THEN
          Add H.SourceIP to Q
        ELSE IF T.Address != H.SourceIP THEN
          Let LMA.NetID be a H.SourceIP.NetID
          Add LMA.NetID||T.Address.high-order 64bits
            to Q as p-MAG
          Add LMA.NetID||T.Address.low-order 64bits
            to Q as c-MAG
        ENDIF
      ELSE
        Discard X
      ENDIF
    ENDIF
ENDIF
```

4   Analysis and Comparison

Table 1 shows qualitative comparison and Table 2 shows quantitative comparison of a proposed mechanism with the existing mechanisms. In Table 2, a signaling mechanism is not mentioned because it uses SPIE.

Table 1. Qualitative comparison of proposed scheme with the exisitsing mechanisms

	iTrace	Hash-based traceback	Signaling mechanism	Proposed mechanism
Management system overhead	Low	High	High	Low
Extensibility	High	Low	Low	High
IPv6 support	Yes	Yes	Yes	Yes
Mobility support	No	No	Yes	Yes

In Table 1, management system overhead means the overhead required for managing the traceback system. The Hash-based traceback and signaling mechanism use SPIE. SPIE has the higher management overhead because use SCARs and STM. But iTrace and proposed traceback mechanism have lower management overhead since they use ICMPv6.

It is difficult to expect high scalability/extensibility for SPIE because the method for construction and management of traceback data and attack path reconstruction process is already determined. The iTrace and proposed mechanism are expected to have high scalability/extensibility since they use ICMPv6.

All of the aforementioned schemes support IPv6 but, they are not considered in aspect of mobile IP environment. SPIE can reconstruct the attack path and signaling mechanism deals with each scenario well but, identifying the moving mobile attacker is not easy. Only proposed mechanism is designed to identify the moving mobile attacker on PMIPv6.

Table 2. Quantitative comparison of proposed scheme with the existing mechanisms

		iTrace	**Hash-based traceback**	**Proposed mechanism**
Network overhead	**Qualitative**	Normal	Low	Normal
	Quantitative	Variable	No-additional overhead	160bits
Router overhead	**Qualitative**	Normal	High	Normal
	Quantitative	Variable	At least 480bits	160bits

In case of network overhead, the schemes using SPIE have no effects. But, the iTrace and proposed mechanism generates additional data traffic since they use ICMPv6. The size of the traceback data for iTrace is variable because iTrace provides many functions and information. The proposed mechanism generates traceback data with fixed size, 160bits.

Router overhead means the overhead required when router constructs and computes a traceback data. SPIE requires DGA module on router. A DGA module requires high overhead for router because it computes at least 480 bits and saves data in bloom filter form. A computed traceback data of iTrace has variable size because the size of traceback data is not fixed. Proposed mechanism computes data of 160bits and hash operation three times.

5   Conclusion

In this paper, we briefly surveyed typical existing traceback mechanisms. However, we have found that they are unable to be applicable to trace the source of mobile attackers in the IPv6 environment. To overcome this difficulty, we propose a novel traceback mechanism that is applicable to IPv6 and PMIPv6 environment. We proved that our proposed mechanism supports traceability for attacker in PMIPv6 as well as IPv6 environment. In addition, our proposed mechanism has high extensibility and comparatively low overhead.

Traceback techniques have to be studied for IPv6 based NGN. Our future work will be focused on simulating our proposed scheme and global standardization work for t traceback mechanisms that are applicable to all-IP environment.

References

1. IETF RFC 3775, Mobility Support in IPv6 (2004)
2. IETF RFC 3213, Proxy Mobile IPv6 (2008)
3. Bellovin, S., Leech, M., Taylor, T.: ICMP Traceback Messages (February 2003)
4. Snoeren, A.C., Partridge, C., Sanchez, L.A., Jones, C.E., Tchakountio, F., Schwartz, B., Kent, S.T., Timothy Strayer, W.: Single-Packet IP Traceback. IEEE/ACM Transactions on Networking, 721–734 (December 2002)
5. Timothy Strayer, W., Jones, C.E., Tchakountio, F., Hain, R.R.: SPIE-IPv6: Single IPv6 Packet Traceback. In: Proceedings of the 29th Annual IEEE International Conference on Local Computer Networks, pp. 118–125 (November 2004)
6. Lee, H.C.J., MA, M., Thing, V.L.L., Xu, Y.: On the Issues of IP Traceback for IPv6 and Mobile IPv6. In: Proceedings of the IEEE International Symposium on Computers and Communication, pp. 582–587 (July 2003)
7. Amin, S.O., Kang, M.S., Hong, C.S.: A Lightweight IP Traceback Mechanism on IPv6. In: Zhou, X., Sokolsky, O., Yan, L., Jung, E.-S., Shao, Z., Mu, Y., Lee, D.C., Kim, D.Y., Jeong, Y.-S., Xu, C.-Z. (eds.) EUC Workshops 2006. LNCS, vol. 4097, pp. 671–680. Springer, Heidelberg (2006)
8. Kim, R.-H., Jang, J.-H., Youm, H.-Y.: An Efficient IP Traceback mechanism for the NGN based on IPv6 Protocol. In: JWIS 2009 (August 2009)
9. IETF RFC-2827, Network Ingress Filtering: Defeating Denial of Service Attacks which employ IP Source Address Spoofing (2000)

Hidden Credential Retrieval without Random Oracles

Atsuko Miyaji[1], Mohammad Shahriar Rahman[1], and Masakazu Soshi[2]

[1] School of Information Science, Japan Advanced Institute of Science and Technology
1-1 Asahidai, Nomi, Ishikawa, Japan 923-1292
{miyaji,mohammad}@jaist.ac.jp
[2] School of Information Sciences, Hiroshima City University
3-4-1, Ozuka-higashi Asa-Minami-Ku, Hiroshima, Japan 731-3194
soshi@hiroshima-cu.ac.jp

Abstract. To address the question of secure and efficient management of the access credentials so that a user can store and retrieve them using a 'short and easy-to-remember' password in a connected world, X. Boyen proposed a user-centric model in ASIACCS'09, named Hidden Credential Retrieval (HCR). The protocol was shown secure under random-oracle model. However, the construction does not explicitly prevent an HCR server from colluding with the third party service provider (i.e., an online bank), which can result into retrieving the hidden credential without the user's participation. In this paper[1], we show the HCR construction without the random-oracles with enhanced properties based on Okamoto's blind signature scheme proposed in TCC'06. For the "Insider attack" model, we provide the attacker (server) with more computational ability in trying to recover the plaintext message from the ciphertext that has been stored in the server by the user, being completely offline. Moreover, we include an explicit notion of identity ID that is useful in practice, so that the server knows whose encrypted credential is to be used in the protocol.

1 Introduction

Digital credentials prove something about their owner. It may contain personal information such as a person's name, birthplace, and birthdate, or biometric information such as a picture or a finger print, or some property, status, or right of its owner without revealing the owner's identity. Credentials are issued by organizations that ascertain the authenticity of the information and can be provided to verifying entities on demand. As the network world is growing in volume offering many services online, concerns also grow about the management of the required credentials to access those services. Various credentials have different formats- from simple to too complex, and it is difficult for the owners to remember or carry all the credentials with them. Here comes the question of

---

[1] This study is partly supported by Grant-in-Aid for Scientific Research (C), 20500075.

Y. Chung and M. Yung (Eds.): WISA 2010, LNCS 6513, pp. 160–174, 2011.

secure and efficient management of the credentials so that a user can store and retrieve them using a 'short and easy-to-remember' password.

Although many existing solutions can be employed to provide such a service, those solutions require certain assumptions on the distribution of the password secure against only a subset of the possible attackers. To solve this, a credential retrieval protocol that provides no explicit success/failure feedback to either party is required such that on the correct password, the user (alone) receives the correct decrypted plaintext, and the user retrieves a pseudo-random string that varies with the password on the incorrect password input. So, the trick is to keep the unauthenticated password-encrypted data on a server, and perform the retrieval and decryption in a single oblivious password-based protocol such that the failure is noticed to no party. When implemented correctly, this strategy offers the best protection against every (computationally-bounded) adversary, for every distribution of the password and the plaintext. It is optimal against both the outsiders who try one password at a time attempting to impersonate one party to the other, and the insiders who can simulate the protocol offline to create a list of plaintexts from the password dictionary. In order to avoid the successful password-recovery by the attacker, it is required that there is no information leaked on success/failure status- thus making the task as hard as exhaustive search. This situation is extremely desirable for security from the user's point of view, assuming low- or no-redundancy secret data. To achieve this, Hidden Credential Retrieval (HCR) has been proposed by X. Boyen in ASIACCS'09 [7] which requires a non-standard discrete-log-type hardness assumption in the random-oracle model. HCR refers to a client-server mechanism whereby the client (a user) can deposit a 'credential', or cryptographic key for some third-party service, on the server, remotely retrievable using a short password. Neither the server nor the communication network are trusted by the client: in particular, the server should not be able to learn either the password or the stored credential.

The whole premise of HCR of [7] is that the thing being hidden/encrypted is the credential that the user needs to use it when interacting with another party for online authentication (for example, the web server of an online bank, but not the server storing the hidden credential, the HCR server). Let us consider a real world scenario when this party colludes with the HCR server to recover the user's credential. This is particularly important for cloud infrastructure where users store their credentials in a server (HCR), and use some service from an online bank which also uses the cloud infrastructure. Now, after the user has stored his credential in an HCR server and has registered with the online bank, the HCR server and the bank may try to collude to retrieve the hidden credential without any participation of that user. Boyen's work have not addressed such a scenario for his proposed HCR scheme explicitly. Also, it is not clear from Boyen's scheme how the HCR identifies an user, and replies to the user's request. This is important for practical implementation where there can be thousands of users registered with an HCR server.

In this paper, we will often have brief visits to Boyen's work as our work follows the basic framework of the original HCR.

1.1 Related Work

In this section, we will have a look at some of the existing techniques that are closely related to the concept of HCR. A detailed discussion and comparison with many of them can be found in [7].

Multi-Party Computation: Two or more parties can compute a public function while keeping their respective inputs secret using general Multi-Party Computation (MPC) [9,14,23]. HCR may be viewed as a special kind of MPC. Where the characterization of HCR as mere MPC fails, is in the existing MPC protocols' difficulty to have the parties reuse their secret inputs, which is essential in HCR due to the need to keep the plaintext hidden from the storage server.

Oblivious Transfer and Private Information Retrieval: Oblivious Transfer (OT) allows a receiver to obtain the messages designated by its indices, "obliviously", i.e., without the sender learning anything about the indices, or the recipient about the remaining messages [3,20]. Private Information Retrieval (PIR) is a type of OT where queries should remain secret from the sender only focusing on the privacy of the recipient [11,13]. The idea of OT and PIR fails to provide a suitable HCR as because of the need to represent the password-to-plaintext map as an explicit database, of size linear in the admissible password space. On the other hand, in Encrypted Keyword Search (EKS), an encrypted data on the server is remotely searchable by the client against pre-programmed keywords using encrypted queries [6,1]. However, it also does not provide a way to construct HCR as the client first needs to commit to a manageable sized password space, and then set up the server with one encrypted searchable string per password.

Password-Authenticated Key Exchange(PAKE): PAKE allows two parties to share a short password for establishing an authenticated secure channel across an adversarially controlled medium allowing the client to keep the password secret from the server [2,16]. These protocols require explicit authentication since their main purpose is to provide mutual authentication in which case notifying the success or failure is necessary, where as HCR does not require this as this can result into an offline password test for the server.

Blind Signatures: The notion of blind signature protocols is such that they allow a user to obtain signatures from a signer on any document in such a manner that the signer learns nothing about the message that is being signed [12,4,21]. Since the concept of blind signatures was introduced by [12], it has been used in many applications including electronic voting and electronic cash. While [12] was based on RSA, and [4] proposed a blind signature based on the bilinear pairings, both of the constructions are showed secure in the random-oracle model from suitable complexity assumptions. On the other hand, [21] proposed a blind signature scheme based on bilinear pairings which is secure without random-oracles from 2SDH assumptions. The blind signature scheme of [21] is much more efficient than the other blind signature schemes in the standard model such as the Camenisch-Koprowski-Warinsch [8] and Juels-Luby-Ostrovsky [15] schemes, and is also almost as efficient as the most efficient blind signature schemes whose security has been analyzed heuristically or in the random oracle model. HCR can be constructed from these blind signatures by setting the message as the password. However, blind signatures provide public verification feature, thus being more powerful than HCR which supports no such verification functions.

Boyen proposed HCR [7] based on Boldyreva's blind signature scheme [4]. The Boldyreva signature is very efficient using a bilinear pairing for its implementation, requiring a GDH assumption for its security reduction, in the random-oracle model. Boyen modified that scheme to build a concrete HCR protocol in prime-order abelian groups under the same assumption without the pairing requirement (since the signing function alone is sufficient to construct an HCR protocol). But it suffers from relying on the random-oracle model (using hash functions). However, the random oracle model cannot be realized in the standard (plain) model. Schemes constructed in random-oracle model do not rule out the possibility of breaking the scheme without breaking the underlying intractability assumption. Nor do they even rule out the possibility of breaking the scheme without finding some kind of weakness in the hash function, as shown by [10]. Moreover, Boyen's HCR does not address the problem when the HCR server and the third party service provider (i.e. online bank) try to collude to retrieve the crdential. Also, it does not clarify how an HCR server can identify a user requesting for her credentials, so that the server knows whose stored ciphertext is to be used in the protocol.

1.2   Our Contribution

In this paper, we show the HCR construction without random-oracles with enhanced properties based on Okamoto's blind signature scheme [22] under 2SDH assumption. For the "Insider attack" model, we provide the attacker (server) with more computational ability in trying to recover the plaintext message from the ciphertext that has been stored in the server by the user, being completely offline. This feature is particularly important to be addressed when the HCR server colludes with the third party service provider in order to retrieve the credential. We also enable the HCR server to identify a requesting user with its ID. Having an explicit notion of identity ID is useful in practice, so that the server knows whose stored ciphertext to use in the protocol. This ID is simple, public, and ideally chosen by the user.

Organization of the paper: The remainder of this paper is organized as follows: Section 2 presents the assumptions and an abstract view on the protocol model. Section 3 describes the security requirements and definitions. Section 4 includes protocol construction and a security analysis. We give some concluding remarks in Section 5.

2   Preliminary

In this section, we will give an outline of our HCR, assumptions, adversarial threat models, and definitions.

2.1   Outlining HCR

The Hidden Credential Retrieval model involves three entities: a preparer $\mathcal{P}$, a querier $\mathcal{Q}$, and a server $\mathcal{S}$. $\mathcal{P}$ and $\mathcal{Q}$ represent a user during the setup (preparing) and the query (retrieval) phases of the protocol. $\mathcal{S}$ is the server having unlimited amount of storage capability, and where a user stores his/her retrievable credentials. In general, HCR consists of the following two protocols:

Store: $\langle \mathcal{P}([P, M], ID), \mathcal{S}[\bot]\rangle \to \langle (C, ID), (C, ID)\rangle$
  This protocol is the initial setup phase, and assumed to be done once over a secure channel. In this phase, a user acts as the preparer $\mathcal{P}$ and $\mathcal{S}$ is the selected storage server. *Store*'s purpose is to set up the long-term secrets, especially that of server's. In a practical setting, a user must have selected a server with which to get services, and must be able to communicate securely with it for the initial setup: this is done in the usual way in HCR where we require an authentic private channel for the setup phase. The reason is to provide $\mathcal{P}$ the ability to limit the disclosure of ciphertext to $\mathcal{S}$ it trusts to act as an insider. By definition, as we will see, the knowledge of ciphertext separates an "insider" from an "outsider". The user $\mathcal{P}$ also registers its id ID. This ID can be public, and ideally chosen by the user. It can be transmitted in the clear later in retrieval phase in the messages, and it plays no role in the security.
  - $\mathcal{P}$ takes two private inputs: a memorable password P and a plaintext credential M. $\mathcal{P}$ also picks its ID on its own choice.
  - $\mathcal{S}$ takes no private input, denoted by the null symbol.
  At the end of the protocol, $\mathcal{S}$ will have acquired a private credential ciphertext C and the ID of user $\mathcal{P}$. Although C is intended for $\mathcal{S}$ alone, $\mathcal{P}$ can learn it too; but nobody else should. ID is simple, plain, and can be known publicly.

Retrieve: $\langle \mathcal{Q}([P'], ID), \mathcal{S}([C'], ID)\rangle \to \langle M', \bot\rangle$
  This protocol can be repeated for any number of times over adversarial channels between the user (named as $\mathcal{Q}$) and the server $\mathcal{S}$.
  - The querier $\mathcal{Q}$ takes one private input: a password P'. It also takes its public value ID.
  - The server $\mathcal{S}$ takes one private input: a ciphertext C'. It also takes the public identifier ID of the requesting querier $\mathcal{Q}$.
  At the end of this protocol, $\mathcal{S}$ learns $\bot$, or nothing at all; whereas $\mathcal{Q}$ retrieves a plaintext M' which is a deterministic function of both parties' inputs. M' must satisfy the following condition with respect to the inputs used by $\mathcal{P}$ and $\mathcal{S}$ in the *Store* protocol:
  $(P' = P) \wedge (C' = C) \Rightarrow (M' = M)$

It is important that, neither of $\mathcal{S}$ and $\mathcal{Q}$ can learn the fact whether $\mathcal{Q}$ could retrieve the correct M from this protocol. We suppose that the password P is always drawn uniformly from a public dictionary D, and that, in the view of the adversary, the prior distribution of the plaintext M is uniform over the whole domain $\{0,1\}^k$ (and which in the concrete protocol is further represented as an element of $\mathbb{G}$). This is because, as we will see in the security definitions, M is drawn from a subset MS about which the adversary has no prior information other than $MS \subseteq \{0,1\}^k$.

2.2   Bilinear Groups

Let $(\mathbb{G}_1, \mathbb{G}_2)$ be bilinear groups as follows:
1. $\mathbb{G}_1$ and $\mathbb{G}_2$ are two cyclic groups of prime order p, where possibly $\mathbb{G}_1=\mathbb{G}_1$,
2. g_1 is a generator of $\mathbb{G}_1$ and g_2 is a generator of $\mathbb{G}_2$,
3. ψ is an isomorphism from $\mathbb{G}_2$ to $\mathbb{G}_1$, with $\psi(g_2) = g_1$,
4. e is a non-degenerate bilinear map $e : \mathbb{G}_1 \times \mathbb{G}_2 \to \mathbb{G}_T$, where $|\mathbb{G}_1| = |\mathbb{G}_2| = |\mathbb{G}_T| = p$, i.e.,
    (a) Bilinear: for all $u \in \mathbb{G}_1$, $v \in \mathbb{G}_2$ and $a, b \in \mathbb{Z}, e(u^a, v^b) = e(u,v)^{ab}$,
    (b) Non-degenerate: $e(g_1, g_2) \neq 1$ (i.e., $e(g_1, g_2)$ is a generator of $\mathbb{G}_T$),
5. e, ψ and the group action in $\mathbb{G}_1, \mathbb{G}_2$ and $\mathbb{G}_T$ can be computed efficiently.

2.3   Assumptions

Here we use the assumption from [22], the 2-variable strong Diffie-Hellman (2SDH) assumption on which the security of the proposed signature scheme (i.e. the HCR) is based.

Variant of q 2-Variable Strong Diffie-Hellman (q-2SDH$_S$) Problem
The q-2SDH$_S$ problem in $(\mathbb{G}_1, \mathbb{G}_2)$ is defined as follows: given a $(3q + 4)$-tuple
$(g_1, g_2, w_2 \leftarrow g_2^x, u_2 \leftarrow g_2^y, g_2^{\frac{y+b_1}{x+a_1}}, \dots, g_2^{\frac{y+b_q}{x+a_q}}, a_1, \dots, a_q, b_1, \dots, b_q)$ as input, output $(\sigma \leftarrow g_1^{\frac{y+d}{\theta x+\rho}}, \alpha \leftarrow g_2^{\theta x+\rho}, d)$ as well as $Test(\alpha) \leftarrow (U, V)$, where $a_1, \dots, a_q, b_1, \dots, b_q, d, \theta, \rho \in \mathbb{Z}_p^*$; $w_1 \leftarrow \psi(w_2), \sigma, U \in \mathbb{G}_1$; $\alpha, V \in \mathbb{G}_2$; and

$$e(\sigma, \alpha) = e(g_1, u_2 g_2^d), \quad e(U, \alpha) = e(w_1, w_2) \cdot e(g_1, V), \quad d \notin \{b_1, \dots, b_q\} \quad (1)$$

Algorithm $\mathcal{A}$ has advantage, $Adv_{2SDH_S}(q)$, in solving q-2SDH$_S$ in $(\mathbb{G}_1, \mathbb{G}_2)$ if

$$Adv_{2SDH_S}(q) \leftarrow Pr[\mathcal{A}(g_1, g_2, w_2, u_2, g_2^{\frac{y+b_1}{x+a_1}}, \dots, g_2^{\frac{y+b_q}{x+a_q}}, a_1, \dots, a_q, b_1, \dots, b_q)$$
$$= (\sigma, \alpha, d, Test(\alpha))] \quad (2)$$

where Eq.(1) holds. The probability is taken over the random choices of $g_2 \in \mathbb{G}_2, x, y, a_1, b_1, \dots, a_q, b_q \in \mathbb{Z}_p^*$, and the coin tosses of $\mathcal{A}$.

Definition 1. *Adversary $\mathcal{A}$ (t, ϵ)-breaks the q-2SDH$_S$ problem if $\mathcal{A}$ runs in time at most t and $Adv_{2SDH_S}(q)$ is at least ϵ. The (q, t, ϵ)-2SDH$_S$ assumption holds if no adversary $\mathcal{A}$ (t, ϵ)-breaks the q-2SDH$_S$ problem.*

We occasionally drop q, t, ϵ, S and refer to the 2SDH assumption rather than the (q, t, ϵ)-2SDH$_S$ assumption denoting a polynomial number of q, a polynomial-time of t and negligible probability of ϵ in security parameter n. A detailed discussion on the assumption can be found in [22].

3   Security Requirements

In this section, we first have a brief look at the threat model informally. Then we will provide game-based definitions to formalize the security requirements capturing all the required properties. To state informally:

- Passive eavesdroppers should gain no computational advantage in recovering M or P by observing arbitrarily many protocol execution transcripts between the two honest players $\mathcal{Q}$ and $\mathcal{S}$.
- An active adversary impersonates $\mathcal{Q}$ or $\mathcal{S}$, or modifies messages between $\mathcal{Q}$ and $\mathcal{S}$. Allowed with maximum one guess test per protocol execution, it should gain no advantage in learning anything other than whether a particular password guess P' is correct or not.
- Even though the server $\mathcal{S}$ is entrusted with the ciphertext C, recovering the corresponding plaintext M efficiently should not be possible more than by running a brute-force offline dictionary attack against the encryption password P. Even arbitrarily many protocol executions with the user $\mathcal{Q}$ should not enable $\mathcal{S}$ to recover M.
- The retrieval protocol itself should be blind, i.e., keep the password invisible to the server.
- The retrieval protocol should also be oblivious, i.e., not disclose its success to either party.
- The encrytion of message M into ciphertext C has to be redundancy-free.

If the plaintext M is a random access key for a separate third-party service, then under the above conditions, it will be impossible for the server to recover the password (or the plaintext) in an offline dictionary attack. We assume that the server $\mathcal{S}$ is partially trusted, and we explicitly allow it to misbehave. On the other hand, the user is ultimately trusted, since all the data belong to him.

3.1   Oracles for Validity Tests

In this model, the attacker will not know a priori the set $MS \subseteq \{0, 1\}^k$ of admissible plaintexts from which the correct message M is to be drawn uniformly. We have the following oracles:

- $\mathcal{TO}_1$ captures the offline recognition of a potentially valid plaintext on the basis of its intrinsic redundancy: $\mathcal{TO}_1[M'] = 1$ means that M' is well-formed, i.e., it is in the set MS, though it is not necessarily correct.
- $\mathcal{TO}_2$ requires an online component and the cooperation of a third party to run an expensive but perfectly accurate validity check: $\mathcal{TO}_2[M'] = 1$ indicates that M' is usable in stead of the correct M with the third party, and thus typically that M' is the correct M.

- $\mathcal{TO}_3$ captures the feature that being offline and given a valid C, runs an expensive validity check: $\mathcal{TO}_3[M''] = 1$ indicates that any M'' is usable in stead of the correct M. $\mathcal{TO}_3$ makes sense when a third party colludes with the HCR server to recover the user's credential. This oracle is only available to the "Insider".

3.2 Outsider Security

We define the privacy model against outsider attacks. It is based on the following game, played between an adversary $\mathcal{A}$ and a challenger $\mathcal{B}$. The challenger simulates all the parties in the HCR protocol. We consider $\mathcal{Q}$ and $\mathcal{S}$, and exclude $\mathcal{P}$ from consideration as it communicates with $\mathcal{S}$ over a secure channel. The outsider adversary acts passively when it makes requests for transcripts of *Retrieve* protocol between $\mathcal{Q}$ and $\mathcal{S}$.

Besides passive eavesdropping, the adversary can also actively impersonate $\mathcal{Q}$ to $\mathcal{S}$, or $\mathcal{S}$ to $\mathcal{Q}$, by interfering the concurrent but independent protocol executions. (It cannot corrupt or read the internal state of any of the actual players.) The following is the attack game analogous to the attack game in [7]:

Game 1:

- **Initialization:** $\mathcal{B}$ privately simulates an execution of the *Store* protocol between $\mathcal{P}$ and $\mathcal{S}$, for a random password $P \in \{0,1\}^n$ and a random message $M \in \{0,1\}^n$.

The distribution of M is assumed to be uniform over some subset $MS \subseteq \{0,1\}^k$, such that $\forall m \in \{0,1\}^k$: $m \in MS \Leftrightarrow \mathcal{TO}_1[m] = 1$. MS is thus the set of well-formed plaintexts, and is a parameter of the game but is not given to $\mathcal{A}$. This is to force $\mathcal{A}$ to make accountable calls to the $\mathcal{TO}_1$-oracle if it wants to test candidate messages for membership to MS.

- **Eavesdropping queries:** $\mathcal{A}$ can adaptively request to see the transcript of a random execution between $\mathcal{Q}$ and $\mathcal{S}$, in which $\mathcal{Q}$ uses the correct password $P' = P$.

- **Impersonation queries:** $\mathcal{A}$ can adaptively send messages to $\mathcal{S}$ or to $\mathcal{S}$; it immediately obtains the corresponding reply if any reply is due.

- **Offline validity tests:** $\mathcal{A}$ can make adaptive calls to the offline oracle $\mathcal{TO}_1$ on any string of its choice. The response indicates whether the string belongs in MS.

- **Online validity tests:** $\mathcal{A}$ can make adaptive calls to the online oracle $\mathcal{TO}_2$ on any string of its choice. The response indicates whether the string is the correct message M.

- **Message guess:** $\mathcal{A}$ eventually outputs one guess $\tilde{M}$ for the value of M.

- **Adjudication:** The adversary wins if $\tilde{M} = M$.

Definition 2. *The advantage of an adversary $\mathcal{A}$ in a (w, q, t_1, t_2)-outsider attack is defined as the probability that $\mathcal{A}$ wins the Game 1, when $\mathcal{A}$ makes a total of w passive eavesdropping queries, q active impersonation queries, and t_1 and t_2 calls to $\mathcal{TO}_1$ and $\mathcal{TO}_2$, respectively.*

3.3   Insider Security

The user ($\mathcal{P}$ or $\mathcal{Q}$) is trusted, and the only possible insider attacker is $\mathcal{S}$ (or any entity that has managed to acquire C from $\mathcal{S}$, and which is thus equivalent to $\mathcal{S}$). This game is played between a malicious server $\mathcal{A}_S$ and a challenger $\mathcal{B}$. $\mathcal{B}$ simulates the trusted user $\mathcal{P}$ and $\mathcal{Q}$. As in the full protocol, the attack may have two phases. The first one contains a single execution of the *Store* protocol between $\mathcal{P}$ and $\mathcal{A}_S$; the second may be run by the adversary as many number of independent executions of *Retrieve* between $\mathcal{Q}$ and $\mathcal{A}_S$ as it wants, and in which $\mathcal{Q}$ will use the correct password $P' = P$. $\mathcal{A}_S$ wants to recover M. In our definition, the notion of insider security adds the fact to the original definition that the adversary tries to guess the valid (M, P) pair right after the *Store* phase by interacting with $\mathcal{TO}_3$.

The insider attack game proceeds as follows:

Game 2:

- **Storage interaction:** $\mathcal{B}$, acting on behalf of $\mathcal{P}$, picks a random password $P \in \{0,1\}^n$ and a random message $M \in MG \subseteq \{0,1\}^k$, and engages in the *Store* protocol with the adversary $\mathcal{A}_S$.

- **Offline recovery tests:** $\mathcal{A}_S$ can make adaptive calls to the offline oracle $\mathcal{TO}_3$ on stored ciphertext C and any string M'' of its choice. The response indicates whether the string is usable instead of the correct M.

- **Retrieval interactions:** $\mathcal{B}$, acting on behalf of $\mathcal{Q}$, initiates the *Retrieve* protocol multiple times with the adversary $\mathcal{A}_S$, using the correct access password $P' = P$.

- **Offline validity tests:** $\mathcal{A}_S$ can make adaptive calls to the offline oracle $\mathcal{TO}_1$ on any string of its choice. The response indicates whether the string belongs in MS.

- **Online validity tests:** $\mathcal{A}_S$ can make adaptive calls to the online oracle $\mathcal{TO}_2$ on any string of its choice. The response indicates whether the string is the correct message M.

- **Message guess:** $\mathcal{A}_S$ eventually outputs one guess $\tilde{M}$ for the value of M.
- **Adjudication:** The adversary wins if $\tilde{M} = M$.

Definition 3. *The advantage of an adversary $\mathcal{A}_S$ in a (z, t_1, t_2, t_3)-insider attack is defined as the probability that $\mathcal{A}_S$ wins the preceding game, after a total of z initiated instances of the Retrieve protocol, and a total of t_1, t_2, and t_3 oracle calls to $\mathcal{TO}_1$, $\mathcal{TO}_2$, and $\mathcal{TO}_3$, respectively.*

Analogous definitions on the password recovery can also be stated in a similar game-based approach.

Definition 4. *An HCR is fully secure if the advantages of $\mathcal{A}$ winning (w, q, t_1, t_2)-outsider attack game, and $\mathcal{A}_S$ winning the (z, s, t_1, t_2)-insider attack game, respectively, are negligible.*

4   The Proposed HCR Scheme

We have already referred to a generic transformation from blind signature protocols into HCR protocols without random oracles. We refer to two secure blind signature schemes that have been presented without random oracle model [8,15] other than [21,22]. However, the construction of [15] is based on a general two-party protocol and is thus extremely inefficient. The solution of [8] is much more efficient than that of [15], but it is still much less efficient than the secure blind signature schemes in the random oracle model. To construct our HCR schme, we use the signature scheme of [21,22] since this is almost as efficient as the most efficient blind signature schemes whose security has been analyzed heuristically or in the random oracle model. The blind signature scheme is also secure for polynomially many synchronized (or constant-depth concurrent) attacks, but not for general concurrent attacks. The [21,22] blind signatures actually require a bilinear pairing for their implementation, but that is because the pairing is needed for signature verification. The blind signature strategy is mainly applied in the retrieval phase. The signing function alone is sufficient to construct an HCR protocol, therefore our construction will not need a pairing (however, the scheme remains compatible with pairing-friendly groups).

Moreover, the HCR server requires to store the *ID* of the user along with the user's other values in the *Store* phase. Having an explicit notion of user *ID* is very useful in practical implementation, so that the server knows whose C to use in the *Retrieve* protocol. There are a number of efficient database search algorithms in the literature [17,19]. Many other searching algorithms can be found in [18]. We leave it to the designers to pick up the most efficient and convenient searching algorithm.

4.1   Protocol Construction

Let $(\mathbb{G}_1, \mathbb{G}_2)$ be bilinear groups as shown in Section 2.2. Here, we also assume that the password P to be blindly signed is an element in $\mathbb{Z}_p^*$ (analogous to message m in [21]), but the domain can be extended to all of $\{0,1\}^*$ by using a collision resistant hash function $H : \{0,1\}^* \rightarrow \mathbb{Z}_p^*$, as mentioned in [5]. We follow the constructions of [22] - the extended version of [21].

Key Generation: Randomly select generators $g_2, u_2, v_2 \in \mathbb{G}_2$ and set $g_1 \leftarrow \psi(g_2)$, $u_1 \leftarrow \psi(u_2)$, and $v_1 \leftarrow \psi(v_2)$. Randomly select $x \in \mathbb{Z}_p^*$ and compute $w_2 \leftarrow g_2^x \in \mathbb{G}_2$. The public and secret keys are:

Public key: g_1, g_2, w_2, u_2, v_2
Secret key: x

Store: $\langle \mathcal{P}[P, M], \mathcal{S}[\perp] \rangle \rightarrow \langle \perp, C \rangle$
   where $P \in \mathbb{Z}_p^*$ and M is in $\mathbb{G}_1$

   1. $\mathcal{P}$ picks a generator g_1

2. $\mathcal{P}$ randomly picks $t \in \mathbb{Z}_p^*$, and computes

$$\zeta \leftarrow (g_1^{Pt})^{1/x}$$

3. $\mathcal{P}$ computes

$$\gamma \leftarrow \zeta^{-1} M$$

4. $\mathcal{P}$ chooses its id ID
5. $\mathcal{P}$ sends x, γ, its id ID, and other public values to $\mathcal{S}$
6. $\mathcal{S}$ stores x, γ, ID, and other public values of $\mathcal{P}$ in its database so that it knows whose γ and public values to use in the retrieve protocol.

Retrieve: $\langle \mathcal{Q}[P'], \mathcal{S}[C'] \rangle \rightarrow \langle M', \perp \rangle$
   where $P' \in \mathbb{Z}_p^*$

1. $\mathcal{Q}$ sends the retrieval request along with its ID to $\mathcal{S}$.
2. $\mathcal{S}$ searches in its database the requesting ID. If it finds an entry for the ID, then it sends $\mathcal{Q}$ the public values along with γ.
3. $\mathcal{Q}$ randomly selects $s \in \mathbb{Z}_p^*$, and computes

$$X \leftarrow g_1^{P't} u_1^t v_1^{st}$$

and sends the blinded request to $\mathcal{S}$. In addition, $\mathcal{Q}$ proves to $\mathcal{S}$ that $\mathcal{Q}$ knows $(P't \bmod p, t, st \bmod p)$ for X using the witness indistinguishable proof as follows:
(a) $\mathcal{Q}$ randomly selects a_1, a_2, a_3 from $\mathbb{Z}_p^*$, computes

$$W \leftarrow g_1^{a_1} u_1^{a_2} v_1^{a_3},$$

and sends W to $\mathcal{S}$.
(b) $\mathcal{S}$ randomly selects $\eta \in \mathbb{Z}_p^*$ and sends η to $\mathcal{Q}$
(c) $\mathcal{Q}$ computes

$$b_1 \leftarrow a_1 + \eta P't \bmod p, \quad b_2 \leftarrow a_2 + \eta t \bmod p, \quad b_3 \leftarrow a_3 + \eta st \bmod p,$$

and sends (b_1, b_2, b_3) to $\mathcal{S}$.
(d) $\mathcal{S}$ checks whether the following equation holds or not:

$$g_1^{b_1} u_1^{b_2} v_1^{b_3} = W X^\eta$$

After checking the equation, $\mathcal{S}$ moves on to next steps.
4. $\mathcal{S}$ randomly selects $r \in \mathbb{Z}_p^*$. In the unlikely event that $x + r = 0 \pmod{p}$, $\mathcal{S}$ tries again with a different random r. $\mathcal{S}$ also randomly selects $l \in \mathbb{Z}_p^*$, computes

$$Y \leftarrow (X v_1^l)^{1/(x+r)}$$

and sends (Y, r, l) to $\mathcal{Q}$.
   Here $Y = (X v_1^l)^{1/(x+r)} = (g_1^{P't} u_1^t v_1^{st+l})^{1/(x+r)} = (g_1^{P'} u_1 v_1^{s + \frac{l}{t}})^{t/(x+r)}$
5. $\mathcal{Q}$ randomly selects $f, \lambda \in \mathbb{Z}_p^*$, and computes

$$\tau = (ft)^{-1} \bmod p, \ \sigma \leftarrow Y^\tau, \ \alpha \leftarrow w_2^f g_2^{rf}, \ \beta \leftarrow s + \frac{l}{t} \bmod p$$

Compute $Test(\alpha) \leftarrow (U, V)$ as follows:

$$U \leftarrow w_1^{1/f} g_1^\lambda, \ V \leftarrow w_2^{f\lambda+r} g_2^{fr\lambda}$$

Here, $\sigma = (g_1^{P'} u_1 v_1^{s+\frac{l}{t}})^{1/(fx+fr)} = (g_1^{P'} u_1 v_1^\beta)^{1/(fx+fr)}$, and $\alpha = w_2^f g_2^{fr} = g_2^{fx+fr}$.

6. $(\sigma, \alpha, \beta, Test(\alpha))$ is the blind signature of P'.

Now, since $\mathcal{Q}$ has got all the secrets and public values, it unblinds and decrypts to retrieve the plaintext. Recall that $\mathcal{Q}$ does not need to verify the validity of the signature, it needs to decrypt and recover the exact message. In order to do so, $\mathcal{Q}$ does the following computations:

$$\sigma^{\frac{1}{\tau}} = g_1^{P't} u_1^t v^{st+l} = (Xv_1)^{\frac{1}{x+r}}$$
$$\Rightarrow \sigma^{\frac{(x+r)}{\tau}} = Xv_1^l$$
$$\Rightarrow \sigma^{\frac{(x+r)}{\tau}} v_1^{-l} = g_1^{P't} u_1^t v_1^{st}$$
$$\Rightarrow \sigma^{\frac{(x+r)}{\tau}} v_1^{-l} u_1^{-t} v_1^{-st} = g_1^{P't}$$
$$\Rightarrow \sigma^{\frac{(x+r)}{\tau}} v_1^{-\frac{(l+st)}{x}} u_1^{-\frac{t}{x}} = (g_1^{P't})^{\frac{1}{x}} = \zeta'$$
$$M' \leftarrow \zeta'\gamma$$

4.2 Security of the Proposed HCR

The blinding in the *Retrieve* phase is perfectly blind and unforgeable because of the two following theorems from [22] provided that the 2SDH assumption holds in $(\mathbb{G}_1, \mathbb{G}_2)$:

Theorem 1. *The blind signature is perfectly blind.*

Theorem 2. *If the (q_S, t', ϵ')-2SDH assumption holds in $(\mathbb{G}_1, \mathbb{G}_2)$, the blind signature is (q_S, t, ϵ)-unforgeable against an L-interval synchronized run of adversaries, provided that*

$$\epsilon' \le \frac{1 - 1/(L+1)}{16} \cdot \epsilon \text{ and } t' \ge O\left(\frac{24Lln(L+1)}{\epsilon} \cdot t\right) + \Theta(q_S T)$$

The definition of $L - interval\ synchronized\ run$, and the proofs of the theorems can be found in [22].

Before going to provide the adversaries'(Insider and Outsider) success probability, we provide some notations. We have already stated that t_1, t_2 and t_3 are the number of unique valid queries to $\mathcal{TO}_1$, $\mathcal{TO}_2$, and $\mathcal{TO}_3$ respectively. We define n_1, n_2, n_3 as the number of negative responses to those queries, so that $n_1 \le t_1$, $n_2 \le t_2$ (and $n_2 \ge t_2 - 1$), and $n_3 \le t_3$. It is also assumed that each query to $\mathcal{TO}_1$ is always followed by an identical query to $\mathcal{TO}_2$ such that if the query to $\mathcal{TO}_1$ returns negative answer, the query to $\mathcal{TO}_2$ is not made. Furthermore queries $\mathcal{TO}_1$ then $\mathcal{TO}_2$ are systematically made on the final guess M' output by $\mathcal{A}$. As we have said earlier, $\mathcal{TO}_3$ is only available to the "Insider" attacker($\mathcal{A}_S$) only right after the *Store* phase.

Proposition 1. *(Outsider Security:)* In this setting, suppose that the 2SDH complexity assumption holds in $(\mathcal{G}_1, \mathcal{G}_2)$, for some chosen security parameter n for the class of all PPT algorithms running in time t. Then, no (w, q, t_1, t_2)-outsider adversary $\mathcal{A}$ running in time t can recover the stored message M with a probability that exceeds the following bound:

$$Pr[\mathcal{A}^{\mathcal{TO}_1, \mathcal{TO}_2} wins] \leq \frac{min\{q, t_2\}}{|D| - min\{q, n_1\}} + \frac{t_2}{2^k - n_1} + negl[n]$$

Proposition 2. *(Insider Security)* In this setting, without random oracles and without any computational hardness assumption, every (z, t_1, t_2, t_3)-insider adversary $\mathcal{A}_S$ that recovers the stored message $M \in MS$, succeeds with probability at most:

$$Pr[\mathcal{A}_S^{\mathcal{TO}_1, \mathcal{TO}_2, \mathcal{TO}_3} wins] \leq \frac{t_2}{|D| - n_1} + \frac{t_2}{2^k - n_1} + \frac{t_3}{2^{k-1} - n_3}$$

The probability bound of recovering the user password P can be derived similarly without random oracle model.

Note that the parameters w and r are not included in the adversaries' success probability bounds. In the "Outsider" attack, w is the number of sessions being passively eavesdropped upon, which looks random to a computationally bounded adversary. Similarly, r is the number of sessions the "Insider" attacker conducts with the user, but we know that the server receives no feedback from the user in the protocol.

Also note that the "Insider" security includes the success probability of the attacker when it is completely offline, targeting to extract the valid message M by using its own M'' from the stored ciphertext C. The attacker in this case is even stronger than that in [7], since it is allowed to make attempts being in purely offline state. The protocol provides unconditional security for the user password against insider attackers, even against dictionary attacks if furthermore the plaintext lacks redundancy, and this is arguably the most important consideration for password reusability.

Theorem 3. *The proposed HCR is fully secure without random oracles as the advantages of $\mathcal{A}$ winning the (w, q, t_1, t_2)-outsider attack game, and $\mathcal{A}_S$ winning the (z, t_1, t_2, t_3)-insider attack games, respectively, are negligible.*

Reducing the Required Computation: Step 5. in the *Retrieve* phase can be avoided to reduce the required computation, since we need to decrypt the received ciphertext instead of computing pairing. As for security, it is still based on discrete-log-type hardness assumption without random oracles.

5   Conclusion

In this paper, for the first time, we show the HCR construction without random oracles with enhanced properties. Our construction is based on Okamoto's blind signature scheme [22] with some modifications. Our construction does not use the signature verification steps of [22]. The security of credential and/or password against "Outsider attacker" is achieved based on 2SDH assumption. Although our 2SDH assumption is stronger than that of Boyen's HCR (GDH), it is still a reasonable assumption. For the "Insider attack" model, we provide the attacker (server) with more computational ability in trying to recover the message from the ciphertext that has been stored in the server by the user, being completely offline. This feature is particularly important to be addressed when the HCR server colludes with the third party service provider in order to retrieve the credential. We also enable the HCR server to identify a requesting user with its ID. Having an explicit notion of identity ID is useful in practice, so that the server knows whose stored ciphertext is to be used in the protocol. Still our protocol provides unconditional security for the user password against "Insider attackers". An HCR with refined security model under relaxed assumptions, and/or with different properties are interesting open problems.

References

1. Baek, J., Naini, R.S., Susilo, W.: Public Key Encryption with Keyword Search Revisited. In: Gervasi, O., Murgante, B., Laganà, A., Taniar, D., Mun, Y., Gavrilova, M.L. (eds.) ICCSA 2008, Part I. LNCS, vol. 5072, pp. 1249–1259. Springer, Heidelberg (2008)
2. Bellovin, S.M., Merritt, M.: Encrypted key exchange: Password-based protocols secure against dictionary attacks. In: IEEE Symposium on Security and Privacy-SP 1992, pp. 72–84 (1992)
3. Bellare, M., Micali, S.: Non-interactive oblivious transfer and applications. In: Brassard, G. (ed.) CRYPTO 1989. LNCS, vol. 435, pp. 547–557. Springer, Heidelberg (1990)
4. Boldyreva, A.: Threshold signatures, multisignatures and blind signatures based on the gap-Diffie-Hellman-group signature scheme. In: Desmedt, Y.G. (ed.) PKC 2003. LNCS, vol. 2567, pp. 31–46. Springer, Heidelberg (2002)
5. Boneh, D., Boyen, X.: Short Signatures Without Random Oracles. In: Cachin, C., Camenisch, J.L. (eds.) EUROCRYPT 2004. LNCS, vol. 3027, pp. 56–73. Springer, Heidelberg (2004)
6. Boneh, D., Crescenzo, G.D., Ostrovsky, R., Persiano, G.: Public key encryption with keyword search. In: Cachin, C., Camenisch, J.L. (eds.) EUROCRYPT 2004. LNCS, vol. 3027, pp. 506–522. Springer, Heidelberg (2004)
7. Boyen, X.: Hidden Credential Retrieval from a Reusable Password. In: The Proceedings of the 4th International Symposium on ACM Symposium on Information, Computer and Communications Security, ASIACCS 2009, pp. 228–238 (2009)
8. Camenisch, J., Koprowski, M., Warinschi, B.: Efficient Blind Signatures without Random Oracles. In: Blundo, C., Cimato, S. (eds.) SCN 2004. LNCS, vol. 3352, pp. 134–148. Springer, Heidelberg (2005)
9. Canetti, R., Feige, U., Goldreich, O., Naor, M.: Adaptively Secure Multi-Party Computation. In: The Proceedings of the 28th Annual ACM Symposium on Theory of Computing, STOC 1996, pp. 639–648 (1996)
10. Canetti, R., Goldreich, O., Halevi, S.: The Random Oracle Methodology, Revisited. In: The Proceedings of the 30th ACM Symposium on Theory of Computing, STOC 1998, pp. 209–218 (1998)

11. Cachin, C., Micali, S., Stadler, M.: Computationally private information retrieval with polylogarithmic communication. In: Stern, J. (ed.) EUROCRYPT 1999. LNCS, vol. 1592, pp. 402–414. Springer, Heidelberg (1999)
12. Chaum, D.: Blind signatures for untraceable payments. In: McCurley, K.S., Ziegler, C.D. (eds.) Advances in Cryptology 1981 - 1997. LNCS, vol. 1440, pp. 199–203. Springer, Heidelberg (1999)
13. Chor, B., Goldreich, O., Kushilevitz, E., Sudan, M.: Private information retrieval. In: IEEE Symposium on Foundations of Computer Science, FOCS 1995, pp. 41–51 (1995)
14. Goldreich, O., Micali, S., Wigderson, A.: How to Play any Mental Game. In: The 19th Annual ACM Symposium on the Theory of Computing, STOC 1987, pp. 218–229 (1987)
15. Juels, A., Luby, M., Ostrovsky, R.: Security of blind digital signatures. In: Kaliski Jr., B.S. (ed.) CRYPTO 1997. LNCS, vol. 1294, pp. 150–164. Springer, Heidelberg (1997)
16. Katz, J., Ostrovsky, R., Yung, M.: Efficient password-authenticated key exchange using human-memorable passwords. In: Kilian, J. (ed.) CRYPTO 2001. LNCS, vol. 2139, pp. 475–494. Springer, Heidelberg (2001)
17. Kimelfeld, B., Sagiv, Y.: Efficient engines for keyword proximity search. In: WebDB 2005 (2005)
18. Knuth, D.: The Art of Computer Programming: Sorting and Searching, 3rd edn., vol. 3. Addison-Wesley, Reading (1997)
19. Liu, F., Yu, C., Meng, W., Chowdhury, A.: Effective keyword search in relational databases. In: Proceedings of the 2006 ACM SIGMOD 2006, pp. 563–574 (2006)
20. Naor, M., Pinkas, B.: Oblivious transfer with adaptive queries. In: Wiener, M. (ed.) CRYPTO 1999. LNCS, vol. 1666, pp. 573–590. Springer, Heidelberg (1999)
21. Okamoto, T.: Efficient Blind and Partially Blind Signatures Without Random Oracles. In: Halevi, S., Rabin, T. (eds.) TCC 2006. LNCS, vol. 3876, pp. 80–99. Springer, Heidelberg (2006)
22. Okamoto, T.: Efficient Blind and Partially Blind Signatures Without Random Oracles. Cryptology ePrint Archive: Report 2006/102, http://eprint.iacr.org/2006/102
23. Yao, A.: How to Generate and Exchange Secrets. In: The 27th Annual IEEE Symposium on the Foundations of Computer Science, FOCS 1986, pp. 162–167 (1986)

Combined Side-Channel Attacks

M. Abdelaziz Elaabid[1,2], Olivier Meynard[1,3],
Sylvain Guilley[1,4], and Jean-Luc Danger[1,4]

[1] Institut TELECOM / TELECOM ParisTech, CNRS LTCI (UMR 5141)
Département COMELEC, 46 rue Barrault, 75 634 Paris Cedex 13, France
[2] Université de Paris 8, Équipe MTII, Laga
2 rue de la liberté, 93 526 Saint-Denis Cedex, France
[3] DGA/MI (CELAR), La Roche Marguerite, 35 174 Bruz, France
[4] Secure-IC S.A.S., 37/39 rue Dareau, 75 014 Paris, France
{elaabid,meynard,guilley,danger}@TELECOM-ParisTech.fr

Abstract. The literature about side-channel attacks is very rich. Many side-channel distinguishers have been devised and studied; in the meantime, many different side-channels have been identified. Also, it has been underlined that the various samples garnered during the same acquisition can carry complementary information. In this context, there is an opportunity to study how to best combine many attacks with many leakages from different sources or using different samples from a single source. This problematic has been evoked as an open issue in recent articles. In this paper, we bring two concrete answers to the attacks combination problem. First of all, we experimentally show that two partitionings can be constructively combined. Then, we explore the richness of electromagnetic curves to combine several timing samples in such a way a sample-adaptive model attack yields better key recovery success rates than a mono-model attack using only a combination of samples (via a principal component analysis).

Keywords: Side-channel analysis; leakage models; attacks combination; multi-partitioning attacks; multi-modal leakage.

1 Introduction

Trusted computing platforms resort to secure components to conceal and manipulate sensitive data. Such components are in charge of implementing cryptographic protocols; for instance, the component is typically asked to encrypt the data with a cryptographic key. The secret key is protected against a direct readout from the circuit thanks to tamper-proof techniques. In general, the component is shielded by coatings to protect it from malevolent manipulations (active or passive micro-probing [1], modification, *etc.*). However, it has been noted that despite this protection, some externally measurable quantities can be exploited without touching the component. Typically, without special care, internal data are somehow modulating the computation timing, the instant current drawn from the power supply, and the radiated fields. Thus, those unintentional

Y. Chung and M. Yung (Eds.): WISA 2010, LNCS 6513, pp. 175–190, 2011.
© Springer-Verlag Berlin Heidelberg 2011

physical emanations can be analyzed in a view to derive from them some sensitive information. Such analyses are referred to as side-channel attacks. The way the observed measurements are affected by the internal data is *a priori* unknown by the attacker, although in some cases an hypothetical, hence imperfect, physical model can be assumed. The link between the data and the side-channel is called the leakage model.

Most side-channel attacks start by a tentative partitioning of the measurements, indexed by key hypotheses [2]. Then, the adversary assesses the quality of each partitioning. This information is typically summarized by a figure of merit. This figure of merit can be a difference of means (in case there are only two partitions [3]), a correlation (case of the CPA [4]), a likelihood (case of template attacks [5]) or a mutual information (case of the MIA [6]), to cite only the few most widespread. Such figures of merit are often referred to as distinguishers, as they are able to successfully distinguish between the key candidates to select the correct one. The comparison of these distinguishers on the same acquisitions has been already discussed in some papers [7–11]. It appears that for a given partitioning, some distinguishers are better than the others to rank the correct key first, some other distinguishers are better than the others to optimize the average rank of the correct key [10]. Moreover, the conclusions depend on the target, since the leakage structure is inherent to each device. The definition of new distinguishers is an active research area; indeed, every new distinguisher contributes to feed a battery of attacks suitable to be launched in parallel on a device under test.

Another research direction is to attempt to make the most of the existing distinguishers. One interesting option is to constructively combine the wealth of cited attacks on common side-leakage traces. Another option consists in combining different samples of traces or even different traces acquired concomitantly.

The rest of the paper is structured as follows. The section 2 tackles the question of the multiple-partitioning attacks. The section 3 reports an original multi-sample electromagnetic (EM) trace, where the leakage model depends on the sample within the trace. We investigate attacks that could take advantage of this originally rich leakage and show that a combined attack indeed outperforms classical ones. The conclusions and the perspectives are in Sec. 4.

2 Combined Attacks and Metrics Based on Multiple Partitions

We explore in this section the combination of multiple partitionings on template attacks. Indeed, some "comparison" attacks that require a physical model of the leakage fail if the leakage function does not match enough the leaking modality of the device.

In [12], a framework is presented in order to evaluate the security of a cryptographic device. This approach relies on two different views: on the one hand the robustness of a circuit against a leakage function, and on the other the strength of an adversary. The information theory and specially the conditional entropy is chosen to quantify the information leaked during encryption. This very concept is thus promoted in order to measure the robustness. Indeed, the more the circuit is leaking the more it is vulnerable. The strength of the adversary is determined for example by its success rate to retrieve the encryption key.

2.1   Information Theoretic Metric

We adopt the idea that the quality of a circuit is assessed by the amount of information given by a leakage function. Thus, if S_K is the random variable representing the secret (ideally the key values), and $\mathbf{L}$ is the random variable representing the values of the leakage function.

The residual uncertainty on S_K knowing $\mathbf{L}$ is given by $\mathbf{H}(S_K \mid L)$. $\mathbf{H}$ is the conditional entropy introduced by Claude E. Shannon [12, 13]. Note that this value will depend on sensitive variables chosen, and thus the quality of the leakage function. The more the sensitive variable leaks, the smaller is the entropy and more vulnerable is the circuit.

2.2   Template Attacks

Template attacks are among the most powerful forms of side channel attacks. They are able to break implementations and countermeasures which assumes that the attacker cannot get more than a very small number of samples extracted from the attacked device. To this end, the adversary needs a hardware identical to the target, which allows him to obtain some information under the form of leakage realizations. The main step is to perform a modeling process; its goal is to build classes for side-channel traces that will help identify the secret values during the on-line phase of the attack. Said differently, the information provided by profiling are used to classify some part of encryption key. Actually, the full round key has obviously too many bits to be guessed in one go by exhaustive search. In general, the key bits at entering substitution boxes (sboxes) are targeted. In fact, they all contribute to activate the same logic, which explains why it is beneficial to guess them together. An adversary can also select other key bits if they are more vulnerable. In other words, the attacker itself selects the bits of the key best for his attack. Guessing the correct key is a problem of decision theory. To solve it, we introduce a statistical model that is directly applicable in principle to the problem of classification. This application is mainly based on Bayes' rule, which allows to evaluate an *a posteriori* probability (that is after the effective observation), knowing the conditional probability distributions *a priori* (*i.e.* independent of any constraint on observed variables). The maximum likelihood approach helps provide the most appropriate model.

2.2.1   Profiling Process

For this step, we need a set of traces $\mathcal{S}_o, o \in [0, N'[$ corresponding to each N' operation that are also values of the sensitive variable. Traces, denoted by t, are vectors of N dimensions related to random values of plaintext and keys needed to algorithm encryption. These observations are then classified according to functions of leakage $\mathcal{L}$. These leakage functions must depend on the configuration of the circuit, and of the implemented algorithm. This provides a framework for the estimation of the leakage during encryption. For each set $\mathcal{S}_o, o \in [0, N'[$ the attacker computes the average $\mu_o = \frac{1}{|\mathcal{S}_o|} \sum_{t \in \mathcal{S}_o} t$ and the covariance matrix $\Sigma_o = \frac{1}{|\mathcal{S}_o|-1} \sum_{t \in \mathcal{S}_o} (t - \mu_o)(t - \mu_o)^\mathsf{T}$. The ordered pair (μ_o, Σ_o) associated with value o of the leakage function outputs, is called *template* and will be used in the attack to retrieve subkeys. It allows to build the ideal probability density function (PDF) of a multivariate Gaussian distribution.

2.2.2 Principal Component(s) Analysis

One of the main contributions of the template attack is that an adversary may use all the information given by any trace. However, he is confronted with enormous data he has on hand, especially the covariance matrices. This poses some difficulties for calculations, since, because of algorithmic noise, large covariance matrices are poorly conditioned. For this purpose, the principal component analysis (PCA) is used to get round those drawbacks. It allows to analyze the structure of the covariance matrix (variability, dispersion of data). The aim of PCA is to reduce the data to $q \ll N$ new descriptors, that summarize a large part of (if not all) the variability. Also, it allows to better visualize the data in 2 or 3 dimensions (if $q = 2$ or 3).

These new descriptors are given by the data projection on the most significant eigenvectors given by PCA. Let EV be the matrix containing the eigenvectors classified according to the decreasing eigenvalues. The mean traces and covariance matrices are then expressed in this basis by: $p\mu_o = (EV)^\mathsf{T} \mu_o$ and $P\Sigma_o = (EV)^\mathsf{T} \Sigma_o (EV)$.

2.2.3 Online Attack and Success Rate

The *online attack* consists in first capturing one trace t of the target device during an encryption using the secret key κ. Knowing that each trace corresponds to one leakage value, the secret key will be retrieved from this trace by using maximum likelihood: $\kappa = \mathrm{argmax}_{s_{Kc}} Pr(s_{Kc} \mid t)$, where s_{Kc} is the candidate key. Indeed, for each key candidate, we estimate the value of leakage by using the message or the ciphertext that are *a priori* known. The success rate is given by the average number of times where the adversary succeeds to retrieve the key $s_{Kc} = \kappa$. For each attempt the adversary can use one trace corresponding to one query, or a set of traces corresponding to different queries.

2.3 Sensitive Variables

In the paper [13] a study is made on the choice of the best suited sensitive variable for an adversary attacking publicly available traces [14]. From a comparison between five different models, it is shown that the most appropriate model for the targeted circuit is the Hamming distance between two registers. However, "partitioning attacks" (in the sense of [2]) on various sensitive values (such as the linear and nonlinear functions inputs) also allows an adversary to recover the key, but with many more traces. The knowledge of circuit architecture provides definitely much more information about the main leakage function. In this article we elaborate by combining these models to retrieve the key with fewer traces, and watch the behavior of entropy as a function of the number of eigenvectors retained in the attack.

2.3.1   Combined Models

The goal is to combine two partitionings. The security of the resulting compound model is evaluated by template attacks; identically, the robustness of the circuit is measured under this new model. Can an adversary that combines models be considered as "higher order" [15]? Is he able to recover the secret key faster? The experiment described in this section attempts to address these issues. Let

1. **Model M1** be the value of the first round corresponding to the fanout of the first sbox. It is a 4-bit model, and
2. **Model M2** be the first bit transition of model M1. It is a mono-bit model, belonging to the general class of "Hamming distance" models.

From those two models, we derive a third one referred to as **Model M3**. M3 combines the 4-bit model M1 and the 1-bit model M2. In other words, M3 is considered as a "bit-field structure" where the value of the most significant bit (MSB) is the model M2. The others 4 bits correspond to the model M1. M3 is the concatenation of MA and M2, and we note $M3 \doteq (M1, M2)$. Hence M3 is a $4 + 1 = 5$ bit model, which means that M3 is based on 32 partitions. Said differently, the partitioning for M3 is equal to the Cartesian product of that of M1 and M2.

The fair comparison between the models is not a trivial operation. Typically, the number of templates for models M1, M2 and M3 differs. Basically, regarding the training (*i.e.* templates building) phase:

1. either the adversary has an equal number of traces by classes,
2. or the adversary has an equal number of traces for all the set of classes.

The choice will influence the success rate as we will see in the forthcoming experiment. The first case is the most realistic: it consists in saying that the precharacterization time is almost unbounded; the valuable asset being the traces taken on-line from the attacked device. We model this situation by taking the same number of traces for each partition. Therefore, in total, much less training traces are used for mono-partition models; but this really represents the case where models are evaluated with as identical conditions as possible. The second one reflects the case where the precharacterization cost is non-negligible. Under this assumption, the advantage of combined attacks is less clear, since the number of available traces to estimate each template gets lower. Thus, in a single-model attack, the greater accuracy of the templates will certainly compensate the loss of benefit conveyed by the combination.

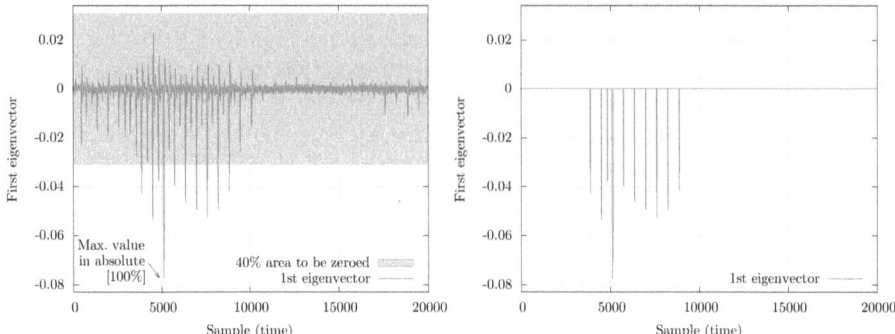

Fig. 1. Main eigenvector without thresholding (*left*), and the same with a 40% thresholding level (*right*)

2.3.2   First Choice: Matching-Limited Evaluation

We use an equal number of traces per class. In our experiment we take 1,000 traces per class for models **M1**, **M2**, and **M3**. The comparison is made with and without the use of the thresholding method as presented in [13]. This method consists in accelerating the estimation of the principal directions in a PCA by forcing to zero the samples that are too small in the eigenvectors. The Fig. 1 illustrates the method. The idea is that most samples with low amplitude would actually be equal to zero with more traces in the estimation of the PCA. The thresholding allows to filter those samples out, so that they do not bring noise to the protection. In the same time, the thresholding keeps the samples with the greatest variance, which makes it a good tool to separate POIs from others. There is of course a trade-off in the choice for the best threshold. A too small threshold keeps too many irrelevant samples, whereas a too large threshold filters out even some weak POIs. For the implementation studied in this section, we found that a value of 40 % is a fair compromise. The figure 2 shows the success rate of the template attacks with the three models. We recall that the higher the success rate, the better the attack. We see in Fig. 2 that in the case of non-thresholding, the template attack based on the combined model is better than that on other models. It is much better than model **M1**, and slightly better than model **M2**.

Incidentally, when we resort to thresholding, the model M2 and M3 are equivalent and obviously always better than M1, that models in a less appropriate way the leakage function. The fact only the first PCA eigenvector is used in the comparison accounts for the equivalence between M2 and M3. Indeed, the other eigenvectors among the 31 possible in the case of combined model M3 also contain information, while the model M2 has only one significant direction.

2.3.3   Second Choice: Training-Limited Evaluation

If we follow the first option, we take 32,000 traces in general. Thus, for a constant number of traces per class, we have $32,000/16 = 2,000$ traces by class for model **M1** and $32,000/2 = 16,000$ traces by class for **M2**. The combined model **M3**

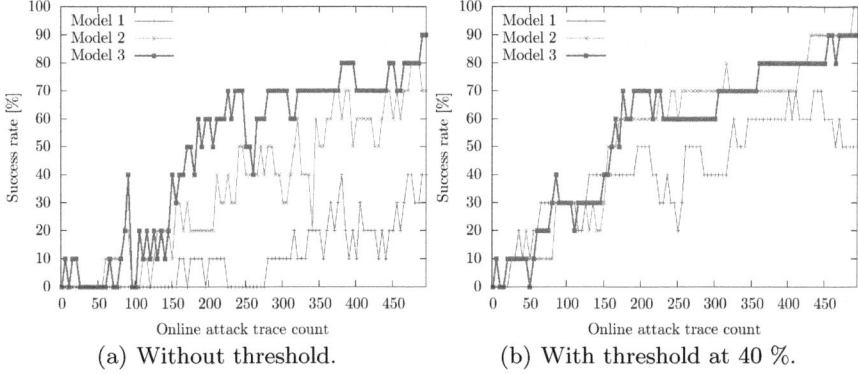

Fig. 2. Success rate comparison between mono-partitioning models M1, M2 and combined model M3 for two different thresholds and 1,000 traces per class

corresponds therefore to an amount of $32,000/32 = 1,000$ traces by class. In this second case, we use systematically 32,000 for the training of all models M1, M2 and M3. As a consequence, model M2, that has the fewer number of partitions, will have its template evaluated more accurately than M1 and M3.

The two plots in Fig. 3 show that the models combination does not so much gain on the attack. Indeed, the success rate of model M3 is very close to the success rate of the model M1.

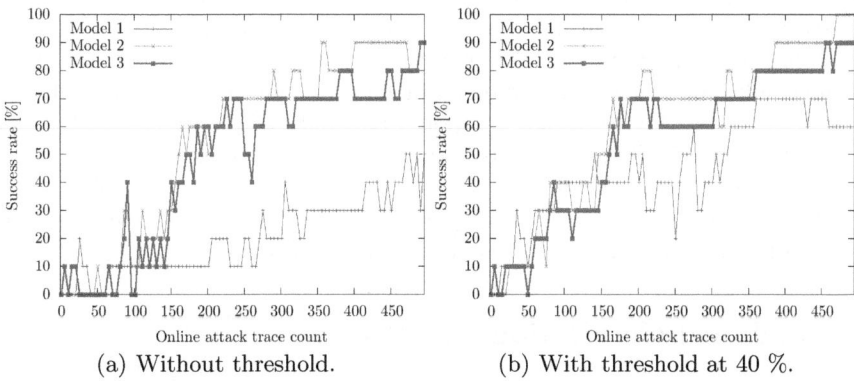

Fig. 3. Success rate comparison between mono-partitioning models M1, M2 and combined model M3 for two different thresholds and 32,000 traces in total for the training (to be divided between respectively 16, 2 and 32 classes)

2.4   Conditional Entropy

As explained above in Sec. 2.1, the conditional entropy gives an idea about the robustness of the circuit, irrespective of any attack. The value of the conditional entropy tends to a limit value in function to the number of traces used for profiling [13]. For our experiment, we took a large number of traces during the profiling phase to have an approximation of this limit value. This will help us compare the circuit robustness against attacks using models M1, M2 or M3. Is our circuit very vulnerable against an attacker who combines model? The figure 4 attempts to answer this question.

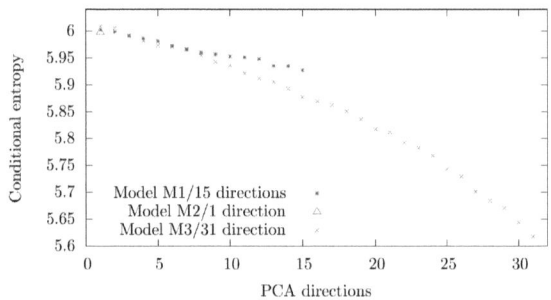

Fig. 4. Conditional entropy comparison between different models

The use of PCA provides new directions corresponding to different eigenvectors. The number of these directions depends on the cardinality of the sensitive variable. For example, in this study, we have 15 directions for the model M1, 1 direction for the model M2, and 31 directions for model M3. The first direction summarizes a large percentage of variance of data. Making a comparison of robustness using only this first direction may seem satisfactory, but this study shows that the more directions, the greatest the estimated leakage (*i.e.* the smallest the conditional entropy). Combined models are thus an opportunity to discover new leakage modes, as already noted for multi side-channel (power+EM) combination in [16]. This noting is actually a warning to the security evaluators: the robustness of an implementation can be underestimated if the models are either inappropriate (since incomplete, and thus should be completed with another or some other models) or contain too few partitions.

3   Combined Correlation Attacks

One difficulty for improving the side channel analysis or the template attack in presence of large noise is to identify the leaking samples, also called *Points Of Interest* (POIs). They correspond to the dates when the sensitive data is indeed processed and leaking the most. As already mentioned in the previous section when discussing the thresholding method, there is an obvious trade-off in the selection process for POIs. The more of them are selected, the more information is collected, but the more noise is kept. The difficult task consists in separating the signal from the noise.

Several techniques have been proposed to identify the POIs. The *Sum Of Squared pairwise (T-)Differences* (or sosd [17] and sost in [18]), the mutual information (MI [19]) and the *Principal Component Analysis* (PCA [20]) are four widespread examples. In this section, we study these methods and compare their efficiency, by applying them on two sets of measurements, one at short distance from the chip and another, one more noisy, at 25 cm from the chip. For these experiments we used a SASEBO-G board [21] embedding an AES hardware implementation. For these two sets of electromagnetic measurements $\mathbf{O}(t)$ we notice that a CPA can be successfully performed, by using the Hamming distance model between the penultimate and the last round state of the AES.

3.1   Techniques for Revealing the POIs

3.1.1   The sosd *versus* sost *versus* MI

The computation of the sosd leakage indicator metric requires to average the traces in a given partitioning. In the original proposal [17], the partitioning concerns all the 256 values of an AES state byte. The SASEBO-G implementation is known to leak the Hamming distance between the penultimate and the last round. Indeed, we succeed CPA for the both sets of measurements in this model. Therefore, we decide to restrict the values of the leakages to the interval $[0,8]$, according to $\mathcal{L} = HW(\text{state}_9[sbox] \oplus \text{ciphertext}[sbox])$, where $sbox \in [0,16[$ is the substitution box index. If we denote $o_i(t)$ all the samples (t) of the ith realization of observation $\mathbf{O}(t)$, then the averages $\mu_j(t)$ in each class $j \in [0,8]$ is given by the mean of set $\{o_i(t) \mid l_i = j\}$. Then their squared pairwise difference is summed up to yield the sosd.

The sost is based on the T-Test, which is a standard statistical tool to meet the challenge of distinguishing noisy signals. This method has the advantage to consider not only the difference between their means $\mu_j, \mu_{j'}$ but as well their variability $(\sigma_j^2, \sigma_{j'}^2)$ in relation to the number of samples $(n_j, n_{j'})$. The definition of the sosd and sost is given below:

$$\text{sosd} \doteq \sum_{j,j'=0}^{8} (\mu_j - \mu_{j'})^2 \qquad \text{and} \qquad \text{sost} \doteq \sum_{j,j'=0}^{8} \left(\frac{\mu_j - \mu_{j'}}{\sqrt{\frac{\sigma_j^2}{n_j} + \frac{\sigma_{j'}^2}{n_{j'}}}} \right)^2 .$$

The sosd and the sost for the two EM observation campaigns are plotted in Fig. 5. We notice that the correlation trace, the sosd and sost curves are matching for the measurement at 0 cm. But, although we use for the partitioning the same leakage function $\mathcal{L}$ and although we find the right key with a CPA on the measurement at 25 cm, the sosd curve does not highlight the right time sample, *i.e.* that where the key can be retrieved by CPA. This figure 5 shows that the sosd metric is not always an efficient metric for revealing the points of interest. Indeed, we have tried to execute CPAs on the samples highlighted, but they all fail. Regarding the sost on the measurement at 25 cm, several POIs are revealed among samples that are not related to the secret data. Thus sost is neither a trustworthy tool to identify POIs.

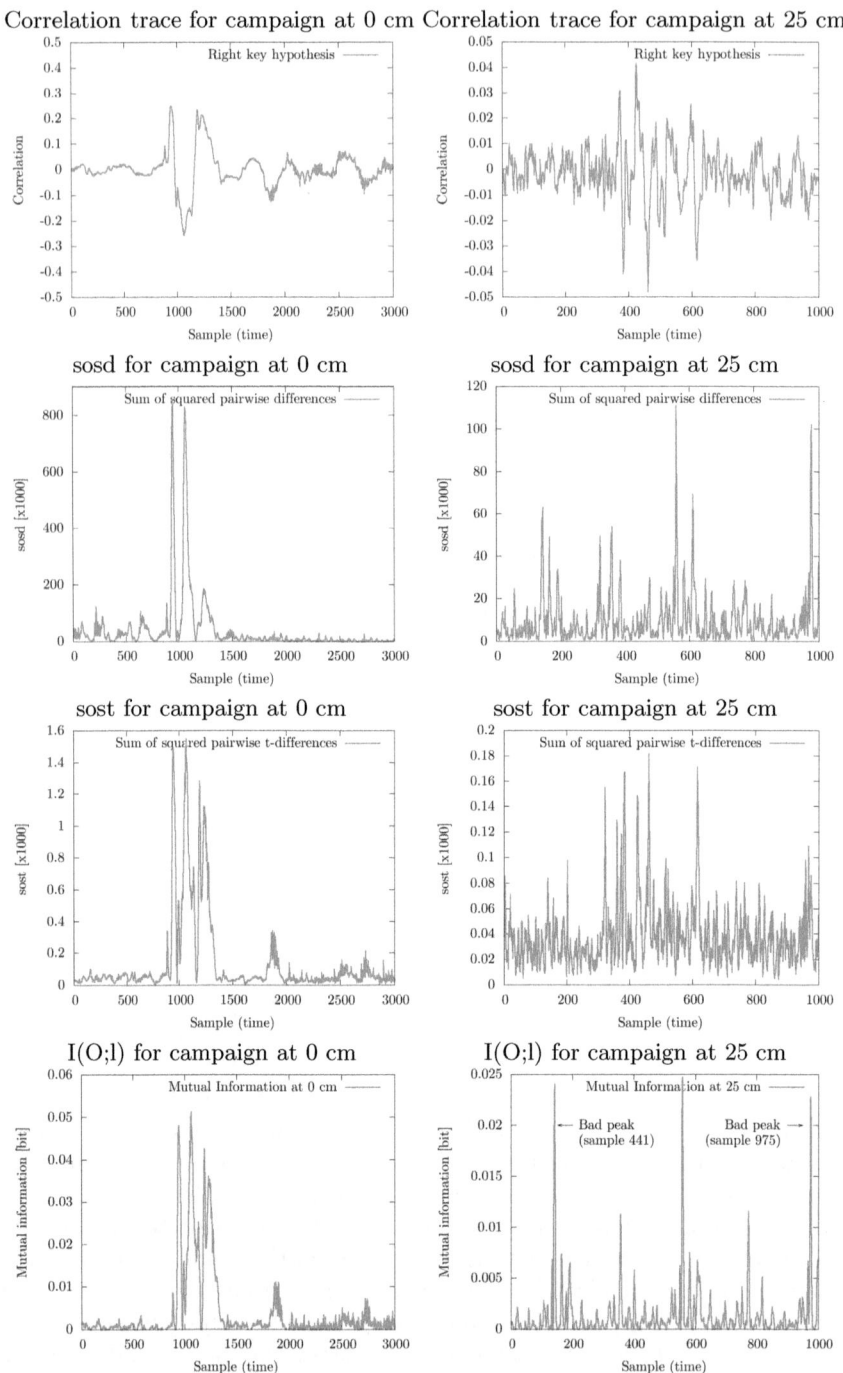

Fig. 5. Correlation traces, sosd, sost and MI obtained for the right key hypothesis

Regarding the MI, also plotted in Fig. 5, it matches well the sost at short distances, but features peaks with no information (notably the samples 441 and 975). It is thus not a reliable tool. The principal reason is that the PDFs are poorly estimated in the presence of large amounts of noise.

3.1.2   The PCA

As previously explained in section 2.2.2, the PCA aims at providing a new description of the measurements by projection on the most significant eigenvector(s) of the empirical covariance matrix of (μ_j). If we compare the success rate of the CPA, applied after a PCA, we can notice, that in the case of the campaign at distance, featuring a high level of noise, the eigenvector corresponding to the greatest eigenvalue is not necessarily suitable. The success rate of the CPA after a projection onto each of the nine eigenvectors is given in Fig. 6. At 25 cm, we notice that the projection onto the first eigenvector is not necessarily the most suitable, since it does not yield the best attack success rate. The projection onto the third eigenvector turns out, quite surprisingly, to be more efficient. At the opposite, when the noise level is low and the electromagnetic probe set at short distance, the projection onto the first vector is indeed more efficient.

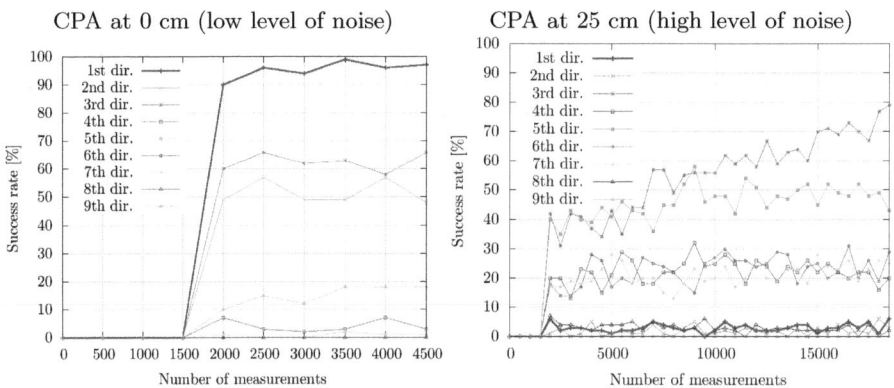

Fig. 6. Success rate of the CPA after PCA pre-processing

This phenomena can be explained by the fact that the number of curves in the sub-set corresponding to the Hamming distances 0 and 8 are in same proportion, nevertheless the level of noise is higher, since they contain the fewest number of traces. Indeed, the proportion of traces available for the training is equal to $\frac{1}{2^8} \cdot \binom{8}{l}$, which is lowest for $l = 0$ or 8. The estimation of those classes is thus less accurate.

In order to improve the PCA, we have reduced the number of partitions from 9 to 7 sub-sets depending on the Hamming distance $HD \in [1,7] = [0,8] \backslash \{0,8\}$. We observe that, under this restriction, the best success rate is obtained for the projection on the first eigenvector. In the meantime, the condition number of the empirical covariance matrix decreases, which confirms that the weakly populated classes $l \in \{0, 8\}$ added more noise than signal to the PCA. Amazingly enough, this approach is antinomic with the multi-bit DPA of Messerges [22]. If we transpose from DES to AES, Messerges suggests at the opposite to get rid of the classes $l = [1, 7]$ and to retain only $l = \{0, 8\}$. Those extremal samples have two ambivalent properties. They convey the most information, as shown in Tab. 1, but also are the rarest samples, and thus are the most noisy coefficient in the covariance matrix. As Messerges does not make use of extra-diagonal coefficients, his attack is not concerned by this fact.

Table 1. Information and probability of the Hamming weight of an 8-bit uniformly distributed random variable

Class index l	0	1	2	3	4	5	6	7	8
Information [bit]	8.00	5.00	3.19	2.19	1.87	2.19	3.19	5.00	8.00
Probability [%]	0.4	3.1	10.9	21.9	27.3	21.9	10.9	3.1	0.4

3.2 Combining Time Samples

3.2.1 Observations
The correlation trace obtained for the right key with measurements at distance is given in Fig. 7. We observe that the correlation traces are extremely noisy. Moreover for some time samples, identified in as Sample{1,2,3,4} in Fig. 7, the magnitude of the correlation trace obtained for the right key is clearly higher than the magnitude of the correlation traces for bad key hypotheses. These samples are all located within the same clock period that corresponds to the last round of the AES. At the four identified dates, the sample are undoubtedly carrying secret information.

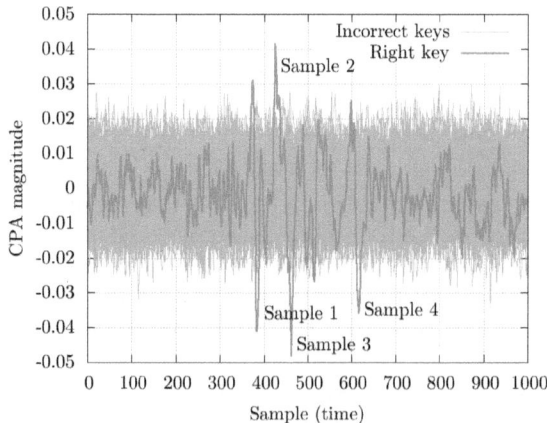

Fig. 7. Correlation traces obtained for the right key hypotheses and for incorrect key hypotheses at 25 cm

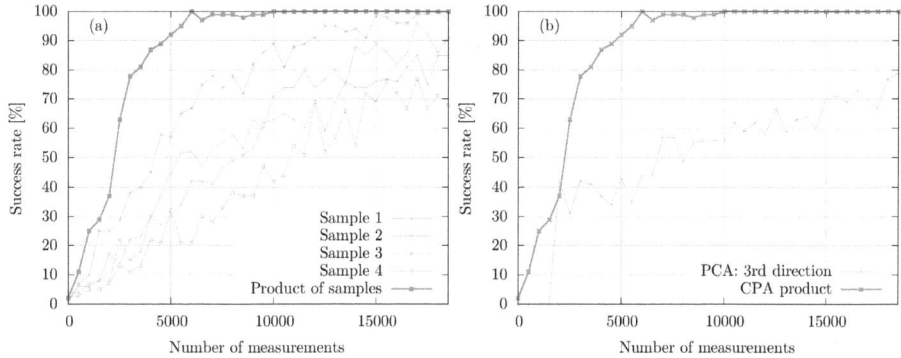

Fig. 8. (a)–*left*: Success rate of the mono-sample attack, and product of correlations attack; (b)–*right*: Comparison between a CPA using the pre-treatment by PCA and our product of correlation, introduced in Eqn. (1)

3.2.2 Sample Combination Principle and Results

We aim at showing that there is a gain in combining the leaks from the four identified dates. First of all, we confirm that the four samples of peak CPA are actually POIs. To do so, we perform successful CPAs at these time samples. The result is shown in Fig. 8: all four attacks pass over a success rate of 50 % after 12,000 traces. Second, we devise a method to attack that exploits at once all those samples. Similar methods have already be introduced in the context of combining samples in order defeat masking countermeasures [23]. In [24], Chari *et al.* suggest to use the product of two leakage models. In [25], Joye *et al.* recommend to combine two samples with the absolute value of the difference. As in our case we intend to combine more than two samples, we resort to the product for the combination function. We apply it to Pearson empirical correlation coefficients $\hat{\rho}_t$, where t are the four identified dates. The new distinguisher we promote is thus:

$$\hat{\rho}_{\text{combined}} \doteq \prod_{t \in \text{Sample}\{1,2,3,4\}} \hat{\rho}_t. \tag{1}$$

This technique applies well to the Pearson correlation coefficients, that are already centered by design. Thus it indeed puts forward the simultaneous coincidences of high correlation, while it demotes incorrect hypotheses for which at least one $\hat{\rho}_t$ is close to zero. As shown in Fig. 8(a), the success rate of this new attack is greater than that for mono-samples attacks. Additionally, we confirm in Fig. 8(b) that our combination defined in Eqn. (1), although simple in its setup, clearly outperforms a PCA after performing PCA.

However, we have only shown that when knowing some POIs in the curve, a powerful combining multi-sample attack can be devised. Now, for the time being, the only method to exhibit those POIs has been to apply a successful attack (a

CPA in our case). Therefore, an open question is to locate those POIs without knowing the key beforehand or without conducting another less powerful attack. We suggest two solutions to spot the POIs: either online or by precharacterization on an open sample assuming the position of the POIs do not depend on the secret key.

4   Conclusion and Perspectives

In this paper, we have studied two examples of side-channel attacks combinations. The first contribution is the demonstration of a constructive multi-partitioning attack. We show that two partitioning can enhance the convergence of the success rate to one hundred percent; such attacks benefit from an exhaustive pre-characterization, since the number of templates increases, and that the training phase length is the product of the training phase for each partitioning. The second contribution is to highlight the existence of the leakage model in far field EM signals. We show how the leakage of each sample can be combined better than usual leakage reduction methods (*e.g.* the sosd, the sost or the PCA). This improvement comes from the fact each sample features a leakage of different nature that can be exploited individually, which is out of the reach of global techniques that consist in identifying points with large variation. Our improved combining distinguisher consists in multiplying the Pearson correlation coefficients for several POIs. Although this attack leads to better success rates than other attacks using different state-of-the-art pre-processing, we do think it can still be enhanced by another method to identify the points of interest accurately even when the side-channel observations are extremely noisy. As a perspective, we intend to apply those ideas to an online only attack, typically the MIA.

References

1. Gammel, B.M., Mangard, S.: On the duality of probing and fault attacks. Cryptology ePrint Archive, Report 2009/352 (2009), http://eprint.iacr.org/
2. Standaert, F.X., Gierlichs, B., Verbauwhede, I.: Partition vs. Comparison Side-Channel Distinguishers: An Empirical Evaluation of Statistical Tests for Univariate Side-Channel Attacks against Two Unprotected CMOS Devices. In: Lee, P.J., Cheon, J.H. (eds.) ICISC 2008. LNCS, vol. 5461, pp. 253–267. Springer, Heidelberg (2009)
3. Kocher, P.C., Jaffe, J., Jun, B.: Differential Power Analysis. In: Wiener, M. (ed.) CRYPTO 1999. LNCS, vol. 1666, pp. 388–397. Springer, Heidelberg (1999)
4. Brier, É., Clavier, C., Olivier, F.: Correlation Power Analysis with a Leakage Model. In: Joye, M., Quisquater, J.-J. (eds.) CHES 2004. LNCS, vol. 3156, pp. 16–29. Springer, Heidelberg (2004)
5. Chari, S., Rao, J.R., Rohatgi, P.: Template Attacks. In: Kaliski Jr., B.S., Koç, Ç.K., Paar, C. (eds.) CHES 2002. LNCS, vol. 2523, pp. 13–28. Springer, Heidelberg (2003)

6. Gierlichs, B., Batina, L., Tuyls, P., Preneel, B.: Mutual information analysis. In: Oswald, E., Rohatgi, P. (eds.) CHES 2008. LNCS, vol. 5154, pp. 426–442. Springer, Heidelberg (2008)
7. Coron, J.S., Kocher, P.C., Naccache, D.: Statistics and Secret Leakage. In: Frankel, Y. (ed.) FC 2000. LNCS, vol. 1962, pp. 157–173. Springer, Heidelberg (2001)
8. Mangard, S., Oswald, E., Popp, T.: Power Analysis Attacks: Revealing the Secrets of Smart Cards, p. 338. Springer, Heidelberg (2006), http://www.springer.com/
9. Le, T.H., Canovas, C., Clédière, J.: An overview of side channel analysis attacks. In: ASIACCS, ASIAN ACM Symposium on Information, Computer and Communications Security, Tokyo, Japan, pp. 33–43 (2008), doi:10.1145/1368310.1368319
10. Gierlichs, B., De Mulder, E., Preneel, B., Verbauwhede, I.: Empirical comparison of side channel analysis distinguishers on DES in hardware. In: IEEE (ed.) ECCTD. European Conference on Circuit Theory and Design, Antalya, Turkey, pp. 391–394 (2009)
11. Veyrat-Charvillon, N., Standaert, F.X.: Mutual Information Analysis: How, When and Why? In: Clavier, C., Gaj, K. (eds.) CHES 2009. LNCS, vol. 5747, pp. 429–443. Springer, Heidelberg (2009)
12. Standaert, F.X., Malkin, T., Yung, M.: A Unified Framework for the Analysis of Side-Channel Key Recovery Attacks. In: Joux, A. (ed.) EUROCRYPT 2009. LNCS, vol. 5479, pp. 443–461. Springer, Heidelberg (2009)
13. Elaabid, M.A., Guilley, S.: Practical improvements of profiled side-channel attacks on a hardware crypto-accelerator. In: Bernstein, D.J., Lange, T. (eds.) AFRICACRYPT 2010. LNCS, vol. 6055, pp. 243–260. Springer, Heidelberg (2010), doi:10.1007/978-3-642-12678-9_15
14. TELECOM ParisTech SEN research group: DPA Contest, 1st edn. (2008-2009), http://www.DPAcontest.org/
15. Messerges, T.S.: Using Second-Order Power Analysis to Attack DPA Resistant Software. In: Paar, C., Koç, Ç.K. (eds.) CHES 2000. LNCS, vol. 1965, pp. 238–251. Springer, Heidelberg (2000)
16. Standaert, F.X., Archambeau, C.: Using Subspace-Based Template Attacks to Compare and Combine Power and Electromagnetic Information Leakages. In: Oswald, E., Rohatgi, P. (eds.) CHES 2008. LNCS, vol. 5154, pp. 411–425. Springer, Heidelberg (2008)
17. Gierlichs, B., Batina, L., Tuyls, P., Preneel, B.: Mutual information analysis. In: Oswald, E., Rohatgi, P. (eds.) CHES 2008. LNCS, vol. 5154, pp. 426–442. Springer, Heidelberg (2008)
18. Gierlichs, B., Lemke-Rust, K., Paar, C.: Templates vs. stochastic methods. In: Goubin, L., Matsui, M. (eds.) CHES 2006. LNCS, vol. 4249, pp. 15–29. Springer, Heidelberg (2006)
19. Macé, F., Standaert, F.X., Quisquater, J.J.: Information theoretic evaluation of side-channel resistant logic styles. In: Paillier, P., Verbauwhede, I. (eds.) CHES 2007. LNCS, vol. 4727, pp. 427–442. Springer, Heidelberg (2007)
20. Archambeau, C., Peeters, É., Standaert, F.X., Quisquater, J.J.: Template Attacks in Principal Subspaces. In: Goubin, L., Matsui, M. (eds.) CHES 2006. LNCS, vol. 4249, pp. 1–14. Springer, Heidelberg (2006)
21. Satoh, A.: (Side-channel Attack Standard Evaluation Board, SASEBO) Project of the AIST – RCIS (Research Center for Information Security), http://www.rcis.aist.go.jp/special/SASEBO/

22. Messerges, T.S., Dabbish, E.A., Sloan, R.H.: Investigations of Power Analysis Attacks on Smartcards. In: USENIX — Smartcard 1999, Chicago, Illinois, USA, pp. 151–162 (1999)
http://www.usenix.org/publications/library/proceedings/smartcard99/messerges.html
23. Prouff, E., Rivain, M., Bevan, R.: Statistical Analysis of Second Order Differential Power Analysis. IEEE Trans. Computers 58, 799–811 (2009)
24. Chari, S., Jutla, C.S., Rao, J.R., Rohatgi, P.: Towards Sound Approaches to Counteract Power-Analysis Attacks. In: Wiener, M. (ed.) CRYPTO 1999. LNCS, vol. 1666, p. 398. Springer, Heidelberg (1999)
25. Joye, M., Paillier, P., Schoenmakers, B.: On Second-Order Differential Power Analysis. In: Rao, J.R., Sunar, B. (eds.) CHES 2005. LNCS, vol. 3659, pp. 293–308. Springer, Heidelberg (2005)

Correlation Power Analysis Based on Switching Glitch Model

Hongying Liu[1], Guoyu Qian[1], Satoshi Goto[1], and Yukiyasu Tsunoo[2]

[1] Graduate School of Information Production and Systems, Waseda University, Japan
[2] Common Platform Software Research Laboratories, NEC Corp., Kawasaki, Japan
liuhongying@fuji.waseda.jp

Abstract. Power analysis attacks are based on analyzing the power consumption of the cryptographic devices while they perform the encryption operation. Correlation Power Analysis (CPA) attacks exploit the linear relation between the known power consumption and the predicted power consumption of cryptographic devices to recover keys. It has been one of the effective side channel attacks that threaten the security of CMOS circuits. However, few works consider the leakage of glitches at the logic gates. In this paper, we present a new power consumption model, namely Switching Glitch (SG) model, which not only considers the data dependent switching activities but also including glitch power consumptions in CMOS circuits. Additionally, from a theoretical point of view, we show how to estimate the glitch factor. The experiments against AES implementation validate the proposed model. Compared with CPA based on Hamming Distance model, the power traces of recovering keys have been decreased by as much as 28.9%.

Keywords: side channel attacks, correlation power analysis (CPA), power leakage model, glitches, AES, Hamming Distance.

1 Introduction

Side channel attacks are any attacks that reveal the keys of cryptographic devices by exploiting its physical implementation information. Unlike the conventional cryptanalysis, it is not only based on the mathematical analysis but also observing and monitoring the running of encryption algorithms. It has posed a serious threat to the security of cryptographic devices. The power consumption, electromagnetic emission and timing information, as well as the variance of cache content of a cryptographic module might be investigated by adversaries to recover the keys. Power analysis attacks are based on analyzing the power consumption of the module while it performs the encryption operation. This kind of attack was introduced by Kocher [1]. After that, researchers pay much attention to such kind of side channel information. There are basically two sorts of power analysis attacks. Simple Power Analysis (SPA) attacks rely on detailed knowledge of the cryptographic algorithm being implemented

Y. Chung and M. Yung (Eds.): WISA 2010, LNCS 6513, pp. 191–205, 2011.
© Springer-Verlag Berlin Heidelberg 2011

and visual inspection of the power consumption curves, to extract cryptographic keys. Differential Power Analysis (DPA) attacks are more powerful based on SPA. It adds statistical techniques to separate signal from noise, and requires less detailed knowledge of the implementation of cryptographic algorithm. In 2004, aimed at improving Hamming Weight leakage model, Brier et al. [2] proposed the correlation power analysis (CPA) attack which uses the correlation factor between Hamming Distance and measured power to guess keys. Then Le et al. [3] enhanced the performance of CPA by restricting the normalization factor in the proposed Partitioning Power Analysis method. The key screening techniques [4] were used to reduce the key estimation time. Furthermore, in 2007, the Switching Distance model was suggested by Peeters et al [5]. They mounted the simulated attacks on an 8-bit PIC16F877 microprocessor against S-box output. All these challenge the implementation algorithms on cryptographic devices, such as Data Encryption Standard (DES) and so on.

Advanced Encryption Standard (AES), also named Rijndael, was published by the National Institute of Standards and Technology (NIST) of United States in 2001 [6]. It has become one of the most popular symmetrical encryption algorithms. AES is designed to be easy to implement on hardware and software, as well as in restricted environments and offer good defenses against various attack techniques. While plenty of research work are carried out on the security examination of AES. Mangard et al. [7] implemented SPA against AES key expansions. The simulated measurements and real power measurements are both been used on ASIC implementation of DPA attack [8]. Additionally, abundant work is done on AES implementations with various countermeasures.

Glitch is the unnecessary signal transition due to the unbalanced path delays to the inputs of a logic gate. Glitch power can account for 20% to 70% of the dynamic switching power in CMOS circuits [9]. Raghunathan et al.[10] demonstrate that glitches form a significant component of the switching activity at signals in typical register-transfer level circuits. So it cannot be overlooked in the analysis of side channel information leakage. However, since glitch power dissipation strongly depends on both circuit topology and technology, there are limited publications about its analysis in side channel attacks. The SPICE-based simulation of masked gates is shown by Mangard et al. [11]. They also point out that glitches in masked circuits pose the highest threat to masked hardware implementations [12]. And Saeki et al.[13] discussed the glitches in DPA-resistance of masked circuits. Suzuki et al.[14] propose Random Switching Logic (RSL) to suppress the propagation of glitches at the logic level .

In CPA, which is based on the widely used leakage models, such as Hamming Weight and Hamming Distance, glitch effects are not involved. In this paper, we propose a new model, named as Switching Glitch model, for CPA in general cases while taking into account of the glitch power consumption.

The remainder of this paper is organized as follows. Section 2 describes the related background knowledge. Section 3 presents the proposed model. Section 4 shows the measurement setup. Section 5 explains CPA experiments and results in detail. Section 6 draws conclusions.

2 Background

In this section, the necessary background about CPA attacks and leakage models are introduced.

2.1 CPA Attacks

The process of conducting a CPA is as follows.

Step 1, selection. One specific intermediate point of the cryptographic device for an encryption algorithm is selected. This point must be a function of the known variable (e.g. the output of S-box) and secret keys K.

Step 2, measuring. The real power consumption of the cryptographic device is measured when it executes encryption algorithm. The digital oscilloscope can be a good candidate to acquire the power transformations. One such sampling data recorded during one round encryption is also called one power trace.

Step 3, assumption. An assumption is made about the power consumption with certain leakage model based on the selected function in Step 1. For example, the Hamming Weight or Hamming Distance is usually used to predict the power consumption of the specific point.

Step 4, computation. The correlation between the power assumption and the measured data is computed. The value which leads to the highest correlation coefficient corresponds to the correct key guess.

2.2 Leakage Models

For an n-bit processor, in Hamming Weight model, it is assumed that the power consumption is proportional to the number of bits that are set in the processed data value, expressed in Eq.1, where x_i is the value of (i+1)th bit of the processing data value X.

$$HW(X) = \sum_{i=0}^{n-1} x_i, \ x_i \in \{0,1\} \tag{1}$$

Based on the relation between the power consumption of static CMOS circuit and state changing process of the gate circuit, Brier et al. proposed the Hamming Distance model, in Eq.2. X and X' are two consecutive intermediate values of a running algorithm during a target implementation. a denotes the scalar gain between the Hamming Distance and power consumption Y, b denotes the offsets, time dependent components and noise. It assumes that the power consumption Y is proportional to the transitions of the intermediate values not the value been processed.

$$Y = HD(X, X') = a \ HW(X \ X') + b \tag{2}$$

$$Y = a E + b \tag{3}$$

Our work follows the Hamming Distance model whereas considering a more accurate description to the data dependent power dissipation. Since there is a linear relationship between the power consumption Y of the cryptographic device and the assumed power consumption E, shown by Eq.3, the more accurate the assumed power, the more legible this relation appears. The approach to calculate E will be presented in next section.

3 SG Model

The proposed switching glitch model is explained in detail after some preliminaries in this section.

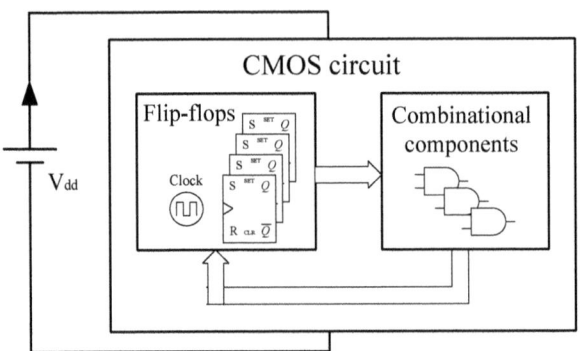

Fig. 1. Simplified structure of CMOS circuit

3.1 Preliminaries

To simplify the problem, the following conditions are satisfied: the cryptographic device is built of CMOS logic gates and edge-triggered flip-flops, and is synchronous. The power supply and ground voltage are fixed on the chip. The simplified structure of a typical CMOS circuit is shown in Fig.1. During the clock ticking, the flip-flops and the combinational components together process the input signals to complete certain functions, such as encryption and so on. So the total power dissipation during this process should include both the flip-flops and combinational components.

The transition probability will be used to aid the analysis of power consumption. Its definition is as follows:

Transition probability [15] for a logic gate or flip-flop X: The average fraction of clock cycles in which the value of X at the end of the cycle is different from its initial value.

The power consumption of a circuit includes two parts: The dynamic power P_{dyn} and the static power P_{stat}. The latter is calculated by Eq.4. V_{dd} is the voltage of the power supply. I_{leak} is the leakage current.

$$P_{stat} = V_{dd} I_{leak} \qquad (4)$$

The dynamic power occurs when the logic gates or flip-flops perform output transitions. One type of this power comes from a short-circuit current. When a signal transition occurs at a gate output, both the pull-up and pull-down transistors can be conducting simultaneously for a short period of time. This causes the short-circuit power consumption P_{sc}. The average power of P_{sc} is expressed by Eq.5. $P_{sc}(t)$ is the instantaneous short-circuit power consumed by one flip-flop or logic gate.

$$P_{sc} = \frac{1}{t} \int_0^t P_{sc}(t)dt \tag{5}$$

Table 1. Power consumption of CMOS circuit

		Flip-flop		$0.5V_{dd}^2 fC_x P(x)$	
Dynamic	Switching activity	Combinational components	Normal Transition	$0.5V_{dd}^2 f \sum_{i=1}^n C_{xi} P(x_i)$	
			glitch	$V_{dd}^2 fC_{av} N_{glch}$	
	Short-circuit	$\frac{1}{t} \int_0^t P_{sc}(t)dt$			
Static	$V_{dd} I_{leak}$				

The other type of dynamic power is consumed by the transition activities of logic gates and flip-flops. For flip-flops, which are the main components of sequential elements of the circuit, the power of one flip-flop can be computed by Eq.6. f denotes the clock frequency. C_x is the total capacitance at one flip-flop output. $P(x)$ is the transition probabilities. In Eq.7, P_{norm} expresses the power consumption of logic gates when they perform normal signal transitions to finish required logic functions. C_{xi} denotes the total capacitance at one gate. $P(x_i)$ is the transition probabilities. n is the total number of logic gates in the circuit. For logic gates, which constitute combinational elements of the circuit, besides the power of P_{norm}, glitch power P_{glch} may occur.

$$P_{flip} = 0.5V_{dd}^2 fC_x P(x) \tag{6}$$

$$P_{norm} = 0.5V_{dd}^2 f \sum_{i=1}^n C_{xi} P(x_i) \tag{7}$$

$$P_{glch} = V_{dd}^2 fC_{av} N_{glch} \tag{8}$$

Glitch or hazard is the temporary states of the output of a combinational component because of the different arrival times of the input signals. Glitch power is a significant portion of the dynamic power consumption. On account of the indeterminate property, a probabilistic modeling is adopted to characterize the glitch power P_{glch}. The power dissipation due to input glitches [16, 17] is shown in Eq.8. C_{av} is the average capacitance at logic gates. N_{glch} expresses the number of generated glitches within a circuit. The total power consumption of a CMOS circuit is summarized in Table1.

3.2 The New Leakage Model

In power analysis, the data dependent and operation dependent power consumption are of the main interest of research. However, in general cases, operation dependent power consumption are more relied on specific cryptographic devices and it is totally black box for attackers. While the short-circuit and static power are negligible [18]. When the logic states change on the arrival of clock cycle, the intermediate value or cipher is stored in flip-flops, and the combinational components perform switching activities. During this period, glitches take place at some logic gates. The dissipated power which is related to data P_{data} is the sum of the power consumed by flip-flops and combinational components, shown as follows.

$$P_{data} = P_{flip} + P_{norm} + P_{glch} \tag{9}$$

For an encryption circuit, it is costly to compute the exact value of each part of P_{data} by the equation in Table1. But quantitatively, from the equations in Table 1, we can conclude that the power consumption of flip-flops and combinational components is in a close magnitude. In other words, a number of flip-flops could consume similar power with the normal combinational components except the little difference of load capacitances. So we can simplify this proportional with some factors.

From a high level of perspective, the estimated energy E of encryption, namely SG model, is shown as follows.

$$E = E_{sf} + \beta \tag{10}$$

$$E_{sf} = N_{01} + \alpha \, N_{10} \tag{10.1}$$

E_{sf} denotes the power of normal switching activities of combinational gates and flip-flops. While glitch factor β describes the glitch power which is circuit and algorithm specific. For different chips and encryption data paths, the glitch factors vary a lot. N_{01} and N_{10} are the number of switches performed by the circuit from 0 to 1 and 1 to 0 respectively. α is switching factor, it characterizes the difference of such transitions. The existence of switching factor is based on the fact that these two kinds of transitions consume different power in normal switching activities. Our ways to estimate glitch factor β are as follows.

$$E_{sf} / \beta = P_{norm} / P_{glch} = 0.5 V_{dd}^2 f \sum\nolimits_{i=1}^{n} C_{xi} P(x_i) \Big/ V_{dd}^2 \, fC_{av} N_{glch} \tag{11}$$

Suppose that the total capacitance at each gate C_{xi} equals to C_{av}, and then the expression is simplified to Eq.12.

$$E_{sf} / \beta = 0.5 \sum\nolimits_{i=1}^{n} P(x_i) \Big/ N_{glch} \tag{12}$$

For an encryption circuit, the value of $P(x_i)$ depends on the input data. Furthermore, if we know the relation between the number of generated glitches N_{glch} and the logic gates n, then β can be expressed by some expression of E_{sf}. In fact, because of the complexity of the design technologies and detailed processing techniques of CMOS circuits, it seems that this relation is unpredictable without CAD simulation tool. We will make a further reckon and verify it through experiments.

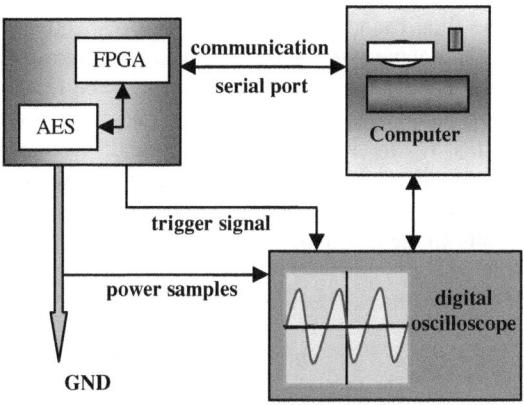

Fig. 2. Experiment environment

4   Measurement Setup

In this section, we describe the process of conducting CPA. As an example, our CPA is against AES implementations on SASEBO [19], which is provided by AIST and Tohoku University [20].

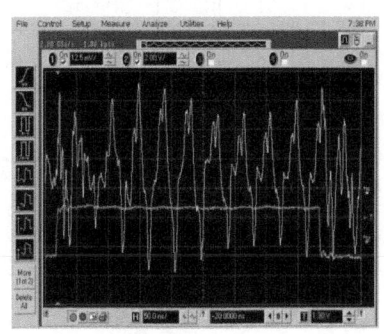

Fig. 3. Power signals   **Fig. 4.** Sampling power curves

Firstly, we select one specific point for the attack. According to the architecture of the AES on ASIC, we choose the output of the final round of encryption function AddRoundKey as a target.

Secondly, the encryption process is measured. The experimental environment is shown in Fig.2.The computer randomly generates 128-bit plaintext in 10k groups, which are transmitted to the FPGA through RS-232 serial ports, and then upon receipt of the plaintext, the FPGA control the ASIC to implement AES encryption program. At the same time, the execution signal on ASIC triggers the digital oscilloscope to start sampling, and thus the oscilloscope obtains power signals through its probe, shown in Fig.3. The sampled data is transmitted to computer through LAN. After the encryption is finished, the cipher text is transmitted to computer. So we obtain 10k groups of plaintext, corresponding cipher text as well as 10k power traces Y. The power curves of 1, 50,1k and 10k for the final round are shown in Fig.4 respectively, where "PT" represents "Power Trace", "k" denotes "thousand". They are almost overlapped.

Then we make estimation about the power consumption of the final round encryption. The cipher texts C are picked up to compute with guessed keys K by inverse-shift rows, inverse-sub bytes, C' are induced. Thus N_{01}' and N_{10}' can be calculated respectively. With our proposed model, we predict that the power consumption of final round encryption is $E_{est} = (N_{01}' + \alpha\ N_{10}') + \beta$. If α and β are determined, we could conduct this CPA continually to the last step.

Table 2. Number of power traces to recover all the key bytes at different SF

	1	2	3	4	5	6	7	8	9	10	11	12	13	14	15	16	Sacu
SF3.5	42	62	34	16	29	74	30	37	46	36	39	48	100	22	63	63	-132
SF3.0	42	61	34	16	29	74	30	35	41	35	28	49	90	21	51	50	-75
SF2.5	42	57	16	16	29	74	31	32	38	34	29	48	90	21	51	54	-53
SF2.0	42	54	34	11	31	55	32	35	37	33	22	48	41	21	50	50	13
SF1.8	42	52	17	11	31	55	32	35	38	34	22	48	41	22	50	50	29
SF1.7	43	51	15	11	29	58	36	35	33	34	21	51	40	21	50	48	35
SF1.6	35	51	16	15	31	56	40	24	32	32	28	48	41	21	50	47	42
SF1.5	35	51	16	15	31	56	40	24	28	32	28	47	38	20	50	47	51
SF1.3	35	54	16	15	28	75	55	31	31	29	38	58	38	15	49	28	14
SF1.1	35	65	16	15	46	76	55	21	26	35	23	64	37	15	49	28	3
SF0.9	38	70	15	20	46	93	67	21	38	39	31	66	40	25	50	28	-72
SF0.8	35	70	15	20	46	93	67	21	28	41	34	66	43	23	50	26	-66
HD	35	65	16	15	46	76	55	24	26	35	23	64	37	15	49	28	0

Finally, the correlation coefficient of the real power consumption Y and the predicted power consumption E_{est} is calculated according to Eq. 13 and Eq.14. Since the predicted power consumption contains key guesses, when the correct key guess appears, the correlation coefficient is supposed to be largest.

$$\rho\ (Y, E_{est}) = \frac{Cov(Y, E_{est})}{\sqrt{Var(Y)}\sqrt{Var(E_{est})}} \tag{13}$$

$$Cov\ (Y, E_{est}) = \frac{1}{n} \sum_{i=1}^{n} [Y_i - \overline{Y}][E_{est\,j} - \overline{E_{est}}] \tag{14}$$

ρ is the correlation coefficient between the power traces and estimated power consumption, V_{ar} is the mathematical Variance of Y and E_{est} respectively. $\overline{Y}$ and $\overline{E_{est}}$ are the average values of Y and E_{est} respectively. n denotes the n_{th} point in power traces, $1 =< i <= n$, j denotes the j_{th} guess of keys.

5 Experiments

In this section, we will further explain the SG model through experiments.

5.1 CPA without Glitches

Notably, we focus on E_{sf} part of SG model, shown in Eq.10.1. The aim of this analysis without considering the power consumption of glitches is to determine the switching factor α (in short, SF). With the acquired power trace curves, which is from the execution of AES with composite field S-box (In Table3, AES1), we conducted CPA on a PC.

When the value of α is set to range from 0.8 to 3.5, the number of power traces used to recover all the 16- byte (128-bit) keys of AES is shown in Table 2. Some identical lines are omitted. For example, when SF is 1.4, the number of power traces is the same as SF1.3. Note that, all the numbers are in unit 100. For instance, when switching factor is 3.5, the first bytes of AES keys can be recovered at 4200 power traces.

In order to find the optimal switching factor, the results of different SF-based analysis are compared with Hamming Distance (HD) model. At the last line of Table 2, the results of CPA using the same power curves with HD model are listed. To quantitatively explore which SF is better, we define "accumulation factor" S_{acu}, shown by Eq. 15. For switching factor N, the accumulative numbers of power traces of all the 16 bytes is the sum of the differences of each byte. It expresses the improved accumulative number of power traces compared with HD.

$$S_{acu}(N) = \sum_{i=1}^{16}(X_{HDi} - X_{Sfi}) \tag{15}$$

When S_{acu} is positive, that means the number of power traces is decreased. While the negative S_{acu} stands for an increase of power traces. For HD itself, this value is 0. So

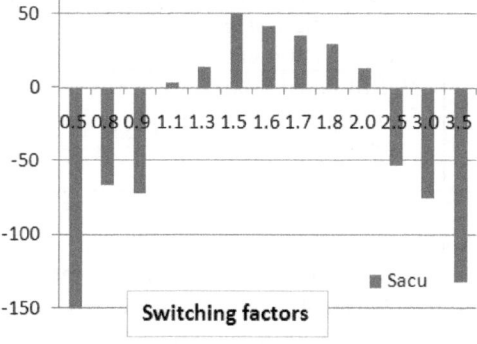

Fig. 5. S_{acu} of different switching factor

the larger this value is, the better the performance is improved. The last column of Table 2 shows the S_{acu} of each SF. Fig.5 gives a more clear vision of S_{acu} at different SF. We can see that the S_{acu} is the largest when SF is 1.5. Therefore, for AES encryption on ASIC, when switching factor is set to 1.5, the 16-byte keys can be recovered with least power traces.

5.2 CPA with Glitches

The purpose of the following experiments is to estimate the glitch factor β in SG model, thus further improve CPA performances. From Eq.15, β can be expressed by Eq.16.

$$\beta = E_{sf} \, N_{glch} / 0.5 \sum_{i=1}^{n} P(x_i) \tag{16}$$

In our experiment, since the plaintext is randomized, the transition probability of the logic gates can be estimated with value 0.5. Then Eq.17 is derived.

$$\beta = E_{sf} \, N_{glch} / 0.25 \, N_{gats} \tag{17}$$

N_{gats} denotes the number of logic gates in encryption circuit. For one byte input data, with switching factor α 1.5, E_{sf} is in 10 magnitude. Suppose that the average generation rate of glitches at the logic gates is 0.1, and then β can be calculated from Eq.17 at 1.0 magnitude.

Table 3. AES Cryptographic circuits on ASIC

Name	Implementation	Gate No.	Area (μm^2)
AES1	Composite field S-box with encryption only	12059	61408
AES2	S-box with Look Up Table	20639	105097
AES3	Positive Prime Reed Muler (PPRM)based S-box using 1-stage AND-XOR logic.	61801	314702
AES4	PPRM-based S-box using 3-stage AND-XOR logic.	16541	84230

However, in our experiment, different values of this glitch factor are attempted. We find that 1.0E-1 is the optimal value rather than the theoretical value 1.0. That is to say, when β is set at 1.0E-1, the number of power traces becomes least.

Since the value of switching factor α and glitch factor β are both computed, the CPA experiments with glitches are continued. We tested CPA against different AES hardware structures based on HD model and SG model on the same chip, which is named IC_a. The cryptographic core uses 0.13μm TSMC standard library of CMOS process technology. The detailed information of each AES is shown in Table 3. Throughout the experiments, the initial encryption 16-byte keys are set as hexadecimal numbers: 12 34 56 78 90 AB CD EF 12 34 56 78 90 AB CD EF. The final round encryption keys are: C3 BE 32 F4 60 A9 B3 4E F7 43 61 57 F2 B9 19 D8.

Table 4. Comparison of CPA on IC_a

Name	Glitch Factor	HD (K)	SG Without Glitch (K)	Reduction Rate (%)	SG With Glitch (K)	Reduction Rate (%)
AES1	0.1	7.6	5.6	26.3	5.4	28.9
AES2	0.09	3.5	3.1	11.4	2.9	17.1
AES3	0.09	3.2	2.9	9.3	2.8	12.5
AES4	0.2	4.9	4.0	18.4	3.8	22.4

In Table 4, we list the glitch factor and the least number of power traces used to recover 16-byte keys by HD model and SG model respectively as well as the power trace reduction rate, where K denotes 1000. For example, the first line of Table4 means: For AES1 implementation on IC_a, the HD-based CPA uses 7.6k power traces to recover16-byte keys. The SG-based CPA without glitches can recover these keys at 5.6k power traces. And the power traces have been reduced by 26.3% compared with HD-based CPA. While the SG model with glitches can recover these keys with 5.4k power traces. And the power traces have been reduced by 28.9%. For different AES implementations, the glitch factors vary. But they are almost in the same magnitude about 1.0E-1. Notably, the reduction rates of power trace also differ a lot.

The correlation coefficient ρ of recovering all the key bytes are calculated from Eq.13. In Fig.6, the computation process of 13th byte key "F2" is exemplified. The largest correlation coefficient peaks at the guess value of F2. In Fig.7, the correct key appears clearly from 10k power traces.

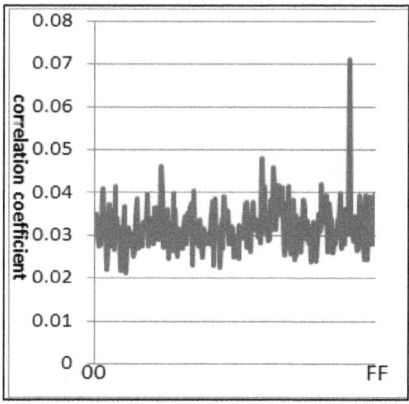

Fig. 6. The correlation coefficient of recovering the 13th key

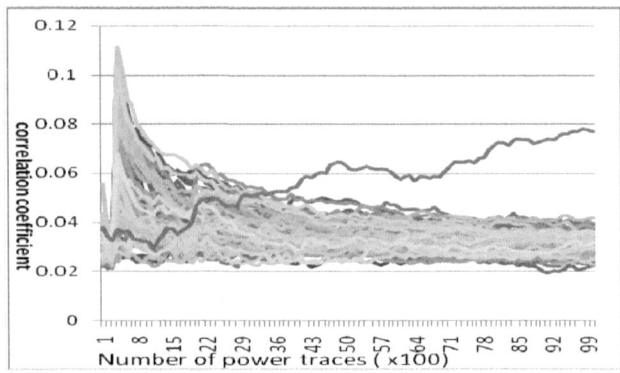

Fig. 7. The appearing of correlation coefficient for correct key

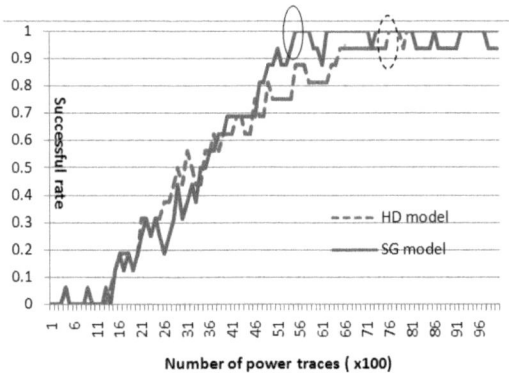

Fig. 8. The successful rates of CPA against AES1 on IC_a

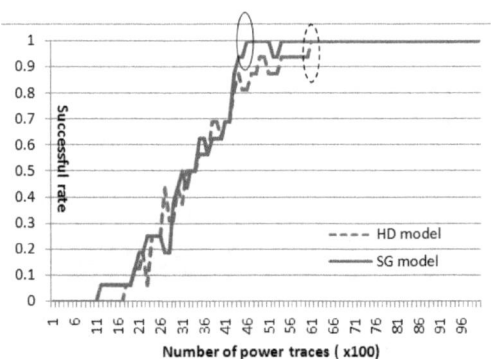

Fig. 9. The successful rates of CPA against AES1on IC_b

Table 5. Power Comparison of CPA on IC_b

Name	Glitch Factor	HD (K)	SG Without Glitch (K)	Reduction Rate (%)	SG With Glitch (K)	Reduction Rate (%)
AES1	0.1	6.1	5.1	16.4	4.6	24.5
AES2	0.09	3.0	2.7	10.0	2.6	14.4
AES3	0.09	2.3	2.1	8.7	2.0	13.0
AES4	0.2	3.4	2.9	14.7	2.7	20.6

The successful rates [21] of HD-based and SG-based CPA against AES1 are illustrated in Fig.8. Successful rates express the number of power traces when all the keys can be recovered. With HD model, 100% appears at 7.6k power traces, which is circled in the Fig. But with the proposed SG model, 100% appears at 5.4k power traces, which means the power traces of recovering keys have been decreased by 28.9%.

To verify the SG model, the same experiments are repeated on another chip, namely IC_b, which is produced with the same technology. The results are listed in Table5. The same glitch factor is used for each AES implementation. Surprisingly, the SG with glitches can further cut the number of power traces from 5.1k to 4.6k, which means the glitch power leakage leads to a reduction rate of 8.1%, namely (24.5-16.4) %. That is much than expected. The greatest reduction rate of power trace is 24.5%, which occurs at CPA against AES1. The successful rates are also compared with HD-based CPA in Fig.9.With HD model, 100% appears at 6.1k power traces, which is circled in the Fig. But with SG model, 100% appears at 4.6k power traces. The power traces of recovering keys have been reduced by 24.5%.

From results of Table 4 and Table 5, the glitch effects contribute a lot to CPA. The power traces are reduced because that a more accurate model which including the power consumption of glitches is built.

6   Conclusions

In this paper, a new power consumption model, namely Switching Glitch model, is proposed, which characterizes the power consumption of cryptographic devices more accurately. The distinguishing of two different dynamic switching activities and the power consumption of glitches are both included. Compared with CPA based on Hamming Distance model, it can reduce the number of power traces by as much as 28.9%. However the switching factor and glitch factor are experimentally represented from AES implementation on ASIC after theoretical derivations. Theoretically, these two factors can be applied to other CPA not confined to against AES and ASIC chip. The future work is to evaluate more encryption implementations based on the Switching Glitch model.

Acknowledgment

This work was supported by "Global COE program" of MEXT and CREST of JST in Japan.

References

1. Kocher, P., Jaffe, J., Jun, B.: Differential Power Analysis. In: CRYPTO 1999. LNCS, vol. 1666, pp. 388–397. Springer, Heidelberg (1999)
2. Brier, E., Clavier, C., Olivier, F.: Correlation Power Analysis with a Leakage Model. In: Joye, M., Quisquater, J.-J. (eds.) CHES 2004. LNCS, vol. 3156, pp. 16–29. Springer, Heidelberg (2004)
3. Le, T., Clédière, J., Canovas, C., et al.: A proposition for correlation power analysis enhancement. In: Goubin, L., Matsui, M. (eds.) CHES 2006. LNCS, vol. 4249, p. 174. Springer, Heidelberg (2006)
4. Katashita, T., Satoh, A., Sugawara, T., et al.: Enhanced Correlation Power Analysis Using Key Screening Technique. In: Proceedings of Reconfigurable Computing and FPGAs (ReConFig 2008), December 3-5, pp. 403–408 (2008)
5. Peeters, E., Standaert, F.X., Quisquater, J.J.: Power and electromagnetic analysis: Improved model, consequences and comparisons. Integration, the VLSI Journal 40(1), 52–60 (2007)
6. National Institute of Standards and Technology (NIST) of U.S. Department of Commerce: FIPS 197: Advanced Encryption Standard (2001)
7. Mangard, S.: A simple power analysis attack on implementation of the AES expansion. In: Lee, P.J., Lim, C.H. (eds.) ICISC 2002. LNCS, vol. 2587, pp. 343–358. Springer, Heidelberg (2003)
8. Ors, S.B., Gurkaynak, F., Oswald, E., et al.: Power-Analysis Attack on an ASIC AES implementation. In: Proceedings of ITCC 2004, Las Vegas, April 5-7 (2004)
9. Lu, Y., Agrawal, V.D.: CMOS Leakage and Glitch Minimization for Power-Performance Tradeoff. Journal of Low Power Electronics 2(3), 1–10 (2006)
10. Raghunathan, A., Dey, S., Jha, N.K.: High-level macro-modeling and estimation techniques for switching activity and power consumption. IEEE Transactions on Very Large Scale Integration (VLSI) Systems 11(4), 538–557 (2003)
11. Mangard, S., Popp, T., Gammel, B.M.: Side-channel Leakage of Masked CMOS Gates. In: Menezes, A. (ed.) CT-RSA 2005. LNCS, vol. 3376, pp. 351–365. Springer, Heidelberg (2005)
12. Mangard, S., Schramm, K.: Pinpointing the side-channel leakage of masked AES hardware implementations. In: Goubin, L., Matsui, M. (eds.) CHES 2006. LNCS, vol. 4249, pp. 76–90. Springer, Heidelberg (2006)
13. Saeki, M., Suzuki, D., Ichikawa, T.: Leakage analysis of DPA Countermeasures at the Logic Level. IEICE transactions on fundamentals of electronics, communications and computer sciences E90-A(1), 169–178 (2007)
14. Suzuki, D., Saeki, M., Ichikawa, T.: Random Switching Logic: A New Countermeasure against DPA and Second-Order DPA at the Logic Level. IEICE transactions on fundamentals of electronics, communications and computer sciences E90-A(1), 160–168 (2007)
15. Najm, F.N.: Power estimation techniques for integrated circuits. In: Proceedings of the International Conference on Computer-Aided Design, California, United States, pp. 492–499 (1995)
16. Liu, X., Papaefthymiou, M.C.: A statistical model of input glitch propagation and its application in power macromodeling. Journal of Power 10, 10
17. Liu, X., Papaefthymiou, M.C.: Incorporation of input glitches into power macromodeling. In: Proceedings of IEEE International Symposium on Circuits and Systems (2002)
18. Chari, S., Jutla, C.S., Rao, J.R., et al.: Towards sound approaches to counteract power analysis attacks. In: Wiener, M. (ed.) CRYPTO 1999. LNCS, vol. 1666, pp. 398–412. Springer, Heidelberg (1999)

19. Research Center for Information Security (RCIS) of AIST: Side-channel Attack Standard Evaluation Board (SASEBO),
    http://www.rcis.aist.go.jp/special/SASEBO/index-en.html
20. Computer Structures Laboratory of Tohoku University.: Cryptographic Hardware Project,
    http://www.aoki.ecei.tohoku.ac.jp/crypto
21. Qian, G., Zhou, Y., Xing, Y., et al.: A Weighted Statistical Analysis of DPA Attack on an ASIC AES Implementation. In: Proceedings of IEEE 8th International Conference on ASIC (ASICON 2009), Changsha, China, October 20-23 (2009)

Appendix

A.   AES Implementation on ASIC

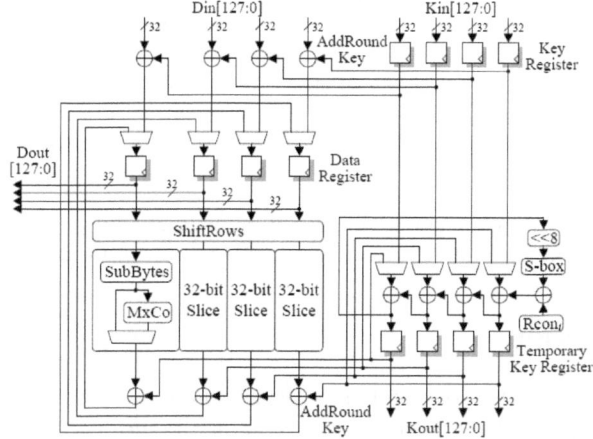

B. CPA Experiment Environment

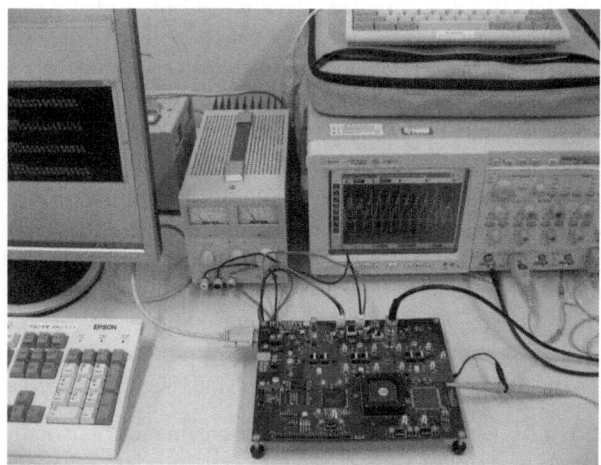

Vulnerabilities of Wireless Key Exchange Based on Channel Reciprocity

Nico Döttling, Dejan Lazich*,
Jörn Müller-Quade, and Antonio Sobreira de Almeida

Karlsruhe Institute of Technology, Institute of Cryptography and Security,
Faculty of Informatics, Am Fasanengarten 5, 76131 Karlsruhe, Germany
{ndoett,lazic,muellerq,almeida}@ira.uka.de

Abstract. Wireless key exchange on the physical layer is a key exchange protocol independent of computational assumptions. It relies only on the physical properties of the wireless channels to generate a common secret key between two parties. Precise conditions, however, for such a key exchange to be secure remain unclear. An argument why unconditional security does not hold for general scenarios is provided. Finally, a novel side-channel attack against such key exchange schemes is described and experimentally validated.

Keywords: Wireless key exchange, physical layer, channel reciprocity, joint randomness, antenna reradiation, side-channel attacks.

1 Introduction

The ubiquitous presence of wireless networks has renewed the interest in key exchange schemes on the physical layer. One of the most promising techniques to generate cryptographic keys on the physical layer is based on the concept of reciprocity of wireless channels. Wireless channels exhibit a phenomenon called multipath interference or multipath fading. In such channels, emitted radio signals are scattered and reflected from various physical obstacles such as cars, buildings, trees, and many others. Thus a receiver will receive the original signal superposed with several echoes caused by reflections. Reciprocity states that the channel, characterized by its channel impulse response, will remain the same if the roles of sender and receiver are exchanged. Therefore a sender-receiver system consisting of two physically separated transceivers, Alice and Bob, can extract joint randomness by measuring the impulse response of the wireless channel between them. The randomness comes from unknown and dynamic electromagnetic characteristics of the physical environment that surrounds them. As during the coherence time the measured channel impulse response is the same for Alice and Bob, it can be processed to a common secret key. Crucial for this concept to be secure is that any further eavesdropping receiver, sufficiently physically separated from the legitimate protocol parties, will receive uncorrelated

---

* Dejan Lazich is now with the Institute of Telecommunications and Applied Information Theory, University of Ulm, Germany (email: dejan.lazich@uni-ulm.de)

Y. Chung and M. Yung (Eds.): WISA 2010, LNCS 6513, pp. 206–220, 2011.

measurements. In this paper we consider such key exchange protocols based on multipath interference and the reciprocity of wireless channels.

After Section 2, where we summarize previous results about wireless key exchange, we will introduce the concepts necessary for reciprocity-based key exchange in Section 3. The basic protocol to generate a common key from a fading channel will be described. Furthermore, we will demonstrate an aspect of reciprocity-based key exchange that has so far been neglected. More precisely, a model scenario for fading channels will be provided in which a passive eavesdropping adversary can reconstruct a key generated by two protocol parties Alice and Bob. In Section 4, a new side-channel attack against reciprocity-based key exchange will be described. This side-channel attack is based on the phenomenon of passive signal reradiation that occurs in receiving antennas. An exhaustive analysis is then presented and the conditions under which this attack can be mounted are identified in detail. Upper theoretical bounds for the feasibility of this attack are derived. In Section 5 we present one experimental study that validates this attack and we conclude in Section 6.

2   Previous Work

Wireless security on the physical layer is an extensively studied subject. Wireless secret key exchange can be based on several principles.

Noise-based methods rely on the assumption that both the legitimate user's channel noise and the eavesdropper's channel noise are uncorrelated. Wyner introduced the famous wiretap channel model in [Wyn75], which is extended to a gaussian wiretap channel in [LYCH78]. Other information-theoretic approaches extending Maurer's paper [Mau93] considered the secrecy capacity of wireless channels, as described in [BBRM08]. It is stated that information-theoretic security is achievable even when the eavesdropper's channel has a better average signal-to-noise ratio (SNR) than the main channel, given quasi-static Rayleigh fading channels.

Reciprocity-based approaches use the fact that channel characteristics are identical when sender and receiver are exchanged. The idea of using the wireless channel as a keying variable first came up in the Hershey, Hassan and Yarlagadda landmark paper [HHY95], which is extended in [HSHC96] and [KHC00]. In this setup, two receivers located far enough from each other in a complex enough environment receive uncorrelated signals [OOKF68] due to reflections and interference of signals propagating through different paths. Rapid spatial decorrelation is the basis of a few schemes used for key exchange. Some rules-of-thumb were established in order to characterize how far both receivers should be separated from each other and how complex the environmental conditions should be. Unconditional security from fading channels is also exploited in [TM01]. Further key establishment schemes claiming unconditional security have been proposed in [MTM+08, YMR+09].

Channel reciprocity can also be used to detect spoofing attacks [LXMT06]. In [ASKMY07] another method for reciprocity-based key exchange is introduced.

Other alternatives were also described in order to achieve a secure key exchange even when the environment is not complex enough or does not change sufficiently over time. In this context, the use of a very peculiar time-varying radiation pattern antennas (ESPAR antennas) was reported, as described in [AHT+05, Ohi05, SHOK04]. The working principle of these antennas is presented in [SHOK04].

More recently, new methods using *multiple-input multiple-output (MIMO)* systems were proposed to enhance security [KV08]. It has been suggested to use the inherent properties of MIMO channels, as well as some characteristics from the different parties, to ensure security under certain conditions, as described in detail in [GN05], [KV08] and [LHR06].

Jamming-based methods make use of a usually "bad intentional" technique in order to obtain secrecy. They try to degrade the eavesdropper's channel in order to achieve a higher SNR for the legitimate users than for the eavesdropper, as exposed in [JYK+07]. Further *jamming-based* techniques are presented in [XTZW05] and [TY07].

3   The Key Exchange Protocol and Security Guarantees

In communications engineering, radio channels are usually represented by their impulse response. We will assume that the channels we consider are quasi-static during the time period of the key exchange. We will thus consider time-invariant impulse responses $h_{AB}(t)$ of a multipath fading channel between a sender Alice and a receiver Bob. The impulse response $h_{AB}(t)$ of the multipath fading channel is given by an impulse train

$$h_{AB}(t) = \sum_{i=1}^{n} \rho_i \delta(t - \tau_i),$$

where the τ_i are the latencies and the coefficients ρ_i are the phasors of the direct and scattered signal components. The scattered components are assumed to arise by reflections of the sent signal, caused by reflective objects like buildings, cars, etc. Reciprocity states that the channel characteristics are the same during the coherence time of the channel if the roles of sender and receiver are exchanged, thus

$$h_{BA} = h_{AB} = h$$

Typical coherence times for fading channels are around 2.5 ms [TV05]. It was observed in [HHY95] that the mutual information that can be extracted from the common channel impulse response h might be used to generate a common secret between Alice and Bob. Some practical implementations have already been designed, e.g. [MTM+08], [LXMT06] and [ASKMY07].

The elementary requirement for reciprocity-based key exchange to be secure is the presence of a fading channel that decorrelates spatially. More precisely, the channel responses h_{AE} and h_{BE} an eavesdropper measures should be uncorrelated to $h_{AB} = h_{BA}$. Usually the spatial decorrelation is implicitly assumed in models describing fading channels. The most common stochastic processes used to model the randomness of fading channels are the Rayleigh and Rician processes. They have been shown to be appropriate to model fading channels in urban or rural areas [OOKF68]. Such models are successfully utilized to analyze and estimate typical error patterns in wireless communication. However, they fail to model how much uncorrelated randomness can be extracted from multipath fading channels. Still, this was commonly assumed in recent work [MTM$^+$08, YMR$^+$09]. However, it is infeasible to give worst case guarantees for wireless key exchange. We want to motivate this by providing a model that instantiates a fading channel for which the reciprocity-based key exchange protocols become insecure under some reasonable assumptions. Even though this model is overly idealized, it demonstrates the fundamental intricacies of wireless key exchange. This model exhibits the following properties:

- The environment is planar. There is only a finite (and small) number of point-shaped specular reflectors with isotropic reflection characteristics. Each reflector R_i has its distinct attenuation factor α_i, which is chosen uniformly from $(0, 1]$;
- There are three parties: two legitimate parties Alice and Bob, who each send and receive one signal, and an adversary (eavesdropper) Eve who only receives signals. Each of them has one antenna;
- We shall only consider first order reflections of signals. Furthermore, in order to simplify the analysis, we neglect noise.

We demand that the adversary Eve knows the positions p_A of Alice and p_B of Bob relative to her own position p_E. This might, for instance, be the case if Alice is an access point and Bob is a static user terminal [HIU$^+$08]. If just one signal s is sent, for instance from Alice to Bob, Bob will measure $h_{AB} * s$, whereas Eve will measure $h_{AE} * s$. To simplify our considerations we will assume that Eve can recover h_{AE} such that the peaks of h_{AE} can still be separated. The information Eve learns from h_{AE} is insufficient to retrieve significant information about Bob's measurement or h_{AB}, as, from her view, Bob's measurement is indetermined by several degrees of freedom. So, Bob's measurement is subject to a significant amount of uncertainty for Eve. The bottom line, however, is that, in this model, given the channel impulse responses h_{AE} between Alice and Eve and h_{BE} between Bob and Eve, Eve is enabled to uniquely recover the channel impulse response h_{AB} within the scope of her measuring accuracy. We will briefly paraphrase how this attack works. Let

$$h_{AE}(t) = \sum_{i=1}^{n} \rho_i \delta(t - \tau_i).$$

We assume that the first peak $\rho_1 \delta(t - \tau_1)$ of the channel impulse response h_{AE} represents the direct path between Alice and Eve. All further multipath components $\rho_i \delta(t - \tau_i)$, $i > 1$ have traversed a distance

$$d_i = d(p_A, p_E) + (\tau_i - \tau_1) \cdot c,$$

where c is the vacuum speed of light. So,

$$d_i = d(p_A, p_{R_i}) + d(p_E, p_{R_i}) \tag{1}$$

defines an equation for some reflector R_i that accounts for this multipath component. The set of solutions for p_{R_i} of (1) is an ellipse. Likewise every multipath component of h_{BE} provides an ellipse equation. The possible loci of the reflectors lie at the intersections of the ellipses obtained from h_{AE} and h_{BE}. We can check for each point of intersection p_S if it is a valid position for a reflector by testing whether it has roughly the same attenuation factor α on both assumed paths. In a final step, the adversary Eve simulates the signal propagation from Alice to Bob in her reconstructed environment to obtain h_{AB}. To obtain accuracy bounds, we have implemented this model in MATLAB and run simulations with several parameter sets. See the Appendix A.1 for simulation results. This argument demonstrates the principal unreliability of implicitly assuming spatial uncorrelatedness of joint measurements.

4   Reradiation Side-Channel

In this section, a new attack against the wireless key exchange on the physical layer, called *reradiated wireless side-channel (RRW-SC)* attack, is presented and analyzed.

The following paragraphs will introduce basic concepts which are necessary for obtaining a method for the derivation of upper bounds on the distance to a receiving antenna where it is still practically possible for an adversary to recover an useful amount of information by considering only the reradiation of the receiving antenna in use.

The general model for an antenna in the receiving mode is described in [Bal97]. This Thévenin equivalent model consists of a simple electrical circuit with the antenna impedance $Z_A = R_A + jX_A$ and the input impedance of the receiver $Z_R = R_R + jX_R$ serially connected to the voltage generator V_R representing the induced voltage by the incident wave. In general, the resistive part $R_A = R_r + R_L$ of Z_A consists of two components, where R_r represents the reradiation resistance and R_L the loss resistance of the antenna. In a conjugate matching condition ($R_r + R_L = R_R$ and $X_A = -X_R$) between the antenna and the receiver, the maximum amount of power is transmitted to the receiver. In this case, expressions for powers P_R, P_r, and P_L delivered to R_R, R_r, and R_L, respectively, as well as the collected (induced) power P_c can be simply calculated. From these expressions follows that from the total amount of power P_c induced in the antenna, half is transmitted to the receiver (P_R) and the other half is partly reradiated (P_r) and partly dissipated as heat (P_L). The ratio $\rho = P_r/P_c$ is called *reradiating factor*. In practice, ρ usually ranges between 0,4 and 0,8.

The previous analysis clearly shows that the amount of power reradiated is an important phenomenon that can leak information about the received signal. Let's consider the following example: Eve has a measuring receiver with a high-gain antenna directed towards Bob's receiver in line-of-sight. When Bob gets the signal (containing information about the secret key) coming from Alice, it will be partially reradiated. Eve will try to capture this signal in order to recover the key. Therefore, Bob and Alice should make Eve's intentions more difficult to achieve by implementing appropriate countermeasures.

In order to estimate the real threat of the RRW-SC and to evaluate the efficiency of the countermeasures, the concept of the *maximal attacking range* (MAR), D_m, using RRW-SC can be introduced. MAR represents the maximal distance d_{BE} between Bob and Eve at which Eve has a practical chance to recover the secret key coming from Alice by only using information obtained from the RRW-SC. The first step in the MAR estimation is the expression of average energy per bit at the receiver, E_{bR}, which is caused by free space propagation of electromagnetic waves. In terms of the average energy per bit at the transmitter, E_{bT}, this *range equation* [Bla90] has the following form:

$$E_{bR} = aE_{bT} = \frac{G_T}{4\pi} \frac{\lambda^2 G_R}{4\pi} \frac{E_{bT}}{d^2} = \frac{\alpha A_R E_{bT}}{d^2}. \tag{2}$$

G_T and G_R are the gains of the transmitting and receiving antennas in the direction of propagation, d is the range from transmitter (Tx) to receiver (Rx) and λ the wavelength of the electromagnetic radiation (EMR). The equation (2) can also be expressed in terms of average power, S, rather than of average energy by replacing E_{bR} and E_{bT} by S_{bR} and S_{bT}. The factor a in (2) represents the *energy (power) attenuation* of EMR between Rx and Tx, which can be expressed by the product of the effective area of the receiving antenna $A_R = \frac{\lambda^2 G_R}{4\pi}$ and the spherical density of the transmitting antenna gain $\alpha = \frac{G_T}{4\pi}$.

Any receiver at absolute temperature T_R will always contaminate the received signal with additive white Gaussian noise (AWGN) of power spectral density $N_0 = kT_R$, where k is the Boltzmann constant (k = 1,38x10^{-23} joule per degree Kelvin). This thermal noise is due to unavoidable thermal fluctuations of electrons in the first stage of amplification at electronic receivers. Actual receivers will have a somewhat larger value of thermal noise power spectral density expressed as

$$N_0 = FkT_R, \tag{3}$$

where F is a number known as the noise figure of the receiver. Ideally, $F = 1$, but in practice it is larger. For a high-quality receiver, it is in the range of 2 to 5.

Generally, the quality of digital communication can be expressed by the average *bit error rate* (BER, denoted by P_{be}) in the received data. In wireless communication systems it depends on numerous influencing factors. The most important are: implemented modulation/demodulation and error control encoding/decoding techniques, the information bit rate R_b, the average power S_T of Tx, the occupied frequency bandwidth W around the carrier frequency f_c, as well as EMR interferences, obstacles and reflectors in the influenceable zone around Tx and Rx. By considering only the ubiquitous influencing factors, the *signal-to-noise ratio* (SNR) in the presence of the AWGN, given by $\frac{S_R}{S_{AWGN}}$, can be expressed as

$$SNR = \frac{S_R}{WN_0} = \frac{aS_T}{WN_0}, \tag{4}$$

where $S_R = aS_T$ is the average signal power and $S_{AWGN} = WN_0$ the thermal noise power at the input of Rx. By introducing (2) and (3) in (4)

$$SNR = \frac{\alpha A_R}{FkT_R}\frac{S_T}{Wd^2} = Q\frac{S_T}{Wd^2}, \tag{5}$$

where $Q = \frac{\alpha A_R}{FkT_R}$ represents the *basic quality* of the wireless AWGN channel. In practice, there are many other influencing factors that degrade Q, like the conduction and dielectric efficiency of antennas, taking in account losses at the input terminals and within the structure of antenna. Such degradation factors are very difficult to model and compute, but they can be determined experimentally. Thus, the practical basic quality Q_p of a wireless channel has always a smaller value than Q and can be expressed by the experimental corrective factor $e < 1$ as $Q_p = eQ$.

For example, the basic quality of an omnidirectional wireless channel ($G_R = G_T = 1$) in the 433 MHz ISM-band (*Industrial, Scientific, and Medical* radio bands) with the carrier signal wavelength $\lambda = 0,7$ m and a receiver at room temperature and noise figure $F = 2$ amounts $Q = 0,384\mathrm{x}10^{18}$ $[m^2/J]$. The basic quality of the wireless channel decreases with the growing carrier frequency. For example, in the 2,4 GHz ISM-band an omnidirectional wireless channel ($G_R = G_T = 1$) with the carrier signal wavelength $\lambda = 0,125$ m and a receiver at room temperature and noise figure F = 2 has a basic quality of $Q = 1,223\mathrm{x}10^{16}$ $[m^2/J]$. When using a transmitter with average power of $S_T = 100$ mW and a bandwidth $W = 1$ MHz in the 433 MHz ISM-band the dependence of SNR on the Tx – Rx distance d can be, according to (5), expressed as $SNR = 3,84\mathrm{x}10^{10}d^{-2}$. For a channel in the 2,4 GHz ISM-band and the same values of S_T and W, this dependency is given by $SNR = 1,22\mathrm{x}10^9 d^{-2}$.

The most adequate detection technique for modelling the secret key extraction in the wireless key exchange on the physical layer is the detection of an M-ary amplitude shift keying signal (M-ASK, also called pulse amplitude modulation M-PAM). The exact average word (symbol) error probability (WER, denoted by P_{we}) in dependence of SNR for the M-ASK detection is given by [J.G02]

$$P_{we} = \frac{(M-1)}{M}erfc(\sqrt{\frac{3SNR}{2(M^2-1)}}), \tag{6}$$

where erfc(x) denotes the complementary error-function and M the number of chosen amplitude levels in a signal sample labeled by $q = log_2 M$ key bits. For example, from (5) and (6) and for above chosen values of S_T, W, λ, F, G_R and G_T in the 433 MHz ISM-band the value $WER = 10^{-2}$ will be attained at the distance of $d = 17$ km, while in the 2,4 GHz ISM-band the same value of WER will be attained at the distance $d = 2$ km, if the number of detected amplitude levels is, for example, $M = 8$.

We can now estimate the maximal attacking range D_m for a RRW-SC as the distance between Eve and Bob at which Eve receives the secret key signal coming from Alice with a given acceptable BER (or WER) denoted by P_{be}^* (or P_{we}^*) by using only the passive reradiation from Bob's receiving antenna, i.e. the RRW-SC. Under above conditions, the $SNR(d_{AB})$ at Bob's receiver for the signal coming from Alice is according to (5)

$$SNR(d_{AB}) = Q_{AB} \frac{S_{TA}}{W_{AB} d_{AB}^2}, \tag{7}$$

where Q_{AB} is the basic quality of the wireless channel between Alice and Bob, S_{TA} the average power of Alice's transmitter, and W_{AB} the bandwidth used on this channel. The $SNR(d_{BE})$ at Eve's receiving antenna for the signal reradiated from Bob's receiving antenna with a reradiating factor ρ is according to (5)

$$SNR(d_{BE}) = \rho Q_{BE} \frac{S_{RB}}{W_{BE} d_{BE}^2}, \tag{8}$$

where Q_{BE} is the basic quality of the wireless channel between Bob and Eve, S_{RB} the average power of Alice's signal at Bob's antenna, and W_{BE} the bandwidth used on the RRW-SC. Using (4) and some other expressions defined above, the term S_{RB} in (8) can be replaced by $SNR(d_{AB}) W_{AB} N_{0AB}$ so that

$$SNR(d_{BE}) = \rho \frac{G_{TA} G_{RB} G_{rrB} G_{RE}}{F_E k T_R} (\frac{\lambda}{4\pi})^4 \frac{S_{TA}}{W_{BE} d_{AB}^2 d_{BE}^2}, \tag{9}$$

where G_{TA} is the gain of Alice's transmitting antenna, G_{RB} the gain of Bob's receiving antenna, G_{rrB} the reradiating gain of Bob's receiving antenna, G_{RE} the gain of Eve's receiving antenna, F_E the noise figure of Eve's receiver, and T_{RE} the absolute temperature of the first stage amplification circuit in Eve's receiver. Finally, (9) can be written as

$$SNR(d_{BE}) = Q_{rr} \frac{S_{TA}}{W_{BE}} \frac{1}{d_{AB}^2 d_{BE}^2}, \tag{10}$$

where Q_{rr} represents the basic quality of the RRW-SC.

Alice and Bob's interest will be to reduce Q_{rr}, while Eve tries to improve it. Eve can increase G_{RE} of her antenna connecting it to a high quality receiver (with small noise figure F_E) whose first stage of amplification is cooled. The best possible practical improvement of Q_{rr} in this way can be attained by choosing the following *best quality parameters* of a RRW-SC: highest reradiation factor of $\rho = 1$, receiving antenna gain of $G_{RE} = 1000$ obtained using a high quality reflector antenna connected to the perfect receiver with $F_E = 2$, whose first stage of amplification is cooled in liquid helium up to $T_R = 4$ degree Kelvin. Since Alice and Bob usually do not know each other's position, they will use omnidirectional antennas, which means that the following values of $G_{TA} = G_{RB} = G_{rrB} = 1$ can be assumed for best quality parameters. On the other hand, Eve will be confronted with some unavoidable disturbances. The coincidental radiation of Alice's transmitter as well as other ubiquitous EMR interferences will more or less decrease the basic quality Q_{rr} of the RRW-SC. By replacing the best quality parameters in (9) and by omitting the influences of all degradation factors on Q_{rr}, the best SNR value, SNR^*, on the RRW-SC, for given λ, S_{TA}, W_{BE}, d_{AB} and d_{BE} can be calculated. Replacing the SNR^* in (6) directly gives the word error probability with which Eve recovers the secret key under best achievable conditions above assumed.

If in (6) the WER is determined by some chosen value P^*_{we} and d_{BE} is taken as a free variable, an upper bound D^*_m on the maximal attacking range (MAR) D_m on a RRW-SC can be obtained. The value of $P^*_{we} = 0,5$ determines the capacity of the digital communication channel using ASK signaling (without using of any kind of error control codes). In this case, D^*_m represents an information-theoretic bound assuring that Eve has no (even theoretical) chance to obtain any relevant information about the secret key if she performs her attack using only one antenna from a distance greater than D^*_m. However, the reradadiation side-channel can be always improved by using many synchronized receivers placed on different positions around Bob's receiver. This kind of attack will not be considered here.

In order to illustrate the magnitude of D^*_m in practice, two examples are evaluated. In the 433 MHz ISM-band, with $\lambda = 0,7$ m, $S_{TA} = 100$ mW, $W_{AB} = W_{BE} = 1$ MHz, and best quality parameters of the RRW-SC, the upper bound on the MAR is $D^*_m = 700$ m when Alice and Bob are $d_{AB} = 1000$ m apart and the number of key extraction levels is $M = 8$. For values of $M = 16$, $M = 4$, and $M = 2$, the upper bound on the MAR, D^*_m, alters to 350 m, 1650 m, and 6300 m respectively. Because of symmetry in (10), d_{AB} and D^*_m can be exchanged. For example, if d_{AB} amounts 700 m, than is $D^*_m = 1000$ m for $M = 8$. In the 2,4 GHz ISM-band, with $\lambda = 0,125$ m, $S_{TA} = 100$ mW, $W_{AB} = W_{BE} = 1$ MHz, and best quality parameters of the RRW-SC, the upper bound on the MAR is $D^*_m = 230$ m if the distance between Alice and Bob is $d_{AB} = 100$ m and $M = 8$. For other values of $M = 16$, $M = 4$, and $M = 2$, D^*_m amounts 100 m, 540 m, and 2000 m respectively.

The above analysis clearly shows that the passive reradiation side-channel represents a serious threat for the wireless key exchange on the physical layer. In realistic scenarios the ranges for successfully attacking the wireless key exchange could be significantly smaller, however the threat should not be neglected. For this reason, some countermeasures should be taken into consideration. The development of effective countermeasures against reradiation side-channel attacks remains an open problem. Possible candidate countermeasures include the use of reradiation supressing electrical and opto-electrical antennas or different jamming techniques.

5   Validation Using Anechoic Chamber

In this Section, our experimental efforts to measure the reradiation side-channel are described. We tried to practically confirm that Bob's antenna leaks enough information that can be captured and properly used by Eve. Due to the fact that the energy of the reradiated signal is predictably very low, an experimental setup that maximizes the reradiated power and minimizes all other signals' interferences is designed. This means that our setup must basically satisfy two conditions:

- minimize the power of the signals arriving to Eve originated in sources other than Bob's antenna, i.e. the signal coming from Alice in line-of-sight and all signals coming from Alice through reflections or scattering;
- maximize the energy of Alice's signal reradiated by Bob's antenna, which means that the pairs Alice and Bob, as well as Bob and Eve, should be in line-of-sight positions.

In order to fulfill these requirements, we performed our experiments using an anechoic chamber as described in 5.1. This chamber is made of ferrite walls, which have the property of absorbing the incident electromagnetic waves within a certain frequency range, strongly reducing the reflection and scattering components [FRA].

5.1   Experiment Setup

In our experimental setup, Alice consisted of a USRP2 transmitter [USR] and a corresponding controlling laptop, as shown in Fig. 1a. Eve was equipped with a directional antenna [ANT] (Fig. 1b) pointed towards Bob's antenna (Fig. 1c). In order to collect the measurment traces, Eve's antenna was connected to an oscilloscope with 2.5 GSamples/s of sampling rate.

Three experiments were performed:

1. Alice was placed inside the anechoic chamber in position A' (Fig. 2); nothing was placed in position B (Fig. 2); Eve just measured the received signal;
2. Alice was placed outside the anechoic chamber in position A; nothing was placed in position B and Eve's antenna (point E) was pointed towards point B. This way, points A and B are in line-of-sight position, as well as points B and E; however, A and E have no line-of-sight between them;
3. a $\lambda/4$ dipole antenna (Fig. 1c) was placed at point B without any other Bob's receiver components (i.e. antenna in open circuit). Alice and Eve remained as described in the previous item.

(a) Alice's USRP2 transmitter with laptop

(b) Eve's directional antenna

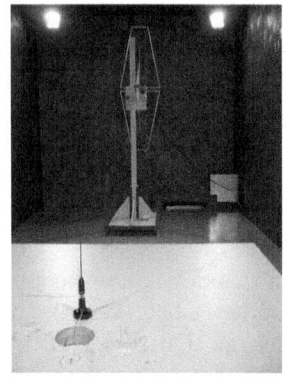

(c) Eve measuring Bob's omnidirectional antenna (on the table) reradiation

Fig. 1. Alice, Bob and Eve's experimental setup

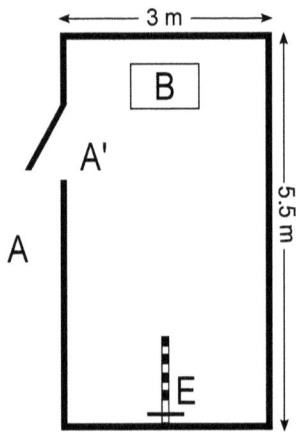

Fig. 2. Schematics of the anechoic chamber with positions of Alice (A or A'), Bob (B) and Eve (E)

Table 1. Eve's measured Energy

Exp.	Alice	Bob	Energy
1	A'	None	3.9675
2	A	None	$2.436 \cdot 10^{-3}$
3	A	Antenna	$2.950 \cdot 10^{-3}$

For all the experiments, we collected the signals measured by Eve when Alice emitted a 430 MHz sinusoidal signal of 100 mW power. This frequency value is within the range where ferrite absorbent material is more effective. Each trace measurement had a duration of 50 μs. Assuming that the ferrite walls absorbed the majority of the energy, Eve would be able to detect Bob's reradiated signal superimposed with unavoidable residual reflection and diffraction components. For each experiment, we gathered a set of traces. With those traces, the resulting average signal was calculated. It is worth noting that all traces were aligned in both axis, due to the uprising trigger set up (x-axis alignement) and due to the DC component extraction (y-axis alignement). Table 1 shows the energy measured from those traces.

5.2 Discussion

According to Table 1, when comparing the results of the experiments 1 and 2, it can be concluded that, as expected, the anechoic chamber absorbes a great part of the signal energy coming from Alice. From the experiments 2 and 3, it becomes clear that the insertion of an antenna at point B (the extreme case of a reradiating receiving antenna in open circuit) is responsible for a significant increase (about 17%) of the energy received by Eve. Thus, we also experimentally demonstrated that reradiation is a side-channel that must be taken into consideration in the development of key exchange protocols based on the channels' physical properties.

6 Conclusions

In certain applications, key exchange on the physical layer seems to be a promising and viable alternative to key exchange protocols whose security is based solely on computational assumptions. However, the conditions under which it can be securely implemented are still to be rigorously defined. In this work, the security of such schemes was examined in detail and two new attacks against this physical primitive were presented. The first attack is strictly based on the potential simplicity of the wireless channel. Under too simple environment conditions, an eavesdropper can reconstruct the environment and, therefore, extract the common secret key established between the two legitimate parties. The other attack is based on the wireless systems physical properties and is considered to be a side-channel attack to reciprocity-based schemes. We theoretically established under which conditions an eavesdropper equipped with a receiver system has some chance to recover a common key from the observation of the reradiated signal emitted from one of the protocol parties. We also presented the results of our efforts to experimentally prove the feasibility of this attack.

Acknowledgements

The authors would like to thank Micronas GmbH for letting us use the anechoic chamber and particularly Marco Bauer for his excellent technical support.

References

[AHT+05]   Aono, T., Higuchi, K., Taromaru, M., Ohira, T., Komiyama, B., Sasaoka, H.: Wireless secret key generation exploiting the reactance-domain scalar response of multipath fading channels. IEEE Transactions on Antennas and Propagation, 3776–3784 (November 2005)

[ANT]   Frankonia antennas, `http://www.frankonia-emv.com/data_sheets/`
             `emc_test_equipment/for_emission_measurements/Antennas_BTA.pdf`
[ASKMY07]   Azimi-Sadjadi, B., Kiayias, A., Mercado, A., Yener, B.: Robust key gen-
             eration from signal envelopes in wireless networks. In: ACM conference
             on Computer and Communications Security, pp. 401–410 (October 2007)
[Bal97]   Balanis, C.A.: Antenna Theory: analysis and design. John Wiley and
             Sons, Chichester (1997)
[BBRM08]   Bloch, M., Barros, J., Rodrigues, M.R.D., McLaughlin, S.W.: Wireless
             information-theoretic security. IEEE Transactions on Information The-
             ory 54(6), 2515–2534 (2008)
[Bla90]   Blahut, R.E.: Digital Transmission of Information. Addison-Wesley,
             Reading (1990)
[FRA]   Frankonia emc test-systems, `http://www.frankonia-emv.com/`
[GN05]   Goel, S., Negi, R.: Secret communication in presence of colluding eaves-
             droppers. In: Proc. IEEE Military Communication (MILCOM), vol. 3,
             pp. 1501–1506 (October 2005)
[HHY95]   Hershey, J.E., Hassan, A.A., Yarlagadda, R.: Unconventional crypto-
             graphic keying variable management. IEEE Transactions on Communi-
             cations 43, 3–6 (1995)
[HIU$^+$08] Hashimoto, T., Itoh, T., Ueba, M., Iwai, H., Sasaoka, H., Kobara, K.,
             Imai, H.: Comparative studies in key disagreement correction process on
             wireless key agreement system. In: Information Security Applications,
             pp. 173–187 (January 2008)
[HSHC96]   Hassan, A.A., Stark, W.E., Hershey, J.E., Chennakeshu, S.: Crypto-
             graphic key agreement for mobile radio. Digital Signal Processing 6,
             207–212 (1996)
[J.G02]   Proakis, J.G.: Communication Systems Engineering, ch. 7.6. Prentice
             Hall, Englewood Cliffs (2002)
[JYK$^+$07] Jørgensen, M., Yanakiev, B., Kirkelund, G., Popovski, P., Yomo, H.,
             Larsen, T.: Shout to secure: Physical-layer wireless security with known
             interference. In: Global Telecommunications Conference, GLOBECOM
             2007, pp. 33–38. IEEE, Los Alamitos (November 2007)
[KHC00]   Koorapaty, H., Hassan, A.A., Chennakeshu, S.: Secure information
             transmission for mobile radio. IEEE Communication Letters 4, 52–55
             (2000)
[KV08]   Kim, H., Villasenor, J.D.: Secure MIMO communications in a system
             with equal number of transmit and receive antennas. IEEE Communi-
             cation Letters 12, 386–388 (2008)
[LHR06]   Li, X., Hwu, J., Paul Ratazzi, E.: Array redundancy and diversity for
             wireless transmissions with low probability of interception. In: IEEE
             International Conference on Acoustics, Speech and Signal Processing,
             ICASSP Proceedings, vol. 4, pp. 525–528 (May 2006)
[LXMT06]   Li, Z., Xu, W., Miller, R., Trappe, W.: Securing wireless systems via
             lower layer enforcements. In: Proceedings of the 5th ACM Workshop on
             Wireless Security, pp. 33–42 (2006)
[LYCH78]   Leung-Yan-Cheong, S.K., Hellman, M.E.: The gaussian wiretap channel.
             IEEE Trans. Inform. Theory 24, 451–456 (1978)
[Mau93]   Maurer, U.M.: Secret key agreement by public discussion from common
             information. IEEE Transactions on Information Theory 39(3), 733–742
             (1993)

[MTM⁺08]   Mathur, S., Trappe, W., Mandayam, N.B., Ye, C., Reznik, A.: Radio-
            telepathy: extracting a secret key from an unauthenticated wireless chan-
            nel. In: Garcia-Luna-Aceves, J.J., Sivakumar, R., Steenkiste, P. (eds.)
            MOBICOM, pp. 128–139. ACM, New York (2008)
[Ohi05]   Ohira, T.: Secret key generation exploiting antenna beam steering and
            wave propagation reciprocity. In: European Microwave Conference ,
            vol. 1 (October 2005)
[OOKF68]   Okumura, Y., Ohmori, E., Kawano, T., Fukuda, K.: Field strength and
            its variability in vhf and uhf land mobile radio services (1968)
[SHOK04]   Sun, C., Hirata, A., Ohira, T., Karmakar, N.C.: Fast beamforming of
            electronically steerable parasitic array radiator antennas: Theory and
            experiment. IEEE Transactions on Antennas and Propagation, 1819–
            1832 (July 2004)
[TM01]   Tope, M.A., McEachen, J.C.: Unconditionally secure communications
            over fading channels. In: Military Communications Conference, Com-
            munications for Network-Centric Operations: Creating the Information
            Force, MILCOM 2001, vol. 1, pp. 54–58 (2001)
[TV05]   Tse, D., Viswanath, P.: Fundamentals of Wireless Communication. Cam-
            bridge University Press, Cambridge (2005)
[TY07]   Tekin, E., Yener, A.: The gaussian multiple access wire-tap channel:
            wireless secrecy and cooperative jamming. In: Information Theory and
            Applications Workshop, pp. 404–413 (February 2007)
[USR]   Ettus research, http://www.ettus.com/
[Wyn75]   Wyner, A.D.: The wire-tap channel. Bell Syst. Tech. J. 54, 1355–1387
            (1975)
[XTZW05]   Xu, W., Trappe, W., Zhang, Y., Wood, T.: The feasibility of launching
            and detecting jamming attacks in wireless networks. In: Proceedings of
            the 6th ACM International Symposium on Mobile ad hoc Networking
            and Computing, pp. 46–57 (2005)
[YMR⁺09]   Ye, C., Mathur, S., Reznik, A., Shah, Y., Trappe, W., Mandayam, N.B.:
            Information-theoretically secret key generation for fading wireless chan-
            nels. CoRR, abs/0910.502 (2009)

A   Appendix

A.1   Simulation of the Environment Reconstruction

Alice and Bob transmit the same test-signal. Bob measures h_{AB}, Alice h_{BA} and Eve the two channel impulse responses h_{AE} and h_{BE}. The power delay profiles of the channels are shown in Figure 3b.

Eve can now separate the peaks that correspond to different reflectors in the received h_{AE} and h_{BE}. When a direct path is present, the primary peak represents that path in each impulse response. Using the delay times between the primary peak and the reflected components, Eve can estimate the lengths of the signal paths of the reflected components, as described in Section 3. Using the reconstructed environment, Eve can now simulate the key exchange between Alice and Bob and, thereby, recover the impulse response h_{AB}, as shown in Fig. 4b.

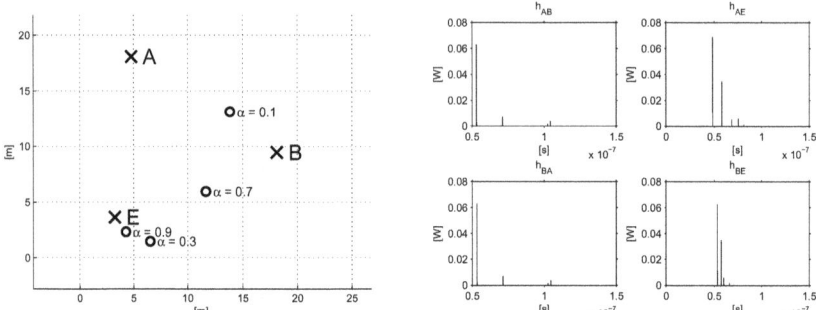

(a) Randomly generated environment with reflectors. The circles indicate the positions of the reflectors, the numbers next to the reflectors are their attenuation factors.

(b) Power delay profiles at A, B and E.

Fig. 3. Environment and received signals by Alice (A), Bob (B) and Eve (E)

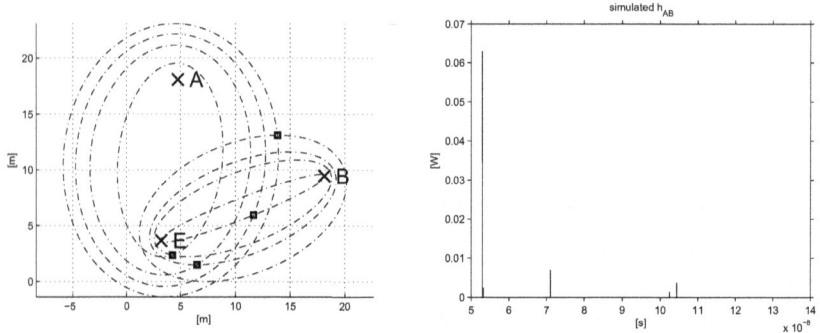

(a) Environment estimated by Eve.

(b) Power delay profile of Eve's simulated channel impulse response between Alice an Bob.

Fig. 4. Eve's performed attack

Collusion Attack on a Self-healing Key Distribution with Revocation in Wireless Sensor Networks

Kehua Bao and Zhenfeng Zhang

State Key Laboratory of Information Security, Institute of Software,
Chinese Academy of Sciences, Beijing, 100190, China
baokh@is.iscas.ac.cn, zfzhang@is.iscas.ac.cn

Abstract. A self-healing key distribution enables non-revoked users to recover the lost session keys on their own from the received broadcast messages and their private information. It decreases the load on the group manager and is very suitable for the unreliable wireless sensor networks. In 2008, Du and He [5] proposed a self-healing key distribution with revocation in wireless sensor networks which is claimed to resist to the collusion attack. In this paper, we show that the scheme 2 in [5] is not secure against the collusion attack. A newly joined user colluding with a revoked user can recover the group session keys that are not supposed to be known to them. Then the scheme will be improved and the modified one, through the analysis, is able to resist the collusion attack. Moreover, the modified scheme has the properties of constant storage, long life-span, forward secrecy and backward secrecy.

Keywords: Collusion attack, self-healing, constant storage, wireless sensor networks.

1 Introduction

Recently, wireless sensor networks (WSN) is attracting more and more research interests because of its wide applications such as military operations, rescue missions and scientific explorations. WSN is composed of a large number of sensor nodes with limited power, storage and communication capabilities. Currently, there are many security challenges in WSN such as limited resource of sensor nodes, unreliable wireless networks and high risk of physical attacks to the sensor nodes.

In 2002, Staddon *et al.* [11] first proposed self-healing key distribution schemes with revocation capability in WSN. These schemes enable non-revoked users to recover the lost session keys on their own from the received broadcast messages and their private information. The group manager does not need to retransmit lost packets and reduces the communication overhead. The technique of secret

Y. Chung and M. Yung (Eds.): WISA 2010, LNCS 6513, pp. 221–233, 2011.

sharing [12] is used to guarantee that revoked users can not recover group session keys. However, the constructions in [11] still suffer from high storage and communication overhead. Blundo *et al.* [2] found an attack on the construction 1 of [11], and showed that an adversary could recover the group session key with just broadcast messages. Later on many self-healing key distribution schemes [17,7,14,4,10,15,13,18] with revocation in wireless sensor networks are proposed.

In 2003, Liu *et al.* [9] generalized the formal definitions and security models presented in [11] and proposed a novel method by combining the key distribution scheme with the self-healing technique to improve the performance. Blundo *et al.* [3] analyzed the definitions of self-healing key distribution in [11] and [9] and gave a lower bound on the user memory storage and communication complexity required for implementing such schemes. In 2007, a constant storage self-healing key distribution scheme was proposed by Dutta *et al.* [6]. The storage of the scheme is constant compared with the previous schemes [1,11,9] and [8]. However, the scheme in [6] was found insecure in [5] and [16]. They showed that a user can recover group manager's secret polynomial which he should not know. So the scheme in [6] can not guarantee forward secrecy and backward secrecy. In 2008, Xu and He [16] proposed two kinds of improved schemes to overcome the weakness of [6]. Both of the schemes are efficient and secure according to their analysis. However, they did not consider the collusion between the revoked user and the newly joined user. Later on Du and He [5] proposed a self-healing key distribution with revocation in wireless sensor networks which is claimed to resist to the collusion attack.

Based on the existing schemes, a practical key distribution scheme in WSN is expected to have the following properties: (1) self-healing capability, where users can recover the group session keys that they missed on their own with their personal secrets and current broadcast messages; (2) forward and backward secrecy, where revoked users can not get any information about the future session keys and newly joined users cannot get any information about the previous session keys; (3) constant storage, which means that the quantity of the information that users need to store is constant; (4) acceptable communication load, there the communication overhead should satisfy the requirements in different applications; (5) long life-span, which means that the secrets of users are not limited to the current m sessions and can be reused in next m sessions; (6) collusion attack resistance, where a newly joined user colluding with a revoked user should not get any information about the group session keys between the sessions that they actually participated.

Our Contribution: In this paper, we show that the scheme 2 in [5] is vulnerable to the collusion attack. A newly joined user colluding with a revoked user can recover the group session keys that they should not know. Then we modify the scheme so that it can resist the collusion attack. Moreover, the modified scheme has the properties of constant storage, long life-span, forward secrecy and backward secrecy.

2   Overview of the Du-He Scheme

In this section, we briefly overview the Du *et al.* 's scheme 2 in [5] (denoted as Du-He scheme in this paper) as well as the security definitions. The notations used in this paper are as follows.

Table 1. Notations

U	the set of universal users in wireless sensor networks
U_i	user i in U
GM	the group manager
n	the total number of users in U, a positive integer
m	the maximum of the session numbers, a positive integer
t	the maximum number of compromised users, a positive integer
F_q	a finite field with order q and q is a large prime number $(q > n)$
r_j	a random number which GM selects for the user who joins in session j
α_j	a random number which GM selects for the user who joins in session j
s_i	the personal secret of user U_i
$f_j(x)$	the secret polynomial for session j, which is randomly chosen by GM
B_j	the broadcast message generated by GM for session j
K_j	the group session key in session j generated by GM and $K_j = K_j^{j-1}$
K_j^0	the seed of the hash key chain in session j
$K_j^{j'-1}$	the j-th key in the key chain of session j generated by GM
$G_j^{j'}$	the masking key of the key $K_j^{j'-1}$
β_j	the self-healing key randomly chosen by GM for session j
R_j	the set of revoked users in and before session j and $R_j \subseteq U$
J_j	the set of users which join in session j and $J_j \subseteq U$
H_1	a one-way hash function and $H_1 : \{0,1\}^* \to F_q$
H	a one-way hash function and $H : \{0,1\}^* \to F_q$
$E_k(\cdot)$	a symmetric encryption function
$D_k(\cdot)$	a symmetric decryption function
$\Lambda_j(x)$	the revocation polynomial in j-th session
$A_j(x)$	the access polynomial in j-th session

2.1   Security Definitions

Definition 1: (self-healing key distribution with t-revocation capability). A key distribution scheme is a self-healing key distribution with t-revocation capability if the following conditions are satisfied.

(a) For each non-revoked user in session j, the group session key K_j is determined by the broadcast message B_j and the user's own secret.

(b) What the non-revoked users learn from B_j or their own personal secret alone cannot determine the group session key K_j.

(c) (t-revocation capability) For each session j, let R_j denotes a set of revoked users in and before session j, such that $|R_j| \leq t$, the group manager can generate a broadcast message B_j such that all the revoked users in R_j cannot recover the group session key K_j.

(d) (self-healing property) Every U_i who joins in or before session j_1 and not revoked before session j_2 ($j_1 < j_2$) can recover all the keys K_j ($j = j_1, \cdots, j_2$) from broadcast B_{j_1} and B_{j_2}.

Definition 2: (t-wise forward secrecy). A key distribution scheme guarantees t-wise forward secrecy if for any set $R \subseteq U$, where $|R| \leq t$, and all $U_i \in R$ are revoked in session j, the members in R together cannot get any information about K_j, even with the knowledge of group session keys before session j.

Definition 3: (t-wise backward secrecy). A group session key distribution guarantees t-wise backward secrecy if for any set J, where $|J| \leq t$, and all $U_i \in J$ join after session j, the members in J together cannot get any information about K_j, even with the knowledge of group session keys after session j.

Definition 4: (resistance to the collusion attack). Let $B \subseteq R_r \cup R_{r-1} \cup \cdots \cup R_1$ be a coalition of users revoked before session r and let $C \subseteq J_s \cup J_{s+1} \cup \cdots$ be a coalition of users who join the group from session s, where $r < s$. Let $|B \cup C| \leq t$ and $B \cup C \subseteq U$. Then, such a coalition does not get any information about keys K_j, for any $r \leq j < s$.

2.2   Review of the Du-He Scheme

Assume $U = \{U_1, U_2, \cdots, U_n\}$, be a set of users in wireless sensor networks. The scheme is divided into four phases.

Phase 1 - Setup. GM first chooses m polynomials of degree t at random, say $f_1(x), \cdots, f_m(x) \in F_q[x]$, and randomly chooses m numbers $r_1, \cdots, r_m \in F_q$ and keep them as his secret.

Second, GM randomly chooses numbers $\alpha_1, \cdots, \alpha_m \in F_q$ for each session.

Third, GM sends in a secure manner, for $i = 1, \cdots, n$, to user U_i as personal key $s_i = \{\alpha_{j'}, r_{j'} \cdot f_{j'}(i), \cdots, r_{j'} \cdot f_m(i)\}$ (j' denotes the session number which the user joins the group and $\alpha_{j'} \in \{\alpha_1, \cdots, \alpha_m\}$, $r_{j'} \in \{r_1, \cdots, r_m\}$). Specifically, a user U_v who joins in session 1, will receive $s_v = \{\alpha_1, r_1 \cdot f_1(v), \cdots, r_1 \cdot f_m(v)\}$ while a user U_k who joins in session j will receive $s_k = \{\alpha_j, r_j \cdot f_j(k), \cdots, r_j \cdot f_m(k)\}$.

GM then chooses a prime key seeds $K_0 \in F_q$ and keeps it secret, and randomly chooses m number $\beta_1, \cdots, \beta_m \in F_q$ as the self-healing keys.

GM computes m key seeds and the corresponding m key chains by using two one-way hash functions $H_1(\cdot)$ and $H(\cdot)$. For session 1, the key seed is $K_1^0 = H_1(K_0, \beta_1)$ and the key chain is $\{K_1^0\}$. For session 2, the key seed is $K_2^0 = H_1(K_1, \beta_2)$ and key chain is $\{K_2^0, K_2^1\}$. For $1 \leq j \leq m$, the key seed of session j is

$$K_j^0 = H_1(K_{j-1}, \beta_j) \qquad (1)$$

and the key chain of session j is

$$\{K_j^0, K_j^1, K_j^2, \cdots, K_j^{j-1}\}_{j=1,\cdots,m} \tag{2}$$

where $K_j^1 = H(K_j^0), K_j^2 = H(K_j^1) = H^2(K_j^0), \cdots$, and $K_j = K_j^{j-1} = H(K_j^{j-2}) = \cdots = H^{j-1}(K_j^0)$, and $H^i(\cdot)$ denotes applying i times hash operation. The group session key in session j is $K_j = K_j^{j-1}$.

It is easy to see that the size of key chain equals to the session number.

Phase 2 - Broadcast. Assume that $R_j = \{U_{r_1}, \cdots, U_{r_{w_j}}\} \subseteq U$ is the set of revoked users in and before session j, and $r_1, \cdots, r_{w_j}$ is the IDs of the revoked users, such that $|R_j| = w_j \leq t$. GM then generates a masking key sequence $\{G_j^1, G_j^2, \cdots, G_j^{j-1}, G_j^j\}$ of size j for session j by applying XOR on both $\alpha_{j'}$ and every key from the one-way hash key chain, where

$$G_j^{j'} = K_j^{j'-1} \oplus \alpha_{j'} \qquad (j = 1, \cdots, m; j' = 1, \cdots, j), \tag{3}$$

and $\alpha_{j'}$ denotes the secret of the users who join the group in session j'.

In session j, GM broadcasts the following message:

$$B_j = R_j \cup \{z_j^{j'}(x) = \Lambda_j(x)G_j^{j'} + r_{j'} \cdot f_j(x)\}_{j'=1,\cdots,j}$$

$$\cup \{E_{K_j^0}(\beta_1), E_{K_j^1}(\beta_2), \cdots, E_{K_j^{j-1}}(\beta_j)\}, \tag{4}$$

where $\Lambda_j(x) = (x - r_1)(x - r_2) \cdots (x - r_{w_j})$ is called revocation polynomial, and $r_{j'} \cdot f_j(x)$ performs the role of masking polynomial which hides the information of $G_j^{j'}$. Note that $\Lambda_j(i) = 0$ for $U_i \in R_j$.

Phase 3 - Group Session Key and Self-Healing Key Recovery. If a non-revoked user $U_i (1 \leq i \leq n)$ who joins the group in session j' receives the broadcast message B_j $(1 \leq j' < j)$, the user U_i can recover the group session key and self-healing key of session j as follows:

First, U_i calculates the value of $z_j^{j'}(x)$ and $\Lambda_j(x)$ at point i from (4), and then computes the masking key $G_j^{j'} = \frac{z_j^{j'}(i) - r_{j'} \cdot f_j(i)}{\Lambda_j(i)}$, where $\Lambda_j(i) \neq 0$ and $r_{j'} \cdot f_j(i) \in s_i$.

According to Equation (3), U_i can compute $K_j^{j'-1}$ as follows:

$$K_j^{j'-1} = G_j^{j'} \oplus \alpha_{j'}, \tag{5}$$

where $\alpha_{j'}$ is the secret of user U_i when he joins the group in session j'.

Then U_i computes all the future keys $\{K_j^{j'}, \cdots, K_j^{j-1}\}$ in the key chain of session j by using one-way hash function $H(\cdot)$, and obtains the current group session key as $K_j = K_j^{j-1} = H^{j-j'}(K_j^{j'-1})$.

Now, in view of (4), U_i can decrypt $\{E_{K_j^{j'-1}}(\beta_{j'}), \cdots, E_{K_j^{j-1}}(\beta_j)\}$ by using the corresponding keys $\{K_j^{j'-1}, \cdots, K_j^{j-1}\}$ in the current key chain to get the corresponding self-healing keys $\{\beta_{j'}, \cdots, \beta_j\}$. If U_i has already obtained $K_{j'}$ from $B_{j'}$, he can recover all the session keys K_l $(j' < l < j)$ with the self-healing keys $\{\beta_{j'}, \cdots, \beta_j\}$ and $K_{j'}$ by equations (1) and (2).

A revoked user who receives the broadcast message can recover neither the current group session key nor the self-healing keys, since $\Lambda_j(i) = 0$ for any $U_i \in R_j$.

Phase 4 - Add Group Members. When GM wants to add a new user starting from session j, it chooses a unique identity $v \in \{1, 2, \cdots, n\}$ for U_v, which is never used before. Then GM sends the personal key $s_v = \{\alpha_j, r_j \cdot f_j(v), \cdots, r_j \cdot f_m(v)\}$ to U_v through the secure communication channel between them. Notice that if a user is revoked in session j, it means that it must be revoked in all future sessions.

3   Collusion Attack

In this section, we show that the scheme described in section 2 can not resist to the collusion attack.

Consider a set of users $B \subseteq R_{j_1+1} \cup R_{j_1} \cup R_{j_1-1} \cup \cdots \cup R_1$ who revoked in or before session $j_1 + 1$, and a set of users $C \subseteq J_{j_2} \cup J_{j_2+1} \cup \cdots$ who join from session j_2 $(B \cup C \subseteq U)$. B and C are disjoint and $|B \cup C| \leq t$.

We will show that a user $U_p \in B$ colluding with a user $U_q \in C$, is able to recover $K_j = K_j^{j-1}$ for $j_1 < j < j_2$ from the message B_{j_1} and B_{j_2}.

For simplicity, we assume U_p joins in session j_1 and revokes after this session, and U_q joins in session j_2. The personal secrets of U_p and U_q received from GM are $s_p = \{\alpha_{j_1}, r_{j_1} \cdot f_{j_1}(p), \cdots, r_{j_1} \cdot f_m(p)\}$ and $s_q = \{\alpha_{j_2}, r_{j_2} \cdot f_{j_2}(q), \cdots, r_{j_2} \cdot f_m(q)\}$ respectively. Specifically, U_p and U_q have $\alpha_{j_1}, r_{j_1} \cdot f_{j_1}(p), r_{j_1} \cdot f_{j_2}(p) \in s_p$ and $\alpha_{j_2}, r_{j_2} \cdot f_{j_2}(q) \in s_q$ which will be used in the following attack.

Let $R_{j_2} = \{U_{r_1}, \cdots, U_{r_{w_{j_2}}}\} \subseteq U$ be the set of revoked users in and before session j_2 such that $|R_{j_2}| = w_{j_2} \leq t$, and $r_1, \cdots, r_{w_{j_2}}$ be the IDs of the revoked users.

In session j_2, U_q receives the broadcast message $B_{j_2} = R_{j_2} \cup \{z_{j_2}^{j'}(x) = \Lambda_{j_2}(x)G_{j_2}^{j'} + r_{j'} \cdot f_{j_2}(x)\}_{j'=1,\cdots,j_2} \cup \{E_{K_{j_2}^0}(\beta_1), E_{K_{j_2}^1}(\beta_2), \cdots, E_{K_{j_2}^{j_2-1}}(\beta_{j_2})\}$.

For the equation $z_{j_2}^{j_2}(x) = \Lambda_{j_2}(x)G_{j_2}^{j_2} + r_{j_2} \cdot f_{j_2}(x)$, U_q computes $z_{j_2}^{j_2}(q)$. Note that $\Lambda_{j_2}(q) = (q - r_1)(q - r_2)\cdots(q - r_{w_{j_2}}) \neq 0$ since $U_q \notin R_{j_2}$. Then he can derive $G_{j_2}^{j_2} = \frac{z_{j_2}^{j_2}(q) - r_{j_2} \cdot f_{j_2}(q)}{\Lambda_{j_2}(q)}$, where $r_{j_2} \cdot f_{j_2}(q) \in s_q$ is the personal secret of U_q, and obtain the session key $K_{j_2} = K_{j_2}^{j_2-1} = G_{j_2}^{j_2} \oplus \alpha_{j_2}$ by Equation (5).

For the equation $r_{j_2} \cdot f_{j_2}(x) = z_{j_2}^{j_2}(x) - \Lambda_{j_2}(x) \cdot G_{j_2}^{j_2}$, U_p and U_q can compute $r_{j_2} \cdot f_{j_2}(p) = z_{j_2}^{j_2}(p) - \Lambda_{j_2}(p) \cdot G_{j_2}^{j_2} = z_{j_2}^{j_2}(p)$ (note that U_p has revoked in session j_2, so $\Lambda_{j_2}(p) = 0$). Combined with U_p's personal secret $r_{j_1} \cdot f_{j_2}(p) \in s_p$, the value of $\frac{r_{j_1}}{r_{j_2}} = \frac{r_{j_1} \cdot f_{j_2}(p)}{r_{j_2} \cdot f_{j_2}(p)}$ will be obtained.

Therefore, U_q is able to get $r_{j_1} \cdot f_{j_2}(q)$ by calculating $\frac{r_{j_1}}{r_{j_2}} \cdot r_{j_2} \cdot f_{j_2}(q)$, where $r_{j_2} \cdot f_{j_2}(q) \in s_q$.

For the equation $z_{j_2}^{j_1}(x) = \Lambda_{j_2}(x)G_{j_2}^{j_1} + r_{j_1} \cdot f_{j_2}(x)$ from the broadcast message B_{j_2}, U_q can also compute $G_{j_2}^{j_1} = \frac{z_{j_2}^{j_1}(q) - r_{j_1} \cdot f_{j_2}(q)}{\Lambda_{j_2}(q)}$, and then derive $K_{j_2}^{j_1-1} = G_{j_2}^{j_1} \oplus \alpha_{j_1}$ by Equation (5) with U_p's secret α_{j_1}.

Then U_q computes all the future keys $\{K_{j_2}^{j_1}, \cdots, K_{j_2}^{j_2-1}\}$ by running hash function $H(\cdot)$ on $K_{j_2}^{j_1-1}$, and decrypts $\{E_{K_{j_2}^{j_1-1}(\beta_{j_1})}, \cdots, E_{K_{j_2}^{j_2-1}(\beta_{j_2})}\}$ to get the self-healing keys $\{\beta_{j_1}, \cdots, \beta_{j_2}\}$.

Because U_p can obtain the session key K_{j_1} from the message B_{j_1} as U_q gets K_{j_2} from B_{j_2}. With the self-healing keys $\{\beta_{j_1}, \cdots, \beta_{j_2}\}$ and K_{j_1}, U_p and U_q can recover the session keys K_j for $j_1 < j < j_2$ by Equation (1) and (2), which they should not know according to the definition 4.

So, Du-He scheme [5] is not resistant to the collusion attack.

4   Improvement

In order to resist to the collusion attack and realize the constant storage for users, an improvement of [5] is proposed as follows.

Phase 1 - Setup. GM chooses a random secret value $t_i \in F_q$ for user U_i and t_i is different from each other. The user U_i's personal key will be replaced by $s_i = \{t_i, \alpha_{j'}, f_{j'}(t_i)\}$ (j' denotes the session number which the user joins the group and $\alpha_{j'} \in \{\alpha_1, \cdots, \alpha_m\}$). Note that $r_{j'}$ is not needed here, so $\{r_1, \cdots, r_m\}$ will be omitted in the improvements. Other parameters are the same as the original scheme of [5].

Phase 2 - Broadcast. The access polynomial [17,16] will be used in stead of the revocation polynomial. Let $\mathcal{U}_{act_j} = \{U_{act_1}, \cdots, U_{act_{a_j}}\}$ be the set of all active users for j-th session, where a_j is the number of active user in session j. Let $\mathcal{T}_{act_j} = \{t_{act_1}, \cdots, t_{act_{a_j}}\}$ be the set of all active users' secret values in j-th session.

In session j, the GM broadcasts the following message:
$$B_j = \{z_j^{j'}(x) = A_j^{j'}(x)G_j^{j'} + f_{j'}(x)\}_{j'=1,\cdots,j}$$

$$\cup\{E_{K_j^0}(\beta_1), E_{K_j^1}(\beta_2), \cdots, E_{K_j^{j-1}}(\beta_j)\}, \tag{6}$$

where $A_j^{j'}(x) = (S_j^{j'} \cdot x - T_j)\prod_{i=1}^{a_j}(x - t_{act_i}) + 1$ is an access polynomial. The GM also randomly picks $S_j^{j'} \in F_q$ ($j' = 1, \cdots, j$) to mask $G_j^{j'}$, otherwise $z_j^{j'}(x)$ will leak the information of $G_j^{j'}$ when the degree of $A_j^{j'}(x)$ is greater than $f_{j'}(x)$. And $T_j \in F_q$ is randomly selected for session j such that $\frac{T_j}{S_j^{j'}}$ ($j' = 1, \cdots, j$) is different from all users' secret values. When an active user U_{act_i} receives the j-th broadcast message B_j, U_{act_i} can evaluate $A_j^{j'}(t_{act_i})$ by using its secret value

t_{act_i}, as $A_j^{j'}(t_{act_i}) = 1$ $(j' = 1, \cdots, j)$. However, for a revoked user U_l, the $A_j^{j'}(t_l)$ $(j' = 1, \cdots, j)$ is a random value.

Phase 3 - Group Session Key and Self-Healing Key Recovery. A non-revoked user U_i who joins in the group in session j' and not revoked in session j $(1 \leq j' \leq j)$ can recover the group session key K_j from the broadcast message B_j as follows:

(1) U_i computes $G_j^{j'} = z_j^{j'}(t_i) - f_{j'}(t_i)$ from Equation (6), where $f_{j'}(t_i) \in s_i$ and $A_j^{j'}(t_i) = 1$.

(2) By Equation (5), U_i evaluates $K_j^{j'-1} = G_j^{j'} \oplus \alpha_{j'}$, where $\alpha_{j'} \in s_i$.

(3) If $j' < j$, U_i can compute all the future keys $\{K_j^{j'}, \cdots, K_j^{j-1}\}$ by using one-way hash function $H(\cdot)$, otherwise (i.e. $j' = j$) one can get K_j^{j-1} from step (2) already and thus the group session key $K_j = K_j^{j-1} = H^{j-j'}(K_j^{j'-1})$ for session j.

(4) From Equation (6), U_i can decrypt $\{E_{K_j^{j'-1}}(\beta_{j'}), \cdots, E_{K_j^{j-1}}(\beta_j)\}$ by using the corresponding keys $\{K_j^{j'-1}, \cdots, K_j^{j-1}\}$ to get the corresponding self-healing keys $\{\beta_{j'}, \cdots, \beta_j\}$.

A revoked user who receives the broadcast message can recover neither the current group session key nor the self-healing keys. Because for any revoked user U_l, $A_j^{j'}(t_l)$ is a random value.

Phase 4 - Add Group Members. If a new user wants to join in the group in session j, the GM chooses a unique identity $v \in \{1, 2, \cdots, n\}$ for U_v, which is never used before. Then GM selects a random secret value $t_v \in F_q$ and sends the personal key $s_v = \{t_v, \alpha_j, f_j(t_v)\}$ to U_v in a secure manner.

5   Analysis of the Modified Scheme

In this section, we show that the improved scheme in section 4 achieves self-healing property, forward security, backward security and resistance to the collusion attack.

5.1   Self-healing Property

Assume $U_i \in U$ joins the group in session j_1 and revoked after session j_2 $(j_1 < j_2)$. According to the improvements in section 4, its personal key is $s_i = \{t_i, \alpha_{j_1}, f_{j_1}(t_i)\}$. U_i has received the broadcast messages B_{j_1} and B_{j_2} $(1 \leq j_1 < j_2)$, but lost the broadcast message B_j $(j_1 < j < j_2)$. It will be shown that U_i can still recover all the lost group session keys $K_j = K_j^{j-1}$ $(j_1 < j < j_2)$ as follows:

(1) From the broadcast message B_{j_1} and B_{j_2}, U_i evaluates $G_{j_1}^{j_1} = Z_{j_1}^{j_1}(t_i) - f_{j_1}(t_i)$ and $G_{j_2}^{j_1} = Z_{j_2}^{j_1}(t_i) - f_{j_1}(t_i)$, as $A_{j_1}^{j_1}(t_i) = A_{j_2}^{j_1}(t_i) = 1$ by Equation (6) in section 3.

(2) U_i can compute the group session key $K_{j_1} = K_{j_1}^{j_1-1} = G_{j_1}^{j_1} \oplus \alpha_{j_1}$ for session j_1 and the key $K_{j_2}^{j_1-1} = G_{j_2}^{j_1} \oplus \alpha_{j_1}$ in the key chain of session j_2.

(3) By using the hash function and $K_{j_2}^{j_1-1}$ (see Equation (2)), U_i can compute all future keys $\{K_{j_2}^{j_1}, K_{j_2}^{j_1+1}, \cdots, K_{j_2}^{j_2-1}\}$ in j_2-th one-way hash key chain and the last one in the key chain $K_{j_2} = K_{j_2}^{j_2-1}$ is the group session key for session j_2.

(4) In order to get the self-healing keys $\{\beta_{j_1}, \cdots, \beta_{j_2}\}$ between session j_1 and session j_2, U_i decrypts the $\{E_{K_{j_2}^{j_1-1}}(\beta_{j_1}), \cdots, E_{K_{j_2}^{j_2-1}}(\beta_{j_2})\}$ by using $\{K_{j_2}^{j_1-1}, \cdots, K_{j_2}^{j_2-1}\}$.

(5) With K_{j_1} and the self-healing keys $\{\beta_{j_1}, \cdots, \beta_{j_2}\}$, U_i can recover all the missed group session keys $K_j = K_j^{j-1}$ $(j_1 < j < j_2)$ by Equation (1) and (2).

Therefore the modified scheme achieves the self-healing property.

5.2   Forward Secrecy

Let R_j be the set of the users revoked in and before session j, where $R_j \subseteq U, |R| \leq t$, and $U_i \in R_j$ revoked in session j. Then we show that neither a single user in R_j nor a set of users in R_j can get any information about the group session key $K_l (l = j, \cdots, m)$, even with the previous group session keys and their personal secrets. From the broadcast message by Equation (6), the way users in R_j to get the j-th group session key $K_j = K_j^{j-1}$ divides into two kinds. The one is to get the corresponding self-healing key β_j which is randomly chosen. Then one can use Equation (1) and (2) to obtain K_j. And the other is to get an active user U_q's secret. However, it will be shown that both of the two ways are impossible.

Firstly, the self-healing keys β_j is encrypted by the corresponding group session key $K_j = K_j^{j-1}$ which is equal to $G_j^j \oplus \alpha_j$. But users in R_j cannot evaluate the masking keys G_j^j, because for any $U_i \in R_j$, $A_j^{j'}(t_i)$ $(j' = 1, \cdots, j)$ is a random value. Moreover, users in R_j do not have α_j. Therefore, the users in R_j cannot obtain the future group session keys by getting the values of the self-healing keys.

Secondly, assume the active user U_q joins in session j' $(j' \leq j)$ and U_q's secret is $\{t_q, \alpha_{j'}, f_{j'}(t_q)\}$. $f_{j'}(x)$ is a t-degree polynomial which needs $t + 1$ points to recover. But users in R_j $(|R_j| \leq t)$ can get at most t points on each polynomial $f_{j'}(x)$. So it is impossible for users in R_j to recover any of the secret polynomial $f_{j'}(x)$ $(1 \leq j' \leq j)$. Moreover, the secret value t_q of U_q is selected randomly by GM. Users in R_j also can not get t_q.

The above analysis shows that the improved scheme is forward secure.

5.3   Backward Secrecy

Let $J_{j+1} \subseteq U$ be the set of users which join in session $j + 1$. Then it will be shown that neither a single user in J_{j+1} nor a set of users in J_{j+1} can get any information about the previous session key K_j even with all the future session keys and their personal secret keys.

On one hand, users in J_{j+1} can only get the current group session key K_{j+1} which is the last key in the one-way hash key chain from the broadcast B_{j+1}, therefore user in J_{j+1} can only get the current self-healing key β_{j+1}. One can get $K_{j+1} = K_{j+1}^j = H(K_{j+1}^{j-1}) = \cdots = H^j(K_{j+1}^0)$ and $K_{j+1}^0 = H_1(K_j, \beta_{j+1})$ by Equation (1) and (2), where $H_1(\cdot)$ and $H(\cdot)$ are two one-way hash functions, it is computationally infeasible for any user in J_{j+1} to compute the previous session key K_j with K_{j+1} and β_{j+1}.

On the other hand, it will be shown that it is also impossible for users in J_{j+1} to recover the personal secret polynomials $f_j(x)$. $f_j(x)$ is a t-degree polynomial which needs at least $t+1$ points on the polynomial $f_j(x)$ to recover. However, users in J_{j+1} do not have any information about $f_j(x)$. Thus no matter how many users in J_{j+1}, it is impossible for them to recover the secret polynomial $f_j(x)$. Furthermore, even users in J_{j+1} can recover $f_j(x)$, they still can not recover $K_j = K_j^{j-1} = G_j^j \oplus \alpha_j$ without α_j.

The above analysis shows that the modified scheme is backward secure.

5.4   Resistance to a Collusion Attack

Consider a set of users $B \subseteq R_{j_1+1} \cup R_{j_1} \cup R_{j_1-1} \cup \cdots \cup R_1$ who revoked in or before session j_1+1 and a set of users $C \subseteq J_{j_2} \cup J_{j_2+1} \cup \cdots$ who join from session j_2 ($B \cup C \subseteq U$). B and C are disjoint and $|B \cup C| \le t$. It will be shown that users in B colluding with users in C, can not recover $K_j = K_j^{j-1}(j_1 < j < j_2)$ from the message B_{j_1} and B_{j_2}.

$B \cup C$ require the self-healing keys between β_{j_1} and β_{j_2} to recover $K_j = K_j^{j-1}(j_1 < j < j_2)$. For the equation $z_{j_2}^{j_1}(x) = A_{j_2}^{j_1}(x)G_{j_2}^{j_1} + f_{j_1}(x)$ from B_{j_2}, $U_q \subseteq C$ which joins in session j_2 needs the value of $f_{j_1}(t_q)$ to obtain $G_{j_2}^{j_1}$. Then U_q can get $K_{j_2}^{j_1-1}$ with U_p's secret α_{j_1} by Equation(5) (assume that U_p joins in session j_1). Finally, U_q and U_p can get $\{K_{j_2}^{j_1-1}, \cdots, K_{j_2}^{j_2-1}\}$ and $\{\beta_{j_1}, \cdots, \beta_{j_2}\}$ by Equation (2) and (6). However, users in $B \cup C$ cannot obtain $f_{j_1}(t_q)$ unless they can recover the secret polynomial $f_{j_1}(x)$. As the analysis in section 5.2 and 5.3, it impossible to recover the polynomial $f_{j_1}(x)$. Therefore, users in $B \cup C$ cannot recover the self-healing keys between β_{j_1} and β_{j_2}.

Moreover, for one thing, the newly joined users from C can only get the group session key $K_l = K_l^{l-1}$ ($l \ge j_2$) and corresponding self-healing key β_l ($l \ge j_2$). For another thing, users from B who are revoked before session j_1+1 can only get the group session keys $K_l = K_l^{l-1}$ ($l \le j_1$) and β_l ($1 \le l \le j_1$). Therefore, they can not get any self-healing key between β_{j_1} and β_{j_2} with all the information they have, thus they cannot get the group session keys $K_j = K_j^{j-1}(j_1 < j < j_2)$ without the corresponding self-healing keys.

Therefore, the modified scheme can resist to the collusion attack.

6   Efficiency

In this section, the modified scheme will be compared with other similar schemes. Table 2 compares the modified scheme with the previous ones in several aspects, such as storage overhead, communication overhead, long life-span, resistance to the collusion attack etc.

Storage Overhead. The storage overhead in the modified scheme comes only from users' personal secrets. U_i who joins in the session j only needs to store $s_i = \{t_i, \alpha_j, f_j(t_i)\}$ as his secret. So the storage overhead in the modified scheme is $3 \log q$ bits, which is a constant storage overhead. In table 2, others schemes except [6,16] do not have constant storage.

Communication Overhead. In order to resist to the collusion attack, GM broadcasts j polynomials for the users who join in different sessions. This increases communication load on GM, and the communication complexity is $(\max\{a_j + 2, t + 1\} \cdot j + j) \log q$, where t is maximum number of revoked users, a_j is the number of active users in session j. However, the communication overhead of the modified scheme is still acceptable comparing to the previous approaches such as construction 3 in [11], scheme 3 in [9] and Du-He scheme [5]. A tradeoff is worthwhile between communication complexity and resistance to the collusion attack, because the sensor nodes are vulnerable to physical attacks and an attacker can launch a collusion attack easily by compromising an revoked node and a newly joined one.

Long Life-span. The life-time of the personal secret of the modified scheme is long-lived and not limited in a fixed m session. The personal secret of a user can be reused to the next m sessions without any alteration in the modified schemes. A user's secret in the modified scheme is not related to the number of sessions. So it can be reused in next sessions. In contrast, users in the schemes such as construction 3 in [11], scheme 3 in [9] and Du-He scheme [5] need to store their secrets which is related to m. If a user in these schemes wants to continue to communicate with GM normally after m sessions, it needs more secrets from GM.

Forward Secrecy & Backward Secrecy. Dutta *et al.*'s scheme [6] was found attacks in [5] and [16]. A user can recover GM secret polynomial $\psi(x)$ easily. So it can not guarantee forward secrecy and backward secrecy.

Resistance to Collusion Attack. A collusion attack on the Du-He scheme [5] was found in section 3. Dutta *et al.*'s scheme [6] and the scheme 1 in [16] can not resist to the collusion attack either. The modified scheme is secure against the collusion attack as the analysis in section 5.4.

Table 2. Comparison between different schemes

Scheme	Storage Overhead	Communication Overhead	Long life-span	Forward Secrecy	Backward Secrecy	Collusion attack resistance
Scheme 3 [11]	$(m - j - 1)^2 \log q$	$(mt^2 + 2mt + m + t) \log q$	No	Yes	Yes	Yes
Scheme 3 [9]	$(m - j + 1) \log q$	$(2tj + j) \log q$	No	Yes	Yes	Yes
[6]	$3 \log q$	$(t + 1 + j) \log q$	Yes	No	No	No
Scheme 1 [16]	$4 \log q$	$\max\{t+j+1, a_j + j + 2\} \log q$	Yes	Yes	Yes	No
Du-He [5]	$(m - j + 2) \log q$	$[(t+1)j + j] \log q$	No	Yes	Yes	No
Our scheme	$3 \log q$	$(\max\{a_j + 2, t + 1\} \cdot j + j) \log q$	Yes	Yes	Yes	Yes

7 Conclusions

In this paper, a collusion attack was found on the Du-He scheme [5] which is designed to resist to such an attack. Then we propose an improvement with the access polynomial to resist the collusion attack. Moreover, the modified scheme has the properties of constant storage, long life-span, forward secrecy and backward secrecy. Through the comparison with previous schemes, the modified scheme is an efficient and secure scheme for wireless sensor networks.

The access polynomial which is applied to resist to the collusion attack also increases the communication load on the group manager. How to reduce the communication overhead is the main concern in future works.

Acknowledgment

The work is supported by the National Natural Science Foundation of China (60873261), the National Basic Research Program (973) of China (2007CB311202), and the National High-Technology Research and Development Program (863) of China (2008AA01Z417).

References

1. Blundo, C., D'Arco, P., Santis, A.D., Listo, M.: Design of Self-healing Key Distribution Schemes. Des. Codes Cryptography 32, 15–44 (2004)
2. Blundo, C., D'Arco, P., Listo, M.: A Flaw in a Self-Healing Key Distribution Scheme. In: Proc. of Information Theory Workshop, Paris, pp. 163–166 (2003)
3. Blundo, C., D'Arco, P., Santis, A., Listo, M.: Definitions and Bounds for Self-healing Key Distribution. In: Díaz, J., Karhumäki, J., Lepistö, A., Sannella, D. (eds.) ICALP 2004. LNCS, vol. 3142, pp. 234–245. Springer, Heidelberg (2004)

4. Chadha, A., Liu, Y.H., Das, S.K.: Group Key Distribution via Local Collaboration in Wireless Sensor Networks. In: 2nd Annual IEEE Communications Society Conference on Sensor and Ad Hoc Communications and Networks, pp. 46–54 (2005)

5. Du, W., He, M.X.: Self-healing Key Distribution with Revocation and Resistance to the Collusion Attack in Wireless Sensor Networks. In: Baek, J., Bao, F., Chen, K., Lai, X. (eds.) ProvSec 2008. LNCS, vol. 5324, pp. 345–359. Springer, Heidelberg (2008)

6. Dutta, R., Wu, Y.D., Mukhopadhyay, S.: Constant Storage Self-Healing Key Distribution with Revocation in Wireless Sensor Network. In: IEEE International Conference on Communications, pp. 1323-1332 (2007)

7. Dutta, R., Chang, E., Mukhopadhyay, S.: Efficient Self-healing Key Distribution with Revocation for Wireless Sensor Networks Using One Way Hash Chains. In: Katz, J., Yung, M. (eds.) ACNS 2007. LNCS, vol. 4521, pp. 385–400. Springer, Heidelberg (2007)

8. Hong, D., Kang, J.: An Efficient Key Distribution Scheme with Self-healing Property. IEEE Communication Letters 9, 759–761 (2005)

9. Liu, D., Ning, P., Sun, K.: Efficient Self-healing Key Distribution with Revocation Capability. In: Proc. of the 10th ACM CCS 2003, pp. 27–31 (2003)

10. More, S., Malkin, M., Staddon, J.: Sliding-window Self-healing Key Distribution with Revocation. In: ACM Workshop on Survivable and Self-regenerative Systems, pp. 82–90 (2003)

11. Staddon, J., Miner, S., Franklin, M., Balfanz, D., Malkin, M., Dean, D.: Self-healing Key Distribution with Revocation. In: Proc. of IEEE Symposium on Security and Privacy, pp. 241–257 (2002)

12. Shamir, A.: How to Share a Secret. Communications of ACM 22, 612–613 (1979)

13. Sáez, G.: Self-healing key distribution schemes with sponsorization. In: Dittmann, J., Katzenbeisser, S., Uhl, A. (eds.) CMS 2005. LNCS, vol. 3677, pp. 22–31. Springer, Heidelberg (2005)

14. Sáez, G.: On Threshold Self-healing Key Distribution Schemes. In: Smart, N.P. (ed.) Cryptography and Coding 2005. LNCS, vol. 3796, pp. 340–354. Springer, Heidelberg (2005)

15. Tian, B.M., He, M.X.: A Self-healing Key Distribution Scheme with Novel Properties. International Journal of Network Security 7(1), 115–120 (2008)

16. Xu, Q.Y., He, M.X.: Improved Constant Storage Self-healing Key Distribution with Revocation in Wireless Sensor Network. In: Chung, K.-I., Sohn, K., Yung, M. (eds.) WISA 2008. LNCS, vol. 5379, pp. 41–55. Springer, Heidelberg (2009)

17. Zou, X.K., Dai, Y.S.: A Robust and Stateless Self-Healing Group Key Management Scheme. In: International Conference on Communication Technology, ICCT 2006, vol. 28, pp. 455–459 (2006)

18. Zhu, S.C., Setia, S., Jajodia, S.: Adding reliable and self-healing key distribution to the subset difference group rekeying method for secure multicast. In: Stiller, B., Carle, G., Karsten, M., Reichl, P. (eds.) NGC 2003 and ICQT 2003. LNCS, vol. 2816, pp. 107–118. Springer, Heidelberg (2003)

Full-Round Differential Attack on TWIS Block Cipher

Bozhan Su, Wenling Wu, Lei Zhang, and Yanjun Li

State Key Laboratory of Information Security,
Institute of Software, Chinese Academy of Sciences, Beijing 100190, P.R. China
Graduate University of Chinese Academy of Sciences, Beijing 100049, P.R. China
{subozhan,wwl,zhanglei1015,liyanjun}@is.iscas.ac.cn

Abstract. The 128-bit block cipher TWIS was proposed by Ojha et al in 2009. It is a lightweight block cipher and its design is inspired from CLEFIA. In this paper, we first study the properties of TWIS structure, and as an extension we also consider the generalized TWIS-type structure named G-TWIS cipher whose block size and round number are $4m$ and n repectively, where n and m are any positive integers. Then we present a series of 10-round differential distinguishers for TWIS and an n-round differential distinguisher for G-TWIS whose probabilities are all equal to 1. It shows that 10-round TWIS cipher and n-round G-TWIS cipher can be distinguished efficiently from random permutation.

Keywords: Block Cipher, TWIS, G-TWIS, Differential Distinguisher, Differential Cryptanalysis.

1 Introduction

Recently, researches on the design of lightweight cryptography have received lots of attention. Lightweight cryptography mainly deals with designing ciphers for extremely resource constrained environments, such as applications of RFID tags and sensor networks. Considering that conventional algorithms such as AES although quite secure, are not suitable for such environments, hence a number of new symmetric lightweight block ciphers have been proposed in the open literature, such as DESL [6], PRESENT [2], HIGHT [5], LCASE [10], Cobra [9] and TWIS [7] et al.

TWIS is a lightweight block cipher designed by Ojha et al in 2009. Both of its block size and key size are 128-bit and the total number of rounds is 10. The overall structure of TWIS is a 2-branch generalized Feistel structure which employs key whitening at the beginning and at the end of the cipher.

In this paper, we first study the properties of TWIS structure, and as an extension we also considered the generalized TWIS-type structure which can be called G-TWIS cipher, whose block size is $4m$-bits and consists of n rounds encryption in all, where n and m are any positive integers. Then we evaluate the security of TWIS and G-TWIS against differential cryptanalysis respectively. Our main results include: we present 7 differential distinguishers for 10-round

Y. Chung and M. Yung (Eds.): WISA 2010, LNCS 6513, pp. 234–242, 2011.

TWIS cipher and a differential distinguisher for n-round G-TWIS cipher whose probabilities are both equal to 1. It shows that 10-round TWIS cipher and n-round G-TWIS cipher can be distinguished efficiently from random permutation. Since our analysis does not depend on any weak-key or weak-subkey assumptions, these attacks can both be independent of the key schedule algorithm.

The rest of this paper is organized as follows. Section 2 gives a brief description of TWIS first and then gives the specification of G-TWIS cipher. Section 3 and Section 4 present the differential attack on the full TWIS cipher and on the full G-TWIS cipher respectively. Finally, Section 5 summarizes the paper.

2 Descriptions of TWIS and G-TWIS

TWIS is a 128-bit block cipher which uses key of size 128-bit. It employs a 2-branch Generalized Feistel structure and consists of 10 rounds. Each round of TWIS uses two rounds of Feistel network which involves a 64-bit round function called G-function. Furthermore, key whitening layers are employed both at the beginning and at the end of the encryption procedure. Since the key scheduling is not involved in out attack, we will omit the description of key schedule algorithm here and interested readers can refer to [7] for more details.

As an extension of TWIS, we construct a generalized TWIS-type cipher called G-TWIS. Its block size can be $4m$-bit and consists of n rounds, where m and n are any positive integers. Similar to the round function of TWIS, in each round of G-TWIS we also use two rounds of Feistel network which involves a $2m$-bit round function called G'-function. In the following, we will give detailed descriptions of the encryption procedures of TWIS and G-TWIS.

2.1 Notation

In this subsection, we first introduce the following notations which are used throughout this paper.

- Z_2^m: the set of m-bit words.
- $a \oplus b$: bitwise XOR of a and b.
- $a \wedge b$: bitwise AND of a and b.
- $a|b$: concatenation of a and b.
- $\lll i$: left rotation by i bits.
- $\ggg i$: right rotation by i bits.

2.2 Encryption Procedure of TWIS

For the encryption procedure of TWIS, let $P = (P_0, P_1, P_2, P_3) \in (Z_2^{32})^4$ denote a 128-bit plaintext, and $C = (C_0, C_1, C_2, C_3) \in (Z_2^{32})^4$ denote the corresponding ciphertext. Let $RK_i \in Z_2^{32}$ ($i = 0, 1, \ldots, 10$) denote the round subkeys provided by the key scheduling part. First of all, two 32-bit whitening subkeys RK_0 and RK_1 are XORed to P_0 and P_3 respectively, and the resulted intermediate value is denoted as (T_0, T_1, T_2, T_3). Then the same round transformation is iterated for 10 times, and the operations in each round is defined as follows.

> For the i−th round, $1 \leq i \leq 10$
>   a) $X_0|X_1 \leftarrow G\_function(RK_{i-1}, T_0|T_1)$
>   b) $T_2 \leftarrow X_0 \oplus T_2, \quad T_3 \leftarrow X_1 \oplus T_3$
>   c) $T_1 \leftarrow T_1 \lll 8, \quad T_3 \leftarrow T_3 \ggg 1$
>   d) $T_0|T_1|T_2|T_3 \leftarrow T_2|T_3|T_0|T_1$
>   e) $X_0|X_1 \leftarrow G\_function(RK_i, T_0|T_3)$
>   f) $T_1 \leftarrow X_0 \oplus T_1, \quad T_2 \leftarrow X_1 \oplus T_2$
>   g) $T_2 \leftarrow T_2 \ggg 1, \quad T_3 \leftarrow T_3 \lll 8$

In the end, two whitening subkeys RK_2 and RK_3 are XORed to T_0 and T_3 respectively, and the result is just the ciphertext $C = (C_0, C_1, C_2, C_3)$. The detailed encryption procedure of TWIS is illustrated in Fig. 1.

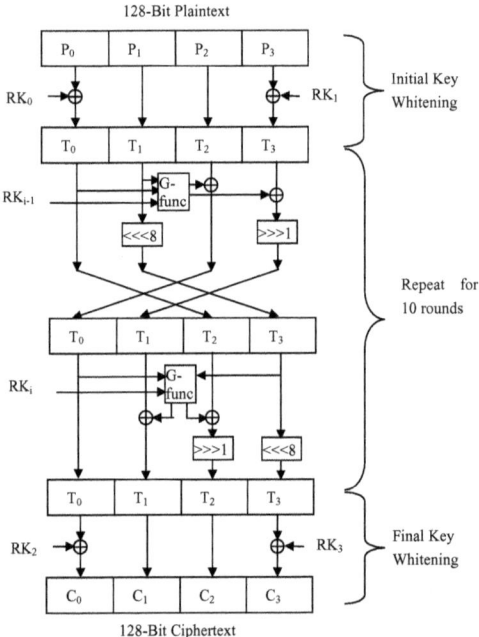

Fig. 1. The Encryption Process of TWIS

For the G-function used in each round, it is defined as follows. It takes 64-bit data $X_0|X_1$ and 32-bit round subkey RK as inputs and produces 64-bit output, and this transformation can be written as the following expressions. The procedure of G-function is despicted in Fig. 2.

1. $T_0|T_1 \leftarrow X_0|X_1$
2. $T_0 \leftarrow T_1 \oplus$ F_function(RK, T_0)
3. $Y_0|Y_1 \leftarrow T_1|T_0$

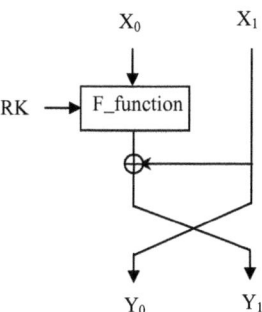

Fig. 2. The G-function

Here it calls another transformation named $F\_function$ which takes 32-bit intermediate state X and 32-bit round subkey RK as inputs, and produces 32-bit output Y. The transformation of $F\_function$ is defined as follows:

1. $T_0|T_1|T_2|T_3 \leftarrow RK \oplus X$
2. $T_0 \leftarrow Sbox(T_0 \wedge 0x3f)$
   $T_1 \leftarrow Sbox(T_1 \wedge 0x3f)$
   $T_2 \leftarrow Sbox(T_2 \wedge 0x3f)$
   $T_3 \leftarrow Sbox(T_3 \wedge 0x3f)$
3. $Y_0|Y_1|Y_2|Y_3 \leftarrow T_2|T_3|T_0|T_1$

Note that the Sbox used in $F\_function$ takes 6-bit input and yields 8-bit output, and the specific Sbox table can be obtained in [7].

2.3 Encryption Procedure of G-TWIS

As an extension of TWIS, we construct a generalized TWIS-type cipher called G-TWIS. Its block size can be $4m$-bit and consists of n rounds, where m and n are any positive integers. Let $P = (P_0, P_1, P_2, P_3) \in (Z_2^m)^4$ and $C = (C_0, C_1, C_2, C_3) \in (Z_2^m)^4$ denote the plaintext and its corresponding ciphertext respectively. Let $RK_i \in Z_2^m$ $(i = 0, \ldots, n-1)$ denote the round subkeys provided by the key scheduling part. The key whitening layers at the beginning and at the end of G-TWIS are exactly the same with TWIS, and the round transformation used in each round is defined as follows. The encryption procedure of G-TWIS is also illustrated in Fig. 3.

For the G'-function used in each round, it takes $2m$-bit data and m-bit round subkey as inputs and produces $2m$-bit output. Similar to the G-function in TWIS, G'-function can be written as the following expressions.

For the i−th round, $1 \leq i \leq n$
   a) $X_0|X_1 \leftarrow G'\text{-}function(RK_{i-1}, T_0|T_1)$
   b) $T_2 \leftarrow X_0 \oplus T_2, \qquad T_3 \leftarrow X_1 \oplus T_3$
   c) $T_1 \leftarrow T_1 \lll r_0, \qquad T_3 \leftarrow T_3 \ggg r_1$
   d) $T_0|T_1|T_2|T_3 \leftarrow T_2|T_3|T_0|T_1$
   e) $X_0|X_1 \leftarrow G'\text{-}function(RK_i, T_0|T_3)$
   f) $T_1 \leftarrow X_0 \oplus T_1, \qquad T_2 \leftarrow X_1 \oplus T_2$
   g) $T_2 \leftarrow T_2 \ggg r_2, \qquad T_3 \leftarrow T_3 \lll r_3$

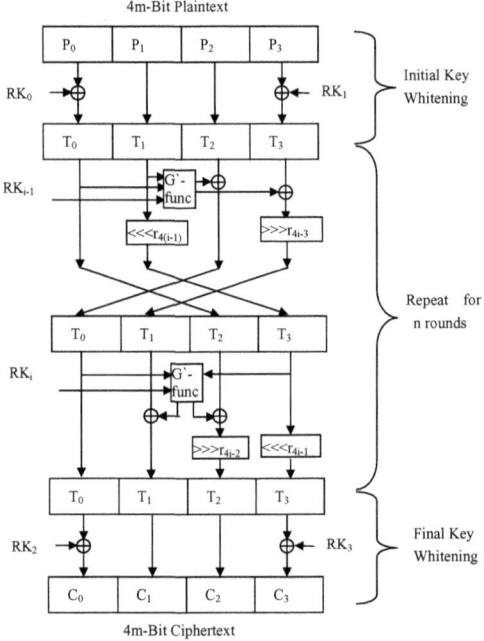

Fig. 3. The Encryption Process of G-TWIS

1. $T_0|T_1 \leftarrow X_0|X_1$
2. $T_0 \leftarrow T_1 \oplus F'\text{-}function(RK, T_0)$
3. $Y_0|Y_1 \leftarrow T_1|T_0$

Here it calls $F'\text{-}function$ which takes m-bit intermediate state X and m-bit round subkey RK as inputs, and produces m-bit output Y.

$$F'\text{-}function = \begin{cases} \{0,1\}^m \times \{0,1\}^m \to \{0,1\}^m, \\ (RK, X) \mapsto Y \end{cases}$$

3   10-Round Differential Distinguishers for TWIS

In this section, we present seven 10-round differential distinguishers for TWIS whose probabilities are all equal to 1. These differential distinguishers are mainly based on the following one-round iterative differential characteristic with probability 1. Fig. 4 illustrates this kind of one-round iterative differential characteristic in detail.

Note here we denote the $F\_function$ of the two $G\_function$ in each round as $F_0\_function$ and $F_1\_function$, respectively. We choose both the input and output differences of the i-th round as $\Delta X = (\Delta X_0, \Delta X_1, \Delta X_2, \Delta X_3) \in (Z_2^{32})^4$ which denotes a 128-bit nonzero difference. Then the input and output differences of $F_0\_function$ are equal to ΔX_0 and $\Delta X_1 \oplus (\Delta X_1 \oplus (\Delta X_1 \lll 8)) \lll 1 \oplus \Delta X_3$ respectively. Similarly, the input and output differences of $F_1\_function$ are equal to ΔX_0 and $\Delta X_0 \oplus (\Delta X_2 \lll 1) \oplus (\Delta X_1 \lll 8)$ respectively. Furthermore, we can obtain the following equations.

$$\Delta X_1 \lll 16 = \Delta X_3 \tag{1}$$
$$\Delta X_1 \oplus \Delta X_2 = \Delta X_0 \tag{2}$$

If we set the input and output differences of $F_0\_function$ and $F_1\_function$ be zero, then we can obtain the following three equations.

$$\Delta X_0 \wedge 0x3f3f3f3f = 0 \tag{3}$$
$$\Delta X_1 \oplus (\Delta X_1 \oplus (\Delta X_1 \lll 8)) \lll 1 \oplus \Delta X_3 = 0 \tag{4}$$
$$\Delta X_0 \oplus (\Delta X_2 \lll 1) \oplus (\Delta X_1 \lll 8) = 0 \tag{5}$$

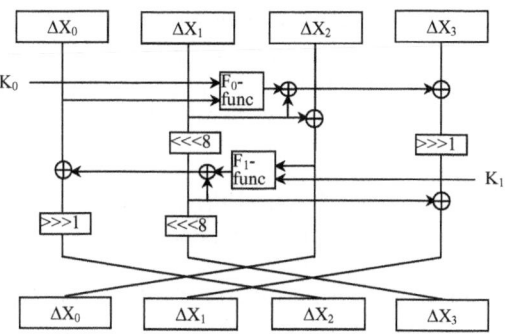

Fig. 4. One-round iterative differential characteristic of TWIS

As we can see, equations (1)-(5) are linear over GF(2). So a 160×128 binary matrix can be derived from a linear system of the above equations. Making a program for solving the above linear system using Gauss Elimination, we obtain that the rank of the matrix is equal to 125. So the number of all solutions is $2^3 = 8$ including the zero solution. The program produces 7 nonzero solutions which is listed in Table 1. Since all these solutions satisfy that the input and output differences of F_0-$function$ and F_1-$function$ equal to zero, we can construct seven 1-round iterative differential characteristics which all hold with probability 1. Then by iterating this kind of 1-round differential characteristic 10 times, we can obtain seven 10-round differential distinguishers for TWIS whose probabilities are all equal to 1. We verify the probability of these differentials by a computer algorithm, and the experimental result also consists with the theoretical analysis.

Table 1. One-round iterative differential characteristics for TWIS

No.	$\Delta X = \Delta X_0, \Delta X_1, \Delta X_2, \Delta X_3$	$\Pr(\Delta X \rightarrow \Delta X)$
1	(0x0c0c0c0c0, 0xc0c0c0c0, 0x00000000, 0xc0c0c0c0)	1
2	(0x80808080, 0x80808080, 0x00000000, 0x80808080)	1
3	(0x40404040, 0x40404040, 0x00000000, 0x40404040)	1
4	(0x40404040, 0xbfbfbfbf, 0xffffffff, 0xbfbfbfbf)	1
5	(0x80808080, 0x7f7f7f7f, 0xffffffff, 0x7f7f7f7f)	1
6	(0xc0c0c0c0, 0x3f3f3f3f, 0xffffffff, 0x3f3f3f3f)	1
7	(0x00000000, 0xffffffff, 0xffffffff, 0xffffffff)	1

4 n-Round Differential Distinguisher for G-TWIS

In this section, we present an n-round differential distinguisher for G-TWIS whose probability is also equal to 1. This n-round differential distinguisher is based on the following one-round iterative differential characteristic with probability 1.

Similar to the analysis in Sect. 3, we also choose the input and output differences of the i-th round as $\Delta X = (\Delta X_0, \Delta X_1, \Delta X_2, \Delta X_3) \in (Z_2^m)^4$, which denotes a $4m$-bit nonzero difference. Then the input and output differences of F_0'-$function$ are equal to $(\Delta X_0, \Delta X_1 \oplus (\Delta X_1 \oplus (\Delta X_1 \lll r_0)) \lll r_1 \oplus \Delta X_3)$, and the input and output differences of F_1'-$function$ are equal to $(\Delta X_0, \Delta X_0 \oplus (\Delta X_2 \lll r_2) \oplus (\Delta X_1 \lll r_0))$ respectively. Similarly, we can obtain the following equations.

$$\Delta X_1 \lll (r_0 + r_3) = \Delta X_3 \tag{6}$$
$$\Delta X_1 \oplus \Delta X_2 = \Delta X_0 \tag{7}$$

Then by setting the input and output differences of F_0'-$function$ and F_1'-$function$ as zero, we can obtain the following equations.

$$\Delta X_0 = 0 \tag{8}$$
$$\Delta X_1 \oplus (\Delta X_1 \oplus (\Delta X_1 \lll r_0)) \lll r_1 \oplus \Delta X_3 = 0 \tag{9}$$
$$\Delta X_0 \oplus (\Delta X_2 \lll r_2) \oplus (\Delta X_1 \lll r_0) = 0 \tag{10}$$

Considering the above system of equations (6)-(10), it is easy to see that $(0, \alpha, \alpha, \alpha)$ is a solution of the system, where $\alpha = \underbrace{11 \ldots 1}_{m}$. Hence we can construct an iterative differential characteristic $(0, \alpha, \alpha, \alpha) \rightarrow (0, \alpha, \alpha, \alpha)$ where $\alpha = \underbrace{11\ldots1}_{m}$, and it holds with probability 1. Then by iterating this differential characteristic n times, we can obtain the following n-round differential distinguisher for G-TWIS whose probability is equal to 1.

$$(0, \alpha, \alpha, \alpha) \xrightarrow{n\ R} (0, \alpha, \alpha, \alpha). \quad \alpha = \underbrace{11\ldots1}_{m}$$

The following Fig. 5 illustrates this one-round iterative differential characteristic of G-TWIS in detail.

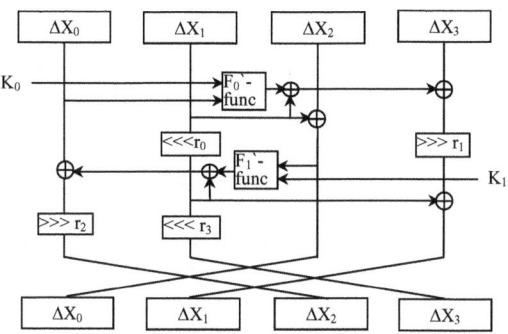

Fig. 5. One-round iterative differential characteristic of G-TWIS

5   Summary

In this paper, we first study the properties of TWIS structure, and as an extension we also consider the generalized TWIS-type structure which can be called G-TWIS cipher whose block size and round number are $4m$ and n, where m and n can be any positive integers. Then we present seven 10-round differential distinguishers for TWIS and an n-round differential distinguisher for G-TWIS whose probabilities are all equal to 1. It shows that 10-round TWIS and n-round G-TWIS are distinguished efficiently from an ideal cipher.

Our results demonstrate that the design of TWIS-type structure has fatal weakness, and no matter how secure the internal building blocks such as Sbox and diffusion matrix are and even how many rounds are used, the overall cipher is still vulnerable to differential attack. Furthermore, the reuse of whitening subkeys as round subkeys may endanger the cipher, too. Therefore, we suggest that this kind of TWIS-type cipher should be carefully used in a cryptographic system.

Acknowledgment

The authors would like to thank the anonymous referees for their valuable comments. Furthermore, this work is supported by the National Natural Science Foundation of China (No. 60873259, and No. 60903212) and the Knowledge Innovation Project of The Chinese Academy of Sciences.

References

1. Biham, E., Shamir, A.: Differential Cryptanalysis of DES-like Cryptosystems. Journal of Cryptology 4(1), 3–72 (1991)
2. Bogdanov, A., Knudsen, L.R., Leander, G., Paar, C., Poschmann, A., Robshaw, M.J.B., Seurin, Y., Vikkelsoe, C.: PRESENT: An Ultra-Lightweight Block Cipher. In: Paillier, P., Verbauwhede, I. (eds.) CHES 2007. LNCS, vol. 4727, pp. 450–466. Springer, Heidelberg (2007)
3. Daemen, J.: Cipher and Hash Function Design Strategies Based on Linear and Differential Cryptanalysis. Doctoral Dissertation. K.U.Leuven (March 1995)
4. Daemen, J., Rijmen, V.: The Design of Rijndael- AES, the Advanced Encryption Standard. Springer, Heidelberg (2002)
5. Hong, D., Sung, J., Hong, S., Lim, J., Lee, S., Koo, B., Lee, C., Chang, D., Lee, J., Jeong, K., Kim, H., Kim, J., Chee, S.: HIGHT: A New Block Cipher Suitable for Low-Resource Device. In: Goubin, L., Matsui, M. (eds.) CHES 2006. LNCS, vol. 4249, pp. 46–59. Springer, Heidelberg (2006)
6. Leander, G., Paar, C., Poschmann, A., Schramm, K.: New Lightweight DES Variants. In: Biryukov, A. (ed.) FSE 2007. LNCS, vol. 4593, pp. 196–210. Springer, Heidelberg (2007)
7. Ojha, S., Kumar, N., Jain, K., Lal, S.: TWIS - A Lightweight Block Cipher. In: Prakash, A., Sen Gupta, I. (eds.) ICISS 2009. LNCS, vol. 5905, pp. 280–291. Springer, Heidelberg (2009)
8. Shirai, T., Shibutani, K., Akishita, T., Moriai, S., Iwata, T.: The 128-bit block cipher CLEFIA. In: Biryukov, A. (ed.) FSE 2007. LNCS, vol. 4593, pp. 181–195. Springer, Heidelberg (2007)
9. Sklavos, N., Moldovyan, N.A., Koufopavlou, O.: High Speed Networking Security: Design and Implementation of Two New DDP-Based Ciphers. In: Mobile Networks and Applications 10, pp. 219–231. Springer, Heidelberg (2005)
10. Tripathy, S., Nandi, S.: LCASE: Lightweight Cellular Automata-based Symmetrickey Encryption. International Journal of Network Security 8(2), 243–252 (2009)

Improved Trace-Driven Cache-Collision Attacks against Embedded AES Implementations

Jean-François Gallais[1], Ilya Kizhvatov[1], and Michael Tunstall[2]

[1] Université du Luxembourg
6, rue Richard Coudenhove-Kalergi, L-1359 Luxembourg
{jean-francois.gallais,ilya.kizhvatov}@uni.lu
[2] Department of Computer Science, University of Bristol
Merchant Venturers Building, Woodland Road
Bristol BS8 1UB, United Kingdom
tunstall@cs.bris.ac.uk

Abstract. In this paper we present two attacks that exploit cache events, which are visible in some side channel, to derive a secret key used in an implementation of AES. The first is an improvement of an adaptive chosen plaintext attack presented at ACISP 2006. The second is a new known plaintext attack that can recover a 128-bit key with approximately 30 measurements to reduce the number of key hypotheses to 2^{30}. This is comparable to classical Differential Power Analysis; however, our attacks are able to overcome certain masking techniques. We also show how to deal with unreliable cache event detection in the real-life measurement scenario and present practical explorations on a 32-bit ARM microprocessor.

Keywords: Side channel attacks, power analysis, cache attacks, AES.

1 Introduction

Fetching data from the random access memory or non-volatile memory in embedded microprocessors can take a significant number of clock cycles and a processor is unable to perform any further instructions while it waits. The use of cache memory aims to decrease the cost of memory accesses. Cache memory is a memory held within the core of the microprocessor that can be accessed rapidly. When data is accessed the line of data holding this address is moved to the cache, where the amount of data moved is dictated by the architecture of the cache. This is based on the assumption that when a certain address is accessed it is likely that the data around this address is also likely to be accessed in the near future.

It has been noted that the power consumption of a microprocessor is dependent on the instruction being executed and on any data being manipulated [8,14]. An attacker can, therefore, observe where functions, and sequences of functions, occur in a power consumption trace. This could, potentially, allow an attacker to derive information on cryptographic keys if an observed sequence is affected by the value of the key. It has also been observed that the electromagnetic field around a microprocessor also has this property [12,22].

Y. Chung and M. Yung (Eds.): WISA 2010, LNCS 6513, pp. 243–257, 2011.
© Springer-Verlag Berlin Heidelberg 2011

In this paper we consider the effect of a cache on an instantiation of AES. Given the above observation, cache accesses should be visible in the power consumption or electromagnetic emanations. The location of these cache accesses during the computation of AES has been shown to reveal information on the secret key used [3,10]. In this paper we present an attack that represents a significant improvement over the adaptive chosen plaintext trace-driven attack [10] with a new adaptive algorithm for choosing plaintexts for recovering of 60 bits of the key from an expected 14.5 acquisitions. We also present a new known-plaintext attack requiring only 30 traces and an exhaustive search in 2^{30} hypotheses. Both attacks can tolerate uncertainties in observing a sequence of cache events, and a partially preloaded cache, as described in [7]. We described some experiments on a 32-bit ARM microcontroller, while all the previous works on trace driven attacks considered simulations of cache accesses [15,1,7,24] or of the power consumption [3].

We consider the implementation of an AES that would be used in a secure microprocessor. That is, an implementation that only uses one lookup table to 256 bytes that can be written to RAM as a masked random ordered table. This would prevent an attacker from being able to apply differential power analysis [16]. This would not be practical in an implementation that uses so-called T-tables that allow a fast implementation on x86 microprocessors. Previous work on observing traces of cache events has primarily been involved in attacking implementations that use T-tables [15,1,7,24]. Our approach assumes that lookup tables used are aligned with the cache, which will be the case for an optimized implementation, as opposed to the recent work [24] that presented a trace-driven attack exploiting cache misalignment. We present our attacks for the cache organized in 16-byte lines, however the attacks are easily adaptable to other cache line sizes.

The rest of this paper is organized as follows. In Sect. 2 we describe the cache mechanism and previous work in analyzing cache access. We present an improved adaptive attack in Sect. 3, and extend this to a known plaintext attack in Sect. 4. In Sect. 5 we then present the results of practical explorations on a 32-bit ARM microcontroller, and explain how to conduct our attacks where a detected sequence of cache hits and misses may be incorrect.

2   Generalities and Previous Work

2.1   Caching and Performance

The gap between the increased speed at which modern microprocessors treat data and the comparatively slow latencies required to fetch the data from the Non-Volatile Memories to the registers raise performance issues. To reduce the "distance" between the CPU and the NVM, i.e. the number of wasted clock cycles for which the CPU has to wait for the data, the solution is to keep them quickly accessible in a faster memory. Faster, however, typically means more expensive, hence this choice affects the size of available fast storage memory, the so-called *cache memory*. Examples of embedded devices with cache memory are the microprocessors of the widespread ARM9 family and of the subsequent ARM families.

Concretely, modern microprocessors typically come with a SRAM cache memory. When a byte of data must be paged in during the computation, the processor first looks for in the cache. If present in the cache, this results in a **cache hit**, the data is brought to the registers within a single clock cycle without stalling the pipeline. If not present in the cache, this results in the **cache miss**, and the desired data fetched from Non-Volatile Memory (NVM), and the entire line containing the desired data is loaded into the cache. As suggested by the different technologies used in the cache and main memory, a cache miss typically takes more clock cycles and consumes more energy than a cache hit.

2.2   Cache-Based Attacks against AES

Following the pioneering articles of Kelsey *et al.* [13] and Page [20], several notorious attacks have been published involving the cache mechanism and targeting AES. Cache-based attacks fall into three different types. *Time-driven attacks* exploit the dependence of the execution time of an algorithm on the cache accesses. Bernstein described a simple cache-timing attack leading to a complete key recovery on a remote server [2]. In *access-driven attacks* presented in [17,19], an attacker learns which cache lines were accessed during the execution by preloading the cache with the chosen data.

Here, we elaborate on *trace-driven attacks*. In this type of cache attacks an adversary derives information from individual cache events from the side-channel trace of an execution, such as registered power consumption or electromagnetic emanations. Trace-driven attacks pose a particular threat to embedded devices since the latter are exposed to a high risk of power or electromagnetic analysis, as opposed to desktop and server implementations that are a usual target in access- and time-driven cache attacks (however, a cache-timing attack on embedded AES implementation was presented recently in [5]).

Previous work on trace-driven attacks was described in [3,15,1,10,24]. However, most of these works target an optimized AES implementation that uses large lookup tables, as described in the original Rijndael proposal [9]. Here we focus on a conventional 256-byte lookup table since this would often be the choice in a constrained device, e.g. in a smart card, for the reasons outlined above in the Introduction. Also, previous works did not tackle the unreliable cache event detection, at most considering the setting when a lookup table is partially preloaded into the cache [7]. In [3,15,1,7], the effect of cache organization, and in particular the cache line size, on the attack was considered. Here we develop our attacks assuming the cache line size is 16 bytes, but they can be easily adapted to other sizes. Another popular cache line size is 32 bytes; in this case our attack will be more complex (however, the dependency of the attack complexity on the cache organization is not straightforward, as detailed in [7]).

We also note that there is a similarity between cache attacks and side channel collision attacks [23,4], as already observed in [15], hence the name *cache-collision* attacks.

2.3   Notation

We denote the most significant nibble of a byte b with $\hat{b}$. In the same manner, the least significant nibble of b is denoted $\check{b}$. We denote the input of the SubByte function in the first AES round as x_i, equal to $p_i \oplus k_i$, where p_i and k_i respectively represent a byte of plaintext and key in blocks of 16 bytes. We index the bytes row-wise and *not* column-wise as in the AES specification [25,9], *i.e.* in our notation p_0, p_1, p_2, p_3 is the first row of a 16-bit plaintext. We assume that in an embedded software AES implementation S-Box lookups are performed row-wise, and indexing bytes in the order of S-Box computation simplifies description of our algorithms. We denote addition and multiplication over $GF(2^8)$ by $\oplus$ and $\bullet$ respectively.

2.4   Adaptive Chosen Plaintext Attack

In this section we recall the trace-driven cache-collision attack presented in [10]. It uses an adaptive chosen plaintext strategy, i.e. each plaintext is chosen according to the result of the analysis done beforehand.

The method presented in [10] targets the AES block cipher with the SubByte function implemented as a single lookup table. It is assumed that the cache contains no AES data before the encryption. This can easily be done by resetting the device. During the AES encryption, the AddRoundKey adds the bytes of the key $K = (k_0, k_1, \ldots, k_{15}) \in (\mathbb{F}_{2^8})^{16}$ and the plaintext $P = (p_0, p_1, \ldots, p_{15}) \in (\mathbb{F}_{2^8})^{16}$. The state produced is $(x_0, x_1, \ldots, x_{15}) = (k_0 \oplus p_0, k_1 \oplus p_1, \ldots, k_{15} \oplus p_{15})$. The SubByte function denoted $S(\cdot)$ is a permutation over $\mathbb{F}_{2^8}$ and its elements are pre-computed and stored in Non-Volatile Memory (NVM). It is performed using a lookup table containing 16 lines with 16 entries, each line being associated to the most significant nibble of the input byte (as detailed in [25]). Because the cache is assumed to contain no AES data, the entire line indexed by the upper nibble of x_0 is loaded from the NVM to the cache, inducing a first cache miss. The second lookup, indexed by x_1, will be a cache hit with probability $\frac{1}{16}$, as there is 1 chance over 16 that the values $S(x_0)$ and $S(x_1)$ belong to the same line. If a cache hit occurs, then we have :

$$\widehat{k_0 \oplus p_0} = \widehat{k_1 \oplus p_1}$$

By rearranging the terms in the equation, we obtain :

$$\widehat{k_0 \oplus k_1} = \widehat{p_0 \oplus p_1}$$

An attacker can try to search among the 16 possible values for the upper nibble of p_1 and find the one inducing a cache hit within an expected number of $\sum_{i=1}^{16} \frac{i}{16} = 8.5$ acquisitions. Once the correct value for the second lookup is found, she can reiterate the process for the 14 other lookups. She will end up with the trace MHH...H and thus with the actual values for $\widehat{k_0 \oplus k_1}, \widehat{k_0 \oplus k_2}, \ldots, \widehat{k_0 \oplus k_{15}}$ which reduces the key search space by 60 bits. Expected number of plaintexts (traces) is $15 \times 8.5 = 127.5$, the worst-case complexity is $16 \times 15 = 240$ traces.

3   Improved Chosen Plaintext Attack

In this section, we show that the adaptive chosen plaintext attack described in [10] does not optimally exploit the adaptive scenario. We present an improved adaptive strategy that significantly reduces the number of required plaintexts.

We observe that in the adaptive algorithm of [10] the plaintexts at each step are chosen *independently* of the plaintexts in the previous steps. More precisely, ignored are the events located in the cache trace to the right of the current event (for which the plaintext nibble is being chosen). Below we show that by observing these events we can drastically reduce the total number of plaintexts required to achieve the desired trace MHH...H.

We make use of the fact that a miss at position i, $0 < i < 16$, indicates that $\widehat{p_j \oplus k_j} \neq \widehat{p_i \oplus k_i}$ for all j such that $0 \leqslant j < i$ and event at position j is a miss. This means that any plaintext with the particular difference $\widehat{p_j \oplus p_i}$ between the nibbles in positions j and i will not lead to the desired trace MHH...H. So the plaintexts with this difference can be omitted from the subsequent queries. On the other hand, if there is a hit at position i, the plaintext nibble in this position may already be the one which we are searching for, i.e. satisfying $\widehat{p_0 \oplus k_0} = \widehat{p_i \oplus k_i}$. So we cannot do better than keeping it for the next query, changing it only if the event in position i becomes a miss in subsequent queries. The formal description of our improved strategy is given in [11].

We have simulated this attack with 10^5 random keys both for the original algorithm of [10] and our improved algorithm. The results are shown in Figure 1. The improvement is drastic: on average 14.5 plaintexts for our improved attack to obtain a 60-bit reduction against 127.5 for the original attack. These figures are for the case of absolutely reliable cache event detection. In Sect. 5.3 we show that our improved algorithm has a good error tolerance.

4   Known Plaintext Attack

The improved attack in Sect. 3 requires adaptively chosen plaintexts. In this section, we present a known plaintext trace-driven cache-collision attack on AES-128 that enables full key recovery. The attack consists of two steps, namely, analyses of the first and second round cache access patterns.

4.1   Analysis of the First AES Round

We first analyze the cache events occurring in the first encryption round of AES with a sieve. The inputs to the sieve are N plaintexts and the corresponding cache traces that are obtained from N acquisitions. In a q-th acquisition, a plaintext $P^{(q)}$ is a 16-byte array and a cache trace $(CT)^{(q)}$ is the array of the cache accesses observed in the first round of AES, while encrypting $P^{(q)}$ under the unknown key K. The output of the sieve is a set of linear equations in the high nibbles of k_i, $i \in \{0, 15\}$ that decreases the entropy of the key search space by 60 bits.

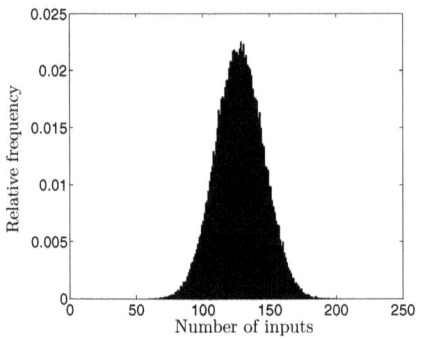

(a) Original chosen plaintext attack [10]

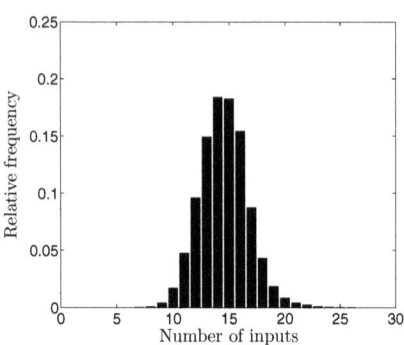

(b) Improved chosen plaintext attack

Fig. 1. Distribution of the number of plaintexts required to obtain a 60-bit reduction of the key search space

In our strategy, the unknowns are defined as high nibbles of the XOR-difference between the first key byte and the 15 other key bytes. Hence, we aim to recover $\widehat{k_0 \oplus k_i}$ for which we define the set of possible initial values: $\kappa_{0,i} = \{0, \ldots, 15\}$, $1 \leqslant i \leqslant 15$.

We recall from Sects. 2.4 and 3 that the cache events observed in a power trace allow an attacker to determine whether at a certain lookup the S-Box input belongs to a previously loaded line of the lookup table or not.

If a cache hit occurs at the i-th lookup, one can state that the high nibble of the input of the S-box is equal to the high nibble of one and only one of the previous inputs that caused a cache miss. Hence the following statement holds:

$$CT_i = H \implies \exists! j \in \Gamma, \ \widehat{k_i \oplus p_i} = \widehat{k_j \oplus p_j}$$

where Γ denotes the set of indices where a cache miss previously occurred in a trace.

Similarly, if a cache miss occurs at the i-th lookup, the high nibble of the input of the S-box is not equal to the high nibble of any of the previous inputs that caused a cache miss. Thus the statement:

$$CT_i = M \implies \forall j \in \Gamma, \ \widehat{k_i \oplus p_i} \neq \widehat{k_j \oplus p_j}$$

Since $\widehat{k_i \oplus k_j} = \widehat{k_i \oplus k_0} \oplus \widehat{k_0 \oplus k_j}$, the terms in the above equations and inequations can be rearranged and we obtain:

$$CT_i = H \implies \exists! j \in \Gamma, \ \widehat{k_i \oplus k_0} = \widehat{p_i \oplus p_j} \oplus \widehat{k_j \oplus k_0}$$

and

$$CT_i = M \implies \forall j \in \Gamma, \ \widehat{k_i \oplus k_0} \neq \widehat{p_i \oplus p_j} \oplus \widehat{k_j \oplus k_0}$$

The sieve we developed uses the above statements to reduce the possibilities for $\widehat{k_i \oplus k_0}$. This is executed particularly efficiently if the right-hand sides of the equations are known, while the left-hand sides are the unknowns. This suggests to fix the lookup i and gain through the analysis of the plaintexts and cache events indexed from 0 to i the most information available on $\widehat{k_i \oplus k_0}$ so that only one possibility remains for this nibble. This can be achieved for a large enough number of traces (see Figure 2). Once done, one can continue the analysis for the next values of i until 15. At the end, an attacker is left with only one possibility for each $\widehat{k_i \oplus k_0}$. The sieve is explicitly detailed in [11].

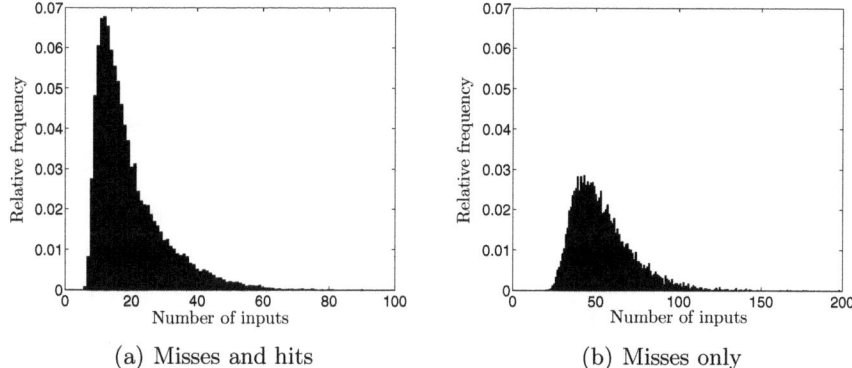

(a) Misses and hits   (b) Misses only

Fig. 2. Distribution of the required number of plaintexts to obtain a 60-bit reduction of the key search space in the known plaintext attack

To estimate the number of traces required to determine 60 bits, we ran the sieve for 10^5 simulated attacks, each with a random key. Figure 2(a) presents the results of this simulation. On average 19.43 acquisitions are required to reduce the entropy of the key to 68 bits. We note that this is less than for the original adaptive *chosen plaintext* attack of [10].

Our strategy also works if we do not take into account the information available from the cache hits, that is, if $\kappa_{0,i}$ is not modified when a cache hit is observed in a cache trace at the i-th lookup. The resulting analysis is less efficient than the one of the misses and the hits, as depicted in the plotted distribution of the number of required inputs (Figure 2(b)). Indeed, the average number of inputs required to perform a 60-bit reduction of the entropy of the key is in this case 54.19. However, we explain in Sect. 5.5 how this 'Misses-only' analysis can be useful if we assume a scenario where the cache already contains AES data before the encryption.

4.2   Analysis of the Second AES Round

After the first round analysis with our sieve we are left with 68 unknown key bits. In this section we show how to recover these remaining bits by analyzing the cache events occurring during the second AES encryption round. Our approach in general resembles that of [10], however we exploit the cache events much more efficiently. Similar approach was briefly sketched in [1], however they did not present the analysis for the number of traces required, whereas we perform theoretical analysis in [11]. We assume that the round keys are pre-computed and pre-stored, thus no access to the S-Box lookup table occurs between the encryption rounds[1].

The analysis of the second round consists of 3 phases:

1. From the first lookup, recover the following nibbles of the key: $\widehat{k}_0$, $\check{k}_0$, $\check{k}_5$, $\check{k}_7$, $\check{k}_{10}$, $\check{k}_{15}$, 24 bits in total.
2. From the second lookup, recover the following nibbles of the key: $\check{k}_1$, $\check{k}_6$, $\check{k}_{11}$, $\check{k}_{12}$, 16 bits in total.
3. Recover the remaining 28 bits by an exhaustive search over.

These phases re-use the known inputs from the first round analysis (we assume that a 2-round cache trace is acquired for each input) but in most cases require additional known inputs.

For simplicity and due to space limitations we will describe the analysis exploiting misses only, but hits can be exploited similarly, leading to an even more efficient attack. We describe our algorithm and then analyze its complexity in terms of required traces and computational workload.

First Lookup of the Second Round. In this step we will exploit the traces of the form M**...*|M, i.e. having a miss in the first lookup of the second round. This lookup is indexed by

$$y_0 = 2 \bullet s(x_0) \oplus 3 \bullet s(x_5) \oplus s(x_{10}) \oplus s(x_{15}) \oplus s(k_7) \oplus k_0 \oplus 1.$$

The fact that this lookup is a miss leads to the following system of inequations:

$$\begin{cases} \widehat{y}_0 \neq \widehat{x}_{j_1} \\ \dots \\ \widehat{y}_0 \neq \widehat{x}_{j_L} \end{cases}, \quad j_1, \dots, j_L \in \Gamma,$$

where Γ is set of indices of misses observed in the 16 previous lookups (i.e. in the first round), $|\Gamma| = L$. After rearranging the terms the system becomes

$$2 \bullet s(x_0) \oplus 3 \bullet s(x_5) \overline{\oplus s(x_{10})} \oplus s(x_{15}) \oplus s(k_7) \neq \begin{cases} \widehat{\delta}_{j_1} \\ \dots \\ \widehat{\delta}_{j_L} \end{cases}, \quad j_1, \dots, j_L \in \Gamma, \quad (1)$$

where $\widehat{\delta}_j$ are some known values depending on the plaintext bytes and the key byte nibbles recovered in the first part of the analysis.

---

[1] Meanwhile, the strategy presented here would be straightforward to adapt to an AES implementation with an on-the-fly key schedule, and a similar strategy can be applied using xtimes operation of AES MixColumns transform in case the former is implemented as a lookup table (see [10] for using xtimes in an adaptive attack).

We have only 24 unknown bits in the left part of (1) since from the first round analysis we know the high nibble of the XOR difference between any two bytes of the key. Solving (1) for a single trace by exhaustive search over 2^{24} candidates for these bits will leave us with some fraction of these candidates. The next trace will result in a different system of the form (1) and thus further reduce the amount of candidates. After several traces of the form M**...*|M we will remain with the k_0, k_5, k_{10}, k_{15} completely recovered. However, up to 4 candidates will remain for k_7. Indeed, for a given input high nibble of the SubByte table, 1, 2, 3 or 4 input low nibbles yield the same output high nibble. Hence it is not possible to distinguish the correct one among them. For simplicity we omit to consider this possible multiplicity of candidates in the rest of the description, but mention that it increases the cost of the exhaustive search by a factor of up to 4. We perform the analysis of the required number of traces in [11].

Second Lookup of the Second Round. Once done with the analysis of the first lookup, we can exploit traces of the form M**...*|*M, i.e. having a miss in the second lookup of the second round. This lookup is indexed by

$$y_1 = 2 \bullet s(x_1) \oplus 3 \bullet s(x_6) \oplus s(x_{11}) \oplus s(x_{12}) \oplus s(k_7) \oplus k_0 \oplus k_1 \oplus 1$$

The fact that this lookup is a miss leads to the following system of inequations (after rearranging the terms):

$$2 \bullet s(x_1) \oplus 3 \bullet s(\widehat{x_6}) \oplus s(x_{11}) \oplus s(x_{12}) \neq \begin{cases} \widehat{\delta_{j_1}} \\ \dots \\ \widehat{\delta_{j_R}} \end{cases} , \quad j_1, \dots, j_R \in \Gamma, \quad (2)$$

where Γ is set of indices of misses observed in the 17 previous lookups (i.e. in the first round and in the first lookup of the second round), $|\Gamma| = R$, and $\widehat{\delta_j}$ are some known values depending on the plaintext bytes and the previously recovered nibbles of key bytes. Note that if the first lookup of the second round is a miss, one of the inequations in (2) emerges from $\widehat{y_1} \neq \widehat{y_0}$. From the analysis of the first lookup we already know y_0 and thus can consider this inequation here.

We have only 16 unknown bits in the left part of (2), namely the nibbles $\check{k}_1$, $\check{k}_6, \check{k}_{11}$ and $\check{k}_{12}$, the rest having been recovered in the previous steps. Solving (2) for several traces of the form M**...*|*M, we will get a single candidate for these unknown nibbles. Analysis of the required number of traces for this step is performed in [11].

Brute Force over 2^{30} Key Candidates. After the analysis of the first and second lookups of the second round the remaining unknown key chunks are $\check{k}_2$, $\check{k}_3, \check{k}_4, \check{k}_8, \check{k}_9, \check{k}_{13}, \check{k}_{14}$. They comprise 28 bits in total and therefore can be recovered by exhaustive search.

Theoretical analysis performed in [11] shows that about 50 traces and 2^{30} AES encryptions are required for the second round attack to succeed.

As already mentioned earlier, the second round attack can exploit hits in a similar way as described above for misses, which leads to a reduction in the number of traces. Our estimations for the second round attack exploiting both hits and misses, done like in [11], show that an average of 28.15 traces is required in the analysis of the first lookup, and 19.59 traces (re-using the available ones) in the analysis of the second lookup.

The simulated attacks we conducted on 2000 random keys led to the average numbers of required traces of 26.86 and 19.47 for the first and second lookups respectively and thus confirm our theoretical estimations.

Thus, for the full AES-128 key recovery we require about 30 known plaintexts with the corresponding side-channel traces and an exhaustive search of 2^{30} (considering the possible multiplicity of candidates for k_7). The attack will work in the same way for AES decryption. In the next section we demonstrate that our attacks can be performed in a real-life noisy environment.

5   Dealing with Detection Errors

In this section, we address the issue of detecting cache events in a real-life noisy environment. First, we show a practical example of distinguishing cache events in a power consumption trace of a 32-bit ARM microcontroller. Then we outline our general approach of dealing with detection errors and propose error-tolerant versions of our two attacks presented in Sects. 3 and 4.

5.1   Practical Explorations

In order to demonstrate that one could observe a series of cache hits and misses in the power consumption, the AES was implemented on NXP LPC2124 [18], an ARM7TDMI microprocessor. Though ARM7 family devices do not normally feature a cache, this particular microprocessor features a Memory Acceleration Module (MAM). The MAM is in fact a cache that increases the efficiency of accesses to the flash memory. A series of power consumption traces were acquired during the computation of the SubByte function. Two examples of these acquisitions are shown in Figure 3.

Each trace shows the first three memory accesses required to compute the SubByte function. In Figure 3(a) one can observe three memory accesses, as peaks in the power consumption, in the right hand side of the figure. In Figure 3(b), the power consumption during the same three memory accesses in the SubByte function is shown. One can see that the second peak in the power consumption is not visible, which corresponds to a cache hit. Note also that the amount of clock cycles is distinctly different, though not that clear from the picture as the difference in the power consumption.

From this we can observe that one can distinguish a cache hit from a cache miss in a straightforward manner. Recording a series of cache hits and misses

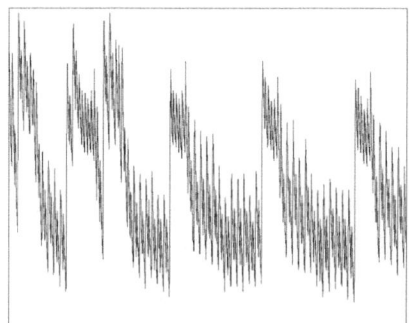

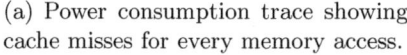

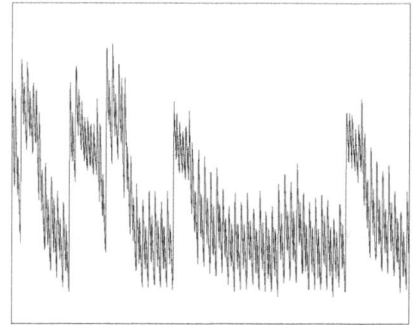

(a) Power consumption trace showing cache misses for every memory access.

(b) Power consumption trace showing a cache hit on second memory access.

Fig. 3. Power consumption during the first three memory accesses of the SubByte function

could be automated by something as simple as setting a threshold and observing whether the power consumption passes this threshold.

Unfortunately, our ARM7TDMI microprocessor is not suitable for implementing the attack described in this paper, since the cache (MAM) consists of one line of 16 bytes. An attack would be possible where cache hits show where two adjacent memory accesses load the same cache line, but this is beyond the scope of this paper.

5.2   General Approach to Distinguishing Cache Events

We assume that we can measure some statistic in a side-channel trace like the height of the peak in the cycles corresponding to the table look-up, the value of the statistic being larger in case of a cache miss and smaller in case of a cache hit. In Sect. 5.1 we have shown that this is a sound assumption that holds in practice. We further assume that the statistic for hits and misses will follow the distributions that are close to normal (due to the noise that is usually Gaussian). Distinguishing between hits and misses is then a task of distinguishing between the two distributions.

A simple distinguishing solution would be in fixing a single threshold for the value of the statistic, like in practical collision detection of [6]. This will result in an unavoidable trade-off between Type I and Type II errors. However, in our algorithms both taking a miss for a hit and a hit for a miss will lead to the incorrect key recovery. Therefore, our approach is in fixing 2 thresholds t_H and t_M, $t_H \leq t_M$. In this setting, we distinguish between three types of events.

1. If the statistic is smaller than t_H we consider the event to be a hit.
2. If the statistic is larger than t_M, we consider the event to be a miss.
3. If the value of the statistic falls between the thresholds, we consider the event to be "uncertain".

We assume that the thresholds t_H and t_M are chosen such that it is highly unlikely for a miss to be misinterpreted as a hit and vice versa. We denote the probability of the "uncertain event" by error probability p. Below we show how the additional "uncertain" category helps in making our algorithms resistant to errors when p is non-zero. Obviously, our error-tolerant attacks require more traces in order to succeed in the presence of errors.

5.3   Error-Tolerant Improved Adaptive Chosen Plaintext Attack

To make our attack of Sect. 3 error-tolerant, we keep the plaintext nibbles unchanged if the event is "uncertain" since we cannot do anything better than wait for another trace. In the forward positions, this means that the errors are treated just as hits. In the current position, where a hit leads to the desired equation and thus to proceeding to the next position, in case of an "uncertain" event we keep the current plaintext nibble and proceed with the next trace. In fact, our improved algorithm from Sect. 3 does not need to be changed: it automatically implements the described strategy when the cache trace includes 3 event types: Miss, Hit, Uncertain.

We performed 10^4 simulated attacks with random keys in the presence of detection errors. The results show that our improved algorithm tolerates errors very well. For the error probability 0.2 it requires 22.6 traces on average, and for the the error probability 0.5 – 47.2 traces on average. Note that this is better than for the original adaptive algorithm of [10] without detection errors.

5.4   Error-Tolerant Known Plaintext Attack

The analysis presented in Sect. 4.1 can also be adapted in order to find the linear dependencies between the upper nibbles of the key in the presence of uncertain cache events. The cache traces are now considered as arrays of 16 events, among the misses M, the hits H and the uncertain accesses U (being in the reality either M or H).

At the i-th lookup, if an uncertain event occurs in the q-th trace, $\kappa_{0,i}$ is not modified and the analysis continues for i with the next input.

Then for another lookup $i' > i$ and the same trace q, κ' is computed and eventually will miss the value $\widehat{p_i \oplus p_i} \oplus \kappa_{0,i}$ if the uncertain event $CT_i^{(q)}$ was actually a cache miss. For the uncertain cache accesses in the q-th trace, another set $\kappa*$ is computed, containing the value $\widehat{p_i \oplus p_i} \oplus \kappa_{0,i}$ involving the uncertain lookup i.

- If $CT_i^{(q)} = M$, the sieve proceeds with subtracting κ' from κ_i. Since κ' is eventually smaller than it should be, there are no chances of evicting the correct value for $\widehat{k_i \oplus k_0}$ from $\kappa_{0,i}$.
- If $CT_i^{(q)} = H$, the sieve intersects κ_i with $\kappa' \cup \kappa*$, such that the correct value, if ever present in $\kappa*$ will not be evicted from $\kappa_{0,i}$.
- If $CT_i^{(q)} = U$, no action is performed on $\kappa_{0,i}$, like previously done at the i-th lookup in the q-th input.

Our known plaintext strategy for the first AES round analysis in the presence of uncertain cache events is explicitly written in [11]. Simulated attacks were conducted for 10^4 random keys when the probability of uncertain events is 0.2 and 0.5. The average required numbers of traces are respectively 24.63 and 39.82. Note that for a probability equal to 0.5 the figure is less than that for the adaptive known plaintext attack reported above in Sect. 5.3.

The analysis of the second AES round can be adapted to be tolerant to uncertainties by treating them in the same manner.

5.5   Attacks with Partially Pre-loaded Cache

Our attacks can tolerate the setting when the cache already contains some S-Box lines at the beginning of the first AES round in a manner similar to [7]. If the lookup table is partially loaded in the cache prior to the encryption, the cache trace will result in having more H than one could have got with a clean cache.

Our adaptive algorithm from Sect. 3 straightforwardly tolerates this setting because it exploits only misses, and a partially preloaded cache means that some misses will not be observed. This does not lead to an incorrect key recovery since we will not exclude the correct key hypotheses from our set but only leave some additional incorrect key hypotheses.

In the case of our known plaintext attack, the claims from Sect. 4.1 when a hit occurs at the i-th lookup are no longer true: there does not necessarily exist an index $j \in \Gamma$ such that $\widehat{x}_i = \widehat{x}_j$. If one applies the sieve described in Sect. 4.1 to such inputs, when $CT_i = H$, the set $\kappa_{0,i}$ will be intersected with a set κ' possibly not containing the correct value for $\widehat{k_i \oplus k_o}$, thus evicting the latter from $\kappa_{0,i}$. However, when $CT_i = M$, one can subtract κ' from $\kappa_{0,i}$ because the former contains only incorrect values for $\widehat{k_0 \oplus k_i}$, although κ' may be smaller than if the cache did not contain any lines prior to the encryption. This suggests, in order to avoid a failure in the key recovery, that the sieve should be adapted as mentioned in Sect. 4.1, i.e. to perform an action on $\kappa_{0,i}$ only when misses occur. The analysis of the second round can exploit misses only in the same manner to tolerate the partially preloaded cache.

We performed simulated attacks with 10^4 random keys, when the cache is filled with 4, 8 and 12 lines of the lookup table, before the encryption starts. The average numbers of known inputs required for a 60-bit reduction of the key entropy are respectively 92.03, 158.02 and 271.10. We finally mention that in case a noisy environment is combined with a partially pre-loaded cache, our solutions described in Sects. 5.4 and 5.5 are perfectly compatible, though requiring a higher number of inputs.

6   Conclusion

In this paper, we describe side channel analysis that can be applied to implementations of AES on embedded devices featuring a cache mechanism. We have improved the adaptive chosen plaintext attack described in [10] and presented a new known plaintext attack that recovers a 128-bit AES key with approximately 30 measurements and with an exhaustive search with 2^{30} remaining hypotheses. We have shown that both our attacks can tolerate the errors in determining cache events from a side channel trace that occur in a noisy environment, as well as the partially pre-loaded cache.

We stress that the complexity of our attacks is comparable to that of the first order Differential Power Analysis on unprotected software implementations. At the same time, cache-collision attacks are resistant to Boolean masking in the case where all S-Boxes share the same random mask, as detailed in [10]. When such a masking scheme is used, our attacks will outperform higher order DPA attacks that typically require thousands of traces.

The countermeasures against trace-driven cache-collision attacks have been discussed in the previous works on the subject [3,15,10,7] and are similar to the countermeasures against cache attacks in general [21]. They include pre-fetching the lookup table into the cache prior to encryption and shuffling the order of table lookup computations.

Acknowledgements

The authors would like to thank the anonymous reviewers from CHES 2010 for their thorough comments and valuable suggestions. The work described in this paper has been supported in part by the European Commission IST Programme under Contract ICT-2007-216676 ECRYPT II and EPSRC grant EP/F039638/1 "Investigation of Power Analysis Attacks".

References

1. Acıiçmez, O., Koç, Ç.K.: Trace-driven cache attacks on AES (short paper). In: Ning, P., Qing, S., Li, N. (eds.) ICICS 2006. LNCS, vol. 4307, pp. 112–121. Springer, Heidelberg (2006)
2. Bernstein, D.J.: Cache-timing attacks on AES (2004),
   http://cr.yp.to/antiforgery/cachetiming-20050414.pdf
3. Bertoni, G., Zaccaria, V., Breveglieri, L., Monchiero, M., Palermo, G.: AES power attack based on induced cache miss and countermeasure. In: ITCC 2005, vol. 1, pp. 586–591. IEEE, Los Alamitos (2005)
4. Bogdanov, A.: Improved side-channel collision attacks on AES. In: Adams, C., Miri, A., Wiener, M. (eds.) SAC 2007. LNCS, vol. 4876, pp. 84–95. Springer, Heidelberg (2007)
5. Bogdanov, A., Eisenbarth, T., Paar, C., Wienecke, M.: Differential cache-collision timing attacks on AES with applications to embedded CPUs. In: Pieprzyk, J. (ed.) CT-RSA 2010. LNCS, vol. 5985, pp. 235–251. Springer, Heidelberg (2010)
6. Bogdanov, A., Kizhvatov, I., Pyshkin, A.: Algebraic methods in side-channel collision attacks and practical collision detection. In: Chowdhury, D.R., Rijmen, V., Das, A. (eds.) INDOCRYPT 2008. LNCS, vol. 5365, pp. 251–265. Springer, Heidelberg (2008)
7. Bonneau, J.: Robust final-round cache-trace attacks against AES. Cryptology ePrint Archive, Report 2006/374 (2006), http://eprint.iacr.org/2006/374

8. Brier, E., Clavier, C., Olivier, F.: Correlation power analysis with a leakage model. In: Joye, M., Quisquater, J.-J. (eds.) CHES 2004. LNCS, vol. 3156, pp. 16–29. Springer, Heidelberg (2004)
9. Daemen, J., Rijmen, V.: The Design of Rijndael: AES – The Advanced Encryption Standard. Springer, Heidelberg (2002)
10. Fournier, J., Tunstall, M.: Cache based power analysis attacks on AES. In: Batten, L.M., Safavi-Naini, R. (eds.) ACISP 2006. LNCS, vol. 4058, pp. 17–28. Springer, Heidelberg (2006)
11. Gallais, J.F., Kizhvatov, I., Tunstall, M.: Improved trace-driven cache-collision attacks against embedded AES implementations. Cryptology ePrint Archive, Report 2010/408 (2010), http://eprint.iacr.org/2010/408
12. Gandolfi, K., Mourtel, C., Olivier, F.: Electromagnetic analysis: Concrete results. In: Koç, Ç.K., Naccache, D., Paar, C. (eds.) CHES 2001. LNCS, vol. 2162, pp. 251–261. Springer, Heidelberg (2001)
13. Kelsey, J., Schneier, B., Wagner, D., Hall, C.: Side channel cryptanalysis of product ciphers. Journal of Computer Security 8, 141–158 (2000)
14. Kocher, P., Jaffe, J., Jun, B.: Differential power analysis. In: Wiener, M. (ed.) CRYPTO 1999. LNCS, vol. 1666, pp. 388–397. Springer, Heidelberg (1999)
15. Lauradoux, C.: Collision attacks on processors with cache and countermeasures. In: Wolf, C., Lucks, S., Yau, P.W. (eds.) WEWoRC 2005. Lecture Notes in Informatics, vol. P-74, pp. 76–85. Gesellschaft für Informatik, Bonn (2005)
16. Mangard, S., Oswald, E., Popp, T.: Power Analysis Attacks: Revealing the Secrets of Smart Cards. Springer, Heidelberg (2007)
17. Neve, M., Seifert, J.P.: Advances on access-driven cache attacks on AES. In: Biham, E., Youssef, A.M. (eds.) SAC 2006. LNCS, vol. 4356, pp. 147–162. Springer, Heidelberg (2007)
18. NXP B.V.: LPC2114/2124 single-chip 16/32-bit microcontrollers (2007), http://www.nxp.com/documents/data_sheet/LPC2114_2124.pdf
19. Osvik, D.A., Shamir, A., Tromer, E.: Cache attacks and countermeasures: The case of AES. In: Pointcheval, D. (ed.) CT-RSA 2006. LNCS, vol. 3860, pp. 1–20. Springer, Heidelberg (2006)
20. Page, D.: Theoretical use of cache memory as a cryptanalytic side-channel. Technical report CSTR-02-003, University of Bristol (2002)
21. Page, D.: Defending against cache-based side-channel attacks. Information Security Technical Report 8(P1), 30–44 (2003)
22. Quisquater, J.J., Samyde, D.: Electromagnetic analysis (EMA): Measures and counter-measures for smart cards. In: Attali, S., Jensen, T. (eds.) E-smart 2001. LNCS, vol. 2140, pp. 200–210. Springer, Heidelberg (2001)
23. Schramm, K., Leander, G., Felke, P., Paar, C.: A collision-attack on AES: Combining side channel- and differential-attack. In: Joye, M., Quisquater, J.-J. (eds.) CHES 2004. LNCS, vol. 3156, pp. 163–175. Springer, Heidelberg (2004)
24. Zhao, X.J., Wang, T.: Improved cache trace attack on AES and CLEFIA by considering cache miss and S-box misalignment. Cryptology ePrint Archive, Report 2010/056 (2010), http://eprint.iacr.org/2010/056
25. FIPS PUB 197: Specification for the Advanced Encryption Standard (2001), http://www.csrc.nist.gov/publications/fips/fips197/fips-197.pdf

Combination of SW Countermeasure and CPU Modification on FPGA against Power Analysis*

Daisuke Nakatsu, Yang Li, Kazuo Sakiyama, and Kazuo Ohta

The University of Electro-Communications,
1-5-1, Chofugaoka, Chofu, Tokyo 182-8585, Japan
{nakatsu_d,liyang,saki,ota}@ice.uec.ac.jp

Abstract. This paper presents a design flow for secure software (SW) implementations of cryptographic algorithms against Side-Channel Attacks (SCAs) by using a CPU modification. The development of countermeasures to increase resistance against the SCAs in SW implementations is a topic of ongoing research. Researchers have proposed SW-level countermeasures in order to defeat the SCAs. However, we notice that more secure SW implementations are possible with an additional support from a hardware (HW) level countermeasure such as partial CPU modifications. This paper proposes a co-design approach of SW-level countermeasures and CPU modifications to defeat the SCAs on Field Programmable Gate Arrays (FPGA). As a case study of evaluating an effectiveness of the combination of our SW-/HW-level countermeasures, the S-box algorithm proposed by Coron *et al.* [1] is used. According to our experimental results, we find that the algorithm can be performed with a higher resistance against power analysis by applying our countermeasures. Our proposed design flow is applicable to various kinds of algorithms as well.

Keywords: SCA, co-design, CPU modification, masking.

1 Introduction

Advanced Encryption Standard (AES) [2] is one of the standardized symmetric block ciphers, which is used in many smart cards that are, in general, based on an embedded processor (i.e. CPU). These devices such as the smart cards must be secure, even if an attacker can obtain physical information leakage (e.g. power dissipation and electromagnetic radiation) during the execution of cryptographic operations. In this paper, we focus on power analysis which is one type of the SCAs based on information leakage via. In order to defeat the SCAs, the cryptographic operations running on a CPU need to be protected by SW-level countermeasures. However, more secure SW implementations are possible with an additional support from HW-level countermeasures such as logic-level countermeasures (e.g. Wave Dynamic Differential Logic (WDDL) [3] and Random Switching Logic (RSL) [4]). In general, a countermeasure causes penalties

---

* This research was partially supported by Strategic International Cooperative Program (Joint Research Type), Japan Science and Technology Agency.

Y. Chung and M. Yung (Eds.): WISA 2010, LNCS 6513, pp. 258–272, 2011.

such as cost increase and performance degradation. Specifically, applying only HW-level countermeasures results in a significant cost increase, while only SW-level countermeasures cause the degradation of the speed performance. Hence, it is important to combine the SW- and HW-level countermeasures aiming to an efficient and secure implementation.

In previous work, to optimize the cost and performance of public-key cryptosystems, SW/HW co-designs have been proposed in [5,6]. However, the SCA resistance is not considered. On the contrary, what we propose in this paper is a secure SW/HW co-design, which enhances the security of SW implementations while also taking into consideration the trade-off between the cost and performance. More details of our contributions of this paper are as follows.

First, in order to improve a security of cryptographic algorithms against the SCAs, we propose not only to apply SW-level countermeasures but also to apply HW-level countermeasures such as a CPU modification. A case study of a CPU modification is shown in Sect. 3.2.

Second, this paper introduces a design flow for secure SW implementations by using a combination of SW- and HW-level countermeasures. Section 3 shows that flaws against the SCAs are pointed out and they could be eliminated by using our design flow. Note that our design flow could be applied to various kinds of algorithms and CPUs.

Finally, we investigate a relationship between applied SW-/HW-level countermeasures and changes in some factors that are HW cost, speed performance and SCAs resistance. Namely, according to our experimental results by using an FPGA, we evaluate the SCAs resistance in Sect. 5. Then we study cost increase and performance degradation corresponding our countermeasures in Sect. 6.

The rest of this paper is organized as follows. Section 2 shows a possible flaw against SCAs in SW implementations. Section 3 explains our countermeasures to the flaw. In Sect. 4, our countermeasures are applied to the S-box algorithm proposed by Coron *et al.* (hereafter, we call this the algorithm by Coron *et al.*) as a case study [1]. Section 5 shows our experimental results to evaluate the security improvement. The resistance against Differential Power Analysis (DPA) [7], cost and performance of the algorithm by Coron *et al.* and our improved version is shown in Sect. 6. Section 7 concludes this paper.

2 Vulnerable Operation against Power Analysis in SW Implementations

In general, there is possible vulnerability against SCAs in straightforward SW implementations. We expect that a major possible flaw could be concentrated on a difference (e.g. power consumption and calculation time) based on the secret value. Thus, this paper focuses on the branch operation because it could cause the difference based on the branch condition. The basic algorithm of the branch operation is shown in Alg. 1.

Algorithm 1 could cause vulnerability against the SCAs depending on CPUs. Generally, CPUs belong to one of two types as follows: on one type, the branch operation causes the different calculation time, while on the other type, it does

---

Algorithm 1. An example algorithm of the branch operation

Input: A secret value s ($s \in \{0, 1\}$).
Output: z.

1: **if** $s = 0$ **then**
2:     $z \leftarrow$ instruction A;
3: **else**
4:     $z \leftarrow$ instruction B;
5: **end if**
6: **Return** z;

---

not cause the different calculation time. For example, when Alg. 1 is operated on the former type, instructions A and B are finished at different timings. Thus, Timing Attack (TA) introduced by Kocher [8] can be successful. On the other hand, when Alg. 1 is operated on the latter type, they are finished at the same timing. Thus, the TA is unsuccessful.

However in the latter type, each instruction may have a different influence on power consumption. Thus, power analysis attacks [7,9] still may succeed due to the different power consumption caused by executing the different instructions. In this paper, a soft CPU, called PicoBlaze [10] on Xilinx FPGA, is used. Because a source code of PicoBlaze is opened so that we could modify the CPU architecture as a case study of our HW-level countermeasure. Specifically, PicoBlaze belongs to the latter type. In following sections, the resistance against power analysis is focused when using PicoBlaze. However, even if other CPUs are used, we expect that the resistance is increased as well as PicoBlaze.

3 Countermeasures against Power Analysis to Vulnerability of Branch Operation

In this section, we show two SW-level countermeasures and one HW-level countermeasure to defeat the vulnerability of the branch operation. Since HW modifications require time and effort, we will apply SW-level countermeasures to thwart SCAs. However, only SW-level countermeasures cannot defeat the vulnerability of the branch operation perfectly. We show that an additional support of the HW-level countermeasure can be used to defeat it. In the following sections, our approaches will be discussed.

3.1 SW-Level Countermeasures against Power Analysis

For the branch operation in the step 1 of Alg. 1, two different instructions, which are executed at the same timing, may have a different power consumption. Therefore, the branch operation causes the vulnerability against power analysis. In order to apply a countermeasure to this vulnerability, we apply a well-known countermeasure so that two instructions could be executed for every trial. This countermeasure is called *branch treatment* in this paper. Algorithm 2, where $Z[0]$ and $Z[1]$ mean two registers, shows the result after applying the branch

---

Algorithm 2. An algorithm with the branch treatment to Alg. 1

Input: A secret value s $(s \in \{0, 1\})$.
Output: z.

1: $Z[0] \leftarrow$ instruction A;
2: $Z[1] \leftarrow$ instruction B;
3: $z \leftarrow Z[s]$;
4: **Return** z;

Algorithm 3. An algorithm with the address randomization to Alg. 2

Input: A secret value s $(s \in \{0, 1\})$.
Output: z.

1: Generate a random bit r;
2: $Z[r] \leftarrow$ instruction A; (r:random number)
3: $Z[\overline{r}] \leftarrow$ instruction B;
4: $z \leftarrow Z[s \oplus r]$;
5: **Return** z;

---

treatment against Alg. 1. In Alg. 2, instructions A and B are operated at a different timing for every trial, which leads to a higher resistance against the power analysis attacks at the expense of the speed performance.

However, a different type of vulnerability is caused by the branch treatment. That is the different power consumption caused by executing the different instructions disappears, while the different addresses appear in the step 3 of Alg. 2 may cause a new vulnerability. Since the different addresses may have a different influence on power consumption, the power analysis attacks will be successful. In order to eliminate the vulnerability caused by the different addresses, we mask the addresses by random numbers as our second SW-level countermeasure [11]. This countermeasure is called *address randomization* in this paper. It can also be applied at the HW level so that the degradation of the speed performance (e.g. increasing the number of needed cycles for a calculation of the addresses) can be suppressed. However, it is easy to apply the address randomization at the SW level compared with the HW level.

Algorithm 3 shows the result after applying the address randomization to Alg. 2. The step 4 of Alg. 3, where the value in the register $Z[s \oplus r]$ is loaded, uses a masked address $s \oplus r$. Thus, the different power consumption caused by the different addresses in the step 4 of Alg. 3 will disappear. As a result of applying our SW-level countermeasures, Alg. 3 is expected to be secure against power analysis.

3.2 HW-Level Countermeasure against Power Analysis

The previous section shows that Alg. 3 is expected to be secure against power analysis. However, when the security of Alg. 3 is scrutinized, it is not yet secure perfect in the step 4, where an assignment of data are executed. In Alg. 3, the instructions A and B potentially have biased intermediate values. If the

---

Algorithm 4. The algorithm by Coron *et al.* [1]

Input: A masked value $\tilde{Z} = Z \oplus R_1$ and the mask R_1 ($\tilde{Z}$ and R_1 are n bits).

Output: The 3-tuple $\left(\left((-1)^{R_2} F(Z) + R_3 \right) \bmod 2^n, R_3, R_2 \right)$ (R_2 is 1 bit and R_3

is n bits).

1: Generate a random bit R_2;
2: Generate two n-bit random R_3 and R_4;
3: $result \leftarrow 2^n R_3 + R_4$;
4: **for** i from 0 to $2^n - 1$ **do**
5:     $T_1 \leftarrow \mathrm{SP}(i, \tilde{Z})$;   ($\mathrm{SP}(i,\tilde{Z})$: $i \cdot \tilde{Z}$)
6:     $T_1 \leftarrow T_1 \oplus R_2$;
7:     $T_2 \leftarrow \mathrm{SP}(i, R_1)$;
8:     $T_1 \leftarrow T_1 \oplus T_2$;
       /-branch operation(begin)-/
9:     $T_1 \leftarrow \mathrm{SFT}(i, T_1)$;   ($\mathrm{SFT}(i,T_1)$: $\hat{F}(i)(-1)^{T_1}$)
10:    $result \leftarrow result \boxplus T_1$;   ($result \leftarrow result \boxminus \hat{F}i$ or $result \boxplus \hat{F}i$)
       /-branch operation(end)-/
11: **end for**
12: $result \leftarrow result \gg n$;
13: **Return** $(result, R_3, R_2)$;

---

different power consumption caused by the biases in the intermediate values can be detected in the step 4, the power analysis attacks can be successful. In order to eliminate the biases, we apply the masking countermeasure [12,13] to the Arithmetic Logic Unit (ALU) in the CPU. This countermeasure is called *processor modification* in this paper. Although, this countermeasure can also be implemented at the SW level, it causes a significant cost increase and performance degradation. Additionally, it is difficult to control the intermediate values, i.e. to mask and unmask them. A solution of the problems is applying the masking countermeasure to the instructions at the HW level. We apply the masking countermeasure to the ALU corresponding to the instructions of PicoBlaze on FPGA. Because the masking countermeasure does not need to treat a circuit layout, while a hiding countermeasure needs to treat it such as WDDL. Thus, our countermeasures using the masking countermeasure can be applied to many platforms. Although an FPGA has less flexibility as for the circuit layout, the masking countermeasure can be applicable. Naturally, since Application Specific Integrated Circuit (ASIC) is more flexible about the circuit layout than FPGA, the masking countermeasure can also be applied to ASIC.

4   Case Study of Algorithm by Coron *et al.*

In order to verify that our countermeasures can improve the security against power analysis, the algorithm by Coron *et al.* (Alg. 4) is used as a case study.

Algorithm 5. Our version based on the algorithm by Coron *et al.*

Input: A masked value $\tilde{Z} = Z \oplus R_1$ and the mask R_1 ($\tilde{Z}$ and R_1 are n bits).

Output: The 3-tuple $\left(\left((-1)^{R_2} F(Z) + R_3 \right) \bmod 2^n, R_3, R_2 \right)$ (R_2 is 1 bit and R_3 is n bits).

1: Generate a random bit R_2 and R_5;   (R_5: for the address randomization)
2: Generate two n-bit random R_3 and R_4;
3: Generate $2n$-bit random R_A and R_B;   (R_A, R_B: for the processor modification)

4: $result \leftarrow 2^n R_3 + R_4$;
5: $result \leftarrow result \oplus R_A$;   (additional process: masking for applying the processor modification)
6: **for** i from 0 to $2^n - 1$ **do**
7:     $T_1 \leftarrow \mathrm{SP}(i, \tilde{Z})$;   ($\mathrm{SP}(i,\tilde{Z})$: $i \cdot \tilde{Z}$)
8:     $T_1 \leftarrow T_1 \oplus R_2$;
9:     $T_2 \leftarrow \mathrm{SP}(i, R_1)$;
10:     $T_1 \leftarrow T_1 \oplus T_2$;
11:     $T_2 \leftarrow \mathrm{SFT}(i, T_1)$;   ($\mathrm{SFT}(i,T_1)$: $\hat{F}(i)(-1)^{T_1}$)
12:     $result \leftarrow result \oplus R_B$;   (additional process: remaking for applying
13:     $result \leftarrow result \oplus R_A$;   the processor modification)
14:     $res[R_5] \leftarrow result \boxplus_{RSL} T_2$;   (additional process: the address randomization
15:     $res[\overline{R_5}] \leftarrow result \boxminus_{RSL} T_2$;   and processor modification are applied then
16:     $result \leftarrow res[R_5 \oplus T_1]$;   each res are already masked by R_A on RSL)
17: **end for**
18: $result \leftarrow result \oplus R_A$;   (additional process: unmasking for applying the processor modification)
19: $result \leftarrow result \gg n$;
20: **Return** $(result, R_3, R_2)$;

4.1 Vulnerability in Algorithm by Coron *et al.* against Power Analysis

Algorithm 4 shows the algorithm by Coron *et al.*, which has vulnerability pointed out by Li *et al.* [14]. We denote the scalar product function $X, Y \longmapsto X \cdot Y$ by SP and the function $X, Y \longmapsto \hat{F}(X)(-1)^Y$ by SFT. The operation $\boxplus$ denotes addition modulo 2^{2n}. The value $\hat{F}(i)$ takes a fixed value of the array $\hat{F}$, which is calculated based on discrete Fourier transform, corresponding to i. The steps 9 and 10 in Alg. 4 could have the vulnerability because they may be implemented by the branch operation using the secret value T_1 like Alg. 1. Since the different instructions (i.e. addition and subtraction) are executed corresponding to the branch condition in the steps 9 and 10, the power analysis attacks can be successful. In order to evaluate the effectiveness of our countermeasures, we will discuss our version (Alg. 5) in the next section.

4.2 Our Countermeasures to Algorithm by Coron *et al.*

Since addition and subtraction are executed as the different instructions which cause the different power consumption, the masking countermeasure is applied

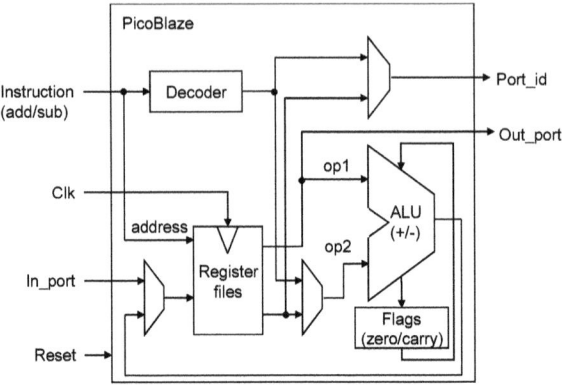

Fig. 1. The architecture in the original PicoBlaze

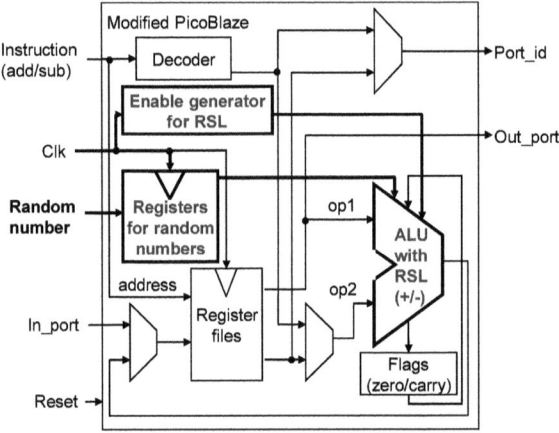

Fig. 2. The architecture in the modified PicoBlaze based on the processor modification

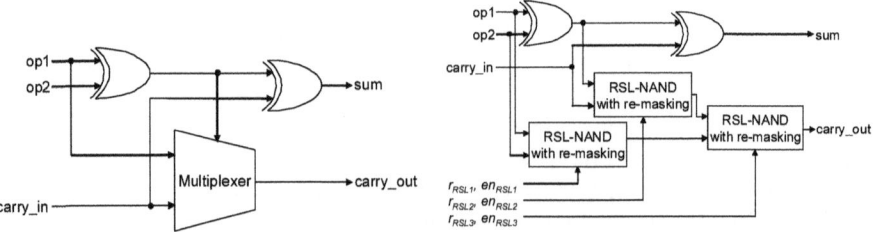

(a) The architecture in a part of the ALU in Fig. 1.

(b) The architecture in a part of the ALU in Fig. 2.

Fig. 3. The architecture in the ALU

Table 1. Evaluation environment

Target FPGA	Xilinx Virtex-II Pro Series XC2VP7-5FG456C
Frequency	8MHz
Oscilloscope	Agilent DSO7032A
Differential probe	Yokogawa 701920

to the adder logics, which is a part of the ALU in the CPU, as the processor modification. Specifically, a masked logic called RSL proposed by Suzuki and Saeki and Ichikawa [4] is applied to the adder. It can suppress glitches in the circuit by controlling an enable signal which becomes 1 after decision of the output in RSL. When the enable signal is 0, the output in RSL is 0. As a result of applying RSL to the ALU, the architecture of PicoBlaze is modified from the architecture shown in Fig. 1 to one shown in Fig. 2. The architecture in the ALU in Figs. 1 and 2 is drawn in Figs. 3(a) and 3(b). An enable generator and registers for random numbers in Fig. 2 are implemented to apply RSL. The enable generator generates an enable signal to suppress a glitch signal and the registers store random numbers for masking and unmasking. This paper refers to [15] for the construction of RSL-NAND with re-masking in Fig. 3(b). The values r_{RSL1}, r_{RSL2} and r_{RSL3} in Fig. 3(b) denote random numbers for RSL. The values en_{RSL1}, en_{RSL2} and en_{RSL3} in Fig. 3(b) denote enable signals for RSL. Although the RSL logics and controller of the enable signals increase the CPU cost and degradation of the maximum operating frequency, the power analysis attacks could be unsuccessful.

Algorithm 5, where $res[R_5]$ and $res[\overline{R_5}]$ mean two registers, shows our improved version which combines the SW-/HW-level countermeasures such as the branch treatment, address randomization and processor modification. The RSL operations $\boxplus_{RSL}$ and $\boxminus_{RSL}$ denote addition and subtraction modulo 2^{2n}, respectively. The values R_A and R_B are two random numbers used for RSL, where R_A masks the output of the adder and R_B re-masks the input of the adder. Since such new random numbers are needed for RSL, necessary cycles for the execution of Alg. 5 could be increased compared with that of Alg. 4. The value R_5 masks the address. The security of our improved version is evaluated in the next section.

5   Results of Our Evaluation Experiment

Following sections show our experimental results to evaluate the resistance against DPA for each of our countermeasures. In order to evaluate the security, an averaged differential power consumption corresponding to the secret value T_1 is used. In every evaluation experiment, 30 000 power traces are used to calculate the averaged differential power consumption.

5.1   Experimental Environment

Table 1 shows our evaluation environment in this paper. We implement the CPU on a cryptographic FPGA of SASEBO-G, which is one of the side-channel attack

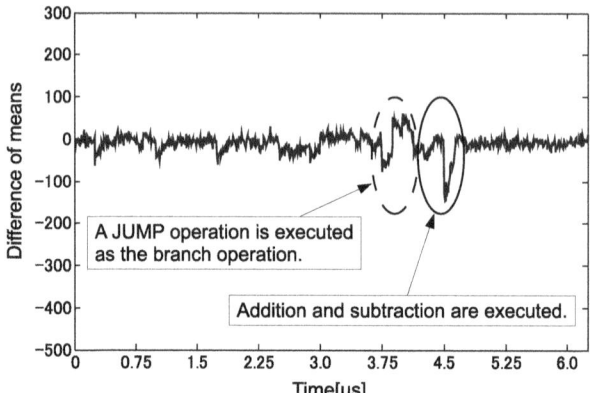

Fig. 4. Without our countermeasures, the averaged differential power trace

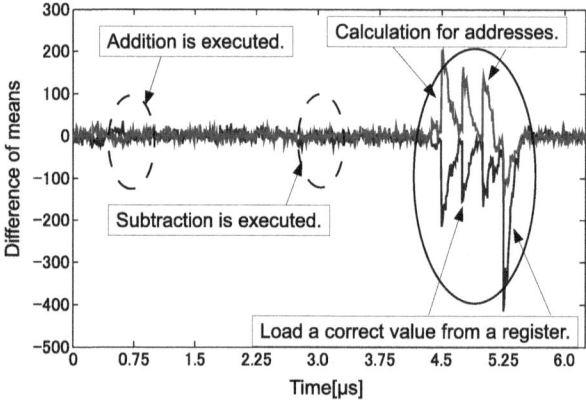

Fig. 5. With the branch treatment, the averaged differential power trace

standard evaluation boards [16]. Every random number used for the masking countermeasure is generated by MATLAB. In this paper, we assume that the random number generator by MATLAB is not target of attack. Then the random numbers are sent to the module via an RS232C cable. In order to evaluate the resistance against DPA, the power traces are obtained by measuring a voltage drop of a resistor inserted between VDD pins of the cryptographic FPGA and the ground of the board.

5.2   Experimental Result without Countermeasures

The security evaluation of the algorithm by coron *et al.* without our counter-measures is shown in this section. Figure 4 shows the averaged differential power consumption after grouping the power traces by T_1. In a circle of a continuous line of Fig. 4, the different instructions are executed at the same timing. Thus,

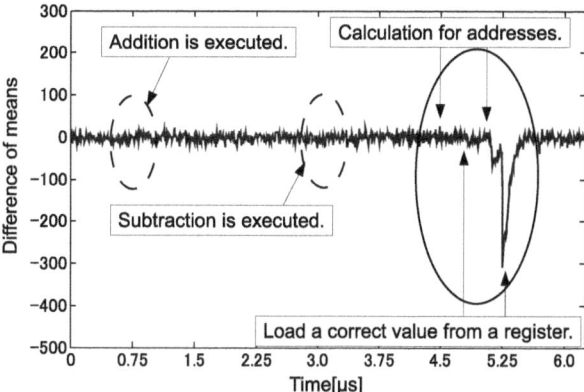

Fig. 6. With adding the address randomization, the averaged differential power trace

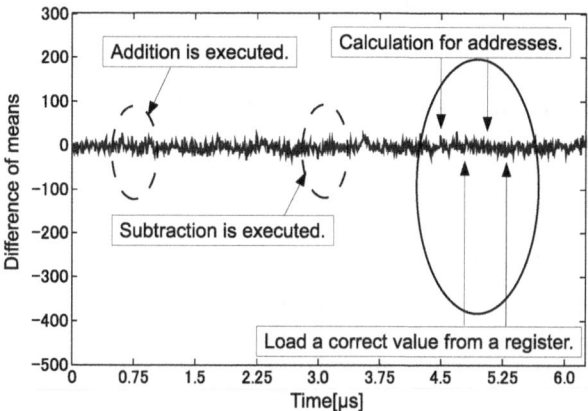

Fig. 7. With adding the processor modification, the averaged differential power trace

peaks in the circle are caused by the different instructions. In other words, Fig. 4 shows that the different instructions have the different influence on power consumption. Therefore, the power analysis attacks can be successful. Additionally, since an operation corresponding to the branch operation using T_1 are executed in a circle of a dash line of Fig. 4, other peaks appear there.

5.3 Experimental Result with the Branch Treatment

This section shows that the peaks disappear by applying the branch treatment to the algorithm by Coron *et al.* Figure 5 shows the averaged differential power consumption after grouping the power traces by T_1. In Fig. 5, a continuous and dash lines denote the experimental results using the reverse address for each other. Since the different instructions are executed for every trial, the power analysis attacks using the different power consumption caused by executing the different instructions become unsuccessful. However, other peaks are detected during calculation depending on the addresses. Thus, the power analysis attacks still can be successful.

5.4   Experimental Result with Adding the Address Randomization

As a result of the address randomization, the peaks, which are detected in Fig. 5, disappear in Fig. 6. Thus, the address randomization can thwart power analysis by exploiting the different addresses. However, around 5.25 μs in the horizontal axis of Fig. 6, there are peaks caused by the biases in the intermediate values. Therefore, the power analysis attacks still can be successful.

5.5   Experimental Result with Adding the Processor Modification

In Fig. 7, as a result of the processor modification, the peaks caused by the biases disappear. Therefore, the processor modification can eliminate the different power consumption caused by the biases. In a word, we show that our SW-/HW-level countermeasures can defeat the power analysis attacks.

6   Comparison of Security, Cost and Performance

This section explains the security, cost and performance of the original algorithm by Coron *et al.* and our improved version based on it.

6.1   Security Evaluation of Masking Version

Before comparing the security, cost and performance, we show how we evaluate the security against DPA in this paper. In order to verify the security against DPA, this paper refers to [1,17] for information about a relation between the bias of random numbers and a number of essential traces to attack. The DPA attacks, which are based on a relation between the power consumption and the intermediate values, need to execute the target algorithm many times, say N. By using a target bit of the intermediate value b for DPA, a leakage Δ_k is calculated by

$$\Delta_k = \frac{\sum_{i=1}^{N}(b_i \oplus r_i) \times l_i}{\sum_{i=1}^{N}(b_i \oplus r_i)} - \frac{\sum_{i=1}^{N}(1 - (b_i \oplus r_i)) \times l_i}{\sum_{i=1}^{N}(1 - (b_i \oplus r_i))} \tag{1}$$

$$= \left(\frac{\sum_{i:r_i=0} b_i \times l_i}{\sum_{i:r_i=0} b_i} - \frac{\sum_{i:r_i=0}(1 - b_i) \times l_i}{\sum_{i:r_i=0}(1 - b_i)} \right)$$

$$- \left(\frac{\sum_{i:r_i=1}(1 - b_i) \times l_i}{\sum_{i:r_i=1}(1 - b_i)} - \frac{\sum_{i:r_i=1} b_i \times l_i}{\sum_{i:r_i=1} b_i} \right), \tag{2}$$

where the leakage l_i denotes the power consumption on the i-th trial. The target bit b_i, which is masked by the random number r_i, is calculated by a public value and a predicted key k. Note that the bias of the random number ϵ is calculated

$$\epsilon = \left| \frac{1}{2} - \frac{\#(r_i = 0)}{N} \right|, \tag{3}$$

Table 2. Comparison of a version without countermeasures and final version with bias, cost and performance

	Bias of random number (ϵ)	CPU cost (Slice/LUT)	Program cost	Cycles	Max operating frequency[MHz]
Original version	2.5%	744/618	2088 bit	1696	200
With the branch treatment	15.8%	744/618	2322 bit	1968	200
With adding the address randomization	10.7%	744/618	2394 bit	2354	200
Final version	0.8%	1313/686	2790 bit	2572	30

according to the Eq. (2), when the predicted key k is the correct key k^*, an expectation of Δ_{k^*} is calculated by

$$E[\Delta_{k^*}] = \left(\frac{1}{2} + \epsilon\right)(E[L(1)] - E[L(0)])$$

$$+ \left(\frac{1}{2} - \epsilon\right)(E[L(0)] - E[L(1)]) \tag{4}$$

$$= 2\epsilon \times (E[L(1)] - E[L(0)]), \tag{5}$$

where the leakage $L(0)$ and $L(1)$ denote the power consumption corresponding to the value $b = 0$ and $b = 1$, respectively. Thus, $E[\Delta_{k^*}]$ is divided by $\frac{1}{2\epsilon}$, compared to no masking version in which ϵ takes $\frac{1}{2}$. Same with [1], we use the relation between the bias of random numbers and the number of the essential traces proposed by Clavier, Coron and Dabbous [17]. According to [17], the Eq. (5) leads that the relation is expressed as:

$$A = C \times \left(\frac{1}{2\epsilon}\right)^2, \tag{6}$$

where the value A denotes the number of the essential traces. The constant value C, which is dependent on the experimental environment, denotes the number of the essential traces in no masking version. In our experiment, a practical attack was not executed to calculate the value C because we just check the relation between the number of the essential traces of the original algorithm by Coron *et al.* and that of our improved version. Since the Eq. (6) is only based on experimental results of [1,17], it is necessary to check the relationship in detail in the future.

6.2   Investigation of Changes in Bias, Cost and Performance

Table 2 shows the bias, cost and performance corresponding to each version. The CPU cost includes a cost of a random number generator, which is based on [18]. In Table 2, the bias of the random number denotes the probability that the random number is distinguished from the power traces. In order to evaluate

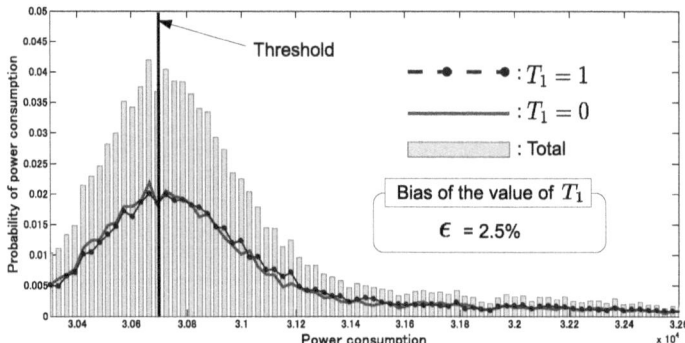

(a) The probability distributions of power consumption of the original version.

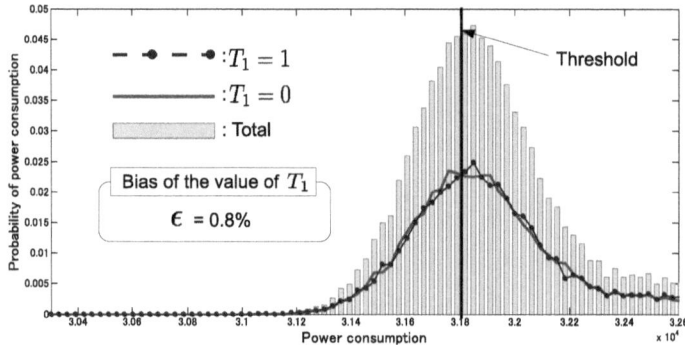

(b) The probability distributions of power consumption of the final version.

Fig. 8. The probability distributions of power consumption during the executions of addition and subtraction

the bias of the random number, the power consumption during the execution of an operation using the random number T_1 is used. Figures 8(a) and 8(b) show probability distributions of the power consumption in the circle of the continuous line of Figs. 4 and 7, respectively. For example, in order to calculate each bias, the power traces are separated into two groups by a threshold in Figs. 8(a) and 8(b). As a result of separating the power traces, each bias is shown in Table 2. Table. 2 also shows the relationship between each countermeasure and the changes in the cost, speed performance and bias. Specifically, the SW countermeasures cause increasing the program cost and the number of the cycles, while the CPU modification causes the degradation of the max operating frequency and increasing the CPU cost. Also, Table. 2 shows that a halfway countermeasure could cause the degeneration of the resistance against the SCAs. However, our version which accumulates every countermeasure proposed in this paper can reduce the bias by 2%, compared with the original algorithm by Coron *et al.* Thus, the number of the essential traces for DPA of our improved version is timed by ten compared to that of the original version, assuming the Eq. (6) can be used for our experimental environment. Even though from a security point of view it is advisable to use our improved version, our countermeasures degenerate the cost and performance. In order to suppress the degeneration of the cost and performance, the rest of this section shows an example to improve them.

In the process of improving the cost and performance, a support of a HW-level countermeasure is used. Especially as stated in Sect. 3.1, the address randomization can also be applied at the HW level. By applying the address randomization at the HW level, the operations, which mask and calculate the address at the SW level, become unnecessary. Specifically, according to a rough estimation based on our implementation, the SW program cost can be decreased by 200 bits and the cycle number can be decreased by 350 cycles. However, the CPU cost increases due to the masking logic, which is used for the address randomization at the HW level. The maximum operating frequency will be unchanged because the adder has the critical path delay.

7 Conclusion

This paper presented how to overcome the major possible flaw in SW implementations by using the combination of SW-/HW-level countermeasures. We also showed the design flow of the combination of the SW-/HW-level countermeasures which could support more secure implementations compared with only SW-level countermeasures. Specifically, as an additional support from the HW level countermeasure, we proposed the modification of the Arithmetic Logic Unit of PicoBlaze, which is one of the CPUs as a case study. In order to evaluate the effectiveness of our countermeasures, they are applied to the S-box algorithm proposed by Coron et al. [1] as a case study. As a result of the evaluation, the security improvement of the S-box algorithm was shown. In addition, the significant degeneration of the cost and speed performance was shown. Thus, it is necessary to investigate the method of the better combination for the cost, speed performance and security. Also we showed that the halfway countermeasure (i.e. applying only branch treatment) could cause the degeneration of the resistance against the SCAs. Therefore, in order to improve the SCAs resistance, we found that it is necessary to apply all of our countermeasures. We expect that our countermeasures can support the security improvement of various kinds of algorithms which have the vulnerability shown in this paper such as the different instructions, addresses and biases of the intermediate values.

References

1. Coron, J.-S., Giraud, C., Prouff, E., Rivain, M.: Attack and Improvement of a Secure S-Box Calculation Based on the Fourier Transform. In: Oswald, E., Rohatgi, P. (eds.) CHES 2008. LNCS, vol. 5154, pp. 1–14. Springer, Heidelberg (2008)
2. National Institute of Standards and Technology (NIST), FIPS PUB 197: the official AES standard,
   http://www.csrc.nist.gov/publications/fips/fips197/fips-197.pdf

3. Tiri, K., Verbauwhede, I.: A Logic Level Design Methodology for a Secure DPA Resistant ASIC or FPGA Implementation. In: Proceedings of the Conference on Design, Automation and Test in Europe, DATE 2004, pp. 246–251. IEEE Computer Society, Los Alamitos (2004)
4. Suzuki, D., Saeki, M., Ichikawa, T.: Random Switching Logic: A Countermeasure against DPA Based on Transition Probability. Cryptology ePrint Archive (2004)
5. Batina, L., Hwang, D., Hodjat, A., Preneel, B., Verbauwhede, I.: Hardware/ Software Co-design for Hyperelliptic Curve Cryptography (HECC) on the 8051μP. In: Rao, J.R., Sunar, B. (eds.) CHES 2005. LNCS, vol. 3659, pp. 106–118. Springer, Heidelberg (2005)
6. Sakiyama, K., Batina, L., Preneel, B., Verbauwhede, I.: Superscalar Coprocessor for High-Speed Curve-Based Cryptography. In: Goubin, L., Matsui, M. (eds.) CHES 2006. LNCS, vol. 4249, pp. 415–429. Springer, Heidelberg (2006)
7. Kocher, P., Jaffe, J., Jun, B.: Differential Power Analysis. In: Wiener, M. (ed.) CRYPTO 1999. LNCS, vol. 1666, pp. 388–397. Springer, Heidelberg (1999)
8. Kocher, P.: Timing Attacks on Implementations of Diffie-Hellman, RSA, DSS, and Other Systems. In: Koblitz, N. (ed.) CRYPTO 1996. LNCS, vol. 1109, pp. 104–113. Springer, Heidelberg (1996)
9. Messerges, T.S.: Using Second-Order Power Analysis to Attack DPA Resistant Software. In: Paar, C., Koç, Ç.K. (eds.) CHES 2000. LNCS, vol. 1965, pp. 238–251. Springer, Heidelberg (2000)
10. XILINX, PicoBlaze 8-bit Embedded Microcontroller User Guide, http://www.xilinx.com/support/documentation/ip_documentation/ug129.pdf
11. Itoh, K., Izu, T., Takenaka, M.: A Practical Countermeasure against Address-Bit Differential Power Analysis. In: Walter, C.D., Koç, Ç.K., Paar, C. (eds.) CHES 2003. LNCS, vol. 2779, pp. 382–396. Springer, Heidelberg (2003)
12. Coron, J.-S., Goubin, L.: On Boolean and Arithmetic Masking against Differential Power Analysis. In: Paar, C., Koç, Ç.K. (eds.) CHES 2000. LNCS, vol. 1965, pp. 231–237. Springer, Heidelberg (2000)
13. Goubin, L.: A Sound Method for Switching between Boolean and Arithmetic Masking. In: Koç, Ç.K., Naccache, D., Paar, C. (eds.) CHES 2001. LNCS, vol. 2162, pp. 3–15. Springer, Heidelberg (2001)
14. Li, Y., Sakiyama, K., Kawamura, S., Komano, Y., Ohta, K.: Security Evaluation of a DPA-Resistant S-box Based on the Fourier Transform. In: International Conference on Information and Communications Security. LNCS, vol. 5927, pp. 3–16. Springer, Heidelberg (2009)
15. Suzuki, D., Saeki, M., Ichikawa, T.: Random Switching Logic: A New Countermeasure against DPA and Second-Order DPA at the Logic Level. IEICE Trans. Fundamentals E90-A(1), 160–168 (2007)
16. National Institute of Advanced Industrial Science and Technology (AIST), Side-channel Attack Standard Evaluation Board (SASEBO), http://www.rcis.aist.go.jp/special/SASEBO/index-en.html
17. Clavier, C., Coron, J.-S., Dabbous, N.: Differential Power Analysis in the Presence of Hardware Countermeasures. In: Paar, C., Koç, Ç.K. (eds.) CHES 2000. LNCS, vol. 1965, pp. 252–263. Springer, Heidelberg (2000)
18. Dichtl, M., Golić, J.D.: High-Speed True Random Number Generation with Logic Gates Only. In: Paillier, P., Verbauwhede, I. (eds.) CHES 2007. LNCS, vol. 4727, pp. 45–62. Springer, Heidelberg (2007)

Face Image Retrieval Using Sparse Representation Classifier with Gabor-LBP Histogram*

Hansung Lee[1], Yunsu Chung[1], Jeongnyeo Kim[1], and Daihee Park[2,**]

[1] Electronics and Telecommunications Research Institute, Korea
{mohan,yoonsu,jnkim}@etri.re.kr
[2] Dept. of Computer and Information Science, Korea University, Korea
dhpark@korea.ac.kr

Abstract. Face image retrieval is an important issue in the practical applications such as mug shot searching and surveillance systems. However, it is still a challenging problem because face images are fairly similar due to the same geometrical configuration of facial features. In this paper, we present a face image retrieval method which is robust to the variations of face image condition and with high accuracy. Firstly, we choose the Gabor-LBP histogram for face image representation. Secondly, we use the sparse representation classification for the face image retrieval. Using the Gabor-LBP histogram and sparse representation classifier, we achieved effective and robust retrieval results with high accuracy. Finally, experiments are conducted on ETRI and XM2VTS database to verify a proposed method. It showed rank 1 retrieval accuracy rate of 98.9% on ETRI face set, and of 99.3% on XM2VTS face set, respectively.

Keywords: face retrieval, face recognition, Gabor filter, local binary patterns, sparse representation classifier.

1 Introduction

With the growing popularity of digital image, the numbers of collections of digital image databases have recently exploded. Consequently, it is more difficult to retrieve the image in manual way from large image databases. Therefore, the content-based image retrieval with query by example has been important research subject since the early 1990's [1]. In particular, face image retrieval (FIR) is a significant research issue in many practical applications such as mug shot searching and surveillance systems. FIR is still a challenging problem because face images are fairly similar due to the same geometrical configuration of facial features [1]. This makes FIR more

---

* This research was financially supported by the Electronics and Telecommunications Research Institute (ETRI) through the project of "Development of CCTV Face Recognition and Identification Technology under Unconstrained Environment"; This research was partially supported by the Ministry of Education, Science Technology (MEST) and Korea Industrial Technology Foundation (KOTEF) through the Human Resource Training Project for Regional Innovation.
** Corresponding author.

Y. Chung and M. Yung (Eds.): WISA 2010, LNCS 6513, pp. 273–280, 2011.

difficult than traditional content based image retrieval. To resolve aforementioned difficulty in FIR, in general, human face recognition (HFR) techniques are employed in FIR.

HFR is an automated biometric method to verify or recognize the identities of persons based on their physiological characteristics. Because of its non-aggressive and non-intrusive nature, the HFR has been the subject of extensive research over the past decades and it spans numerous fields and disciplines [2]. HFR models can be broadly divided into two categories: global approach and component based approach. Global approach methods use the whole face region as the raw input to a face recognition system. In general, these methods apply dimensionality reduction to raw input and then conduct subspace analysis. One of the most widely used methods is based on principal component analysis (PCA) and linear discriminant analysis (LDA). Most of the contemporary subspace analysis methods are either inspired or an improvements of these original works [2-4]. Global approach works well for classifying frontal face images. However, much of these methods fail in case of varying illuminations and are not robust to pose and expression changes [2-4]. An alternative method to the global approach is component based method. These methodologies extract local features or landmark such as the eyes, nose, nostrils, and corner of mouth from face image and apply statistical modeling for face recognition. Component based methods are invariant to similarity transformations, and robust to pose, illumination, and expression changes. However, it is very difficult to detect exact landmarks of face image and it is time consuming process [2-4].

According to the recent literature, unlike the mainstream approaches of face representation based on statistical learning such as subspace analysis, SVM, and Adaboost, there are many ongoing attempts to represent the face image based on non statistical learning methods. Gabor filter and local binary patterns (LBP) based methods have been successfully applied to many face recognition applications [5-8]. In particular, hybrid methods with combining Gabor filter and LBP recently attract significant attention in face recognition and retrieval. These methods are invariant to illumination and expressional variability [6-8].

On the other hand, supervised classification framework based on sparse representation, viz. sparse representation classifier (SRC), is recently proposed for face recognition [9-10]. The sparsity is an important way to encode the domain knowledge, thus generally improve the generalization capability of the model [11]. J. Wright et al. [10] showed that the classifier based on sparse representation is remarkably effective and achieves the best recognition rate on some face database. Especially, it is robust to partial occlusion and corruption of face images.

In this paper, we propose a hybrid method for face retrieval, which is not only robust to the variations of imaging condition but also with high accuracy. We choose Gabor-LBP histogram for face image representation and SRC for the face image retrieval. The proposed face image retrieval system is given in Fig. 1. It consists of the following three stages: face detection, face representation, and face image retrieval. In this paper, we focus on the second and last stages. Using the Gabor-LBP histogram and sparse representation classifier, we achieved effective and robust retrieval results with high accuracy. To evaluate the performance of our proposed method, we conduct experiments on ETRI and XM2VTS face database. Our experiments show that the retrieval accuracy at rank 1 approaches 98.9% on ETRI face set and 99.3% on XM2VTS face set, respectively.

The rest of this paper is organized as follows. In Section 2, we describe the face image representation with Gabor-LBP histogram. A sparse representation classifier based face image retrieval method is presented in Section 3. In Section 4, we show experimental results. Finally, in Section 5, we conclude with a brief summary and suggest future research directions.

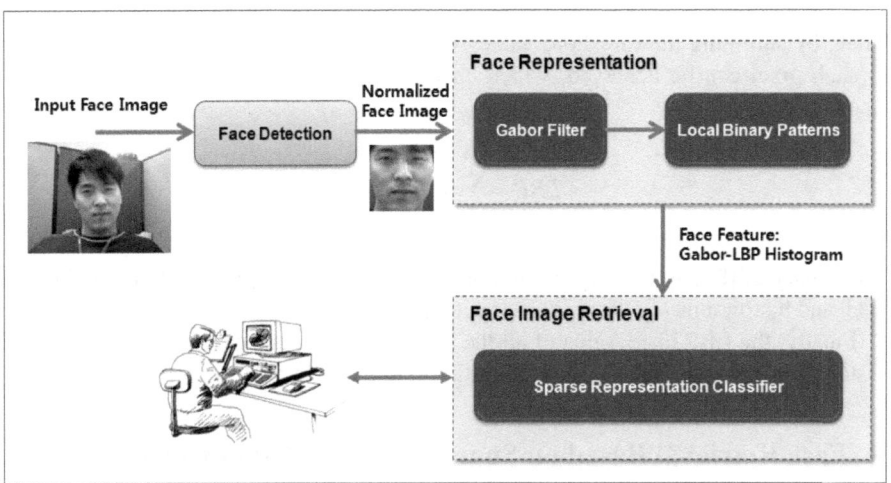

Fig. 1. Architecture of proposed face image retrieval system

2   Face Representation with Gabor-LBP Histogram

In this Section, we describe the face representation based on Gabor filter and LBP. Gabor feature based face representations have been well known as one of the most successful methods. Recently, with the success of LBP, there are ongoing attempts to combine Gabor feature and LBP for the face description [6-8].

In this paper, we employ the face representation method that is proposed in [8]. It is robust to noise and local image transformations due to variations of lighting, occlusion and pose. Combining Gabor and LBP enhances the representation power of the spatial histogram. A face image is presented as a histogram sequence by the following steps [8]: First, an input face image is normalized and then transformed to multiple Gabor images by convolving the face image with Gabor filters. Let $f(x, y)$ be the face image. Its convolution with a Gabor filter $\psi_{o,s}(z)$ is defined as follows

$$G_{\psi f}(x, y, o, s) = f(x, y) * \psi_{o,s}(z) \tag{1}$$

where o and s are orientation and scale of the Gabor filters, $z = (x, y)$, and $*$ denotes the convolution operator. Five scales and eight orientations Gabor filters are used.

Second, each Gabor image is converted to local binary patterns map using LBP operator. The LBP operator labels the image pixels by thresholding the 3×3-neighborhood of each pixel $p_i (i = 0, 1, \cdots, 7)$ with the center value p_c and considering the result as a binary number [8].

$$S(p_i - p_c) = \begin{cases} 1, & p_i \geq p_c \\ 0, & p_i < p_c \end{cases} \tag{2}$$

Then, by summing the threshold values weighted by power of two, the LBP patterns at each pixel can be achieved, which characterizes the spatial structure of the local image texture.

$$LBP = \sum_{i=0}^{7} S(p_i - p_c) \cdot 2^i \tag{3}$$

Third, each LBP map is divided into non-overlapping sub-regions with predefined bin size, and histograms of sub-regions are computed.

Finally, the LBP histograms of all the LBP maps are concatenated to form the final histogram sequence as the face representation (or description).

3 Face Retrieval Based on Sparse Representation Classifier

In this Section, we present the face image retrieval method based on sparse representation classifier. Sparse representation (SR) was firstly proposed for signal representation. In the past few years, SR has successfully applied in many practical applications such as signal compression and coding, image de-noising, and compressive sensing. Recently, supervised classification methods based on sparse representation, viz. sparse representation classifier (SRC), is proposed for face recognition. It is especially robust to partial occlusion and corruption of face images [9-11].

The problem of face image classification based on sparse representation can be formulated as follows [10-11]: Given a face image with vector pattern $y \in R^m$, and a matrix $A = [x_1, x_2, \cdots, x_n] \in R^{m \times n}$, the objective of SR is to represent y using as few entries of A as possible. This can be formally expressed as follows:

$$x_0 = \arg\min \|x\|_0 \quad \text{subject to} \quad y = Ax \tag{4}$$

where $x \in R^n$ is the coefficient vector. Unfortunately, finding the sparsest solution of (4) is NP-hard. It can be shown that if the solution x_0 is sparse enough, the solution of l_0 minimization problem is equal to the solution of l_1 minimization problem [10-11].

$$x_1 = \arg\min \|x\|_1 \quad \text{subject to} \quad y = Ax \tag{5}$$

This problem can be solved in polynomial time by standard linear programming methods [10].

Given a new test data y from one of the classes in the training set, its sparse representation x_1 is computed by (5). The nonzero entries in the estimate x_1 will be associated with the columns of A from a single object class i, and we can easily assign the test sample y to that class.

In the context of face image retrieval, we assume that training images and test images are taken under different conditions, e.g., change of illumination, hair style, facial hair, shape, facial expression and presence or absence of glasses. This may lead to nonzero entries associated with multiple object classes. Therefore, in general, face image retrieval system outputs the retrieved results in sorted order according to the score value. In this paper, we use the coefficient value in the solution x_1 of l_1 minimization problem as the score value. Algorithm 1 below summarizes the face image retrieval procedure.

Algorithm 1. Face Image Retrieval based on Sparse Representation

1. Input: a matrix of training samples

$A = [A_1, A_2, \cdots, A_k] \in R^{m \times n}$ for k classes, a test sample $y \in R^m$.

2. Normalize the columns of A to have unit l_2 norm.

3. Solve the l_1 minimization problem:

$x_1 = \arg\min \|x\|_1 \quad \text{subject to} \quad y = Ax$

4. Compute the mean coefficient value of each class.

$mc_i = \dfrac{1}{n_i} \sum_1^{n_i} \delta_i(x_1) \text{ for } i = 1, 2, \cdots, k$

mc_i : mean coefficient value of i -th class; n_i : number of elements in i -th class;

$\delta_i(x_1)$: characteristic function that selects the coefficients associated with the

i -th class.

5. Sort the class in descending order according with mean coefficient value of classes.

6. Output: p face images which have large mean coefficient value.

4   Experimental Results

To evaluate the performance of our proposed method, we conducted experiments on the Electronics and Telecommunications Research Institute (ETRI) and XM2VTS face database. The ETRI face database contains images of 55 different subjects with 20 images of each subject. We used 10 images per subject as training dataset and the rest of images as test dataset. The XM2VTS database is one of standard bench mark data set which consists of 295 subjects. The database contains eight images for each subject. We used four images per subject as training dataset and the rest of images as test dataset. The proposed system has been realized by using Matlab, and SparseLab [12] is used as a sparse representation solver. To show the efficiency of proposed method, we compared our method with typical subspace analysis based method such as PCA and NMF. For this experiment, we use the k neighborhood classifier for face image retrieval.

The experimental results for ETRI face database are shown in Fig. 2. It shows that the proposed method has the best retrieval accuracy rate of 98.9% at rank 1 on ETRI face set. The proposed method and NMF find exact person before rank 10.

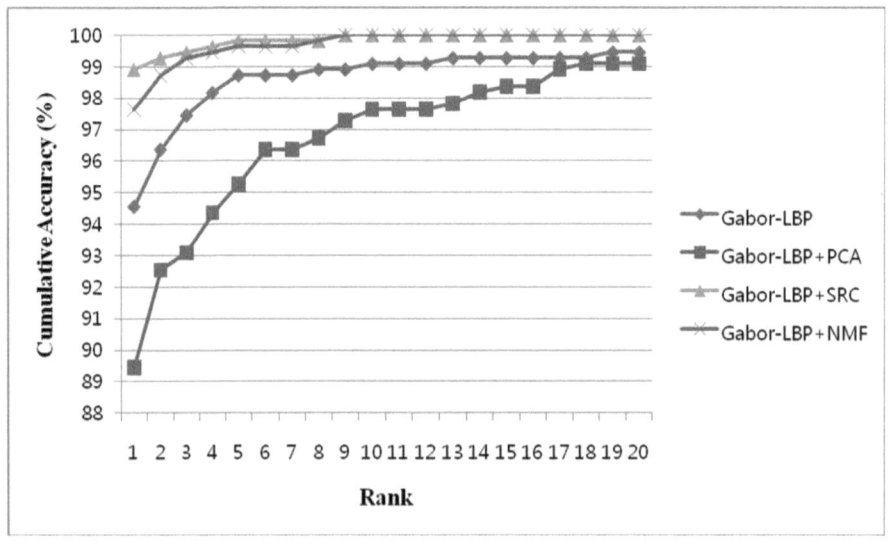

Fig. 2. Cumulative accuracy of retrieval on ETRI faceset

Figure 3 shows the experimental results for XM2VTS face database. It achieves rank 1 retrieval accuracy rate of 99.3% on XM2VTS face set. For XM2VTS face set, the proposed method and NMF show similar performance.

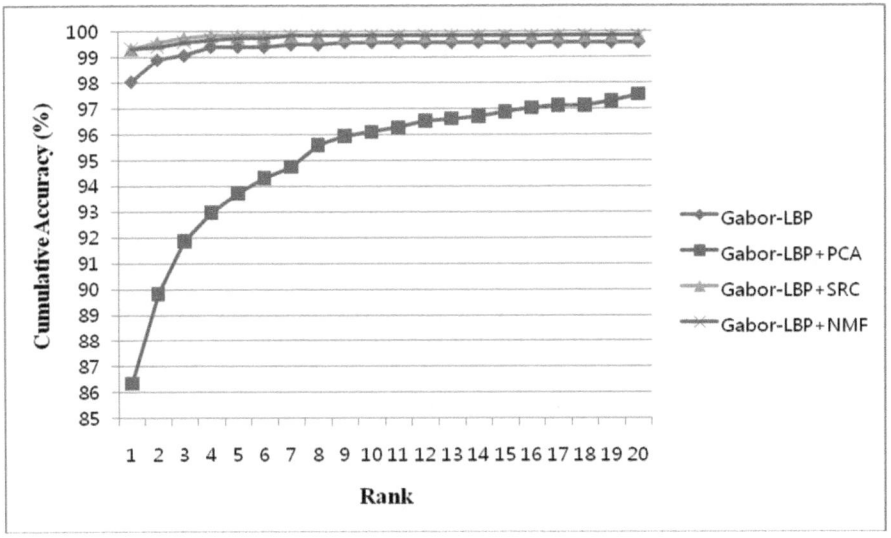

Fig. 3. Cumlative accuracy of retrieval on XM2VTS faceset

5 Conclusions

In this paper, we introduced a face image retrieval method which is not only robust to the variations of face image condition but also with high accuracy. Firstly, we used the Gabor-LBP histogram for face image representation. Secondly, we adopted the sparse representation classification for the face image retrieval. Using the Gabor-LBP histogram and sparse representation classifier, we achieved effective and robust retrieval results with high accuracy. To evaluate the performance of our proposed method, we conducted experiments on ETRI and XM2VTS face database. Our experiments showed that the retrieval accuracy at rank 1 approaches 98.9% on ETRI face set and 99.3% on XM2VTS face set, respectively.

For the future work, we are planning to develop a prototype system based on the proposed mechanism for face image recognition and retrieval from large face image database.

References

1. Megherbi, D.B., Miao, Y.: A Distributed Technique for Recognition and Retrieval of Faces with Time-Varying Expressions. In: IEEE International Conference on Computational Intelligence for Measurement Systems and Applications, pp. 8–13. IEEE Press, Hong Kong (2009)
2. Tolba, A.S., El-Baz, A.H., El-Harby, A.A.: Face Recognition: A Literature Review. International Journal of Signal Processing 2(2), 88–103 (2006)
3. Zhao, W.: Face Recognition: A Literature Survey. ACM Computing Surveys 35(4), 339–458 (2003)

4. Vikram, T.N., Chidananda, G.K., Guru, D.S., Shalini, R.U.: Face Indexing and Retrieval by Spatial Similarity. In: International Congress on Image and Signal Processing, pp. 543–547. IEEE Press, Hainan (2008)
5. Shen, L., Bai, L.: A Review on Gabor Wavelets for Face Recognition. Pattern Anal. Applic. 9, 273–292 (2006)
6. Xie, S., Shan, S., Chen, X., Chen, J.: Fusing Local Patterns of Gabor Magnitude and Phase for Face Recognition. IEEE Trans. on Image Processing 19(5), 1349–1361 (2010)
7. Gao, T., He, M.: A Novel Face Description by Local Multi-Channel Gabor Histogram Sequence Binary Pattern. In: International Conference on Audio, Language and Image Processing, Shanghai, China, pp. 1240–1244 (2008)
8. Zhang, W., Shan, S., Gao, W., Chen, X., Zhang, H.: Local Gabor Binary Pattern Histogram Sequence (LGBPHS): A Novel Non-Statistical Model for Face Representation and Recognition. In: International Conference on Computer Vision, Beijing, China, vol. 1, pp. 786–791 (2005)
9. Yang, A.Y., Wright, J., Ma, Y., Sastry, S.S.: Feature Selection in Face Recognition: a Sparse Representation Perspective. UC Berkeley Technical Report UCB/EECS-2007-99 (2007)
10. Wright, J., Yang, A.Y., Ganesh, A., Sastry, S.S., Ma, Y.: Robust Face Recognition via Sparse Representation. IEEE Trans. on Pattern Analysis and Machine Intelligence 31(2), 210–227 (2009)
11. Qiao, L., Chen, S., Tan, X.: Sparsity Preserving Projections with Applications to Face Recognition. Pattern Recognition 43, 331–341 (2010)
12. Stanford SparseLab, http://sparselab.stanford.edu/

Fingerprint Liveness Detection Based on Multiple Image Quality Features

Changlong Jin, Shengzhe Li, Hakil Kim, and Ensoo Park

School of Information and Communication Engineering, INHA University,
253, Yonghyun-dong, Nam-gu, 402-751, Incheon, Korea
{cljin,szli}@vision.inha.ac.kr,
hikim@inha.ac.kr, espark@vision.inha.ac.kr

Abstract. Recent studies have shown that the conventional fingerprint recognition systems are vulnerable to fake attacks, and there are many existing systems that need to update their anti-spoofing capability inexpensively. This paper proposes an image quality-based fake detection method to address this problem. Three effective fake/live quality measures, spectral band energy, middle ridge line and middle valley line, are extracted firstly, and then, these features are fused and tested on a fake/live dataset using SVM and QDA classifiers. Experimental results demonstrate that the proposed method is promising in increasing the security of the existing fingerprint authentication system by only updating the software.

Keywords: Liveness detection, spectral band energy, middle ridge line, middle valley line.

1 Introduction

In spite of their advantages, fingerprint systems are vulnerable to attacks. Studies [1, 2] have shown that artificial fingers made by silicone, gelatin or other materials can spoof most of the existing fingerprint sensors including optical sensor, capacitive sensor, etc. Liveness detection can be performed in a biometric device either at the acquisition stage or at the processing stage. Therefore, it is generally implemented into a system in one of two ways: add an auxiliary sensor to detect vitality either at the acquisition stage or extract features of fake/live fingerprints at the image processing stage. That is, the countermeasures to fake fingerprint attacks can be categorized into hardware-based approaches and software-based approaches.

The hardware-based approaches add extra hardware to obtain the live signals by detecting the intrinsic properties and/or involuntary signals of a living body. The hardware-based approaches take advantage of these explicit physiological features, but are expensive, bulky and not always as effective as people would expect. Furthermore, it is not suitable in the existing fingerprint authentication system.

The software-based approaches detect the live signals by using the information already captured by the sensor. The existing approaches can be broadly categorized into

Y. Chung and M. Yung (Eds.): WISA 2010, LNCS 6513, pp. 281–291, 2011.

three classes: 1) perspiration-based method, 2) skin deformation-based method, and 3) image quality-based method.

The main idea of the Perspiration-based approaches [2] is to recognize the fake fingerprint images by measuring the perspiration signals along the middle ridge line. However, two important issues limit this theory to the commercial application: one is perspiration period and the other one is pressure when the test fingers including both live and fake are presented on the scanners. Ohhashi et al. [3] have reported that the average sweat secreting time is about 3sec to 4ecs under a strong stimulation of a loud noise, namely, the perspiration phenomenon is hard to obtain in a short time under normal conditions. Fig. 1 illustrates the qualitative observations of the pressure's affects. This figure shows that the fake fingerprint with constant pressure produces lower middle ridge line signals than that of the live fingerprint as the perspiration-based approaches proposed. However, the middle ridge line signals of the fake fingers with increasing pressure are largely higher than that of live fingers with constant pressure.

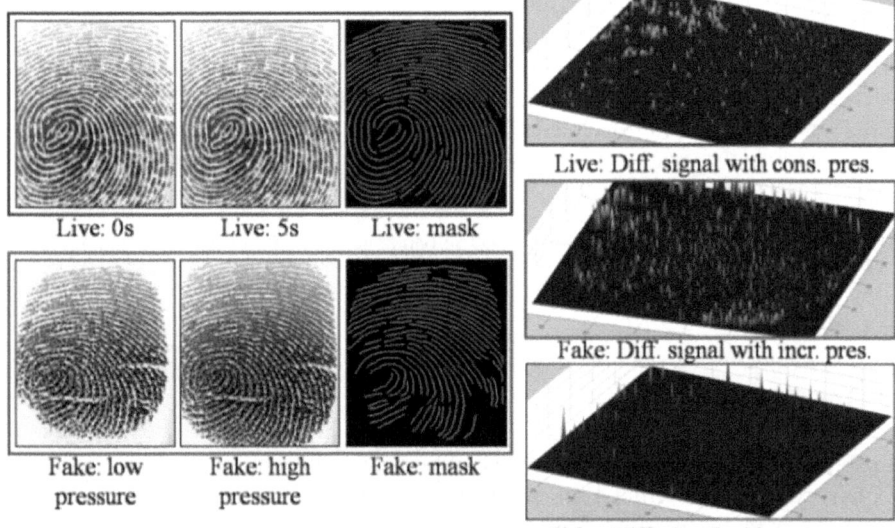

Live: 0s   Live: 5s   Live: mask

Fake: low pressure   Fake: high pressure   Fake: mask

Live: Diff. signal with cons. pres.

Fake: Diff. signal with incr. pres.

Fake: Diff. signal with cons. pres.

Fig. 1. Differential middle ridge line signal under different pressures

The rationale behind Skin distortion-based approaches [4-6] is to measure the elasticity difference between the live finger and the fake finger by performing additional actions so as to produce different live signals and it is utilized to detect the fake fingerprint from the real ones. The key point of these methods is the difference of the material elasticity. Thus, these methods may perform poorly when the hardness of fake material is similar to live skin, such as soft silicone or silicone film.

The quality-based approaches mainly utilize the fingerprint image quality difference between fake and live. These approaches includes Power spectrum energy [7], ridgelet transform-based [8], statistical features of fingerprint texture [9, 10], middle valley signal analysis [11, 12] and gray-intensity analysis [13]. The drawback of the quality-based approaches is that it is difficult to extract robust measures for each single feature. Therefore, feature fusion can increase the detection performance. Furthermore, the existing quality-based methods only detect the fake fingerprint in the identification mode instead of considering an individual character as in the verification mode.

Intended to increase the security of the existing fingerprint system in anti-spoofing, this paper proposes a software-based method which utilizes multiple image quality features in the verification mode, not in the identification mode. Firstly, global fingerprint texture is analyzed and three effective fake/live quality measures are extracted and fused to detect fake from live fingerprints. The advantages of the proposed method are: a) it needs only one fingerprint to detect liveness, b) error rate can be decreased by updating the template database continuously, c) benefit in the designing of simple classifier, d) Existing fingerprint sensors can easily use this software-based approach by just updating the software.

2 Proposed Method

The term, fingerprint quality, refers to the differences of ridge/valley texture between live and fake fingerprints, such as, clarity of ridge/valley structure, smoothness of foreground contour, pore spot, image intensity, the differences of middle ridge line signal, etc., whereas it is used to measure the minutia extractability in fingerprint recognition. The fake fingerprints show a lot of differences to the live fingerprints.

2.1 Fingerprint Texture Analysis and Quality Hypothesis

Generally, it is difficult to make fake a fingerprint image comparable or a better image quality than the corresponding live fingerprint for the same period. There are many quality related differential features between live and fake fingerprints, such as image intensity, foreground contour, ridge/valley clarity, pore spot (generally appeared in light area of live fingerprint as a black dot), foreground area size, ridge/valley texture, etc. Therefore, the fake fingerprints can be identified based on these features. These differences are summarized in table 1.

Some features, such as foreground contour, pore spot, foreground area size, and fingerprint image intensity, are not stable, they take place occasionally. Therefore, these features are not included in this study. The clarities of ridge/valley structures are different for the fake and live fingerprints. The differences can be measured by the energy concentration of the annulus pattern in spectral domain. This is the first measure used in this study.

Because the fake fingerprints are hard to copy the pores along the ridges, the middle ridge line signals of fake fingerprints have fewer periodic peaks than that of live fingerprints. Moreover, because the elasticity, valley depths, and shapes of fake fingertips, the gray-scale values of the middle valley signals of fake fingerprints are lower than that of live fingerprints. Thus, these two features are employed as the second and the third measure in this paper.

Table 1. Global texture characteristics of live and fake fingerprint images

Text characteristics	Live	Fake	Comment
Clarity of ridge/ valley structure	Generally clearer than the fake fingerprint	More blurred than the live fingerprint	This feature can be quantified by a spectral band of energy measure
Foreground contour	Has a smooth and convex foreground	Has many concave boundaries	This feature takes place occasionally, so it is not included in this study
Pore spot	Dark spots in the light area which is caused by the perspiration phenomenon	Usually does not have this feature	Especially for a live dry fingerprint
Middle ridge line signal	Since the live fingerprints have pores along the middle ridge, this feature has more periodic peaks than the fake one	Since it is difficult to copy pores, especially for gelatin, this feature has fewer periodic peaks than the live one	Depending on fingertip and fake material
Middle valley line signal	Has clear valleys, therefore less noise in this feature	Usually has noisy valley	Depending on fingertip and fake material
Foreground area size	Has relatively a larger size than the fake	Has relatively a smaller size than the live	Occasionally applicable
Fingerprint image intensity	Generally drier than the fake one	Generally darker than the live one	Depending on environment and fingertip skin type

2.2 Live Sample-Based Calibration

In general, live fingerprints have better quality than fake fingerprints. This assertion can be proved by all the samples posted in the liveness detection related papers.

Furthermore, live fingertips can easily produce the fingerprints with similar quality, but it is not true for fake fingertips, because the quality of fake fingerprint heavily depends on many factors such as the maker's skill, the materials etc. Therefore, a hypothesis is adopted: the quality of a fake is comparable or less than that of a live. Assume that the qualities have a normal distribution, then the hypothesis can also expressed by Eq. 1.

$$\sigma_{fake} > \sigma_{live}; \quad \mu_{fake} < \mu_{live} \tag{1}$$

There are existing quality differences between live and fake fingerprints. However, the qualities of fake fingerprints depend on the creative skill and the skin quality of the fingertip, namely, the fake fingerprint qualities of good fingertip skin may be better than that of poor fingertip skin. That is, the live/fake related quality is a relative term. Therefore, the calibration procedure is necessary in the fingerprint image quality-based method. Fig. 2 demonstrates the live sample-based quality calibration.

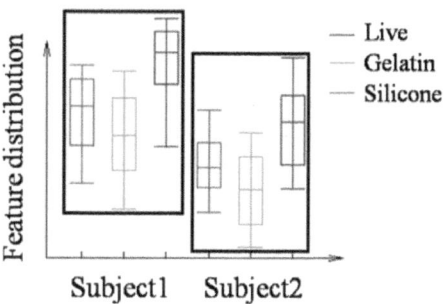

Fig. 2. Sketch map of live sample-based calibration

2.3 Feature Extraction

Due to the characteristics of the fake material and the duplication skill, the live fingertip cannot be copied exactly. Thus, there are differences in the captured fingerprint images. Intuitively, the fake fingerprints look a little blurred compared to the corresponding live fingerprints, and there are more incipient ridges in the valleys. Furthermore, many pores fade away when compared to the corresponding live fingerprints. These features can be quantitatively measured by spectral band energy, middle ridge line signal and middle valley signal.

The algorithm flowchart of spectral band energy is shown in Fig. 3. In this study, the spectral energy is divided into fifteen bands excluding the DC component. The energies from the 1st band to the 4th band represent the low frequency energy. Since the fake fingerprint has much more noise and the ridge/valley textures blurred than the corresponding live fingerprint, the low frequency energies of the fake tend to have a higher value than that of the live. The bands position of ridge energy depends on the characteristics of ridge width. And since the ridge width of the fake fingerprint is

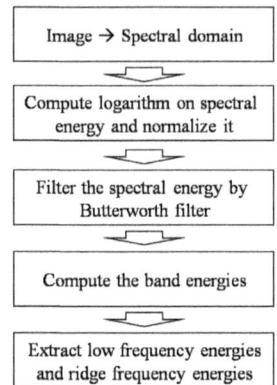

Fig. 3. Algorithm flowchart of spectral energy measure

different from that of the live, the peak of ridge energy of the fake will differ from that of live.

Fig. 4 shows the distributions of DC-removed fifteen-band energies. The middle-band energies from the 7th band to the 11th band represent the ridge energy. The highest band energy of gelatin and silicone are occur between the 8th band and the 12th band, respectively. It is evident that the highest live band energy-based calibration can enhance the discriminating ability of power spectral energy. The 2-D spectral band energy vector is computed by Eq. 2.

$$SE = \begin{bmatrix} \sum_{i=1}^{4} e_i \\ \sum_{i=I_{live}-2}^{I_{live}-2} e_i \end{bmatrix} \tag{2}$$

where $I_{live} = \arg\max_{k}(e_k), \quad 5 < k \leq 15$.

The middle ridge line signal (*MRL*) and the middle valley line signal (*MVL*) are mutual signals. These features reflect the texture difference along the ridges and valleys. Because of the existence of pores in the ridge and incipient ridges in the valley, the *MRL* of a live fingerprint generally has more period peaks than that of a fake fingerprint, and the *MVL* of a live fingerprint has a higher gray-level value than that of a fake fingerprint. These features are effective in distinguishing the live fingerprints from the fake fingerprints.

To extract the *MRL* and *MVL* correctly, the line mask of *MRL* and *MVL* are extracted firstly through the flowchart shown in Fig. 5, and then a 2-D vector comprised of the mean and standard deviation of the 1-D gray-scale signals in the position of the line mask are computed for *MRL* and *MVL*, respectively.

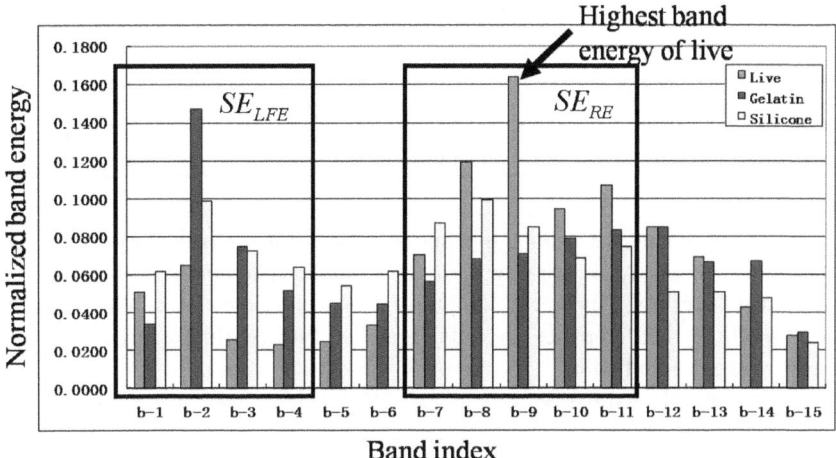

Fig. 4. Spectral band energy and live sample-based calibration

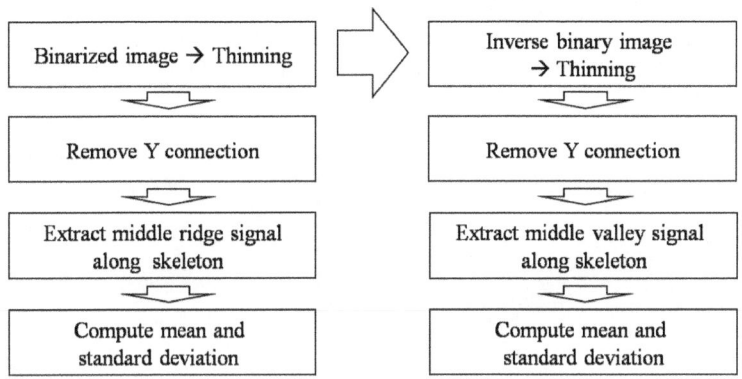

Fig. 5. Algorithm flowchart of *MRL* (left) and *MVL* (right)

3 Experiments and Discussions

The extracted features are tested over a dataset collected by the Biometrics Engineering Research Center (BERC) [10]. Table 1 shows the characteristics of this dataset and this data collection protocol. By considering the effect of fingertip pressure, the datasets are collected in three different pressure levels and three optical sensors (A, B, C) with 500 DPI resolution are adopted in this dataset collection. For the purpose of real simulation, instead of a ten-fold cross verification method, one of third random samples of both the live and the fake are selected in a training procedure, and the rest of the datasets are used to perform a test. This random process is made 10 times and the error rate and standard deviation are recorded.

Table 2. Dataset description

Dataset	Subject	Impression	Total	Samples for each pressure level
Live	46	15	690	Low: 5; middle: 5; high: 5
Gelatin	46	15	690	Low: 5; middle: 5; high: 5
Silicone	46	15	690	Low: 5; middle: 5; high: 5

In this experiment, we assume that spoof detection is not necessary for the imposter matching, that is, if the test fingerprint is accepted as an imposter, then the liveness
detection will follow. Another assumption is that enrollment is conducted in an at-
tended mode so that templates are only from live fingers while queries can be made
by either fake or live fingers.

Five random selected live samples are enrolled as live templates, and three 2-D features: SE, MRL, MVL are extracted from each sample. The average features: $\overline{SE}$,
$\overline{MRL}$, $\overline{MVL}$ are taken as live templates. All of the queries which will be calibrated
by these features, namely, the features, SE_q, MRL_q, MVL_q of query are subtracted
by the live template: $\overline{SE}$, $\overline{MRL}$, $\overline{MVL}$. Fig. 6, 7, and 8 show the sample distributions of spectral energy, middle ridge line signal, and middle valley line signal of the
raw data and the calibrated data. As shown, the calibrated data has higher concentration characteristics.

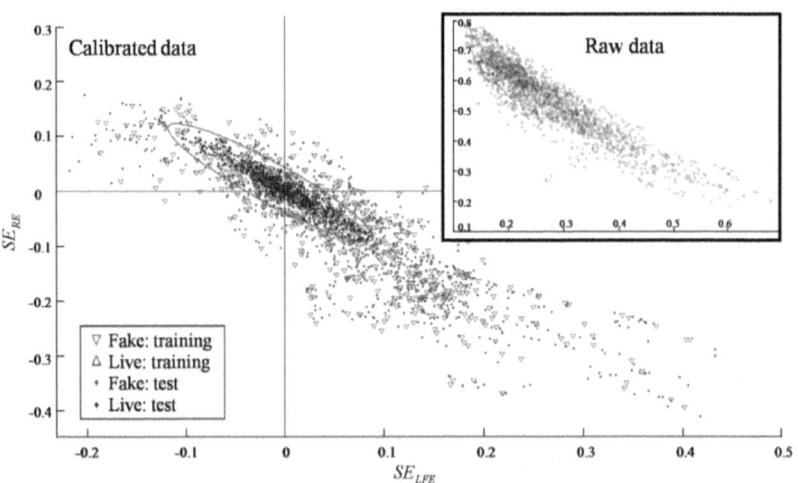

Fig. 6. Sample distribution of spectral energy and the classification result of quadratic discriminant analysis

Two classical classifiers: support vector machine (SVM) and quadratic discriminant analysis (QDA) are used to classify the fake from the live fingerprint according

to the three features. Fig. 9 shows the classification results and an average error rate of 6.5% is obtained. This experiment shows promising results in using multiple quality feature fusion-based spoof detection.

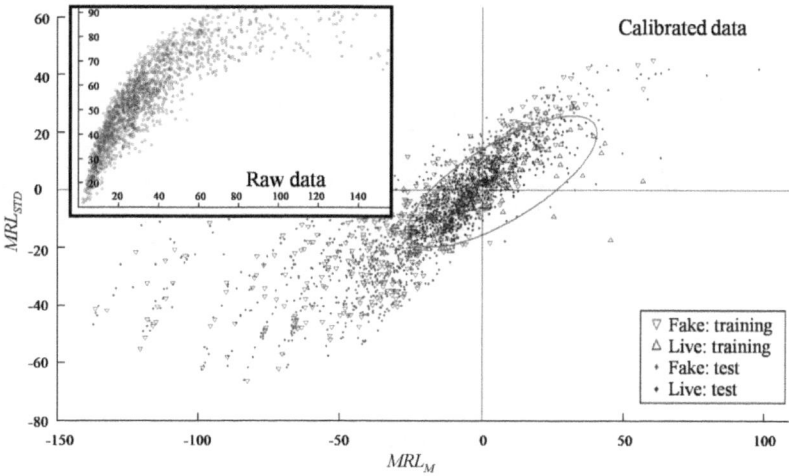

Fig. 7. Sample distribution of middle ridge line signal and the classification result of quadratic discriminant analysis

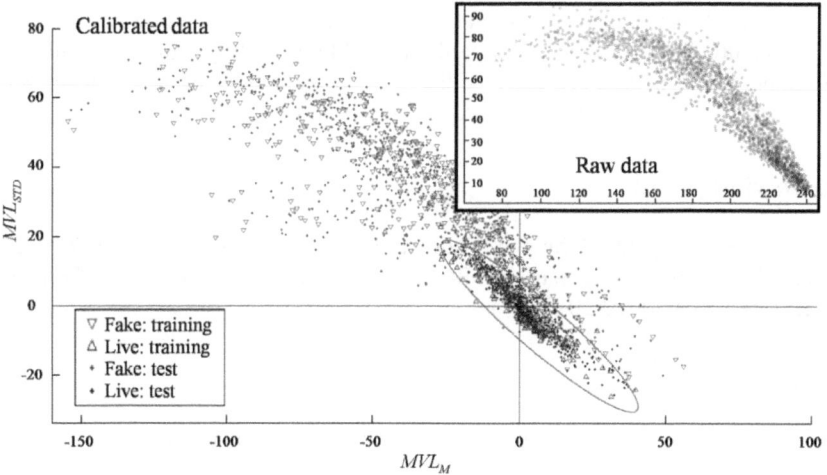

Fig. 8. Sample distribution of middle valley line signal and the classification result of quadratic discriminant analysis

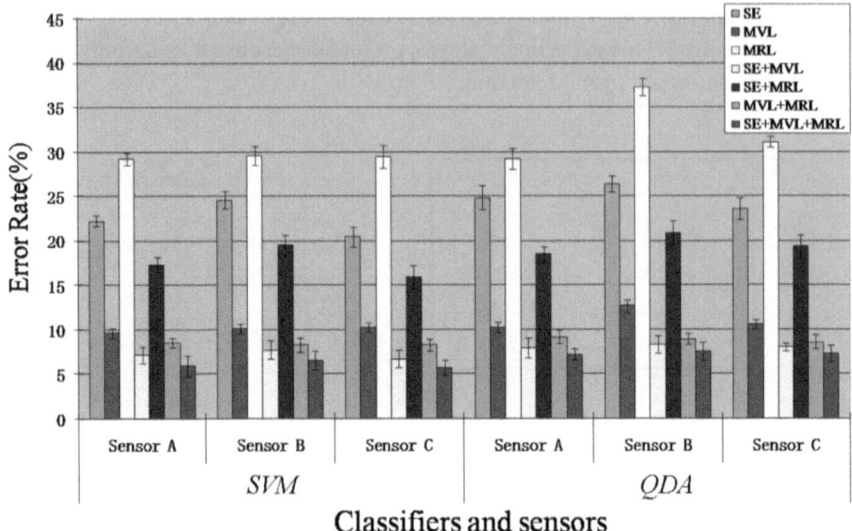

Fig. 9. Classification results

4   Conclusions

Since it is difficult to duplicate a live fingerprint exactly, there are quality differences, hence the qualities of a fake fingerprint are generally lower than that of a live finger-print. The main differences are the ridge clarity, middle ridge line signal and middle valley signal. This paper proposes a fake fingerprint detection method based on image quality feature fusion and live sample-based calibration. Experimental results show that the proposed method can increase the security and can be used in real fingerprint authentication systems since only a single fingerprint is needed.

Acknowledgment

This work was supported by the National Research Foundation of Korea (NRF) through the Biometrics Engineering Research Center (BERC) at Yonsei University. (No.R112002105080010(2010)).

References

[1] Matsumoto, T., Matsumoto, H., Yamada, K., Hoshino, S.: Impact of Artificial. Gummy, Fingers on Fingerprint Systems, presented at Optical Security and Counterfeit Deterrence Techniques IV (2002)
[2] Derakhshani, R., Schuckers, S.A.C., Hornak, L.A., O'Gorman, L.: Determination of vitality from a non-invasive biomedical measurement for use in fingerprint scanners. Pattern Recognition 36, 383–396 (2003)

[3] Ohhashi, T., Sakaguchi, M., Tsuda, T.: Human perspiration measurement. Physiological Measurement 19, 449–461 (1998)

[4] Antonelli, A., Cappelli, R., Maio, D., Maltoni, D.: Fake finger detection by skin distortion analysis. IEEE Transactions on Information Forensics and Security 1, 360–373 (2006)

[5] Chen, Y., Jain, A., Dass, S.: Fingerprint Deformation for Spoof Detection. Presented at Biometrics symposium, Arlington, VA (2005)

[6] Zhang, Y., Tian, J., Chen, X., Yang, X., Shi, P.: Fake Finger Detection Based on Thin-Plate Spline Distortion Model. In: Lee, S.-W., Li, S.Z. (eds.) ICB 2007. LNCS, vol. 4642, pp. 742–749. Springer, Heidelberg (2007)

[7] Coli, P., Marcialis, G., Roli, F.: Power spectrum-based fingerprint vitality detection. Presented at IEEE Workshop on Automatic Identification Advanced Technologies (2007)

[8] Bhausaheb Nikam, S., Agarwal, S.: Ridgelet-based fake fingerprint detection. Neurocomputing 72, 2491–2506 (2008)

[9] Abhyankar, A., Schuckers, S.: Fingerprint Liveness Detection Using Local Ridge Frequencies And Multiresolution Texture Analysis Techniques. Presented at IEEE International Conference on Image Processing (2006)

[10] Choi, H., Kang, R., Choi, K., Jin, A.T.B., Kim, J.: Fake-fingerprint detection using multiple static features. Optical Engineering 48, 1-1-14 (2009)

[11] Tan, B., Schuckers, S.: New approach for liveness detection in fingerprint scanners based on valley noise analysis. Journal of Electronic Imaging 17, 011009-1-011009-9 (2008)

[12] Jia, J., Cai, L.: Fake Finger Detection Based on Time-Series Fingerprint Image Analysis. In: Huang, D.-S., Heutte, L., Loog, M. (eds.) ICIC 2007. LNCS, vol. 4681, pp. 1140–1150. Springer, Heidelberg (2007)

[13] Tan, B., Schuckers, S.A.C.: Liveness Detection using an Intensity Based Approach in Fingerprint Scanners. Presented at Biometrics Symposium, Arlington, VA (2005)

Robust Feature Extraction for Facial Image Quality Assessment

Thi Hai Binh Nguyen, Van Huan Nguyen, and Hakil Kim

Biometrics Engineering Research Center,
Dept. of Information & Communication Engineering, INHA University,
Incheon, Korea
{binh,conghuan}@vision.inha.ac.kr,
hikim@inha.ac.kr

Abstract. With the aim of developing an automatic system to verify if facial images meet ISO/IEC 19794-5 standards and ICAO requirements, this paper proposes a robust method to detect facial features including two eye centers and four lip features. The proposed method restricts the areas where facial features are observed by using the skin color and shape characteristic of faces. Two eye centers are detected independently in the restricted area by means of the circular filters. The use of circular filters makes the algorithm robust to head poses and occlusions, which are the main factors of unsuccessful eye detections. To accurately detect lip features regardless facial expressions and the presence of beard or mustache, the proposed method fuses edge and color information together. An experiment was performed on a subset of the FERET database, and the experimental results demonstrated the accuracy and robustness of the proposed method.

Keywords: Skin modeling, face detection, facial feature detection, facial image quality.

1 Introduction

Biometrics, which refers to a range of technologies that uses unique identifiable attributes of people, such as fingerprint, hand, iris, face, voice, gait, or signature, to identify or authenticate individuals, is a key fundamental security mechanism. Among these identifiable attributes, face images are easy and cheap to obtain, in a non-intrusive manner. Therefore, although reliable face recognition is still a challenge to computer vision and pattern recognition researchers, it is one of the most suitable biometric systems for wide range surveillance and security applications. The wide use of face recognition makes facial image quality assessment be a research topic worthy of studying.

Recently, ePassports, which use face as the primary biometric identifier, has successfully developed and introduced by the International Civil Aviation Organization (ICAO). In order to ensure that facial images, which are stored in

Y. Chung and M. Yung (Eds.): WISA 2010, LNCS 6513, pp. 292–306, 2011.

ePassports, will be useful for both visual and electronic matching, ICAO defines minimal quality requirements for facial images [1,2]. These requirements comply with ISO/IEC19795-5 standards [3]. All requirements defined in ISO/IEC 19794-5 and ICAO are organized into 4 categories [3], namely scene requirements, photographic requirements, digital requirements and format requirements. Each requirement is related to one or several parts of the image. Based on this relationship, all mentioned requirements can be classified into 7 groups. Table 1 summarizes the ISO/IEC requirements and their related checking areas in facial images.

Table 1. ISO/IEC requirements and their related checking areas in facial images

Requirement	ISO/IEC Requirements	Related Areas
Environment	Focus area	Entire face
	Grayscale density	
	Contrast and saturation	
Background	Shadows on BG	Background
	Gradation on BG	
	Lightness of BG	
Eye	Resolution (eye-to-eye distance)	Eye areas
	Eye closed/opened	
	Eye direction	
	Shadows in eye sockets	
Eyeglasses	Sunglasses	
	Transparent lens	
	Flash reflection on lens	
	Glasses frame	
Mouth	Mouth opened/closed	Mouth areas
Head and face	Head pose	Eye, mouth and entire face
	Size and position	Entire face
	Shadows on face	
	Hot spots	
	Unnatural skin color	
Shoulder	Shoulder tilted/portrait style	Shoulder areas

Motivated by developing an automatic system to verify if facial images are in compliance with the ICAO specifications as well as ISO/IEC 19794-5 standards, this paper proposes a robust method to detect necessary features for facial image quality assessment. Specifically, algorithms of detecting faces, eye centers, mouth corners and upper/lower lips are proposed. Those facial features are then used as the inputs for checking the standards about eye, mouth, face (Table 1).

Detecting facial features has been investigated using a variety of different approaches. However, most dominant approaches used facial regions as the prior knowledge. In these approaches, skin areas were first detected by color cues, and then facial features were extracted by evaluating topographic gray-level reliefs [4,5] or analyzing color properties [6,7]. Although this approach is sensitive to head poses and illumination changes, it still gains attention in literature, since it can achieve a low run time that is of key importance in real-time applications. Recently, model-based algorithms have received attention in literature on automatic facial feature extraction [8,9,10]. Mahoor et al. proposed an algorithm that utilized color information to improve the ASM approach for facial feature extraction [9]. Color information was used not only to initialize the ASM, but also to model the local structure of the feature points. In [10], a cascade of model-based facial feature detection was proposed to obtain an optimal performance in both robustness and accuracy. The advantage of these methods is that the important features are represented in a low-dimensional space. Also they are normally invariant to rotation, scaling and illumination. However, there are some difficulties that come from how to build a model that can describe the faces efficiently, how to fit the model to accurately and robustly extract facial features and how to reduce the processing time.

In order to overcome these above drawbacks of the existing algorithms, this paper proposes a robust method to detect facial features including two eye centers, four lip features (mouth corners and upper/lower lips) which are then utilized for assessing the quality of facial images according to the ISO/IEC 19794-5 standard and ICAO specifications. Fig. 1 shows the overall flowchart of the proposed algorithms. The following algorithms are proposed in this paper:

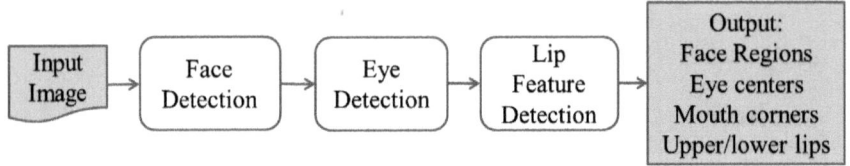

Fig. 1. Overall flowchart of the proposed algorithms

- Face detection: The skin model is estimated by observing the distribution of skin color in the C_bC_r space, which is extracted from the YC_bC_r color model. In addition, a process of shape evaluation is carried out in the result of skin detection using the well-known mean-shift clustering and elliptic fitting to remove fail detections. The C_bC_r space was proved to be effective for modeling skin colors of different ethnic groups. It is also robust to illuminations. The skin-based face detection is independent to rotations, scaling, partial occlusions and resolution changes. The weakness of this method is its results may contain false positives (i.e. non-facial objects are detected as faces). The shape evaluation, that is based on the fact that human faces are like ellipses, is carried out to deal with this weakness. Two eyes are then detected in the face areas so that the false eye detection rate can be reduced, also the running time is lessened.
- Eye detection: The result of the face detection forms a face mask. From the face mask, the grayscale face image is extracted and adaptively thresholded by considering the distribution of the skin tone. Then, a set of circular filters,

which is designed to detect circular shapes in images, is applied to this binary image. An eye-weight mask, generated from the binary face image, is weighted to the filtered image to produce an eye-peaked image. Finally, the eyes are located by searching the peaks in the eye-peaked image. Since the threshold to binarize the face image is determined adaptively, the proposed method shows its robustness to illumination. Using the circular filters to find two eyes independently increases the capability of the proposed method to detect accurately eye centers regardless of head poses.
- Lip feature detection: A small area, restricted by two eye positions, is used for observing lip features. The lip map, that is a combination of edge and color information of the mouth area, is computed for this area. All lip features, including two mouth corners, the centers of the upper and lower lips, are then located by analyzing the lip map. The combination of edge and color information makes the lip feature detection algorithm robust to facial expressions and the existence of beard/mustache as well.

The remaining of this paper is organized as follows: Section 2, 3, 4 describes in detail the algorithms of face, eye and lip feature detection. Section 5 presents experimental results and conclusions are stated in Section 6.

2   Face Detection

In the field of face and facial feature detection, finding all regions that have a high potential of being human faces using skin color as a detection cue has gained in popularity. Skin color has been utilized as an effective cue because it is independent to rotations, scaling and partial occlusions as well as resolution changes. However, using skin color as a cue may result in many false detections (i.e. hair or clothes or background objects are detected as face areas). In order to discard these false detections, a process of shape evaluation is performed. Fig. 2 depicts the overall process of detecting faces.

One of the most important issues in skin color-based face detection is choosing a color space that is suitable for modeling the skin color. The color space has to be able to reduce the overlapping area between the skin and non-skin color distribution. Among the existing color spaces, the C_bC_r subspace is proved to be suitable for detecting skin. The observation shows that the skin color clusters in a condensed region in the C_bC_r subspace whatever the race of skin is. Fig. 3 shows the cluster of skin color in the C_bC_r subspace of different skin races in different taking conditions. The skin samples used to draw the scatters were randomly collected from FERET databases [12] and the Internet. The skin detection rule (1) is determined based on observing the distribution of the skin color in the C_bC_r space.

$$95 \leq C_b \leq 130$$
$$125 \leq C_r \leq 160 \tag{1}$$

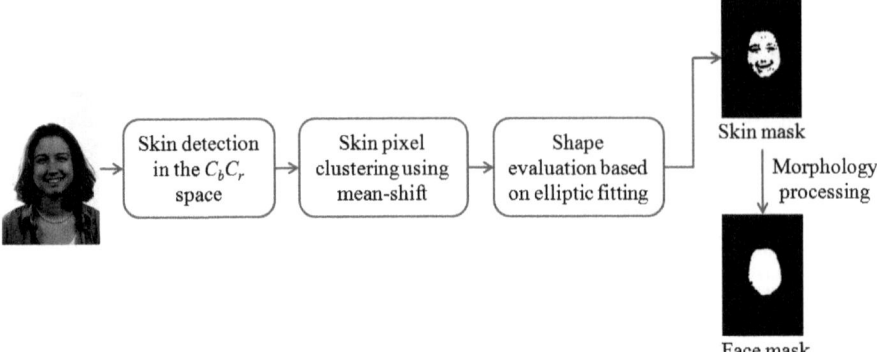

Fig. 2. Overall process of face detection

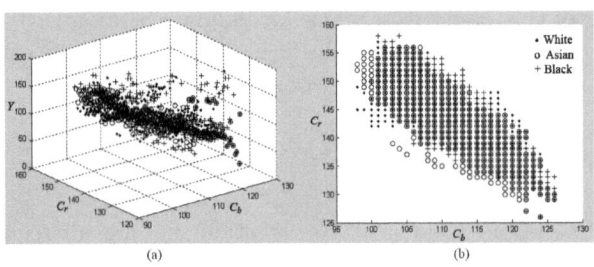

Fig. 3. The cluster of skin tones: (a) in YC_bC_r color model, (b) in C_bC_r subspace

After detecting all skin areas, a process of shape evaluation is carried out so that false detections are removed. The shape evaluation is done by means of the mean-shift clustering and elliptic fitting. Mean shift was first proposed by K. Funkunaga and L.D. Hosteler and applied in pattern recognition problem as a gradient clustering algorithm [14]. It is known as a useful method for clustering, mode seeking and so on.

To cluster detected skin pixels, the values of skin pixels in the C_bC_r subspace are used as a 2-D feature vector. The choice of kernels may differ depending on the task or scene, which the mean shift clustering is applied to. A simple uniform kernel is much faster to calculate, while a non-uniform kernel, i.e. a Gaussian kernel, is less prone to outliers but slower than a uniform kernel [16]. In this paper, the multivariate kernel density estimate obtained with a uniform kernel and window radius $h = 3.25$ is used. The mean-shift algorithm assigns all detected skin pixels into clusters. Fig. 4c shows an example of mean-shift clustering results.

Let $R_1, \ldots, R_n$ be the clusters of skin pixels, n is the number of clusters. Assume that $R_1, \ldots, R_n$ are sorted in a order so that $d_i \leq d_{i+1}, (1 \leq i < n)$ where d_i is the distance from the centroid of the ith cluster to the center of the image. The algorithm of shape evaluation is described below.

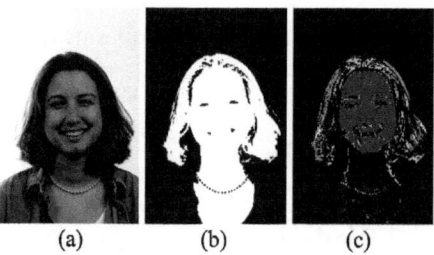

(a)   (b)   (c)

Fig. 4. (a) Input image, (b) Result of skin detection in C_bC_r space, (c) Result of the mean-shift clustering (9 clusters)

```
Input: R₁, ..., Rₙ
Output: S - a group of clusters that forms a "perfect" ellipse
procedure Shape evaluation
S = R₁                    \\ Initial S
Vₘᵢₙ = elliptic(S)
Q ← R                     \\ Q is a priority queue
while Q ≠ φ
    do T ← EXTRACT_ MIN(Q)
        Sₙₑw = S ∪ T
        Vₙₑw = elliptic(Sₙₑw)
        if Vₙₑw < Vₘᵢₙ
            then
                S = Sₙₑw
                Vₘᵢₙ = Vₙₑw
```

In the evaluation function, the *elliptic* function is called as a nested function to measure the similarity between an area and an ellipse. This function contains two steps. Firstly, the best fitting ellipse of the area A is estimated using the least-squares method [13]. The best fitting ellipse is defined by its center (x_0, y_0), the length a and b of its major and minor axes and its orientation θ. The detailed fitting algorithm was described in [13,17]. Secondly, a template is generated from the estimated ellipse. The value of each pixel (x, y) of the template $\mathcal{E}$ is defined as in (2).

$$\mathcal{E}(x,y) = \begin{cases} 1 & \text{if } \frac{(x-x_0)\cos\theta + (y-y_0)\sin\theta}{a^2} + \frac{-(x-x_0)\sin\theta + (y-y_0)\cos\theta}{b^2} \leq 1 \\ 0 & \text{otherwise} \end{cases} \quad (2)$$

A measure is performed to assess how well the area A is similar to its best fitting ellipse through (3).

$$V = 1 - \frac{\sum_{(x,y)\in\mathcal{E}} \mathcal{E}(x,y) \oplus \mathcal{B}}{m \times n} \quad (3)$$

where $\mathcal{B} = \begin{cases} 1 & \text{if } (x,y) \in A \\ 0 & \text{otherwise} \end{cases}$, $\oplus$ is the XOR operator, $m \times n$ is the size of the input image. The higher the value of V is, the more the area A becomes an ellipse.

The skin mask is defined as following:

$$M_S(i,j) = \begin{cases} 1 & \text{if } (i,j) \in S \\ 0 & \text{otherwise} \end{cases} \tag{4}$$

where (i,j) is the pixel position, S is the result of the shape evaluation. The skin mask is then processed by several mophological operations (close and region filling) to obtain the face mask.

3   Eye Detection

3.1   Circular Filter

Circular filters are designed to detect circular shapes in digital images in conjunction with a binarization method which uses of 1 and -1 instead of 0 and 1 as usual. The circular filter is defined in (5).

$$C(i,j) = \begin{cases} 1 & \text{if } (i,j) \text{ within the circle } ([\frac{s}{2}, \frac{s}{2}], r = \frac{s}{\sqrt{2\pi}}) \\ 0 & \text{otherwise} \end{cases} \tag{5}$$

where C is the matrix representing the filter of size $s \times s$, and r is the radius of the filter.

In applying the circular filters to finding different sizes of circular regions, the following measure is defined to select the most suitable filter in term of its size:

$$k = \frac{\text{Max}(I_f)}{S_C^2} \qquad (\in [-1,1]) \tag{6}$$

where $\text{Max}(I_f)$ is the maximum value in the filtered image and S_C is the size of the filter. The filter, whose size is corresponding to the largest k, is selected.

3.2   Eye Center Detection

The overall diagram of eye detection taking advantage of the face mask M_F and the skin mask M_S, which are computed in the face map construction step, is given in Fig. 5. Using the face mask, the face grayscale image is extracted, and simultaneously, the skin grayscale is extracted from the skin mask as follows:

$$\begin{aligned} I_F(i,j) &= I_{gr}(i,j) * M_F(i,j) \\ I_S(i,j) &= I_{gr}(i,j) * M_S(i,j) \end{aligned} \tag{7}$$

where I_{gr} is the grayscale image converted from the input image, and I_F, I_S are the grayscale face image and the grayscale skin image, respectively.

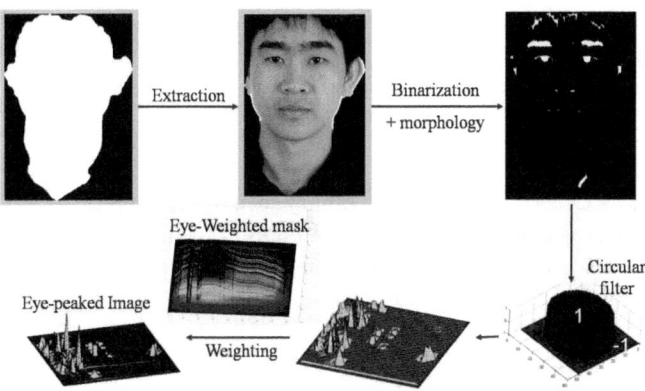

Fig. 5. Overall process of eye detection

Let μ_S, σ_S be the mean and the standard deviation of the distribution of the skin intensities in the grayscale skin image. The binary face image is then defined as follows:

$$F_b(i,j) = \begin{cases} 1 & \text{if } I_F(i,j) > \mu_S - 3\sigma_S \\ 0 \text{ OR } M_S(i,j) & \text{otherwise} \end{cases} \qquad (8)$$

Eq. 8 is expected to include all non-skin pixels that have low intensity values to the binary face image. In order to eliminate the reflection on eyes, some morphological operations (opening and closing) with small size structuring elements are utilized. The binary face image shown in Fig. 5 is an inversion of the original binary image for the purpose of a better visualization.

The binary face image is then convolved with circular filters. Different filters at different sizes (namely, $S_c = 7, 9, 11, 13$ in our experiments) are assessed. Using the measure (6), the best-fitting filter to the iris region is selected. Subsequently, the radius of the selected filter is considered as the radius of the iris region.

As a characteristic of the circular filter, the values of the on-and-near boundary in filtered images are pretty large. However, the eyes are not expected to appear near the face boundary except the case of profile faces. Furthermore, if dense eyebrows or heavy beards are present, the eyes may be located at these areas. In order to solve that problem, an eye-weighted mask is generated from the binary face image as follows:

$$\begin{aligned} v(j) &= \sum_{i=1}^{m} F_b(i,j), \ j=1,..,n \\ h(i) &= \sum_{j=1}^{n} F_b(i,j), \ i=1,..,m \\ M_{m\times n} &= h \times v' \end{aligned} \qquad (9)$$

where M is the eye-weight mask, F_b is the binary face image and $m \times n$ is the size of F_b. The eye-weighted mask puts less weight on the dense eyebrows, beards (if present) and the face boundary. Moreover, the valley of the eyebrows in the eye-weighted mask is deeper or shallower depending on the denseness of the eyebrows.

The eye-peaked image is then defined as:

$$I_E(i,j) = I_C(i,j) \times M(i,j) \tag{10}$$

where $I_C = F_b \times C$ is the result of the binary face image convolved with a circular filter. In the eye-peaked image, two local maximum distinctive peaks that have maximum k' ratios (defined for a position (i,j) as in (11) are considered as the centers of the left and right eyes if:

$$\begin{aligned} k'_j &= \frac{I_f(i,j)}{S_C^2} \ (j = 1, 2) \\ k'_1 &> t \\ k'_2 &> t \end{aligned} \tag{11}$$

The threshold t is to guarantee that the selected eyes have at least a $t \times 100\%$ overlap over the circular filter.

4   Lip Feature Detection

In this paper, four lip features, including two mouth corners, the inner upper and lower lips are defined. Fig. 6 shows two examples of lip features in the cases of mouth closed and opened.

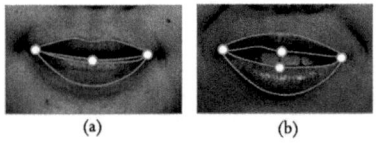

(a)   (b)

Fig. 6. The lip features in the case of: (a) mouth closed, (b) mouth opened

Before locating lip features, the face is rotated by its tilting angle around the center between two eyes. The tilting angle is estimated using two detected eyes. The mouth area where four lip features are observed is defined in (12). The edge lip map, color lip map and lip map are computed for the extracted area. The lip map will be used to locate mouth corners and upper/lower lips. Fig. 7 describes the overall flowchart of detecting lip features.

$$W = \left\{ (x,y) \ \middle| \ \begin{array}{l} x_E + 0.6 \times D \le x \le x_E + 1.6 \times D \\ y_E - 0.6 \times D \le y \le y_E + 0.6 \times D \end{array} \right\} \tag{12}$$

where (x_E, y_E) is the midpoint of the line segment joining two eyes, D is the distance between two eyes.

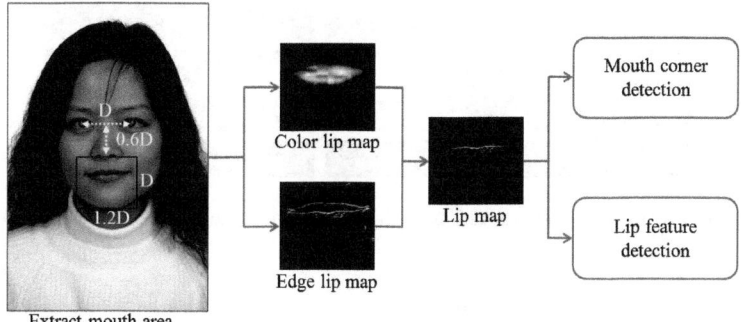

Fig. 7. Overall process of detecting lip features

4.1 Lip Map Construction

The proposed method uses a lip map computed by combining edge and color information of the mouth image to locate all lip features (i.e. mouth corners, upper and lower lips).Since the lip feature points normally lay on the horizontal line between the upper and lower lips, the horizontal edge information can be used to locate these features. In this paper, the horizontal Sobel filter is applied to extract edge information. The image obtained by convolving the grayscale mouth image with the horizontal Sobel filter is called *edge lip map*.

However, edge lip maps usually contain noise caused by the presence of a beard or mustache. The color information of the mouth area is taken into account to eliminate these noise. The color information of a mouth area is reflected in the *color lip map* that is adopted from Hsu's work [7].

$$I_{color\_lip\_map}(i, j) = C_r^2 (C_r^2 - \eta C_r / C_b)^2 \tag{13}$$

where C_r, C_b, which are normalized to [0, 255], are the values in C_r, C_b components of the YC_bC_r color model, η represents a ratio of the average C_r^2 to the average C_r/C_b. The combination of edge and color information is carried out by the fusion operation (14).

$$\mathcal{I}_{lip\_map} = \mathcal{I}_{edge\_lip\_map} \odot \mathcal{I}_{color\_lip\_map} \tag{14}$$

where $\mathcal{I}_{edge\_lip\_map}$ and $\mathcal{I}_{color\_lip\_map}$ are the edge and color lip map mentioned above, $\odot$ is the entry-by-entry product of two matrices.

The higher value a pixel has in the lip map, the more likely it belongs to the lip area; thus, the fusion operation (14) will emphasize the edges caused by two lips and abate the edges caused by non-lip objects. Fig. 8 exhibits the effect of the fusing process. The images in the first row are extracted mouth areas. The second and third row contain the corresponding color lip maps and edge lip maps, respectively. The results of the fusion operation (14) are shown in the last row.

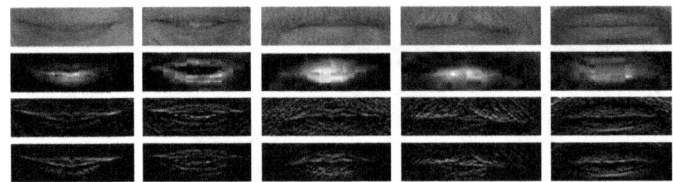

Fig. 8. Examples of extracted mouth areas and the corresponding lip maps

4.2 Mouth Corner Detection

After extracting the mouth area from the input image, the lip map is computed for this area and then divided into left and right parts based on the vertical line through the center of two eyes. Each part is binarized by an adaptive threshold (15).

$$T_0 = \mu_L - \tau\sigma_L \tag{15}$$

where μ_L, σ_L are the mean and standard deviation of the distribution of all pixel values in the left (or right) part, respectively; τ is a constant (it is 2 in the experiments).

By scanning the binary image, the first-left edge pixel of the longest edge in the left part is identified as the left corner (x_L, y_L). Similarly, the right corner (x_R, y_R) is detected.

4.3 Upper/Lower Lip Detection

To detect upper and lower lips, the lip map is filtered by an average filter. The differentiation signal $\mathcal{F}$ is computed for the filtered lip map as in (16).

$$\mathcal{F}(i) = \sum_{j=1}^{n} \mathcal{I}_{lip\_map}(i+1, j) - \mathcal{I}_{lip\_map}(i, j), \quad 1 \leq i < m \tag{16}$$

where $\mathcal{I}_{lip\_map}(i, j)$ is the pixel value in the lip map, $m \times n$ is the size of the input image. The upper and lower lips are located at the first two peaks of the signal $\mathcal{F}$.

5 Experimental Results

To evaluate the accuracy and robust of the proposed method, the algorithms were tested on 720 images collected from the FERET database [12]. The images were taken in different illumination conditions as well as different lighting directions. There are also many variations in colors of hair and clothes, as well as in facial expressions and appearances. The performance of the detection algorithms is summarized in Table 2. And several examples of successful detection are shown in Fig. 9.

Table 2. Summary of the proposed algorithm performance

Facial Features	Successful Detection	Successful Rate
Eye centers	628/720	87.22
Lip features[1]	608/628	96.82
All features[2]	608/720	84.44

[1] Do not include the failure cases caused by wrongly locating of two eye centers.
[2] Include two eye centers, four lip features.

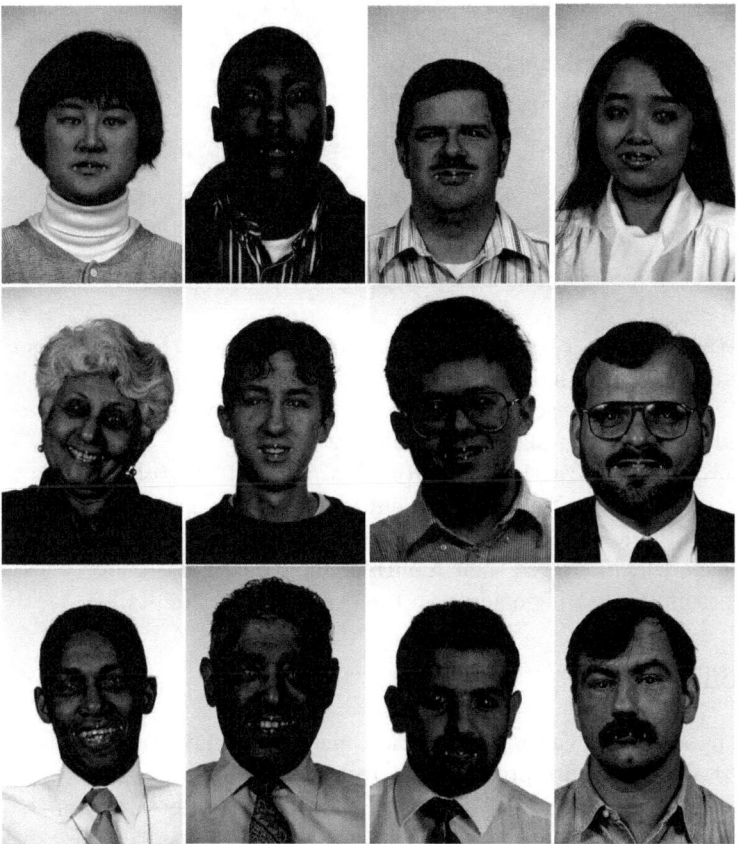

Fig. 9. Successful Facial Feature Detection

As regards the eye detection algorithm, the proposed method was proved to be independent to eye colors as well as skin races. Also, it works well with the image taken in low illumination condition. However, the algorithm could not

Fig. 10. Examples of unsuccessful eye detections

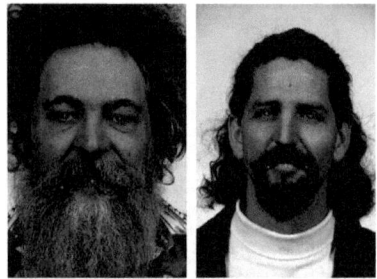

Fig. 11. Examples of unsuccessful lip feature detections

work correctly when two eyes did not show up clearly (i.e. two eyes closed or eyes were covered by hair, eyeglasses frames ...). And the heavy reflections on eyeglasses lens also cause false detections. Fig. 10 shows several images that the proposed eye detection algorithm could not handle.

The process of extracting lip features is proved to be robust. It is robust to different facial expressions, different subjects' appearances, and different illumination conditions. The failure cases only appeared when the subject had beard or mustache which covered their mouth or mouth corners. The weakest point of this algorithm is that it depends on the eye detection results.

6   Conclusions

In this paper, facial feature extraction algorithms have been developed. The proposed algorithms are proved to be robust and efficient to detect eye and lip features. By utilizing skin color in the C_bC_r space and facial shape characteristic, the searching space of facial features is reduced. Thus, the false positives of detecting these features are reduced. The C_bC_r space was proved to be suitable for modeling skin colors of different ethnic groups. It is also robust to illuminations. The skin-based face detection is independent to rotations, scaling, partial occlusions and resolution changes. The weakness of this method is its results may contain false positives (i.e. non-facial objects are detected as faces). The shape evaluation, that is based on the fact that human faces are like ellipses, is carried out to deal with this weakness. Regarding eye detection, by choosing an adaptive threshold to binarize the face image, the proposed method shows its robustness to illumination. Using the circular filter increases the capability of the proposed method to find accurately eye centers regardless of head poses. The algorithms of detecting lip features were demonstrated robust to different ethnic groups as well as the variances in facial expressions and appearances. By fusing the lip color and edge information, the algorithm can locate lip features accurately even when the beard or mustache is present. However, restricting the searching space of lip features by two eye positions increases the false detection rate. In the future, the algorithms will be improved so that eyes and mouth can be detected independently and the eye-mouth relationship will be used to reduce the false detections.

Acknowledgment

Portions of the research in this paper use the FERET database of facial images collected under the FERET program, sponsored by the DOD Counterdrug Technology Development Program Office.

References

1. International Civil Aviation Organization: Machine readable travel documents, part 1, vol. 1 (2006)
2. International Civil Aviation Organization: Machine readable travel documents, part 1, vol. 2 (2006)
3. The International Organization for Standardization: Text of 2nd working draft revision 19794-5, biometric data interchange format - part 5: Face image data (2008)
4. Alattar, A.M., Rajala, S.A.: Facial features localization in front view head and shoulders images. In: IEEE International Conference on Acoustics, Speech, and Signal Processing, pp. 3557–3560. IEEE Computer Society, Washington (1999)
5. Baskan, S., Bulut, M.M., Atalay, V.: Projection Based Method for Segmentation of Human Face and Its Evaluation. Pattern Recogn. Lett. 23, 1623–1629 (2002)
6. Chiang, C.C., Huang, C.J.: A Robust Method for Detecting Arbitrarily Tilted Human Faces in Color Images. Pattern Recogn. Lett. 26, 2518–2536 (2005)
7. Hsu, R.L., Mottaleb, M.A., Jain, A.K.: Face Detection in Color Images. IEEE Trans. Pattern Anal. Mach. Intell. 24, 696–706 (2002)
8. Hammal, Z., Eveno, N., Caplier, A., Coulon, P.: Parametric Models for Facial Features Segmentation. Signal Process 86, 399–413 (2006)
9. Mahoor, M., Abdel-Mottaleb, M.: Facial Feature Extraction in Color Images Using Enhanced Active Shape Model. In: 7th International Conference on Automatic Face and Gesture Recognition, pp. 144–148. IEEE Computer Society, Washington (2006)
10. Zuo, F., de With, P.H.N.: Facial Feature Extraction by A Cascade of Model-Based Algorithms. Image Commun. 23, 194–211 (2008)
11. Chai, D., Ngan, K.N.: Locating facial region of a head-and-shoulders color image. In: 3rd. International Conference on Face & Gesture Recognition, pp. 124–129. IEEE Computer Society, Washington (1998)

12. Phillips, P.J., Wechsler, H., Huang, J., Rauss, P.J.: The FERET database and evaluation procedure for face-recognition algorithms. Image & Vision Comput. 16, 295–306 (1998)
13. Gander, W., Golub, G.H., Strebel, R.: Least squares fitting of circles and ellipses. BIT 34, 558–578 (1994)
14. Fukunaga, K., Hostetler, L.D.: The Estimation of the Gradient of a Density Function, with Applications in Pattern Recognition. IEEE Trans. Inform. Theory 21, 32–40 (1975)
15. Luo, Q., Khoshgoftaar, T.M.: Efficient Image Segmentation by Mean Shift Clustering and MDL-Guide Region Merging. In: 16th IEEE International Conference on Tools with Artificial Intelligence, pp. 337–343 (2004)
16. Sutor, S., Rohr, R., Pujolle, G., Reda, R.: Efficient Mean Shift Clustering Using Exponential Integral Kernels. World Academic of Science, Engineering and Technology 26, 376–380 (2008)
17. Fitzgibbon, A., Pilu, M., Fisher, R.B.: Direct Least Square Fitting of Ellipses. IEEE Trans. Pattern Anal. Mach. Intell. 21, 476–480 (1999)

Round-Optimal Deniable Ring Authentication in the Presence of Big Brother

Rafael Dowsley[1], Goichiro Hanaoka[2],
Hideki Imai[2], and Anderson C.A. Nascimento[1]

[1] Department of Electrical Engineering, University of Brasília
Campus Universitário Darcy Ribeiro, Brasília, CEP: 70910-900, Brazil
`rafaeldowsley@redes.unb.br, andclay@ene.unb.br`
[2] National Institute of Advanced Industrial Science and Technology (AIST)
1-18-13, Sotokanda, Chyioda-ku, 101-0021, Tokyo, Japan
`hanaoka-goichiro@aist.go.jp, h-imai@aist.go.jp`

Abstract. In this work we propose a Deniable Ring Authentication scheme secure against a powerful Big Brother type of adversary and yielding an optimal number of communication rounds. Our scheme is based on an infra-structure assumption: the existence of verifiable Broadcast Encryption. Particularly, our solution can be instantiated by using the Broadcast Encryption protocol of Boneh, Gentry and Waters (CRYPTO 2005), resulting in a Deniable Ring Authentication protocol with constant message size.

Keywords: Deniable Ring Authentication, Broadcast Encryption, Big Brother.

1 Introduction

Digital Signatures [5] play a very important role in modern cryptography and are used in applications ranging from e-commerce to contract signing and secure email communication. In signature schemes one usually desires non-repudiation of messages: the receiver of a signed message can convince anyone that the sender actually signed that message. However, non-repudiation can be highly undesirable in many applications, for example, consider the situation when the receiver is paying for the authentication as in the case of software distribution. Deniable Authentication [9] has been proposed to cope with the cases where non-repudiation is a problem. It is an authentication protocol that convinces a receiver of the authenticity of a given message but does not allow he/she to prove this authenticity to other parties.

In [18], Naor combined Deniable Authentication and Ring Signatures [22] to obtain Deniable Ring Authentication in which it is possible to convince any receiver (a.k.a. verifier) that a sender (a.k.a. prover) that is member of some *ad hoc* subset of the parties (a ring) is authenticating a message M without revealing the identity of the prover and in such way that the verifier cannot convince other parties of this authentication. In the same paper, Naor provided a Deniable Ring Authentication protocol that assumes the existence of a Public Key

Y. Chung and M. Yung (Eds.): WISA 2010, LNCS 6513, pp. 307–321, 2011.

Infrastructure, has four rounds of communication (since deniable authentication is stronger than ZKIP, it requires at least four rounds [12]) and has message size proportional to the number of ring's members. Naor also considered a different scenario where the protocol security must be proven against a powerful adversary which knows all the secret keys (called a Big Brother). This properly models attacks against Deniable Ring Authentication protocols based on Identity Based Encryption infrastructure [23,2] and on Broadcast Encryption [10,3], where a center provides keys to the users. In this stricter scenario, Naor obtained a secure protocol based on the existence of Identity Based Encryption infrastructure and Broadcast Encryption. The resulting protocol had six rounds of communication in total.

1.1 Motivation

We obtain a practical deniable ring authentication schemes secure against a Big Brother adversary yielding

- Optimal communication rounds (4 rounds).
- Constant message size.

Our solution assumes the existence of a Broadcast Encryption Infrastructure with one additional requirement: verifiability. This property can be found in the protocol of [3], for example. By assuming this infra-structure assumption, we present a Deniable Ring Authentication protocol that is secure in the presence of Big Brother and has four rounds of communication (round-optimal). When instantiated with the particular protocol proposed in [3], the resulting scheme has constant message size (i.e., it does not dependent on the number of ring's members). Thus assuming a Broadcast Encryption Infrastructure instead of a Public Key Infrastructure, we obtain a protocol that has the same four rounds as Naor's protocol for Public Key Infrastructure, but has constant message size instead of message size linear in the number of ring's members. In comparison to Naor's protocol that is secure in the presence of Big Brother, our protocol saves two rounds of communication.

1.2 Background

Deniable Authentication. Deniable authentication is a stronger notion of zero knowledge interactive proof system in which the transcript of the interaction cannot be an evidence for enforcing non-repudiation of the sender. Note that in the security proof of ZKIPs we construct a simulator which can create the same transcript without using the witness, but this does not immediately imply deniability.

In Naor's paper "Deniable Ring Authentication" [18], he extends this notion to the context of Rivest, Shamir, Tauman's ring signature framework [22]. Ring signature is a very similar notion to Group signature except for:

- There exists no authority who can violate the user's anonymity.
- It should be setup free, i.e. we can use only existing infrastructures (e.g. PKI) which are used for common purposes, e.g. normal encryption or authentication.

Ring authentication is an interactive version of ring signatures.

Broadcast Encryption. Broadcast Encryption (BE) is an encryption scheme in which the messages have multiple recipients. The first non-trivial solution was present in [10] by Fiat and Naor. Naor et al. [19] obtained a more efficient scheme to broadcast encrypted messages for large subsets of the system parties (i.e., only a small fraction of the users can be revoked). Other schemes of BE for large sets were proposed in [20,14,6,7,13]. Boneh, Gentry and Waters [3] constructed the first fully collusion resistant BE protocol that has constant size for ciphertext and decryption keys.

1.3   Outline of the Paper

In section 2 we define Deniable Ring Authentication, Broadcast Encryption and the computational assumptions used in this paper. In section 3 we present Naor's Deniable Ring Authentication protocol. We present our new protocol in section 4. Section 5 describes an efficient implementation of our protocol using Boneh-Gentry-Waters' Broadcast Encryption protocol. The conclusions are in section 6.

2   Preliminaries

In this section we introduce the definitions of Deniable Ring Authentication and Broadcast Encryption. We also present the computational assumptions used in the scheme of section 5. We closely follow the lines of [18] in the description of Deniable Ring Authentication and the lines of [3] in the description of Broadcast Encryption and computational assumptions.

2.1   Deniable Ring Authentication

In the Deniable Ring Authentication model, we assume that the set of possible provers (each having an unique id $i \in \{1, 2, \ldots, n\}$) has access to some infrastructure, either Public Key Infrastructure or Broadcast Encryption. A ring $\mathcal{S}$ is any subset of $\{1, 2, \ldots, n\}$.

An honest authenticator $\mathcal{P} \in \mathcal{S}$ executes an interactive protocol with a verifier $\mathcal{V}$ to authenticate a message M. We do not require that the verifier be part of the PKI/BE in question, we only require that the verifier and the prover know the public keys of all members of $\mathcal{S}$. We assume that messages are routed anonymously and that the message M to be authenticated is known previously by the prover and the verifier. The adversary $\mathcal{A}$ controls some parties of the system and knows the secret keys of all players (i.e., we assume the Big Brother model). The Deniable Ring Authentication should be complete and secure as defined below.

Let $\text{Output}(\mathcal{S}, \mathcal{P}, \mathcal{V}, M)$ denote the result of executing the Deniable Ring Authentication protocol between the verifier $\mathcal{V}$ and the prover $\mathcal{P}$ that tries to prove that some member of the ring $\mathcal{S}$ is authenticating the message M. Similarly, let $\text{View}(\mathcal{S}, \mathcal{P}, \mathcal{V}, M)$ denote the transcript of such execution.

Definition 1 (Completeness). *A Deniable Ring Authentication protocol is complete if for any valid ring $\mathcal{S}$, any honest prover $\mathcal{P} \in \mathcal{S}$, any honest verifier $\mathcal{V}$, and any message M, we have that $\text{Output}(\mathcal{S}, \mathcal{P}, \mathcal{V}, M) = $ accept with overwhelming probability.*

A Deniable Ring Authentication protocol is secure if it satisfy three requirements described below: Soundness (Existential Unforgeability), Source Hiding and Zero-Knowledge (Deniability).

To an adversary $\mathcal{A}$ trying to forge a message we associate the following game. $\mathcal{A}$ initially knows the identities and the public keys of all possible provers. It also chooses a target ring $\mathcal{S}$ (which we call *honest provers*), and is given all private keys of $\{1, ..., n\} \backslash \mathcal{S}$.

Query Phase: $\mathcal{A}$ adaptively chooses messages $M_1, M_2, \ldots$, rings $\mathcal{S}_1, \mathcal{S}_2, \ldots$ and honest provers $\mathcal{P}_1, \mathcal{P}_2, \ldots$ such that $\mathcal{P}_i \in \mathcal{S}_i$. The honest prover $\mathcal{P}_i$ executes the protocol authenticating the message M_i as been sent by some member of $\mathcal{S}_i$ ($\mathcal{A}$ controls the verifiers in these protocol executions).

Output Phase: $\mathcal{A}$ playing the role of the prover $\mathcal{P}$ chooses a message M, and executes the authentication protocol with an honest verifier $\mathcal{V}$. $\mathcal{A}$ wins if $\text{Output}(\mathcal{S}, \mathcal{P}, \mathcal{V}, M) = $ accept, $(\mathcal{S}, M) \notin \{\mathcal{S}_i, M_i\}_{i=1,2,\ldots}$.

Definition 2 (Soundness - Existential Unforgeability). *A Deniable Ring Authentication protocol meets the Soundness requirement if for any probabilistic polynomial time adversary $\mathcal{A}$, we have that its winning probability in the previous game is negligible.*

To an adversary $\mathcal{A}$ trying to discover the identity of the prover we associate the following game. $\mathcal{A}$ initially knows the identities and the keys (both public and private) of all possible provers.

Challenge Phase: $\mathcal{A}$ (that is given <u>all secrets in the system</u> and plays the role of the verifier $\mathcal{V}$) chooses a ring $\overline{\mathcal{S}}$, two honest provers $\mathcal{P}_0, \mathcal{P}_1 \in \mathcal{S}$ and a message M and sends this information to the challenger. The challenger randomly chooses $b \in \{0, 1\}$ and executes the authentication protocol with $\mathcal{P}_b$ as the prover.

Output Phase: $\mathcal{A}$ outputs its guess $b' \in \{0, 1\}$. $\mathcal{A}$ wins the game if $b' = b$.

Definition 3 (Source Hiding:). *A Deniable Ring Authentication protocol is Source Hiding, if for all probabilistic polynomial time adversary $\mathcal{A}$, the probability that $\mathcal{A}$ wins the game above is negligibly close to $\frac{1}{2}$.*

Definition 4 (Zero-Knowledge - Deniability). *Consider an adversary $\mathcal{A}$ that initially knows the identities and the keys (both public and private) of all* *possible provers. A protocol meets the Zero-Knowledge requirement if for any transcript* View$(\mathcal{S}, \mathcal{P}, \mathcal{V}, M)$ *generated by a protocol execution in which a member* $\mathcal{P}$ *of* $\mathcal{S}$ *acted as the prover and authenticated the message* M *to* $\mathcal{V}$*, there exists a polynomial-time simulator* $\mathcal{Z}$ *that knowing only* $\mathcal{S}, \mathcal{V}, M$ *and the public keys generates an indistinguishable transcript (to every one but the sender).*

2.2   Broadcast Encryption

We present the definitions of our main tool for obtaining our result: Broadcast Encryption. We define Broadcast Encryption as a key encapsulation mechanism (the key generated by this protocol can be used in a One-time Symmetric Key Encryption protocol to encrypt the message M [4]). It is constituted of three algorithms:

Setup: Takes as input the number of parties n and outputs the public key PK and the private keys $d_1, \ldots, d_k$ (one for each party).

Encrypt: Takes as input the public key PK, a set $\mathcal{S} \subseteq \{1, \ldots, n\}$ of receivers of the broadcast and local randomness *coin*. It outputs a header H and a key of a symmetric encryption scheme K.

The key K is then used in a symmetric key encryption scheme to encrypt the message M obtaining a ciphertext L. The message broadcasted to the users is $C = (\mathcal{S}, H, L)$. We will denote the result of executing this algorithm by $C = \text{Enc}_{PK,\mathcal{S},coin}(M)$.

Decrypt: Takes as input a public key PK, an user id $i \in \{1, \ldots, n\}$, the private key d_i and a ciphertext C (constituted of a header H, a set $\mathcal{S} \subseteq \{1, \ldots, n\}$ and a ciphertext L of a symmetric encryption scheme). If $i \in \mathcal{S}$, it outputs a key of a symmetric encryption scheme K.

The key K is then used to decrypt L in the symmetric key encryption scheme obtaining the message M.

For all $\mathcal{S} \subseteq \{1, \ldots, n\}$ and all $i \in \mathcal{S}$, if the public and private keys were correctly generated by the Setup algorithm and the ciphertext was generated following the procedures of the Encrypt algorithm, then the output obtained by i executing correctly the Decrypt algorithm must be M with overwhelming probability.

We define security against a static adversary that selects the parties that it will attack before the execution of the Setup procedure. Security of a broadcast encryption scheme is defined as a game between a challenger and an adversary $\mathcal{A}$ who chooses some subset of the parties to attack and controls all the other parties. The game proceeds in the sequence below.

Initialization: $\mathcal{A}$ outputs a set $\mathcal{S}^* \subseteq \{1, \ldots, n\}$ of the parties that it will attack.

Setup: The challenger runs the setup algorithm of the scheme and obtains the public key and the privates keys. It sends to $\mathcal{A}$ the keys of the parties that $\mathcal{A}$ controls (i.e., all the parties that are not members of $\mathcal{S}^*$).

Query Phase 1: $\mathcal{A}$ adaptively sends decryption queries to the challenger. Each decryption query consists of triple $(i, \mathcal{S}, H)$ such that $\mathcal{S} \subseteq \mathcal{S}^*$ and $i \in \mathcal{S}$. The challenger executes the decryption procedure using the private key of party i and sends the output (i.e., the symmetric key) to $\mathcal{A}$.

Challenge: For the set $\mathcal{S}^*$, the challenger using the Encrypt algorithm generates a header H^* and a key K^* of the symmetric encryption scheme. It chooses randomly $b \in \{0, 1\}$, sets $K_b = K$ and chooses randomly a key K_{1-b}. It sends (H^*, K_0, K_1) to $\mathcal{A}$.

Query Phase 2: $\mathcal{A}$ adaptively sends decryption queries to the challenger. Each decryption query consists of triple $(i, \mathcal{S}, H)$ such that $\mathcal{S} \subseteq \mathcal{S}^*$, $i \in \mathcal{S}$ and $H \neq H^*$. The challenger executes the decryption procedure using the private key of party i and sends the output (i.e., the symmetric key) to $\mathcal{A}$.

Output: $\mathcal{A}$ outputs its guess $b' \in \{0, 1\}$. $\mathcal{A}$ wins the game if $b' = b$.

If the adversary is adaptive, we have to modify the above game as follows: (1) there is no Initialization phase, (2) the adversary can corrupt the parties adaptively, (3) $\mathcal{A}$ only fix the set of honest parties that it will attack, $\mathcal{S}^*$, in the Challenge phase.

We now define what it means for a broadcast encryption to be CCA2 secure [21].

Definition 5 (CCA2 Security). *The Broadcast Encryption protocol is CCA2 secure, if for all probabilistic polynomial time adversary $\mathcal{A}$, the probability that $\mathcal{A}$ wins the game is negligibly close to $\frac{1}{2}$.*

2.3 Verifiability in Broadcast Encryption Schemes

Now we explain the definition of verifiability for broadcast encryption schemes that we consider in this paper. Verifiability is a property that allows the valid receivers to check that each recipient of the broadcasted encrypted message received the same message (i.e., it must be possible to verify the equality of the messages that each recipient decrypts). The definition is identical to that proposed by Hanaoka and Kurosawa in a recent paper [15]. There are two types of verifiability: public and private.

We say that a BE scheme is publicly verifiable if each valid receiver of the broadcasted message can verify without using its decryption key that the message received by each receiver is the same one.

For public verifiability, we define the advantage of an adversary $\mathcal{A}$ as

$$\text{AdvVfy}_{\mathcal{A}} = \Pr[\exists i, j \in \mathcal{S}, \text{Decrypt}(PK, i, d_i, C) \neq \text{Decrypt}(PK, j, d_j, C)|$$
$$((d_1, \ldots, d_n), PK) \leftarrow \text{Setup}(n); C \leftarrow \mathcal{A}((d_1, \ldots, d_n), PK)]$$

Definition 6. *A Broadcast Encryption scheme is publicly verifiable if for all probabilistic polynomial time adversary $\mathcal{A}$, $\text{AdvVfy}_{\mathcal{A}}$ is negligible.*

2.4 The Bilinear Diffie-Hellman Exponent Assumption

We use the same the notation as [16,17,2,3] for bilinear maps and bilinear map groups. Let $\mathbb{G}$ and $\mathbb{G}_1$ be two (multiplicative) cyclic groups of prime order p. Let g be a generator of $\mathbb{G}$. A bilinear map is a map $e : \mathbb{G} \times \mathbb{G} \to \mathbb{G}_1$ with the following properties

- (Bilinear) for all $u, v \in \mathbb{G}$ and $a, b \in \mathbb{Z}$, we have that $e(u^a, v^b) = e(u, v)^{ab}$.
- (Non-degenerate) $e(g, g) \neq 1$.

A group $\mathbb{G}$ is bilinear if the group operation in $\mathbb{G}$ can be computed efficiently and there exists a group $\mathbb{G}_1$ and an efficiently computable bilinear map as described above.

We will use the computational assumption known as Bilinear Diffie-Hellman Exponent (BDHE) assumption [1,3]. Let $\mathbb{G}$ be a bilinear group of prime order p (p is a security parameter), let g and h be random generators in $\mathbb{G}$ and let α be random in $\mathbb{Z}_p^*$. The decision l-BDHE states that given the vector

$$y_{g,\alpha,l} = (g^{(\alpha)}, g^{(\alpha^2)}, \ldots, g^{(\alpha^l)}, g^{(\alpha^{l+2})}, \ldots, g^{(\alpha^{2l})}) \in \mathbb{G}^{2l-1},$$

no probabilistic polynomial time algorithm has non-negligible advantage, in the security parameter p, in distinguishing the inputs $(g, h, y_{g,\alpha,l}, e(g^{(\alpha^{l+1})}, h))$ and $(g, h, y_{g,\alpha,l}, T)$, where T is a random element of $\mathbb{G}_1$. The advantage is computed over the random choice of g, h, α, T and the random bits used by the algorithm.

We will use henceforth the notation g_i to denote $g^{(\alpha^i)}$.

3   Previous Work: Naor's Scheme

In this section, as an important previous work, we review Naor's Deniable Ring Authentication protocol.

3.1   Naor's Idea

Naor started his scheme [18] from Dwork, Naor, and Sahai's authentication scheme [9] (which is an extension of Dolev, Dwork, Naor's scheme [8]). Dwork-Naor-Sahai scheme (with a single sender) is as follows:

Let (dk, PK) be a PKE key-pair of the prover. We assume that this PKE scheme is CCA2 [21]. Let M be the message to be authenticated. We assume that M is already known to both prover and verifier. We denote by $\mathrm{Enc}_{PK,coin}(M)$ the result of executing the PKE's encryption algorithm with message M, public key PK and local randomness $coin$. The authentication protocol for proving possession of dk is carried out as

Protocol 1 (Deniable Authentication)

1. $\mathcal{V}$ sends $C = \mathrm{Enc}_{PK,coin}(M||R)$ to $\mathcal{P}$ where R is a random number.
2. $\mathcal{P}$ decrypts C (using its private key dk) to obtain R and sends $C' = \mathrm{Enc}_{PK,coin'}(R)$ to $\mathcal{V}$.
3. $\mathcal{V}$ sends R and $coin$ to $\mathcal{P}$. $\mathcal{P}$ re-encrypts $M||R$ using the same $coin$ and verifies whether $\mathrm{Enc}_{PK,coin}(M||R) = C$ holds or not.
4. $\mathcal{P}$ sends R and $coin'$ to $\mathcal{V}$. $\mathcal{V}$ re-encrypts R using the same $coin'$ and verifies whether $\mathrm{Enc}_{PK,coin'}(R) = C'$ holds or not.

The above protocol is provably deniable and existentially unforgeable (for single-user setting).

In Sec. 5 of Naor's paper, he presents a ring authentication version of the above protocol. The essential idea of Naor's protocol is the following. For each member of S, we run a independent parallel copy of the above protocol using the same R. However, there is a delicate point which has to be carefully handled in order to guarantee source hiding, and therefore, Naor also fixes this issue by splitting R into $R = R_1 + \ldots + R_n$ and encrypt them separately in Step 2. For a set S such that the members public keys are $PK_1, \ldots, PK_n$, the protocol is executed as follows

Protocol 2 (Naor's Deniable Ring Authentication Scheme)

1. $\mathcal{V}$ generates a random R and sends $(C_1, \ldots, C_n) = (\text{Enc}_{PK_1, coin_1}(M\|R), \ldots, \text{Enc}_{PK_n, coin_n}(M\|R))$ to $\mathcal{P}$.
2. $\mathcal{P}$ extracts R from C_i (using its secret key dk_i), chooses random $R_1, \ldots, R_n$ such that $R = R_1 + \ldots + R_n$ and sends $(C_1', \ldots, C_n') = (\text{Enc}_{PK_1, coin_1'}(R_1), \ldots, \text{Enc}_{PK_n, coin_n'}(R_n))$ to $\mathcal{V}$.
3. $\mathcal{V}$ sends R and $(coin_1, \ldots, coin_n)$ to $\mathcal{P}$. $\mathcal{P}$ verifies if the ciphertexts from Step 1 were properly formed.
4. $\mathcal{P}$ sends $(R_1, \ldots, R_n)$ and $(coin_1', \ldots, coin_n')$ to $\mathcal{V}$. $\mathcal{V}$ verifies if the ciphertexts from Step 2 were properly formed and if $R = R_1 + \ldots + R_n$.

The main issue of this scheme is that the communication complexity of the above scheme is linear in n, and this is considered not very efficient.

3.2   Modified Naor's Scheme from Broadcast Encryption

In Sec. 7 of the same paper, Naor addresses an interesting and efficient variant of the above-mentioned scheme by using Broadcast Encryption (BE). In this variant, we assume that there exists a dedicated infrastructure of BE (for contents distribution or something like that). If you want to prove that you are a member of a specific subset of the set of all users, you can use the BE system by replacing it with the PKE scheme in the above protocol. Then, we can have a deniable ring authentication with "setup-free" property since we already have a BE infrastructure (which would be commonly established in our real life).

However, in a strict sense, the above simple modification is not sufficient. Namely, in a BE system, there exists the *center* who knows all users' secrets, and he can violate any user's anonymity.

Here, we omit the concrete method for revealing anonymity. But, anyway, if one knows all users' secrets, he (i.e. *center*) can easily reveal it by using invalid ciphertexts at Step 1 of the protocol. More specifically (for the two parties case), if it (invalidly) consists of

$$(C1, C2) = (\text{Enc}_{PK_1, coin_1}(M\|R), \text{Enc}_{PK_2, coin_2}(M\|R'))$$

in Step 1 and if the returned message from $\mathcal{P}$ at Step 2 consists of

$$(C1', C2') = (\text{Enc}_{PK_1, coin_1'}(R_1), \text{Enc}_{PK_2, coin_2'}(R_2)),$$

such that $R_1 + R_2 = R'$, then $\mathcal{V}$ can immediately know that $\mathcal{P}$ has $dk2$.

Therefore, Naor further modifies the scheme for protecting against the above attack. The final scheme is presented in Sec. 7 on Naor's paper and has two extra rounds of communication in comparison to the protocol using PKE.

From the above results, we see that if we use the standard PKE infrastructure, transmission data size of the resulting ring authentication protocol becomes linear in the size of the ring (but its round complexity is optimal, i.e. four rounds), and if we use BE infrastructure, the round complexity becomes not optimal, i.e. six rounds (but transmission data can be shorter than that from the standard PKE infrastructure). Hence, a deniable ring authentication scheme (with setup-free property) which yields both constant transmission data size and optimal round complexity has not been known.

4   Our Scheme

In this section we introduce our deniable ring authentication protocol that is based on a broadcast encryption scheme.

4.1   Discussion: Essential Problem of the Naive Scheme

Here, we discuss the essential problem in the above faulty scheme (see section 3.2). The main point is that the verifier $\mathcal{V}$ can reveal $\mathcal{P}$'s anonymity by encrypting two different random numbers R and R' in the first step of the protocol and using the fact that it knows the private keys of all parties in order to discover which party encrypted the message sent to the verifier in the second step. So the verifier can violate the anonymity taking advantage of its ability of sending different messages to the members of the ring.

Naor solved this problem using a non-malleable commitment with respect to the encryptions of the first step, this way he protects the protocol against everyone (see [18] for details). But this approach adds two rounds of communication to the protocol.

We follow a different approach and use a broadcast encryption protocol that is verifiable to construct our deniable ring authentication protocol. In a verifiable broadcast encryption protocol it is possible to the prover to check if the verifier sent the same message to all recipients of the first step message, and so the attack above does not work any more.

4.2   Our Scheme

Our idea is very simple. We just use a verifiable BE system in the above protocol instead of an ordinary one in order to assure that the verifier sends the same message to all members of the ring in the first step of the protocol. Despite the simplicity of this idea, it solves the problem of the above faulty scheme since it forces the verifier to send the same message to all members of the ring. Interestingly, the Boneh-Gentry-Waters (BGW) BE system [3], which is considered as the "basic" BE scheme, originally has verifiability, and therefore, it is not very unnatural to assume a verifiable BE infrastructure.

Our protocol is similar to protocol 1, but it uses BE to the members of the ring instead of using public key encryption with prover's keys. Letting $\text{Enc}_{PK,\mathcal{S},coin}(M)$ denote encryption of plaintext M for users $\mathcal{S}$ under public key PK of the underlying BE with local randomness $coin$, for any ring $\mathcal{S}$ such that the prover $\mathcal{P} \in \mathcal{S}$ (where $\mathcal{S}$ is a subset of all users), $\mathcal{P}$ can prove that he is member of $\mathcal{S}$ as follows:

Protocol 3 (Our Deniable Ring Authentication Protocol)

1. $\mathcal{V}$ sends $C = \text{Enc}_{PK,\mathcal{S},coin}(M||R)$ to $\mathcal{P}$ where R is a random number.
2. $\mathcal{P}$ verifies if all the receivers of the broadcasted encrypted messages received the same message (using the verifiability of the broadcast encryption scheme) and stops the protocol if C is invalid. $\mathcal{P}$ decrypts C to obtain R and sends $C' = \text{Enc}_{PK,\mathcal{S},coin'}(R)$ to $\mathcal{V}$.
3. $\mathcal{V}$ sends R and $coin$ to $\mathcal{P}$. $\mathcal{P}$ re-encrypts $M||R$ using the same $coin$ and checks whether $\text{Enc}_{PK,\mathcal{S},coin}(M||R) = C$ holds or not.
4. $\mathcal{P}$ sends R and $coin'$ to $\mathcal{V}$. $\mathcal{V}$ re-encrypts R using the same $coin'$ and checks whether $\text{Enc}_{PK,\mathcal{S},coin'}(R) = C'$ holds or not.

Since the deniability requirement implies that the deniable ring authentication protocols should be zero-knowledge, these protocols are stronger than ZKIP. Therefore these protocols requires at least four rounds, because ZKIP is impossible with three rounds [12]. Hence, the above protocol is round optimal.

4.3   Security of the Protocol

We now proof the security of the above protocol following the definitions of security described in section 2 and assuming that the Broadcast Encryption protocol used is CCA2 secure and verifiable and that the One-time Symmetric Key Encryption is CCA2 secure. I.e., we argue that the protocol meets the four requirements described previously: completeness, soundness, source hiding and deniability.

Theorem 1. *Assume that the Broadcast Encryption scheme is verifiable and CCA2 secure, and that the One-time Symmetric Key Encryption scheme is CCA2 secure. Then the Deniable Ring Authentication protocol presented above is secure according to the definitions of Sec. 2.*

We briefly sketch the proof of security of our scheme. Due to space constraints, we leave the complete proof to a full version of this paper.

Completeness: The Broadcast Encryption and the One-time Symmetric Key Encryption schemes used within our protocol must be correct in the sense that if the parties follow the procedures of the protocol, then the original message is decrypted correctly with overwhelming probability in the random choices of the procedure. Therefore the completeness requirement follows easily from this property of the Broadcast Encryption and the One-time Symmetric Key Encryption schemes, since the valid prover decrypts correctly the message $M||R$ and learns the correct R in first step with overwhelming probability, and from the fact that the rest of the execution for honest parties is correct if the first step is.

Soundness - Existential Unforgeability: As the Key Encapsulation Mechanism (i.e., the Broadcast Encryption) and the One-time Symmetric Key Encryption schemes are CCA2 secure, it follows that the Hybrid Encryption scheme is also CCA2 secure [4]. So the Hybrid Encryption scheme is non-malleable. The soundness of our protocol follows from the fact that the ciphertext $C' = \mathrm{Enc}_{PK,\mathcal{S},coin'}(R)$, which the prover sends in the second step of the protocol, is a non-malleable commitment to the random value R that the verifier sends in the first step. The access to the authentication oracle essentially means that the can make decryption queries in the Hybrid scheme. The adversary cannot take advantage of its access to the authentication oracle in order to forge a message with non-negligible probability, since this would imply in a non-negligible advantage against the Hybrid Encryption scheme contradicting the assumption that the Broadcast Encryption and One-time Symmetric Key Encryption schemes are CCA2 secure.

Source Hiding: The verifiability property of the Broadcast Encryption protocol guarantees that the actual prover can check if all possible provers in the current ring (i.e., all the receivers of the broadcasted encrypted message) received the same message in the first step of the protocol. Due to the verifiability of the Broadcast Encryption scheme, this tests fails only with negligible probability. Therefore the actual prover has the guarantee that all possible honest provers in the ring would encrypt the same value R (and so send indistinguishable messages) in the second step of the protocol with overwhelming probability, and so the source hiding property is satisfied by our protocol.

Zero-Knowledge - Deniability: We run the simulator with the prover $\mathcal{P}$ encrypting a random value R' in the second step of the protocol. If the verifier $\mathcal{V}$ opens R in the third step, the simulator rewind to just after step 1 and run the protocol again with the prover encrypting the correct value R in the second step.

To deal with verifiers that do not open the random value in third step, we use the fact that the Broadcast Encryption and the One-time Symmetric Key Encryption used are CCA2 secure, so the message in the second step is a secure commitment to R' and the verifier cannot learn non-negligible information about R'.

As our scheme meets the security requirements for deniable ring authentication schemes described in section 2, it is a secure deniable ring authentication scheme.

5   Efficient Implementation from BGW Protocol

5.1   BGW Protocol

Here, we review an efficient CCA2 secure variant of BGW protocol [3] which is secure under the Bilinear Diffie-Hellman Exponent (BDHE) assumption, which is due to Hanaoka and Kurosawa [15]. As mentioned in [3], the BGW can also be modified using a signature scheme and a collision resistant hash function to become CCA2 secure.

Let $\mathbb{G}$ and $\mathbb{G}_1$ be multiplicative cyclic groups with prime order p, and $e : \mathbb{G} \times \mathbb{G} \to \mathbb{G}_1$ be a bilinear mapping such that for all $a, b \in \mathbb{Z}$ and $u, v \in \mathbb{G}$, we have that $e(u^a, v^b) = e(u, v)^{ab}$ and for a generator $g \in \mathbb{G}$ we have that $e(g, g) \neq 1$.

The CCA2 secure variant of BGW protocol is as follows:

Setup: Choose $\ell \in \mathbb{N}$ such that $2\ell C_\ell \geq p$. Let $\mathbb{G}$ be a bilinear group with prime order p. Pick a random generator $g \in \mathbb{G}$ and random $\alpha \in \mathbb{Z}_p$. Compute $g_i = g^{(\alpha^i)} \in \mathbb{G}$ for $i = 1, 2, ..., n + 2\ell, n + 2\ell + 2, ..., 2(n + 2\ell)$. Pick a injective mapping $\mathsf{INJ} : \mathbb{G} \to \mathcal{P}$, where $\mathcal{P}$ is the set of all $\Delta\mathcal{S} \subseteq \{n + 1, ..., n + 2\ell\}$ with $|\Delta\mathcal{S}| = \ell$. Pick a random $\gamma \in \mathbb{Z}_p$ and set $v = g^\gamma \in \mathbb{G}$. Set $Z = e(g_{n+2\ell+1}, g)$ where $g_{n+2\ell+1} = g^{\alpha^{n+2\ell+1}}$. The public key is $PK = (g, g_1, ..., g_{n+2\ell}, g_{n+2\ell+2}, ..., g_{2(n+2\ell)}, v, Z, \mathsf{INJ})$, and the decryption keys for user $i \in \{1, ..., n\}$ is set as $d_i = g_i^\gamma \in \mathbb{G}$. Output $(d_1, ..., d_n, PK)$.

Encrypt: Pick a random $t \in \mathbb{Z}_p$, and set $K = Z^t \in \mathbb{G}_1$. Compute $\Delta\mathcal{S} = \mathsf{INJ}(g^t)$, and output (ψ, K) where $\psi = (g^t, (v \cdot \prod_{j \in \mathcal{S} \cup \Delta\mathcal{S}} g_{n+2\ell+1-j})^t) \in \mathbb{G}^2$.

Decrypt: Letting $\psi = (C_0, C_1)$, compute $\Delta\mathcal{S} = f(C_0)$, and check whether

$$e(g, C_1) \overset{?}{=} e(v \cdot \prod_{j \in \mathcal{S} \cup \Delta\mathcal{S}} g_{n+2\ell+1-j}, C_0),$$ and if not, output $\bot$. Otherwise, output $K = e(g_i, C_1)/e(d_i \cdot \prod_{j \in \mathcal{S} \cup \Delta\mathcal{S} \setminus \{i\}} g_{n+2\ell+1-j+i}, C_0)$.

The security of the above scheme is addressed as follows:

Theorem 2. *Let $\mathbb{G}$ be a bilinear group with prime order p, and INJ be an injective mapping. Then, for any positive integers n, the above scheme is CCA2 secure under the BDHE assumption on $\mathbb{G}$ such that $2\ell C_\ell \geq p$.*

As explained in [15] (see the full version of the paper), BGW protocol can be slightly modified to add verifiability. To add verifiability to their protocol, we only have to check in the beginning of the decryption procedure if

$$e(g, C_1) \overset{?}{=} e(v \cdot \prod_{j \in \mathcal{S} \cup \Delta\mathcal{S}} g_{n+2\ell+1-j}, C_0)$$

and output an error symbol if they are not equal.

By applying this scheme to our generic construction in the previous section, we have the *first* deniable ring authentication with constant transmission data size and optimal round complexity.

5.2   Implementing Our Protocol from BGW

Assuming that the parties have access to a Broadcast Encryption infrastructure which is based on (CCA2 secure variant of) BGW protocol, one can carry out Deniable Ring Authentication protocol as follows:

1. $\mathcal{V}$ picks a random $t \in \mathbb{Z}_p$ and computes the header H and the symmetric key K. $\mathcal{V}$ uses an One-Time Symmetric Key Encryption protocol with the key K and randomness Z to encrypt $M||R$ (where R is a random number) and obtain a ciphertext L. It sends $C = (\mathcal{S}, H, L)$ to $\mathcal{P}$.

2. $\mathcal{P}$ verifies if $e(g, C_1) \stackrel{?}{=} e(v \cdot \prod_{j \in \mathcal{S} \cup \Delta \mathcal{S}} g_{n+2\ell+1-j}, C_0)$ and stops the protocol if it is not equal. $\mathcal{P}$ decrypts H to obtain the symmetric key K, and then uses K to decrypt $M \| R$ and obtain R. $\mathcal{P}$ picks a random $t' \in \mathbb{Z}_p$ and computes the header H' and the symmetric key K'. $\mathcal{P}$ encrypts R uses an One-Time Symmetric Key Encryption protocol with the key K' and randomness Z' to encrypt R and obtain a ciphertext L'. It sends $C' = (\mathcal{S}, H', L')$ to $\mathcal{V}$.
3. $\mathcal{V}$ sends R, t and Z to $\mathcal{P}$. $\mathcal{P}$ re-encrypts $M \| R$ using the same t and Z. It checks whether the result is equal to $C = (\mathcal{S}, H, L)$ or not, and stops if it is not.
4. $\mathcal{P}$ sends R, t' and Z' to $\mathcal{V}$. $\mathcal{V}$ re-encrypts R using the same t' and Z'. It checks whether the result is equal to $C' = (\mathcal{S}, H', L')$ or not, and stops if it is not.

Theorem 3. *The above protocol is a secure Deniable Ring Authentication protocol under the BDHE assumption on $\mathbb{G}$ in the sense of the definitions of Sec. 2.*

It should be noticed that the above protocol requires only constant transmission data size (which is independent of the size of the ring) and four rounds (which is optimal).

5.3   A Drawback of This Scheme

There is one unsolved issue in our scheme. Namely, its security can be proven against only static adversaries since the BGW scheme has only static security. More specifically, before the setup phase, the adversary has to first commit to a subset $\mathcal{S}^*$ for which it wants to compromise the soundness property (the goal of adversary is to pretend to be a member of $\mathcal{S}^*$ without using no valid decryption keys). Obviously, this security notion is weaker than the adaptive adversarial model in which the adversary can adaptively choose $\mathcal{S}^*$ after the setup phase.

One possible solution would be to prove the verifiability of some adaptively secure BE system with constant ciphertext size. One possible candidate is the scheme recently proposed by Gentry and Waters [11].

6   Conclusion

We have constructed a practical deniable ring authentication schemes which has optimal communication rounds and constant message size. To the best of our knowledge, this is the first solution meeting those properties against a Big Brother like adversary. In our scheme we assumed the existence of a verifiable Broadcast Encryption protocol. Our solution can be implemented using the Boneh-Gentry-Waters' protocol [3]. Since their protocol has been proven secure only against adversaries that selects the set of parties that it wants to attack prior to the setup phase of the broadcast encryption scheme, this implementation of our scheme can be proven secure only against this static type of adversary.

One open problem is to prove the verifiability of some practical broadcast encryption protocol that has constant message size and that has been proven secure against adversaries that adaptively selects the participants that it wants to attack. Such protocol can be used with our construction to obtain a deniable ring authentication protocol secure against adversaries that adaptively corrupts the parties.

We also suggest as a future research direction to investigate further uses of broadcast encryption with the extra verifiability property.

References

1. Boneh, D., Boyen, X., Goh, E.: Hierarchical Identity Based Encryption with Constant Size Ciphertext. In: Cramer, R. (ed.) EUROCRYPT 2005. LNCS, vol. 3494, pp. 440–456. Springer, Heidelberg (2005)
2. Boneh, D., Franklin, M.: Identity-Based Encryption from the Weil Pairing. In: Kilian, J. (ed.) CRYPTO 2001. LNCS, vol. 2139, pp. 213–229. Springer, Heidelberg (2001)
3. Boneh, D., Gentry, C., Waters, B.: Collusion Resistant Broadcast Encryption with Short Ciphertexts and Private Keys. In: Shoup, V. (ed.) CRYPTO 2005. LNCS, vol. 3621, pp. 258–275. Springer, Heidelberg (2005)
4. Cramer, R., Shoup, V.: Design and Analysis of Practical Public-Key Encryption Schemes Secure against Adaptive Chosen Ciphertext Attack. SIAM Journal of Computing 33, 167–226 (2003)
5. Diffie, W., Hellman, M.E.: New Directions in Cryptography. IEEE Trans. on Info. Theory IT-22, 644–654 (1976)
6. Dodis, Y., Fazio, N.: Public Key Broadcast Encryption for Stateless Receivers. In: Feigenbaum, J. (ed.) DRM 2002. LNCS, vol. 2696, pp. 61–80. Springer, Heidelberg (2003)
7. Dodis, Y., Fazio, N.: Public Key Broadcast Encryption Secure Against Adaptive Chosen Ciphertext Attack. In: Desmedt, Y.G. (ed.) PKC 2003. LNCS, vol. 2567. Springer, Heidelberg (2002)
8. Dolev, D., Dwork, C., Naor, M.: Non-malleable Cryptography. SIAM J. Comput. 30(2), 391–437 (2000)
9. Dwork, C., Naor, M., Sahai, A.: Concurrent Zero-Knowledge. In: STOC 1998, pp. 409–418 (1998)
10. Fiat, A., Naor, M.: Broadcast Encryption. In: Stinson, D.R. (ed.) CRYPTO 1993. LNCS, vol. 773, pp. 480–491. Springer, Heidelberg (1994)
11. Gentry, C., Waters, B.: Adaptive Security in Broadcast Encryption Systems (with Short Ciphertexts). In: Joux, A. (ed.) EUROCRYPT 2009. LNCS, vol. 5479, pp. 171–188. Springer, Heidelberg (2009)
12. Goldreich, O., Oren, Y.: Definitions and Properties of Zero-Knowledge Proof Systems. J. Cryptology 7(1), 1–32 (1994)
13. Goodrich, M.T., Sun, J.Z., Tamassia, R.: Efficient Tree-based Revocation in Groups of Low-state Devices. In: CRYPTO 2004. LNCS, vol. 2204, Springer, Heidelberg (2004)
14. Halevy, D., Shamir, A.: The LSD Broadcast Encryption Scheme. In: Yung, M. (ed.) CRYPTO 2002. LNCS, vol. 2442, pp. 47–60. Springer, Heidelberg (2002)

15. Hanaoka, G., Kurosawa, K.: Efficient Chosen Ciphertext Secure Public Key En-cryption under the Computational Diffie-Hellman Assumption. In: Pieprzyk, J. (ed.) ASIACRYPT 2008. LNCS, vol. 5350, pp. 308–325. Springer, Heidelberg (2008), http://eprint.iacr.org/2008/211

16. Joux, A.: A One Round Protocol for Tripartite Diffie-Hellman. In: Bosma, W. (ed.) ANTS 2000. LNCS, vol. 1838, pp. 385–394. Springer, Heidelberg (2000)

17. Joux, A., Nguyen, K.: Separating Decision Diffie-Hellman from Computational Diffie-Hellman in Cryptographic Groups. J. Cryptology 16(4), 239–247 (2003)

18. Naor, M.: Deniable Ring Authentication. In: Yung, M. (ed.) CRYPTO 2002. LNCS, vol. 2442, pp. 481–498. Springer, Heidelberg (2002)

19. Naor, D., Naor, M., Lotspiech, J.: Revocation and Tracing Schemes for Stateless Receivers. In: Kilian, J. (ed.) CRYPTO 2001. LNCS, vol. 2139, pp. 41–62. Springer, Heidelberg (2001)

20. Naor, M., Pinkas, B.: Efficient trace and revoke schemes. In: Frankel, Y. (ed.) FC 2000. LNCS, vol. 1962, pp. 1–20. Springer, Heidelberg (2001)

21. Rackoff, C., Simon, D.R.: Non-interactive zero-knowledge proof of knowledge and chosen ciphertext attack. In: Feigenbaum, J. (ed.) CRYPTO 1991. LNCS, vol. 576, pp. 433–444. Springer, Heidelberg (1992)

22. Rivest, R.L., Shamir, A., Tauman, Y.: How to Leak a Secret. In: Boyd, C. (ed.) ASIACRYPT 2001. LNCS, vol. 2248, pp. 552–565. Springer, Heidelberg (2001)

23. Shamir, A.: Identity-Based Cryptosystems and Signature Schemes. In: Blakely, G.R., Chaum, D. (eds.) CRYPTO 1984. LNCS, vol. 196, pp. 47–53. Springer, Heidelberg (1985)

Cross-Realm Password-Based
Server Aided Key Exchange

Kazuki Yoneyama

NTT Information Sharing Platform Laboratories
yoneyama.kazuki@lab.ntt.co.jp

Abstract. In this paper, we extend password-based server aided key exchange (PSAKE) to the cross-realm setting which two clients in two different realms with different passwords can exchange a session key through their corresponding servers, i.e., there are two servers. We cannot simply apply the previous security model of PSAKE to cross-realm setting because there is the difference between security properties which can be captured in the previous setting and in the new setting. Therefore, we define a new formal security model of cross-realm PSAKE. Our model captures all desirable security requirements, like resistance to leakage of ephemeral private keys, to key-compromise impersonation and to undetectable on-line dictionary attack. Furthermore, we propose a concrete construction of cross-realm PSAKE with the optimal number of rounds for a client, which is secure in the sense of our model. Our scheme assumes no pre-established secure channels between different realms unlike previous schemes, but just authenticated channels between different realms.

Keywords: password-based authenticated key exchange, leakage of internal states, undetectable on-line dictionary attack.

1 Introduction

The rapid growth of user created contents advances *client-to-client* communication. When a client wants to communicate securely with another client, the client typically execute an authenticated key exchange (AKE) protocol with the peer in order to establish the secure channel. Especially, password-based AKE (PAKE) protocols are used in a practical sense because clients do not need any pre-shared cryptographic secret key or support from a trusted third party, i.e., PAKE needs only pre-shared human memorable password.

However, since PAKE requires that clients have to share a same password in advance, it is not suitable for client-to-client setting. Thus, in this setting, it is desirable to be able to exchange the session key even if clients have different passwords. Hence, several schemes have been presented to provide PAKE between two clients with their different passwords, called client-to-client PAKE (C2C-PAKE). In C2C-PAKE, clients carry out key exchange with the assistance of intermediate servers because clients have no secret common information.

Y. Chung and M. Yung (Eds.): WISA 2010, LNCS 6513, pp. 322–336, 2011.

The first construction of C2C-PAKE was introduced by Steiner et al. [1] in the *single-server* setting. In the single-server setting, the model consists of two clients A and B (or n clients) and a server S, where clients are in the same realm as the server S. Cliff et al. [2] proposed a variant of C2C-PAKE, called the password-based server aided key exchange (PSAKE), which has the similar setting of previous C2C-PAKE schemes except the server uses encryption based authenticators and password. The encryption based authenticator in PSAKE means that a client has the server's public-key as well as the password shared with the server, and the server has clients' passwords and his private-key. They also proved security of PSAKE in the standard model, i.e., without the random oracle. By helping of the encryption based authenticator, PSAKE satisfies strong security like resistance to leakage of ephemeral private keys of servers (LEP) (i.e., Even if all the session specific ephemeral private key of *servers* in a session is compromised, secrecy of the session key is not compromised. This property is not guaranteed when the ephemeral private key of a client of a session is revealed even if the session key of the session is not revealed. In such a case, password of the client is easily derived by the off-line dictionary attack since the session key deterministically depends on the client's ephemeral key, static password, and communication received from the other party. So, we only consider resistance to LEP of servers.) and resistance to key-compromise impersonation (KCI) (i.e., When a client's password is compromised, this event does not enable an outside adversary to impersonate other entities to the client.), which cannot be guaranteed in password-only setting C2C-PAKE schemes. Also, Yoneyama [3] proposed a stronger security model of PSAKE than Cliff et al.'s, which captures resistance to undetectable on-line dictionary attacks (UDonDA) [4] (i.e., The adversary attempts to use a guessed password in an on-line transaction. He verifies the correctness of his guess using responses of servers. If his guess fails then he can start a new transaction with servers using another guessed password. By computing requests to servers which a failed guess cannot be detected and logged by servers, the adversary makes servers be not able to depart an honest request from a malicious request. So, the adversary can obtain enough information to guess the password and finds the proper one.) Besides PSAKE, though several schemes embrace the single-server setting [5,6,7], there is a problem that it is unrealistic that all clients trying to agree their session key are registered in a common single server.

From this viewpoint, C2C-PAKE in the *cross-realm* setting (cross-realm C2C-PAKE) is studied, which two clients are in two different realms and hence there exists two servers involved. Cross-realm C2C-PAKE schemes consist of two clients A and B, and two servers SA and SB, where A and B are clients of SA and SB respectively. Thus, two clients can agree the session key if they are not registered by a common server.

1.1 Prior Related Works

The first construction of cross-realm C2C-PAKE is proposed by Byun et al. [8]. However, some attacks are found against this scheme by Chen [9] which showed an off-line dictionary attack (offDA) (i.e., The adversary guesses a password and verifies his guess off-line. No participation of servers is required, so servers don't notice the attack. If his guess fails the adversary tries again with another password, until he finds the proper one.) by a malicious server in a different realm, Wang et al. [10] which showed three different dictionary attacks and Kim et al. [11] which showed Denning-Sacco-style attack (a variant of dictionary attack) by an insider with knowledge of the password of a client in a different realm. Though Kim et al. also proposed an improved cross-realm C2C-PAKE in [11], Phan and Goi [12] presented two unknown-key share (UKS) attacks [13] (i.e., A client C including a malicious client insider interferes with the session establishment between two honest parties A and B such that at the end of the attack both parties compute the same session key (which C may not learn), yet while A is convinced that the key is shared with B, B believes that the peer to the session has been C.) on it. To shake off vicious circle of attack-and-remedy procedures, Byun et al. [14] introduced a provably secure cross-realm C2C-PAKE scheme. However, it is also shown by Phan and Goi [15] that this scheme falls to an UDonDA by any adversary and a successful man-in-the-middle (MIM) attack (i.e., The adversary impersonates an honest client to the other client of the session without the client's password.) by malicious servers. On all above schemes in the cross-realm setting, clients use their corresponding servers to obtain information for authentication and directly communicate for establishing their session key after obtaining these information. So, we call these schemes have *direct communication structure*. On the other hand, there are cross-realm C2C-PAKE schemes which have another structure, called *indirect communication structure*. Clients communicate only through their corresponding servers in the indirect communication structure. The advantage of schemes which have the indirect communication structure is to be able to reduce the *optimal* number of rounds for a client, i.e, 2-rounds, than the existing schemes which have the direct communication structure, i.e., 4-rounds, and to remove communications of a client across different realms. So, the indirect communication structure can reduce loads of clients. Yin and Bao [16] proposed a cross-realm C2C-PAKE scheme (YB scheme) which has the indirect communication structure and provable security. However, despite its provable security, defects of their security model (YB model) caused two attacks, an UDonDA by any adversary and an UKS attack by a malicious client insider, which are found by Phan and Goi [15]. Wang and Zhang [17] defined a stronger model (WZ model) than the YB model and proposed a construction of secure cross-realm C2C-PAKE in the sense of the WZ model. However, their construction (WZ construction) needs the large number of rounds for a client, i.e., 4-rounds. Wu and Zhu [18] proposed a cross-realm C2C-PAKE scheme under the CDH assumption, but, their scheme still needs 3-rounds for a client. All above cross-realm C2C-PAKE schemes are password-only setting, i.e., secret information of clients and servers is only passwords. Thus, it is impossible to avoid some complicated attacks, e.g., LEP, KCI and UDonDAs. Indeed, the WZ model (the previous strongest model) does not capture resistance to KCI and LEP. Feng and Xu [19] gave a first cross-realm C2C-PAKE scheme secure against KCI by use of public-key crypto by servers. However, their scheme needs the enormous number of rounds for a client, i.e., 7-rounds. Jin and Xu [20] also proposed a cross-realm C2C-PAKE scheme secure against KCI by use of smart cards. Their scheme still needs 4-rounds for a client.

1.2 Our Contribution

We extend PSAKE to cross-realm setting in order to obtain strong security properties which are not guaranteed in previous cross-realm C2C-PAKE schemes. We call this extension *cross-realm PSAKE*.

First, we define a security model of cross-realm PSAKE in order to capture strong security properties. The major difference between our model and previous models of cross-realm C2C-PAKE consists in adversary's available oracle queries, specifically, obtaining of static secret or ephemeral secret separately, and in adversary's capability in the target session, i.e., the adversary can obtain static secrets of all entities and ephemeral secrets of servers in the target session. Therefore, our model can represent resistance to complicated attacks which is cannot captured in previous C2C-PAKE models. Our model is based on the recent formal model of AKE [21] and that of PSAKE [3].

Also, we give a concrete construction of cross-realm PSAKE which has the indirect communication structure. Our scheme only needs the optimal number of rounds for clients and servers (i.e., 2-rounds between a client and a server, and 2-rounds between servers) as the YB scheme. So, our scheme is more efficient than the WZ construction [17] from the viewpoint of communication complexity. By applying the technique of [2] and [3] (i.e., use of public-key crypto by servers), the UDonDA and the UKS attack to the YB scheme don't work for our scheme. Furthermore, we show that our scheme is secure in the sense of our model. Thus, our scheme also satisfies resistance to LEP to KCI and to UKS attacks. Though most previous C2C-PAKE schemes which have indirect communication structure assume pre-established secure channels between servers, we can prove security of our scheme by assuming only pre-established *authenticated* channels between servers. The comparison among previous schemes and our scheme is shown in Table 1.[1]

2 Insecurity of Previous Schemes

2.1 Attacks on the YB Scheme

The protocol of the YB scheme [16] appears in Figure 1. Besides the UKS attack and the UDonDA in [15], we show a KCI attack and an offDA with LEP of servers to the YB scheme.

---

[1] Due to space limitations, we will show concrete insecurity of schemes of [19] and [20] against LEP of servers in the full version of this paper.

Table 1. Comparison among previous schemes and our scheme

	setting	# of rounds for clients	UDonDA	LEP of servers	KCI	channel between servers
[16]	password-only	2	insecure	insecure	insecure	secure channel
[17]	password-only	2 + P	secure	insecure	insecure	secure channel
[19]	password and public-key crypto	7	secure	insecure	secure	none
[20]	password and smart cards	4	secure	insecure	secure	none
Ours	password and public-key crypto	2	secure	secure	secure	authenticated channel

Where P denote the number of moves of a secure 2-party PAKE.

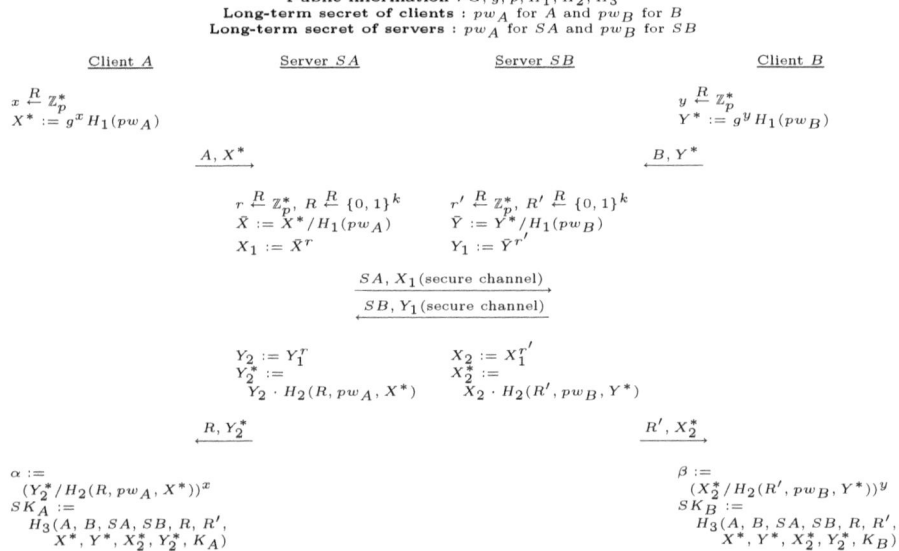

Fig. 1. YB scheme

KCI Attack. The adversary $\mathcal{A}$ obtains pw_A of the client A and tries to impersonate a honest client B to A. When A sends A, X^* to SA and SA sends reply R, Y_2^* to A, $\mathcal{A}$ interferes it, chooses $\tilde{r} \in \mathbb{Z}_p^*$, and sends $R, \tilde{Y}_2^* = g^{\tilde{r}} \cdot H_2(R, pw_A, X^*)$ to A as SA's reply. Then, $\mathcal{A}$ computes $\alpha := (\tilde{Y}_2^*/H_2(R, pw_A, X^*))^x = g^{x\tilde{r}}$ and $\mathcal{A}$ can also compute $g^{x\tilde{r}}$. Thus, $\mathcal{A}$ successfully impersonates B to A.

offDA with LEP of Servers. The adversary $\mathcal{A}$ obtains ephemeral private keys r and r' of the servers SA and SB in a session, and tries to obtain pw_A and pw_B of the client A and B. $\mathcal{A}$ watches the transcript of the session, guesses passwords

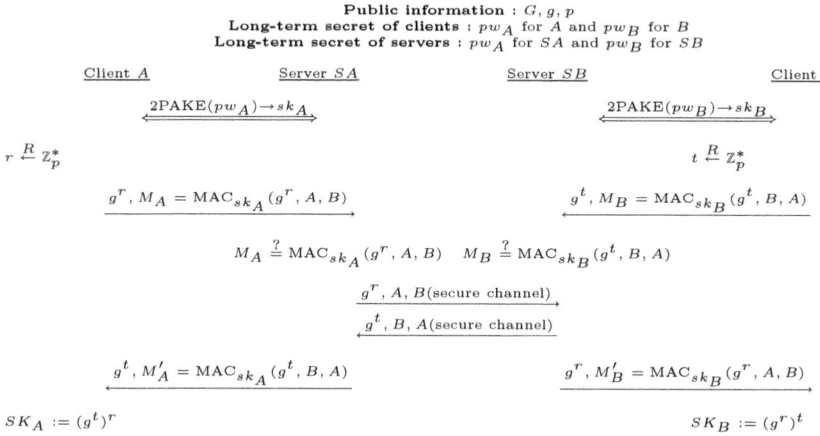

Public information : G, g, p
Long-term secret of clients : pw_A for A and pw_B for B
Long-term secret of servers : pw_A for SA and pw_B for SB

Client A	Server SA	Server SB	Client B

$$\xleftrightarrow{\text{2PAKE}(pw_A) \to sk_A} \qquad\qquad \xleftrightarrow{\text{2PAKE}(pw_B) \to sk_B}$$

$$r \xleftarrow{R} \mathbb{Z}_p^* \qquad\qquad\qquad\qquad\qquad\qquad\qquad t \xleftarrow{R} \mathbb{Z}_p^*$$

$$\xrightarrow{g^r, M_A = \text{MAC}_{sk_A}(g^r, A, B)} \qquad\qquad \xrightarrow{g^t, M_B = \text{MAC}_{sk_B}(g^t, B, A)}$$

$$M_A \overset{?}{=} \text{MAC}_{sk_A}(g^r, A, B) \qquad M_B \overset{?}{=} \text{MAC}_{sk_B}(g^t, B, A)$$

$$\xrightarrow{g^r, A, B(\text{secure channel})}$$
$$\xleftarrow{g^t, B, A(\text{secure channel})}$$

$$\xleftarrow{g^t, M_A' = \text{MAC}_{sk_A}(g^t, B, A)} \qquad\qquad \xrightarrow{g^r, M_B' = \text{MAC}_{sk_B}(g^r, A, B)}$$

$$SK_A := (g^t)^r \qquad\qquad\qquad\qquad\qquad\qquad SK_B := (g^r)^t$$

Fig. 2. WZ construction

$p\tilde{w}_A$ and $p\tilde{w}_B$, and checks that both $X^*/H_1(p\tilde{w}_A) = (X_2^*/H_2(R', pw_B, Y^*))^{-rr'}$ and $Y^*/H_1(p\tilde{w}_B) = (Y_2^*/H_2(R, pw_A, X^*))^{-rr'}$ hold. Since the password dictionary is small enough, $\mathcal{A}$ successfully obtains pw_A and pw_B.

Weakness of the YB Model. From the attacks, it is clear that resistances to KCI, UKS, LEP and UDonDA cannot be captured in the YB model. Also, forward secrecy cannot be represented since the adversary capabilities do not include any query for corruption of parties.

2.2 Attacks on the WZ Construction

The protocol of the WZ construction [17] appears in Figure 2. 2PAKE means a secure 2-party PAKE which outputs a temporary session key sk and MAC means a secure message authentication code with the key sk. We show a KCI attack and an offDA with LEP of servers to the WZ construction.

KCI Attack. The attack is very simple. By revealing pw_A, the adversary $\mathcal{A}$ can impersonate SA to A in the 2PAKE part and share the temporary session key sk_A with A. $\mathcal{A}$ chooses $\tilde{r} \in \mathbb{Z}_p^*$, and sends $g^{\tilde{r}}$, $\text{MAC}_{sk_A}(g^{\tilde{r}}, B, A)$ to A as SA's reply. Then, A computes $SK_A = (g^{\tilde{r}})^r$ and $\mathcal{A}$ can also compute $(g^r)^{\tilde{r}}$. Thus, $\mathcal{A}$ successfully impersonates B to A.

offDA with LEP of Servers. If SA's ephemeral private key is revealed, pw_A is easily derived by the off-line dictionary attack since the temporary session key sk_A deterministically depends on SA's ephemeral private key, pw_A, and communication received from A. Thus, $\mathcal{A}$ successfully obtains pw_A.

Weakness of the WZ Model. From the attacks, it is clear that resistances to KCI and LEP cannot be captured in the WZ model. Also, forward secrecy cannot be represented since the adversary capabilities do not include any query for corruption of parties.

3   New Model: Cross-Realm PSAKE Security

3.1   Cross-Realm C2C-PAKE and PSAKE

Cross-realm C2C-PAKE schemes contain four parties (two clients and two servers) who will engage in the protocol. In cross-realm setting, each client is in a realm and has a corresponding server belonging to the realm. We denote the set of servers by $\mathcal{S}$ and the set of clients by $\mathcal{U}$. Let each password be pre-shared between a client and a corresponding server and be uniformly and independently chosen from fixed low-entropy dictionary $\mathcal{D}$ of the size $|\mathcal{D}|$. Note that clients do not need to share passwords with other clients. In addition, in cross-realm PSAKE, the server pre-establishes his public-key and private-key pair and goes public the public-key. We denote with U^l the lth instance that clients $U \in \mathcal{U}$ runs. Also, we denote with S^l the lth instance that server $S \in \mathcal{S}$ runs. All instances finally output *accept* symbol and halt if their specified execution is correctly finished. The session identifier $\text{sid}_P^{l_i}$ of an instance P^{l_i} is represented via matching conversations, i.e., concatenations of messages which are sent and received between clients in the session, along with their identity strings, (initialized as *null*). Note that, we say that two instances $P_i^{l_i}$ and $P_j^{l_j}$ are *partnered*, and this session is *matching* if both $P_i^{l_i}$ and $P_j^{l_j}$ share the same sid but not *null*, and the partner identification set for $P_i^{l_i}$ coincides with the one for $P_j^{l_j}$.

3.2   Adversary Capabilities

An outside adversary or a malicious insider can obtain and modify messages on unauthenticated-links channels. Furthermore, the adversary is given oracle access to client and server instances. We remark that unlike the standard notion of an "oracle", in this model instances maintain state which is updated as the protocol progresses.

- Execute$(U_1^{l_1}, U_2^{l_2}, S_1^{l_3}, S_2^{l_4})$: This query models passive attacks. The output of this query consists of messages that were exchanged during the honest execution of the protocol among $U_1^{l_1}$, $U_2^{l_2}$, $S_1^{l_3}$ and $S_2^{l_4}$.
- SendClient(U^l, m) : This query models active attacks against a client. The output of this query consists of the message that the client instance U^l would generate on receipt of message m.
- SendServer(S^l, m) : This query models active attacks against servers. The output of this query consists of the message that the server instance S^l would generate on receipt of message m.

- SessionReveal(U^l) : This query models the misuse of session keys. The output of this query consists of the session key held by the client instance U^l if the session is completed for U^l. Otherwise, return $\perp$.
- StaticReveal(P) : This query models leakage of the static secret of P (i.e., the password between the client and the corresponding server, or the private information for the server). The output of this query consists of the static secret of P. Note that, there is no giving the adversary full control of P or revealing any ephemeral private information.
- EphemeralReveal(P^l) : This query models leakage of all session-specific information (ephemeral key) used by P^l. The output of this query consists of the ephemeral key of the instance P^l.
- EstablishParty(U^l, pw_U) : This query models the adversary to register a static secret pw_U on behalf of a client. In this way the adversary totally controls that client. Clients against whom the adversary did not issue this query are called *honest*.
- Test(U^l) : This query does not model the adversarial ability, but indistinguishability of the session key. At the beginning a hidden bit b is chosen. If no session key for the client instance U^l is defined, then return the undefined symbol $\perp$. Otherwise, return the session key for the client instance U^l if $b = 1$ or a random key from the same space if $b = 0$. Note that, the adversary can only one Test query at any time during the experiment. The target session is called the test session.
- TestPassword(U, pw') : This query does not model the adversarial ability, but no leakage of the password. If the guessed password pw' is just the same as the client U's password pw, then return 1. Otherwise, return 0. Note that, the adversary can only one TestPassword query at any time during the experiment.

3.3 Indistinguishability

Firstly, we consider the notion of indistinguishability. This notion provides security properties with respect to session keys, i.e., known-key security, key privacy against passive server, forward secrecy, resistance to MIM, resistance to KCI, resistance to UKS and resistance to LEP. Note that, to capture notions of forward secrecy and resistance to KCI, an adversary can obtain static keys in the test session.

The adversary is considered successful if it correctly guesses whether the challenge is the true session key or a random key. The adversary is allowed to make Execute, SendClient, SendServer, SessionReveal, StaticReveal, EphemeralReveal and Test queries, and outputs a guess bit b'. Let Succ^{ind} denote the event that $b' = b$ where b is the random bit chosen in the Test(U^l) query. Let $\bar{U}^{l'}$ be the partnered client of U^l in the test session. Note that, we restrict the adversary such that none of the following freshness conditions holds:

1. The adversary obtains the session key of sid_U^l or of $\text{sid}_{\bar{U}}^{l'}$.
2. The adversary asks no SendClient(U^l, m) or SendClient($\bar{U}^{l'}, m'$) query. Then the adversary either makes queries:

    – EphemeralReveal(U^l) or EphemeralReveal($\bar{U}^{l'}$).

3. There exists the partnered client $\bar{U}^{l'}$ and the adversary asks SendClient($\bar{U}^{l'}, m$) query. Then the adversary either makes queries:
    – StaticReveal(U),StaticReveal(SU), StaticReveal($S\bar{U}$), EphemeralReveal(U^i) for any session i or EphemeralReveal($\bar{U}^{l'}$).

4. The adversary asks SendClient(U^l, m) query. Then the adversary either makes queries:
    – StaticReveal($\bar{U}$), StaticReveal($S\bar{U}$), StaticReveal(SU), EphemeralReveal(U^l) or EphemeralReveal($\bar{U}^i$) for any session i.

Now, the adversary $\mathcal{A}$'s advantage is formally defined by:

$$\mathsf{Adv}^{ind}(\mathcal{A}) = |2 \cdot \Pr[\mathsf{Succ}^{ind}] - 1| \quad \text{and} \quad \mathsf{Adv}^{ind}(t, R) = \max_{\mathcal{A}}\{\mathsf{Adv}^{ind}(\mathcal{A})\},$$

where the maximum is over all $\mathcal{A}$ with time-complexity at most t and using the number of queries to its oracle at most R.

We say a cross realm PSAKE satisfies indistinguishability of the session key if the advantage Adv^{ind} is only negligibly larger than $n \cdot q_{send}/|\mathcal{D}|$, where n is a constant and q_{send} is the number of send queries, and parties who complete matching sessions compute the same session key.

Capturing Security Properties. First, in the freshness condition 3 and 4, if the adversary poses SendClient query for a client in the test session, we have to prohibit the adversary from posing EphemeralReveal query for the peer of the client for any session because the adversary can obtain the static private key by offDA if an ephemeral private key of a session is leaked. That is, EphemeralReveal query for a session has the same effect as StaticReveal query. If both the static private key and the ephemeral private key of a client in the test session are leaked, we cannot guarantee any security in the test session trivially. Thus, these restrictions are needed. The condition of known-key security is represented as the adversary can obtain session keys except one of the test session by SessionReveal query. The condition of forward secrecy and key privacy against passive servers is represented as the freshness condition 2, that is, the adversary can obtain static and ephemeral private key of servers by StaticReveal and EphemeralReveal query but no SendClient query and EphemeralReveal query to clients for the test session. This condition can be understood that the adversary has the same capability as passive servers, and so it corresponds to key privacy against passive servers. On the other hand, this condition can be understood that the adversary try to obtain information of previously established session key (i.e., no SendClient query) by using static secrets of the client and the corresponding server, and so it corresponds to forward secrecy. MIM is represented as the freshness condition 3, that is, the adversary can freely eavesdrop messages, obtain ephemeral private key of servers, and send any message to honest clients by Execute and SendClient queries but no StaticReveal query to the target client and its corresponding server. KCI is also represented as the freshness condition 4, that is, the adversary can obtain the password of the target client by StaticReveal query but cannot ask SendClient query or StaticReveal query to the partnered client and its corresponding server. LEP is represented as the adversary can obtain ephemeral keys of servers on the test session by EphemeralReveal query.

By the definition of indistinguishability, we can guarantee to prevent these attacks in our model.

3.4   Password Protection

Next, we consider the notion of password protection. This notion provides security properties with respect to passwords, i.e., resistance to UDonDA and to offDA. Beyond the notion of indistinguishability, the notion of password protection is needed because we have to consider security for passwords against attacks by insiders (i.e., the partnered client and its corresponding server) which can trivially know the session key. So, just the notion of indistinguishability cannot capture insider attacks. Also, we cannot allow the adversary to obtain ephemeral private keys of the target client. Given the ephemeral key the target password is easily derived by offDA because the session key in a session deterministically depends on the client's ephemeral key, the password, and communication received from the other party.

The adversary is considered successful if it correctly guesses the password between a client and the corresponding server. The adversary is allowed to make Execute, SendClient, SendServer, SessionReveal, StaticReveal, EphemeralReveal and TestPassword queries. Let Succ^{pw} denote the event that $\mathsf{TestPassword}(U)$ outputs 1. Note that, we restrict the adversary such that none of the following freshness condition holds:

- We suppose that S is a corresponding server of U. Then the adversary either makes queries:
  - $\mathsf{StaticReveal}(U)$, $\mathsf{StaticReveal}(S)$ or $\mathsf{EphemeralReveal}(U^i)$ for any session i.

Now, the adversary $\mathcal{A}$'s advantage is formally defined by:

$$\mathsf{Adv}^{pw}(\mathcal{A}) = \Pr[\mathsf{Succ}^{pw}] \quad \text{and} \quad \mathsf{Adv}^{pw}(t, R) = \max_{\mathcal{A}}\{\mathsf{Adv}^{pw}(\mathcal{A})\},$$

where the maximum is over all $\mathcal{A}$ with time-complexity at most t and using the number of queries to its oracle at most R.

We say a cross realm PSAKE satisfies password protection if the advantage Adv^{pw} is only negligibly larger than $n \cdot q_{send}/|\mathcal{D}|$, where n is a constant and q_{send} is the number of send queries which messages are found as "invalid" by a server. "Invalid" message means the message which is not generated according to the protocol description.

Capturing Security Properties.   UDonDA is represented as the adversary can unlimitedly use SendClient and SendServer queries as far as the party does not find that the query is "invalid". offDA is represented as the adversary can be the insider by SessionReveal, StaticReveal and EphemeralReveal queries except the target client and her corresponding server.

By the definition of password protection, we can guarantee to prevent these attacks in our model.

3.5   Mutual Authentication

Finally, we consider the notion of mutual authentication. This notion provides the security property with respect to authentication, i.e., resistance to UKS. The notion of mutual authentication is needed because the adversary may try to corrupt just authentication between clients without knowing any information of the session key and password in UKS scenario. The adversary can play a malicious insider by EstablishParty query.

The adversary is allowed to make Execute, SendClient, SendServer, SessionReveal, StaticReveal, EphemeralReveal and EstablishParty queries. Let Succ^{ma} denote the event that some honest client U accepts a session and shares a common session key with another honest client $\bar{U}$, but it has no partner and there is no matching session. Note that, we restrict that none of the following freshness condition holds:

- We suppose that SU and $S\bar{U}$ are corresponding servers of clients U and $\bar{U}$. Then the adversary either makes queries:
  - StaticReveal(U), StaticReveal($\bar{U}$), StaticReveal(SU), StaticReveal($S\bar{U}$), EphemeralReveal(U^i) for any session i or EphemeralReveal($\bar{U}^i$) for any session i.

Now, the adversary $\mathcal{A}$'s advantage is formally defined by:

$$\text{Adv}^{ma}(\mathcal{A}) = \Pr[\text{Succ}^{ma}] \quad \text{and} \quad \text{Adv}^{ma}(t, R) = \max_{\mathcal{A}}\{\text{Adv}^{ma}(\mathcal{A})\},$$

where the maximum is over all $\mathcal{A}$ with time-complexity at most t and using the number of queries to its oracle at most R.

We say a cross realm PSAKE satisfies password protection if the advantage Adv^{ma} is only negligible.

Capturing Security Properties.   UKS is represented as the condition that honest parties who compute the same session key are not partnered. That is, the adversary can establish a malicious insider by EstablishParty query and try to make a honest client A which thinks that he shares the session key with the insider share the session key with an another honest client B.

By the definition of mutual authentication, we can guarantee to prevent this attack in our model.

4   Proposed Scheme

In this section, we show our cross-realm PSAKE scheme.

4.1   Notation

Let p and q be large primes such that $p = 2q + 1^2$ and let g be a generator of a finite cyclic group G of prime order p. $A, B \in \mathcal{U}$ are identities of two clients

---

[2] Such a safe prime is needed to prevent small subgroup confinement attacks [22].

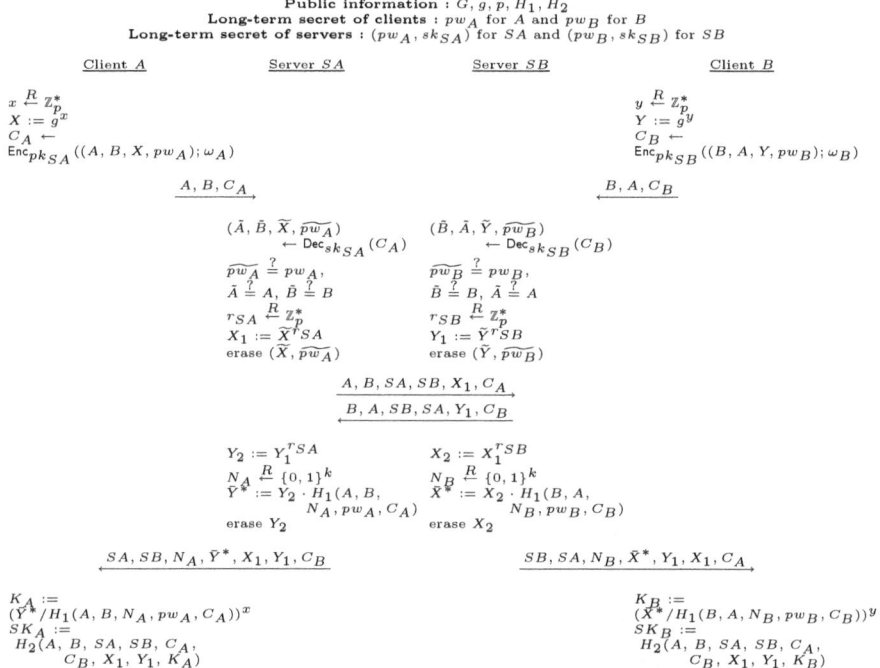

Public information : G, g, p, H_1, H_2
Long-term secret of clients : pw_A for A and pw_B for B
Long-term secret of servers : (pw_A, sk_{SA}) for SA and (pw_B, sk_{SB}) for SB

Fig. 3. Our protocol

in two different realms, and $SA, SB \in \mathcal{S}$ are identities of their corresponding servers respectively. (Gen, Enc, Dec) is a public-key encryption scheme, where $\mathsf{Gen}(1^k)$ is key generation algorithm, $\mathsf{Enc}_{pk}(m; \omega)$ is encryption algorithm of a message m using a public key pk and randomness ω, and $\mathsf{Dec}_{sk}(c)$ is decryption algorithm of a cipher-text c using a private key sk. A and SA (resp. B and SB) have shared common secret password pw_A (resp. pw_B), and SA and SB have pre-established their private keys sk_{SA} and sk_{SB} with their public keys pk_{SA} and pk_{SB}. We assume that there is an authenticated channel between SA and SB.[3] $H_1 : \{0,1\}^* \to G$ and $H_2 : \{0,1\}^* \to \{0,1\}^k$ are hash functions modeled as random oracles, where $Cspace$ is the space of a cipher-text for (Gen, Enc, Dec) and k is a sufficiently large security parameter.

For simplicity, we omit "(mod p)" in this paper when computing the modular exponentiation. "$v \xleftarrow{R} V$" means randomly choosing an element v of a set V.

Here, we show the construction of our cross-realm PSAKE scheme. Our protocol has the indirect communication structure as YB scheme. To guarantee resistance to resistance to KCI, we apply public-key encryption for servers like PSAKE scheme in [2]. Our protocol appears in Figure 3.

---

[3] In the YB scheme and the WZ construction, they assume authenticated private communication channel between servers. Thus, our assumption of channel is relaxed than previous cross-realm C2C-PAKE schemes.

4.2 Design Principles

Our protocol can be viewed as an extension of YB scheme. The main difference consists in use of public-key encryption. Thus, as Cliff et al.'s C2C-PAKE scheme [2], our scheme is not password-only setting on the whole. However, our scheme is password-only setting for clients since clients can keep only passwords.

First, upon receiving an input from a client the corresponding server verifies the validity of encrypted password of the client and him. Such an explicit verification prevents UDonDA and KCI. We cannot do an explicit verification with password only (i.e., without public-key techniques) because passwords have low-entropy and then the adversary trivially obtain the password by an offDA. This setting plays the same role as the encryption based authenticator in Cliff et al.'s C2C-PAKE scheme. Applying servers' public-keys may put a burden on clients because they have to verify servers' public-keys in advance, and the certificate infrastructure is needed. However, we can easily resolve this problem by applying *certificateless encryption* [23] for servers instead of standard public-key encryption for servers. Since clients can encrypt messages by using only corresponding servers' ID and servers' public-key without certificate, clients need no verifying servers' public-keys. If we replace use of public-key encryption to use of certificateless encryption, security of our scheme is not changed.

Next, erasing ephemeral states except necessary states is needed for resistance to LEP as the technique of [21]. Even if EphemeralReveal query is asked, information of passwords and the session key do not leak from leakage information since all critical states are deleted immediately when these states are used.

Finally, when a client blinds X with his password, we make the client include the identities of both clients into the computation of the ciphertext. This procedure prevents KCI and UKS by a malicious client insider as the technique of Choo et al. [24].

5 Security of Our Scheme

In this section, we show security properties of our scheme.

5.1 Building Blocks

We recall the definition of the decisional Diffie-Hellman assumptions which we use in the security proof of our scheme. Let p be a prime and let g be a generator of a finite cyclic group G of prime order p.

Decisional Diffie-Hellman Assumption (DDH). We can define the DDH assumption by defining two experiments, $\mathsf{Exp}_{g,p}^{ddh\text{-}real}(\mathcal{I})$ and $\mathsf{Exp}_{g,p}^{ddh\text{-}rand}(\mathcal{I})$. For a distinguisher $\mathcal{I}$, inputs (g, g^u, g^v, Z) are provided, where $(u,v) \in_R (\mathbb{Z}_p)^2$. $Z = g^{uv}$ in $\mathsf{Exp}_{g,p}^{ddh\text{-}real}(\mathcal{I})$ and $Z = g^w$ in $\mathsf{Exp}_{g,p}^{ddh\text{-}rand}(\mathcal{I})$, where $w \in_R \mathbb{Z}_p$. Let $(g, g^u, g^v, g^{uv}) \in \mathbf{D}$ be the tuple in $\mathsf{Exp}_{g,p}^{ddh\text{-}real}(\mathcal{I})$ and $(g, g^u, g^v, Z = g^w) \in \mathbf{R}$ be the tuple in $\mathsf{Exp}_{g,p}^{ddh\text{-}rand}(\mathcal{I})$. We say that the (t, ϵ)-DDH assumption on G holds if the maximum value of $|\Pr[\mathsf{Exp}_{g,p}^{ddh\text{-}real}(\mathcal{I}) = 1] - \Pr[\mathsf{Exp}_{g,p}^{ddh\text{-}rand}(\mathcal{I}) = 1]|$ over all $\mathcal{I}$ with a time-complexity at most t is equal or less than ϵ.

5.2 Main Theorems

Theorem 1. *Assuming the DDH problem is hard and* (Gen, Enc, Dec) *is a semantically secure public-key encryption scheme, then our scheme satisfies indistinguishability of the session key.*

Theorem 2. *Assuming* (Gen, Enc, Dec) *is a semantically secure public-key encryption scheme, then our scheme satisfies password protection.*

Theorem 3. *Assuming the DDH problem is hard and* (Gen, Enc, Dec) *is a semantically secure public-key encryption scheme, then our scheme satisfies mutual authentication.*

Due to space considerations, the proofs of Theorem 1, 2 and 3 will be shown in the full version of this paper.

6 Conclusion

This paper showed an extension of PSAKE to the cross-realm setting. Firstly, we pointed out that previous security definitions of cross-realm C2C-PAKE cannot capture all desirable security requirements for cross-realm PSAKE. Next, we proposed a formal security definition of cross-realm PSAKE which captures all desirable security requirements. Finally, we introduced a cross-realm PSAKE protocol with optimal rounds for client and proved its security in the sense of our definition.

Our scheme uses the public-key encryption as a building block in order to guarantee resistance to KCI, LEP and UDonDA. However, public-key encryption schemes are time-consuming. Thus, a remaining problem of further researches is more efficient construction which satisfies strong security.

References

1. Steiner, M., Tsudik, G., Waidner, M.: Refinement and Extension of Encrypted Key Exchange. ACM Operating Systems Review 29(3), 22–30 (1995)
2. Cliff, Y., Tin, Y.S.T., Boyd, C.: Password Based Server Aided Key Exchange. In: Zhou, J., Yung, M., Bao, F. (eds.) ACNS 2006. LNCS, vol. 3989, pp. 146–161. Springer, Heidelberg (2006)
3. Yoneyama, K.: Efficient and Strongly Secure Password-Based Server Aided Key Exchange. In: Chowdhury, D.R., Rijmen, V., Das, A. (eds.) INDOCRYPT 2008. LNCS, vol. 5365, pp. 172–184. Springer, Heidelberg (2008)
4. Ding, Y., Horster, P.: Undetectable On-line Password Guessing Attacks. Operating Systems Review 29(4), 77–86 (1995)
5. Lin, C.L., Sun, H.M., Hwang, T.: Three-party Encrypted Key Exchange: Attacks and A Solution. ACM Operating Systems Review 34(4), 12–20 (2000)
6. Abdalla, M., Fouque, P.-A., Pointcheval, D.: Password-Based Authenticated Key Exchange in the Three-Party Setting. In: Vaudenay, S. (ed.) PKC 2005. LNCS, vol. 3386, pp. 65–84. Springer, Heidelberg (2005)
7. Abdalla, M., Pointcheval, D.: Interactive Diffie-Hellman Assumptions with Applications to Password-Based Authentication. In: S. Patrick, A., Yung, M. (eds.) FC 2005. LNCS, vol. 3570, pp. 341–356. Springer, Heidelberg (2005)

8. Byun, J.W., Jeong, I.R., Lee, D.H., Park, C.S.: Password-Authenticated Key Exchange between Clients with Different Passwords. In: Deng, R.H., Qing, S., Bao, F., Zhou, J. (eds.) ICICS 2002. LNCS, vol. 2513, pp. 134–146. Springer, Heidelberg (2002)
9. Chen, L.: A Weakness of the Password-Authenticated Key Agreement between Clients with Different Passwords Scheme. In: ISO/IEC JTC 1/SC27 N3716 (2003)
10. Wang, S., Wang, J., Xu, M.: Weaknesses of a Password-Authenticated Key Exchange Protocol between Clients with Different Passwords. In: Jakobsson, M., Yung, M., Zhou, J. (eds.) ACNS 2004. LNCS, vol. 3089, pp. 414–425. Springer, Heidelberg (2004)
11. Kim, J., Kim, S., Kwak, J., Won, D.: Cryptanalysis and Improvement of Password Authenticated Key Exchange Scheme between Clients with Different Passwords. In: Laganá, A., Gavrilova, M.L., Kumar, V., Mun, Y., Tan, C.J.K., Gervasi, O. (eds.) ICCSA 2004. LNCS, vol. 3043, pp. 895–902. Springer, Heidelberg (2004)
12. Phan, R.C.W., Goi, B.M.: Cryptanalysis of an Improved Client-to-Client Password-Authenticated Key Exchange (C2C-PAKE) Scheme. In: Ioannidis, J., Keromytis, A.D., Yung, M. (eds.) ACNS 2005. LNCS, vol. 3531, pp. 33–39. Springer, Heidelberg (2005)
13. Diffie, W., van Oorschot, P.C., Wiener, M.J.: Authentication and Authenticated Key Exchanges. Des. Codes Cryptography 2(2), 107–125 (1992)
14. Byun, J.W., Lee, D.H., Lim, J.: Efficient and Provably Secure Client-to-Client Password-Based Key Exchange Protocol. In: Zhou, X., Li, J., Shen, H.T., Kitsuregawa, M., Zhang, Y. (eds.) APWeb 2006. LNCS, vol. 3841, pp. 830–836. Springer, Heidelberg (2006)
15. Phan, R.C.W., Goi, B.M.: Cryptanalysis of Two Provably Secure Cross-Realm C2C-PAKE Protocols. In: Barua, R., Lange, T. (eds.) INDOCRYPT 2006. LNCS, vol. 4329, pp. 104–117. Springer, Heidelberg (2006)
16. Yin, Y., Bao, L.: Secure Cross-Realm C2C-PAKE Protocol. In: Batten, L.M., Safavi-Naini, R. (eds.) ACISP 2006. LNCS, vol. 4058, pp. 395–406. Springer, Heidelberg (2006)
17. Wang, F., Zhang, Y.: A New Security Model for Cross-Realm C2C-PAKE Protocol. In: Cryptology ePrint Archive: 2007/342 (2007)
18. Wu, S., Zhu, Y.: Password-Authenticated Key Exchange between Clients in a Cross-Realm Setting. In: Cao, J., Li, M., Wu, M.-Y., Chen, J. (eds.) NPC 2008. LNCS, vol. 5245, pp. 94–104. Springer, Heidelberg (2008)
19. Feng, D., Xu, J.: A New Client-to-Client Password-Authenticated Key Agreement Protocol. In: Chee, Y.M., Li, C., Ling, S., Wang, H., Xing, C. (eds.) IWCC 2009. LNCS, vol. 5557, pp. 63–76. Springer, Heidelberg (2009)
20. Jin, W., Xu, J.: An Efficient and Provably Secure Cross-Realm Client-to-Client Password-Authenticated Key Agreement Protocol with Smart Cards. In: Garay, J.A., Miyaji, A., Otsuka, A. (eds.) CANS 2009. LNCS, vol. 5888, pp. 299–314. Springer, Heidelberg (2009)
21. LaMacchia, B.A., Lauter, K., Mityagin, A.: Stronger Security of Authenticated Key Exchange. In: Susilo, W., Liu, J.K., Mu, Y. (eds.) ProvSec 2007. LNCS, vol. 4784, pp. 1–16. Springer, Heidelberg (2007)
22. Lim, C.H., Lee, P.J.: A Key Recovery Attack on Discrete Log-based Schemes Using a Prime Order Subgroup. In: Kaliski Jr., B.S. (ed.) CRYPTO 1997. LNCS, vol. 1294, pp. 249–263. Springer, Heidelberg (1997)
23. Dent, A.W.: A survey of certificateless encryption schemes and security models. Int. J. Inf. Sec. 7(5), 349–377 (2008)
24. Choo, K.-K.R., Boyd, C., Hitchcock, Y.: Examining Indistinguishability-Based Proof Models for Key Establishment Protocols. In: Roy, B. (ed.) ASIACRYPT 2005. LNCS, vol. 3788, pp. 585–604. Springer, Heidelberg (2005)

A Two-Party Protocol with Trusted Initializer for Computing the Inner Product

Rafael Dowsley[1], Jeroen van de Graaf[2],
Davidson Marques[3], and Anderson C.A. Nascimento[1]

[1] Department of Electrical Engineering, University of Brasília
Campus Universitário Darcy Ribeiro, Brasília, CEP: 70910-900, Brazil
rafaeldowsley@redes.unb.br, andclay@ene.unb.br
[2] Department of Computer Science, Universidade Federal de Ouro Preto
Ouro Preto, Minas Gerais, CEP: 35400-000, Brazil
jvdg@iceb.ufop.br
[3] Department of Computer Science, Universidade Federal de Minas Gerais,
Belo Horizonte, Minas Gerais, CEP 31270-901, Brazil
rodrigue@dcc.ufmg.br

Abstract. We propose the first protocol for securely computing the inner product modulo an integer m between two distrustful parties based on a trusted initializer, i.e. a trusted party that interacts with the players solely during a setup phase. We obtain a very simple protocol with universally composable security. As an application of our protocol, we obtain a solution for securely computing linear equations.

1 Introduction

Situations in which two parties wish to perform some joint computation arise naturally. Internet auctions are a well-known example. There are also many situations in which two organizations would like to compare their data bases, but privacy regulation, or the fact them being competitors, does not allow the simple solution: just sharing the data and do the computation.

There are many results showing that *any* function can be computed between two parties, by transforming the algorithm to a Boolean circuit and then emulating this circuit cryptographically [13]. Unfortunately, the cost of this emulation is prohibitively high, and the evaluation of even modest functions is often impractical. For this reason it is interesting to search for cryptographic primitives that efficiently implement the evaluation of some function f, in which f is not merely a Boolean, but some higher level primitive.

In this paper the primitive we study is computing the inner product modulo an arbitrary integer m. In other words, Alice provides an input vector $\overrightarrow{x}$, Bob provides an input vector $\overrightarrow{y}$, and they want to compute the inner product $\langle \overrightarrow{x} \cdot \overrightarrow{y} \rangle \bmod m = \sum_{i=1}^{n} x_i y_i \bmod m$. This is an interesting primitive since it is sufficiently high-level to

Y. Chung and M. Yung (Eds.): WISA 2010, LNCS 6513, pp. 337–350, 2011.

have some immediate applications. It pops up in two-party protocols for linear alge-
bra, statistical analysis, computational geometry and data mining. Additionally, we also
propose a protocol for securely solving linear systems based on our secure solution for
computing the inner product.

It is well-known that two-party computation is only possible with some additional
assumption, either about the computational resources available to the parties (e.g. polynomial time, bounded memory), either about the channel available between them (e.g.
a noisy channel, oblivious transfer), or some trust assumption (e.g. the help of some
trusted party or honest majority in a multiparty scenario). Here we study the inner product protocol under the assumption that a trusted initializer is available. This is a party
who sends two different, but correlated, messages to the parties *before* the protocol
starts, then he leaves. This model has appeared in many places in the literature, but was
first formalized by Beaver in [1]

There are situations in which this model, with a trusted initializer, is realistic. For
instance, suppose two hospitals want to do some combined statistical analysis on their
data, but privacy legislation prohibits them to compare patient records directly. Con-
ceivably, some third, neutral entity (say, the Association of All Hospitals) could help
them to bootstrap the protocol in some session with all the three parties present. The
third entity creates two DVDs with the correlated data, then, witnessed by the two others, wipes (or destroys) the platform that was used to create these DVDs, erasing all
data.

In a somewhat looser trust model, we can suppose that the parties do not meet, but
that parties buy their correlated data on the internet as originally proposed by Beaver
in [1].

Observe that in the context of digital certificates such providers exist already. There
they are called certification authorities.

Comparison with Other Work

We briefly relate our work to previous results stated in the literature.

Even tough the commodity based model (where parties receive cryptographic com-
modities/data from off-line servers before the protocol starts) was formalized just in [1],
it has appeared in different flavors throughout the literature. For instance, in some sense,
a Key Distribution Center can be interpreted as a trusted initializer for the task of private
communication between two parties [7]. In [11], Rivest shows how to do Bit Commitment and Oblivious Transfer with a trusted initializer.

These protocols were generalized to oblivious polynomial evaluation and linear functional evaluation [9], verifiable secret sharing and two party computation of a multiplication in a field of characteristic p [10]. Another interesting primitive is oblivious linear
function evaluation [8]. As far as we know, no work has been published on the inner
product with a trusted initializer.

However, the inner product has been studied in other models. In fact, it attracted a
lot of attention from the data mining community. See for instance the work of [12, 3]
and of [5]. Unfortunately, many of the protocols proposed (including for other functions, not just for inner product) are seriously flawed, as already has been noted by
others, see [5, 6]. To repair the situation, Goethals et al. propose a protocol using

homomomorphic encryption and provide a security proof [5]. We show that the commodity based framework provides a way to obtain an efficient, simple and elegant solution for the secure two-party inner product problem and for solving linear equations. Moreover, we also show that it is possible to obtain this result in the strictest model of security available nowadays, that presented by the universal composability model [2].

Our Contributions

In this paper, we present a protocol for computing the inner product modulo any integer m with a trusted initializer, and prove it secure in the universal composability framework [2]. We restrict our analysis to the case of static adversaries.

We also show that the problems of solving linear equations securely can use the inner product protocol as a subprotocol:

Solving linear equation. Alice input a matrix X and a vector $\overrightarrow{x}$, Bob inputs a matrix Y and a vector $\overrightarrow{y}$. They want the vector $\overrightarrow{z}$ that solves the equation $(X+Y)\cdot\overrightarrow{z} = \overrightarrow{x}+\overrightarrow{y}$

It should be emphasized that this last protocols can only be proven secure assuming that we use some finite field $\mathbb{F}$ of cardinality $m = p^k$. The reason is that solving linear equations requires the ability to compute inverse elements, which are only well-defined over fields. In addition, our techniques are only able to suitable for *finite* fields.

The Thesis of Du

An important starting point for this research was the Ph.D. thesis of Du. Here, a strong point is made for the need of practical two-party computations, with several interesting applications to privacy-preserving data mining and statistical computing.

It quickly became obvious that the thesis leaves much to be desired from a theoretical point of view: no formal model is presented, and no formal security proofs are given. However, it took several months to realize that the situation was much more serious.

In the first place, often it is not defined to which set the values used in the protocols belong. Almost always there are several auxiliary variables that take on a random value, i.e. that are randomly chosen. However, in most cases the underlying set is assumed to be $\mathbb{Z}$, which does not allow a uniform distribution. For this reason, any attempt to prove security fails and the protocols are insecure. In some situations this can be remedied choosing a large modulus M and performing the computations mod M. For instance, the inner product protocol can be modified in this way, and the result is secure.

In the second place, Du proposes a division protocol in $\mathbb{Z}$ that is not secure. This was shown in [6], which presents another, much more elaborate, division protocol. One can think: no problem, we will do our computations in a finite field. But that almost never resolve the problem. $\mathbb{Z}$ and $\mathbb{Q}$ are well-ordered sets, but finite fields are not. For instance, in $\mathbb{Q}$ one knows that $x < y$ implies $1/x > 1/y$, but in a finite field this does not make sense, they have no notion of small and large.

In the case of the protocol for solving a linear equation over a finite field, it *does* make sense to consider this question over $\mathbb{F}_q$. But it is not clear how to extend this protocol to

$\mathbb{Z}$ or $\mathbb{Q}$. Here, choosing a large (prime) modulus does not work. This reduces severely the applicability of this protocol. The situation for several other protocols is worse. For instance, restricting the protocol for linear programming to $\mathbb{F}_q$ does not make sense, and in $\mathbb{Z}$ the protocol proposed is hopelessly insecure.

2   The Universal Composability Framework

The objective of the UC framework is to allow the truly modular design of cryptographic protocols. The crux of the UC framework is the introduction of an environment, $\mathcal{Z}$, who supplies input to the parties, Alice, Bob and the Adversary, $\mathcal{A}$, and receives there outputs.

In order to prove security of a specific protocol implementation, we will compare it with some idealized version of the protocol and show that $\mathcal{Z}$ cannot tell the difference. This idealized version is called the (ideal) *functionality*, and can be seen as some black box that does exactly what the protocol is supposed to do, i.e. follow the protocol specification faithfully. Observe that the functionality must also deal with invalid inputs or other unexpected behavior from the parties, because even in the idealized model we have to assume that parties can be corrupted and behave dishonestly, by changing their inputs, for instance.

The whole purpose of the UC security definition is to avoid the existence of attacks possible in the real protocol implementation that do not exist in the ideal model. In other words, we want that each attack against the real protocol corresponds to an attack against the ideal protocol. This proves that the real protocol is at least as secure as the ideal functionality, so, assuming the latter is well-defined, we obtain a secure protocol implementation.

More precisely, we want to show that for every adversary in the real protocol, denoted $\mathcal{A}$, there exists an ideal adversary in the ideal protocol, denotes $\mathcal{S}$, such that no environment exists that can tell the difference:

$$\forall \mathcal{A} \; \exists \mathcal{S} \; \forall \mathcal{Z} \; : \; \text{REAL}_{\pi, \mathcal{A}, \mathcal{Z}} \equiv \text{IDEAL}_{\mathcal{F}_{\langle \overrightarrow{x} \cdot \overrightarrow{y} \rangle}, \mathcal{S}, \mathcal{Z}}$$

In this expression REAL stands for $\mathcal{Z}$'s output, defined as a single bit, after observing the real Alice and Bob running the protocol imlementation with real adversary $\mathcal{A}$, whereas IDEAL stands for $\mathcal{Z}$'s single bit output, after observing the ideal Alice and Bob running the functionality with ideal adversary $\mathcal{S}$. The probability distribution is taken over all the parties' random tapes. Observe that $\mathcal{Z}$ acts as a distinguisher, trying to tell the real and ideal model apart. The universal quantifier guarantees that this is impossible. Indistinguishability between families of probability distributions comes in various flavors: perfect, statistical and computational indistinguisability. In this paper we will only use perfect indistinguisability, meaning that the two distributions are identical.

3   The Inner Product Protocol

3.1   Protocol Specification and Notation

We briefly describe the players inputs and outputs specified by the protocol. In the following, we denote by $\mathbb{Z}_m$ the set $\{1, \cdots, m - 1\}$, by $\mathbb{Z}_m^n$ the space of all n-tuples of elements of $\mathbb{Z}_m$. The act of randomly choosing an element $\vec{x}$ from $\mathbb{Z}_m^n$ is represented by $\vec{x} \in_R \mathbb{Z}_m^n$. The players are conveniently named Alice and Bob, while the trusted initializer is called TI.

	Alice	Bob
input	$\vec{x} \in \mathbb{Z}_m^n$	$\vec{y} \in \mathbb{Z}_m^n$
output	$r \in \mathbb{Z}_m$	$\langle \vec{x} \cdot \vec{y} \rangle - r \in \mathbb{Z}_m$

3.2   Ideal Functionality for the Inner Product

We describe the ideal functionality for securely computing the inner product.

- Upon receiving an (ASENDSINPUT, $\vec{x}$, sid) message from A:

Ignore any subsequent ASENDSINPUT messages. If $\vec{x} \notin \mathbb{Z}_m^n$, then send an INVALIDINPUT message to A and B and stop. If no BSENDSINPUT message has been received from B, then store $\vec{x}$ and sid, and send the public delayed output (AINPUTRECEIVED, sid) to B; else choose $r \in_R \mathbb{Z}_m$, set $u := r$ and $v := \langle \vec{x} \cdot \vec{y} \rangle - r$, send the public delayed outputs (AGETSOUTPUT, u, sid) to A and (BGETSOUTPUT, v, sid) to B.

- Upon receiving a (BSENDSINPUT, $\vec{y}$, sid) message from B:

Ignore any subsequent BSENDSINPUT messages. If $\vec{y} \notin \mathbb{Z}_m^n$, then send an INVALIDINPUT message to A and B and stop. If no ASENDSINPUT message has been received from A, then store $\vec{y}$ and sid, and send the public delayed output (BINPUTRECEIVED, sid) to A; else choose $r \in_R \mathbb{Z}_m$, set $u := r$ and $v := \langle \vec{x} \cdot \vec{y} \rangle - r$, send the public delayed outputs (AGETSOUTPUT, u, sid) to A and (BGETSOUTPUT, v, sid) to B.

It is interesting to observe that, depending on the security parameters, the ideal functionality might leak a lot of information on the players inputs. For instance, if n, the size of the vectors) is very low, and m, the modulus is very high, both parties can deduce the other's input. On the other hand, for $m = 2$ the protocol only gives the parity of the inner product, which is already meaningful for $n = 1$ in which case it reduces to the matchmaking problem.

3.3   Trusted Initializer Functionality

We also define an ideal functionality modeling the behavior of the trusted initializer.

- When first activated, choose $\vec{x_0} \in_R \mathbb{Z}_m^n$, $\vec{y_0} \in_R \mathbb{Z}_m^n$, compute $s_0 := \langle \vec{x_0} \cdot \vec{y_0} \rangle$ and distribute $\vec{x_0}$ to Alice and $(\vec{y_0}, s_0)$ to Bob.

3.4   Protocol Implementation

	Alice	Bob
TI	$\overrightarrow{x_0} \in_R \mathbb{Z}_m^n$	$\overrightarrow{y_0} \in_R \mathbb{Z}_m^n;$ $s_0 := \langle \overrightarrow{x_0} \cdot \overrightarrow{y_0} \rangle$
data sent by TI	$\mu_A := \overrightarrow{x_0}$	$\mu_B := (\overrightarrow{y_0}, s_0)$
input	$\overrightarrow{x} \in \mathbb{Z}_m^n$	$\overrightarrow{y} \in \mathbb{Z}_m^n$
protocol		(1) $\overrightarrow{y_1} := \overrightarrow{y} - \overrightarrow{y_0} \in \mathbb{Z}_m^n$ Send $\mu_1 := (\overrightarrow{y_1})$ to Alice
	(2) If μ_1 is invalid then abort $\overrightarrow{x_1} := \overrightarrow{x} + \overrightarrow{x_0} \in \mathbb{Z}_m^n$ $r \in_R \mathbb{Z}_m$ $r_1 := \langle \overrightarrow{x} \cdot \overrightarrow{y_1} \rangle - r$ Send $\mu_2 := (\overrightarrow{x_1}, r_1)$ to Bob	
		If μ_2 is invalid then abort
output	$u := r$	$v := \langle \overrightarrow{x_1} \cdot \overrightarrow{y_0} \rangle + r_1 - s_0$

It is straightforward to check the correctness of the protocol.

$$
\begin{aligned}
v := & \langle \overrightarrow{x_1} \cdot \overrightarrow{y_0} \rangle + r_1 - s_0 \\
= & \langle (\overrightarrow{x} + \overrightarrow{x_0}) \cdot \overrightarrow{y_0} \rangle + (\langle \overrightarrow{x} \cdot (\overrightarrow{y} - \overrightarrow{y_0}) \rangle - r) - \langle \overrightarrow{x_0} \cdot \overrightarrow{y_0} \rangle \\
= & \langle \overrightarrow{x} \cdot \overrightarrow{y_0} \rangle + \langle \overrightarrow{x_0} \cdot \overrightarrow{y_0} \rangle + \langle \overrightarrow{x} \cdot \overrightarrow{y} \rangle - \langle \overrightarrow{x} \cdot \overrightarrow{y_0} \rangle - r - \langle \overrightarrow{x_0} \cdot \overrightarrow{y_0} \rangle \\
= & \langle \overrightarrow{x} \cdot \overrightarrow{y} \rangle - r
\end{aligned}
$$

4   Security Proof

For clarity we write Alice and Bob in the proofs, to avoid confusion with the adversary $\mathcal{A}$. $\mathcal{S}$ runs A' internally. We will also denote all variables in the simulated environment with a prime $'$.

4.1   Alice Corrupted, Bob Honest

Simulation. $\mathcal{S}$ runs an internal (embedded) copy of $\mathcal{A}$ called A'. Observe that Alice is corrupted, so $\mathcal{S}$ has access to Alice's input $\overrightarrow{x}$. The interactions of A' with $\mathcal{S}$ are those of Alice in the real protocol with the other parties, $\mathcal{Z}$, the TI, and Bob. We now show how $\mathcal{S}$ acts when such interactions take place:

# Events	S's actions
1 Onset of the Simulation	Choose $\overrightarrow{x_0}' \in_R \mathbb{Z}_m^n$ and send $\mu_A' := \overrightarrow{x_0}'$ to A'
2 Get input $\overrightarrow{x}$	S forwards $\overrightarrow{x}$ from $\mathcal{Z}$, i.e. $\overrightarrow{x}' := \overrightarrow{x}$
3 Message (BINPUTRECEIVED, sid)	S feeds $\mu_1' := \overrightarrow{y_1}' \in_R \mathbb{Z}_m^n$ to A'
4 Message μ_2'	If A' sends $(\overrightarrow{x_1}', r_1')$ as message μ_2', then S sends a message (ASENDSINPUT, $\overrightarrow{x}$, sid) to $\mathcal{F}_{\langle \overrightarrow{x} \cdot \overrightarrow{y} \rangle}$. If A' sends something invalid in μ_2', then S sends something invalid to $\mathcal{F}_{\langle \overrightarrow{x} \cdot \overrightarrow{y} \rangle}$.
5 Output u';	As long as no reponse from $\mathcal{F}_{\langle \overrightarrow{x} \cdot \overrightarrow{y} \rangle}$ is received, S does nothing, even if this means waiting forever.
	When an INVALIDINPUT message is received, S forwards it to $\mathcal{Z}$.
	When an AGETSOUTPUT message is received, S does the following: It lets the functionality deliver the message (BGETSOUTPUT, v, sid). S also intercepts the simulated output $u' = r'$ and verifies if this value is consistent with the input $\overrightarrow{x}$, and the simulated messages μ_A', μ_1' and μ_2'. If consistent, S substitutes the simulated output u' for the real output u obtained from $\mathcal{F}_{\langle \overrightarrow{x} \cdot \overrightarrow{y} \rangle}$ by setting $u_S = u$; else it sets $u_S = u'$. Then u_S is sent to $\mathcal{Z}$ through Alice's interface.

Indistinguishability. We make the following observations:

1. Independent of $\mathcal{A}$, $\mathcal{Z}$ can make Bob send no input or an invalid input. In the simulation, S behavior after sending the message copies this perfectly.
2. Whatever A''s strategy is, it either sends a valid or an invalid message μ_2'. If the message is invalid, both the simulated and the ideal protocol will send INVALIDINPUT to the two parties, which will be forwarded to $\mathcal{Z}$.
3. Even if A' sent a valid message μ_2', it can still deviate from the protocol by sending a completely different output. Here, deviate means to send an output u' that is not consistent with the input $\overrightarrow{x}' = \overrightarrow{x}$ and the messages μ_A', μ_1' and μ_2'. In the case A' did deviate, S detects this and does nothing, i.e. it forwards the output produced by A' directly to $\mathcal{Z}$.
4. In the case A' did follow the protocol, S substitutes A''s output u_s for the output $u_{\mathcal{F}}$ obtained from $\mathcal{F}_{\langle \overrightarrow{x} \cdot \overrightarrow{y} \rangle}$.

If we consider A' (and $\mathcal{A}$) as deterministic algorithms whose probabilism comes from a random tape, it follows that A' behavior is completely determined by these random bits, called s_A, the incoming message μ_A', the input $\overrightarrow{x}$ and the incoming message μ_1'. We already know that the random bits s_A and the input $\overrightarrow{x}$ have the same distribution in the real and ideal protocol, because of the way the model is defined.

So in order to show that $\forall \mathcal{A} \ \exists S \ \forall \mathcal{Z} \ : \text{REAL}_{\pi, \mathcal{A}, \mathcal{Z}} \equiv \text{IDEAL}_{\mathcal{F}_{\langle \overrightarrow{x} \cdot \overrightarrow{y} \rangle}, S, \mathcal{Z}}$, it suffices to show that the incoming message μ_A' produced by S has the same distribution as the incoming message μ_A produced by the TI in the real protocol. But this is trivial, since both are generated from the same distribution, the uniform distribution on $\mathbb{Z}_m^n$.

In addition, we must show that μ'_1 produced by $\mathcal{S}$ and μ_1 sent by Bob have the same distribution. Observe that $\mu_1 := \overrightarrow{y_1} := \overrightarrow{y} - \overrightarrow{y_0}$, with $\overrightarrow{y_0} \in_R \mathbb{Z}_m^n$. Since both TI and Bob are honest in the real protocol, it follows that both μ'_1 and μ_1 are generated according to the uniform distribution on $\mathbb{Z}_m^n$.

So we conclude that A'''s incoming messages in the simulated protocol have a distribution identical to $\mathcal{A}$'s incoming message in the real protocol. It follows therefore that the ideal and real protocol distributions are perfectly indistinguishable from $\mathcal{Z}$ point of view, which completes the proof.

4.2 Alice Honest, Bob Corrupted

The proof of this case is very much along the same lines as the previous case: $\mathcal{S}$ runs an internal (embedded) copy of $\mathcal{A}$ called B'. Observe that Bob is corrupted, so $\mathcal{S}$ has access to Bob's input $\overrightarrow{y}$. The interactions of B' with $\mathcal{S}$ are those of Bob in the real protocol with the other parties, $\mathcal{Z}$, the TI, and Alice. We give an overview how $\mathcal{S}$ acts

# Events	$\mathcal{S}$'s actions
1 Onset of the Simulation	$\mathcal{S}$ sets $\overrightarrow{y_0}' \in_R \mathbb{Z}_m^n$, $s'_0 \in_R \mathbb{Z}_m$ and feeds $\mu'_B := (\overrightarrow{y_0}', s'_0)$ to B'
2 Get input $\overrightarrow{y}$;	$\mathcal{S}$ forwards $\overrightarrow{y}$ from $\mathcal{Z}$, i.e. $\overrightarrow{y}' := \overrightarrow{y}$
3 Message μ'_1	If B' sends $\overrightarrow{y_1}'$ as message μ'_1, then $\mathcal{S}$ sends a message (BSENDSINPUT, $\overrightarrow{y}$, $bsid$) to $\mathcal{F}_{\langle \overrightarrow{x} \cdot \overrightarrow{y} \rangle}$. If B' sends something invalid in μ'_1, then $\mathcal{S}$ sends something invalid to $\mathcal{F}_{\langle \overrightarrow{x} \cdot \overrightarrow{y} \rangle}$. $\mathcal{S}$ lets the functionality deliver the message (BINPUTRECEIVED, sid)
4 Message (BGETSOUTPUT, v, sid)	$\mathcal{S}$ sets $(\overrightarrow{x_1}' \in_R \mathbb{Z}_m^n, r'_1 \in_R \mathbb{Z}_m^n$ and feeds $\mu'_2 := (\overrightarrow{x_1}', r'_1)$ to B'; $\mathcal{S}$ lets the functionality deliver the message (AGETSOUTPUT, u, sid) to A. $\mathcal{S}$ intercepts the simulated output $v' = \langle \overrightarrow{x_1}' \cdot \overrightarrow{y_0}' \rangle + r'_1 - s'_0$ and verifies if this value is consistent with the input $\overrightarrow{y}$, and the simulated messages μ'_B, μ'_1 and μ'_2. If consistent, $\mathcal{S}$ substitutes the simulated output v' with the real output v obtained from $\mathcal{F}_{\langle \overrightarrow{x} \cdot \overrightarrow{y} \rangle}$ by setting $v_{\mathcal{S}} = v$; else it sets $v_{\mathcal{S}} = v'$. As long as no v' from B' is received, $\mathcal{S}$ does not forward the message BGETSOUTPUT, even if this means waiting forever. Then $v_{\mathcal{S}}$ is sent to $\mathcal{Z}$ through Bob's interface.

The proof of indistinguishability is almost identical to the previous case and is omitted.

4.3 Alice and Bob Honest

If neither party is corrupted, $\mathcal{A}$ simulates the Trusted Initializer Functionality, sees a transcript of the message sent between Alice and Bob and let the functionality send the public delayed outputs in the ideal protocol when $\mathcal{A}$ deliver the respective messages in the simulated execution.

4.4   Alice and Bob Corrupted

The protocol is a deterministic function of the parties' inputs and random tapes. When both Alice and Bob are corrupted, $\mathcal{S}$ has full access to this information and can simulate perfectly.

5   Solving Linear Equations

We now show how to use the previously proposed protocol for computing the inner product in order to obtain a new protocol for securely solving linear equations. Before we introduce the ideal functionalities related to this task, we briefly introduce the notation used in the protocol description.

In the following, we denote by $\mathbb{F}_q$ the finite field of order q, by $\mathbb{F}_q^n$ the space of all n-tuples of elements of $\mathbb{F}_q$. The act of randomly choosing an element $\vec{x}$ from $\mathbb{F}_q^n$ is represented by $\vec{x} \in_R \mathbb{F}_q^n$. $\mathbb{F}_q^{n \times n}$ represents the space of all $n \times n$ matrices with elements belonging to $\mathbb{F}_q$, while $SL(\mathbb{F}_q)$ represents the set of all non-singular $n \times n$ matrices with elements belonging to $\mathbb{F}_q$. Sum, multiplication and multiplication by scalar for vectors and matrices are defined as usual.

5.1   Ideal Functionality

- Upon receiving an (ASENDSINPUT, $\vec{x}$, X, sid) message from A:
Ignore any subsequent ASENDSINPUT messages. If $\vec{x} \notin \mathbb{Z}_m^n$ or $X \notin SL(\mathbb{F}_q)$, then send an INVALIDINPUT message to A and B and stop. If no BSENDSINPUT message has been received from B, then store $\vec{x}$, X and sid, and send the public delayed output (AINPUTRECEIVED, sid) to B; else find $\vec{z}$ such that $(X + Y)\vec{z} = \vec{x} + \vec{y}$ and send the public delayed output (BGETSOUTPUT, $\vec{z}$, sid) to B.

- Upon receiving a (BSENDSINPUT, $\vec{y}$, Y, sid) message from B:
Ignore any subsequent BSENDSINPUT messages. If $\vec{y} \notin \mathbb{Z}_m^n$ or $Y \notin SL(\mathbb{F}_q)$, then send an INVALIDINPUT message to A and B and stop. If no ASENDSINPUT message has been received from A, then store $\vec{y}$, Y and sid, and send the public delayed output (BINPUTRECEIVED, sid) to A; else find $\vec{z}$ such that $(X + Y)\vec{z} = \vec{x} + \vec{y}$ and send the public delayed output (BGETSOUTPUT, $\vec{z}$, sid) to B.

5.2   Protocol Implementation

Our approach is based on Du's approach [3]. The solution $\vec{z}$ to the linear equation $(X + Y)\vec{z} = \vec{x} + \vec{y}$ is equal to the solution $\vec{z}$ in $P(X + Y)QQ^{-1}\vec{z} = P(\vec{x} + \vec{y})$, in which P and Q are random, invertible matrices over $\mathbb{F}_q$ only known by Bob. In the protocol, we let Alice solve the blinded equation $P(X + Y)Q\vec{t} = P(\vec{x} + \vec{y})$, so $\vec{t} = Q^{-1}\vec{z}$. In other words, the solution that Alice gets to see is the final solution $\vec{z}$, blinded with a random invertible matrix Q^{-1}. To allow Alice to compute $P(X + Y)Q$ and $P(\vec{x} + \vec{y})$ without her learning Y or y, we use the inner product as a subprotocol, since matrix multiplication is nothing but the inner products of the right rows and columns.

Note that we can do all subprotocols in parallel since we have proven it UC. Note also that we can modify the previous protocol (without affecting its security) so that the value r can be is chosen randomly by TI and pre-distributed. Though the protocol notation below seems to suggest otherwise, it should be pointed out that the initialization phase for the main protocol and the subprotocols takes place at the same time. The Trusted Initializer Functionality is similar to the previous one, but in addition to the data used by the inner product protocols, it also pre-distributes the other data needed by the protocol below.

In the following, $(R; [PX - R]) := \Pi_{\langle \vec{x} \cdot \vec{y} \rangle}(X; P)$ denotes a protocol where Alice inputs the matrix X, Bob inputs the matrix P, Alice receives a random R as output while Bob receives $PX - R$. As stated previously, such a protocol for secure multiplication of matrices is clearly implementable given our protocol for computing the inner product.

Trusted Initializer	$Q, R \in_R SL(\mathbb{F}_q)$	
	$U \in_R \mathbb{F}_q^{n \times n}$	
	$\vec{s} \in_R \mathbb{F}_q^n$	
Data sent by TI	$\mu_A := (R, V = RQ + U, \vec{s})$	$\mu_B := (Q, U)$
	Alice	**Bob**
Input	$X \in SL(\mathbb{F}_q), \vec{x} \in \mathbb{F}_q^n$	$Y \in SL(\mathbb{F}_q), \vec{y} \in \mathbb{F}_q^n$
Step 1:		$P \in_R SL(\mathbb{F}_q)$
Call subprotocol $\Pi_{\langle \vec{x} \cdot \vec{y} \rangle}$	$(R; [PX - R]) := \Pi_{\langle \vec{x} \cdot \vec{y} \rangle}(X; P)$	
Call subprotocol $\Pi_{\langle \vec{x} \cdot \vec{y} \rangle}$	$(\vec{s}; [P\vec{x} - \vec{s}]) := \Pi_{\langle \vec{x} \cdot \vec{y} \rangle}(\vec{x}; P)$	
		$M := [PX - R]Q + PYQ - U$
		$\vec{c} := [P\vec{x} - \vec{s}] + P\vec{y}$
		Send $\mu_1 := (M, \vec{c})$ to Alice
Step 2:	If μ_1 is invalid then abort	
	$N := M + V$	
	$\vec{d} := \vec{c} + \vec{s}$	
	Find $\vec{t}$ such that $N\vec{t} = \vec{d}$	
	Send $\mu_2 := (\vec{t})$ to Bob	
Step 3:		Compute $\vec{z} = Q^{-1}\vec{t}$
Output	$u := \varepsilon$	$v := \vec{z}$

The correctness of the protocol is trivially verified:

$$N := M + V = [PX - R]Q + PYQ - U + RQ + U = P(X + Y)Q$$
$$\vec{d} := \vec{c} + \vec{s} = [P\vec{x} - \vec{s}] + P\vec{y} + \vec{s} = P(\vec{x} + \vec{y})$$

so Alice solves the equaltion $P(X + Y)Q\vec{t} = P(\vec{x} + \vec{y})$.

In order to find the solution to $(X + Y)\vec{z} = \vec{x} + \vec{y}$, Bob must compute $\vec{z} = Q^{-1}\vec{t}$.

6   Security Proof

6.1   Alice Corrupted, Bob Honest

Simulation. $\mathcal{S}$ runs an internal (embedded) copy of $\mathcal{A}$ called A$'$. Observe that Alice is corrupted, so $\mathcal{S}$ has access to Alice's inputs $\vec{x}$ and X. The interactions of A$'$ with $\mathcal{S}$ are those of Alice in the real protocol with the other parties, $\mathcal{Z}$, the TI, and Bob. We now show how $\mathcal{S}$ acts when such interactions take place (the simulation deals with the inner products in the same way as explained previously, and so these steps will be omitted):

# Events	$\mathcal{S}$'s actions
1 Onset of the Simulation	Choose the pre-distributed data following the correct procedures of the Trusted Initializer Functionality and sends Alice's pre-distributed data to A$'$.
2 Get input $\vec{x}$ and X	$\mathcal{S}$ forwards $\vec{x}$ and X from $\mathcal{Z}$, i.e. $\vec{x}' := \vec{x}$ and $X' = X$. $\mathcal{S}$ also chooses $\vec{y}' \in_R \mathbb{F}_q^n$, $Y' \in_R SL(\mathbb{F}_q)$ and $P' \in_R SL(\mathbb{F}_q)$.
3 Message (BINPUTRECEIVED, sid)	$\mathcal{S}$ computes M' and $\vec{c}'$, and sends $\mu_1' := (M', \vec{c}')$ to A$'$
4 Message μ_2'	If A$'$ sends $\vec{t}'$ as message μ_2', then $\mathcal{S}$ sends a message (ASENDSINPUT, $\vec{x}$, X, sid) to $\mathcal{F}_{\langle \vec{x} \cdot \vec{y} \rangle}$. If A$'$ sends something invalid in μ_2', then $\mathcal{S}$ sends something invalid to $\mathcal{F}_{\langle \vec{x} \cdot \vec{y} \rangle}$.
5 Message (BGETSOUTPUT, $\vec{z}$, sid)	$\mathcal{S}$ lets the functionality deliver the message (BGETSOUTPUT, v sid).

Indistinguishability. We make the following observations:

1. Independent of $\mathcal{A}$, $\mathcal{Z}$ can make Bob send no input or an invalid input. In the simulation, $\mathcal{S}$ behavior after sending the message copies this perfectly.
2. Whatever A$''$s strategy is, it either sends a valid or an invalid message μ_2'. If the message is invalid, both the simulated and the ideal protocol will send INVALIDINPUT to the two parties, which will be forwarded to $\mathcal{Z}$.

If we consider A$'$ (and $\mathcal{A}$) as deterministic algorithms whose probabilism comes from a random tape, it follows that A$'$ behavior is completely determined by these random bits, called s_A, the pre-distributed data, the inputs $\vec{x}$ and X, and the incoming message

μ'_1. We already know that the random bits s_A and the inputs $\overrightarrow{x}$ and X have the same distribution in the real and ideal protocol, because of the way the model is defined.

So in order to show that $\forall \mathcal{A} \exists \mathcal{S} \forall \mathcal{Z} :$ REAL$_{\pi,\mathcal{A},\mathcal{Z}} \equiv$ IDEAL$_{\mathcal{F}_{\langle \overrightarrow{x} \cdot \overrightarrow{y} \rangle},\mathcal{S},\mathcal{Z}}$, it suffices to show that the pre-distributed data produced by $\mathcal{S}$ has the same distribution as the pre-distributed data produced by the TI in the real protocol. But this is trivial, since $\mathcal{S}$ generate these data using the same distribution that the TI uses in the real protocol.

In addition, we must show that μ'_1 produced by $\mathcal{S}$ and μ_1 sent by Bob have the same distribution. Observe that $M := [PX - R]Q + PYQ - U$ with $U \in_R \mathbb{F}_q^{n \times n}$ and $\overrightarrow{c} := [P\overrightarrow{x} - \overrightarrow{s}] + P\overrightarrow{y}$ with $P \in_R SL(\mathbb{F}_q)$. Since both TI and Bob are honest in the real protocol, it follows that both μ'_1 and μ_1 are generated according to the uniform distribution.

So we conclude that A''s incoming messages in the simulated protocol have a distribution identical to $\mathcal{A}$'s incoming message in the real protocol. It follows therefore that the ideal and real protocol distributions are perfectly indistinguishable from $\mathcal{Z}$ point of view, which completes the proof.

6.2 Alice Honest, Bob Corrupted

The proof of this case is very much along the same lines as the previous case: $\mathcal{S}$ runs an internal (embedded) copy of $\mathcal{A}$ called B'. Observe that Bob is corrupted, so $\mathcal{S}$ has access to Bob's input $\overrightarrow{y}$. The interactions of B' with $\mathcal{S}$ are those of Bob in the real protocol with the other parties, $\mathcal{Z}$, the TI, and Alice. We give an overview how $\mathcal{S}$ acts

# Events	$\mathcal{S}$'s actions
1 Onset of the Simulation	Choose the pre-distributed data following the correct procedures of the Trusted Initializer Functionality and sends Bob's pre-distributed data to B'.
2 Get input $\overrightarrow{y}$ and Y	$\mathcal{S}$ forwards $\overrightarrow{y}$ and Y from $\mathcal{Z}$, i.e. $\overrightarrow{y}' := \overrightarrow{y}$ and $Y' = Y$. $\mathcal{S}$ also chooses $\overrightarrow{x}' \in_R \mathbb{F}_q^n$ and $X' \in_R SL(\mathbb{F}_q)$.
3 Message μ'_1	If B' sends $(M', \overrightarrow{c}')$ as message μ'_1, then $\mathcal{S}$ sends a message (BSENDSINPUT, $\overrightarrow{y}$, Y, $bsid$) to $\mathcal{F}_{\langle \overrightarrow{x} \cdot \overrightarrow{y} \rangle}$. If B' sends something invalid in μ'_1, then $\mathcal{S}$ sends something invalid to $\mathcal{F}_{\langle \overrightarrow{x} \cdot \overrightarrow{y} \rangle}$. $\mathcal{S}$ lets the functionality deliver the message (BINPUTRECEIVED, sid)
4 Message (BGETSOUTPUT, v, sid)	$\mathcal{S}$ computes N', $\overrightarrow{y}'$, finds $\overrightarrow{t}'$ and sends $\mu'_2 := (\overrightarrow{t}')$ to B'; $\mathcal{S}$ intercepts the simulated output v' and verifies if this value is consistent with the values used in this simulated execution (note that $\mathcal{S}$ knows all these values as it plays the role of the Trusted Initializer). If consistent, $\mathcal{S}$ substitutes the simulated output v' with the real output v obtained from $\mathcal{F}_{\langle \overrightarrow{x} \cdot \overrightarrow{y} \rangle}$ by setting $v_{\mathcal{S}} = v$; else it sets $v_{\mathcal{S}} = v'$. As long as no v' from B' is received, $\mathcal{S}$ does not forward the message BGETSOUTPUT, even if this means waiting forever. Then $v_{\mathcal{S}}$ is sent to $\mathcal{Z}$ through Bob's interface.

The proof of indistinguishability is almost identical to the previous case and is omitted.

6.3   Alice and Bob Honest

If neither party is corrupted, $\mathcal{A}$ simulates the Trusted Initializer Functionality, sees a transcript of the message sent between Alice and Bob and let the functionality send the public delayed outputs in the ideal protocol when $\mathcal{A}$ deliver the respective messages in the simulated execution.

6.4   Alice and Bob Corrupted

The protocol is a deterministic function of the parties' inputs and random tapes. When both Alice and Bob are corrupted, $\mathcal{S}$ has full access to this information and can simulate perfectly.

7   Conclusions

We have presented a protocol for computing the inner product between two vectors defined over $\mathbb{Z}_m$. We proved our solution secure in the UC framework. As an application of our protocol, we built on top of it another protocol that securely solves linear equations over finite fields.

We believe that the commodity/ trusted initializer model, where parties receive pre-distributed data during a setup phase from a trusted source and then go on and proceed with their secure computations without further interaction with this trusted source, provides a practical and interesting framework for secure two-party computations. The solutions obtained usually demand a large (but not prohibitively with today's technology) storage capability, but are otherwise very efficient from a computational point of view.

We hope our protocols presented here are used to provide more complex tasks, such as secure data mining and so on. Generalizations for approximately solving linear equations over the reals are also an interesting sequel to this work [4].

References

1. Beaver, D.: Commodity-based cryptography (extended abstract). In: STOC 1997: Proceedings of the Twenty-Ninth Annual ACM Symposium on Theory of Computing, pp. 446–455. ACM, New York (1997)
2. Canetti, R.: Universally composable security: A new paradigm for cryptographic protocols. In: FOCS, p. 136. IEEE Computer Society, Los Alamitos (2001)
3. Du., W.: A study of several specific secure two-party computation problems. PhD thesis, Purdue University, West-Lafayette, Indiana (2001)
4. Feigenbaum, J., Ishai, Y., Malkin, T.G., Nissim, K., Strauss, M.J., Wright, R.N.: Secure multiparty computation of approximations. In: Yu, Y., Spirakis, P.G., van Leeuwen, J. (eds.) ICALP 2001. LNCS, vol. 2076, pp. 927–938. Springer, Heidelberg (2001)

5. Goethals, B., Laur, S., Lipmaa, H., Mielikäinen, T.: On private scalar product computation for privacy-preserving data mining. In: Park, C.-s., Chee, S. (eds.) ICISC 2004. LNCS, vol. 3506, pp. 104–120. Springer, Heidelberg (2005)
6. Kiltz, E., Leander, G., Malone-Lee, J.: Secure computation of the mean and related statistics. In: Kilian, J. (ed.) TCC 2005. LNCS, vol. 3378, pp. 283–302. Springer, Heidelberg (2005)
7. Matsumoto, T., Imai, H.: On the key predistribution system: A practical solution to the key distribution problem. In: Pomerance, C. (ed.) CRYPTO 1987. LNCS, vol. 293, pp. 185–193. Springer, Heidelberg (1988)
8. Meier, R., Przydatek, B., Wullschleger, J.: Robuster combiners for oblivious transfer. In: Vadhan, S.P. (ed.) TCC 2007. LNCS, vol. 4392, pp. 404–418. Springer, Heidelberg (2007)
9. Nascimento, A., Tonicelli, R., Otsuka, A., Hanaoka, G., Imai, H., Winter, A.: Information Theoretically Secure Oblivious Polynomial Evaluation: Model, Bounds and Constructions (2008) (manuscript)
10. Nascimento, A.C.A., Müller-Quade, J., Otsuka, A., Hanaoka, G., Imai, H.: Unconditionally non-interactive verifiable secret sharing secure against faulty majorities in the commodity based model. In: Jakobsson, M., Yung, M., Zhou, J. (eds.) ACNS 2004. LNCS, vol. 3089, pp. 355–368. Springer, Heidelberg (2004)
11. Rivest, R.: Unconditionally Secure Commitment and Oblivious Transfer Schemes Using Private Channels and a Trusted Initializer (1999),
http://people.csail.mit.edu/rivest/Rivest-commitment.pdf
12. Vaidya, J., Clifton, C.: Privacy preserving association rule mining in vertically partitioned data. In: Proceedings of the Eighth ACM SIGKDD International Conference on Knowledge Discovery and Data Mining, Edmonton, Alberta, Canada, July 23-26, pp. 639–644. ACM, New York (2002)
13. Yao, A.C.-C.: Protocols for secure computations (extended abstract). In: 23rd Annual Symposium on Foundations of Computer Science, Chicago, Illinois, EUA, November 3-5, pp. 160–164. IEEE, Los Alamitos (1982)

Author Index

GPSR Compliance

The European Union's (EU) General Product Safety Regulation (GPSR) is a set of rules that requires consumer products to be safe and our obligations to ensure this.

If you have any concerns about our products, you can contact us on ProductSafety@springernature.com

In case Publisher is established outside the EU, the EU authorized representative is:

Springer Nature Customer Service Center GmbH
Europaplatz 3
69115 Heidelberg, Germany

Batch number: 09474024

Printed by Printforce, the Netherlands